ESSENTIALS

of the **Theory of Fiction**

ESSENTIALS

of the Theory of Fiction

edited by MICHAEL J. HOFFMAN

and PATRICK D. MURPHY

—— [**THIRD EDITION**] ——

Duke University Press

Durham and London

2005

2nd printing, 2007

© 2005 Duke University Press

All rights reserved

Printed in the United States of

America on acid-free paper ∞

Designed by Amy Ruth Buchanan

Typeset in Janson by Keystone

Typesetting, Inc.   Library of Congress

Cataloging-in-Publication Data appear

on the last printed page of this book.

—[CONTENTS]—

When in the mid-1980s we began to think about this book, we did some research into our potential competition. We discovered at that time that no collection of essays on the theory of fiction had been published for more than ten years and that all the older editions were now out of print. There were a number of anthologies of literary theory, which often included an essay or two on the theory of fiction, but there were no collections that served serious students of fiction who were interested in covering that field or wanted a text that their own students could use in a course on the novel.

It seemed clear then, and it remains so now, that there is a serious need for such a text, given the proliferation of courses on prose fiction at colleges and universities and because the theory of fiction is a burgeoning subdivision in the study of literary theory. What we have tried to provide in *Essentials of the Theory of Fiction* is a single text that contains the best and most current essays written on the major topics in the theory of fiction so that readers can experience that field at its highest level.

We conceive of our audience as consisting of educated general readers as well as scholars. Our criteria of selection are (1) those texts traditionally considered "classics," (2) those that reflect the concerns of the most important scholars and critics, (3) those that are the best in their quality of thought and exposition, and (4) those that are the most readable and well written. The reader should know that we have excluded essays that we found needlessly obscure or poorly written, no matter how much they might have represented the most "advanced" ideas.

Within these strictures, our focus in all three editions of *Essentials* has been both historical and topical, so we present the essays in chronological order of their publication. We have also tried to represent those topics that have defined the field, and in an attempt to stay current with that discussion, we have in each edition replaced almost a third of the essays that appeared in the previous one.

Some readers may wish to read the book straight through in order to follow the field's historical development; others may wish to dip in here and there, following their interests of the moment. Instructors may wish to use the essays to introduce fictional topics in conjunction with the reading of specific stories, novellas, or novels. Experience also shows that the book can be used in an advanced undergraduate or graduate course that stresses the historical development of fiction and its accompanying criticism.

In the introduction, we introduce readers to the field, state something about its history, and describe some of the categories and terms under which discussion of narrative theory has taken place. Unlike the introductions to many anthologies, ours says comparatively little about each of the essays we have chosen or about their authors, letting the essays speak for themselves. Nonetheless, careful readers will note that in a discipline like this one, such essays always exist in a kind of dialogue — occasionally explicit, perhaps most often implicit — with one another.

Having worked together for almost twenty years on three editions of this book, we have experienced both the joys and the synergy connected with collaboration. This is certainly a better book than either of us could have produced alone. In addition, however, there are others who deserve a word of thanks. In particular, we are grateful to Reynolds Smith, our editor at Duke University Press, for all three versions of *Essentials*. His enthusiastic support and thoughtful editing have made our job a pleasure. Patrick Murphy wishes to thank Danielle Impellitier, who, as his graduate research assistant, helped locate potential new essays for the third edition. We both would like to thank all the professors and students who have provided comments about the first two editions that have helped us to improve and update *Essentials* with this third edition.

Who was the first storyteller? A lonely hunter consoling his fellows on a cold northern evening far from home? A mother calming a frightened child with tales of gods and demigods? A lover telling his intended of fantastic exploits, designed to foster his courtship? The reader can multiply the number of possibilities, but we will never know the answer, for the impulse to tell stories is as old as the development of speech, far older than the invention of writing. It has deep psychological springs we do not fully comprehend, but the need to make up characters, and to place them in worlds that are parallel to our own or are perhaps wildly at variance with it, is part of the history of all peoples, cultures, and countries; there is no known human group that has not told tales.

Oral cultures are great sources for students of the theory of fiction. Researchers have established that in those that still exist, the storyteller (or bard) is highly revered for the ability to relate from memory a number of verse narratives of enormous length, told within the regularities of meter and conventional figures of language that aid the memory, containing the stories of characters known to listeners who share in a common folklore and myth. These stories, about familiar characters in recognizable situations, do not engage their audience in the mysteries of an unresolved plot, for the listeners know the story already, have heard it told before, and are often as familiar with its events as they are with events in their own lives. Then why do they listen? Beyond the story itself, the audience concerns itself with the voice and manner of the teller of the tale; the texture and density of the story's material; the fit of the characters with the audience's expectations about how human beings, gods, demigods, and mythic heroes behave in a world something like their own. For such people — as for ourselves — fictions have an extraordinary explanatory power; they make clear why, for instance, there are seasons, why there is an underworld for the spirits of dead ancestors, why there is one royal line of descent and not another.

We begin this collection of essays on the theory of fiction with a discussion of so-called primitive origins because we believe that the impulse to tell tales and listen to them is akin to the impulse in "literate" cultures to write stories and read them, and as the anthropologist Claude Lévi-Strauss has shown us in *The Savage Mind*, the science of primitive peoples is as sophisticated in its own purposes as the science in literate cultures; so too are the fictions. Tribal members in oral cultures may or may not engage in detailed discussions of the nature and forms of their fictions, but clearly they do make judgments about the adequacy of the telling of stories, and the act of judgment is, after all, an act of criticism. Questions of judgment and interpretation, in fact, inform human discourse everywhere.

While we do not suggest that the theory of fiction claims much attention from tribal scholars, we do note that the interpretation of works of literature, and in particular of fictional creation, is part of the written record of all literate cultures. It has constituted an extremely large and important part of literature since the times of the ancient Hebrews and Greeks, with its beginnings in Midrashic texts and in the writings of Plato and the sophists and, ultimately, in the most important literary critical text of Western antiquity, the *Poetics* of Aristotle.

The study of literature and literary theory — by which we mean the use of social-science, philosophical, rhetorical, linguistic, and structural analysis as means of interpreting texts — has, therefore, a long tradition in Western intellectual history, one employed quite heavily during certain periods and certainly appearing during the past century as a principal form of literate intellectual activity. In its forms of analysis, literary theory has been defined to a great extent by the kinds of texts to which it has been applied. In the *Poetics* Aristotle was concerned primarily with discussing the epic poem and the two dominant modes of drama, comedy and tragedy. For the most part, these were the most important forms, along with lyric poetry, written by the ancient Greek authors that Aristotle studied. The fictions about which Aristotle could have written were therefore composed in verse or dialogue, and the forms were not the prose fictional genres that dominate our time: the novel, the novella, and the short story.

Historians of literature have argued at length about which prose fictions might qualify as the first novels. There were certainly prominent examples of lengthy prose fictions in the ancient world, with *The Golden Ass* of Apuleius and Petronius's *Satyricon* coming to mind. But while these are extended narratives in prose, they do not, for most critics, fulfill the criteria for defining a novel formally in terms of the development of plot and character. Both tales are products of the Roman Empire and were followed by more than a millennium in which the long fictional forms consisted mainly of verse epics and romances whose subject matter was the conventional material of shared folklore and myth. Indeed, with some exceptions such as the Icelandic sagas and Giovanni Boccaccio's *Decameron*, extended prose fictions did not begin to flourish in England and on the European continent until the sixteenth century, in the writings of Thomas Nashe and John Lyly in England, François Rabelais in France, and Miguel de Cervantes in Spain. Some critics have called Cervantes's *Don Quixote*, published during the early years of the seventeenth century, the first European novel, but although the adventures of the man of La Mancha have been extraordinarily influential on later forms of prose fiction, Cervantes did not found a tradition in which the writers who came after him self-consciously thought of themselves as writing "novels." Rather, Cervantes's book summed up and parodied the tradition of medieval and Renaissance romance, with all its chivalric and courtly conventions. The self-conscious establishment of a tradition of novel writing did not come about with any lasting force until more than a century later, in an increasingly mercantile and industrial Europe where the middle classes were rapidly expanding. The rising literacy that always accompanies trade and technology created an expanded reading public hungry for stories of people like themselves, in prose like that of the newspapers, journals, and scientific treatises that had come to dominate the new technology of print. For the middle classes, poetry was identified with the aristocracy, except for such didactic verse as they sang in church.

England in the first half of the eighteenth century was a country dominated increasingly by trade and a mercantile class who used their great prosperity to purchase for themselves the perquisites hitherto reserved for the landed aristocracy. The earliest British novels dramatized the rise of this new class. In addition, the development of a literate population, helped by the technology of print, made it possible for the first time for writers to earn a living through the sale of their printed works rather than through receiving patronage from a wealthy person of noble birth.

This new technology created a veritable writing industry in London, producing not only great masses of publications for science and various trades but also the first newspapers, biographies, "confessions" of famous criminals, travel books, and ostensibly "true" accounts of how successful individuals found ways to thrive in the developing bourgeois culture. The works of Daniel Defoe are representative of this tendency; the ones we still read today were written as serious parodies of the forms developed in the popular press: *Robinson Crusoe* (1719), *A Journal of the Plague Year* (1722), and *Moll Flanders* (1722). All are written in a "nonliterary" prose of great lucidity and apparent functional utility. *Moll Flanders* and *Crusoe* are often called the great precursors of the British novel and are taught in courses on that genre. The other great precursor of this period, Jonathan Swift's *Gulliver's Travels* (1728), uses the form of the travel tale to parody the society of England by placing it in various guises in exotic fictional settings.

While the works of Defoe and Swift are surely wonderful exercises of the fictional imagination, they were not written by authors working self-consciously in a new literary form. Not until two decades after the appearance of Lemuel Gulliver's *Travels into Several Remote Regions of the World* did the works of two writers, Samuel Richardson and Henry Fielding, announce the development of a new form. Richardson's epistolary novels, *Pamela* (1741) and *Clarissa* (1747–1748), caught the imagination of England and much of Europe because of their sympathetic and extended treatment of character and their fashionable excesses of feeling. Fielding's work as a novelist began with a parody of Richardson's *Pamela* in a travesty called *Shamela* (1741). Having found his gift for comedy, Fielding then produced two of the best early novels in British literature: *Joseph Andrews* (1742) and *Tom Jones* (1749), in each of which, but especially in the latter, he wrote justifications of his use of the new form. Calling his books comic epics in prose and rationalizing his procedures through reference to the works of classic Greek and Roman authors, Fielding more than anyone else wrote the first essays on the theory of fiction in British literature.

Although the tradition of the novel was established quite quickly and has ultimately come to dominate the common conception of literature for the reading public, no corresponding tradition of writings on the theory of fiction arose to follow Fielding's lead in that area. Works on literary theory continued to concentrate, as they had since Aristotle, on poetry and drama, and the main practitioners in the eighteenth century were primarily poets, such as John Dryden and Alexander Pope. The one major exception to that rule, Samuel Johnson — that extraordinary man of letters who worked in many forms, including the novel — wrote little about fiction in his theoretical writings.

Well into the nineteenth century, the novel remained for critics the stepchild among literary forms, popular with the mass reading public but not considered *serious* in the way of the lyric or the long poem. Major British critics continued to be poets, such as Samuel Taylor Coleridge and Matthew Arnold, but again neither had much to say about the novel. In France and Russia, however, critics including Charles Augustin Sainte-Beuve and

Vassarion Belinsky and the novelists Honoré de Balzac and Stendhal (Marie Henri Beyle) did begin to write seriously about fiction. Nonetheless, the first writer to develop an extensive and lasting body of writing in English on the theory of fiction was the novelist Henry James, who — in a lengthy series of essays written over more than four decades and in the prefaces he wrote to the New York Edition (1907–1909) of his collected works — practically invented the field, along with many of the terms and concepts still most frequently used by people who write about fiction. Indeed, for instance, the Jamesian dictum about the importance of the single point of view, as well as his belief that authors should not "intrude" by "telling" but should drama-tize action, became an almost tyrannical force in critical theory and novelis-tic practice during the first half of the twentieth century — as Wayne Booth demonstrates in *The Rhetoric of Fiction* (1961).

It may well be, however, that the most important example set by James's writings on fictional theory, as well as by his own work as an artist, is to show that the writing of fiction is not simply a form of entertainment but a seri-ous art form, to be ranked with the lyric, the epic, and the drama and to be taken just as seriously by its practitioners. James's monastic commit-ment to writing, along with his belief that the exercise of craft is a form of moral commitment — a belief he learned from Gustave Flaubert and Ivan Turgenev — was so powerful that the theory of fiction has been dominated ever since by an emphasis on craft with less thought in general given to subject matter. It seems only fitting, then, to begin our collection of essays with James's "The Art of Fiction" (1884), an essay that reads like a manifesto for the position just summarized.

The nineteenth century has come to seem the great age of narrative, particularly in the realistic novel. Even though the theory of fiction in England had to await the advent of James, by the time of his death in 1916, fiction had come to be seen as the central act of literary creation — the area of real artistic commitment. In his early essays, for instance, Ezra Pound claimed that it was again time for poets to take their craft as seriously as the novelists take theirs. While for a time poet-critics such as Pound and T. S. Eliot continued to dominate literary theory — both of them strongly in-fluenced by the *example* of James as an artist — from the 1920s on, ma-jor contributions were made to the theory of fiction by both scholars and practitioners.

As a result, a study of recent contributions made to the theory of fiction indicates the field to be a microcosm of both the concerns of literary theory and the general study of literature — particularly because the entire field of literature has become more and more a part of the academic enterprise. As, for instance, the study of poetry moved away from a concern with the poet's biography and the poem's subject matter, so did the study of fiction focus more on the ways the novel or story is constructed rather than on how facts of the author's life relate to details in the fiction.

While readers of this collection may wish to seek analogies between the concerns expressed in these essays and those expressed throughout the previous century in the study of poetry, drama, language, and rhetoric, the editors wish to focus the remainder of this introduction on the central concerns of the theory of fiction and on how they have evolved since the time of James.

Genre

A number of the following essays treat an issue that has occupied many writers on fiction: that of defining the nature of each of the fictional genres. The first issue lies in deciding which works fall under the purview of the theory of fiction, as distinct from theories of poetry and drama. Most writers draw the line between works written in prose and those written in verse — which is certainly the case with most of the essays in this collection. Still, some critics have claimed that Homer's *Iliad* and Chaucer's *Troilus and Criseyde* are, for instance, almost "perfect" novels, even though they are both long poems in the epic or romance traditions. Major theorists like Georg Lukács and Mikhail Bakhtin see the lines of fictional tradition as running from the epic to the novel; their major task then becomes to show how the two forms differ. For Bakhtin the fact that one form is written in verse, the other in prose, seems almost incidental. For other critics this distinction is crucial. Does the final distinction here become a cultural one, for example, between historical cultures that use one form of discourse rather than another? Is there a difference in the way the world appears through the lenses of prose and verse?

Making distinctions among the prose fictional forms of the novel, novella, and short story has also occupied recent critics. Are these distinctions simply ones of length between forms of up to 15,000 words, up to 50,000 words, or more than 50,000 words? Do these arbitrary word lengths impose formal constraints on authors, so that novels, novellas, and short stories differ in their basic characters? The short story is in fact an older form, attracting critical attention at least as early as the 1840s, in Edgar Allan Poe's classical essay on his countryman Nathaniel Hawthorne's *Twice-Told*

Tales, whereas the novella did not emerge as a self-consciously viable form until the latter part of the nineteenth century. What does the actual word limit of the various forms mean to a writer when composing a work of fiction? What advantages does each form give writers that they cannot take advantage of in the others?

Narrative Voice and Point of View

Since the time of Henry James the related matters of narrative voice and point of view have played a major role in the discussion of fiction. It is important to remember that both concepts are metaphoric, that the figure of point of view has to do with how the action is seen or experienced and that the figurative narrative voice is really silent and requires us to suppose from the words on the page how that voice might sound if someone were actually speaking them. Although they are figurative concepts, these notions have long had a powerful explanatory power for critics and readers, enabling us to understand that all narrative is written from a certain perspective and that one major fictional device is working to make the reader share in the experience from that perspective.

Henry James codified the concept of point of view by insisting that the narrative voice be purified of the kind of authorial commentary that he claimed interfered with the narrative flow. Moral judgments were to become implicit rather than explicit, and a single narrative perspective was to be carried through the story — either that of a character in the tale or that of a narrator whose voice was to become the flexible instrument that sustained a distance between the author and the fictional matter. Authors were not to demean their tasks by pretending that novels were merely "made up" and that they could cavalierly intervene anytime they wished to make a comment. The author was to become invisible, to be — as in James Joyce's famous formulation in *A Portrait of the Artist as a Young Man* — "like the God of the creation, who remains within or behind or beyond or above his handiwork, invisible, refined out of existence, indifferent, paring his fingernails."

Such extraordinary narrative purity remained an ideal throughout much of the twentieth century, motivating the work of writers such as Joyce, Ernest Hemingway, William Faulkner, and Virginia Woolf. So strongly did this concept take hold of critics that it was not seriously challenged until Booth's *Rhetoric of Fiction*, mentioned earlier, which pointed out that not only had some of the greatest novels never striven for such purity but that in no work of fiction did the author *ever* disappear; judgments were always present in the narrative tone and in all the various kinds of irony available to the narrator and the "implied author." Booth's influence has not only opened up earlier novels for our greater appreciation but also made more accessible to us a whole host of "postmodern" novels that make no attempt to hide the fact that they were written — that, in fact, make a fetish of their artificiality. Our collection includes several essays that focus on the varied narrative dimensions of fiction, a field that has received increasing attention from critics. The concerns include feminist narratology, the African American strategy of "signifying," and the computer-generated uses of hypertext.

Plot

Discussions of plot have become much more sophisticated in recent criticism. Instead of simply seeing plot as a succession of events taking place in a narrative, critics have now begun to make important distinctions. They understand that major differences exist among the story embedded in the narrative, the actual narrative sequence (which is frequently *not* in the story's chronological order), and the various tensions between the two orders that authors have always self-consciously exploited.

In addition, there are many different types of plots, ranging from idyllic love stories to stories of war, murder, and mayhem to stories of ritual and religion to stories that are primarily intellectual discussions of ideas. And to advance the many different kinds of plots, novelists employ many devices, including "flashes" forward and backward, involutions of temporal sequence, and telling the story more than once from the points of view of different characters, as in William Faulkner's *The Sound and the Fury*. Gérard Genette has established a critical method with his structuralist analysis of temporal strategies within narrative, and Peter Brooks has argued for reestablishing the centrality of plot to any narrative.

Character

What exactly is a character? Is it simply that entity which, for the most part, retains the same name from the beginning to the end of the work of fiction? Are fictional characters obliged to obey the same rules of human behavior as living people of flesh and blood? If so, then why, for instance, do we identify with the characters in novels such as George Orwell's *Animal Farm*, in which animals speak and act like human beings?

What constitutes a good character? To borrow terminology from E. M. Forster's *Aspects of the Novel*, can we claim that "rounded" characters are more vivid and memorable than "flat" ones? Forster himself makes no such claim, but some of his followers have misread him in suggesting that he did. Can we really say that Leo Tolstoy's Anna Karenina (a rounded character) is more memorable than Herman Melville's Captain Ahab (a flat one) — to take two tragic characters as examples? Hardly. But the question does point out that fictional characters are defined not so much by what they are as by how they are used. The functions to which characters are put determine whether we will see only one side of them or experience their many-sidedness. Captain Ahab's obsession is what defines him and controls the monomaniacal nature of the quest for Moby-Dick. To see him much outside of this defining obsession would soften him too much and would allow the momentum of the quest to flag. Anna Karenina's role, on the other hand, demands that we see her much more completely within a set of social situations and in many moods, for her fate is tied up with the mores of a large society, and she does not assume the dominant role in it that Captain Ahab does in his. But with all their differences, both characters rank among the most memorable in the history of fiction.

The problem is made to seem even more complex when we consider comic characters, who are more often flat (Don Quixote) than round (Leopold Bloom in *Ulysses*), and characters in more recent fiction who are frequently both serious and comic, round and flat (e.g., the nameless narrator in Ralph Ellison's *Invisible Man*).

And what, then, do we think of the arguments made by post–World War II practitioners of the French *nouveau roman* such as Alain Robbe-Grillet and Nathalie Sarraute, who recently claimed that the notion of character was passé, and that a new conception of the novel would have to be developed in which character no longer played a role as we know it? In such a new novel, the writer could only record phenomena. What, then, is character: a speaking voice, a thinking mind, a feeling of spirit? The essays here trace the development of this continuing argument.

Fiction and Reality

The relationship of fictional worlds to those inhabited by readers has long been a subject for discussion in the theory of fiction. Are novels primarily representations of reality, or are they all "made up"? How obliged are novelists to make what happens in their texts compare with what might have happened had the same events occurred in the real world? Is verisimilitude, for instance, an obligation for a writer?

Lionel Trilling once claimed that realism is the basic drive behind all fictional creation, that the lives of individuals in society have provided the stuff out of which novels have always been made. Other writers have identified realism more closely with certain periods of history (the nineteenth century) than with others (the twentieth century). Even, however, in modernist novels as different as Joyce's *Ulysses* and Faulkner's *Absalom, Absalom!* one of the main thematic problems in each concerns the relatedness of fictional events to those of a specific moment in history, a single day (June 16, 1904), as in *Ulysses*, or a more lengthy period (from the 1830s to the 1930s), as in *Absalom, Absalom!*

But can we think of fictional reality in the same terms we use in thinking about history or about our own lives? Lives in fiction are surely more carefully determined than those that are lived by people who read books. Few lives conform to a satisfying plot or reveal an understandable meaning. Novels do not have to end in death the way all lives and most biographies do. Nonetheless we do not find fictional characters to be well portrayed or developed unless some event or early action in the novel has prepared us for what happens to them later. In this way novels are predictable and predetermined in ways unlike the randomness we all experience when living in a contingent world.

It seems, then, that we demand that novels and stories be plausible within the terms of their own fictional world, and that such plausibility be measured not against whether that universe is truly a "represented" world but whether it is analogous to our own — that if some things happen, then other things will follow, just as they might were we living in a universe constructed like the one in that made-up world. This, it seems to us, is as true about works of fiction written in the great age of realism of Charles Dickens, George Eliot, Stendhal, or Fyodor Dostoyevsky as it is of the more contrived but still essentially realistic novels of Joyce, Woolf, Faulkner, and Gabriel García Márquez — as well as works using fantastic worlds, which often provide far more "realistic" or everyday details of their world than many avant-garde fictions. The latter part of the twentieth century saw the development of new forms such as the documentary novel, which forces us to establish the border between fact and fiction; magical realism, which mingles realism and the fantastic; and science fiction and fantasy, which often posit an alternative universe.

Time and Space

Prose fiction is a temporal medium. It takes time for the reader of a novel to absorb its words, assimilate its concepts, and perceive its various elements. Characters are developed, and plots unfold in time. Like a symphony, a novel frequently shifts from one moment to the next, and the development of a given passage depends on other passages that have preceded it.

Novelists have often manipulated a story's temporal unfolding by telling a tale out of chronological order, and in that way exploiting the tension among story, narrative, and plot—a tension that we mentioned earlier. Even in fictions characterized primarily by straightforward, continuous chronology, the time of reading is almost always at variance with the time the plot takes to unfold: almost all novels cover a longer period of time than the number of hours even a slow reader might take to finish the book. (The occasional novel that tries to match reading and narrative time exactly goes therefore against the reader's expectations.) Exploitation of this tension becomes yet another device through which authors define the rhythms of their narratives.

Another concern of recent critics (e.g., Joseph Frank) has been to describe the ways in which certain novels attempt to use spatial means to achieve certain effects. As applied to fiction, space is even more metaphoric than the concept of time. Painting and sculpture are spatial forms, and because they exist in space (as does an unopened book), they can be experienced "all at once" in a single and instantaneous visual perception. A painting (as distinguished from one's understanding of it) does not unfold in time; it is all there at every moment, and its parts are not sequential but physically connected.

Many modernist novels have demanded that readers experience them all at once — an obviously impossible demand, given the temporal nature of the reading experience. But like a cubist painting, whose various elements are related simply by contiguity, novels like *Ulysses* or Faulkner's *The Sound and the Fury* can be understood only when they are perceived "all at once," for the various elements unfold not chronologically but in a fashion that seems at first to be almost random. It is often said that you cannot read such novels for the first time unless you have already read them. In other words, you must have their facts and their stories in your head (as you would when looking at a painting) before you can understand them as their narratives unfold. All students of fiction must therefore come to terms with the different conceptions of time conveyed in a nineteenth-century novel (like Dickens's *Great Expectations* or Leo Tolstoy's *War and Peace*), with its emphasis on historical continuity, and the more fragmented modernist novel as it breaks with seemingly old-fashioned concepts such as causality and relatedness.

We hope this discussion of certain major topics in the theory of fiction will prove helpful to students, teachers, and scholars alike. Those topics and many others like them — metaphor, myth, setting, symbolism — are raised in much greater detail in the collection of texts that follow.

As prose fiction has developed from the early experiments of Cervantes's parodies, Richardson's epistolary works, and Hawthorne's sketches to the sophisticated experiments of modernism and postmodernism, literary criticism has also evolved. It has become more sophisticated as the result of efforts by critics to explain how fictions work their magic. The essays that follow, drawn from the past 120 years, and displaying that growth and change, are essential to any study of fiction at the beginning of our new century.

The Art of Fiction · HENRY JAMES

The only obligation to which in advance we may hold a novel, without incurring the accusation of being arbitrary, is that it be interesting. That general responsibility rests upon it, but it is the only one I can think of. The ways in which it is at liberty to accomplish this result (of interesting us) strike me as innumerable, and such as can only suffer from being marked out or fenced in by prescription. They are as various as the temperament of man, and they are successful in proportion as they reveal a particular mind, different from others. A novel is in its broadest definition a personal, a direct impression of life: that, to begin with, constitutes its value, which is greater or less according to the intensity of the impression. But there will be no intensity at all, and therefore no value, unless there is freedom to feel and say. The tracing of a line to be followed, of a tone to be taken, of a form to be filled out, is a limitation of that freedom and a suppression of the very thing that we are most curious about. The form, it seems to me, is to be appreciated after the fact: then the author's choice has been made, his standard has been indicated; then we can follow lines and directions and compare tones and resemblances. Then in a word we can enjoy one of the most charming of pleasures, we can estimate quality, we can apply the test of execution. The execution belongs to the author alone; it is what is most personal to him, and we measure him by that. The advantage, the luxury, as well as the torment and responsibility of the novelist, is that there is no limit to what he may attempt as an executant — no limit to his possible experiments, efforts, discoveries, successes. Here it is especially that he works, step by step, like his brother of the brush, of whom we may always say that he has painted his picture in a manner best known to himself. His manner is his secret, not necessarily a jealous one. He cannot disclose it as a general thing if he would; he would be at a loss to teach it to others. I say this with a due recollection of having insisted on the community of method of the artist who paints a picture and the artist who writes a novel. The painter *is* able to teach the rudiments of his practice, and it is possible, from the study of good work (granted the aptitude), both to learn how to paint and to learn how to write. Yet it remains true, without injury to the *rapprochement*, that the literary artist would be obliged to say to his pupil much more than the other, "Ah, well, you must do it as you can!" It is a question of degree, a matter of delicacy. If there are exact sciences, there are also exact arts, and the grammar of painting is so much more definite that it makes the difference.

I ought to add, however, that if Mr. Besant says at the beginning of his essay that the "laws of fiction may be laid down and taught with as much precision and exactness as the laws of harmony, perspective, and proportion," he mitigates what might appear to be an extravagance by applying his remark to "general" laws, and by expressing most of these rules in a manner with which it would certainly be unaccommodating to disagree. That the novelist must write from his experience, that his "characters must be real and such as might be met with in actual life"; that "a young lady brought up in a quiet country village should avoid descriptions of garrison life," and "a writer whose friends and personal experiences belong to the lower middle-class should carefully avoid introducing his characters into society"; that one should enter one's notes in a common-place book; that one's figures should be clear in outline; that making them clear by some trick of speech or of carriage is a bad method, and "describing them at length" is a worse one; that English Fiction should have a "conscious moral purpose"; that "it is almost impossible to estimate too highly the value of careful workman-ship — that is, of style"; that "the most important point of all is the story," that "the story is everything": these are principles with most of which it is surely impossible not to sympathize. That remark about the lower middle-class writer and his knowing his place is perhaps rather chilling; but for the rest I should find it difficult to dissent from any one of these recommenda-tions. At the same time, I should find it difficult positively to assent to them, with the exception, perhaps, of the injunction as to entering one's notes in a common-place book. They scarcely seem to me to have the quality that Mr. Besant attributes to the rules of the novelist — the "precision and exactness" of "the laws of harmony, perspective, and proportion." They are suggestive, they are even inspiring, but they are not exact, though they are doubtless as much so as the case admits of: which is a proof of that liberty of in-terpretation for which I just contended. For the value of these different injunctions — so beautiful and so vague — is wholly in the meaning one attaches to them. The characters, the situation, which strike one as real will be those that touch and interest one most, but the measure of reality is very difficult to fix.

. . . . Experience is never limited, and it is never complete; it is an immense sensibility, a kind of huge spider-web of the finest silken threads suspended in the chamber of consciousness, and catching every air-borne particle in its tissue. It is the very atmosphere of the mind; and when the mind is imaginative — much more when it happens to be that of a man of genius — it takes to itself the faintest hints of life, it converts the very pulses of the air into revelations. The young lady living in a village has only to be a damsel upon whom nothing is lost to make it quite unfair (as it seems to me) to declare to her that she shall have nothing to say about the military. Greater miracles have been seen than that, imagination assisting, she should speak the truth about some of these gentlemen. I remember an English novelist, a woman of genius,[1] telling me that she was much commended for the impression she had managed to give in one of her tales of the nature and way of life of the French Protestant youth. She had been asked where she learned so much about this recondite being, she had been congratulated on her peculiar opportunities. These opportunities consisted in her having once, in Paris, as she ascended a staircase, passed an open door where, in the household of a *pasteur*, some of the young Protestants were seated at table round a finished meal. The glimpse made a picture; it lasted only a moment, but that moment was experience. She had got her direct personal impression, and she turned out her type. She knew what youth was, and what Protestantism; she also had the advantage of having seen what it was to be French, so that she converted these ideas into a concrete image and produced a reality. Above all, however, she was blessed with the faculty which when you give it an inch takes an ell, and which for the artist is a much greater source of strength than any accident of residence or of place in the social scale. The power to guess the unseen from the seen, to trace the implication of things, to judge the whole piece by the pattern, the condition of feeling life in general so completely that you are well on your way to knowing any particular corner of it — this cluster of gifts may almost be said to constitute experience, and they occur in country and in town, and in the most differing stages of education. If experience consists of impressions, it may be said that impressions *are* experience, just as (have we not seen it?) they are the very air we breathe. Therefore, if I should certainly say to a novice, "Write from experience and experience only," I should feel that this was rather a tantalizing monition if I were not careful immediately to add, "Try to be one of the people on whom nothing is lost!"

I am far from intending by this to minimize the importance of exactness — of truth of detail. One can speak best from one's own taste, and I may therefore venture to say that the air of reality (solidity of specification) seems to me to be the supreme virtue of a novel — the merit on which all its other merits (including that conscious moral purpose of which Mr. Besant speaks) helplessly and submissively depend. If it be not there they are all as nothing, and if these be there, they owe their effect to the success with which the author has produced the illusion of life. The cultivation of this success, the study of this exquisite process, form, to my taste, the beginning and the end of the art of the novelist. . . . That his characters "must be clear in outline," as Mr. Besant says — he feels that down to his boots; but how he shall make them so is a secret between his good angel and himself. It would be absurdly simple if he could be taught that a great deal of "description" would make them so, or that on the contrary the absence of description and the cultivation of dialogue, or the absence of dialogue and the multiplication of "incident," would rescue him from his difficulties. Nothing, for instance, is more possible than that he be of a turn of mind for which this odd, literal opposition of description and dialogue, incident and description, has little meaning and light. People often talk of these things as if they had a kind of internecine distinctness, instead of melting into each other at every breath, and being intimately associated parts of one general effort of expression. I cannot imagine composition existing in a series of blocks, nor conceive, in any novel worth discussing at all, of a passage of description that is not in its intention narrative, a passage of dialogue that is not in its intention descriptive, a touch of truth of any sort that does not partake of the nature of incident, or an incident that derives its interest from any other source than the general and only source of the success of a work of art — that of being illustrative. A novel is a living thing, all one and continuous, like any other organism, and in proportion as it lives will it be found, I think, that in each of the parts there is something of each of the other parts. The critic who over the close texture of a finished work shall pretend to trace a geography of items will mark some frontiers as artificial, I fear, as any that have been known to history. There is an old-fashioned distinction between the novel of character and the novel of incident which must have cost many a smile to the intending fabulist who was keen about his work. It appears to me as little to the point as the equally celebrated distinction between the novel and the romance — to answer as little to any reality. There are bad novels and good novels, as there are bad pictures and good pictures; but that is the only distinction in which I see any meaning, and I can as little imagine speaking of a novel of character as I can imagine speaking of a picture of character. When one says picture one says of character, when one says novel one says of incident, and the terms may be transposed at will. What is character but the determination of incident? What is incident but the illustration of character? What is either a picture or a novel that is *not* of character? What else do we seek in it and find in it? It is an incident for a woman to stand up with her hand resting on a table and look out at you in a certain way; or if it be not an incident I think it will be hard to say what it is. At the same time it is an expression of character. If you say you don't see it (character in *that — allons donc!*), this is exactly what the artist who has reasons of his own for thinking he *does* see it undertakes to show you. When a young man makes up his mind that he has not faith enough after all to enter the church as he intended, that is an incident, though you may not hurry to the end of the chapter to see whether perhaps he doesn't change once more. I do not say that these are extraordinary or startling incidents. I do not pretend to estimate the degree of interest proceeding from them, for this will depend upon the skill of the painter. It sounds almost puerile to say that some incidents are intrinsically much more important than others, and I need not take this precaution after having professed my sympathy for the major ones in remarking that the only classification of the novel that I can understand is into that which has life and that which has it not.

The novel and the romance, the novel of incident and that of character — these clumsy separations appear to me to have been made by critics and readers for their own convenience, and to help them out of some of their occasional queer predicaments, but to have little reality or interest for the producer, from whose point of view it is of course that we are attempting to consider the art of fiction. . . . If we pretend to respect the artist at all, we must allow him his freedom of choice, in the face, in particular cases, of innumerable presumptions that the choice will not fructify. Art derives a considerable part of its beneficial exercise from flying in the face of presumptions, and some of the most interesting experiments of which it is capable are hidden in the bosom of common things. Gustave Flaubert has written a story[2] about the devotion of a servant-girl to a parrot, and the production, highly finished as it is, cannot on the whole be called a success. We are perfectly free to find it flat, but I think it might have been interesting; and I, for my part, am extremely glad he should have written it; it is a contribution to our knowledge of what can be done — or what cannot. Ivan Turgenev has written a tale about a deaf and dumb serf and a lap-dog[3] and the thing is touching, loving, a little masterpiece. He struck the note of life where Gustave Flaubert missed it — he flew in the face of a presumption and achieved a victory.

So that it comes back very quickly, as I have said, to the liking: in spite of M. Zola, who reasons less powerfully than he represents, and who will not reconcile himself to this absoluteness of taste, thinking that there are certain things that people ought to like, and that they can be made to like. I am quite at a loss to imagine anything (at any rate in this manner of fiction) that people *ought* to like or dislike. Selection will be sure to take care of itself, for it has a constant motive behind it. That motive is simply experience. As people feel life, so they will feel the art that is most closely related to it. This closeness of relation is what we should never forget in talking of the effort of the novel. Many people speak of it as a factitious, artificial form, a product of ingenuity, the business of which is to alter and arrange the things that surround us, to translate them into conventional, traditional moulds. This, however, is a view of the matter which carries us but a very short way, condemns the art to an eternal repetition of a few familiar *clichés*, cuts short its development, and leads us straight up to a dead wall. Catching the very note and trick, the strange irregular rhythm of life, that is the attempt whose strenuous force keeps Fiction upon her feet. In proportion as in what she offers us we see life *without* rearrangement do we feel that we are touching the truth; in proportion as we see it *with* rearrangement do we feel that we are being put off with a substitute, a compromise and convention. It is not uncommon to hear an extraordinary assurance of remark in regard to this matter of rearranging, which is often spoken of as if it were the last word of art. Mr. Besant seems to me in danger of falling into the great error with his rather unguarded talk about "selection." Art is essentially selection, but it is a selection whose main care is to be typical, to be inclusive. . . .

Mr. Besant has some remarks on the question of "the story" which I shall not attempt to criticize, though they seem to me to contain a singular ambiguity, because I do not think I understand them. I cannot see what is meant by talking as if there were a part of a novel which is the story and part of it which for mystical reasons is not — unless indeed the distinction be made in a sense in which it is difficult to suppose that any one should attempt to convey anything. "The story," if it represents anything, represents the subject, the idea, the *donnée* of the novel; and there is surely no "school" — Mr. Besant speaks of a school — which urges that a novel should be all treatment and no subject. There must assuredly be something to treat; every school is intimately conscious of that. This sense of the story being the idea, the starting-point, of the novel, is the only one that I see in which it can be spoken of as something different from its organic whole; and since in proportion as the work is successful the idea permeates and penetrates it, informs and animates it, so that every word and every punctuation-point contribute directly to the expression, in that proportion do we lose our sense of the story being a blade which may be drawn more or less out of its sheath. The story and the novel, the idea and the form, are the needle and thread, and I never heard of a guild of tailors who recommended the use of the thread without the needle, or the needle without the thread. . . .

There is one point at which the moral sense and the artistic sense lie very near together; that is in the light of the very obvious truth that the deepest quality of a work of art will always be the quality of the mind of the producer. In proportion as that intelligence is fine will the novel, the picture, the statue partake of the substance of beauty and truth. To be constituted of such elements is, to my vision, to have purpose enough. No good novel will ever proceed from a superficial mind; that seems to me an axiom which, for the artist in fiction, will cover all needful moral ground: If the youthful aspirant take it to heart it will illuminate for him many of the mysteries of "purpose." There are many other useful things that might be said to him, but I have come to the end of my article, and can only touch them as I pass. The critic in the *Pall Mall Gazette*, whom I have already quoted, draws attention to the danger, in speaking of the art of fiction, of generalizing. The danger that he has in mind is rather, I imagine, that of particularizing, for there are some comprehensive remarks which, in addition to those embodied in Mr. Besant's suggestive lecture, might without fear of misleading him be addressed to the ingenuous student. I should remind him first of the magnificence of the form that is open to him, which offers to sight so few restrictions and such innumerable opportunities. The other arts, in comparison, appear confined and hampered; the various conditions under which they are exercised are so rigid and definite. But the only condition that I can think of attaching to the composition of the novel is, as I have already said, that it be sincere. This freedom is a splendid privilege, and the first lesson of the young novelist is to learn to be worthy of it.

Notes

1. Probably Anne Thackeray, Lady Ritchie, daughter of Thackeray, whose first novel *The Story of Elizabeth* corresponds to James's description.
2. *Un coeur simple.*
3. *Mumu.*

Mr. Bennett and Mrs. Brown · VIRGINIA WOOLF

It seems to me possible, perhaps desirable, that I may be the only person in this room who has committed the folly of writing, trying to write, or failing to write, a novel. And when I asked myself, as your invitation to speak to you about modern fiction made me ask myself, what demon whispered in my ear and urged me to my doom, a little figure rose before me — the figure of a man, or of a woman, who said, "My name is Brown. Catch me if you can."

Most novelists have the same experience. Some Brown, Smith, or Jones comes before them and says in the most seductive and charming way in the world, "Come and catch me if you can." And so, led on by this will-o'-the-wisp, they flounder through volume after volume, spending the best years of their lives in the pursuit, and receiving for the most part very little cash in exchange. Few catch the phantom; most have to be content with a scrap of her dress or a wisp of her hair.

My belief that men and women write novels because they are lured on to create some character which has thus imposed itself upon them has the sanction of Mr. Arnold Bennett. In an article from which I will quote he says, "The foundation of good fiction is character-creating and nothing else. . . . Style counts; plot counts; originality of outlook counts. But none of these counts anything like so much as the convincingness of the characters. If the characters are real the novel will have a chance; if they are not, oblivion will be its portion. . . . " And he goes on to draw the conclusion that we have no young novelists of first-rate importance at the present moment, because they are unable to create characters that are real, true, and convincing.

These are the questions that I want with greater boldness than discretion to discuss tonight. I want to make out what we mean when we talk about "character" in fiction; to say something about the question of reality which Mr. Bennett raises; and to suggest some reasons why the younger novelists fail to create characters, if, as Mr. Bennett asserts, it is true that fail they do. This will lead me, I am well aware, to make some very sweeping and some very vague assertions. For the question is an extremely difficult one. Think how little we know about character — think how little we know about art. But, to make a clearance before I begin, I will suggest that we range Edwardians and Georgians into two camps; Mr. Wells, Mr. Bennett, and Mr. Galsworthy I will call the Edwardians; Mr. Forster, Mr. Lawrence, Mr. Strachey, Mr. Joyce, and Mr. Eliot I will call the Georgians. And if I speak in the first person, with intolerable egotism, I will ask you to excuse me. I do not want to attribute to the world at large the opinions of one solitary, ill-informed, and misguided individual.

My first assertion is one that I think you will grant — that every one in this room is a judge of character. Indeed it would be impossible to live for a year without disaster unless one practised character-reading and had some skill in the art. Our marriages, our friendships depend on it; our business largely depends on it; every day questions arise which can only be solved by its help. And now I will hazard a second assertion, which is more disputable perhaps, to the effect that on or about December, 1910, human character changed.

I am not saying that one went out, as one might into a garden, and there saw that a rose had flowered, or that a hen had laid an egg. The change was not sudden and definite like that. But a change there was, nevertheless; and, since one must be arbitrary, let us date it about the year 1910. The first signs of it are recorded in the books of Samuel Butler, in *The Way of All Flesh* in particular; the plays of Bernard Shaw continue to record it. In life one can see the change, if I may use a homely illustration, in the character of one's cook. The Victorian cook lived like a leviathan in the lower depths, formidable, silent, obscure, inscrutable; the Georgian cook is a creature of sunshine and fresh air; in and out of the drawing-room, now to borrow the *Daily Herald*, now to ask advice about a hat. Do you ask for more solemn instances of the power of the human race to change? Read the *Agamemnon*, and see whether, in process of time, your sympathies are not almost entirely with Clytemnestra. Or consider the married life of the Carlyles and bewail the waste, the futility, for him and for her, of the horrible domestic tradition which made it seemly for a woman of genius to spend her time chasing beetles, scouring saucepans, instead of writing books. All human relations have shifted — those between masters and servants, husbands and wives, parents and children. And when human relations change there is at the same time a change in religion, conduct, politics, and literature. Let us agree to place one of these changes about the year 1910.

I have said that people have to acquire a good deal of skill in character-reading if they are to live a single year of life without disaster. But it is the art of the young. In middle age and in old age the art is practised mostly for its uses, and friendships and other adventures and experiments in the art of reading character are seldom made. But novelists differ from the rest of the world because they do not cease to be interested in character when they have learnt enough about it for practical purposes. They go a step further, they feel that there is something permanently interesting in character in itself. When all the practical business of life has been discharged, there is something about people which continues to seem to them of overwhelming importance, in spite of the fact that it has no bearing whatever upon their happiness, comfort, or income. The study of character becomes to them an absorbing pursuit; to impart character an obsession. And this I find it very difficult to explain: what novelists mean when they talk about character, what the impulse is that urges them so powerfully every now and then to embody their view in writing.

So, if you will allow me, instead of analysing and abstracting, I will tell you a simple story which, however pointless, has the merit of being true, of a journey from Richmond to Waterloo, in the hope that I may show you what I mean by character in itself; that you may realize the different aspects it can wear; and the hideous perils that beset you directly you try to describe it in words.

One night some weeks ago, then, I was late for the train and jumped into the first carriage I came to. As I sat down I had the strange and uncomfortable feeling that I was interrupting a conversation between two people who were already sitting there. Not that they were young or happy. Far from it. They were both elderly, the woman over sixty, the man well over forty. They were sitting opposite each other, and the man, who had been leaning over and talking emphatically to judge by his attitude and the flush on his face, sat back and became silent. I had disturbed him, and he was annoyed. The elderly lady, however, whom I will call Mrs. Brown, seemed rather relieved. She was one of those clean, threadbare old ladies whose extreme tidiness — everything buttoned, fastened, tied together, mended and brushed up — suggests more extreme poverty than rags and dirt. There was something pinched about her — a look of suffering, of apprehension, and, in addition, she was extremely small. Her feet, in their clean little boots, scarcely touched the floor. I felt that she had nobody to support her; that she had to make up her mind for herself; that, having been deserted, or left a widow, years ago, she had led an anxious, harried life, bringing up an only son, perhaps, who, as likely as not, was by this time beginning to go to the bad. All this shot through my mind as I sat down, being uncomfortable, like most people, at travelling with fellow passengers unless I have somehow or other accounted for them. Then I looked at the man. He was no relation of Mrs. Brown's I felt sure; he was of a bigger, burlier, less refined type. He was a man of business I imagined, very likely a respectable corn-chandler from the North, dressed in good blue serge with a pocket-knife and a silk handkerchief, and a stout leather bag. Obviously, however, he had an unpleasant business to settle with Mrs. Brown; a secret, perhaps sinister business, which they did not intend to discuss in my presence.

"Yes, the Crofts have had very bad luck with their servants," Mr. Smith (as I will call him) said in a considering way, going back to some earlier topic, with a view to keeping up appearances.

"Ah, poor people," said Mrs. Brown, a trifle condescendingly. "My grandmother had a maid who came when she was fifteen and stayed till she was eighty" (this was said with a kind of hurt and aggressive pride to impress us both perhaps).

"One doesn't come across that sort of thing nowadays," said Mr. Smith in conciliatory tones.

Then they were silent.

"It's odd they don't start a golf club there — I should have thought one of the young fellows would," said Mr. Smith, for the silence obviously made him uneasy.

Mrs. Brown hardly took the trouble to answer.

"What changes they're making in this part of the world," said Mr. Smith, looking out of the window, and looking furtively at me as he did so.

It was plain, from Mrs. Brown's silence, from the uneasy affability with which Mr. Smith spoke, that he had some power over her which he was exerting disagreeably. It might have been her son's downfall, or some painful episode in her past life, or her daughter's. Perhaps she was going to London to sign some document to make over some property. Obviously against her will she was in Mr. Smith's hands. I was beginning to feel a great deal of pity for her, when she said, suddenly and inconsequently:

"Can you tell me if an oak-tree dies when the leaves have been eaten for two years in succession by caterpillars?"

She spoke quite brightly, and rather precisely, in a cultivated, inquisitive voice.

Mr. Smith was startled, but relieved to have a safe topic of conversation given him. He told her a great deal very quickly about plagues of insects. He told her that he had a brother who kept a fruit farm in Kent. He told her what fruit farmers do every year in Kent, and so on, and so on. While he talked a very odd thing happened. Mrs. Brown took out her little white handkerchief and began to dab her eyes. She was crying. But she went on listening quite composedly to what he was saying, and he went on talking, a little louder, a little angrily, as if he had seen her cry often before; as if it were a painful habit. At last it got on his nerves. He stopped abruptly, looked out of the window, then leant towards her as he had been doing when I got in, and said in a bullying, menacing way, as if he would not stand any more nonsense:

"So about that matter we were discussing. It'll be all right? George will be there on Tuesday?"

"We shan't be late," said Mrs. Brown, gathering herself together with superb dignity.

Mr. Smith said nothing. He got up, buttoned his coat, reached his bag down, and jumped out of the train before it had stopped at Clapham Junction. He had got what he wanted, but he was ashamed of himself; he was glad to get out of the old lady's sight.

Mrs. Brown and I were left alone together. She sat in her corner opposite, very clean, very small, rather queer, and suffering intensely. The impression she made was overwhelming. It came pouring out like a draught, like a smell of burning. What was it composed of — that overwhelming and peculiar impression? Myriads of irrelevant and incongruous ideas crowd into one's head on such occasions; one sees the person, one sees Mrs. Brown, in the centre of all sorts of different scenes. I thought of her in a seaside house, among queer ornaments: sea-urchins, models of ships in glass cases. Her husband's medals were on the mantelpiece. She popped in and out of the room, perching on the edges of chairs, picking meals out of saucers, indulging in long, silent stares. The caterpillars and the oak-trees seemed to imply all that. And then, into this fantastic and secluded life, in broke Mr. Smith. I saw him blowing in, so to speak, on a windy day. He banged, he slammed. His dripping umbrella made a pool in the hall. They sat closeted together.

And then Mrs. Brown faced the dreadful revelation. She took her heroic decision. Early, before dawn, she packed her bag and carried it herself to the station. She would not let Smith touch it. She was wounded in her pride, unmoored from her anchorage; she came of gentlefolks who kept servants — but details could wait. The important thing was to realize her character, to steep oneself in her atmosphere. I had no time to explain why I felt it somewhat tragic, heroic, yet with a dash of the flighty and fantastic, before the train stopped, and I watched her disappear, carrying her bag, into the vast blazing station. She looked very small, very tenacious; at once very frail and very heroic. And I have never seen her again, and I shall never know what became of her.

The story ends without any point to it. But I have not told you this anecdote to illustrate either my own ingenuity or the pleasure of travelling from Richmond to Waterloo. What I want you to see in it is this. Here is a character imposing itself upon another person. Here is Mrs. Brown making someone begin almost automatically to write a novel about her. I believe that all novels begin with an old lady in the corner opposite. I believe that all novels, that is to say, deal with character, and that it is to express character — not to preach doctrines, sing songs, or celebrate the glories of the British Empire, that the form of the novel, so clumsy, verbose, and undramatic, so rich, elastic, and alive, has been evolved. To express character, I have said; but you will at once reflect that the very widest interpretation can be put upon those words. For example, old Mrs. Brown's character will strike you very differently according to the age and country in which you happen to be born. It would be easy enough to write three different versions of that incident in the train, an English, a French, and a Russian. The English writer would make the old lady into a "character"; he would bring out her oddities and mannerisms; her buttons and wrinkles; her ribbons and warts. Her personality would dominate the book. A French writer would rub out all that; he would sacrifice the individual Mrs. Brown to give a more general view of human nature; to make a more abstract, proportioned, and harmonious whole. The Russian would pierce through the flesh; would reveal the soul — the soul alone, wandering out into the Waterloo Road, asking of life some tremendous question which would sound on and on in our ears after the book was finished. And then besides age and country there is the writer's temperament to be considered. You see one thing in character, and I another. You say it means this, and I that. And when it comes to writing each makes a further selection on principles of his own. Thus Mrs. Brown can be treated in an infinite variety of ways, according to the age, country, and temperament of the writer.

But now I must recall what Mr. Arnold Bennett says. He says that it is only if the characters are real that the novel has any chance of surviving. Otherwise, die it must. But, I ask myself, what is reality? And who are the judges of reality? A character may be real to Mr. Bennett and quite unreal to me. For instance, in this article he says that Dr. Watson in *Sherlock Holmes* is real to him: to me Dr. Watson is a sack stuffed with straw, a dummy, a figure of fun. And so it is with character after character — in book after book. There is nothing that people differ about more than the reality of characters, especially in contemporary books. But if you take a larger view I think that Mr. Bennett is perfectly right. If, that is, you think of the novels which seem to you great novels — *War and Peace, Vanity Fair, Tristram Shandy, Madame Bovary, Pride and Prejudice, The Mayor of Casterbridge, Villette* — if you think of these books, you do at once think of some character who has seemed to you so real (I do not by that mean so lifelike) that it has the power to make you think not merely of it itself, but of all sorts of things through its eyes — of religion, of love, of war, of peace, of family life, of balls in country towns, of sunsets, moonrises, the immortality of the soul. There is hardly any subject of human experience that is left out of *War and Peace* it seems to me. And in all these novels all these great novelists have brought us to see whatever they wish us to see through some character. Otherwise, they would not be novelists; but poets, historians, or pamphleteers.

But now let us examine what Mr. Bennett went on to say — he said that there was no great novelist among the Georgian writers because they cannot create characters who are real, true, and convincing. And there I cannot agree. There are reasons, excuses, possibilities which I think put a different colour upon the case. It seems so to me at least, but I am well aware that this is a matter about which I am likely to be prejudiced, sanguine, and nearsighted. I will put my view before you in the hope that you will make it impartial, judicial, and broad-minded. Why, then, is it so hard for novelists at present to create characters which seem real, not only to Mr. Bennett, but to the world at large? Why, when October comes round, do the publishers always fail to supply us with a masterpiece?

Surely one reason is that the men and women who began writing novels in 1910 or thereabouts had this great difficulty to face — that there was no English novelist living from whom they could learn their business. Mr. Conrad is a Pole; which sets him apart, and makes him, however admirable, not very helpful. Mr. Hardy has written no novel since 1895. The most prominent and successful novelists in the year 1910 were, I suppose, Mr. Wells, Mr. Bennett, and Mr. Galsworthy. Now it seems to me that to go to these men and ask them to teach you how to write a novel — how to create characters that are real — is precisely like going to a boot maker and asking him to teach you how to make a watch. Do not let me give you the impression that I do not admire and enjoy their books. They seem to me of great value, and indeed of great necessity. There are seasons when it is more important to have boots than to have watches. To drop metaphor, I think that after the creative activity of the Victorian age it was quite necessary, not only for literature but for life, that someone should write the books that Mr. Wells, Mr. Bennett, and Mr. Galsworthy have written. Yet what odd books they are! Sometimes I wonder if we are right to call them books at all. For they leave one with so strange a feeling of incompleteness and dissatisfaction. In order to complete them it seems necessary to do something — to join a society, or, more desperately, to write a cheque. That done, the restlessness is laid, the book finished; it can be put upon the shelf, and need never be read again. But with the work of other novelists it is different. *Tristram Shandy* or *Pride and Prejudice* is complete in itself; it is self-contained; it leaves one with no desire to do anything, except indeed to read the book again, and to understand it better. The difference perhaps is that both Sterne and Jane Austen were interested in things in themselves; in character, in itself; in the book in itself. Therefore everything was inside the book, nothing outside. But the Edwardians were never interested in character in itself; or in the book in itself. They were interested in something outside. Their books, then, were incomplete as books, and required that the reader should finish them, actively and practically, for himself.

. . . . With all his powers of observation, which are marvellous, with all his sympathy and humanity, which are great, Mr. Bennett has never once looked at Mrs. Brown in her corner. There she sits in the corner of the carriage — that carriage which is travelling, not from Richmond to Waterloo, but from one age of English literature to the next, for Mrs. Brown is eternal, Mrs. Brown is human nature, Mrs. Brown changes only on the surface, it is the novelists who get in and out — there she sits and not one of the Edwardian writers has so much as looked at her. They have looked very powerfully, searchingly, and sympathetically out of the window; at factories, at Utopias, even at the decoration and upholstery of the carriage; but never at her, never at life, never at human nature. And so they have developed a technique of novel-writing which suits their purpose; they have made tools and established conventions which do their business. But those tools are not our tools, and that business is not our business. For us those conventions are ruin, those tools are death.

You may well complain of the vagueness of my language. What is a convention, a tool, you may ask, and what do you mean by saying that Mr. Bennett's and Mr. Wells's and Mr. Galsworthy's conventions are the wrong conventions for the Georgians? The question is difficult: I will attempt a short cut. A convention in writing is not much different from a convention in manners. Both in life and in literature it is necessary to have some means of bridging the gulf between the hostess and her unknown guest on the one hand, the writer and his unknown reader on the other. The hostess bethinks her of the weather, for generations of hostesses have established the fact that this is a subject of universal interest in which we all believe. She begins by saying that we are having a wretched May, and, having thus got into touch with her unknown guest, proceeds to matters of greater interest. So it is in literature. The writer must get into touch with his reader by putting before him something which he recognizes, which therefore stimulates his imagination, and makes him willing to co-operate in the far more difficult business of intimacy. And it is of the highest importance that this common meeting-place should be reached easily, almost instinctively, in the dark, with one's eyes shut. Here is Mr. Bennett making use of this common ground in the passage which I have quoted. The problem before him was to make us believe in the reality of Hilda Lessways. So he began, being an Edwardian, by describing accurately and minutely the sort of house Hilda lived in, and the sort of house she saw from the window. House property was the common ground from which the Edwardians found it easy to proceed to intimacy. Indirect as it seems to us, the convention worked admirably, and thousands of Hilda Lessways were launched upon the world by this means. For that age and generation, the convention was a good one.

But now, if you will allow me to pull my own anecdote to pieces, you will see how keenly I felt the lack of a convention, and how serious a matter it is when the tools of one generation are useless for the next. The incident had made a great impression on me. But how was I to transmit it to you? All I could do was to report as accurately as I could what was said, to describe in detail what was worn, to say, despairingly, that all sorts of scenes rushed into my mind, to proceed to tumble them out pell-mell, and to describe this vivid, this overmastering impression by likening it to a draught or a smell of burning. To tell you the truth, I was also strongly tempted to manufacture a three-volume novel about the old lady's son, and his adventures crossing the Atlantic, and her daughter, and how she kept a milliner's shop in Westminister, the past life of Smith himself, and his house at Sheffield, though such stories seem to me the most dreary, irrelevant, and humbugging affairs in the world.

But if I had done that I should have escaped the appalling effort of saying what I meant. And to have got at what I meant I should have had to go back and back and back; to experiment with one thing and another; to try this sentence and that, referring each word to my vision, matching it as exactly as possible, and knowing that somehow I had to find a common ground between us, a convention which would not seem to you too odd, unreal, and far-fetched to believe in. I admit that I shirked that arduous undertaking. I let my Mrs. Brown slip through my fingers. I have told you nothing whatever about her. But that is partly the great Edwardians' fault. I asked them — they are my elders and betters — How shall I begin to describe this woman's character? And they said: "Begin by saying that her father kept a shop in Harrogate. Ascertain the rent. Ascertain the wages of shop assistants in the year 1878. Discover what her mother died of. Describe cancer. Describe calico. Describe—" But I cried: "Stop! Stop!" And I regret to say that I threw that ugly, that clumsy, that incongruous tool out of the window, for I knew that if I began describing the cancer and the calico, my Mrs. Brown, that vision to which I cling though I know no way of imparting it to you, would have been dulled and tarnished and vanished for ever.

That is what I mean by saying that the Edwardian tools are the wrong ones for us to use. They have laid an enormous stress upon the fabric of things. They have given us a house in the hope that we may be able to deduce the human beings who live there. To give them their due, they have made that house much better worth living in. But if you hold that novels are in the first place about people, and only in the second about the houses they live in, that is the wrong way to set about it. Therefore, you see, the Georgian writer had to begin by throwing away the method that was in use at the moment. He was left alone there facing Mrs. Brown without any method of conveying her to the reader. But that is inaccurate. A writer is never alone. There is always the public with him — if not on the same seat, at least in the compartment next door. Now the public is a strange travelling companion. In England it is a very suggestible and docile creature, which, once you get it to attend, will believe implicitly what it is told for a certain number of years. If you say to the public with sufficient conviction: "All women have tails, and all men humps," it will actually learn to see women with tails and men with humps, and will think it very revolutionary and probably improper if you say: "Nonsense. Monkeys have tails and camels humps. But men and women have brains, and they have hearts; they think and they feel," — that will seem to it a bad joke, and an improper one into the bargain.

In view of these facts — with these sounds in my ears and these fancies in my brain — I am not going to deny that Mr. Bennett has some reason when he complains that our Georgian writers are unable to make us believe that our characters are real. I am forced to agree that they do not pour out three immortal masterpieces with Victorian regularity every autumn. But, instead of being gloomy, I am sanguine. For this state of things is, I think, inevitable whenever from hoar old age or callow youth the convention ceases to be a means of communication between writer and reader, and becomes instead an obstacle and an impediment. At the present moment we are suffering, not from decay, but from having no code of manners which writers and readers accept as a prelude to the more exciting intercourse of friendship. The literary convention of the time is so artificial — you have to talk about the weather and nothing but the weather throughout the entire visit — that, naturally, the feeble are tempted to outrage, and the strong are led to destroy the very foundations and rules of literary society. Signs of this are everywhere apparent. Grammar is violated; syntax disintegrated; as a boy staying with an aunt for the week-end rolls in the geranium bed out of sheer desperation as the solemnities of the sabbath wear on. The more adult writers do not, of course, indulge in such wanton exhibitions of spleen. Their sincerity is desperate, and their courage tremendous; it is only that they do not know which to use, a fork or their fingers. Thus, if you read Mr. Joyce and Mr. Eliot you will be struck by the indecency of the one, and the obscurity of the other. Mr. Joyce's indecency in *Ulysses* seems to me the conscious and calculated indecency of a desperate man who feels that in order to breathe he must break the windows. At moments, when the window is broken, he is magnificent. But what a waste of energy! And, after all, how dull indecency is, when it is not the overflowing of a superabundant energy or savagery, but the determined and public-spirited act of a man who needs fresh air! Again, with the obscurity of Mr. Eliot. I think that Mr. Eliot has written some of the loveliest single lines in modern poetry. But how intolerant he is of the old usages and politenesses of society — respect for the weak, consideration for the dull! As I sun myself upon the intense and ravishing beauty of one of his lines, and reflect that I must make a dizzy and dangerous leap to the next, and so on from line to line, like an acrobat flying precariously from bar to bar, I cry out, I confess, for the old decorums, and envy the indolence of my ancestors who, instead of spinning madly through mid-air, dreamt quietly in the shade with a book. Again, in Mr. Strachey's books, *Eminent Victorians* and *Queen Victoria*, the effort and strain of writing against the grain and current of the times is visible too. It is much less visible, of course, for not only is he dealing with facts, which are stubborn things, but he has fabricated, chiefly from eighteenth-century material, a very discreet code of manners of his own, which allows him to sit at table with the highest in the land and to say a great many things under cover of that exquisite apparel which, had they gone naked, would have been chased by the men-servants from the room. Still, if you compare *Eminent Victorians* with some of Lord Macaulay's essays, though you will feel that Lord Macaulay is always wrong, and Mr. Strachey always right, you will also feel a body, a sweep, a richness in Lord Macaulay's essays which show that his age was behind him; all his strength went straight into his work; none was used for purposes of concealment or of conversion. But Mr. Strachey has had to open our eyes before he made us see; he has had to search out and sew together a very artful manner of speech; and the effort, beautifully though it is concealed, has robbed his work of some of the force that should have gone into it, and limited his scope.

For these reasons, then, we must reconcile ourselves to a season of failures and fragments. We must reflect that where so much strength is spent on finding a way of telling the truth, the truth itself is bound to reach us in rather an exhausted and chaotic condition. Ulysses, Queen Victoria, Mr. Prufrock—to give Mrs. Brown some of the names she has made famous lately—is a little pale and dishevelled by the time her rescuers reach her. And it is the sound of their axes that we hear—a vigorous and stimulating sound in my ears—unless of course you wish to sleep, when, in the bounty of his concern, Providence has provided a host of writers anxious and able to satisfy your needs.

Thus I have tried, at tedious length, I fear, to answer some of the questions which I began by asking. I have given an account of some of the difficulties which in my view beset the Georgian writer in all his forms. I have sought to excuse him. May I end by venturing to remind you of the duties and responsibilities that are yours as partners in this business of writing books, as companions in the railway carriage, as fellow travellers with Mrs. Brown? For she is just as visible to you who remain silent as to us who tell stories about her. In the course of your daily life this past week you have had far stranger and more interesting experiences than the one I have tried to describe. You have overheard scraps of talk that filled you with amazement. You have gone to bed at night bewildered by the complexity of your feelings. In one day thousands of ideas have coursed through your brains; thousands of emotions have met, collided, and disappeared in astonishing disorder. Nevertheless, you allow the writers to palm off upon you a version of all this, an image of Mrs. Brown, which has no likeness to that surprising apparition whatsoever. In your modesty you seem to consider that writers are different blood and bone from yourselves; that they know more of Mrs. Brown than you do. Never was there a more fatal mistake. It is this division between reader and writer, this humility on your part, these professional airs and graces on ours, that corrupt and emasculate the books which should be the healthy offspring of a close and equal alliance between us. Hence spring those sleek, smooth novels, those portentous and ridiculous biographies, that milk and watery criticism, those poems melodiously celebrating the innocence of roses and sheep which pass so plausibly for literature at the present time.

Your part is to insist that writers shall come down off their plinths and pedestals, and describe beautifully if possible, truthfully at any rate, our Mrs. Brown. You should insist that she is an old lady of unlimited capacity and infinite variety; capable of appearing in any place; wearing any dress; saying anything and doing heaven knows what. But the things she says and the things she does and her eyes and her nose and her speech and her silence have an overwhelming fascination, for she is, of course, the spirit we live by, life itself.

But do not expect just at present a complete and satisfactory presentment of her. Tolerate the spasmodic, the obscure, the fragmentary, the failure. Your help is invoked in a good cause. For I will make one final and surpassingly rash prediction — we are trembling on the verge of one of the great ages of English literature. But it can only be reached if we are determined never, never to desert Mrs. Brown.

3

Flat and Round Characters · E. M. FORSTER

We may divide characters into flat and round.

Flat characters were called "humorous" in the seventeenth century, and are sometimes called types, and sometimes caricatures. In their purest form, they are constructed round a single idea or quality: when there is more than one factor in them, we get the beginning of the curve towards the round. The really flat character can be expressed in one sentence such as "I never will desert Mr. Micawber." There is Mrs. Micawber—she says she won't desert Mr. Micawber, she doesn't, and there she is. Or: "I must conceal, even by subterfuges, the poverty of my master's house." There is Caleb Balderstone in *The Bride of Lammermoor.* He does not use the actual phrase, but it completely describes him; he has no existence outside it, no pleasures, none of the private lusts and aches that must complicate the most consistent of servitors. Whatever he does, wherever he goes, whatever lies he tells or plates he breaks, it is to conceal the poverty of his master's house. It is not his *idée fixe,* because there is nothing in him into which the idea can be fixed. He is the idea, and such life as he possesses radiates from its edges and from the scintillations it strikes when other elements in the novel impinge. Or take Proust. There are numerous flat characters in Proust, such as the Princess of Parma, or Legrandin. Each can be expressed in a single sentence, the Princess's sentence being, "I must be particularly careful to be kind." She does nothing except to be particularly careful, and those of the other characters who are more complex than herself easily see through the kindness, since it is only a by-product of the carefulness.

One great advantage of flat characters is that they are easily recognized whenever they come in—recognized by the reader's emotional eye, not by the visual eye, which merely notes the recurrence of a proper name. In Russian novels, where they so seldom occur, they would be a decided help. It is a convenience for an author when he can strike with his full force at once, and flat characters are very useful to him, since they never need re-introducing, never run away, have not to be watched for development, and provide their own atmosphere — little luminous disks of a pre-arranged size, pushed hither and thither like counters across the void or between the stars; most satisfactory.

A second advantage is that they are easily remembered by the reader afterwards. They remain in his mind as unalterable for the reason that they were not changed by circumstances; they moved through circumstances, which gives them in retrospect a comforting quality, and preserves them when the book that produced them may decay. The Countess in *Evan Harrington* furnishes a good little example here. Let us compare our memories of her with our memories of Becky Sharp. We do not remember what the Countess did or what she passed through. What is clear is her figure and the formula that surrounds it, namely, "Proud as we are of dear papa, we must conceal his memory." All her rich humour proceeds from this. She is a flat character. Becky is round. She, too, is on the make, but she cannot be summed up in a single phrase, and we remember her in connection with the great scenes through which she passed and as modified by those scenes — that is to say, we do not remember her so easily because she waxes and wanes and has facets like a human being. All of us, even the sophisticated, yearn for permanence, and to the unsophisticated permanence is the chief excuse for a work of art. We all want books to endure, to be refuges, and their inhabitants to be always the same, and flat characters tend to justify themselves on this account.

All the same, critics who have their eyes fixed severely upon daily life — as were our eyes last week — have very little patience with such renderings of human nature. Queen Victoria, they argue, cannot be summed up in a single sentence, so what excuse remains for Mrs. Micawber? One of our foremost writers, Mr. Norman Douglas, is a critic of this type, and the passage from him which I will quote puts the case against flat characters in a forcible fashion. The passage occurs in an open letter to D. H. Lawrence, with whom he is quarrelling: a doughty pair of combatants, the hardness of whose hitting makes the rest of us feel like a lot of ladies up in a pavilion. He complains that Lawrence, in a biography, has falsified the picture by employing "the novelist's touch," and he goes on to define what this is:

> It consists, I should say, in a failure to realize the complexities of the ordinary human mind; it selects for literary purposes two or three facets of a man or woman, generally the most spectacular, and therefore useful ingredients of their character and disregards all the others. Whatever fails to fit in with these specially chosen traits is eliminated — must be eliminated, for other-

wise the description would not hold water. Such and such are the data: everything incompatible with those data has to go by the board. It follows that the novelist's touch argues, often logically, from a wrong premise: it takes what it likes and leaves the rest. The facets may be correct as far as they go but there are too few of them: what the author says may be true and yet by no means the truth. That is the novelist's touch. It falsifies life.

Well, the novelist's touch as thus defined is, of course, bad in biography, for no human being is simple. But in a novel it has its place: a novel that is at all complex often requires flat people as well as round, and the outcome of their collisions parallels life more accurately than Mr. Douglas implies. The case of Dickens is significant. Dickens's people are nearly all flat (Pip and David Copperfield attempt roundness, but so diffidently that they seem more like bubbles than solids). Nearly every one can be summed up in a sentence, and yet there is this wonderful feeling of human depth. Probably the immense vitality of Dickens causes his characters to vibrate a little, so that they borrow his life and appear to lead one of their own. It is a conjuring trick; at any moment we may look at Mr. Pickwick edgeways and find him no thicker than a gramophone record. But we never get the sideway view. Mr. Pickwick is far too adroit and well-trained. He always has the air of weighing something, and when he is put into the cupboard of the young ladies' school he seems as heavy as Falstaff in the buck-basket at Windsor. Part of the genius of Dickens is that he does use types and caricatures, people whom we recognize the instant they re-enter, and yet achieves effects that are not mechanical and a vision of humanity that is not shallow. Those who dislike Dickens have an excellent case. He ought to be bad. He is actually one of our big writers, and his immense success with types suggests that there may be more in flatness than the severer critics admit.

Or take H. G. Wells. With the possible exceptions of Kipps and the aunt in *Tono Bungay*, all Wells's characters are as flat as a photograph. But the photographs are agitated with such vigour that we forget their complexities lie on the surface and would disappear if it were scratched or curled up. A Wells character cannot indeed be summed up in a single phrase; he is tethered much more to observation, he does not create types. Nevertheless his people seldom pulsate by their own strength. It is the deft and powerful hands of their maker that shake them and trick the reader into a sense of depth. Good but imperfect novelists, like Wells and Dickens, are very clever at transmitting force. The part of their novel that is alive galvanizes the part that is not, and causes the characters to jump about and speak in a convincing way. They are quite different from the perfect novelist who touches all his material directly, who seems to pass the creative finger down every sentence and into every word. Richardson, Defoe, Jane Austen, are perfect in this particular way; their work may not be great but their hands are always upon it; there is not the tiny interval between the touching of the button and the sound of the bell which occurs in novels where the characters are not under direct control.

For we must admit that flat people are not in themselves as big achievements as round ones, and also that they are best when they are comic. A serious or tragic flat character is apt to be a bore. Each time he enters crying "Revenge!" or "My heart bleeds for humanity!" or whatever his formula is, our hearts sink. One of the romances of a popular contemporary writer is constructed round a Sussex farmer who says, "I'll plough up that bit of gorse." There is the farmer, there is the gorse; he says he'll plough it up, he does plough it up, but it is not like saying "I'll never desert Mr. Micawber," because we are so bored by his consistency that we do not care whether he succeeds with the gorse or fails. If his formula were analysed and connected up with the rest of the human outfit, we should not be bored any longer, the formula would cease to be the man and become an obsession in the man; that is to say he would have turned from a flat farmer into a round one. It is only round people who are fit to perform tragically for any length of time and can move us to any feelings except humour and appropriateness.

So now let us desert these two-dimensional people, and by way of transition to the round, let us go to *Mansfield Park*, and look at Lady Bertram, sitting on her sofa with pug. Pug is flat, like most animals in fiction. He is once represented as straying into a rosebed in a cardboard kind of way, but that is all, and during most of the book his mistress seems to be cut out of the same simple material as her dog. Lady Bertram's formula is, "I am kindly, but must not be fatigued," and she functions out of it. But at the end there is a catastrophe. Her two daughters come to grief—to the worst grief known to Miss Austen's universe, far worse than the Napoleonic wars. Julia elopes; Maria, who is unhappily married, runs off with a lover. What is Lady Bertram's reaction? The sentence describing it is significant: "Lady Bertram did not think deeply, but, guided by Sir Thomas, she thought justly on all important points, and she saw therefore in all its enormity, what had happened, and neither endeavoured herself, nor required Fanny to advise her, to think little of guilt and infamy." These are strong words, and they used to worry me because I thought Jane Austen's moral sense was getting out of hand. She may, and of course does, deprecate guilt and infamy herself, and she duly causes all possible distress in the minds of Edmund and Fanny, but has she any right to agitate calm, consistent Lady Bertram? Is not it like giving pug three faces and setting him to guard the gates of Hell? Ought not her ladyship to remain on the sofa saying, "This is a dreadful and sadly exhausting business about Julia and Maria, but where is Fanny gone? I have dropped another stitch"?

I used to think this, through misunderstanding Jane Austen's method — exactly as Scott misunderstood it when he congratulated her for painting on a square of ivory. She is a miniaturist, but never two-dimensional. All her characters are round, or capable of rotundity. Even Miss Bates has a mind, even Elizabeth Eliot a heart, and Lady Bertram's moral fervour ceases to vex us when we realize this: the disk has suddenly extended and become a little globe. When the novel is closed, Lady Bertram goes back to the flat, it is true; the dominant impression she leaves can be summed up in a formula. But that is not how Jane Austen conceived her, and the freshness of her reappearances are due to this. Why do the characters in Jane Austen give us a slightly new pleasure each time they come in, as opposed to the merely repetitive pleasure that is caused by a character in Dickens? Why do they combine so well in a conversation, and draw one another out without seeming to do so, and never perform? The answer to this question can be put in several ways: that, unlike Dickens, she was a real artist, that she never stooped to caricature, etc. But the best reply is that her characters though smaller than his are more highly organized. They function all round, and even if her plot made greater demands on them than it does, they would still be adequate. Suppose that Louisa Musgrove had broken her neck on the Cobb. The description of her death would have been feeble and ladylike — physical violence is quite beyond Miss Austen's powers — but the survivors would have reacted properly as soon as the corpse was carried away, they would have brought into view new sides of their character, and though *Persuasion* would have been spoiled as a book, we should know more than we do about Captain Wentworth and Anne. All the Jane Austen characters are ready for an extended life, for a life which the scheme of her books seldom requires them to lead, and that is why they lead their actual lives so satisfactorily. Let us return to Lady Bertram and the crucial sentence. See how subtly it modulates from her formula into an area where the formula does not work. "Lady Bertram did not think deeply." Exactly: as per formula. "But guided by Sir Thomas she thought justly on all important points." Sir

Thomas' guidance, which is part of the formula, remains, but it pushes her ladyship towards an independent and undesired morality. "She saw therefore in all its enormity what had happened." This is the moral fortissimo — very strong but carefully introduced. And then follows a most artful decrescendo, by means of negatives. "She neither endeavoured herself, nor required Fanny to advise her, to think little of guilt or infamy." The formula is reappearing, because as a rule she does try to minimize trouble, and does require Fanny to advise her how to do this; indeed Fanny has done nothing else for the last ten years. The words, though they are negatived, remind us of this, her normal state is again in view, and she has in a single sentence been inflated into a round character and collapsed back into a flat one. How Jane Austen can write! In a few words she has extended Lady Bertram, and by so doing she has increased the probability of the elopements of Maria and Julia. I say probability because the elopements belong to the domain of violent physical action, and here, as already indicated, Jane Austen is feeble and ladylike. Except in her schoolgirl novels, she cannot stage a crash. Everything violent has to take place "off" — Louisa's accident and Marianne Dashwood's putrid throat are the nearest exceptions — and consequently all the comments on the elopement must be sincere and convincing, otherwise we should doubt whether it occurred. Lady Bertram helps us to believe that her daughters have run away, and they have to run away, or there would be no apotheosis for Fanny. It is a little point, and a little sentence, yet it shows us how delicately a great novelist can modulate into the round.

All through her works we find these characters, apparently so simple and flat, never needing reintroduction and yet never out of depth — Henry Tilney, Mr. Woodhouse, Charlotte Lucas. She may label her characters "Sense," "Pride," "Sensibility," "Prejudice," but they are not tethered to those qualities.

As for the round characters proper, they have already been defined by implication and no more need be said. All I need do is to give some examples of people in books who seem to me round so that the definition can be tested afterwards:

All the principal characters in *War and Peace*, all the Dostoevsky characters, and some of the Proust — for example, the old family servant, the Duchess of Guermantes, M. de Charlus, and Saint Loup; Madame Bovary — who, like Moll Flanders, has her book to herself, and can expand and secrete unchecked; some people in Thackeray — for instance, Becky and Beatrix; some in Fielding — Parson Adams, Tom Jones; and some in Charlotte Brontë, most particularly Lucy Snowe. (And many more — this is not a catalogue.) The test of a round character is whether it is capable of surprising in a convincing way. If it never surprises, it is flat. If it does not convince, it is a flat pretending to be round. It has the incalculability of life about it — life within the pages of a book. And by using it sometimes alone, more often in combination with the other kind, the novelist achieves his task of acclimatization and harmonizes the human race with the other aspects of his work.

4

Epic and Novel · M. M. BAKHTIN

The study of the novel as a genre is distinguished by peculiar difficulties. This is due to the unique nature of the object itself: the novel is the sole genre that continues to develop, that is as yet uncompleted. The forces that define it as a genre are at work before our very eyes: the birth and development of the novel as a genre takes place in the full light of the historical day. The generic skeleton of the novel is still far from having hardened, and we cannot foresee all its plastic possibilities.

We know other genres, as genres, in their completed aspect, that is, as more or less fixed pre-existing forms into which one may then pour artistic experience. The primordial process of their formation lies outside historically documented observation. We encounter the epic as a genre that has not only long since completed its development, but one that is already antiquated. With certain reservations we can say the same for the other major genres, even for tragedy. The life they have in history, the life with which we are familiar, is the life they have lived as already completed genres, with a hardened and no longer flexible skeleton. Each of them has developed its own canon that operates in literature as an authentic historical force.

All these genres, or in any case their defining features, are considerably older than written language and the book, and to the present day they retain their ancient oral and auditory characteristics. Of all the major genres only the novel is younger than writing and the book: it alone is organically receptive to new forms of mute perception, that is, to reading. But of critical importance here is the fact that the novel has no canon of its own, as do other genres; only individual examples of the novel are historically active, not a generic canon as such. Studying other genres is analogous to studying dead languages; studying the novel, on the other hand, is like studying languages that are not only alive, but still young.

This explains the extraordinary difficulty inherent in formulating a theory of the novel. For such a theory has at its heart an object of study completely different from that which theory treats in other genres. The novel is not merely one genre among other genres. Among genres long since completed and in part already dead, the novel is the only developing genre. It is the only genre that was born and nourished in a new era of world history and therefore it is deeply akin to that era, whereas the other major genres entered that era as already fixed forms, as an inheritance, and only now are they adapting themselves — some better, some worse — to the new conditions of their existence. Compared with them, the novel appears to be a creature from an alien species. It gets on poorly with other genres. It fights for its own hegemony in literature; wherever it triumphs, the other older genres go into decline. Significantly, the best book on the history of the ancient novel — that by Erwin Rohde[1] — does not so much recount the history of the novel as it does illustrate the process of disintegration that affected all major genres in antiquity.

The mutual interaction of genres within a single unified literary period is a problem of great interest and importance. In certain eras — the Greek classical period, the Golden Age of Roman literature, the neoclassical period — all genres in "high" literature (that is, the literature of ruling social groups) harmoniously reinforce each other to a significant extent; the whole of literature, conceived as a totality of genres, becomes an organic unity of the highest order. But it is characteristic of the novel that it never enters into this whole, it does not participate in any harmony of the genres. In these eras the novel has an unofficial existence, outside "high" literature. Only already completed genres, with fully formed and well-defined generic contours, can enter into such a literature as a hierarchically organized, organic whole. They can mutually delimit and mutually complement each other, while yet preserving their own generic natures. Each is a unit, and all units are interrelated by virtue of certain features of deep structure that they all have in common.

The great organic poetics of the past — those of Aristotle, Horace, Boileau — are permeated with a deep sense of the wholeness of literature and of the harmonious interaction of all genres contained within this whole. It is as if they literally hear this harmony of the genres. In this is their strength — the inimitable, all-embracing fullness and exhaustiveness of such poetics. And they all, as a consequence, ignore the novel. Scholarly poetics of the nineteenth century lack this integrity: they are eclectic, descriptive; their aim is not a living and organic fullness but rather an abstract and encyclopedic comprehensiveness. They do not concern themselves with the actual possibility of specific genres coexisting within the living whole of literature in a given era; they are concerned rather with their coexistence in a maximally complete anthology. Of course these poetics can no longer ignore the novel—they simply add it (albeit in a place of honor) to already existing genres (and thus it enters the roster as merely one genre among many; in literature conceived as a living whole, on the other hand, it would have to be included in a completely different way).

We have already said that the novel gets on poorly with other genres. There can be no talk of a harmony deriving from mutual limitation and complementariness. The novel parodies other genres (precisely in their role as genres); it exposes the conventionality of their forms and their language; it squeezes out some genres and incorporates others into its own peculiar structure, reformulating and reaccentuating them. Historians of literature sometimes tend to see in this merely the struggle of literary tendencies and schools. Such struggles of course exist, but they are peripheral phenomena and historically insignificant. Behind them one must be sensitive to the deeper and deeper and more truly historical struggle of genres, the establishment and growth of a generic skeleton of literature.

Of particular interest are those eras when the novel becomes the dominant genre. All literature is then caught up in the process of "becoming," and in a special kind of "generic criticism." This occurred several times in the Hellenic period, again during the late middle ages and the Renaissance, but with special force and clarity beginning in the second half of the eighteenth century. In an era when the novel reigns supreme, almost all the remaining genres are to a greater or lesser extent "novelized": drama (for example Ibsen, Hauptmann, the whole of Naturalist drama), epic poetry (for example, *Childe Harold* and especially Byron's *Don Juan*), even lyric poetry (as an extreme example, Heine's lyrical verse). Those genres that stubbornly preserve their old canonic nature begin to appear stylized. In general any strict adherence to a genre begins to feel like a stylization, a stylization taken to the point of parody, despite the artistic intent of the author. In an environment where the novel is the dominant genre, the conventional languages of strictly canonical genres begin to sound in new ways, which are quite different from the ways they sounded in those eras when the novel was *not* included in "high" literature.

Parodic stylizations of canonized genres and styles occupy an essential place in the novel. In the era of the novel's creative ascendency—and even more so in the periods of preparation preceding this era—literature was flooded with parodies and travesties of all the high genres (parodies precisely of genres, and not of individual authors or schools)—parodies that are the precursors, "companions" to the novel, in their own way studies for it. But it is characteristic that the novel does not permit any of these various individual manifestations of itself to stabilize. Throughout its entire history there is a consistent parodying or travestying of dominant or fashionable novels that attempt to become models for the genre: parodies on the chivalric romance of adventure (*Dit d'aventures*, the first such parody, belongs to the thirteenth century), on the Baroque novel, the pastoral novel (Sorel's *Le berger extravagant*),[2] the Sentimental novel (Fielding, and *The Second Grandison*[3] of Musäus) and so forth. This ability of the novel to criticize itself is a remarkable feature of this ever-developing genre.

What are the salient features of this novelization of other genres suggested by us above? They become more free and flexible, their language renews itself by incorporating extraliterary heteroglossia and the "novelistic" layers of literary language, they become dialogized, permeated with laughter, irony, humor, elements of self-parody and finally — this is the most important thing — the novel inserts into these other genres an indeterminacy, a certain semantic open-endedness, a living contact with unfinished, still-evolving contemporary reality (the open-ended present). As we will see below, all these phenomena are explained by the transposition of other genres into this new and peculiar zone for structuring artistic models (a zone of contact with the present in all its open-endedness), a zone that was first appropriated by the novel.

It is of course impossible to explain the phenomenon of novelization purely by reference to the direct and unmediated influence of the novel itself. Even where such influence can be precisely established and demonstrated, it is intimately interwoven with those direct changes in reality itself that also determine the novel and that condition its dominance in a given era. The novel is the only developing genre and therefore it reflects more deeply, more essentially, more sensitively and rapidly, reality itself in the process of its unfolding. Only that which is itself developing can comprehend development as a process. The novel has become the leading hero in the drama of literary development in our time precisely because it best of all reflects the tendencies of a new world still in the making; it is, after all, the only genre born of this new world and in total affinity with it. In many respects the novel has anticipated, and continues to anticipate, the future development of literature as a whole. In the process of becoming the dominant genre, the novel sparks the renovation of all other genres, it infects them with its spirit of process and inconclusiveness. It draws them ineluctably into its orbit precisely because this orbit coincides with the basic direction of the development of literature as a whole. In this lies the exceptional importance of the novel, as an object of study for the theory as well as the history of literature.

Unfortunately, historians of literature usually reduce this struggle between the novel and other already completed genres, all these aspects of novelization, to the actual real-life struggle among "schools" and "trends." A novelized poem, for example, they call a "romantic poem" (which of course it is) and believe that in so doing they have exhausted the subject. They do not see beneath the superficial hustle and bustle of literary process the major and crucial fates of literature and language, whose great heroes turn out to be first and foremost genres, and whose "trends" and "schools" are but second- or third-rank protagonists.

The utter inadequacy of literary theory is exposed when it is forced to deal with the novel. In the case of other genres literary theory works confidently and precisely, since there is a finished and already formed object, definite and clear. These genres preserve their rigidity and canonic quality in all classical eras of their development; variations from era to era, from trend to trend or school to school are peripheral and do not affect their ossified generic skeleton. Right up to the present day, in fact, theory dealing with these already completed genres can add almost nothing to Aristotle's formulations. Aristotle's poetics, although occasionally so deeply embedded as to be almost invisible, remains the stable foundation for the theory of genres. Everything works as long as there is no mention of the novel. But the existence of novelized genres already leads theory into a blind alley. Faced with the problem of the novel, genre theory must submit to a radical restructuring.

Thanks to the meticulous work of scholars, a huge amount of historical material has accumulated and many questions concerning the evolution of various types of novels have been clarified—but the problem of the novel genre as a whole has not yet found anything like a satisfactory principled resolution. The novel continues to be seen as one genre among many; attempts are made to distinguish it as an already completed genre from other already completed genres, to discover its internal canon—one that would function as a well-defined system of rigid generic factors. In the vast majority of cases, work on the novel is reduced to mere cataloging, a description of all variants on the novel—albeit as comprehensive as possible. But the results of these descriptions never succeed in giving us as much as a hint of comprehensive formula for the novel as a genre. In addition, the experts have not managed to isolate a single definite, stable characteristic of the novel—without adding a reservation, which immediately disqualifies it altogether as a generic characteristic.

Some examples of such "characteristics with reservations" would be: the novel is a multilayered genre (although there also exist magnificent single-layered novels); the novel is a precisely plotted and dynamic genre (although there also exist novels that push to its literary limits the art of pure description); the novel is a complicated genre (although novels are mass produced as pure and frivolous entertainment like no other genre); the novel is a love story (although the greatest examples of the European novel are utterly devoid of the love element); the novel is a prose genre (although there exist excellent novels in verse). One could of course mention a large number of additional "generic characteristics" for the novel similar to those given above, which are immediately annulled by some reservation inno-cently appended to them.

Of considerably more interest and consequence are those normative definitions of the novel offered by novelists themselves, who produce a specific novel and then declare it the only correct, necessary and authen-tic form of the novel. Such, for instance, is Rousseau's foreword to his *La nouvelle Héloïse*, Wieland's to his *Agathon*,[4] Wezel's to his *Tobias Knouts*;[5] in such a category belong the numerous declarations and statements of principle by the romantics on *Wilhelm Meister, Lucinde*, and other texts. Such statements are not attempts to incorporate all the possible variants of the novel into a single eclectic definition, but are themselves part and parcel of the living evolution of the novel as a genre. Often they deeply and faith-fully reflect the novel's struggle with other genres and with itself (with other dominant and fashionable variants of the novel) at a particular point in its development. They come closer to an understanding of the peculiar posi-tion of the novel in literature, a position that is not commensurate with that of other genres.

Especially significant in this connection is a series of statements that accompanied the emergence of a new novel-type in the eighteenth century. The series opens with Fielding's reflections on the novel and its hero in *Tom Jones*. It continues in Wieland's foreword to *Agathon*, and the most essential link in the series is Blankenburg's *Versuch über den Roman*.[6] By the end of this series we have, in fact, that theory of the novel later formulated by Hegel. In all these statements, each reflecting the novel in one of its critical stages (*Tom Jones, Agathon, Wilhelm Meister*), the following prerequisites for the novel are characteristic: (1) the novel should not be "poetic," as the word "poetic" is used in other genres of imaginative literature; (2) the hero of a novel should not be "heroic" in either the epic or the tragic sense of the word: he should combine in himself negative as well as positive features, low as well as lofty, ridiculous as well as serious; (3) the hero should not be portrayed as an already completed and unchanging person but as one who is evolving and developing, a person who learns from life; (4) the novel should become for the contemporary world what the epic was for the ancient world (an idea that Blankenburg expressed very precisely, and that was later repeated by Hegel).

All these positive prerequisites have their substantial and productive side — taken together, they constitute a criticism (from the novel's point of view) of other genres and of the relationship these genres bear to reality: their stilted heroizing, their narrow and unlifelike poeticalness, their monotony and abstractness, the prepackaged and unchanging nature of their heroes. We have here, in fact, a rigorous critique of the literariness and poeticalness inherent in other genres and also in the predecessors of the contemporary novel (the heroic Baroque novel and the Sentimental novels of Richardson). These statements are reinforced significantly by the practice of these novelists themselves. Here the novel — its texts as well as the theory connected with it — emerges consciously and unambiguously as a genre that is both critical and self-critical, one fated to revise the fundamental concepts of literariness and poeticalness dominant at the time. On the one hand, the contrast of novel with epic (and the novel's opposition to the epic) is but one moment in the criticism of other literary genres (in particular, a criticism of epic heroization); but on the other hand, this contrast aims to elevate the significance of the novel, making of it the dominant genre in contemporary literature.

The positive prerequisites mentioned above constitute one of the highpoints in the novel's coming to self-consciousness. They do not yet of course provide a theory of the novel. These statements are also not distinguished by any great philosophical depth. They do however illustrate the nature of the novel as a genre no less — if perhaps no more — than do other existing theories of the novel.

I will attempt below to approach the novel precisely as a genre-in-the-making, one in the vanguard of all modern literary development. I am not constructing here a functional definition of the novelistic canon in literary history, that is, a definition that would make of it a system of fixed generic characteristics. Rather, I am trying to grope my way toward the basic structural characteristics of this most fluid of genres, characteristics that might determine the direction of its peculiar capacity for change and of its influence and effect on the rest of literature.

I find three basic characteristics that fundamentally distinguish the novel in principle from other genres: (1) its stylistic three-dimensionality, which is linked with the multi-languaged consciousness realized in the novel; (2) the radical change it effects in the temporal coordinates of the literary image; (3) the new zone opened by the novel for structuring literary images, namely, the zone of maximal contact with the present (with contemporary reality) in all its open-endedness.

These three characteristics of the novel are all organically interrelated and have all been powerfully affected by a very specific rupture in the history of European civilization: its emergence from a socially isolated and culturally deaf semipatriarchal society, and its entrance into international and interlingual contacts and relationships. A multitude of different languages, cultures and times became available to Europe, and this became a decisive factor in its life and thought.

In another work[7] I have already investigated the first stylistic peculiarity of the novel, the one resulting from the active polyglossia of the new world, the new culture and its new creative literary consciousness. I will summarize here only the basic points.

Polyglossia had always existed (it is more ancient than pure, canonic monoglossia), but it had not been a factor in literary creation; an artistically conscious choice between languages did not serve as the creative center of the literary and language process. Classical Greeks had a feeling both for "languages" and for the epochs of language, for the various Greek literary dialects (tragedy is a polyglot genre), but creative consciousness was realized in closed, pure languages (although in actual fact they were mixed). Polyglossia was appropriated and canonized among all the genres.

The new cultural and creative consciousness lives in an actively polyglot world. The world becomes polyglot, once and for all and irreversibly. The period of national languages, coexisting but closed and deaf to each other, comes to an end. Languages throw light on each other: one language can, after all, see itself only in the light of another language. The naive and stubborn coexistence of "languages" within a given national language also comes to an end — that is, there is no more peaceful coexistence between territorial dialects, social and professional dialects and jargons, literary language, generic languages within literary language, epochs in language and so forth.

All this set into motion a process of active, mutual cause-and-effect and interillumination. Words and language began to have a different feel to them; objectively they ceased to be what they had once been. Under these conditions of external and internal interillumination, each given language — even if its linguistic composition (phonetics, vocabulary, morphology, etc.) were to remain absolutely unchanged — is, as it were, reborn, becoming qualitatively a different thing for the consciousness that creates in it.

In this actively polyglot world, completely new relationships are established between language and its object (that is, the real world) — and this is fraught with enormous consequences for all the already completed genres that had been formed during eras of closed and deaf monoglossia. In contrast to other major genres, the novel emerged and matured precisely when intense activization of external and internal polyglossia was at the peak of its activity; this is its native element. The novel could therefore assume leadership in the process of developing and renewing literature in its linguistic and stylistic dimension.

In the above-mentioned work I tried to elucidate the profound stylistic originality of the novel, which is determined by its connection with polyglossia.

Let us move on to the two other characteristics, both concerned with the thematic aspect of structure in the novel as a genre. These characteristics can be best brought out and clarified through a comparison of the novel with the epic.

The epic as a genre in its own right may, for our purposes, be characterized by three constitutive features: (1) a national epic past — in Goethe's and Schiller's terminology the "absolute past" — serves as the subject for the epic;[8] (2) national tradition (not personal experience and the free thought that grows out of it) serves as the source for the epic; (3) an absolute epic distance separates the epic world from contemporary reality, that is, from the time in which the singer (the author and his audience) lives.

Let us now touch upon several artistic features related to the above. The absence of internal conclusiveness and exhaustiveness creates a sharp increase in demands for an *external* and *formal* completedness and exhaustiveness, especially in regard to plot line. The problems of a beginning, an end, and "fullness" of plot are posed anew. The epic is indifferent to formal beginnings and can remain incomplete (that is, where it concludes is almost arbitrary). The absolute past is closed and completed in the whole as well as in any of its parts. It is, therefore, possible to take any part and offer it as the whole. One cannot embrace, in a single epic, the entire world of the absolute past (although it is unified from a plot standpoint) — to do so would mean a retelling of the whole of national tradition, and it is sufficiently difficult to embrace even a significant portion of it. But this is no great loss, because the structure of the whole is repeated in each part, and each part is complete and circular like the whole. One may begin the story at almost any moment, and finish at almost any moment. The *Iliad* is a random excerpt from the Trojan cycle. Its ending (the burial of Hector) could not possibly be the ending from a novelistic point of view. But epic completedness suffers not the slightest as a result. The specific "impulse to end" — How does the war end? Who wins? What will happen to Achilles? and so forth — is absolutely excluded from the epic by both internal and external motifs (the plot-line of the tradition was already known to everyone). This specific "impulse to continue" (what will happen next?) and the "impulse to end" (how will it end?) are characteristic only for the novel and are possible only in a zone where there is proximity and contact; in a zone of distanced images they are impossible.

In distanced images we have the whole event, and plot interest (that is, the condition of not knowing) is impossible. The novel, however, speculates in what is unknown. The novel devises various forms and methods for employing the surplus knowledge that the author has, that which the hero does not know or does not see. It is possible to utilize this authorial surplus in an external way, manipulating the narrative, or it can be used to complete the image of an individual (an externalization that is peculiarly novelistic). But there is another possibility in this surplus that creates further problems.

The distinctive features of the novelistic zone emerge in various ways in various novels. A novel need not raise any problematic questions at all. Take, for example, the adventuristic "boulevard" romance. There is no philosophy in it, no social or political problems, no psychology. Consequently none of these spheres provides any contact with the inconclusive events of our own contemporary reality. The absence of distance and of a zone of contact are utilized here in a different way: in place of our tedious lives we are offered a surrogate, true, but it is the surrogate of a fascinating and brilliant life. We can experience these adventures, identify with these heroes; such novels almost become a substitute for our own lives. Nothing of the sort is possible in the epic and other distanced genres. And here we encounter the specific danger inherent in the novelistic zone of contact: we ourselves may actually enter the novel (whereas we could never enter an epic or other distanced genre). It follows that we might substitute for our own life an obsessive reading of novels, or dreams based on novelistic models (the hero of [Dostoevsky's] *White Nights*); Bovaryism becomes possible, the real-life appearance of fashionable heroes taken from novels — disillusioned, demonic and so forth. Other genres are capable of generating such phenomena only after having been novelized, that is, after having been transposed to the novelistic zone of contact (for example, the verse narratives of Byron).

Yet another phenomenon in the history of the novel — and one of extreme importance — is connected with this new temporal orientation and with this zone of contact: it is the novel's special relationship with extraliterary genres, with the genres of everyday life and with ideological genres. In its earliest stages, the novel and its preparatory genres had relied upon various extraliterary forms of personal and social reality, and especially those of rhetoric (there is a theory that actually traces the novel back to rhetoric). And in later stages of its development the novel makes wide and substantial use of letters, diaries, confessions, the forms and methods of rhetoric associated with recently established courts and so forth. Since it is constructed in a zone of contact with the incomplete events of a particular present, the novel often crosses the boundary of what we strictly call fictional literature — making use first of a moral confession, then of a philosophical tract, then of manifestos that are openly political, then degenerating into the raw spirituality of a confession, a "cry of the soul" that has not yet found its formal contours. These phenomena are precisely what characterize the novel as a developing genre. After all, the boundaries between fiction and nonfiction, between literature and nonliterature and so forth are not laid up in heaven. Every specific situation is historical. And the growth of literature is not merely development and change within the fixed boundaries of any given definition; the boundaries themselves are constantly changing. The shift of boundaries between various strata (including literature) in a culture is an extremely slow and complex process. Isolated border violations of any given specific definition (such as those mentioned above) are only symptomatic of this larger process, which occurs at a great depth. These symptoms of change appear considerably more often in the novel than they do elsewhere, as the novel is a developing genre; they are sharper and more significant because the novel is in the vanguard of change. The novel may thus serve as a document for gauging the lofty and still distant destinies of literature's future unfolding.

But the changes that take place in temporal orientation, and in the zone where images are constructed, appear nowhere more profoundly and inevitably than in the process of restructuring the image of the individual in literature. Within the bounds of the present article, however, I can touch on this great and complex question only briefly and superficially.

The individual in the high distanced genres is an individual of the absolute past and of the distanced image. As such he is a fully finished and completed being. This has been accomplished on a lofty heroic level, but what is complete is also something hopelessly ready-made; he is all there, from beginning to end he coincides with himself, he is absolutely equal to himself. He is, furthermore, completely externalized. There is not the slightest gap between his authentic essence and its external manifestation. All his potential, all his possibilities are realized utterly in his external social position, in the whole of his fate and even in his external appearance; outside of this predetermined fate and predetermined position there is nothing. He has already become everything that he could become, and he could become only that which he has already become. He is entirely externalized in the most elementary, almost literal sense: everything in him is exposed and loudly expressed: his internal world and all his external characteristics, his appearance and his actions all lie on a single plane. His view of himself coincides completely with others' views of him — the view of his society (his community), the epic singer and the audience also coincide.

In this context, mention should be made of the problem of self-praise that comes up in Plutarch and others. "I myself," in an environment that is distanced, exists not *in* itself or for *itself* but for the self's descendents, for the memory such a self anticipates in its descendents. I acknowledge myself, an image that is my own, but on this distanced plane of memory such a consciousness of self is alienated from "me." I see myself through the eyes of another. This coincidence of forms — the view I have of myself as self, and the view I have of myself as other — bears an integral, and therefore naive, character — there is no gap between the two. We have as yet no confession, no exposing of self. The one doing the depicting coincides with the one being depicted.[9]

He sees and knows in himself only the things that others see and know in him. Everything that another person — the author — is able to say about him he can say about himself, and vice versa. There is nothing to seek for in him, nothing to guess at, he can neither be exposed nor provoked; he is all of a piece, he has no shell, there is no nucleus within. Furthermore, the epic hero lacks any ideological initiative (heroes and author alike lack it). The epic world knows only a single and unified world view, obligatory and indubitably true for heroes as well as for authors and audiences. Neither world view nor language can, therefore, function as factors for limiting and determining human images, or their individualization. In the epic, characters are bounded, preformed, individualized by their various situations and destinies, but not by varying "truths." Not even the gods are separated from men by a special truth: they have the same language, they all share the same world view, the same fate, the same extravagant externalization.

These traits of the epic character, shared by and large with other highly distanced genres, are responsible for the exclusive beauty, wholeness, crystal clarity and artistic completedness of this image of man. But at the same time such traits account for his limitations and his obvious woodenness under conditions obtaining in a later period of human existence.

The destruction of epic distance and the transferral of the image of an individual from the distanced plane to the zone of contact with the inconclusive events of the present (and consequently of the future) result in a radical restructuring of the image of the individual in the novel — and consequently in all literature. Folklore and popular-comic sources for the novel played a huge role in this process. Its first and essential step was the comic familiarization of the image of man. Laughter destroyed epic distance; it began to investigate man freely and familiarly, to turn him inside out, expose the disparity between his surface and his center, between his potential and his reality. A dynamic authenticity was introduced into the image of man, dynamics of inconsistency and tension between various factors of this image; man ceased to coincide with himself, and consequently men ceased to be exhausted entirely by the plots that contain them. Of these inconsistencies and tensions laughter plays up, first of all, the comic sides (but not only the comic sides); in the serio-comical genres of antiquity, images of a new order emerge — for example, the imposing, newly and more complexly integrated heroic image of Socrates.

Characteristic here is the artistic structuring of an image out of durable popular masks — masks that had great influence on the novelistic image of man during the most important stages of the novel's development (the serio-comical genres of antiquity, Rabelais, Cervantes). Outside his destiny, the epic and tragic hero is nothing; he is, therefore, a function of the plot fate assigns him; he cannot become the hero of another destiny or another plot. On the contrary, popular masks — Maccus, Pulcinello, Harlequin — are able to assume any destiny and can figure into any situation (they often do so within the limits of a single play), but they cannot exhaust their possibilities by those situations alone; they always retain, in any situation and in any destiny, a happy surplus of their own, their own rudimentary but inexhaustible human face. Therefore these masks can function and speak independent of the plot; but, moreover, it is precisely in these excursions outside the plot proper—in the Atellan *trices*,[10] in the *lazzi*[11] of Italian comedy—that they best of all reveal a face of their own. Neither an epic nor a tragic hero could ever step out in his own character during a pause in the plot or during an intermission: he has no face for it, no gesture, no language. In this is his strength and his limitation. The epic and tragic hero is the hero who, by his very nature, must perish. Popular masks, on the contrary, never perish: not a single plot in Atellan, Italian, or Italianized French comedies provides for, or could ever provide for, the actual death of a Maccus, a Pulcinello, or a Harlequin. However, one frequently witnesses their fictive comic deaths (with subsequent resurrections). These are heroes of free improvisation and not heroes of tradition, heroes of a life process that is imperishable and forever renewing itself, forever contemporary—these are not heroes of an absolute past.

These masks and their structure (the noncoincidence with themselves, and with any given situation—the surplus, the inexhaustibility of their self and the like), have had, we repeat, an enormous influence on the development of the novelistic image of man. This structure is preserved even in the novel, although in a more complex, deeply meaningful and serious (or serio-comical) form.

One of the basic internal themes of the novel is precisely the theme of the hero's inadequacy to his fate or his situation. The individual is either greater than his fate, or less than his condition as a man. He cannot become once and for all a clerk, a landowner, a merchant, a fiancé, a jealous lover, a father and so forth. If the hero of a novel actually becomes something of the sort—that is, if he completely coincides with his situation and his fate (as do generic, everyday heroes, the majority of secondary characters in a novel)—then the surplus inhering in the human condition is realized in the main protagonist. The way in which this surplus will actually be realized grows out of the author's orientation toward form and content, that is, the ways he sees and depicts individuals. It is precisely the zone of contact with an inconclusive present (and consequently with the future) that creates the necessity of this incongruity of a man with himself. There always remains in him unrealized potential and unrealized demands. The future exists, and this future ineluctably touches upon the individual, has its roots in him.

An individual cannot be completely incarnated into the flesh of existing sociohistorical categories. There is no mere form that would be able to incarnate once and forever all of his human possibilities and needs, no form in which he could exhaust himself down to the last word, like the tragic epic hero; no form that he could fill to the very brim, and yet at the same time not splash over the brim. There always remains an unrealized surplus of humanness; there always remains a need for the future, and a place for his future must be found. All existing clothes are always too tight, and thus comical, on a man. But this surplus of un-fleshed-out humanness may be realized not only in the hero, but also in the author's point of view (as, for example, in Gogol). Reality as we have it in the novel is only one of many possible realities; it is not inevitable, not arbitrary, it bears within itself other possibilities.

The epic wholeness of an individual disintegrates in a novel in other ways as well. A crucial tension develops between the external and the internal man, and as a result of the subjectivity of the individual becomes an object of experimentation and representation — and first of all on the humorous familiarizing plane. Coordination breaks down between the various aspects: man for himself alone and man in the eyes of others. This disintegration of the integrity that an individual had possessed in epic (and in tragedy) combines in the novel with the necessary preparatory steps toward a new, complex wholeness on a higher level of human development.

Finally, in a novel the individual acquires the ideological and linguistic initiative necessary to change the nature of his own image (there is a new and higher type of individualization of the image). In the antique stage of novelistic development there appeared remarkable examples of such hero-ideologues — the image of Socrates, the image of a laughing Epicurus in the so-called "Hypocratic" novel, the deeply novelized image of Diogenes in the thoroughly dialogized literature of the cynics and in Menippean satire (where it closely approximates the image of the popular mask), and, finally, the image of Menippius in Lucian. As a rule, the hero of a novel is always more or less an ideologue.

What all this suggests is a somewhat abstract and crude schematization for restructuring the image of an individual in the novel.

We will summarize with some conclusions.

The present, in its all open-endedness, taken as a starting point and center for artistic and ideological orientation, is an enormous revolution in the creative consciousness of man. In the European world this reorientation and destruction of the old hierarchy of temporalities received its crucial generic expression on the boundary between classic antiquity and Hellenism, and in the new world during the late middle ages and Renaissance. The fundamental constituents of the novel as a genre were formed in these eras, although some of the separate elements making up the novel were present much earlier, and the novel's roots must ultimately be sought in folklore. In these eras all other major genres had already long since come to completion, they were already old and almost ossified genres. They were all permeated from top to bottom with a more ancient hierarchization of temporalities. The novel, from the very beginning, developed as a genre that had at its core a new way of conceptualizing time. The absolute past, tradition, hierarchical distance played no role in the formation of the novel as a genre (such spatiotemporal categories did play a role, though insignificant, in certain periods of the novel's development, when it was slightly influenced by the epic—for example in the Baroque novel). The novel took shape precisely at the point when epic distance was disintegrating, when both the world and man were assuming a degree of comic familiarity, when the object of artistic representation was being degraded to the level of a contemporary reality that was inconclusive and fluid. From the very beginning the novel was structured not in the distanced image of the absolute past but in the zone of direct contact with inconclusive present-day reality. At its core lay personal experience and free creative imagination. Thus a new, sober artistic-prose novelistic image and a new critical scientific perception came into being simultaneously. From the very beginning, then, the novel was made of different clay than the other already completed genres; it is a different breed, and with it and in it is born the future of all literature. Once it came into being, it could never be merely one genre among others, and it could not erect rules for interrelating with others in peaceful and harmonious co-existence. In the presence of the novel, all other genres somehow have a different resonance. A lengthy battle for the novelization of the other genres began, a battle to drag them into a zone of contact with reality. The course of this battle has been complex and tortuous.

The novelization of literature does not imply attaching to already completed genres a generic canon that is alien to them, not theirs. The novel, after all, has no canon of its own. It is, by its very nature, not canonic. It is plasticity itself. It is a genre that is ever questing, ever examining itself and subjecting its established forms to review. Such, indeed, is the only possibility open to a genre that structures itself in a zone of direct contact with developing reality. Therefore, the novelization of other genres does not imply their subjection of an alien generic canon; on the contrary, novelization implies their liberation from all that serves as a brake on their unique development, from all that would change them along with the novel into some sort of stylization of forms that have outlived themselves.

I have developed my various positions in this essay in a somewhat abstract way. There have been few illustrations, and even these were taken only from an ancient period in the novel's development. My choice was determined by the fact that the significance of that period has been greatly underestimated. When people talk about the ancient period of the novel they have traditionally had in mind the "Greek novel" alone. The ancient period of the novel is enormously significant for a proper understanding of the genre. But in ancient times the novel could not really develop all its potential; this potential came to light only in the modern world. We indicated that in several works of antiquity, the inconclusive present begins to sense a greater proximity to the future than to the past. The absence of a temporal perspective in ancient society assured that this process of reorientation toward a real future could not complete itself; after all, there was no real concept of a future. Such a reorientation occurred for the first time during the Renaissance. In that era, the present (that is, a reality that was contemporaneous) for the first time began to sense itself not only as an incomplete continuation of the past, but as something like a new and heroic beginning. To re-interpret reality on the level of the contemporary present now meant not only to degrade, but to raise reality into a new and heroic sphere. It was in the Renaissance that the present first began to feel with great clarity and awareness an incomparably closer proximity and kinship to the future than to the past.

The process of the novel's development has not yet come to an end. It is currently entering a new phase. For our era is characterized by an extraordinary complexity and a deepening in our perception of the world; there is an unusual growth in demands on human discernment, on mature objectivity and the critical faculty. These are features that will shape the further development of the novel as well.

Notes

1. Erwin Rohde (1845–1898), *Der griechische Roman und seine Vorläufer* (1876, but many later editions, most recently published by F. Olds [Hildesheim, 1960]), one of the greatest monuments of nineteenth-century classical scholarship in Germany. It has never really been superseded. But see: Ben F. Perry, *The Ancient Romances* (Berkeley, 1967) and Arthur Heiserman, *The Novel before the Novel* (Chicago, 1977). (Translator's note)

2. Charles Sorel (1599–1674), an important figure in the reaction to the *preciosité* of such figures as Honoré d'Urfé (1567–1625), whose *L'Astrée* (1607–1627), a monstrous 5,500-page volume overflowing with highflown language, is parodied in *Le berger ex-*

travagant (1627). The latter book's major protagonist is a dyed-in-the-wool Parisian who reads too many pastoral novels; intoxicated by these, he attempts to live the rustic life as they describe it — with predictably comic results. (Translator's note)

3. Johann Karl August Musäus (1735–1787), along with Tieck and Brentano, one of the great collectors of German folktales and author of several *Kunstmärchen* of his own (translated into English by Carlyle). Reference here is to his *Grandison der Zweite* (1760–1762, rewritten as *Der deutsche Grandison*, 1781–1782), a satire on Richardson. (Translator's note)

4. Christoph Martin Wieland (1733–1813) is the author of *Geschichte des Agathon* (1767, first of many versions), an autobiographical novel in the guise of a Greek romance, considered by many to be the first in the long line of German *Bildungsromane*. (Translator's note)

5. Reference here is to Johann Carl Wezel (1747–1819), *Lebensgeschichte Tobias Knouts, des Weisen, sonst der Stammler genannt* (1773), a novel that has not received the readership it deserves. A four-volume reprint was published by Metzler (Stuttgart, Afterword by Viktor Lange) in 1971. Also see Elizabeth Holzberg-Pfenniger, *Der desorientierte Erzähler: Studien zu J. C. Wezels Lebensgeschichte des Tobias Knauts* (Bern, 1976). (Translator's note)

6. Friedrich von Blankenburg (1744–1796), *Versuch über den Roman* (1774), an enormous work (over 500 pages) that attempts to define the novel in terms of a rudimentary psychology, a concern for *Tugend* in the heroes. A facsimile edition was published by Metzler (Stuttgart) in 1965. Little is known about Blankenburg, who is also the author of an unfinished novel with the imposing title *Beytrage zur Geschichte deutschen Reichs und deutschen Sitten*, the first part of which appeared a year after the *Versuch* in 1775. (Translator's note)

7. Cf. the article "From the Prehistory of Novelistic Discourse" in *The Dialogic Imagination.*

8. Reference here is to "Über epische und dramatische Dichtung," cosigned by Schiller and Goethe, but probably written by the latter in 1797, although not published until 1827. The actual term used by Goethe for what Bakhtin is calling "absolute past" is *vollkommen vergangen*, which is opposed not to the novel, but to drama, which is defined as *vollkommen gegenwärtig*. The essay can be found in Goethe's *Sämtliche Werke* (Stuttgart and Berlin: Jubilaums-Ausgabe, 1902–1907), vol. 36, pp. 149–52. (Translator's note)

9. Epic disintegrates when the search begins for a new point of view on one's own self (without any admixture of others' points of view). The expressive novelistic gesture arises as a departure from a norm, but the "error" of this norm immediately reveals how important it is for subjectivity. First there is a departure from a norm, and then the problematicalness of the norm itself.

10. *Trices* are thought to have been interludes in the action of the Atellanae during which the masks often stepped out of character.

11. *Lazzi* were what we might now call "routines" or "numbers" that were not part of the ongoing action of the plot.

5

Spatial Form in Modern Literature · JOSEPH FRANK

For a study of esthetic form in the modern novel, Flaubert's famous county fair scene in *Madame Bovary* is a convenient point of departure. This scene has been justly praised for its mordant caricature of bourgeois pomposity, its portrayal — unusually sympathetic for Flaubert — of the bewildered old servant, and its burlesque of the pseudo-romantic rhetoric by which Rodolphe woos the sentimental Emma. At present, it is enough to notice the method by which Flaubert handles the scene — a method we might as well call cinematographic, since this analogy comes immediately to mind. As Flaubert sets the scene, there is action going on simultaneously at three levels, and the physical position of each level is a fair index to its spiritual significance. On the lowest plane, there is the surging, jostling mob in the street, mingling with the livestock brought to the exhibition; raised slightly above the street by a platform are the speechmaking officials, bombastically reeling off platitudes to the attentive multitudes; and on the highest level of all, from a window overlooking the spectacle, Rodolphe and Emma are watching the proceedings and carrying on their amorous conversation, in phrases as stilted as those regaling the crowds. Albert Thibaudet has compared this scene to the medieval mystery play, in which various related actions occur simultaneously on different stage levels; but this acute comparison refers to Flaubert's intention rather than to his method. "Everything should sound simultaneously," Flaubert later wrote, in commenting on this scene, "one should hear the bellowing of the cattle, the whisperings of the lovers and the rhetoric of the officials all at the same time."[1]

But since language proceeds in time, it is impossible to approach this simultaneity of perception except by breaking up temporal sequence. And this is exactly what Flaubert does: he dissolves sequence by cutting back and forth between the various levels of action in a slowly-rising crescendo until — at the climax of the scene — Rodolphe's Chateaubriandesque phrases are read at almost the same moment as the names of prize winners for raising the best pigs. Flaubert takes care to underline this satiric similarity by description, as well as by juxtaposition, as if he were afraid the reflexive relations of the two actions would not be grasped: "From magnetism, by slow degrees, Rodolphe had arrived at affinities, and while M. le Président was citing Cincinnatus at his plow, Diocletian planting his cabbages, and the emperors of China ushering in the new year with sowing-festivals, the young man was explaining to the young woman that these irresistible attractions sprang from some anterior existence."

This scene illustrates, on a small scale, what we mean by the spatialization of form in a novel. For the duration of the scene, at least, the time-flow of the narrative is halted: attention is fixed on the interplay of relationships within the limited time-area. These relationships are juxtaposed independently of the progress of the narrative; and the full significance of the scene is given only by the reflexive relations among the units of meaning. In Flaubert's scene, however, the unit of meaning is not, as in modern poetry, a word-group or a fragment of an anecdote, but the totality of each level of action taken as an integer: the unit is so large that the scene can be read with an illusion of complete understanding, yet with a total unawareness of the "dialectic of platitude" (Thibaudet) interweaving all levels, and finally linking them together with devastating irony. In other words, the struggle towards spatial form in Pound and Eliot resulted in the disappearance of coherent sequence after a few lines; but the novel, with its larger unit of meaning, can preserve coherent sequence within the unit of meaning and break up only the time-flow of narrative. (Because of this difference, readers of modern poetry are practically forced to read reflexively to get any literal sense, while readers of a novel like *Nightwood*, for example, are led to expect narrative sequence by the deceptive normality of language sequence within the unit of meaning.) But this does not affect the parallel between esthetic form in modern poetry and the form of Flaubert's scene: both can be properly understood only when their units of meaning are apprehended reflexively, in an instant of time.

Flaubert's scene, although interesting in itself, is of minor importance to his novel as a whole, and is skillfully blended back into the main narrative structure after fulfilling its satiric function. But Flaubert's method was taken over by James Joyce, and applied on a gigantic scale in the composition of *Ulysses*. Joyce composed his novel of an infinite number of references and cross-references which relate to one another independently of the time-sequence of the narrative; and, before the book fits together into any meaningful pattern, these references must be connected by the reader and viewed as a whole. Ultimately, if we are to believe Stuart Gilbert, these systems of references form a complete picture of practically everything under the sun, from the stages of man's life and the organs of the human body to the colors of the spectrum; but these structures are far more important for Joyce, as Harry Levin has remarked, than they could ever possibly be for the reader. Students of Joyce, fascinated by his erudition, have usually applied themselves to exegesis. Unfortunately, such considerations have little to do with the perceptual form of Joyce's novel.

Joyce's most obvious intention in *Ulysses* is to give the reader a picture of Dublin seen as a whole — to re-recreate the sights and sounds, the people and places, of a typical Dublin day, much as Flaubert had re-created his provincial county fair. And, like Flaubert, Joyce wanted his depiction to have the same unified impact, the same sense of simultaneous activity occurring in different places. Joyce, as a matter of fact, frequently makes use of the same method as Flaubert — cutting back and forth between different actions occurring at the same time — and usually does so to obtain the same ironic effect. But Joyce had the problem of creating this impression of simultaneity for the life of a whole teeming city, and of maintaining it — or rather of strengthening it — through hundreds of pages that must be read as a sequence. To meet this problem, Joyce was forced to go far beyond what Flaubert had done; while Flaubert had maintained a clear-cut narrative line, except in the county-fair scene, Joyce breaks up his narrative and transforms the very structure of his novel into an instrument of his esthetic intention.

Joyce conceived *Ulysses* as a modern epic; and in the epic, as Stephen Dedalus tells us in *A Portrait of the Artist as a Young Man*, "the personality of the artist, at first sight a cry or a cadence and then a fluid and lambent narrative, finally refines itself out of existence, impersonalizes itself, so to speak . . . the artist, like the God of creation, remains within or beyond or above his handiwork, invisible, refined out of existence, indifferent, paring his fingernails." The epic is thus synonymous for Joyce with the complete self-effacement of the author; and, with his usual uncompromising rigor, Joyce carries this implication further than anyone had dared before. He assumes — what is obviously not true — that his readers are Dubliners, intimately acquainted with Dublin life and the personal history of his characters. This allows him to refrain from giving any direct information about his characters: such information would immediately have betrayed the presence of an omniscient author. What Joyce does, instead, is to present the elements of his narrative — the relations between Stephen and his family, between Bloom and his wife, between Stephen and Bloom and the Dedalus family — in fragments, as they are thrown out unexplained in the course of casual conversation, or as they lie embedded in the various strata of symbolic reference; and the same is true of all the allusions to Dublin life, history, and the external events of the twenty-four hours during which the novel takes place. In other words, all the factual background — so conveniently summarized for the reader in an ordinary novel — must be reconstructed from fragments, sometimes hundreds of pages apart, scattered through the book. As a result, the reader is forced to read *Ulysses* in exactly the same manner as he reads modern poetry — continually fitting fragments together and keeping allusions in mind until, by reflexive reference, he can link them to their complements.

Joyce intended, in this way, to build up in the reader's mind a sense of Dublin as a totality, including all the relations of the characters to one another and all the events which enter their consciousness. As the reader progresses through the novel, connecting allusions and references spatially, gradually becoming aware of the pattern of relationships, this sense was to be imperceptibly acquired; and, at the conclusion of the novel, it might almost be said that Joyce literally wanted the reader to become a Dubliner. For this is what Joyce demands: that the reader have at hand the same instinctive knowledge of Dublin life, the same sense of Dublin as a huge, surrounding organism, which the Dubliner possesses as a birthright. It is such knowledge which, at any one moment of time, gives him a knowledge of Dublin's past and present as a whole; and it is only such knowledge which might enable the reader, like the characters, to place all the references in their proper context. This, it should be realized, is practically the equivalent of saying that Joyce cannot be read — he can only be re-read. A knowledge of the whole is essential to an understanding of any part; but, unless one is a Dubliner, such knowledge can be obtained only after the book has been read, when all the references are fitted into their proper place and grasped as a unity. Although the burdens placed on the reader by this method of composition may seem insuperable, the fact remains that Joyce, in his unbelievably laborious fragmentation of narrative structure, proceeded on the assumption that a unified spatial apprehension of his work would ultimately be possible.

In a far more subtle manner than with Joyce and Flaubert, the same principle of composition is at work in Marcel Proust. Since Proust himself tells us that, before all else, his novel will have imprinted on it "a form which usually remains invisible, the form of Time," it may seem strange to speak of Proust in connection with spatial form. He has, almost invariably, been considered the novelist of time *par excellence:* the literary interpreter of that

Bergsonian "real time" intuited by the sensibility, as distinguished from the abstract, chronological time of the conceptual intelligence. To stop at this point, however, is to miss what Proust himself considered the deepest significance of his work. Obsessed with the ineluctability of time, Proust was suddenly visited by certain quasi-mystical experiences — described in detail in the last volume of his work, "Le temps retrouvé" — which, by providing him with a spiritual technique for transcending time, enabled him to escape what he considered to be time's domination. By writing a novel, by translating the transcendent, extra-temporal quality of these experiences to the level of esthetic form, Proust hoped to reveal their nature to the world — for they seemed to him a clue to the ultimate secrets of reality. And not only should the world learn about these experiences indirectly, by reading a descriptive account of them, but, through his novel, it would feel their impact on the sensibility as Proust himself had felt it.

To define the method by which this is accomplished, one must first understand clearly the precise nature of the Proustian revelation. Each such experience, Proust tells us, is marked by a feeling that "the permanent essence of things, usually concealed, is set free and our true self, which had long seemed dead but was not dead in other ways, awakes, takes on fresh life as it receives the celestial nourishment brought to it." This celestial nourishment consists of some sound, or odor, or other sensory stimulus, "sensed anew, simultaneously in the present and the past." But why should these moments seem so overwhelmingly valuable that Proust calls them celestial? Because, Proust observes, his imagination could only operate on the past; and the material presented to his imagination, therefore, lacked any sensuous immediacy. But, at certain moments, the physical sensations of the past came flooding back to fuse with the present; and, in these moments, Proust believed that he grasped a reality "real without being of the present moment, ideal but not abstract." Only in these moments did he attain his most cherished ambition — "to seize, isolate, immobilize for the duration of a lightning flash" what otherwise he could not apprehend, "namely: a fragment of time in its pure state." For a person experiencing this moment, Proust adds, the word "death" no longer has meaning. "Situated outside the scope of time, what could he fear from the future?"

The significance of this experience, though obscurely hinted at throughout the book, is made explicit only in the concluding pages which describe the final appearance of the narrator at the reception of the Princesse de Guermantes. The narrator decides to dedicate the remainder of his life to re-creating these experiences in a work of art; and this work will differ essentially from all others because, at its foundation, will be a vision of reality that has been refracted through an extra-temporal perspective. Viewing Proust as the last and most debilitated of a long line of neurasthenic esthetes, many critics have found in this decision to create a work of art merely the final step in his flight from the burdens of reality. Edmund Wilson, ordinarily so discerning, links up this view with Proust's ambition to conquer time, assuming that Proust hoped to oppose time by establishing something—a work of art—impervious to its flux; but this somewhat ingenuous interpretation scarcely does justice to Proust's own conviction, expressed with special intensity in the last volume of his work, that he was fulfilling a prophetic mission. It was not the work of art *qua* work of art that Proust cared about—his contempt for the horde of faddish scribblers was unbounded—but a work of art which should stand as a monument to his personal conquest of time. This his own work could do not simply because it was a work of art, but because it was at once the vehicle through which he conveyed his vision and the concrete substance of that vision shaped by a method which compels the reader to re-experience its exact effect.

The prototype of this method, like the analysis of the revelatory moment, occurs during the reception at the Princesse de Guermantes. After spending years in a sanatorium, losing touch almost completely with the fashionable world of the earlier volumes, the narrator comes out of seclusion to attend the reception. He finds himself bewildered by the changes in social position, and the even more striking changes in character and personality among his former friends. According to some socially minded critics, Proust intended to paint here the invasion of French aristocratic society by the upper bourgeoisie, and the gradual breakdown of all social and moral standards caused by the First World War. No doubt this process is incidentally described at some length; but, as the narrator takes great pains to tell us, it is far from being the most important meaning of the scene. What strikes the narrator, almost with the force of a blow, is this: in trying to recognize old friends under the masks which, as he feels, the years have welded to them, he is jolted for the first time into a consciousness of the passage of time. When a young man addresses the narrator respectfully, instead of familiarly, as if he were an elderly gentleman, the narrator realizes suddenly that he has become an elderly gentleman; but for him the passage of time had gone unperceived up until that moment. To become conscious of time, the narrator begins to understand, it had first been necessary to remove himself from his accustomed environment—or, what amounts to the same thing, from the stream of time acting on that environment—and then to plunge back into the stream after a lapse of years. In so doing, the narrator found himself presented with two images — the world as he had formerly known it, and the world, transformed by time, that he now saw before him; and when these two images are juxtaposed, the narrator discovers, the passage of time is suddenly experienced through its visible effects. Habit, that universal soporific, ordinarily conceals the passage of time from those who have gone their accustomed ways: at any one moment of time the changes are so minute as to be imperceptible: "Other people," Proust writes, "never cease to change places in relation to ourselves. In the imperceptible, but eternal march of the world, we regard them as motionless in a moment of vision, too short for us to perceive the motion that is sweeping them on. But we have only to select in our memory two pictures taken of them at different moments, close enough together however for them not to have altered in themselves — perceptibly, that is to say — and the difference between the two pictures is a measure of the displacement that they have undergone in relation to us." By comparing these two images in a moment of time, the passage of time can be experienced concretely, in the impact of its visible effects on the sensibility, rather than as a mere gap counted off in numbers. And this discovery provides the narrator with a method which, in T. S. Eliot's phrase, is an "objective correlative" to the visionary apprehension of the fragment of "pure time" intuited in the revelatory moment.

When the narrator discovers this method of communicating his experience of the revelatory moment, he decides, as we have already said, to incorporate it in a novel. But the novel the narrator decides to write has just been finished by the reader; and its form is controlled by the method that the narrator has outlined in its concluding pages. The reader, in other words, is substituted for the narrator, and is placed by the author throughout the book in the same position as the narrator occupies before his own experience at the reception of the Princesse de Guermantes. This is done by the discontinuous presentation of character — a simple device which, nevertheless, is the clue to the form of Proust's vast structure. Every reader soon notices that Proust does not follow any of his characters through the whole course of his novel: they appear and reappear, in various stages of their lives, but hundreds of pages sometimes go by between the time they are last seen and the time they reappear; and when they do turn up again, the passage of time has invariably changed them in some decisive way. Instead of being submerged in the stream of time — which, for Proust, would be the equivalent of presenting a character progressively, in a continuous line of development — the reader is confronted with various snapshots of the characters "motionless in a moment of vision," taken at different stages in their lives; and the reader, in juxtaposing these images, experiences the effects of the passage of time exactly as the narrator had done. As he had promised, therefore, Proust does stamp his novel indelibly with the form of time; but we are now in a position to understand exactly what he meant by the promise.

To experience the passage of time, Proust learned, it was necessary to rise above it, and to grasp both past and present simultaneously in a moment of what he called "pure time." But "pure time," obviously, is not time at all — it is perception in a moment of time, that is to say, space. And, by the discontinuous presentation of character, Proust forces the reader to juxtapose disparate images of his characters spatially, in a moment of time, so that the experience of time's passage will be fully communicated to their sensibility. There is a striking analogy here between Proust's method and that of his beloved impressionist painters; but this analogy goes far deeper than the usual comments about the "impressionism" of Proust's style. The Impressionist painters juxtaposed pure tones on the canvas, instead of mixing them on the palette, in order to leave the blending of colors to the eye of the spectator. Similarly, Proust gives us what might be called pure views of his characters — views of them "motionless in a moment of vision" in various phases of their lives — and allows the sensibility of the reader to fuse these views into a unity. Each view must be apprehended by the reader as a unit; and Proust's purpose is only achieved when these units of meaning are referred to each other reflexively in a moment of time. As with Joyce and the modern poets, we see that spatial form is also the structural scaffolding of Proust's labyrinthine masterpiece.

The name of Djuna Barnes is not unknown to those readers who followed, with any care, the stream of pamphlets, books, magazines, and anthologies that poured forth to enlighten America in the feverish days of literary expatriation. Miss Barnes, it is true, must always have remained a somewhat enigmatic figure even to the most attentive reader. Born in New York State, she spent most of her time abroad in England and France; and the glimpses one catches of her in the memoirs of the period are brief and unrevealing. She appears in the *Dial* from time to time with a drawing or a poem; she crops up now and again in some anthology of advance-guard writers — the usual agglomeration of people who are later to become famous, or to sink into the melancholy oblivion of frustrated promise. Before the publication of *Nightwood*, indeed, one might have been inclined to place her name in the latter group. For, while she has a book of short stories and an earlier novel to her credit, neither of them prepares one for the maturity of achievement so conspicuous in every line of her latest work.

Of the fantastical quality of her imagination, of the gift for imagery which, as T. S. Eliot has said, gives one a sense of horror and doom akin to Elizabethan tragedy; of the epigrammatic incisiveness of her phrasing and her penchant, also akin to the Elizabethans, for dealing with the more scabrous manifestations of human fallibility — of all these there is evidence in *Ryder*, Miss Barnes's first novel. But all this might well have resulted only in a momentary flare-up of capricious brilliance, whose radiance would have been as dazzling as it was insubstantial. *Ryder*, it must be confessed, is an anomalous creation from any point of view. Although Miss Barnes's unusual qualities gradually emerge from its kaleidoscope of moods and styles, these qualities are still, so to speak, held in solution, or at best placed in the service of a literary *jeu d'esprit*. Only in *Nightwood* do they finally crystallize into a definitive and comprehensible pattern.

Many critics — not least among them T. S. Eliot himself — have paid tribute to *Nightwood*'s compelling intensity, its head-and-shoulders superiority, simply as a stylistic phenomenon, to most of the works that currently pass for literature. But *Nightwood*'s reputation at present is similar, in many respects, to that of *The Waste Land* in 1922 — it is known as a collection of striking passages, some of breathtaking poetic quality, appealing chiefly to connoisseurs of somewhat gamey literary items. Such a reputation, it need hardly be remarked, is not conducive to intelligent appreciation or understanding. Thanks to critics like F. R. Leavis, Cleanth Brooks, and F. O. Matthiessen, we are now able to approach *The Waste Land* as a work of art, rather than as a battleground for opposing poetic theories or as a curious piece of literary esoterica; and it is time that such a process should be at least begun for *Nightwood*.

Before dealing with *Nightwood* in detail, however, we must make certain broad distinctions between it and the novels already considered. While the structural principle of *Nightwood* is the same as in *Ulysses* and *A la recherche du temps perdu* — spatial form, obtained by means of reflexive reference — there are marked differences in technique that will be obvious to every reader. Taking an analogy from another art, we can say that these differences are similar to the differences between the work of Cézanne and the compositions of a later abstract painter like Braque. What characterizes the work of Cézanne, above all, is the tension between two conflicting but deeply-rooted tendencies: on the one hand, a struggle to attain esthetic form — conceived of by Cézanne as a self-enclosed unity of form-and-color harmonies — and, on the other hand, the desire to create this form through the recognizable depiction of natural objects. Later artists, abandoning Cézanne's efforts to achieve form in terms of natural objects, took over only his preoccupation with formal harmonies, omitting natural objects altogether or presenting them in some distorted manner.

Like Cézanne, Proust and Joyce accept the naturalistic principle, presenting their characters in terms of those commonplace details, those descriptions of circumstance and environment, that we have come to regard as verisimilar. At the same time, we have seen, they intended to control the ebullience of their naturalistic detail by the unity of spatial apprehension. But in *Nightwood*, as in the work of Braque and the later abstract painters, the naturalistic principle is totally abandoned: no attempt is made to convince us that the characters are actual flesh-and-blood human beings. We are asked only to accept their world as we accept an abstract painting or, to return to literature, as we accept a Shakespearian play — as an autonomous pattern giving us an individual vision of reality, rather than what we might consider its exact reflection.

To illustrate the transition that takes place in *Nightwood* let us examine an interesting passage from Proust, where the process can be caught at a rudimentary level. In describing Robert de Saint-Loup, an important character in the early sections of the novel, the narrator tells us that he could see concealed "beneath a courtier's smile his warrior's thirst for action — when I examined him I could see how closely the vigorous structure of his triangular face must have been modelled on that of his ancestors' faces, a face devised rather for an ardent bowman than for a delicate student. Beneath his fine skin the bold construction, the feudal architecture were apparent. His head made one think of those old dungeon keeps on which the disused battlements are still to be seen, although inside they have been converted into libraries." When the reader comes across this passage, he has already learned a considerable number of facts about Saint-Loup. He is, for one thing, a member of the Guermantes family, one of the oldest and most aristocratic in the French nobility and still the acknowledged leaders of Parisian society. Unlike their feudal ancestors, however, the Guermantes have no real influence over the internal affairs of France under the Third Republic. Saint-Loup, for another thing, is by way of being a family black sheep: seemingly uninterested in social success, a devoted student of Nietzsche and Proudhon, we are told that his head was full of "socialistic spoutings," and that he was "imbued with the most profound contempt for his caste." Knowing these facts from earlier sections of the novel, the reader accepts the passage quoted above simply as a trenchant summation of Saint-Loup's character. But so precisely do the images in this passage apply to everything the reader has learned about Saint-Loup, so exactly do they communicate the central impression of his personality, that it would be possible to derive a total knowledge of his character solely from the images without attaching them to a set of external social and historical details.

Images of this kind are commoner in poetry than in prose — more particularly, since we are speaking of character description, in dramatic poetry. In Shakespeare and the Elizabethans, descriptions of character are not "realistic" as we understand the word today: they are not a collection of circumstantial details whose bare conglomeration is assumed to form a definition. The dramatic poet, rather, defined both the physical and psychological aspects of character at one stroke, in an image or series of images. Here is Antony, for example, as Shakespeare presents him in the opening scene of *Antony and Cleopatra:*

> Nay, but this dotage of our general's
> O'erflows the measure: those his goodly eyes
> That o'er the files and musters of the war
> Have glow'd like plated Mars, now bend, now turn,
> The office and devotion of their view
> Upon a tawny front: his captain's heart,
> Which in the scuffles of great fights hath burst
> The buckles on his breast, reneges all temper,
> And is become the bellows and the fan
> To cool a gipsy's lust.

And then, to complete the picture, Antony is contemptuously called "the triple pillar of the world transformed into a strumpet's fool." Or, to take a more modern example, from a poet strongly influenced by the Elizabethans, here is the twentieth-century everyman:

> He, the young man carbuncular, arrives,
> A small house agent's clerk, with one bold stare,
> One of the low on whom assurance sits
> As a silk hat on a Bradford millionaire.

As Ramon Fernandez has remarked of similar character descriptions in the work of George Meredith, images of this kind analyze without dissociating;

they describe character but, at the same time, hold fast to the unity of personality, without splintering it to fragments in trying to seize the secret of its integration.

Writing of this order, charged with symbolic overtones, piercing through the cumbrous mass of naturalistic detail to express the essence of character in an image, is the antithesis to what we are accustomed in the novel. Ordinary novels, as T. S. Eliot justly observes in his preface to *Nightwood*, "obtain what reality they have largely from an accurate rendering of the noises that human beings currently make in their daily simple needs of communication; and what part of a novel is not composed of these noises consists of a prose which is no more alive than that of a competent newspaper writer or government official." Miss Barnes abandons any pretensions to this kind of verisimilitude, just as modern artists have abandoned any attempt at naturalistic representation; and the result is a world as strange to the reader, at first sight, as the world of abstract art was to its first spectators. Since the selection of detail in *Nightwood* is governed, not by the logic of verisimilitude, but by the demands of the *décor* necessary to enhance the symbolic significance of the characters, the novel has baffled even its most fascinated admirers. Perhaps we can clear up some of the mystery by applying our method of reflexive reference, instead of approaching the book, as most of its readers have done, expecting to find a coherent temporal pattern of narrative.

Since *Nightwood* lacks a narrative structure in the ordinary sense, it cannot be reduced to any sequence of action for purposes of explanation. One can, if one chooses, follow the narrator in Proust through the various stages of his social career; one can, with some difficulty, follow Leopold Bloom's epic journey through Dublin; but no such reduction is possible in *Nightwood*. As Dr. O'Connor remarks to Nora Flood, with his desperate gaiety, "I have a narrative, but you will be put to it to find it." Strictly speaking, the doctor is wrong—he has a static situation, not a narrative, and no matter how hard the reader looks he will find only the various facets of this situation explored from different angles. The eight chapters of *Nightwood* are like searchlights, probing the darkness each from a different direction, yet ultimately focusing on and illuminating the same entanglement of the human spirit. In the first four chapters we are introduced to each of the important persons—Felix Volkbein, Nora Flood, Robin Vote, Jenny Petherbridge, and Dr. O'Connor. The next three chapters are, for the most part, long monologues by the doctor, through which the developments of the earlier chapters begin to take on meaning. The last chapter, only a few pages long, has the effect of a coda, giving us what we have already come to feel is the only possible termination. And these chapters are knit together, not by the progress of any action—either physical action, or, as in a stream-of-consciousness novel, the act of thinking—but by the continual reference and cross-reference of images and symbols which must be referred to each other spatially throughout the time-act of reading.

Note

1. This discussion of the county-fair scene owes a good deal to Albert Thibaudet's *Gustave Flaubert*, probably the best critical study yet written on the subject. The quotation from Flaubert's letter is used by Thibaudet and has been translated from his book.

6

Writing and the Novel · ROLAND BARTHES

The Novel and History have been closely related in the very century which witnessed their greatest development. Their link in depth, that which should allow us to understand at once Balzac and Michelet, is that in both we find the construction of an autarkic world which elaborates its own dimensions and limits, and organizes within these its own Time, its own Space, its population, its own set of objects and its myths.

This sphericity of the great works of the nineteenth century found its expression in those long recitatives, the Novel and History, which are, as it were, plane projections of a curved and organic world of which the serial story which came into being at that precise moment, presents, through its involved complications, a degraded image. And yet narration is not necessarily a law of the form. A whole period could conceive novels in letters, for instance; and another can evolve a practice of History by means of analyses. Therefore Narration, as a form common to both the Novel and to History, does remain, in general, the choice or the expression of an historical moment.

Obsolete in spoken French, the preterite, which is the cornerstone of Narration, always signifies the presence of Art; it is a part of a ritual of Letters. Its function is no longer that of a tense. The part it plays is to reduce reality to a point of time, and to abstract, from the depth of a multiplicity of experiences, a pure verbal act, freed from the existential roots of knowledge, and directed towards a logical link with other acts, other processes, a general movement of the world: it aims at maintaining a hierarchy in the realm of facts. Through the preterite, the verb implicitly belongs with a causal chain, it partakes of a set of related and oriented actions, it functions as the algebraic sign of an intention. Allowing as it does an ambiguity between temporality and causality, it calls for a sequence of events, that is, for an intelligible Narrative. This is why it is the ideal instrument for every construction of a world; it is the unreal time of cosmogonies, myths, History and Novels. It presupposes a world which is constructed, elaborated, self-sufficient, reduced to significant lines, and not one which has been sent sprawling before us, for us to take or leave. Behind the preterite there always lurks a demiurge, a God or a reciter. The world is not unexplained since it is told like a story; each one of its accidents is but a circumstance, and the preterite is precisely this operative sign whereby the narrator reduces the exploded reality to a slim and pure logos, without density, without volume, without spread, and whose sole function is to unite as rapidly as possible a cause and an end. When the historian states that the duc de Guise died on December 23rd, 1588, or when the novelist relates that the Marchioness went out at five o'clock,[1] such actions emerge from a past without substance; purged of the uncertainty of existence, they have the stability and outline of an algebra, they are a recollection, but a useful recollection, the interest of which far surpasses its duration.

So that finally the preterite is the expression of an order, and consequently of a euphoria. Thanks to it, reality is neither mysterious nor absurd; it is clear, almost familiar, repeatedly gathered up and contained in the hand of a creator; it is subjected to the ingenious pressure of his freedom. For all the great storytellers of the nineteenth century, the world may be full of pathos but it is not derelict, since it is a grouping of coherent relations, since there is no overlapping between the written facts, since he who tells the story has the power to do away with the opacity and the solitude of the existences which made it up, since he can in all sentences bear witness to a communication and a hierarchy of actions and since, to tell the truth, these very actions can be reduced to mere signs.

The narrative past is therefore a part of a security system for Belles-Lettres. Being the image of an order, it is one of those numerous formal pacts made between the writer and society for the justification of the former and the serenity of the latter. The preterite *signifies* a creation: that is, it proclaims and imposes it. Even from the depth of the most sombre realism, it has a reassuring effect because, thanks to it, the verb expresses a closed, well-defined, substantival act, the Novel has a name, it escapes the terror of an expression without laws: reality becomes slighter and more familiar, it fits within a style, it does not outrun language. Literature remains the currency in use in a society apprised, by the very form of words, of the meaning of what it consumes. On the contrary, when the Narrative is rejected in favour of other literary genres, or when, within the narration, the preterite is replaced by less ornamental forms, fresher, more full-blooded and nearer to speech (the present tense or the present perfect), Literature becomes the receptacle of existence in all its density and no longer of its meaning alone. The acts it recounts are still separated from History, but no longer from people.

We now understand what is profitable and what is intolerable in the preterite as used in the Novel: it is a lie made manifest, it delineates an area of plausibility which reveals the possible in the very act of unmasking it as false. The teleology common to the Novel and to narrated History is the alienation of the facts: the preterite is the very act by which society affirms its possession of its past and its possibility. It creates a content credible, yet flaunted as an illusion; it is the ultimate term of a formal dialectics which clothes an unreal fact in the garb first of truth then of a lie denounced as such. This has to be related to a certain mythology of the universal typifying the bourgeois society of which the Novel is a characteristic product; it involves giving to the imaginary the formal guarantee of the real, but while preserving in the sign the ambiguity of a double object, at once believable and false. This operation occurs constantly in the whole of Western art, in which the false is equal to the true, not through any agnosticism or poetic duplicity, but because the true is supposed to contain a germ of the universal, or to put it differently, an essence capable of fecundating by mere reproduction, several orders of things among which some differ by their remoteness and some by their fictitious character.

It is thanks to an expedient of the same kind that the triumphant bourgeoisie of the last century was able to look upon its values as universal and to carry over to sections of society which were absolutely heterogeneous to it all the Names which were parts of its ethos. This is strictly how myths function, and the Novel — and within the Novel, the preterite — are mythological objects in which there is, superimposed upon an immediate intention, a second-order appeal to a corpus of dogmas, or better, to a pedagogy, since what is sought is to impart an essence in the guise of an artefact. In order to grasp the significance of the preterite, we have but to compare the Western art of the novel with a certain Chinese tradition, for instance, in which art lies solely in the perfection with which reality is imitated. But in this tradition no sign, absolutely nothing, must allow any distinction to be drawn between the natural and the artificial objects: this wooden walnut must not impart to me, along with the image of a walnut, the intention of conveying to me the art which gave birth to it. Whereas on the contrary this is what writing does in the novel. Its task is to put the mask in place and at the same time to point it out.

This ambiguous function disclosed in the preterite is found in another fact relating to this type of writing: the third person in the Novel. The reader will perhaps recall a novel by Agatha Christie in which all the invention consisted in concealing the murderer beneath the use of the first person of the narrative. The reader looked for him behind every "he" in the plot: he was all the time hidden under the "I." Agatha Christie knew perfectly well that, in the novel, the "I" is usually a spectator, and that it is the "he" who is an actor. Why? The "he" is a typical novelistic convention; like the narrative tense, it signifies and carries through the action of the novel; if the third person is absent, the novel is powerless to come into being, and even wills its own destruction. The "he" is a formal manifestation of the myth, and we have just seen that, in the West at least, there is no art which does not point to its own mask. The third person, like the preterite, therefore performs this service for the art of the novel, and supplies its consumers with the security born of a credible fabrication which is yet constantly held up as false.

Less ambiguous, the "I" is thereby less typical of the novel: it is therefore at the same time the most obvious solution, when the narration remains on this side of convention (Proust's work, for instance, purports to be a mere introduction to Literature), and the most sophisticated, when the "I" takes its place beyond convention and attempts to destroy it, by conferring on the narrative the spurious naturalness of taking the reader into its confidence (such is the guileful air of some stories by Gide). In the same way the use of the "he" in a novel involves two opposed systems of ethics: since it represents an unquestioned convention, it attracts the most conformist and the least dissatisfied, as well as those others who have decided that, finally, this convention is necessary to the novelty of their work. In any case, it is the sign of an intelligible pact between society and the author; but it is also, for the latter, the most important means he has of building the world in the way that he chooses. It is therefore more than a literary experiment: it is a human act which connects creation to History or to existence.

In Balzac for instance, the multiplicity of "he"s, this vast network of characters, slight in terms of solid flesh, but consistent by the duration of their acts, reveals the existence of a world of which History is the first datum. The Balzacian "he" is not the end-product of a development starting from some transformed and generalized "I"; it is the original and crude element of the novel, the material, not the outcome, the creative activity: there is no Balzacian history prior to the history of each third person in the novels of Balzac. His "he" is analogous to Caesar's "he": the third person here brings about a kind of algebraic state of the action, in which existence plays the smallest possible part, in favour of elements which connect, clarify, or show the tragedy inherent in human relationships. Conversely — or at any rate previously — the function of "he" in the novel can be that of expressing an existential experience. In many modern novelists the history of the man is identified with the course of the conjugation: starting from an "I" which is still the form which expresses anonymity most faithfully, man and author little by little win the right to the third person, in proportion as existence becomes fate, and soliloquy becomes a Novel. Here the appearance of the "he" is not the starting point of History, it is the end of an effort which has been successful in extracting from a personal world made up of humours and tendencies, a form which is pure, significant, and which therefore vanishes as soon as it is born thanks to the totally conventional and ethereal decor of the third person. This certainly was the course displayed in the first novels of Jean Cayrol, whose case can be taken as an exemplar. But whereas in the classics — and we know that where writing is concerned classicism lasts until Flaubert — the withdrawal of the biological person testifies to the establishment of essential man, in novelists such as Cayrol, the invasion of the "he" is a progressive conquest over the profound darkness of the existential "I": so true it is that the Novel, identified as it is by its most formal signs, is a gesture of sociability; it establishes Literature as an institution.

Maurice Blanchot has shown, in the case of Kafka, that the elaboration of the impersonal narrative (let us notice, apropos of this term, that the "third person" is always presented as a negative degree of the person) was an act of fidelity to the essence of language, since the latter naturally tends towards its own destruction. We therefore understand how "he" is a victory over "I," inasmuch as it conjures up a state at once more literary and more absent. None the less this victory is ceaselessly threatened: the literary convention of the "he" is necessary to the belittling of the person, but runs at every moment the risk of encumbering it with an unexpected density. For Literature is like phosphorus: it shines with its maximum brilliance at the moment when it attempts to die. But as, on the other hand, it is an act which necessarily implies a duration — especially in the Novel — there can never be any Novel independently of Belles-Lettres. So that the third person in the Novel is one of the most obsessive signs of this tragic aspect of writing which was born in the last century, when under the weight of History, Literature became dissociated from the society which consumes it. Between the third person as used by Balzac and that used by Flaubert, there is a world of difference (that of 1848): in the former we have a view of History which is harsh, but coherent and certain of its principles, the triumph of an order; in the latter, an art which in order to escape its pangs of conscience either exaggerates conventions or frantically attempts to destroy them. Modernism begins with the search for a Literature which is no longer possible.

Thus we find, in the Novel too, this machinery directed towards both destruction and resurrection, and typical of the whole of modern art. What must be destroyed is duration, that is, the ineffable binding force running through existence: for order, whether it be that of poetic flow or of narrative signs, that of Terror or plausibility, is always a murder in intention. But what reconquers the writer is again duration, for it is impossible to develop a negative within time, without elaborating a positive art, an order which must be destroyed anew. So that the greater modern works linger as long as possible, in a sort of miraculous stasis, on the threshold of Literature, in this anticipatory state in which the breadth of life is given, stretched but not yet destroyed by this crowning phase, an order of signs. For instance, we have the first person in Proust, whose whole work rests on a slow and protracted effort towards Literature. We have Jean Cayrol, whose acquiescence to the Novel comes only as the very last stage of soliloquy, as if the literary act, being supremely ambiguous, could be delivered of a creation consecrated by society, only at the moment when it has at last succeeded in destroying the existential density of a hitherto meaningless duration.

The Novel is a Death; it transforms life into destiny, a memory into a useful act, duration into an orientated and meaningful time. But this transformation can be accomplished only in full view of society. It is society which imposes the Novel, that is, a complex of signs, as a transcendence and as the History of a duration. It is therefore by the obviousness of its intention, grasped in that of the narrative signs, that one can recognize the path which, through all the solemnity of art, binds the writer to society. The preterite and the third person in the Novel are nothing but the fateful gesture with which the writer draws attention to the mask which he is wearing. The whole of Literature can declare *Larvatus prodeo*[2] "As I walk forward, I point out my mask." Whether we deal with the inhuman experience of the poet, who accepts the most momentous of all breaks, that from the language of society, or with the plausible untruth of the novelist, sincerity here feels a need of the signs of falsehood, and of conspicuous falsehood in order to last and to be consumed. Writing is the product, and ultimately the source, of this ambiguity. This specialized language, the use of which gives the writer a glorious but none the less superintended function, evinces a kind of servitude, invisible at first, which characterizes any responsibility. Writing, free in its beginnings, is finally the bond which links the writer to a History which is itself in chains: society stamps upon him the unmistakable signs of art so as to draw him along the more inescapably in its own process of alienation.

Notes

1. The sentence which for Valéry epitomized the conventions of the novel.
2. *Larvatus prodeo* was the motto of Descartes.

7

Distance and Point of View: An Essay

in Classification · WAYNE BOOTH

"But he [the narrator] little knows what surprises lie in wait for him, if someone were to set about analysing the mass of truth and falsehoods which he has collected here." — "Dr. S.," in *Confessions of Zeno*

Like other notions used in talking about fiction, point of view has proved less useful than was expected by the critics who first brought it to our attention. When Percy Lubbock hailed the triumph of Henry James's dramatic use of the "central intelligence," and told us that "the whole intricate question of method, in the craft of fiction," is governed by "the relation in which the narrator stands to the story," he might have predicted that many critics would, like E. M. Forster, disagree with him. But he could hardly have predicted that his converts would produce, in forty years of elaborate investigations of point of view, so little help to the author or critic who must decide whether this or that technique in a particular work is appropriate to this or that effect. On the one hand we have been given classifications and descriptions which leave us wondering why we have bothered to classify and describe; the author who counted the number of times the word "I" appears in each of Jane Austen's novels may be more obviously absurd than the innumerable scholars who have traced in endless detail the "*Ich-Erzählung*," or "*erlebte Rede*," or "*monologue intérieur*" from Dickens to Joyce or from James to Robbe-Grillet. But he is no more irrelevant to literary judgment. To describe particulars may be interesting but it is only the preliminary to the kind of knowledge that might help us explain the success or failure of individual works.

On the other hand, our efforts at formulating useful principles have been of little more use because they have been overtly prescriptive. If to count the number of times "I" occurs tells us nothing about how many times "I" should occur, to formulate abstract appeals for more "showing" and less "telling," for less authorial commentary and more drama, for more realistic consistency and fewer arbitrary shifts which remind the reader that he is reading a book, gives us the illusion of having discovered criteria when we really have not. While it is certainly true that some effects are best achieved by avoiding some kinds of telling, too often our prescriptions have been for "the novel" entire, ignoring what James himself knew well: there are "5,000,000 ways to tell a story," depending on one's overall purposes. Too many Jamesians have tried to establish in advance the precise degree of realistic intensity or irony or objectivity or "aesthetic distance" his work should display.

It is true that dissenting voices are now heard more and more frequently, perhaps the most important being Kathleen Tillotson's recent inaugural lecture at the University of London, *The Tale and the Teller.* But the clichés about the superiority of dramatic showing over mere telling are still to be found everywhere: in scholarly journals, in the literary quarterlies, in the weekly reviews, in the latest book on how to read a novel, and in dust-jacket blurbs. "The author does not tell you directly but you find out for yourself from their [the characters'] every word, gesture, and act," a Modern Library jacket tells us about Salinger's *Nine Stories.* That this is praise, that Salinger would be in error if he were found telling us anything directly, is taken for granted.

Since the novelist's choices are in fact practically unlimited, in judging their effectiveness we can only fall back on the kind of reasoning used by Aristotle in the *Poetics: if* such-and-such an effect is desired, *then* such-and-such points of view will be good or bad. We all agree that point of view is in some sense a technical matter, a means to larger ends; whether we say that technique is the artist's way of discovering his artistic meaning or that it is his way of working his will upon his audience, we still can judge it only in the light of the larger meanings or effects which it is designed to serve. Though we all at times violate our own convictions, most of us are convinced that we have no right to impose on the artist abstract criteria derived from other kinds of work.

But even when we have decided to put our judgments in the hypothetical "if-then" form, we are still faced with an overwhelming variety of choices. One of the most striking features of our criticism is the casual way in which we allow ourselves to reduce this variety, thoughtlessly, carelessly, to simple categories, the impoverishment of which is evident whenever we look at any existing novel. On the side of effect critics at one time had a fairly large number of terms to play with — terms like tragedy, comedy, tragicomedy, epic, farce, satire, elegy, and the like. Though the neoclassical kinds were often employed in inflexible form, they did provide a frame of discourse which allowed the critic and artist to communicate with each other: "if the effect you want is what we have traditionally expected under the concept 'tragedy,' then your technique here is inadequate." If what we are working for is a first-rate comedy, Dryden tells us in "An Essay of Dramatic Poesy," then here are some rules we can count on; they may be difficult to apply, they may require painstaking discussion, and they will certainly require genius if they are to be made to work, but they can still be of help to artist and critic because they are based on an agreement about a recognized literary effect.

In place of the earlier kinds, we have generally substituted a criticism based on qualities that are supposed to be sought in all works. All novels are said to be aiming for a common degree of realistic intensity; ambiguity and irony are discussed as if they were always beauties, never blemishes. Point of view should always be used "consistently," because otherwise the realistic illusion will be destroyed.

When technical means are related to such simplified ends, it is hardly surprising that they are themselves simplified. Yet we all know that our experience of particular works is more complex than the simple terminology suggests. The prescriptions against "telling" cannot satisfy any reader who has experienced *Tom Jones, The Egoist, Light in August,* or *Ulysses* (the claim that the author does not address us directly in the last of these is one of the most astonishingly persistent myths in modern criticism). They explicitly contradict our experience of dozens of good novels of the past fifteen years which, like Joyce Cary's posthumous *The Captive and the Free,* have rediscovered for us how lively "telling" can be. We all know, of course, that "too much" of the author's voice is, as Aristotle said, unpoetic. But how much is too much? Is there an abstract rule applicable to "the novel," quite aside from the needs of particular works or kinds?

Our experience with the great novels tells us that there is not. Most novels, like most plays, cannot be purely dramatic, entirely shown as taking place in the moment. There are always what Dryden called "relations," narrative summaries of action that takes place "off-stage." And try as we will to ignore the troublesome fact, "some parts of the action are more fit to be represented, some to be related." But related by whom? When? At what length? The dramatist must decide, and his decision will be based in large part on the particular needs of the work in hand. The novelist's case is different mainly in that he has more devices to choose from; he may speak with all of the voices available to the dramatist, and he may also choose — some would say he is also tempted by — some forms of telling not easily adapted to the stage.

Unfortunately our terminology for the author's many voices has been inadequate. If we name over three or four of the great narrators — say Cervantes's Cid, Hamete Benengeli, Tristram Shandy, the "author" of *Middlemarch*, and Strether in *The Ambassadors* (with his nearly effaced "author" using his mind as a reflector of events) — we find again that to describe any of them with conventional terms like "first person" and "omniscient" tells us little about how they differ from each other, and consequently it tells us little about why they succeed while others, described in the same terms, fail. Some critics do, indeed, talk about the problem of "authority," showing that first-person tales produce difficulties in stories which do not allow any one person to know all that goes on; having made this point, which seems so obvious, they are often then driven to find fault with stories like *Moby-Dick*, in which the author allows his narrator to know of events that happen outside his designated sphere of authority.

We can never be sure that enriching our terms will improve our criticism. But we can be quite sure that the terms with which we have long been forced to work cannot help us in discriminating among effects too subtle — as are all actual literary effects — to be caught in such loose-meshed nets. Even at the risk of pedantry, then, it should be worth our while to attempt a richer tabulation of the forms the author's voice can take.

(1) Perhaps the most overworked distinction is that of "person." To say that a story is told in the first or the third person, and to group novels into one or the other kind, will tell us nothing of importance unless we become more precise and describe how the particular qualities of the narrators relate to specific desired effects. It is true that choice of the first person is sometimes unduly limiting; if the "I" has inadequate access to necessary information, the author may be led into improbabilities. But we can hardly expect to find useful criteria in a distinction that would throw all fiction into two, or at most three, heaps. In *this* pile we see *Henry Esmond*, "The Cask of Amontillado," *Gulliver's Travels*, and *Tristram Shandy*. In *that* we have *Vanity Fair*, *Tom Jones*, *The Ambassadors*, and *Brave New World*. But the commentary in *Vanity Fair* and *Tom Jones* is in the first person, often resembling more the intimate effect of *Tristram Shandy* than that of many third person works. And again, the effect of *The Ambassadors* is much closer to that of the great first-person novels, since Strether in large part "narrates" his own story, even though he is always referred to in the third person.

Further evidence that this distinction is ordinarily overemphasized is seen in the fact that all of the following functional distinctions apply to both first- and third-person narration alike.

(2) There are *dramatized* narrators and *undramatized* narrators. The former are always and the latter are usually distinct from the implied author who is responsible for their creation.

(a) *The implied author (the author's "second self"*). Even the novel in which no narrator is dramatized creates an implicit picture of an author who stands behind the scenes, whether as stage manager, as puppeteer, or as an indifferent God, silently paring his fingernails. This implied author is always distinct from the "real man"—whatever we may take him to be—who creates a superior version of himself as he creates his work; any successful novel makes us believe in an "author" who amounts to a kind of "second self." This second self is usually a highly refined and selected version, wiser, more sensitive, more perceptive than any real man could be.

Insofar as a novel does not refer directly to this author, there will be no distinction between him and the implied, undramatized narrator; for example, in Hemingway's *The Killers* there is no narrator other than the implicit second self that Hemingway creates as he writes.

(b) *Undramatized narrators.* Stories are usually not as rigorously scenic as "The Killers"; most tales are presented as passing through the consciousness of a teller, whether an "I" or a "he." Even in drama much of what we are given is narrated by someone, and we are often as much interested in the effect on the narrator's own mind and heart as we are in learning what *else* the author has to tell us. When Horatio tells of his first encounter with the ghost in *Hamlet*, his own character, though never mentioned explicitly as part of the narrative event, is important to us as we listen. In fiction, as soon as we encounter an "I" we are conscious of an experiencing mind whose views of the experience will come between us and the event. When there is no such "I," as in *The Killers*, the inexperienced reader may make the mistake of thinking that the story comes to him unmediated. But even the most naive reader must recognize that something mediating and transforming has come into a story from the moment that the author explicitly places a narrator into the tale, even if he is given no personal characteristics whatever.

One of the most frequent reading faults comes from a naive identification of such narrators with the authors who create them. But in fact there is always a distinction, even though the author himself may not have been aware of it as he wrote. The created author, the "second self," is built up in our minds from our experience with all of the elements of the presented story. When one of those elements is an explicit reference to an experiencing narrator, our view of the author is derived in part from our notion of how the presented "I" relates to what he claims to present. Even when the "I" or "he" thus created is ostensibly the author himself — Fielding, Jane Austen, Dickens, Meredith — we can always distinguish between the narrator and the created author who presents him. But though the distinction is always present, it is usually important to criticism only when the narrator is explicitly dramatized.

(c) *Dramatized narrators.* In a sense even the most reticent narrator has been "dramatized" as soon as he refers to himself as "I," or, like Flaubert, tells us that "we" were in the classroom when Charles Bovary entered. But many novels dramatize their narrators with great fullness. In some works the narrator becomes a major person of great physical, mental, and moral vividness (*Tristram Shandy, Remembrance of Things Past*, and *Dr. Faustus*); in such works the narrator is often radically different from the implied author who creates him, and whose own character is built up in our minds partly by the way in which the narrator is made to differ from him. The range of human types that have been dramatized as narrators is almost as great as the range of other fictional characters — one must say "almost" because there are some characters who are unqualified to narrate or reflect a story.

We should remind ourselves that many dramatized narrators are never explicitly labeled as narrators at all. In a sense, every speech, every gesture, narrates; most works contain disguised narrators who, like Molière's *raisonneurs*, are used to tell the audience what it needs to know, while seeming merely to act out their roles. The most important unacknowledged narrators are, however, the third-person "centers of consciousness" through whom authors filter their narrative. Whether such "reflectors," as James sometimes called them, are highly polished, lucid mirrors reflecting complex mental experience, or the rather turbid, sense-bound "camera eyes" of much fiction since James, they fill precisely the function of avowed narrators.

> Gabriel had not gone with the others. He was in a dark part of the hall gazing up the staircase. A woman was standing near the top of the first flight, in the shadow also. He could not see her face but he could see the terra-cotta and salmon-pink panels of her skirt which the shadow made appear black and white. It was his wife. She was leaning on the banisters, listening to something. Gabriel was surprised at her stillness and strained his ear to listen also. But he could hear little save the noise of laughter and dispute on the front

steps, a few chords struck on the piano and a few notes of a man's voice singing. . . . He asked himself what is a woman standing on the stairs in the shadow, listening to distant music, a symbol of.

The very real advantages of this method, for some purposes, have been a dominant note in modern criticism. Indeed, so long as our attention is on such qualities as naturalness and vividness, the advantages seem overwhelming. It is only as we break out of the fashionable assumption that all good fiction seeks these qualities in the same degree that we are forced to recognize disadvantages. The third-person reflector is only one mode among many, suitable for some effects but cumbersome and even harmful when other effects are desired.

(3) Among dramatized narrators, whether first-person or third-person reflectors, there are mere *observers* (the "I" of *Tom Jones*, *The Egoist*, *Troilus and Criseyde*), and there are *narrator-agents* who produce some measurable effect on the course of events (ranging from the minor involvement of Nick in *The Great Gatsby* to the central role of Tristram Shandy, Moll Flanders, Huckleberry Finn, and — in the third person — Paul Morel in *Sons and Lovers*). Clearly any rules we might discover about observers may or may not apply to narrator-agents, yet the distinction is seldom made in talk about point of view.

(4) All narrators and observers, whether first or third person, can relay their tales to us primarily as *scene* ("The Killers," *The Awkward Age*), primarily as *summary* or what Lubbock called "picture" (Addison's almost completely nonscenic tales in *The Spectator*), or, most commonly, as a combination of the two.

Like Aristotle's distinction between dramatic and narrative manners, the somewhat different modern distinction between telling and showing does cover the ground. But the trouble is that it pays for broad coverage with gross imprecision. Narrators of all shapes and shades must either report dialogue alone or support it with "stage directions" and description of setting. But when we think of the radically different effect of a scene reported by Huck Finn and a scene reported by Poe's Montresor, we see that the quality of being "scenic" suggests very little about literary effect. And compare the delightful summary of twelve years given in two pages of *Tom Jones* (III, i), with the tedious showing of even ten minutes of uncurtailed conversation in the hands of a Sartre when he allows his passion for "durational realism" to dictate a scene when summary is called for. We can only conclude that the contrast between scene and summary, between showing and telling—indeed, between any two dialectical terms that try to cover so much ground—is not prescriptive or normative but loosely descriptive only. And as description, it is likely to tell us very little until we specify the kind of narrator who is providing the scene or the summary.

(5) Narrators who allow themselves to tell as well as show vary greatly depending on the amount and kind of *commentary* allowed in addition to a direct relating of events in scene and summary. Such commentary can, of course, range over any aspect of human experience, and it can be related to the main business in innumerable ways and degrees. To treat of it as if it were somehow a single device is to ignore important differences between commentary that is merely ornamental, commentary that serves a rhetorical purpose but is not part of the dramatic structure, and commentary that is integral to the dramatic structure, as in *Tristram Shandy*.

(6) Cutting across the distinction between observers and narrator-agents of all these kinds is the distinction between *self-conscious narrators*, aware of themselves as writers (*Tom Jones, Tristram Shandy, Barchester Towers, The Catcher in the Rye, Remembrance of Things Past, Dr. Faustus*), and narrators or observers who rarely if ever discuss their writing chores (*Huckleberry Finn*) or who seem unaware that they are writing, thinking, speaking, or "reflecting" a literary work (Camus's *The Stranger*, Lardner's *Haircut*, Bellow's *The Victim*).

(7) Whether or not they are involved in the action as agents, narrators and third-person reflectors differ markedly according to the degree and kind of *distance* that separates them from the author, the reader, and the other characters of the story they relate or reflect. Such distance is often discussed under terms like "irony," or "tone," but our experience is in fact much more diverse than such terms are likely to suggest. "Aesthetic distance" has been especially popular in recent years as a catchall term for any lack of identification between the reader and the various norms in the work. But surely this useful term should be reserved to describe the degree to which the reader or spectator is asked to forget the artificiality of the work and "lose himself" in it; whatever makes him aware that he is dealing with an aesthetic object and not real life increases "aesthetic distance," in this sense. What I am dealing with is more complex and more difficult to describe, and it includes "aesthetic distance" as one of its elements.

In any reading experience there is an implied dialogue among author, narrator, the other characters, and the reader. Each of the four can range, in relation to each of the others, from identification to complete opposition, on any axis or value or judgment: moral, intellectual, aesthetic, and even physical (does the reader who stammers react to the stammering of H. C. Earwicker as I do? Surely not). The elements usually discussed under "aesthetic distance" enter in of course; distance in time and space, differences of social class or conventions of speech or dress — these and many others serve to control our sense that we are dealing with an aesthetic object, just as the paper moons and other unrealistic stage effects of some modern drama have had an "alienation" effect. But we must not confuse these effects with the equally important effects of personal beliefs and qualities, in author, narrator, reader, and all others in the cast of characters. Though we cannot hope to deal with all of the varieties of control over distance that narrative technique can achieve, we can at least remind ourselves that we deal here with something more than the question of whether the author attempts to maintain or destroy the illusion of reality.

(a) The *narrator* may be more or less distant from the *implied author.* The distance may be moral (Jason versus Faulkner; the barber versus Lardner, the narrator versus Fielding in *Jonathan Wild*). It may be intellectual (Twain and Huck Finn, Sterne and Tristram Shandy in the matter of bigotry about the influence of noses, Richardson and Clarissa). It may be physical or temporal: most authors are distant from even the most knowing narrator in that they presumably know how "everything turns out in the end"; and so on.

(b) The *narrator* also may be more or less distant from the *characters* in the story he tells. He may differ, for example, morally, intellectually, and temporally (the mature narrator and his younger self in *Great Expectations* or *Redburn*), morally and intellectually (Fowler the narrator and Pyle the American in Greene's *The Quiet American*, both departing radically from the author's norms but in different directions), or morally and emotionally (Maupassant's "The Necklace," and Huxley's "Nuns at Luncheon," in which the narrators affect less emotional involvement than Maupassant and Huxley clearly expect from the reader).

(c) The *narrator* may be more or less distant from the *reader's* own norms, e.g., physically and emotionally (Kafka's *The Metamorphosis*); morally and emotionally (Pinkie in *Brighton Rock*, the miser in Mauriac's *Knot of Vipers*; the many moral degenerates that modern fiction has managed to make into convincing human beings).

One of the standard sources of plot in modern fiction — often advanced in the name of repudiating plot — is the portrayal of narrators whose characteristics change in the course of the works they narrate. Ever since Shakespeare taught the modern world what the Greeks had overlooked in neglecting character change (compare *Macbeth* and *Lear* with *Oedipus*), stories of character development or degeneration have become more and more popular. But it was not until we had discovered the full uses of the third-person reflector that we found how to show a narrator changing *as he narrates*. The mature Pip, in *Great Expectations*, is presented as a generous man whose heart is where the reader's is supposed to be; he watches his young self move away from the reader, as it were, and then back again. But the third-person reflector can be shown, technically in the past tense but in effect present before our eyes, moving toward or away from values that the reader holds dear. The twentieth century has proceeded almost as if determined to work out all of the permutations and combinations on this effect: start far and end near; start near and end far; start far, move close, but lose the prize and end far; start near, like Pip, move away, but see the light and return close; start far and move farther (many modern "tragedies" are so little tragic because the hero is too distant from us at the beginning for us to care that he is, like Macbeth, even further at the end); start near and end nearer. . . . I can think of no theoretical possibilities that haven't been tried; anyone who has read widely in modern fiction can fill in examples.

(d) The *implied author* may be more or less distant from the *reader*. The distance may be intellectual (the implied author of *Tristram Shandy*, not of course to be identified with Tristram, is more interested in and knows more about recondite classical lore than any of his readers), moral (the works of Sade), and so on. From the author's viewpoint, a successful reading of his book will reduce to zero the distance between the essential norms of his implied author and the norms of the postulated reader. Often enough there is very little distance to begin with; Jane Austen does not have to convince us that pride and prejudice are undesirable. A bad book, on the other hand, is often a book whose implied author clearly asks that we judge according to norms we cannot accept.

(e) The *implied author* (and reader) may be more or less distant from *other characters*, ranging from Jane Austen's complete approval of Jane Fairfax in *Emma* to her contempt for Wickham in *Pride and Prejudice*. The complexity that marks our pleasure in all significant literature can be seen by contrasting the kinds of distance in these two situations. In *Emma*, the *narrator* is noncommittal toward Jane Fairfax, though there is no sign of disapproval. The *author* can be inferred as approving of her almost completely. But the chief *reflector*, Emma, who has the largest share of the job of narration, is definitely disapproving of Jane Fairfax for most of the way. In *Pride and Prejudice*, on the other hand, the narrator is noncommittal toward Wickham for as long as possible, hoping to mystify us; the author is secretly disapproving; and the chief reflector, Elizabeth, is definitely approving for the first half of the book.

It is obvious that on each of these scales my examples do not begin to cover the possibilities. What we call "involvement" or "sympathy" or "identification," is usually made up of many reactions to author, narrators, observers, and other characters. And narrators may differ from their authors or readers in various kinds of involvement or detachment, ranging from deep personal concern (Nick in *The Great Gatsby*, MacKellar in *The Master of Ballantrae*, Zeitblom in *Dr. Faustus*) to a bland or mildly amused or merely curious detachment (Waugh's *Decline and Fall*).

In talk about point of view in fiction, the most seriously neglected of these kinds of distance is that between the fallible or unreliable narrator and the implied author who carries the reader with him as against the narrator. If the reason for discussing point of view is to find how it relates to literary effects, then surely the moral and intellectual qualities of the narrator are more important to our judgment than whether he is referred to as "I" or "he," or whether he is privileged or limited, and so on. If he is discovered to be untrustworthy, then the total effect of the work he relays to us is transformed.

Our terminology for this kind of distance in narrators is almost hopelessly inadequate. For lack of better terms, I shall call a narrator *reliable* when he speaks for or acts in accordance with the norms of the work (which is to say, the implied author's norms), *unreliable* when he does not. It is true that most of the great reliable narrators indulge in large amounts of incidental irony, and they are thus "unreliable" in the sense of being potentially deceptive. But difficult irony is not sufficient to make a narrator unreliable. We should reserve the term unreliable for those narrators who are presented as if they spoke *throughout* for the norms of the book and who do not in fact do so. Unreliability is not ordinarily a matter of lying, although deliberately deceptive narrators have been a major resource of some modern novelists (Camus's *The Fall*, Calder Willingham's *Natural Child*, etc.). It is most often a matter of what James calls *inconscience;* the narrator is mistaken, or he pretends to qualities which the author denies him. Or, as in *Huckleberry Finn*, the narrator claims to be naturally wicked while the author silently praises his virtues, as it were, behind his back.

Unreliable narrators thus differ markedly depending on how far and in what direction they depart from their author's norms; the older term "tone," like the currently fashionable "distance," covers many effects that we should distinguish. Some narrators, like Barry Lyndon, are placed as far "away" from author and reader as possible, in respect to every virtue except a kind of interesting vitality. Some, like Fleda Vetch, the reflector in James's *The Spoils of Poynton*, come close to representing the author's ideal of taste, judgment, and moral sense. All of them make stronger demands on the reader's powers of inference than does reliable narration.

(8) Both reliable and unreliable narrators can be *isolated*, unsupported or uncorrected by other narrators (Gully Jimson in *The Horse's Mouth*, Henderson in Bellow's *Henderson the Rain King*) or supported or corrected (*The Sound and the Fury*). Sometimes it is almost impossible to infer whether or to what degree a narrator is fallible; sometimes explicit corroborating or conflicting testimony makes the inference easy. Support or correction differs radically, it should be noted, depending on whether it is provided from within the action, so that the narrator-agent might benefit (Faulkner's *Intruder in the Dust*) or is simply provided externally, to help the reader correct or reinforce his own view *as against the narrator's* (Graham Greene's *The Power and the Glory*). Obviously the effects of isolation will be radically different in the two cases.

(9) Observers and narrator-agents, whether self-conscious or not, reliable or not, commenting or silent, isolated or supported, can be either *privileged* to know what could not be learned by strictly natural means or *limited* to realistic vision and inference. Complete privilege is what we usually call omniscience. But there are many kinds of privilege, and very few "omniscient" narrators are allowed to know or show as much as their authors know.

We need a good study of the varieties of limitation and their function. Some limitations are only temporary, or even playful, like the ignorance Fielding sometimes imposes on his "I" (as when he doubts his own powers of narration and invokes the Muses for aid, e.g., *Tom Jones* XIII, i). Some are more nearly permanent but subject to momentary relaxation, like the generally limited, humanly realistic Ishmael in *Moby-Dick*, who can yet break through his human limitations when the story requires (" 'He waxes brave, but nevertheless obeys; most careful bravery that!' murmured Ahab" — with no one present to report to the narrator). And some are confined to what their literal condition would allow them to know (first person, Huck Finn; third person, Miranda and Laura in Katherine Anne Porter's stories).

The most important single privilege is that of obtaining an inside view, because of the rhetorical power that such a privilege conveys upon a narrator. A curious ambiguity in our notions of "omniscience" is ordinarily hidden by our terminology. Many modern works that we usually classify as narrated dramatically, with everything relayed to us through the limited views of the characters, postulate fully as much omniscience in the silent author as Fielding claims for himself. Our roving visitation into the minds of sixteen characters in Faulkner's *As I Lay Dying*, seeing nothing but what those minds contain, may seem in one sense not to depend on an omniscient narrator. But this method is omniscience with teeth in it: the implied author demands our absolute faith in his powers of divination. We must never for a moment doubt that he knows everything about each of these sixteen minds, or that he has chosen correctly how much to show of each. In short the choice of the most rigorously limited point of view is really no escape from omniscience — the true narrator is as "unnaturally" all-knowing as he ever was. If evident artificiality were a fault — which it is not — modern narration would be as faulty as Trollope's.

Another way of suggesting the same ambiguity is to look closely at the concept of "dramatic" story-telling. The author can present his characters in a dramatic situation without in the least presenting them in what we normally think of as a dramatic manner. When Joseph Andrews, who has been stripped and beaten by thieves, is overtaken by a stagecoach, Fielding presents the scene in what by some modern standards must seem an inconsistent and undramatic mode. "The poor wretch, who lay motionless a long time, just began to recover his senses as a stage-coach came by. The postilion hearing a man's groans, stopped his horses, and told the coachman, he was certain there was a dead man lying in the ditch. . . . A lady, who heard what the postilion said, and likewise heard the groan, called eagerly to the coachman to stop and see what was the matter. Upon which he bid the postilion alight, and look into the ditch. He did so, and returned, 'That there was a man sitting upright, as naked as ever he was born.'" There follows a splendid description, hardly meriting the name of *scene*, in which the selfish reactions of each passenger are recorded. A young lawyer points out that they might be legally liable if they refuse to take Joseph up. "These words had a sensible effect on the coachman, who was well acquainted with the person who spoke them; and the old gentleman above mentioned, thinking the naked man would afford him frequent opportunities of showing his wit to the lady, offered to join with the company in giving a mug of beer for his fare; till partly alarmed by the threats of the one, and partly by the promises of the other, and being perhaps a little moved with compassion at the poor creature's condition, who stood bleeding and shivering with the cold, he at length agreed." Once Joseph is in the coach, the same kind of indirect reporting of the "scene" continues, with frequent excursions, however superficial, into the minds and hearts of the assembly of fools and knaves, and occasional guesses when complete knowledge seems inadvisable. If to be dramatic is to show characters dramatically engaged with each other, motive clashing with motive, the outcome depending upon the resolution of motives, then this scene is dramatic. But if it is to give the impression that the story is taking place by itself, with the characters existing in a dramatic relationship vis-à-vis the spectator, unmediated by a narrator and decipherable only through inferential matching of word to word and word to deed, then this is a relatively undramatic scene.

On the other hand, an author can present a character in this latter kind of dramatic relationship with the reader without involving that character in any internal drama at all. Many lyric poems are dramatic in this sense and totally undramatic in any other. "That is no country for old men — " Who says? Yeats, or his "mask," says. To whom? To us. How do we know that it is Yeats and not some character as remote from him as Caliban is remote from Browning in "Caliban upon Setebos"? We infer it as the dramatized statement unfolds; the need for the inference is what makes the lyric *dramatic* in this sense. Caliban, in short, is dramatic in two senses; he is in a dramatic situation with other characters and he is in a dramatic situation over-against us. Yeats, or if we prefer "Yeats's mask," is dramatic in only one sense.

The ambiguities of the word dramatic are even more complicated in fiction that attempts to dramatize states of consciousness directly. Is *A Portrait of the Artist as a Young Man* dramatic? In some respects, yes. We are not told about Stephen. He is placed on the stage before us, acting out his destiny with only disguised help or comments from his author. But it is not his actions that are dramatized directly, not his speech that we hear unmediated. What is dramatized is his mental record of everything that happens. We see his consciousness at work on the world. Sometimes what it records is itself dramatic, as when Stephen observes himself in a scene with other characters. But the report itself, the internal record, is dramatic in the second sense only. The report we are given of what goes on in Stephen's mind is a monologue uninvolved in any modifying dramatic context. And it is an *infallible* report, even less subject to critical doubts than the typical Elizabethan soliloquy. We accept, by convention, the claim that what is reported as going on in Stephen's mind really goes on there, or in other words, that Joyce knows how Stephen's mind works. "The equation of the page of his scribbler began to spread out a widening tail, eyed and starred like a peacock's; and, when the eyes and stars of its indices had been eliminated, began slowly to fold itself together again. The indices appearing and disappearing were eyes opening and closing; the eyes opening and closing were stars . . . " Who says so? Not Stephen, but the omniscient, infallible author. The report is direct, and it is clearly unmodified by any "dramatic" context — that is, unlike a speech in a dramatic scene, we do not suspect that the report has here been in any way aimed at an effect on anyone but the reader. We are thus in a dramatic relation with Stephen only in a limited sense — the sense in which a lyrical poem is dramatic.

Indeed, if we compare the act of reporting in *Tom Jones* with the act of reporting in *Portrait*, the former is in one sense considerably more dramatic; Fielding dramatizes himself and his telling, and even though he is essentially reliable we must be constantly on our toes in comparing word to word and word to deed. "It is an observation sometimes made, that to indicate our idea of a simple fellow, we say, he is easily to be seen through: nor do I believe it a more improper denotation of a simple book. Instead of applying this to any particular performance, we choose rather to remark the contrary in this history, where the scene opens itself by small degrees; and he is a sagacious reader who can see two chapters before him." Our running battle to keep up with these incidental ironies in Fielding's narration is matched, in *Portrait*, with an act of absolute, unquestioning credulity.

We should note finally that the author who eschews both forms of artificiality, both the traditional omniscience and the modern manipulation of inside views, confining himself to "objective" surfaces only, is not necessarily identical with the "undramatized author" under (2) above. In *The Awkward Age*, for example, James allows himself to comment frequently, but only to conjecture about the meaning of surfaces; the author is dramatized, but dramatized as partially ignorant of what is happening.

(10) Finally, narrators who provide inside views differ in the depth and the axis of their plunge. Boccaccio can give inside views, but they are extremely shallow. Jane Austen goes relatively deep morally, but scarcely skims the surface psychologically. All authors of stream-of-consciousness narration attempt to go deep psychologically, but some of them deliberately remain shallow in the moral dimension. We should remind ourselves that any sustained inside view, of whatever depth, temporarily turns the character whose mind is shown into a narrator; inside views are thus subject to variations in all of the qualities we have described above, and most importantly in the degree of unreliability. Generally speaking, the deeper our plunge, the more unreliability we will accept without loss of sympathy. The whole question of how inside views and moral sympathy interrelate has been seriously neglected.

Narration is an art, not a science, but this does not mean that we are necessarily doomed to fail when we attempt to formulate principles about it. There are systematic elements in every art, and criticism of fiction can never avoid the responsibility of trying to explain technical successes and failures by reference to general principles. But the question is that of where the general principles are to be found. Fiction, the novel, point of view — these terms are not in fact subject to the kind of definition that alone makes critical generalizations and rules meaningful. A given technique cannot be judged according to its service to "the novel," or "fiction," but only according to its success in particular works or kinds of work.

It is not surprising to hear practicing novelists report that they have never had help from critics about point of view. In dealing with point of view the novelist must always deal with the individual work: which particular character shall tell this particular story, or part of a story, with what precise degree of reliability, privilege, freedom to comment, and so on. Shall he be given dramatic vividness? Even if the novelist has decided on a narrator who will fit one of the critic's classifications — "omniscient," "first person," "limited omniscient," "objective," "roving," "effaced," and so on — his troubles have just begun. He simply cannot find answers to his immediate, precise, practical problems by referring to statements that the "omniscient is the most flexible method," or "the objective the most rapid or vivid," or whatever. Even the soundest of generalizations at this level will be of little use to him in his page-by-page progress through his novel. As Henry James's detailed records show, the novelist discovers his narrative technique as he tries to achieve for his readers the potentialities of his developing idea. The majority of his choices are consequently choices of degree, not kind. To decide that your narrator shall not be omniscient decides practically nothing. The hard question is, just how *inconscient* shall he be? To decide that you will use first-person narration decides again almost nothing. What kind of first person? How fully characterized? How much aware of himself as a narrator? How reliable? How much confined to realistic inference, how far privileged to go beyond realism? At what points shall he speak truth and at what points utter no judgment or even utter falsehood?

There are no doubt *kinds* of effect to which the author can refer — e.g., if he wants to make a scene more amusing, poignant, vivid, or ambiguous, or if he wants to make a character more sympathetic or more convincing, such-and-such practices may be indicated. But it is not surprising that in his search for help in his decisions, he should find the practice of his peers more helpful than the abstract rules of the textbooks: the sensitive author who reads the great novels finds in them a storehouse of precise examples, examples of how *this* effect, as distinct from all other possible effects, was heightened by the proper narrative choice. In dealing with the types of narration, the critic must always limp behind, referring constantly to the varied practice which alone can correct his temptations to overgeneralize.

8

Marxist Aesthetics and Literary Realism

GEORG LUKÁCS

The Marxist philosophy of history is a comprehensive doctrine dealing with the necessary progress made by humanity from primitive communism to our own time and the perspectives of our further advance along the same road. As such, it also gives us indications for the historical future. But such indications—born of the recognition of certain laws governing historical development—are not a cookery book providing recipes for each phenomenon or period; Marxism is not a Baedeker of history, but a signpost pointing the direction in which history moves forward. The final certainty it affords consists in the assurance that the development of mankind does not and cannot finally lead to nothing and nowhere.

Of course, such generalizations do not do full justice to the guidance given by Marxism, a guidance extending to every topical problem of life. Marxism combines a consistent following of an unchanging direction with incessant theoretical and practical allowances for the deviousness of the path of evolution. Its well-defined philosophy of history is based on a flexible and adaptable acceptance and analysis of historical development. This apparent duality—which is in reality the dialectic unity of the materialist worldview—is also the guiding principle of Marxist aesthetics and literary theory.

Those who do not know Marxism at all or know it only superficially or at second hand, may be surprised by the respect for the classical heritage of mankind which one finds in the really great representatives of this doctrine and by their incessant references to that classical heritage. Without wishing to enter into too much detail, we mention as an instance, in philosophy, the heritage of Hegelian dialectics, as opposed to the various trends in the latest philosophies. "But all this is long out of date," the modernists cry. "All this is the undesirable, outworn legacy of the nineteenth century," say those who—intentionally or unintentionally, consciously or unconsciously—support the Fascist ideology and its pseudo-revolutionary rejection of the past, which is in reality a rejection of culture and humanism. Let us look without prejudice at the bankruptcy of the very latest philosophies; let us consider how most philosophers of our day are compelled to pick up the broken and scattered fragments of dialectic (falsified and distorted in this decomposition) whenever they want to say something even remotely touching its essence about present-day life; let us look at the modern attempts at a philosophical synthesis and we shall find them miserable, pitiful caricatures of the old genuine dialectic, now consigned to oblivion.

It is not by chance that the great Marxists were jealous guardians of our classical heritage in their aesthetics as well as in other spheres. But they do not regard this classical heritage as a reversion to the past; it is a necessary outcome of their philosophy of history that they should regard the past as irretrievably gone and not susceptible of renewal. Respect for the classical heritage of humanity in aesthetics means that the great Marxists look for the true highroad of history, the true direction of its development, the true course of the historical curve, the formula of which they know; and because they know the formula they do not fly off at a tangent at every hump in the graph, as modern thinkers often do because of their theoretical rejection of the idea that there is any such thing as an unchanged general line of development.

For the sphere of aesthetics this classical heritage consists in the great arts which depict man as a whole in the whole of society. Again it is the general philosophy (here: proletarian humanism) which determines the central problems posed in aesthetics. The Marxist philosophy of history analyses man as a whole, and contemplates the history of human evolution as a whole, together with the partial achievement, or non-achievement of completeness in its various periods of development. It strives to unearth the hidden laws governing all human relationships. Thus the object of proletarian humanism is to reconstruct the complete human personality and free it from the distortion and dismemberment to which it has been subjected in class society. These theoretical and practical perspectives determine the criteria by means of which Marxist aesthetics establish a bridge back to the classics and at the same time discover new classics in the thick of the literary struggles of our own time. The ancient Greeks, Dante, Shakespeare, Goethe, Balzac, Tolstoy all give adequate pictures of great periods of human development and at the same time serve as signposts in the ideological battle fought for the restoration of the unbroken human personality.

Such viewpoints enable us to see the cultural and literary evolution of the nineteenth century in its proper light. They show us that the true heirs of the French novel, so gloriously begun early in the last century, were not

Flaubert and especially not Zola, but the Russian and Scandinavian writers of the second half of the century. The present volume contains my studies of French and Russian realist writers seen in this perspective.

If we translate into the language of pure aesthetics the conflict (conceived in the sense of the philosophy of history) between Balzac and the later French novel, we arrive at the conflict between realism and naturalism. Talking of a conflict here may sound a paradox to the ears of most writers and readers of our day. For most present-day writers and readers are used to literary fashions swinging to and fro between the pseudo-objectivism of the naturalist school and the mirage-subjectivism of the psychologist or abstract-formalist school. And inasmuch as they see any worth in realism at all, they regard their own false extreme as a new kind of near-realism or realism. Realism, however, is not some sort of middle way between false objectivity and false subjectivity, but on the contrary the true, solution-bringing third way, opposed to all the pseudo-dilemmas engendered by the wrongly posed questions of those who wander without a chart in the labyrinth of our time. Realism is the recognition of the fact that a work of literature can rest neither on a lifeless average, as the naturalists suppose, nor on an individual principle which dissolves its own self into nothingness. The central category and criterion of realist literature is the type, a peculiar synthesis which organically binds together the general and the particular both in characters and situations. What makes a type a type is not its average quality, not its mere individual being, however profoundly conceived; what makes it a type is that in it all the humanly and socially essential determinants are present on their highest level of development, in the ultimate unfolding of the possibilities latent in them, in extreme presentation of their extremes, rendering concrete the peaks and limits of men and epochs.

True great realism thus depicts man and society as complete entities, instead of showing merely one or the other of their aspects. Measured by this criterion, artistic trends determined by either exclusive introspection or exclusive extraversion equally impoverish and distort reality. Thus realism means a three-dimensionality, an all-roundness, that endows with independent life characters and human relationships. It by no means involves a rejection of the emotional and intellectual dynamism which necessarily develops together with the modern world. All it opposes is the destruction of the completeness of the human personality and of the objective typicality of men and situations through an excessive cult of the momentary mood. The struggle against such tendencies acquired a decisive importance in the realist literature of the nineteenth century. Long before such tendencies appeared in the practice of literature, Balzac had already prophetically fore-seen and outlined the entire problem in his tragicomic story *Le chef d'oeuvre inconnu*. Here, experiment on the part of a painter to create a new classic three-dimensionality by means of an ecstasy of emotion and colour quite in the spirit of modern impressionism, leads to complete chaos. Fraunhofer, the tragic hero, paints a picture which is a tangled chaos of colours out of which a perfectly modeled female leg and foot protrude as an almost for-tuitous fragment. Today a considerable section of modern artists has given up the Fraunhofer-like struggle and is content with finding, by means of new aesthetic theories, a justification for the emotional chaos of their works.

The central aesthetic problem of realism is the adequate presentation of the complete human personality. But as in every profound philosophy of art, here, too, the consistent following-up to the end of the aesthetic view-point leads us beyond pure aesthetics: for art, precisely if taken in its most perfect purity, is saturated with social and moral humanistic problems. The demand for a realistic creation of types is in opposition both to the trends in which the biological being of man, the physiological aspects of self-preservation and procreation are dominant (Zola and his disciples), and to the trends which sublimate man into purely mental, psychological pro-cesses. But such an attitude, if it remained within the sphere of formal aesthetic judgments, would doubtless be quite arbitrary, for there is no reason why, regarded merely from the point of view of good writing, erotic conflict with its attendant moral and social conflicts should be rated higher than the elemental spontaneity of pure sex. Only if we accept the concept of the complete human personality as the social and historical task humanity has to solve; only if we regard it as the vocation of art to depict the most important turning points of this process with all the wealth of the factors affecting it; only if aesthetics assign to art the role of explorer and guide, can the content of life be systematically divided up into spheres of greater and lesser importance; into spheres that throw light on types and paths and spheres that remain in darkness. Only then does it become evident that any description of mere biological processes — be these the sexual act or pain and sufferings, however detailed and, from the literary point of view, perfect it may be — results in a leveling-down of the social, historical, and moral being of men and is not a means but an obstacle to such essential artistic expression as illuminating human conflicts in all their complexity and com-pleteness. It is for this reason that the new contents and new media of expression contributed by naturalism have led not to an enrichment but to an impoverishment and narrowing-down of literature.

Apparently similar trains of thought were already put forward in early polemics directed against Zola and his school. But the psychologists, although they were more than once right in their concrete condemnation of Zola and the Zola school, opposed another no less false extreme to the false extreme of naturalism. For the inner life of man, its essential traits and essential conflicts, can be truly portrayed only in organic connection with social and historical factors. Separated from the latter and developing merely its own immanent dialectic, the psychologist trend is no less abstract, and distorts and impoverishes the portrayal of the complete human personality no less than does the naturalist biologism which it opposes.

It is true that, especially regarded from the viewpoint of modern literary fashions, the position in respect of the psychologist school is at the first glance less obvious than in the case of naturalism. Everyone will immediately see that a description in the Zola manner of, say, an act of copulation between Dido and Aeneas or Romeo and Juliet would resemble each other much more closely than the erotic conflicts depicted by Virgil and Shakespeare, which acquaint us with an inexhaustible wealth of cultural and human facts and types. Pure introspection is apparently the diametrical opposite of naturalist leveling-down, for what it describes are quite individual, non-recurring traits. But such extremely individual traits are also extremely abstract, for this very reason of non-recurrence. Here, too, Chesterton's witty paradox holds good, that the inner light is the worst kind of lighting. It is obvious to everyone that the coarse biologism of the naturalists and the rough outlines drawn by propagandist writers deform the true picture of the complete human personality. Much fewer are those who realize that the psychologists' punctilious probing into the human soul and their transformation of human beings into a chaotic flow of ideas destroy no less surely every possibility of a literary presentation of the complete human personality. A Joyce-like shoreless torrent of associations can create living human beings just as little as Upton Sinclair's coldly calculated all-good and all-bad stereotypes.

Owing to lack of space this problem cannot be developed here in all its breadth. Only one important and at present often neglected point is to be stressed here because it demonstrates that the live portrayal of the complete human personality is possible only if the writer attempts to create types. The point in question is the organic, indissoluble connection between man as a private individual and man as a social being, as a member of a community. We know that this is the most difficult question of modern literature today and has been so ever since modern *bourgeois* society came into being.

On the surface the two seem to be sharply divided, and the appearance of the autonomous, independent existence of the individual is all the more pronounced, the more completely modern *bourgeois* society is developed. It seems as if the inner life, genuine "private" life, were proceeding according to its own autonomous laws and as if its fulfillments and tragedies were growing ever more independent of the surrounding social environment. And correspondingly, on the other side, it seems as if the connection with the community could manifest itself only in high-sounding abstractions, the adequate expression for which would be either rhetoric or satire.

An unbiased investigation of life and the setting aside of these false traditions of modern literature lead easily enough to the uncovering of the true circumstances, to the discovery which had long been made by the great realists of the beginning and middle of the nineteenth century and which Gottfried Keller expressed thus: "Everything is politics." The great Swiss writer did not intend this to mean that everything was immediately tied up with politics: on the contrary, in his view — as in Balzac's and Tolstoy's — every action, thought, and emotion of human beings is inseparably bound up with the life and struggles of the community, i.e., with politics; whether the humans themselves are conscious of this, unconscious of it, or even trying to escape from it, objectively their actions, thoughts, and emotions nevertheless spring from and run into politics.

The true great realists not only realized and depicted this situation — they did more than that, they set it up as a demand to be made on men. They knew that this distortion of objective reality (although, of course, due to social causes), this division of the complete human personality into a public and a private sector was a mutilation of the essence of man. Hence they protested not only as painters of reality, but also as humanists, against this fiction of capitalist society, however unavoidable this spontaneously formed superficial appearance. If as writers, they delved deeper in order to uncover the true types of man, they had inevitably to unearth and expose to the eyes of modern society the great tragedy of the complete human personality.

In the works of such great realists as Balzac we can again find a third solution opposed to both false extremes of modern literature, exposing as an abstraction, as a vitiation of the true poesy of life, both the feeble common-places of the well-intentioned and honest propagandist novels and the spurious richness of a preoccupation with the details of private life.

This brings us face to face with the question of the topicality today of the great realist writers. Every great historical period is a period of transition, a contradictory unity of crisis and renewal, of destruction and rebirth; a new social order and a new type of man always come into being in the course of a unified though contradictory process. In such critical, transitional periods the tasks and responsibility of literature are exceptionally great. But only truly great realism can cope with such responsibilities; the accustomed, the fashionable media of expression, tend more and more to hamper literature in fulfilling the tasks imposed by history. It should surprise no one if from this point of view we turn against the individualistic, psychologist trends in literature. It might more legitimately surprise many that these studies express a sharp opposition to Zola and Zolaism.

Such surprise may be due in the main to the fact that Zola was a writer of the left and his literary methods were dominant chiefly, though by no means exclusively, in left-wing literature. It might appear, therefore, that we are involving ourselves in a serious contradiction, demanding on the one hand the politicization of literature and on the other hand attacking insidiously the most vigorous and militant section of left-wing literature. But this contradiction is merely apparent. It is, however, well suited to throw light on the true connection between literature and *Weltanschauung*.

The problem was first raised (apart from the Russian democratic literary critics) by Engels, when he drew a comparison between Balzac and Zola. Engels showed that Balzac, although his political creed was legitimist royalism, nevertheless inexorably exposed the vices and weakness of royalist feudal France and described its death agony with magnificent poetic vigour. This phenomenon, references to which the reader will find more than once in these pages, may at the first glance again — and mistakenly — appear contradictory. It might appear that the *Weltanschauung* and political attitude of serious great realists are a matter of no consequence. To a certain extent this is true. For from the point of view of the self-recognition of the present and from the point of view of history and posterity, what matters is the picture conveyed by the work; the question to what extent this picture conforms to the views of the authors is a secondary consideration.

This, of course, brings us to a serious problem of aesthetics. Engels, in writing about Balzac, called it "the triumph of realism"; it is a problem that goes down to the very roots of realist artistic creation. It touches the essence of true realism: the great writer's thirst for truth, his fanatic striving for reality — or expressed in terms of ethics: the writer's sincerity and probity. A great realist such as Balzac, if the intrinsic artistic development of situations and characters he has created comes into conflict with his most cherished prejudices or even his most sacred convictions, will, without an instant's hesitation, set aside these his own prejudices and convictions and describe what he really sees, not what he would prefer to see. This ruthlessness towards their own subjective world-picture is the hallmark of all great realists, in sharp contrast to the second-raters, who nearly always succeed in bringing their own *Weltanschauung* into "harmony" with reality, that is, forcing a falsified or distorted picture of reality into the shape of their own worldview. This difference in the ethical attitude of the greater and lesser writers is closely linked with the difference between genuine and spurious creation. The characters created by the great realists, once conceived in the vision of their creator, live an independent life of their own: their comings and goings, their development, their destiny is dictated by the inner dialectic of their social and individual existence. No writer is a true realist—or even a truly good writer, if he can direct the evolution of his own characters at will.

All this is however merely a description of the phenomenon. It answers the question as to the ethics of the writer: what will he do if he sees reality in such and such a light? But this does not enlighten us at all regarding the other question: what does the writer see and how does he see it? And yet it is here that the most important problems of the social determinants of artistic creation arise. In the course of these studies we shall point out in detail the basic differences which arise in the creative methods of writers according to the degree to which they are bound up with the life of the community, take part in the struggles going on around them, or are merely passive observers of events. Such differences determine creative processes which may be diametrical opposites; even the experience which gives rise to the work will be structurally different, and in accordance with this the process of shaping the work will be different. The question of whether a writer lives within the community or is a mere observer of it, is determined not by psychological, not even by typological factors; it is the evolution of society that determines (not automatically, not fatalistically, of course), the line the evolution of an author will take. Many a writer of a basically contemplative type has been driven to an intense participation in the life of the community by the social conditions of his time; Zola, on the contrary, was by nature a man of action, but his epoch turned him into a mere observer and when at last he answered the call of life, it came too late to influence his development as a writer.

But even this is as yet only the formal aspect of this problem, although no longer the abstractly formal. The question grows essential and decisive only when we examine concretely the position taken up by a writer. What does he love and what does he hate? It is thus that we arrive at a deeper interpretation of the writer's true *Weltanschauung*, at the problem of the artistic value and fertility of the writer's worldview. The conflict which previously stood before us as the conflict between the writer's worldview and the faithful portrayal of the world he sees, is now clarified as a problem within the *Weltanschauung* itself, as a conflict between a deeper and a more superficial level of the writer's own *Weltanschauung*.

Realists such as Balzac or Tolstoy in their final posing of questions always take the most important, burning problems of the community for their starting-point; their pathos as writers is always stimulated by those sufferings of the people which are the most acute at the time; it is these sufferings that determine the objects and direction of their love and hate and through these emotions determine also what they see in their poetic visions and how they see it. If, therefore, in the process of creation their conscious worldview comes into conflict with the world seen in their vision, what really emerges is that their true conception of the world is only superficially formulated in the consciously held worldview, and the real depth of their *Weltanschauung*, their deep ties with the great issues of their time, their sympathy with the sufferings of the people can find adequate expression only in the being and fate of their characters.

No one experienced more deeply than Balzac the torments which the transition to the capitalist system of production inflicted on every section of the people, the profound moral and spiritual degradation which necessarily accompanied this transformation on every level of society. At the same time Balzac was also deeply aware of the fact that this transformation was not only socially inevitable, but at the same time progressive. This contradiction in his experience Balzac attempted to force into a system based on a Catholic legitimism and tricked out with Utopian conceptions of English Toryism. But this system was contradicted all the time by the social realities of his day and the Balzacian vision which mirrored them. This contradiction itself clearly expressed, however, the real truth: Balzac's profound comprehension of the contradictorily progressive character of capitalist development.

It is thus that great realism and popular humanism are merged into an organic unity. For if we regard the classics of the social development that determined the essence of our age, from Goethe and Walter Scott to Gorki and Thomas Mann, we find *mutatis mutandis* the same structure of the basic problem. Of course every great realist found a different solution for the basic problem in accordance with his time and his own artistic personality. But they all have in common that they penetrate deeply into the great universal problems of their time and inexorably depict the true essence of reality as they see it. From the French Revolution onwards the development of society moved in a direction which rendered inevitable a conflict between such aspirations of men of letters and the literature and public of their time. In this whole age a writer could achieve greatness only in the struggle against the current of everyday life. And since Balzac the resistance of daily life to the deeper tendencies of literature, culture, and art has grown ceaselessly stronger. Nevertheless, there were always writers who in their life work, despite all the resistance of the day, fulfilled the demand formulated by Hamlet: "to hold the mirror up to nature," and by means of such a reflected image aided the development of mankind and the triumph of humanist principles in a society so contradictory in its nature that it on the one hand gave birth to the ideal of the complete human personality and on the other hand destroyed it in practice.

The great realists of France found worthy heirs only in Russia. All the problems mentioned here in connection with Balzac apply in an even greater measure to Russian literary development and notably to its central figure Leo Tolstoy. It is not by chance that Lenin (without having read Engels's remarks about Balzac) formulated the Marxist view of the principles of true realism in connection with Tolstoy. Hence there is no need for us to refer to these problems again here. There is all the more need, however, to call attention to the erroneous conceptions current in respect of the historical and social foundations of Russian realism, errors which in many cases are due to deliberate distortion or concealment of facts. In Britain, as everywhere else in Europe, the newer Russian literature is well known and popular among the intelligent reading public. But as everywhere else, the reactionaries have done all they could to prevent this literature from becoming popular; they felt instinctively that Russian realism, even if each single work may not have a definite social tendency, is an antidote to all reactionary infection.

Only if we have a correct aesthetic conception of the essence of Russian classical realism can we see clearly the social and even political importance of its past and future fructifying influence on literature. With the collapse and eradication of Fascism a new life has begun for every liberated people. Literature has a great part to play in solving the new tasks imposed by the new life in every country. If literature is really to fulfill this role, a role dictated by history, there must be as a natural prerequisite, a philosophical and political rebirth of the writers who produce it. But although this is an indispensable prerequisite, it is not enough. It is not only the opinions that must change, but the whole emotional world of men; and the most effective propagandists of the new, liberating, democratic feeling are the men of letters. The great lesson to be learnt from the Russian development is precisely the extent to which a great realist literature can fructifyingly educate the people and transform public opinion. But such results can be achieved only by a truly great, profound, and all-embracing realism. Hence, if literature is to be a potent factor of national rebirth, it must itself be reborn in its purely literary, formal, aesthetic aspects as well. It must break with reactionary, conservative traditions which hamper it and resist the seeping-in of decadent influences which lead into a blind alley.

In these respects the Russian writers' attitude to life and literature is exemplary, and for this, if for no other reason, it is most important to destroy the generally accepted reactionary evaluation of Tolstoy, and, together with the elimination of such false ideas, to understand the human roots of his literary greatness. And what is most important of all: to show how such greatness comes from the human and artistic identification of the writer with some broad popular movement. It matters little in this connection what popular movement it is in which the writer finds this link between himself and the masses; that Tolstoy sinks his roots into the mass of the Russian peasantry, and Gorki of the industrial workers and landless peasants. For both of them were to the bottom of their souls bound up with the movements seeking the liberation of the people and struggling for it. The result of such a close link in the cultural and literary sphere was then and is today that the writer can overcome his isolation, his relegation to the role of a mere observer, to which he would otherwise be driven by the present state of capitalist society. He thus becomes able to take up a free, unbiased, critical attitude towards those tendencies of present-day culture which are unfavourable to art and literature. To fight against such tendencies by purely artistic methods, by the mere formal use of new forms, is a hopeless undertaking, as the tragic fate of the great writers of the West in the course of the last century clearly shows. A close link with a mass movement struggling for the emancipation of the common people does, on the other hand, provide the writer with the broader viewpoint, with the fructifying subject matter from which a true artist can develop the effective artistic forms which are commensurate with the requirements of the age, even if they go against the superficial artistic fashions of the day.

These very sketchy remarks were required before we could express our final conclusion. Never in all its history did mankind so urgently require a realist literature as it does today. And perhaps never before have the traditions of great realism been so deeply buried under a rubble of social and artistic prejudice. It is for this reason that we consider a revaluation of Tolstoy and Balzac so important. Not as if we wished to set them up as models to be imitated by the writers of our day. To set an example means only: to help in correctly formulating the task and studying the conditions of a successful solution. It was thus that Goethe aided Walter Scott, and Walter Scott aided Balzac. But Walter Scott was no more an imitator of Goethe than Balzac was of Scott. The practical road to a solution for the writer lies in an ardent love of the people, a deep hatred of the people's enemies and the people's own errors, the inexorable uncovering of truth and reality, together with an unshakable faith in the march of mankind and their own people towards a better future.

There is today in the world a general desire for a literature which could penetrate with its beam deep into the tangled jungle of our time. A great realist literature could play the leading part, hitherto always denied to it, in the democratic rebirth of nations. If in this connection we evoke Balzac in opposition to Zola and his school, we believe that we are helping to combat the sociological and aesthetical prejudices which have prevented many gifted authors from giving their best to mankind. We know the potent social forces which have held back the development of both writers and literature: a quarter century of reactionary obscurantism which finally twisted itself into the diabolical grimace of the Fascist abomination.

Political and social liberation from these forces is already an accomplished fact, but the thinking of the great masses is still bedevilled by the fog of reactionary ideas which prevents them from seeing clearly. This difficult and dangerous situation puts a heavy responsibility on the men of letters. But it is not enough for a writer to see clearly in matters political and social. To see clearly in matters of literature is no less indispensable and it is to the solution of these problems that this book hopes to bring its contribution.

9

The Concept of Character in Fiction

WILLIAM H. GASS

I have never found a handbook on the art of fiction or the stage, nor can I imagine finding one, that did not contain a chapter on the creation of character, a skill whose mastery, the author of each manual insists, secures for one the inner secrets of these arts: not, mind you, an easy thing: rather as difficult as the whole art itself, since, in a way, it is the whole art: to fasten in the memory of the reader, like a living presence, some bright human image. All well and good to paint a landscape, evoke a feeling, set a tempest loose, but not quite good enough to nail an author to his immortality if scheming Clarence, fat, foul-trousered Harry, or sweetly terraced Priss do not emerge from the land they huff and rage and eat in fully furnished out by Being; enough alive, indeed, to eat and huff in ours — dear God, more alive than that! — sufficiently enlarged by genius that they threaten to eat up and huff down everything in sight.

Talk about literature, when it is truly talk about something going on in the pages, if it is not about ideas, is generally about the people in it, and ranges from those cries of wonder, horror, pleasure, or surprise, so readily drawn from the innocently minded, to the annotated stammers of the most erudite and nervous critics. But it is all the same. Great character is the most obvious single mark of great literature. The rude, the vulgar, may see in Alyosha nothing more than the image of a modest, God-loving youth; the scholar may perceive through this demeanor a symbolic form; but the Alyosha of the untutored is somehow more real and present to him than the youth on his street whom he's known since childhood, loving of his God and modest too, equally tried, fully as patient; for in some way Alyosha's visionary figure will take lodging in him, make a model for him, so to reach, without the scholar's inflationary gifts, general form and universal height; whereas the neighbor may merely move away, take cold, and forget to write. Even the most careful student will admit that fiction's fruit survives its handling and continues growing off the tree. A great character has an endless interest; its fascination never wanes. Indeed it is a commonplace to say so. Hamlet. Ahab. Julien Sorel. Madame Bovary. There is no end to their tragedy. Great literature is great because its characters are great, and characters are great when they are memorable. A simple formula. The Danish ghost cries to remember him, and obediently—for we are gullible and superstitious clots—we do.

It hasn't always been a commonplace. Aristotle regarded character as a servant of dramatic action, and there have been an endless succession of opinions about the value and function of characters since—all dreary—but the important thing to be noted about nearly every one of them is that whatever else profound and wonderful these theories have to say about the world and its personalities, characters are clearly conceived as living outside language. Just as the movie star deserts herself to put on some press agent's more alluring fictional persona, the hero of a story sets out from his own landscape for the same land of romance the star reached by stepping there from life. These people—Huckleberry Finn, the Snopeses, Prince Myshkin, Pickwick, Molly Bloom—seem to have come to the words of their novels like a visitor to town . . . and later they leave on the arm of the reader, bound, I suspect, for a shabbier hotel, and dubious entertainments.

However, Aristotle's remark was a recommendation. Characters ought to exist for the sake of the action, he thought, though he knew they often did not, and those who nowadays say that given a sufficiently powerful and significant plot the characters will be dominated by it are simply answered by asking them to imagine the plot of *Moby-Dick* in the hands of Henry James, or that of *Sanctuary* done into Austen. And if you can persuade them to try (you will have no success), you may then ask how the heroes and the heroines come out. The same disastrous exercise can be given those who believe that traits make character like definitions do a dictionary. Take any set of traits you like and let Balzac or Joyce, Stendhal or Beckett, loose in a single paragraph to use them. Give your fictional creatures qualities, psychologies, actions, manners, moods; present them from without or from within; let economics matter, breeding, custom, history; let spirit wet them like a hose: all methods work, and none do. The nature of the novel will not be understood at all until this is: *from any given body of fictional text, nothing necessarily follows, and anything plausibly may.* Authors are gods—a little tinny sometimes but omnipotent no matter what, and plausible on top of that, if they can manage it.[1]

Though the handbooks try to tell us how to create characters, they carefully never tell us we are making images, illusions, imitations. Gatsby is not an imitation, for there is nothing he imitates. Actually, if he were a copy, an illusion, sort of shade or shadow, he would not be called a character at all. He must be unique, entirely himself, as if he had a self to be. He is required, in fact, to act *in character*, like a cat in a sack. No, theories of character are not absurd in the way representational theories are; they are absurd in a grander way, for the belief in Hamlet (which audiences often seem to have) is like the belief in God — incomprehensible to reason — and one is inclined to seek a motive: some deep fear or emotional need.

There are too many motives. We pay heed so easily. We are so pathetically eager for this other life, for the sounds of distant cities and the sea; we long, apparently, to pit ourselves against some trying wind, to follow the fortunes of a ship hard beset, to face up to murder and fornication, and the somber results of anger and love; oh, yes, to face up — *in books* — when on our own we scarcely breathe. The tragic view of life, for instance, in Shakespeare or in Schopenhauer, Unamuno, Sartre, or Sophocles, is not one jot as pure and penetratingly tragic as a pillow stuffed with Jewish hair, and if we want to touch life where it burns, though life is what we are even now awash with — futilely, stupidly drawing in — we ought not to back off from these other artifacts (wars, pogroms, poverty: men make them, too). But of course we do, and queue up patiently instead to see Prince Hamlet moon, watch him thrust his sword through a curtain, fold it once again into Polonius, that foolish old garrulous proper noun. The so-called life one finds in novels, the worst and best of them, is nothing like actual life at all, and cannot be; it is not more real, or thrilling, or authentic; it is not truer, more complex, or pure, and its people have less spontaneity, are less intricate, less free, less full.[2]

It is not a single cowardice that drives us into fiction's fantasies. We often fear that literature is a game we can't afford to play — the product of idleness and immoral ease. In the grip of that feeling it isn't life we pursue, but the point and purpose of life — its facility, its use. So Sorel is either a man it is amusing to gossip about, to see in our friends, to puppet around in our dreams, to serve as our more able and more interesting surrogate in further fanciful adventures; or Sorel is a theoretical type, scientifically profound, representing a deep human strain, and the writing of *The Red and the Black* constitutes an advance in the science of — what would you like? sociology?

Before reciting a few helpless arguments, let me suggest, in concluding this polemical section, just how absurd these views are which think of fiction as a mirror or a window onto life — as actually creative of living creatures — for really one's only weapon against Tertullians is ridicule.

There is a painting by Picasso which depicts a pitcher, candle, blue enamel pot. They are sitting, unadorned, upon the barest table. Would we wonder what was cooking in that pot? Is it beans, perhaps, or carrots, a marmite? The orange of the carrot is a perfect complement to the blue of the pot, and the genius of Picasso, neglecting nothing, has surely placed, behind that blue, invisible disks of dusky orange, which, in addition, subtly enrich the table's velvet brown. Doesn't that seem reasonable? Now I see that it must be beans, for above the pot — you can barely see them — are quaking lines of steam, just the lines we associate with boiling beans . . . or is it blanching pods? Scholarly research, supported by a great foundation, will discover that exactly such a pot was used to cook cassoulet in the kitchens of Charles the Fat . . . or was it Charles the Bald? There's a dissertation in that. And this explains the dripping candle standing by the pot. (Is it dripping? no? a pity. Let's go on.) For isn't Charles the Fat himself that candle? Oh no, some say, he's not! Blows are struck. Reputations made and ruined. Someone will see eventually that the pot is standing on a table, not a stove. But the pot has just come from the stove, it will be pointed out. Has not Picasso caught that vital moment of transition? The pot is too hot. The brown is burning. Oh, not *this* table, which has been coated with resistant plastic. Singular genius — blessed man — he thinks of everything.

Here you have half the history of our criticism in the novel. Entire books have been written about the characters in Dickens, Trollope, Tolstoy, Faulkner. But why not? Entire books have been written about God, his cohorts, and the fallen angels.

A character, first of all, is the noise of his name, and all the sounds and rhythms that proceed from him. We pass most things in novels as we pass things on a train. The words flow by like the scenery. All is change.[3] But there are some points in a narrative which remain relatively fixed; we may depart from them, but soon we return, as music returns to its theme. Characters are those primary substances to which everything else is attached. Hotels, dresses, conversations, sausage, feelings, gestures, snowy evenings, faces — each may fade as fast as we read of them. Yet the language of the novel will eddy about a certain incident or name, as Melville's always circles back to Ahab and his wedding with the white whale. Mountains are characters in Malcolm Lowry's *Under the Volcano*, so is a ravine, a movie, mescal, or a boxing poster. A symbol like the cross can be a character. An idea or a situation (the anarchist in *The Secret Agent*, bomb ready in his pocket), or a particular event, an obsessive thought, a decision (Zeno's, for instance, to quit smoking), a passion, a memory, the weather, Gogol's overcoat — anything, indeed, which serves as a fixed point, like a stone in a stream or that soap in Bloom's pocket, functions as a character. Character, in this sense, is a matter of degree, for the language of the novel may loop back seldom, often, or incessantly. But the idea that characters are like primary substances has to be taken in a double way, because if any thing becomes a character simply to the degree the words of the novel qualify it, it also loses some of its substance, some of its primacy, to the extent that it, in turn, qualifies something else. In a perfectly organized novel, every word would ultimately qualify one thing, like the God of the metaphysician, at once the subject and the body of the whole.[4] Normally, characters are fictional human beings, and thus are given proper names. In such cases, to create a character is to give meaning to an unknown X; it is *absolutely* to *define;* and since nothing in life corresponds to these X's, their reality is borne by their name. They *are*, where it *is*.

Most of the words the novelist uses have their meanings already formed. Proper names do not, except in a tangential way. It's true that Mr. Mulholland could not be Mr. Mull, and Mr. Cashmore must bear, as best he can, the curse of his wealth forever, along with his desire for gain. Character has a special excitement for a writer (apart from its organizing value) because it offers him a chance to give fresh meaning to new words. A proper name begins as a blank, like a wall or a canvas, upon which one might paint a meaning, perhaps as turbulent and mysterious, as treacherous and vast, as Moby-Dick's, perhaps as delicate, scrupulous, and sensitive as that of Fleda Vetch.

I cannot pause here over the subject of rhythm and sound, though they are the heartbeat of writing, of prose no less than poetry.

> Their friend, Mr. Grant-Jackson, a highly preponderant pushing person, great in discussion and arrangement, abrupt in overture, unexpected, if not perverse, in attitude, and almost equally acclaimed and objected to in the wide midland region to which he had taught, as the phrase was, the size of his foot — their friend had launched his bolt quite out of the blue and had thereby so shaken them as to make them fear almost more than hope.[5]

Mr. Grant-Jackson is a preponderant pushing person because he's been made by *p*'s, and the rhythm and phrasing of James's writing here prepares and perfectly presents him to us. Certainly we cannot think of Molly Bloom apart from her music, or the gay and rapid Anna Livia apart from hers.

If one examines the texture of a fiction carefully, one will soon see that some words appear to gravitate toward their subject like flies settle on sugar, while others seem to emerge from it. In many works this logical movement is easily discernible and very strong. When a character speaks, the words seem to issue from him and to be acts of his. Description first forms a *nature*, then allows that nature to *perform*. We must be careful, however, not to judge by externals. Barkis says that Barkis is willing, but the expression *functions* descriptively to qualify Barkis, and it is Dickens's habit to treat speech as if it were an attribute of character, like tallness or honesty, and not an act. On the other hand, qualities, in the right context, can be transformed into verbs. Later in the book don't we perceive the whiteness of the whale as a design, an intention of Moby-Dick's, like a twist of his flukes or the smashing of a small boat?

Whether Mr. Cashmore was once real and sat by James at someone's dinner table, or was instead the fabrication of James's imagination,[6] as long as he came into being from the world's direction he once existed outside language. The task of getting him in I shall call the problem of rendering. But it must be stressed (it cannot be stressed too severely) that Mr. Cashmore may never have had a model, and may never have been imagined either, but may have come to be in order to serve some high conception (a Mr. Moneybags) and represent a type, not just himself, in which case he is not a reality *rendered*, but a universal *embodied*.[7] Again, Mr. Cashmore might have had still other parents. Meanings in the stream of words before his appearance might have suggested him, dramatic requirements may have called him forth, or he may have been the spawn of music, taking his substance from rhythm and alliteration. Perhaps it was all of these. In well-regulated fictions, most things are *over-determined*.

So far I have been talking about the function of a character in the direct stream of language, but there are these two other dimensions, the rendered and the embodied, and I should like to discuss each briefly.

If we observe one of J. F. Powers's worldly priests sharpening his eye for the pin by putting through his clerical collar, the humor, with all *its* sharpness, lives in the situation, and quite incidentally in the words.[8] One can indeed imagine Powers thinking it up independently of any verbal formula. Once Powers had decided that it would be funny to show a priest playing honeymoon bridge with his housekeeper, then his problem becomes the technical one of how best to accomplish it. What the writer must do, of course, is not only render the scene, but render the scene inseparable from its language, so that if the idea (the chaste priest caught in the clichés of marriage) is taken from the situation, like a heart from its body, both die. Far easier to render a real cornfield in front of you, because once that rendering has reached its page, the cornfield will no longer exist for literary purposes, no one will be able to see it by peering through your language, and consequently there will be nothing to abstract from your description. But with a "thought up" scene or situation, this is not the case. It comes under the curse of story. The notion, however amusing, is not literary, for it might be painted, filmed, or played. If we inquire further and ask why Powers wanted such a scene in the first place, we should find, I think, that he wanted it in order to embody a controlling "idea" — at one level of abstraction, the worldliness of the church, for instance. If he had nuns around a kitchen table counting the Sunday take and listening to the Cubs, *that* would do it. Father Burner beautifully embodies just such a controlling idea in Powers's celebrated story "The Prince of Darkness." Both rendering and embodying involve great risks because they require working into a scientific order of words what was not originally there. Any painter knows that a contour may only more or less enclose his model, while a free line simply and completely is. Many of the model's contours may be esthetically irrelevant, so it would be unwise to follow them. The free line is subject to no such temptations. Its relevance can be total. As Valéry wrote: There are no details in execution.

Often novelists mimic our ordinary use of language. We report upon ourselves; we gossip. Normally we are not lying; and our language, built to refer, actually does. When these selfsame words appear in fiction, and when they follow the forms of daily use, they create, quite readily, that dangerous feeling that a real Tietjens, a real Nickleby, lives just beyond the page; that through that thin partition we can hear a world at love.[9] But the writer must not let the reader out; the sculptor must not let the eye fall from the end of his statue's finger; the musician must not let the listener dream. Of course, he will; but let the blame be on himself. High tricks are possible: to run the eye rapidly along that outstretched arm to the fingertip, only to draw it up before it falls away in space; to carry the reader to the very edge of every word so that it seems he must be compelled to react as though to truth as told in life, and then to return him, like a philosopher liberated from the cave, to the clear and brilliant world of concept, to the realm of order, proportion, and dazzling construction . . . to fiction, where characters, unlike ourselves, freed from existence, can shine like essence, and purely Be.

Notes

1. This has already been discussed in "Philosophy and the Form of Fiction." In "Mirror, Mirror," I complain that Nabokov's omnipotence is too intrusive. [The essays to which Gass refers in all of these notes appear in W. H. Gass, *Fiction and The Figures of Life*.]

2. I treat the relation of fiction to life in more detail in "In Terms of the Toenail: Fiction and the Figures of Life." The problem is handled in other ways in "The Artist and Society," "Even if, by All the Oxen in the World," and "The Imagination of an Insurrection."

3. Of course nothing prevents a person from feeling that life is like this. See "A Spirit in Search of Itself."

4. There is no reason why every novel should be organized in this way. This method constructs a world according to the principles of Absolute Idealism. See "Philosophy and the Form of Fiction."

5. Henry James, "The Birthplace."

6. Some aspects of this imagination are dealt with in "The High Brutality of Good Intentions," and "In The Cage."

7. See "Philosophy and the Form of Fiction."

8. I enlarge on this aspect of Powers's work in "The Bingo Game at the Foot of the Cross."

9. See "The Medium of Fiction."

10

Time and Narrative in *A la recherche du temps perdu*

GÉRARD GENETTE

I suggest a study of *narrative discourse* or, in a slightly different formulation, of *narrative* [*récit*] as *discourse* [*discours*]. As a point of departure, let us accept the hypothesis that all narratives, regardless of their complexity or degree of elaboration—and Proust's *A la recherche du temps perdu*, the text I shall be using as an example, reaches of course a very high degree of elaboration— can always be considered to be the development of a verbal statement such as "I am walking," or "He will come," or "Marcel becomes a writer." On the strength of this rudimentary analogy, the problems of narrative discourse can be classified under three main headings: the categories of *time* (temporal relationships between the narrative [story] and the "actual" events that are being told [history]); of *mode* (relationships determined by the distance and perspective of the narrative with respect to the history); and of *voice* (rela- tionships between the narrative and the narrating agency itself: narrative situation, level of narration, status of the narrator and of the recipient, etc.). I shall deal only, and very sketchily, with the first category.

The time-category can itself be divided into three sections: the first con- cerned with the relationships between the temporal *order* of the events that are being told and the pseudotemporal order of the narrative; the second concerned with the relationships between the *duration* of the events and the duration of the narrative; the third dealing with relationships of *frequency* of repetition between the events and the narrative, between history and story.

Order

It is well known that the folk tale generally keeps a one-to-one correspon- dence between the "real" order of events that are being told and the order of the narrative, whereas literary narrative, from its earliest beginnings in Western literature, that is, in the Homeric epic, prefers to use the beginning *in medias res*, generally followed by an explanatory flashback. This chrono- logical reversal has become one of the formal *topoi* of the epic genre. The style of the novel has remained remarkably close to its distant origin in this respect: certain beginnings in Balzac, as in the *Duchesse de Langeais* or *César Birotteau*, immediately come to mind as typical examples.

From this point of view, the *Recherche*—especially the earlier sections of the book—indicates that Proust made a much more extensive use than any of his predecessors of his freedom to reorder the temporality of events.

The first "time," dealt with in the six opening pages of the book, refers to a moment that cannot be dated with precision but that must take place quite late in the life of the protagonist: the time at which Marcel, during a period when, as he says, "he often used to go to bed early," suffered from spells of insomnia during which he relived his own past. The first moment in the organization of the narrative is thus far from being the first in the order of the reported history, which deals with the life of the hero.

The second moment refers to the memory relived by the protagonist during his sleepless night. It deals with his childhood at Combray, or, more accurately, with a specific but particularly important moment of this childhood: the famous scene that Marcel calls "the drama of his going to bed," when his mother, at first prevented by Swann's visit from giving him his ritualistic goodnight kiss, finally gives in and consents to spend the night in his room.

The third moment again moves far ahead, probably to well within the period of insomnia referred to at the start, or a little after the end of this period: it is the episode of the *madeleine*, during which Marcel recovers an entire fragment of his childhood that had up till then remained hidden in oblivion.

This very brief third episode is followed at once by a fourth: a second return to Combray, this time much more extensive than the first in temporal terms since it covers the entire span of the Combray childhood. Time segment (4) is thus contemporary with time segment (2) but has a much more extensive duration.

The fifth moment is a very brief return to the initial state of sleeplessness and leads to a new retrospective section that takes us even further back into the past, since it deals with a love experience of Swann that took place well before the narrator was born.

There follows a seventh episode that occurs some time after the last events told in the fourth section (childhood at Combray): the story of Marcel's adolescence in Paris and of his love for Gilberte. From then on, the story will proceed in more closely chronological order, at least in its main articulations.

A la recherche du temps perdu thus begins with a zigzagging movement that could easily be represented by a graph and in which the relationship between the time of events and the time of the narrative could be summarized as follows: N(arrative) 1 = H(istory) 4; N_2 = H_2; N_3 = H_4; N_4 = H_2; N_5 = H_4; N_6 = H_1 (Swann's love); N_7 = H_3. We are clearly dealing with a highly complex and deliberate transgression of chronological order. I have said that the rest of the book follows a more continuous chronology in its main patterns, but this large-scale linearity does not exclude the presence of a great number of anachronisms in the details: *retrospections*, as when the story of Marcel's stay in Paris during the year 1914 is told in the middle of his later visit to Paris during 1916; or *anticipations*, as when, in the last pages of *Du côté de chez Swann*, Marcel describes what has become of the Bois de Boulogne at a much later date, the very year he is actually engaged in writing his book. The transition from the *Côté de Guermantes* to *Sodome et Gomorrhe* is based on an interplay of anachronisms: the last scene of *Guermantes* (announcing the death of Swann) in fact takes place later than the subsequent first scene of *Sodome* (the meeting between Charlus and Jupien).

I do not intend to analyze the narrative anachronisms in detail but will point out in passing that one should distinguish between *external* and *internal* anachronisms, according to whether they are located without or within the limits of the temporal field defined by the main narrative. The external anachronisms raise no difficulty, since there is no danger that they will interfere with the main narrative. The internal anachronisms, on the contrary, create a problem of interference. So we must subdivide them into two groups, according to the nature of this relation. Some function to fill in a previous or later blank (ellipsis) in the narrative and can be called *completive* anachronisms, such as the retrospective story of Swann's death. Others return to a moment that has already been covered in the narrative: they are *repetitive* or apparently redundant anachronisms but fulfill in fact a very important function in the organization of the novel. They function as *announcements* (in the case of prospective anticipations) or as *recalls* (when they are retrospective). Announcements can, for example, alert the reader to the meaning of a certain event that will only later be fully revealed (as with the lesbian scene at Montjouvain that will later determine Marcel's jealous passion for Albertine). Recalls serve to give a subsequent meaning to an event first reported as without particular significance (as when we find that Albertine's belated response to a knock on the door was caused by the fact that she had locked herself in with Andrée), or serve even more often to alter the original meaning — as when Marcel discovers after more than thirty years' time that Gilberte was in love with him at Combray and that what he took to be a gesture of insolent disdain was actually meant to be an advance.

Next to these relatively simple and unambiguous retrospections and anticipations, one finds more complex and ambivalent forms of anachronisms: anticipations within retrospections, as when Marcel remembers what used to be his projects with regard to the moment that he is now experiencing; retrospections within anticipations, as when the narrator indicates how he will later find out about the episode he is now in the process of telling; "announcements" of events that have already been told anticipatively or "recalls" of events that took place earlier in the story but that have not yet been told; retrospections that merge seamlessly with the main narrative and make it impossible to identify the exact status of a given section, etc. Finally, I should mention what is perhaps the rarest but most specific of all instances: structures that could properly be called *achronisms*, that is to say, episodes entirely cut loose from any chronological situation whatsoever. These occurrences were pointed out by J. P. Houston in a very interesting study published in *French Studies* (January 1962) entitled "Temporal Patterns in *À la recherche du temps perdu.*" Near the end of *Sodome et Gomorrhe*, as Marcel's second stay at Balbec draws to a close, Proust tells a sequence of episodes not in the order in which they took place but by following the succession of roadside-stops made by the little train on its journey from Balbec to La Raspelière. Events here follow a geographical rather than a chronological pattern. It is true that the sequence of places still depends on a temporal event (the journey of the train), but this temporality is not that of the "real" succession of events. A similar effect is achieved in the composition of the end of *Combray*, when the narrator successively describes a number of events that took place on the Méséglise way, at different moments, by following the order of their increasing distance from Combray. He follows the temporal succession of a walk from Combray to Méséglise and then, after returning to his spatial and temporal point of departure, tells a sequence of events that took place on the Guermantes way using exactly the same principle. The temporal order of the narrative is not that of the actual succession of events, unless it happens to coincide by chance with the sequence of places encountered in the course of the walk.

I have given some instances of the freedom that Proust's narrative takes with the chronological order of events, but such a description is necessarily sketchy and even misleading if other elements of narrative temporality such as duration and frequency are not also taken into account.

Duration

Generally speaking, the idea of an isochrony between narrative and "history" is highly ambiguous, for the narrative unit which, in literature, is almost always a narrative text cannot really be said to possess a definite duration. One could equate the duration of a narrative with the time it takes to read it, but reading times vary considerably from reader to reader, and an ideal average speed can only be determined by fictional means. It may be better to start out from a definition in the form of a relative quantity, and define isochrony as a uniform projection of historical time on narrative extension, that is, number of pages per duration of event. In this way, one can record variations in the speed of the narrative in relation to itself and measure effects of acceleration, deceleration, stasis, and ellipsis (blank spaces within the narrative while the flow of events keeps unfolding).

I have made some rather primitive calculations of the relative speed of the main narrative articulations, measuring on the one hand the narrative of the *Recherche* by number of pages and on the other hand the events by quantity of time. Here are the results.

The first large section, *Combray* or Marcel's childhood, numbers approximately 180 pages of the Pléiade edition and covers about ten years (let me say once and for all that I am defining the duration of events by general consensus, knowing that it is open to question on several points). The next episode, Swann's love affair with Odette, uses approximately 200 pages to cover about two years. The Gilberte episode (end of *Swann*, beginning of *Jeunes filles en fleurs*) devotes 160 pages to a duration that can be evaluated at two or three years. Here we encounter an ellipsis involving two years of the protagonist's life and mentioned in passing in a few words at the beginning of a sentence. The Balbec episode numbers 300 pages for a three-month-long time-span; then the lengthy section dealing with life in Paris society (*Côté de Guermantes* and beginning of *Sodome et Gomorrhe*) takes up 750 pages for two and a half years. It should be added that considerable variations occur within this section: 110 pages are devoted to the afternoon party at Mme. de Villeparisis's that lasts for about two hours, 150 pages to the dinner of nearly equal length at the Duchesse de Guermantes's, and 100 pages to the evening at the Princesse de Guermantes's. In this vast episode of 750 pages for two and a half years, 360 pages—nearly one-half—are taken up by less than ten hours of social life.

The second stay at Balbec (end of *Sodome*) covers approximately six months in 380 pages. Then the Albertine sequence, reporting the hero's involvement with Albertine in Paris (*La Prisonnière* and beginning of *La Fugitive*), requires 630 pages for an eighteen-month period, of which 300 deal with only two days. The stay in Venice uses 35 pages for a few weeks, followed by a section of 40 pages (astride *La Fugitive* and *Le Temps retrouvé*) for the stay in Tansonville, the return to the country of Marcel's childhood. The first extended ellipsis of the *Recherche* occurs here; the time-span cannot be determined with precision, but it encompasses approximately ten years of the hero's life spent in a rest home. The subsequent episode, situated during the war, devotes 130 pages to a few weeks, followed by another ellipsis of ten years again spent in a rest home. Finally, the concluding scene, the party at the Princesse de Guermantes's, devotes 190 pages to a two- or three-hour-long reception.

What conclusions can be derived from this barren and apparently useless enumeration? First of all, we should note the extensive shifts in relative duration, ranging from one line of text for ten years to 190 pages for two or three hours, or from approximately one page per century to one page per minute. The second observation refers to the internal evolution of the *Recherche* as a whole. It could be roughly summarized by stressing, on the one hand, the gradual slowing down of the narrative achieved by the insertion of longer and longer scenes for events of shorter and shorter duration. This is compensated for, on the other hand, by the presence of more and more extensive ellipses. The two trends can be easily united in one formula: increasing discontinuity of the narrative. As the Proustian narrative moves toward its conclusion, it becomes increasingly discontinuous, consisting of gigantic scenes separated from each other by enormous gaps. It deviates more and more from the ideal "norm" of an isochronic narrative.

We should also stress how Proust selects among the traditional literary forms of narrative duration. Among the nearly infinite range of possible combinations of historical and narrative duration, the literary tradition has made a rather limited choice that can be reduced to the following fundamental forms: (1) the *summary*, when the narrative duration is greatly reduced with respect to the historical duration; it is well known that the summary constitutes the main connective tissue in the classical *récit*; (2) the dramatic scene, especially the dialogue, when narrative and historical time are supposed to be nearly equal; (3) the narrative *stasis*, when the narrative discourse continues while historical time is at a standstill, usually in order to take care of a description; and (4) *ellipsis*, consisting of a certain amount of historical time covered in a zero amount of narrative. If we consider the

Recherche from this point of view, we are struck by the total absence of summarizing narrative, which tends to be absorbed in the ellipses, and by the near-total absence of descriptive stasis: the Proustian descriptions always correspond to an actual observation-time on the part of the character; the time lapse is sometimes mentioned in the text and is obviously longer than the time it takes to read the description (three-quarters of an hour for the contemplation of the Elstir paintings owned by the Duc de Guermantes, when the description takes only four or five pages of the text). The narrative duration is not interrupted — as is so often the case with Balzac — for, rather than *describing*, Proust *narrates* how his hero perceives, contemplates, and experiences a given sight; the description is incorporated within the narrative and constitutes no autonomous narrative form. Except for another effect with which I shall deal at some length in a moment, Proust makes use of only two of the traditional forms of narrative duration: scene and ellipsis. And since ellipsis is a zero point of the text, we have in fact only one single form: the scene. I should add, however, without taking time to develop a rather obvious observation, that the narrative function of this traditional form is rather strongly subverted in Proust. The main number of his major scenes do not have the purely dramatic function usually associated with the classical "scene." The traditional economy of the novel, consisting of summarizing and nondramatic narrative alternating with dramatic scenes, is entirely discarded. Instead, we find another form of alternating movement toward which we must now direct our attention.

Frequency

The third kind of narrative temporality, which has in general received much less critical and theoretical attention than the two previous ones, deals with the relative frequency of the narrated events and of the narrative sections that report them. Speaking once more very schematically, the most obvious form of narration will tell once what happens once, as in a narrative statement such as: "Yesterday, I went to bed early." This type of narrative is so current and presumably normal that it bears no special name. In order to emphasize that it is merely one possibility among many, I propose to give it a name and call it the *singulative* narrative [*récit singulatif*]. It is equally possible to tell several times what happened several times, as when I say: "Monday I went to bed early, Tuesday I went to bed early, Wednesday I went to bed early," etc. This type of anaphoric narrative remains singulative and can be equated with the first, since the repetitions of the story correspond one-to-one to the repetitions of the events. A narrative can also tell several times, with or without variations, an event that happened only once, as in a statement of this kind: "Yesterday I went to bed early, yesterday I went to bed early, yesterday I tried to go to sleep well before dark," etc. This last hypothesis may seem a priori to be a gratuitous one, or even to exhibit a slight trace of senility. One should remember, however, that most texts by Alain Robbe-Grillet, among others, are founded on the repetitive potential of the narrative: the recurrent episode of the killing of the centipede, in *La jalousie*, would be ample proof of this. I shall call *repetitive* narrative this type of narration, in which the story repetitions exceed in number the repetitions of events. There remains a last possibility. Let us return to our second example: "Monday, Tuesday, Wednesday," etc. When such a pattern of events occurs, the narrative is obviously not reduced to the necessity of reproducing it as if its discourse were incapable of abstraction or synthesis. Unless a deliberate stylistic effect is aimed for, even the simplest narration will choose a formulation such as "every day" or "every day of the week" or "all week long." We all know which of these devices Proust chose for the opening sentence of the *Recherche*. The type of narrative in which a single narrative assertion covers several recurrences of the same event or, to be more precise, of several analogical events considered only with respect to what they have in common, I propose to call by the obvious name of *iterative* narrative [*récit itératif*].

My heavy-handed insistence on this notion may well seem out of place, since it designates a purely grammatical concept without literary relevance. Yet the quantitative amount and the qualitative function of the iterative mode are particularly important in Proust and have seldom, to my knowledge, received the critical attention they deserve. It can be said without exaggeration that the entire Combray episode is essentially an iterative narrative, interspersed here and there with some "singulative" scenes of salient importance such as the motherly goodnight kiss, the meeting with the Lady in the pink dress (a retrospective scene), or the profanation of Vinteuil's portrait at Montjouvain. Except for five or six such scenes referring to a single action and told in the historical past [*passé défini*], all the rest, told in the imperfect, deals with what used to happen at Combray regularly, ritualistically, every night or every Sunday, or every Saturday, or whenever the weather was good or the weather was bad, etc. The narrative of Swann's love for Odette will still be conducted, for the most part, in the mode of habit and repetition; the same is true of the story of Marcel's love for Swann's daughter Gilberte. Only when we reach the stay at Balbec in the *Jeunes filles en fleurs* do the singulative episodes begin to predominate, although they remain interspersed with numerous iterative passages: the Balbec outings with Mme. de Villeparisis and later with Albertine, the hero's stratagems at the beginning of *Guermantes* when he tries to meet the Duchess every morning, the journeys in the little train of the Raspelière (*Sodome*, 2), life with Albertine in Paris (the first eighty pages of *La Prisonnière*), the walks in Venice (*La Fugitive*), not to mention the iterative treatment of certain moments within the singulative scenes, such as the conversations about genealogy during the dinner at the Duchess's, or the description of the aging guests at the last Guermantes party. The narrative synthesizes these moments by reducing several distinct occurrences to their common elements: "the *women* were like this . . . the *men* acted like that; *some* did this, *others* that," etc. I shall call these sections *internal iterations*, in contrast with other, more common passages, in which a descriptive-iterative parenthesis begins in the middle of a singulative scene to convey additional information needed for the reader's understanding and which I shall call *external iterations*. An example would be the long passage devoted, in the middle of the first Guermantes dinner, to the more general and therefore necessarily iterative description of the Guermantes wit.

The use of iterative narrative is by no means Proust's invention; it is one of the most classical devices of fictional narrative. But the frequency of the mode is distinctively Proustian, a fact still underscored by the relatively massive presence of what could be called *pseudo-iterations*, scenes presented (mostly by the use of the imperfect tense) as if they were iterative, but with such a wealth of precise detail that no reader can seriously believe that they could have taken place repeatedly in this way, without variations. One thinks for example of some of the conversations between Aunt Léonie and her maid Françoise that go on for page after page, or of conversations in Mme. Verdurin's or Mme. Swann's salon in Paris. In each of these cases, a singular scene has arbitrarily, and without any but grammatical change, been converted into an iterative scene, thus clearly revealing the trend of the Proustian narrative toward a kind of inflation of the iterative.

It would be tempting to interpret this tendency as symptomatic of a dominant psychological trait: Proust's highly developed sense of habit and repetition, his feeling for the *analogy* between different moments in life. This is all the more striking since the iterative mode of the narrative is not always, as in the Combray part, based on the repetitive, ritualistic pattern of a bourgeois existence in the provinces. Contrary to general belief, Proust is less aware of the specificity of moments than he is aware of the specificity of places; the latter is one of the governing laws of his sensibility. His moments have a strong tendency to blend into each other, a possibility which is at the root of the experience of spontaneous recollection. The opposition between the "singularity" of his spatial imagination and, if I dare say so, the "iterativity" of his temporal imagination is nicely illustrated in the following sentence from *Swann*. Speaking of the Guermantes landscape, Proust writes: "[Its] specificity would *at times*, in my dreams, seize upon me with almost fantastical power" ("le paysage dont *parfois*, la nuit dans mes rêves, l'individualité m'étreint avec une puissance presque fantastique"). Hence the highly developed sense of *ritual* (see, for example, the scene of the Saturday luncheon at Combray) and, on the other hand, the panic felt in the presence of irregularities of behavior, as when Marcel, at Balbec, wonders about the complex and secret law that may govern the unpredictable absences of the young girls on certain days.

But we must now abandon these psychological extrapolations and turn our attention to the technical questions raised by the iterative narration.

Every iterative sequence can be characterized by what may be called its *delimitation* and its *specification*. The delimitation determines the confines within the flow of external duration between which the iterative sequence, which generally has a beginning and an end, takes place. The delimitation can be vague, as when we are told that "from a certain year on, Mlle. Vinteuil could never be seen alone" (1:147), or precise, defined — a very rare occurrence in Proust — by a specific date, or by reference to a particular event, as when the break between Swann and the Verdurins puts an end to an iterative sequence telling of Swann's encounters with Odette and starts off a new sequence. The specification, on the other hand, points out the recurring periodicity of the iterative unit. It can be indefinite (as is frequently the case in Proust who introduces an iterative statement by such adverbs of time as "sometimes," "often," "on certain days," etc.) or definite, when it follows an absolute and regular pattern such as: "every day," "every Sunday," etc. The pattern can also be more irregular and relative, as when the walks toward Méséglise are said to take place in bad or uncertain weather, or the walks toward Guermantes whenever the weather is good. Two or more specifications can of course be juxtaposed. "Every summer" and "every Sunday" combine to give "every Sunday in the summer," which is the iterative specification of much of the Combray section.

The interplay between these two dimensions of the iterative narrative varies and enriches a temporal mode threatened, by its very nature, by a degree of abstraction. Provided it has a certain length, an iterative section can very closely resemble an ordinary narrative, except for some grammatical traits. Yet it goes without saying that a narrative such as "Sunday at Combray" that would retain only events that *all* Sundays have in common would run the risk of becoming as dryly schematic as a stereotyped time-schedule. The monotony can be avoided by playing on the internal delimitations and specifications.

Internal delimitations: for instance, the diachronic caesura brought about by the story of the encounter with the "Lady in the pink dress" in the narration of Marcel's Sunday afternoon readings: this encounter will bring about a change of locale, after the quarrel between Marcel's parents and Uncle Adolphe has put the latter's room out of bounds. Another instance would be the change of direction in the hero's dreams of literary glory after his first encounter with the Duchess in the church of Combray. The single scene, in those instances, divides the iterative sequence into a *before* and an *after*, and so diversifies it into two subsequences which function as two *variants*.

Internal specifications: I mentioned the good weather/bad weather pattern which introduces a definite specification in the iterative series of the Sunday walks and determines the choice between Guermantes and Méséglise. Most of the time, however, the iterative narrative is diversified in indefinite specifications introduced by "sometimes . . . " or "one time . . . some other time . . . ," etc. These devices allow for a very flexible system of variations and for a high degree of particularization, without leaving the iterative mode. A characteristic example of this technique occurs toward the end of the *Jeunes filles en fleurs* in a description of Albertine's face (1:946–47). The iterative mode, indeed, applies just as well to the descriptive as to the narrative passages; half of Proust's descriptions make use of this mode:

> *Certains jours*, mince, le teint gris, l'air maussade, une transparence violette descendant obliquement au fond de ses yeux comme il arrive quelquefois pour la mer, elle semblait éprouver une tristesse d'exilée. *D'autres jours*, sa figure plus lisse engluait les désirs à sa surface vernie et les empêchait d'aller au delà; *à moins que* je ne la visse tout à coup de côté, car ses joues mates comme une blanche cire à la surface étaient roses par transparence, ce qui donnait tellement envie de les embrasser, d'atteindre ce teint différent qui se dérobait. *D'autres fois*, le bonheur baignait ces joues d'une clarté si mobile que la peau, devenue fluide et vague, laissait passer comme des regards sous-jacents qui la faisaient paraître d'une autre couleur, mais non d'une autre matière, que les yeux; *quelquefois*, sans y penser, quand on regardait sa figure

ponctuée de petits points bruns et où flottaient seulement deux taches plus bleues; C'était comme on eût fait d'un oeuf de chardonneret, *souvent* comme d'une agate opaline travaillée et polie à deux places seulement où, au milieu de la pierre brune, luisaient, comme les ailes transparentes d'un papillon d'azur, les yeux où la chair devient miroir et nous donne l'illusion de nous laisser, plus qu'en les autres parties du corps, approcher de l'âme. Mais *le plus souvent* aussi elle était plus colorée, et alors plus animée: *quelquefois* seul était rose, dans sa figure blanche, le bout de son nez, fin comme celui d'une petite chatte sournoise avec qui l'on aurait eu envie de jouer; *quelquefois* ses joues étaient si lisses que le regard glissait comme sur celui d'une miniature sur leur émail rose, que faisait encore paraître plus delicat, plus intérieur, le couvercle entr'ouvert et superposé de ses cheveux noirs; *il arrivait que* le teint de ses joues atteignît le rose violacé du cyclamen, et *parfois* même, quand elle était congestionnée ou fiévreuse, et donnant alors l'idée d'une complexion maladive qui rabaissait mon désir à quelque chose de plus sensuel et faisait exprimer à son regard quelque chose de plus pervers et de plus malsain, la sombre pourpre de certaines roses d'un rouge presque noir; et chacune de ces Albertin était différente, comme est différente chacune des apparitions de la danseuse dont sont transmutées les couleurs, la forme, le caractère, selon les jeux innombrablement variés d'un projecteur lumineux. (italics added)[1]

On *certain days*, slim, with grey cheeks, a sullen air, a violet transparency falling obliquely from her such as we notice sometimes on the sea, she seemed to be feeling the sorrows of exile. On *other days* her face, more sleek, caught and glued my desires to its varnished surface and prevented them from going any farther; *unless* I caught a sudden glimpse of her from the side, for her dull cheeks, like white wax on the surface, were visibly pink beneath, which made me anxious to kiss them, to reach that different tint, which thus avoided my touch. *At other times* happiness bathed her cheeks with a clarity so mobile that the skin, grown fluid and vague, gave passage to a sort of stealthy and sub-cutaneous gaze, which made it appear to be of another colour but not of another substance than her eyes; *sometimes*, instinctively, when one looked at her face punctuated with tiny brown marks among which floated what were simply two larger, bluer stains, it was like looking at the egg of a goldfinch — or *often* like an opalescent agate cut and polished in two places only, where, from the heart of the brown stone, shone like the transparent wings of a sky-blue butterfly her eyes, those features in which the flesh becomes a mirror and gives us the illusion that it allows us, more than through the other parts of the body, to approach the soul. But *most often of all* she showed more colour, and was then more animated; *sometimes* the only pink thing in her white face was the tip of her nose, as finely pointed as that of a mischievous kitten with which one would have liked to stop and play; *sometimes* her cheeks were so glossy that one's glance slipped, as over the surface of a miniature, over their pink enamel, which was made to appear still more delicate, more private, by the enclosing though half-opened case of her black hair; *or it might happen that* the tint of her cheeks had deepened to the violet shade of the red cyclamen, and, *at times, even,* when she was flushed or feverish, with a suggestion of unhealthiness which lowered my desire to something more sensual and made her glance expressive of something more perverse and unwholesome, to the deep purple of certain roses, a red that was almost black; and each of these Albertines was different, as in every fresh appearance of the dancer whose colours, form, character, are transmitted according to the innumerably varied play of projected limelight. (1:708; italics added)

The two devices (internal delimitation and internal specification) can be used together in the same passage, as in this scene from *Combray* that deals in a general way with returns from walks. The general statement is then diversified by a delimitation (itself iterative, since it recurs every year) that distinguishes between the beginning and the end of the season. This second sequence is then again diversified by a single indefinite specification: "certains soirs. . . . " The following passage is built on such a system; very simple but very productive:

> Nous rentrions *toujours* de bonne heure de nos promenades, pour pouvoir faire une visite à ma tante Léonie avant le dîner. *Au commencement de la saison,* où le jour finit tôt, quand nous arrivions rue du Saint-Esprit, il y avait encore un reflet du couchant sur les vitres de la maison et un bandeau de pourpre au fond des bois du Calvaire, qui se reflétait plus loin dans l'étang, rougeur qui, accompagnée souvent d'un froid assez vif, s'associait, dans mon esprit, à la rougeur du feu au-dessus duquel rôtissait le poulet qui ferait succéder pour moi au plaisir poétique donné par la promenade, le plaisir de la gourmandise, de la chaleur et du repos. *Dans l'été, au contraire,* quand nous rentrions le soleil ne se couchait pas encore; et pendant la visite que nous faisions chez ma tante Léonie, la lumière qui s'abaissait et touchait la fenêtre, était arrêtée entre les grands rideaux et les embrasses, divisée, ramifiée, filtrée, et, incrustant de petits morceaux d'or le bois de citronnier de la commode, illuminait obliquement la chambre avec la délicatesse qu'elle prend dans les sous-bois. Mais, *certains jours forts rares,* quand nous rentrions, il y avait bien longtemps

que la commode avait perdu ses incrustations momentanées, il n'y avait plus, quand nous arrivions rue du Saint-Esprit, nul reflet de couchant étendu sur les vitres, et l'étang au pied du calvaire avait perdu sa rougeur, quelquefois il était déjà couleur d'opale, et un long rayon de lune, qui allait en s'élargissant et se fendillait de toutes les rides de l'eau, le traversait tout entier. (1:133; italics added)

We used *always* to return from our walks in good time to pay aunt Léonie a visit before dinner. *In the first weeks of our Combray holidays*, when the days ended early, we would still be able to see, as we turned into the Rue du Saint-Esprit, a reflection of the western sky from the windows of the house and a band of purple at the foot of the Calvary, which was mirrored further on in the pond; a fiery glow which, accompanied often by a cold that burned and stung, would associate itself in my mind with the glow of the fire over which, at that very moment, was roasting the chicken that was to furnish me, in place of the poetic pleasure I had found in my walk, with the sensual pleasures of good feeding, warmth and rest. *But in summer*, when we came back to the house, the sun would not have set; and while we were upstairs paying our visit to aunt Léonie its rays, sinking until they touched and lay along her window-sill, would there be caught and held by the large inner curtains and the bands which tied them back to the wall, and split and scattered and filtered; and then, at last, would fall upon and inlay with tiny flakes of gold the lemonwood of her chest-of-drawers, illuminating the room in their passage with the same delicate, slanting, shadowed beams that fall among the boles of forest trees. *But on some days, though very rarely*, the chest-of-drawers would long since have shed its momentary adornments, there would no longer, as we turned into the Rue du Saint-Esprit, be any reflection from the western sky burning along the line of window-panes; the pond beneath the Calvary would have lost its fiery glow, sometimes indeed had changed already to an opalescent pallor, while a long ribbon of moonlight, bent and broken and broadened by every ripple upon the water's surface, would be lying across it, from end to end. (1:102; italics added)

Finally, when all the resources of iterative particularization have been exhausted, two devices remain. I have already mentioned pseudo-iteration (as in the conversations between Françoise and Aunt Léonie); this is admittedly a way of cheating or, at the very least, of stretching the reader's benevolence to the limit. The second device is more honest — if such ethical terminology can have any sense in the world of art — but it represents an extreme case leading out of the actually iterative mode: in the midst of an iterative section the narrator mentions a particular, singular occurrence, either as illustration, or example, or, on the contrary, as an exception to the law of repetition that has just been established. Such moments can be introduced by an expression such as "thus it happened that . . . " ("c'est ainsi que . . . ") or, in the case of an exception, "this time however . . . " ("une fois pourtant . . . "). The following passage from the *Jeunes filles* is an example of the first possibility: "*At times*, a kind gesture of one [of the girls] would awaken within me an expansive sympathy that replaced, for a while, my desire for the others. *Thus it happened that* Albertine, one day . . . " etc. (1:911).[2] The famous passage of the Martinville clock towers is an example of the second possibility. It is explicitly introduced as an exception to the habitual pattern: generally, when Marcel returns from walks, he forgets his impressions and does not try to interpret their meaning. "This time, however" (the expression is in the text), he goes further and composes the descriptive piece that constitutes his first literary work. The exceptional nature of an event is perhaps even more explicitly stressed in a passage from *La Prisonnière* that begins as follows: "*I will put aside*, among the days during which I lingered at Mme. de Guermantes's, one day that was marked by a small incident . . . ," after which the iterative narrative resumes: "*Except for this single incident*, everything went *as usual* when I returned from the Duchess's . . . " (3:54, 55).[3]

By means of such devices, the singulative mode merges, so to speak, with the iterative section and is made to serve it by positive or negative illustrations, either by adhering to the code or by transgressing it—which is another way of recognizing its existence.

The final problem associated with iterative temporality concerns the relationship between the duration or, rather, the internal diachrony of the iterative unit under consideration, and the external diachrony, that is, the flow of "real" and necessarily singulative time between the beginning and the end of the iterative sequence. A unit such as "sleepless night," made up of a sequence that stretches over several years, may very well be told in terms of its own duration from night to morning, without reference to the external passage of years. The typical night remains constant, except for internal specifications, from the beginning to the end of the sequence, without being influenced by the passage of time outside the particular iterative unit. This is, in fact, what happens in the first pages of the *Recherche*. However, by means of internal delimitations, the narrative of an iterative unit may just as readily encompass the external diachrony and narrate, for example, "a Sunday at Combray" by drawing attention to changes in the dominical ritual brought about by the passage of years: greater maturity of the protagonist, new acquaintances, new interests, etc. In the Combray episodes, Proust very skillfully plays upon these possibilities. J. P. Houston claimed that the narrative progresses simultaneously on three levels: with the duration of the day, of the season, and of the years. Things are perhaps not quite as clear and systematic as Houston makes them out to be, but it is true that, in the Sunday scenes, events taking place in the afternoon are of a later date than those taking place in the morning and that, in the narration of the walks, the most recent episodes are assigned to the longest itineraries. For the reader, this creates the illusion of a double temporal progression, as if the hero were a naïve little boy in the morning and a sophisticated adolescent at night, aging several years in the course of a single day or a single walk. We are touching here upon the outer limits of the iterative narrative mode.

Thus Proust appears to substitute for the *summary*, which typifies the classical novel, another form of synthesis, the iterative narrative. The synthesis is no longer achieved by acceleration, but by analogy and abstraction. The rhythm of Proust's narrative is no longer founded, as in the classical *récit*, on the alternating movement of dramatic and summarizing sections, but on the alternating movement of iterative and singular scenes. Most of the time, these alternating sections overlay a system of hierarchical subordinations that can be revealed by analysis. We already encountered two types of such systems: an iterative-explanatory section that is functionally dependent on an autonomous singular episode: the Guermantes wit (iterative) in the midst of a dinner at the duchess's (singular): and a singular-illustrative section dependent on an autonomous iterative sequence (in the scenes used as illustrations or exceptions). The hierarchical systems of interdependence can be more complex, as when a singular scene illustrates an iterative section that is itself inserted within another singulative scene: this happens, for example, when a particular anecdote (such as Oriane's wordplay on Taquin le Superbe) is used to illustrate the famous Guermantes wit: here we have a singulative element (Taquin le Superbe) within an iterative sequence (Guermantes wit) itself included in a singulative scene (dinner at Oriane de Guermantes's). The description of these structural relationships is one of the tasks of narrative analysis.

It often happens that the relationships are less clear and that the Proustian narrative fluctuates between the two modes without visible concern for their respective functions, without even seeming to be aware of the differences. Some time ago, Marcel Vigneron pointed out confusions of this sort in the section dealing with Marcel's love for Gilberte at the Champs-Elysées: an episode would start off in the historical past [*passé défini*], continue in the imperfect, and return to the historical past, without any possibility for the reader to determine whether he was reading a singular or an iterative scene. Vigneron attributed these anomalies to last-minute changes in the manuscript made necessary by publication. The explanation may be correct, but it is not exhaustive, for similar discrepancies occur at other moments in the *Recherche* when no such considerations of expediency can be invoked. Proust probably at times forgets what type of narrative he is using; hence, for example, the very revealing sudden appearance of a historical past within a pseudo-iterative scene (1:104, 722). He was certainly also guided by a secret wish to set the narrative forms free from their hierarchical function, letting them play and "make music" for themselves, as Proust himself said of Flaubert's ellipses. Hence the most subtle and admirable passages of all, of which J. P. Houston has mentioned a few, in which Proust passes from an iterative to a singular passage or uses an almost imperceptible modulation — such as an ambiguous imperfect of which it is impossible to know whether it functions iteratively or singularly, or the interposition of directly reported dialogue without declarative verb and, consequently, without determined mode, or a page of commentary by the narrator, in the present tense — to achieve the opposite effect; such a modulation, lengthily developed and to all appearances carefully controlled, serves as a transition between the first eighty pages of *La Prisonnière* that are in an iterative mode, and the singulative scenes that follow.

I have particularly stressed the question of narrative frequency because it has often been neglected by critics and by theoreticians of narrative technique, and because it occupies a particularly prominent place in the work of Marcel Proust. A paper that deals so sketchily and provisionally with a single category of narrative discourse cannot hope to reach a conclusion. Let me therefore end by pointing out that, together with the daring manipulations of chronology I have mentioned in the first part of my paper and the large-sized distortions of duration described in the second, Proust's predilection for an iterative narrative mode and the complex and subtle manner in which he exploits the contrasts and relations of this mode with a singulative discourse combine to free his narrative forever from the constraints and limitations of traditional narration. For it goes without saying that, in an iterative temporality, the order of succession and the relationships of duration that make up classical temporality are from the very beginning subverted or, more subtly and effectively, *perverted*. Proust's novel is not only what it claims to be, a novel of time lost and recaptured, but also, perhaps more implicitly, a novel of controlled, imprisoned, and bewitched time, a part of what Proust called, with reference to dreams, "the formidable game it plays with Time" ("le jeu formidable qu'il fait avec le Temps").

Notes

1. All citations are from the Pléiade edition of *A la recherche du temps perdu*. The English version of this passage and of the passage on pp. 195–96 is from the translation by C. K. Scott Moncrieff, published by Random House. Translations in the text are by Paul De Man.

2. "*Parfois* une gentille attention de telle ou telle éveillait en moi d'amples vibrations qui éloignaient pour un temps le désir des autres. *Ainsi un jour* Albertine . . . "

3. "*Je mettrai à part*, parmi ces jours ou je m'attardai chez Mme. de Guermantes, un qui fût marqué par un petit incident . . . "; "*Sauf cet incident unique*, tout se passait *normalement* quand je remontais de chez la duchesse . . . "

11

Discourse: Nonnarrated Stories

SEYMOUR CHATMAN

Silence is become his mother tongue.
— Oliver Goldsmith, *The Good-Natured Man*

Every narrative — so this theory goes — is a structure with a content plane (called "story") and an expression plane (called "discourse"). . . . The expression plane is the set of narrative statements, where "statement" is the basic component of the form of the expression, independent of and more abstract than any particular manifestation — that is, the expression's substance, which varies from art to art. A certain posture in the ballet, a series of film shots, a whole paragraph in a novel, or only a single word — any of these might manifest a single narrative statement. I have proposed that narrative statements are of two kinds — process and stasis — corresponding to whether the deep narrative (not the surface linguistic) predicate is in the mode of existence (is) or action (does).

Crosscutting this dichotomy is another: Is the statement directly presented to the audience or is it mediated by someone — the someone we call the narrator? Direct presentation presumes a kind of overhearing by the audience. Mediated narration, on the other hand, presumes a more or less express communication from narrator to audience. This is essentially Plato's distinction between *mimesis* and *diegesis*,[1] in modern terms between showing and telling. Insofar as there is telling, there must be a teller, a narrating voice.

The teller, the transmitting source, is best accounted for, I think, as a spectrum of possibilities, going from narrators who are least audible to those who are most so. The label affixed to the negative pole of narratorhood is less important than its reality in the spectrum. I say "nonnarrated"; the reader may prefer "minimally narrated," but the existence of this kind of transmission is well attested.

The narrator's presence derives from the audience's sense of some demonstrable communication. If it feels it is being told something, it presumes a teller. The alternative is a "direct witnessing" of the action. Of course, even in the scenic arts like drama and the ballet, pure mimesis is an illusion. But the degree of possible analogy varies. The main question is how the illusion is achieved. By what convention does a spectator or reader accept the idea that it is "as if" he were personally on the scene, though he comes to it by sitting in a chair in a theater or by turning pages and reading words. Authors may make special efforts to preserve the illusion that events "literally unfold before the reader's eyes," mostly by restricting the kinds of statements that can occur.

To understand the concept of narrator's voice (including its "absence") we need to consider three preliminary issues: the interrelation of the several parties to the narrative transaction, the meaning of "point of view" and its relation to voice, and the nature of acts of speech and thought as a subclass of the class of acts in general. These topics form a necessary prolegomena to the analysis of narrator's voice, upon which any discussion of narrative discourse rests.

Real Author, Implied Author, Narrator, Real Reader, Implied Reader, Narratee

That it is essential not to confuse author and narrator has become a commonplace of literary theory. As Monroe Beardsley argues, "the speaker of a literary work cannot be identified with the author — and therefore the character and condition of the speaker can be known by internal evidence alone — unless the author has provided a pragmatic context, or a claim of one, that connects the speaker with himself."[2] But even in such a context, the speaker is not the author, but the "author" (quotation marks of "as if"), or better the "author"-narrator, one of several possible kinds.

In addition, there is a demonstrable third party, conveniently dubbed, by Wayne Booth, the "implied author":

As he writes, [the real author] creates not simply an ideal, impersonal "man in general" but an implied version of "himself" that is different from the implied authors we meet in other men's works. . . . Whether we call this implied author an "official scribe," or adopt the term recently revived by Kathleen Tillotson — the author's "second self" — it is clear that the picture the reader gets of this presence is one of the author's most important effects. However impersonal he may try to be, his reader will inevitably construct a picture of the official scribe.[3]

He is "implied," that is, reconstructed by the reader from the narrative. He is not the narrator, but rather the principle that invented the narrator, along with everything else in the narrative, that stacked the cards in this particular way, had these things happen to these characters, in these words or images. Unlike the narrator, the implied author can *tell* us nothing. He, or better, *it* has no voice, no direct means of communicating. It instructs us silently, through the design of the whole, with all the voices, by all the means it has chosen to let us learn. We can grasp the notion of implied author most clearly by comparing different narratives written by the same real author but presupposing different implied authors. Booth's example: the implied author of *Jonathan Wild* "is by implication very much concerned with public affairs and with the effects of unchecked ambition on the 'great men' who attain to power in the world," whereas the implied author "who greets us on page one of *Amelia*" conveys rather an "air of sententious solemnity."[4] The implied author of *Joseph Andrews*, on the contrary, sounds "facetious" and "generally insouciant." Not merely the narrator but the whole design of *Joseph Andrews* functions in a tone quite different from that of *Jonathan Wild* or *Amelia*. Henry Fielding created three clearly different implied authors.

The distinction is particularly evident in the case of the "unreliable narrator" (another of Booth's happy coinages). What makes a narrator unreliable is that his values diverge strikingly from that of the implied author's; that is, the rest of the narrative — "the norm of the work" — conflicts with the narrator's presentation, and we become suspicious of his sincerity or competence to tell the "true version." The unreliable narrator is at virtual odds with the implied author; otherwise his unreliability could not emerge.

The implied author establishes the norms of the narrative, but Booth's insistence that these are moral seems unnecessary. The norms are general cultural codes, whose relevance to story we have already considered. The real author can postulate whatever norms he likes through his implied author. It makes no more sense to accuse the real Céline or Montherlant of what the implied author causes to happen in *Journey to the End of the Night* or *Les Jeunes Filles* than to hold the real Conrad responsible for the reactionary attitudes of the implied author of *The Secret Agent* or *Under Western Eyes* (or, for that matter, Dante for the Catholic ideas of the implied author of the *Divine Comedy*). One's moral fibre cannot really be "seduced" by wily implied authors. Our acceptance of their universe is aesthetic, not ethical. To confound the "implied author," a structural principle, with a certain historical figure whom we may or may not admire morally, politically, or personally would seriously undermine our theoretical enterprise.[5]

There is always an implied author, though there might not be a single real author in the ordinary sense: the narrative may have been composed by committee (Hollywood films), by a disparate group of people over a long period of time (many folk ballads), by random-number generation by a computer, or whatever.[6]

The counterpart of the implied author is the *implied reader*—not the flesh-and-bones you or I sitting in our living rooms reading the book, but the audience presupposed by the narrative itself. Like the implied author, the implied reader is always present. And just as there may or may not be a narrator, there may or may not be a *narratee*.[7] He may materialize as a character in the world of the work: for example, the someone listening to Marlow as he unfolds the story of Jim or Kurtz. Or there may be no overt reference to him at all, though his presence is felt. In such cases the author makes explicit the desired audience stance, and we must give him the benefit of the doubt if we are to proceed at all. The narratee-character is only one device by which implied author informs the real reader how to perform as implied reader, which *Weltanschauung* to adopt. The narratee-character tends to appear in narratives like Conrad's whose moral texture is particularly complex, where good is not easily distinguished from evil. In narratives without explicit narratees, the stance of the implied reader can only be inferred, on ordinary cultural and moral terms. Thus, Hemingway's "The Killers" does not permit us to assume that we too are members of the Mob; the story just will not work if we do. Of course, the real reader may refuse his projected role at some ultimate level—nonbelievers do not become Christians just to read *The Inferno* or *Paradise Lost*. But such refusal does not contradict the imaginative or "as if" acceptance of implied readership necessary to the elementary comprehension of the narrative.

It is as necessary to distinguish among narratees, implied readers (parties immanent to the narrative), and real readers (parties extrinsic and accidental to the narrative) as it is among narrator, implied author, and real author. The "you" or "dear reader" who is addressed by the narrator of *Tom Jones* is no more Seymour Chatman than is the narrator Henry Fielding. When I enter the fictional contract I add another self: I become an implied reader. And just as the narrator may or may not ally himself with the implied author, the implied reader furnished by the real reader may or may not ally himself with a narratee. In *Tom Jones* or *Tristram Shandy* the alliance is reasonably close; in *Les Liaisons dangereuses* or *Heart of Darkness* the distance is great.

The situation of the narratee is parallel to that of the narrator: he ranges from a fully characterized individual to "no one." Again, "absence" or "un-markedness" is put in quotation marks: in some sense every tale implies a listener or reader, just as it implies a teller. But the author may, for a variety of reasons, leave these components unmentioned, indeed, go out of his way to suggest that they do not exist.

We can now diagram the whole narrative-communication situation as follows:

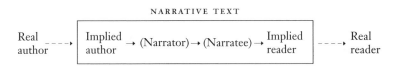

NARRATIVE TEXT

Real author - - - → Implied author → (Narrator) → (Narratee) → Implied reader - - - → Real reader

The box indicates that only the implied author and implied reader are immanent to a narrative, the narrator and narratee are optional (paren-theses). The real author and real reader are outside the narrative trans-action as such, though, of course, indispensable to it in an ultimate practical sense. . . .

Point of View and Its Relation to Narrative Voice

It is the task of narrative theory, like any theory, to deal with the ambiguities and unclarities of terms passed down to it. To understand the concept of narrator's voice — including the case where one is "not" (or minimally) present — we must first distinguish it from "point of view," one of the most troublesome of critical terms. Its plurisignification must give pause to any-one who wishes to use it in precise discussion. At least three senses can be distinguished in ordinary use: (a) literal: through someone's eyes (per-ception); (b) figurative: through someone's worldview (ideology, conceptual system, *Weltanschauung*, etc.); (c) transferred: from someone's interest-vantage (characterizing his general interest, profit, welfare, well-being, etc.). The following sentences will illustrate these distinctions: (a) From John's point of view, at the top of Coit Tower, the panorama of the San Francisco Bay was breathtaking. (b) John said that from his point of view, Nixon's position, though praised by his supporters, was somewhat less than noble. (c) Though he didn't realize it at the time, the divorce was a disaster from John's point of view. In the first sentence, "The panorama of the Bay" is reported as acutally seen by John; he stands at the center of a half-circle of vision. Let us call that his *perceptual* point of view. In the second, there is no reference to his actual physical situation in the real world but to his attitudes or conceptual apparatus, his way of thinking, and how facts and impressions are strained through it. We can call that his *conceptual* point of view. In the third, there is no reference to John's mind at all, either to perceptual or conceptual powers. Since John is unaware of the mentioned consequences, he is not "seeing," in either the actual or the figurative sense; the term then is a simple synonym for "as far as John is concerned." Let us call this his *interest* point of view. What is confusing is that "point of view" may thus refer to an *action* of some kind — perceiving or conceiving — or to a *passive state* — as in the third sense.

Now texts, any kind of text, even ordinary conversation, may entail one or any combination of these senses. A simple description of an experiment or an explorer's account of a new island may convey only the literal perceptions of the author, but it may also entail his *Weltanschauung*, or his practical interests. A philosophical treatise on abstract issues does not usually entail perceptual point of view, but may express quite eloquently the author's personal interests in the matter, along with his ideology.

When we turn to narrative texts, we find an even more complicated situation, since as we have seen there is no longer a single presence, as in expository essays, sermons, political speeches, and so on, but two — character and narrator — not to speak of the implied author. Each of these may manifest one or more kinds of point of view. A character may literally perceive a certain object or event; and/or it may be presented in terms of his conceptualization; and/or his interest in it may be invoked (even if he is unconscious of that interest).[8]

Thus the crucial difference between "point of view" and narrative voice: point of view is the physical place or ideological situation or practical life-orientation to which narrative events stand in relation. Voice, on the contrary, refers to the speech or other overt means through which events and existents are communicated to the audience. Point of view does *not* mean expression; it only means the perspective in terms of which the expression is made. *The perspective and the expression need not be lodged in the same person.*[9] Many combinations are possible. Consider just literal, that is perceptual, point of view. Events and existents may be perceived by the narrator and recounted by him in his own first person: "I felt myself fall down the hill" or "I saw Jack fall down the hill" (in the first case, the narrator is protagonist, in the second, witness). Or the point of view may be assigned to a character who is not the narrator: then the separate narrating voice may or may not make itself heard—"Mary, *poor dear*, saw Jack fall down the hill" versus "Mary saw Jack fall down the hill." Or the event may be presented so that it is not clear who, if anyone, perceived it (or perception is not an issue): "Jack fell down the hill."

The "camera eye" names a convention (an "illusion of mimesis") which pretends that the events just "happened" in the presence of a neutral recorder. To call such narrative transmission "limited third person" is wrong because it specifies only the point of view, not the narrative voice. It is necessary to distinguish between "limited third person point of view voiced by a covert narrator," "limited third person point of view voiced by an overt narrator," and so on.

Perception, conception, and interest points of view are quite independent of the manner in which they are expressed. When we speak of "expression," we pass from point of view, which is only a perspective or stance, to the province of narrative voice, the medium through which perception, conception, and everything else are communicated. Thus point of view is *in* the story (when it is the character's), but voice is always outside, in the discourse. From *A Portrait of the Artist as a Young Man:* "A few moments [later] he found himself on the stage amid the garish gas and the dim scenery." The perceptual point of view is Stephen's, but the voice is the narrator's. Characters' perceptions need not be articulated—Stephen is not saying to himself the *words* "garish gas and dim scenery"; the words are the narrator's. This is a narrator's report. But in " 'He shivered a little, and I beheld him rise slowly as if a steady hand from above had been pulling him out of the chair by the hair' " (*Lord Jim*), not only the voice, but the perceptual point of view is the narrator's, Marlow's, not Jim's. And in "Coffin now. Got here before us, dead as he is. Horse looking round at it with his plume skewways. Dull eye: collar tight on his neck, pressing on a bloodvessel or something. Do they know what they cart out here every day?" ("Hades," *Ulysses*), the perceptual point of view is Leopold Bloom's, and so are the words, but he is no narrator. He is not telling a narratee anything. Indeed, he is not speaking even to himself: the convention argues that he is directly perceiving the coffin and the nag's dull eye, and nothing more. There *is* no narrator.

In all these cases the character perceives: his senses are directed outward upon the story-world. But when that perception is reported, as in the first two examples, there is necessarily presupposed another act of "seeing" with an independent point of view, namely that of the narrator, who has "peered into" the character's mind (metaphors are inevitable) and reports its contents from his *own* point of view. Can this kind of point of view be called "perceptual"? The word sounds strange, and for good reason. It makes sense to say that the character is literally perceiving something within the world of the work ("homodiegetically," as Genette would say). But what the narrator reports from his perspective is almost always outside the story (heterodiegetic), even if only retrospective, that is, temporally distant. Typically, he is looking back at his own earlier perception-as-a-character. But that looking-back is a conception, no longer a perception. The completely external narrator presents an even more purely conceptual view. He never *was* in the world of the work: discourse-time is not a later extension of story-time. He did not "perceive" in the same direct or diegetic sense that any character did. Literally speaking, he cannot have "seen" anything in that other world.

Thus the use of terms like "view" and "see" may be dangerously metaphorical. We "see" issues in terms of some cultural or psychological predisposition; the mechanism is entirely different from that which enables us to see cats or automobiles. Though it is true that preconceptions of various sorts affect our strictly physiological vision too (people may not see what is literally before their noses because they have compelling personal reasons not to), there remains an essential difference between perceptions and conceptions. Further, the narrator's is second-order or heterodiegetic conceptualizing *about* the story — as opposed to the first-order conceptualizing of a character within the story. These distinctions most clearly emerge where the two conflict, where the narrator is operating under a clearly different set of attitudes than those of the character. Then the narrator's conceptual point of view (except when he is unreliable) tends to override the character's, despite the fact that the latter maintains the center of interest and consciousness. An example is Conrad's *The Secret Agent:* the narrator is clearly unsympathetic to Verloc. Or, more precisely, the character has a conceptual point of view undermined by the narrator's manner of depicting it. Verloc's ideology (such as it is) reeks of indolence; the narrator carefully picks words to so characterize it. For example, Verloc does not simply stay in bed, he "wallows" in it. But the narrator (like all Conrad's narrators) is on the side of vigorous achievement. Similarly, he tells us that Verloc "remained undisturbed by any sort of aesthetic doubt about his appearance." From the narrator's conceptual point of view, implicitly communicated, Verloc's physical messiness is reprehensible and a clear analogue to moral sloth and political dishonesty. Or consider the difference between Verloc's and the narrator's attitudes toward female psychology. Verloc's unpleasant encounter with Mr. Vladimir brings him home in a towering rage. Forgetting that his wife is mourning the death of her brother, for which he is responsible, he is disappointed that she does not soothe him. Yet, immediately, he realizes that she is "a woman of few words." But his notion of his relationship with her, his conceptual point of view, is paraphrased in the narrator's superior diction: "[Winnie's] reserve, expressing in a way their profound confidence in each other, introduced at the same time a certain element of vagueness into their intimacy." Though the "profound confidence in each other" is the narrator's expression, not Verloc's, whose verbal style we know to be less elegant, it can only be Verloc's sentiment. His complacency, of course, turns out suicidal.

Disparity between the character's point of view and the narrator's expression of it need not entail ironic opposition. The narrator may verbalize neutrally or even sympathetically what (for reasons of youth, lack of education and intelligence, and so on) the character cannot articulate. This is the whole structural principle of James's *What Maisie Knew*. Maisie's uncertainty about when next she will visit her mother is expressed thusly: "Mama's roof, however, had its turn, this time, for the child, of appearing but remotely contingent. . . . " Clearly these are not phrases in Maisie's vocabulary. We accept them only because a sensitive little girl might have feelings that somehow matched the narrator's elegant terms. That is, we can "translate" into more childlike verbiage — for instance, "I don't expect to be at Mama's again very soon." The diction is sanctioned only by the convention of the "well-spoken narrator."

"Point of view" expressing someone's interests is even more radically distanced, since there is not even a figurative "seeing." The subject may be completely unconscious that events work for or against his interests (welfare, success, happiness). The identification of interest point of view may follow the clear specification of the character's perceptual and conceptual points of view. Once they are established, we continue identifying with his interests, by a process of inertia, even if he is unaware of something. In *The Ambassadors*, the narrator speaks of Maria Gostrey's powers of "pigeon-holing her fellow mortals": "She was as equipped in this particular as Strether was the reverse, and it made an opposition between them which he might well have shrunk from submitting to if he had fully suspected it." The narrator informs us of aspects of Maria's character that Strether does not know, yet it makes perfect sense to say that the sentence is "from his point of view." The focus of attention remains on him. Maria's traits are significant only in their implications for him — even though he is not aware of them.

Access to a character's consciousness is the standard entree to his point of view, the usual and quickest means by which we come to identify with him. Learning his thoughts insures an intimate connection. The thoughts are truthful, except in cases of willful self-deception. Unlike the narrator, the character can only be "unreliable" to himself.

At the same time, interest point of view can be established quite independently. The point of view may reside in a character who is "followed" in some sense, even if there is no reference at all to his thinking. If Jack and Peter are in the first scene, and Jack and Mary in the second, and Jack and Joseph in the third, we identify with Jack simply because he is the one continually on the scene. This has nothing to do with whether or not we care for him on human or other grounds.

The notion of interest point of view is not very meaningfully applied to an external narrator. His only interest is to get the narrative told. Other sorts of interest arise only if he is or was also a character. Then he may use the narrative itself as vindication, expiation, explanation, rationalization, condemnation, or whatever. There are hundreds of reasons for telling a story, but those reasons are the narrator's, not the implied author's, who is without personality or even presence, hence without motivation other than the purely theoretical one of constructing the narrative itself. The narrator's vested interests may be so marked that we come to think of him as unreliable.

The different points of view usually combine, but in important and interesting cases, they do not. Consider "autobiographical" or first-person narration, as in *Great Expectations*. The protagonist-as-narrator reports things from the perceptual point of view of his younger self. His ideology on the other hand tends to be that of his older self. The narrator is older and wiser for his experiences. In other narratives the ideology may not change; the narrator may exhibit substantially the same traits as characterized his earlier self. Where the narrator is a different person than the hero, he may present his own ideology, against which he judges his hero's actions, either overtly, as in *Tom Jones*, or covertly and inferentially, as in *The Ambassadors*. The narrator may utilize a perceptual point of view possible to no character, for example when he describes a bird's-eye view, or a scene with no one present, or what the character did *not* notice.

Notes

1. These terms are revived by Gérard Genette in "Frontières du récit," *Communications* 8 (1966).

2. In *Aesthetics* (New York, 1958), p. 240. Cf. Walker Gibson, "Authors, Speakers, Readers, Mock Readers," *College English* 11 (1950): 265–69; and Kathleen Tillotson, *The Tale and the Teller* (London: Rupert Hart-Davis, 1959).

3. *Rhetoric of Fiction*, pp. 70–71.

4. Ibid., p. 72.

5. There is an interesting discussion of the question in Susan Suleiman, "Ideological Dissent from Works of Fiction: Toward a Rhetoric of the *Roman a thèse*," *Neophilologus* (April 1976): 162–77. Suleiman thinks that the implied author, as well as the narrator, can be unreliable, and thus we can accept imaginatively a narrative that we reject ideologically.

6. Christian Metz, *Film Language: A Semiotics of the Cinema*, trans. Michael Taylor (New York: Oxford University Press, 1974), p. 20.

7. The term was first coined, so far as I know, by Gerald Prince, "Notes Toward a Categorization of Fictional 'Narratees,' " *Genre* 4 (1971): 100–105. Booth's "postulated reader" is what I call the implied reader.

8. Another ambiguity of "point of view" was recognized by Sister Kristin Morrison in "James's and Lubbock's Differing Points of View," *Nineteenth-Century Fiction* 16 (1961): 245–56. Lubbock and his followers used the term in the sense of the narrative perspective of the speaker (the narrator), while James usually used it in the sense of the perspective of the knower or reader. Boris Uspensky in *Poetics of Composition*, trans. Valentina Zavarin and Susan Wittig (Berkeley: University of California Press, 1974), chap. 1, distinguishes various kinds of point of view along lines similar to mine. Some alternatives to "point of view" have been proposed: for instance, James's "central consciousness," Allen Tate's "post of observation," and Todorov's "*vision*" (derived from Jean Pouillon). The latter two continue the confusion between cognition and interest.

9. For example a recent article misreads "Eveline" by confusing character's point of view and narrator's voice (Clive Hart, "Eveline," in *James Joyce's Dubliners: Critical Essays* [London: Faber and Faber, 1969], p. 51). The author argues that Eveline is shallow and incapable of love—which may be true—but supports his argument with questionable evidence: "She over-dramatizes her association with Frank, calls it an 'affair' and him her 'lover'; she thinks of herself in pulp-literature terms as 'unspeakably' weary. But most obvious of all is the strong note of falsity in the language of the passage in which she reasserts her choice to leave: 'As she mused the pitiful vision of her mother's life laid its spell on the very quick of her being. . . . ' Dublin has so paralysed Eveline's emotions that she is unable to love, can think of herself and her situation only by means of a series of tawdry cliches." Surely the objectionable words are not Eveline's but the narrator's. It is he who is parodying pulp-literature sentimentality in tawdry cliches (as does the narrator of the "Nausicaa" section of *Ulysses*). Eveline may indeed feel maudlin sentiments, but "mused," "pitiful vision," "very quick of her being" are not in her vocabulary.

12

Reading as Construction · TZVETAN TODOROV

What is omnipresent is imperceptible. Nothing is more commonplace than the reading experience, and yet nothing is more unknown. Reading is such a matter of course that, at first glance, it seems there is nothing to say about it.

In literary studies, the problem of reading has been posed from two opposite perspectives. The first concerns itself with readers, their social, historical, collective, or individual variability. The second deals with the image of the reader as it is represented in certain texts: the reader as character or as "narratee." There is, however, an unexplored area situated between the two: the domain of the logic of reading. Although it is not represented in the text, it is nonetheless anterior to individual variation.

There are several types of reading. I shall pause here to discuss one of the more important ones: the one we usually practice when we read classical fiction or, rather, the so-called representative texts. This particular type of reading, and only this type, unfolds as a construction.

Although we no longer refer to literature in terms of imitation, we still have trouble getting rid of a certain way of looking at fiction; inscribed in our speech habits, it is a vision through which we perceive the novel in terms of representation, or the transposition of a reality that exists prior to it. This attitude would be problematic even if it did not attempt to describe the creative process. When it refers to the text itself, it is sheer distortion. What exists first and foremost is the text itself, and nothing but the text. Only by subjecting the text to a particular type of reading do we construct, from our reading, an imaginary universe. Novels do not imitate reality; they create it. The formula of the pre-Romantics is not a simple terminological innovation; only the perspective of construction allows us to understand thoroughly how the so-called representative text functions.

Given our framework, the question of reading can be restated as follows: How does a text get us to construct an imaginary world? Which aspects of the text determine the construction we produce as we read? And in what way? Let us begin with basics.

Only referential sentences allow construction to take place; not all sentences, however, are referential. This fact is well known to linguists and logicians, and we need not dwell on it.

Comprehension is a process different from construction. Take for example the following two sentences from *Adolphe:* "Je la sentais meilleure que moi; je me méprisais d'être indigne d'elle. C'est un affreux malheur que de n'être aimé quand on aime; mais c'en est un bien grand d'être aimé avec passion quand on n'aime plus."[1] The first sentence is referential: it evokes an event (Adolphe's feelings); the second sentence is not referential: it is a maxim. The difference between the two is marked by grammatical indices: the maxim requires a third-person present-tense verb, and contains no anaphores (words referring to preceding segments of the same discourse).

A sentence is either referential or nonreferential; there are no intermediary stages. However, the words that make up a sentence are not all alike in this respect; depending on the lexical choice, the results will be very different. Two independent oppositions seem pertinent here: the affective versus the nonaffective, and the particular versus the general. For example, Adolphe refers to his past as "au milieu d'une vie très dissipée." This remark evokes perceptible events but in an extremely general way. One could easily imagine hundreds of pages describing this very same fact. Whereas in the other sentence, "Je trouvais dans mon père, non pas un censeur, mais un observateur froid et caustique, qui souriait d'abord de pitié, et qui finissait bientôt la conversation avec impatience,"[2] we have a juxtaposition of affective versus nonaffective events: a smile, a moment of silence, are observable facts; pity and impatience are suppositions (justified, no doubt) about feelings to which we are denied direct access.

Normally, a given fictional text will contain examples of all these speech registers (although we know that their distribution varies according to period, schools of thought, or even as a function of the text's global organization). We do not retain nonreferential sentences in the kind of reading I call reading as construction (they belong to another kind of reading). Referential sentences lead to different types of construction depending on their degree of generality and on the affectivity of the events they evoke.

The characteristics of discourse mentioned thus far can be identified outside of any context: they are inherent in the sentences themselves. But in reading, we read whole texts, not just sentences. If we compare sentences from the point of view of the imaginary world which they help to construct, we find that they differ in several ways or, rather, according to several parameters. In narrative analysis, it has been agreed to retain three parameters: time, point of view, and mode. Here again, we are on relatively familiar ground (which I have already dealt with in my book *Poétique*); now it is simply a question of looking at the problems from the point of view of reading.

Mode. Direct discourse is the only way to eliminate the differences between narrative discourse and the world which it evokes: words are identical to words, and construction is direct and immediate. This is not the case with nonverbal events, nor with transposed discourse. At one point, the "editor" in *Adolphe* states: "Notre hôte, qui avait causé avec un domestique napolitain, qui servait cet étranger [i.e., Adolphe] sans savoir son nom, me dit qu'il ne voyageait point par curiosité, car il ne visitait ni les ruines, ni les sites, ni les monuments, ni les hommes."[3] We can imagine the conversation between the editor-narrator and the host, even though it is unlikely that the former used words (be it in Italian) identical to those which follow the "he told me that" formula. The construction of the conversation between the host and the servant, which is also evoked, is far less determined; thus we have more freedom if we want to construct it in detail. Finally, the conversations and the other activities common to Adolphe and the servant are completely vague; only a general impression is given.

The remarks of a fictional narrator can also be considered as direct discourse, although on a different (higher) level. This is especially the case if, as in *Adolphe*, the narrator is represented in the text. The maxim, which we previously excluded from reading as construction, becomes pertinent here — not for its value as an "énoncé" (i.e., a statement) but as "énonciation" (i.e., an utterance, implying a speaker and his circumstances). The fact that Adolphe as narrator formulates a maxim on the misery of being loved tells us something about his character, and therefore about the imaginary universe of which he is a part.

Time. The time of the fictional world ("story" time) is ordered chronologically. However, the sentences in the text do not, and as a rule cannot, absolutely respect this order; the reader undertakes therefore, unconsciously, the task of chronological reordering. Similarly, certain sentences evoke several events which are distinct yet similar ("iterative narrative"); in these instances we reestablish the plurality of the events as we construct.

Point of view. The "vision" we have of the events evoked by the text clearly determines our work of construction. For example, in the case of a positively slanted vision, we take into consideration (1) the event recounted, and (2) the attitude of the person who "sees" the event.

Furthermore, we know how to distinguish between information that a sentence gives concerning its object, and the information it gives concerning its subject; thus the "editor" of *Adolphe* can only think of the latter, as he comments on the story we have just read: "Je hais cette vanité qui s'occupe d'elle-même en racontant le mal qu'elle a fait, qui a la prétention de sa faire plaindre en se décrivant, et qui, planant indestructible au milieu des ruines, s'analyse au lieu de se repentir."[4] The editor constructs the subject of the narrative (Adolphe the narrator), and not its object (Adolphe the character, and Ellénore).

We usually do not realize just how repetitive, or rather how redundant, fiction is; we could, in fact, state almost categorically that each event is narrated at least twice. For the most part, these repetitions are modulated by the filters mentioned above: at one point a conversation may be reproduced in its entirety; at another, it may be alluded to briefly; action may be observed from several different points of view; it can be recounted in the future, in the present, and in the past. In addition, all these parameters can be combined.

Repetition plays an important role in the process of construction. We must construct *one* event from *many* accounts of it. The relationship between these different accounts varies, ranging from total agreement to downright contradiction. Even two identical accounts do not necessarily produce the same meaning (a good example of this is seen in Coppola's film *The Conversation*). The functions of these repetitions are equally varied: they help to establish the facts as in a police investigation, or to disprove the facts. Thus in *Adolphe*, the fact that the same character expresses contradictory views on the same subject at two different times which are quite close to each other, helps us to understand that states of mind do not exist in and of themselves, but rather in relationship to an interlocutor, to a partner. Constant himself expressed the law of this universe in the following manner: "L'objet qui nous échappe est nécessairement tout différent de celui qui nous poursuit."[5]

Therefore, if the reader is to construct an imaginary universe through his reading of the text, the text itself must be referential; in the course of reading, we let our imagination go to work, filtering the information we receive through the following types of questions: To what extent is the description of this universe accurate (mode)? When did the events take place (time)? To what extent is the story distorted by the various "centers of consciousness" through whom it is told (vision)? At this point, however, the job of reading has only begun.

Signification and Symbolization

How do we know what happens as we read? Through introspection; and if we want to confirm our own impressions, we can always have recourse to other readers' accounts of their own reading. Nevertheless, two accounts of the same text will never be identical. How do we explain this diversity? By the fact that these accounts describe, not the universe of the book itself, but this universe as it is transformed by the psyche of each individual reader. The stages of this transformation can be diagrammed as follows:

1. The author's account	4. The reader's account
↓	↑
2. The imaginary universe evoked by the author →	3. The imaginary universe constructed by the reader

We could question whether there really is a difference between stages 2 and 3, as is suggested by the diagram. Is there such a thing as nonindividual construction? It is easy to show that the answer must be positive. Everyone who reads *Adolphe* knows that Ellénore first lived with the Comte de p^{xxx}, that she left him, and went to live with Adolphe; they separated; she later joined him in Paris, etc. On the other hand, there is no way to establish with the same certainty whether Adolphe is weak or merely sincere.

The reason for this duality is that the text evokes facts according to two different modes, which I shall call signification and symbolization. Ellénore's trip to Paris is *signified* by the words in the text. Adolphe's (ultimate) weakness is *symbolized* by other factors in the imaginary universe, which are themselves signified by words. For example, Adolphe's inability to defend Ellénore in social situations is signified; this in turn symbolizes his inability to love. Signified facts are *understood:* all we need is knowledge of the language in which the text is written. Symbolized facts are *interpreted;* and interpretations vary from one subject to another.

Consequently, the relationship between stages 2 and 3, as indicated above, is one of symbolization (whereas the relationship between stages 1 and 2, or 3 and 4, is one of signification). In any case, we are not dealing with a single or unique relationship, but rather a heterogeneous ensemble. First, we always abbreviate as we read: stage 4 is (almost) always shorter than stage 1, whence stage 2 is richer than stage 3. Secondly, we often make mistakes. In both cases, studying the relationship between stages 2 and 3 leads to psychological projection: the transformations tell us about the reading subject. Why does he remember (or even add) certain facts and not others? But there are other transformations which provide information about the reading process itself, and these are the ones that will be our main concern here.

It is hard for me to say whether the situation I observe in the most varied kinds of fiction is universal or whether it is historically and culturally determined. Nevertheless, it is a fact that in every case, symbolization and interpretation (the movement from stage 2 to stage 3) imply the determinism of action. Would reading other texts, lyrical poems for example, require an effort of symbolization based on other presuppositions (e.g., universal analogy)? I do not know; the fact remains that in fiction, symbolization is based on the acknowledgment, either implicit or explicit, of the principle of causality. The questions we address, therefore, to the events that constitute the mental image of stage 2 are the following: What is their cause? What is their effect? We then add their answers to the mental image that constitutes stage 3.

Let us admit that this determinism is universal; what is certainly not universal is the form it takes in a given case. The simplest form, although one that we rarely find in our culture as a reading norm, consists in constructing another fact of the same type. A reader might say to himself, "If John killed Peter (a fact present in the story), it's because Peter slept with John's wife (a fact absent from the story)." This type of reasoning, characteristic of courtroom procedures, is not applied seriously to the novel; we assume that the author has not cheated and that he has provided (has signified) all the information we need to understand the story (*Armance* is an exception). The same is true as concerns effects or aftereffects: many books are sequels to others and tell the consequences of events in the imaginary universe represented in the first text; nevertheless, the content of the second book is generally not considered inherent in the first. Here again, reading practices differ from everyday habits.

When we read, we usually base our constructions upon another kind of causal logic; we look for the causes and consequences of a particular event elsewhere, in elements unlike the event itself. Two types of causal construction seem most frequent (as Aristotle already noted): the event is perceived as the consequence (and/or the cause) either of a character trait or of an impersonal or universal law. *Adolphe* contains numerous examples of both types of interpretation, and they are integrated into the text itself. Here is how Adolphe describes his father: "Je ne me souviens pas, pendant mes dix-huit premières années, d'avoir eu jamais un entretien d'une heure avec lui. . . . Je ne savais pas alors ce que c'etait que la timidité."[6] The first sentence signifies a fact (the absence of lengthy conversations). The second makes us consider this fact as symbolic of a character trait—timidity: if the father behaves in this way, it is because he is timid. The character trait is the cause of the action. Here is an example of the second case: "Je me dis qu'il ne fallait rien précipiter, qu'Ellénore était trop peu préparée à l'aveu que je méditais, et qu'il valait mieux attendre encore. Presque toujours, pour vivre en repos avec nous-mêmes, nous travestissons en calculs et en systèmes nos impuissances ou nos faiblesses: cela satisfait cette portion de nous qui est, pour ainsi dire, spectatrice de l'autre."[7] Here, the first sentence describes the event, and the second provides the reason—a universal law of human behavior, not an individual character trait. We might add that this second type of causality is dominant in *Adolphe:* the novel illustrates psychological laws, not individual psychologies.

After we have constructed the events that compose a story, we begin the task of reinterpretation. This enables us to construct not only the "personalities" of the characters but also the novel's underlying system of values and ideas. A reinterpretation of this type is not arbitrary; it is controlled by two series of constraints. The first is contained in the text itself: the author need but take a few moments to teach us how to interpret the events he evokes. This was the case in the passages from *Adolphe* cited earlier: once he has established a few deterministic interpretations, Constant can forgo naming the cause of the subsequent events; we have learned his lesson, and we shall continue to interpret in the way he has taught us. Such explicit interpretations have a double function: on the one hand, they tell us the reason behind a particular fact (exegetic function); on the other hand, they initiate us into the author's own system of interpretation, the one that will operate throughout the course of the text (meta-exegetic function).

The second series of constraints comes from the cultural context. If we read that so-and-so has cut his wife up into little pieces, we do not need textual indications to conclude that this is truly a cruel deed. These cultural constraints, which are nothing but the commonplaces of a society (its "set" of probabilities), change with time. These changes permit us to explain why interpretations differ from one period to another. For example, since extramarital love is no longer considered proof of moral corruption, we have trouble understanding the condemnations heaped upon so many fictional heroines of the past.

Human character and ideas: such entities are symbolized through action, but they can be signified as well. This was precisely the case in the passages from *Adolphe* quoted earlier: action symbolized shyness in Adolphe's father. Later, however, Adolphe signified the same thing, saying: My father was shy; that is also true of the general maxim. Human character and ideas can thus be evoked in two ways: directly and indirectly. During the course of his construction, the reader will compare the various bits of information obtained from each source and will find that they either tally or do not. The relative proportion of these two types of information has varied greatly during the course of literary history, as goes without saying: Hemingway did not write like Constant.

We must, however, differentiate between human character constructed in this way and the characters in a novel as such: not every character has a character, so to speak. The fictional character is a segment of the spatiotemporal universe represented in the text, nothing more; he/she comes into existence the moment referential linguistic forms (proper names, certain nominal syntagms, personal pronouns) appear in the text regarding an anthropomorphic being. In and of itself the fictional character has no content: someone is identified without being described. We can imagine — and there exist — texts where the fictional character is limited to just that: being the agent of a series of actions. But, as soon as psychological determinism appears in the text, the fictional character becomes endowed with character: he acts in a certain way, *because* he is shy, weak, courageous, etc. There is no such thing as character without determinism of this type.

The construction of character is a compromise between difference and repetition. On the one hand, we must have continuity: the reader must construct the *same* character. This continuity is already given in the identity of the proper name, which is its principal function. At this point, any and all combinations become possible: all actions might illustrate the same character trait, or the behavior of a particular character might be contradictory, or he might change the circumstances of his life, or he might undergo profound character modification. . . . So many examples come to mind that it is not necessary to mention them. Here again the choices are more a function of the history of styles than of the idiosyncrasies of individual authors.

Character, then, can be an effect of reading; there exists a kind of reading to which every text can be subjected. But in fact, the effect is not arbitrary; it is no accident that character exists in the eighteenth- and nineteenth-century novel and not in Greek tragedy or the folktale. A text always contains within itself directions for its own consumption.

Construction as Theme

One of the difficulties in studying reading is due to the fact that reading is so hard to observe: introspection is uncertain, psychosociological investigation is tedious. It is therefore with a kind of relief that we find the work of construction represented in fiction itself, a much more convenient place for study.

Construction appears as a theme in fiction simply because it is impossible to refer to human life without mentioning such an essential activity. Based on the information he receives, every character must construct the facts and the characters around him; thus, he parallels exactly the reader who is constructing the imaginary universe from his own information (the text, and his sense of what is probable); thus, reading becomes (inevitably) one of the themes of the book.

The thematics of reading can, however, be more or less emphasized, more or less exploited as a technique in a given text. In *Adolphe*, it is only partially the case: only the ethical undecidability of action is emphasized. If we want to use fiction to study construction, we must choose a text where construction appears as one of the principal themes. Stendhal's *Armance* is a perfect example.

The entire plot of the novel is, in fact, subjugated to the search for knowledge. Octave's erroneous construction functions as the novel's point of departure: based upon Armance's behavior (an interpretation deducing a character trait from an action), Octave believes that Armance is too concerned with money. This initial misunderstanding is barely settled when it is followed by a second one, symmetrical to but the reverse of the first: Armance now believes that Octave is too concerned with money. This initial mix-up establishes the pattern of the constructions that follow. Next, Armance correctly constructs her feelings for Octave, but it takes Octave ten chapters before he discovers that his feelings for Armance are called *love*, not *friendship*. For five chapters Armance believes that Octave doesn't love her; Octave believes that Armance doesn't love him during the book's fifteen main chapters; the same misunderstanding is repeated toward the end of the novel. The characters spend all their time searching for the truth, in other words, constructing the facts and the events around them. The tragic ending of the love relationship is not caused by impotence, as has often been said, but by ignorance. Octave commits suicide because of an erroneous construction: he believes that Armance doesn't love him anymore. As Stendhal says suggestively, "Il manquait de pénétration et non pas de caractère."[8]

We can see from this brief summary that several aspects of the construction process can vary. One can be agent or patient, a sender or receiver of information; one can even be both. Octave is an agent when he pretends or reveals, a patient when he learns or is mistaken. It is also possible to construct a fact ("first-level" construction), or someone else's construction of that same fact ("second-level" construction). Thus, Armance rejects the idea of marrying Octave when she contemplates what others might think of her. "Je passerais dans le monde pour une dame de compagnie qui a séduit le fils de la maison. J'entends d'ici ce que dirait Mme. la duchesse d'Ancre et même les femmes les plus respectables, par exemple la marquise de Seyssins qui voit dans Octave un époux pour l'une de ses filles."[9] Octave likewise rejects the idea of suicide when he envisions the possible constructions of others. "Si je me tue, Armance sera compromise; toute la société recherchera curieusement pendant huit jours les plus petites circonstances de cette soirée; et chacun de ces messieurs qui étaient présents sera autorisé à faire un récit différent."[10]

What we learn above all in *Armance* is the fact that a construction can be either right or wrong; if all right constructions are alike (they are the "truth"), wrong constructions vary, as do the reasons behind them: flaws in the transmitted information. The simplest type is the case of total ignorance: until a certain point in the plot, Octave hides the very existence of a secret concerning him (active role); Armance is also unaware of its existence (passive role). Afterwards, the existence of the secret may be learned, but without any additional information; the receiver may then react by inventing his own "truth" (Armance suspects Octave of having killed someone). Illusion constitutes yet a further degree of faulty information: the agent does not dissemble, but misrepresents; the patient is not ignorant or unknowing, but is in error. This is the most prevalent situation in the novel: Armance camouflages her love for Octave, claiming she will marry someone else; Octave thinks that Armance feels only friendship toward him. One may be both agent and victim of the travesty; thus Octave hides from himself the fact that he loves Armance. Finally, the agent can reveal the truth, and the patient can apprehend it.

Ignorance, imagination, illusion, and truth: here are at least three stages through which the search for knowledge passes before leading a character to a definitive construction. Obviously, the same stages are possible in the reading process. Normally, the construction represented in the text is isomorphic to the one that takes the text as its point of departure. What the characters don't know, the reader doesn't know either; of course, other combinations are possible as well. In the detective novel, a Watson figure constructs like the reader, but a Sherlock Holmes constructs better: the two roles are equally necessary.

Other Readings

The flaws in the reading construction do not in any way undermine its existence: we do not stop constructing because of insufficient or erroneous information. On the contrary, defects such as these only intensify the construction process. Nevertheless, it is possible that construction does not occur, and that other types of reading supersede it.

Discrepancies between readings are not necessarily found where we might expect. For example, there does not seem to be a big difference between construction based on a literary text and construction based on a referential but nonliterary text. This resemblance was implied in the propositions I advanced in the previous section; in other words, the construction of characters (from nonliterary material) is analogous to the reader's construction (from the text of a novel). "Fiction" is not constructed any differently from "reality." Both the historian and the judge, the former on the basis of written documents, the latter on that of oral testimony, reconstitute the facts; in principle, they do not proceed differently from the reader of *Armance*; this does not mean there are no differences as far as details are concerned.

A more difficult question, beyond the scope of this study, concerns the relationship between construction based on verbal information and construction based on other perceptions. From the smell of roast lamb, we construct the roast; similarly for a sound, a view, etc. Piaget calls this phenomenon "the construction of reality." In these instances the differences may be much greater.

We do not have to stray very far from the novel to find material requiring another type of reading. There are many literary texts, nonrepresentative texts, that do not lead to any construction at all. Several types can be distinguished here. The most obvious is a specific type of poetry, generally called lyric poetry, which does not describe events, which evokes nothing exterior to it. The modern novel, in turn, requires a different reading; the text is still referential, but construction does not occur because, in a certain sense, it is undecidable. This effect is obtained by a dismantling of any one of the mechanisms necessary for construction as we have described them. To take just one example: we have seen that a character's identity was a function of the identity and inambiguity of his name. Suppose now that, in a text, the same character is evoked successively by several different names, first "John," then "Peter," then "the man with the black hair," then "the man with the blue eyes," without any indication of co-reference between the two expressions; or, suppose again that "John" designates not one, but three or four characters; each time, the result is the same: construction is no longer possible because the text is representatively undecidable. We see the difference here between such impossibility of construction and the defective constructions mentioned earlier: we shift from the misunderstood to the unknowable. This modern literary practice has its counterpart outside of literature: schizophrenic discourse. Schizophrenic discourse preserves its representative intention, yet through a series of inappropriate procedures (which I have tried to classify elsewhere) it renders construction impossible.

This is not the place to study other types of reading; noting their place beside reading as construction will suffice. To perceive and describe reading as construction is all the more necessary, given that the individual reader, far from being aware of the theoretical nuances it exemplifies, reads the same text in several ways at the same time, or at different times. His activity is so natural to him that it remains imperceptible. Therefore, it is necessary to learn how to construct reading—whether it be as construction or as deconstruction.

Notes

1. "I felt that she was better than I; I scorned myself for being unworthy of her. It is a terrible misfortune not to be loved when one loves; but it is a far greater misfortune to be loved passionately when one no longer loves." All translations from *Adolphe* and *Armance* by Susan Suleiman.

2. "I found in my father not a censor, but a cold and caustic observer who would first smile in pity and soon finish the conversation with impatience."

3. "Our host, who had chatted with a Neapolitan servant who attended on that stranger [i.e., Adolphe] without knowing his name, told me that he was not at all travel-

ing out of curiosity, for he visited neither the ruins, nor the natural sites, nor the monuments, nor his fellow-men."

4. "I hate that vanity which is preoccupied only with recounting the evil it has done, which has the pretension of inspiring pity by describing itself, and which, hovering indestructibly above the ruins, analyzes itself instead of repenting."

5. "The object that escapes us is of necessity altogether different from the one that pursues us."

6. "I cannot recall, during the first eighteen years of my life, ever having had an hour's conversation with him. . . . I did not know then what timidity was."

7. "I told myself that I mustn't be overhasty, that Ellénore was not sufficiently prepared for the confession I was planning and that it was better to wait some more. Almost always, to live in peace with ourselves, we hide our weaknesses and impotence beneath the guise of calculations and systems: this satisfies the part of ourselves which is, as it were, the spectator of the other."

8. "He lacked penetration, not character."

9. "The world would regard me as a lady's companion who seduced the son of the house. I can already hear what the duchesse d'Ancre would say, or even more respectable women like the marquise de Seyssins, who sees in Octave a husband for one of her daughters."

10. "If I kill myself, Armance will be compromised. All of society will spend a week in tracking down the most minute circumstances of this evening; and every one of these gentlemen who were present will be authorized to give a different account of what happened."

13

The Literature of Replenishment · JOHN BARTH

The word is not yet in our standard dictionaries and encyclopedias, but since the end of World War II, and especially in the United States in the latter 1960s and the 1970s, "postmodernism" has enjoyed a very considerable currency, particularly with regard to our contemporary fiction. There are university courses in the American postmodernist novel; at least one quarterly journal is devoted exclusively to the discussion of postmodernist literature; at the University of Tübingen last June (1979), the annual meeting of the Deutsche Gesellschaft für Amerikastudien took as its theme "America in the 1970s," with particular emphasis on American postmodernist writing. Three alleged practitioners of that mode — William Gass, John Hawkes, and myself — were even there as live exhibits. The December annual convention of the Modern Language Association, just held in San Francisco, likewise scheduled a symposium on "the self in postmodernist fiction," a subtopic that takes the larger topic for granted.

From all this, one might innocently suppose that such a creature as postmodernism, with defined characteristics, is truly at large in our land. So I myself imagined when, in preparation for the Tübingen conference, and in response to being frequently labeled a postmodernist writer, I set about to learn what postmodernism is. I had a sense of *déjà vu:* About my very first published fiction, a 1950 undergraduate effort published in my university's quarterly magazine, a graduate-student critic wrote: "Mr. Barth alters that modernist dictum, 'the plain reader be damned': He removes the adjective." Could that, I wondered now, be postmodernism?

What I quickly discovered is that while some of the writers labeled as postmodernists, myself included, may happen to take the label with some seriousness, a principal activity of postmodernist critics (also called "metacritics" and "paracritics"), writing in postmodernist journals or speaking at postmodernist symposia, consists in disagreeing about what postmodernism is or ought to be, and thus about who should be admitted to the club —

or clubbed into admission, depending upon the critic's view of the phenomenon and of particular writers.

Who are the postmodernists? By my count, the American fictionists most commonly included in the canon, besides the three of us at Tübingen, are Donald Barthelme, Robert Coover, Stanley Elkin, Thomas Pynchon, and Kurt Vonnegut, Jr. Several of the critics I read widen the net to include Saul Bellow and Norman Mailer, different as those two writers would appear to be. Others look beyond the United States to Samuel Beckett, Jorge Luis Borges, and the late Vladimir Nabokov as engendering spirits of the "movement"; others yet insist upon including the late Raymond Queneau, the French "new novelists" Nathalie Sarraute, Michel Butor, Alain Robbe-Grillet, Robert Pinget, Claude Simon, and Claude Mauriac, the even newer French writers of the Tel Quel group, the Englishman John Fowles, and the expatriate Argentine Julio Cortázar. Some assert that such filmmakers as Michelangelo Antonioni, Federico Fellini, Jean-Luc Godard, and Alain Resnais are postmodernists. I myself will not join any literary club that doesn't include the expatriate Colombian Gabriel García Márquez and the semi-expatriate Italian Italo Calvino, of both of whom more presently. Anticipations of the "postmodernist literary aesthetic" have duly been traced through the great modernists of the first half of the twentieth century—T. S. Eliot, William Faulkner, André Gide, James Joyce, Franz Kafka, Thomas Mann, Robert Musil, Ezra Pound, Marcel Proust, Gertrude Stein, Miguel de Unamuno, Virginia Woolf—through *their* nineteenth-century predecessors—Alfred Jarry, Gustave Flaubert, Charles Baudelaire, Stéphane Mallarmé, and E. T. A. Hoffmann—back to Laurence Sterne's *Tristram Shandy* (1767) and Miguel de Cervantes's *Don Quixote* (1615).

On the other hand, among certain commentators the sifting gets exceedingly fine. Professor Jerome Klinkowitz of Northern Iowa, for example, hails Barthelme and Vonnegut as the exemplary "postcontemporaries" of the American 1970s and consigns Pynchon and myself to some 1960ish outer darkness. I regard the novels of John Hawkes as examples of fine late modernism rather than of postmodernism (and I admire them no less for that). Others might regard most of Bellow, and Mailer's *The Naked and the Dead*, as comparatively *pre*modernist, along with the works of such more consistently traditionalist American writers as John Cheever, Wallace Stegner, William Styron, or John Updike, for example (the last of whom, however, Ihab Hassan calls a modernist), or those of most of the leading British writers of this century (as contrasted with the Irish), or those of many of our contemporary American women writers of fiction, whose main literary concern, for better or worse, remains the eloquent issuance of what the critic Richard Locke has called "secular news reports." Even among the productions of a given writer, distinctions can be and often are invoked. Joyce Carol Oates writes all over the aesthetical map. John Gardner's first two published novels I would call distinctly modernist works; his short stories dabble in postmodernism; his polemical nonfiction is aggressively reactionary. Italo Calvino, on the other hand, began as an Italian new-realist (in *The Path to the Nest of Spiders* [1947]) and matured into an exemplary postmodernist (with, e.g., *Cosmicomics* [1965] and *The Castle of Crossed Destinies* [1969] who on occasion rises, sinks, or merely shifts to modernism (e.g., *Invisible Cities* [1972]). My own novels and stories seem to me to have both modernist and postmodernist attributes, even occasional premodernist attributes.

One certainly does have a sense of having been through this before. Indeed, some of us who have been publishing fiction since the 1950s have had the interesting experience of being praised or damned in that decade as existentialists and in the early 1960s as black humorists. Had our professional careers antedated the Second World War, we would no doubt have been praised or damned as modernists, in the distinguished company listed above. Now we are praised or damned as postmodernists.

Well, but what *is* postmodernism? When one leaves off the mere recitation of proper names and makes due allowance for the differences among any given author's works, do the writers most often called postmodernist share any aesthetic principles or practices as significant as the differences between them? The term itself, like "postimpressionism," is awkward and faintly epigonic, suggestive less of a vigorous or even interesting new direction in the old art of storytelling than of something anticlimactic, feebly following a very hard act to follow. One is reminded of the early James Joyce's fascination with the word *gnomon* in its negative geometrical sense: the figure that remains when a parallelogram has been removed from a similar but larger parallelogram with which it shares a common corner.

My Johns Hopkins colleague Professor Hugh Kenner, though he does not use the term postmodernist, clearly feels that way in his study of American modernist writers (*A Homemade World* [1975]): After a chapter on William Faulkner entitled "The Last Novelist," he dismisses Nabokov, Pynchon, and Barth with a sort of sigh. The late John Gardner goes even farther in his tract *On Moral Fiction* (1978), an exercise in literary kneecapping that lumps modernists and postmodernists together without distinction and consigns us all to Hell with the indiscriminate fervor characteristic of late converts to the right. Irving Howe (*The Decline of the New* [1970]) and George P. Elliott (*The Modernist Deviation* [1971]) would applaud— Professor Howe perhaps less enthusiastically than Professor Elliott. Professor Gerald Graff of Northwestern University, writing in *Tri-Quarterly* in 1975, takes a position somewhat similar to Kenner's, as the titles of two of his admirable essays make clear: "The Myth of the Postmodernist Breakthrough" (*Tri-Quarterly* 26) and "Babbitt at the Abyss" (*Tri-Quarterly* 33). Professor Robert Alter of Berkeley, in the same magazine, subtitles *his* essay on postmodernist fiction "reflections on the aftermath of modernism." Both critics proceed to a qualified sympathy for what they take to be the postmodernist program (as does Professor Ihab Hassan of the University of Wisconsin-Milwaukee in his 1971 study *The Dismemberment of Orpheus: Towards a Postmodern Literature*), and both rightly proceed *from* the premise that that program is in some respects an extension of the program of modernism, in other respects a reaction against it. The term *postmodernism* clearly suggests both; any discussion of it must therefore either presume that modernism in its turn, at this hour of the world, needs no definition— surely everybody knows what modernism is!—or else must attempt after all to define or redefine that predominant aesthetic of Western literature (and music, painting, sculpture, architecture, and the rest) in the first half of this century.

Professor Alter takes the former course: His aforementioned essay opens with the words: "Over the past two decades, as the high tide of modernism ebbed and its masters died off . . . " and proceeds without further definition to the author's reflections upon the ensuing low tide. Professor Graff, on the other hand, borrowing from Professor Howe, makes a useful quick review of the conventions of literary modernism before discussing the mode of fiction which, in his words, "departs not only from realistic conventions but from modernist ones as well."

It is good that he does, for it is not only *post*modernism that lacks definition in our standard reference books. My *Oxford English Dictionary* attests *modernism* to 1737 (Jonathan Swift, in a letter to Alexander Pope) and *Modernist* to 1588, but neither term in the sense we mean. My *American Heritage Dictionary* (1973) gives as its fourth and last definition of *modernism* "the theory and practice of modern art," a definition which does not take us very far into our American Heritage. My *Columbia Encyclopedia* (1975) discusses modernism only in the theological sense—the reinterpretation of Christian doctrine in the light of modern psychological and scientific discoveries—and follows this with an exemplary entry on *el modernismo*, a nineteenth-century Spanish literary movement which influenced the "Generation of '98" and inspired the *ultraísmo* of which Jorge Luis Borges was a youthful exponent. Neither my *Reader's Encyclopedia* (1950) nor my *Reader's Guide to Literary Terms* (1960) enters *modernism* by any definition whatever, much less *postmodernism*.

Now, as a working writer who cut his literary teeth on Eliot, Joyce, Kafka, and the other great modernists, and who is currently branded as a postmodernist, and who in fact has certain notions, no doubt naive, about what that term might conceivably mean if it is to describe anything very good very well, I am grateful to the likes of Professor Graff for not regarding his categories as self-defining. It is quite one thing to compare a line of Verdi or Tennyson or Tolstoy with a line of Stravinsky or Eliot or Joyce and to recognize that you have put the nineteenth century behind you: "Happy families are all alike; every unhappy family is unhappy in its own way" (Leo Tolstoy, *Anna Karenina*, trans. Constance Garnett). " . . . riverrun, past Eve's and Adam's, from swerve of shore to bend of bay, brings us by a commodius vicus of recirculation back to Howth Castle and Environs" (James Joyce, *Finnegans Wake*). It is quite another thing to characterize the differences between those two famous opening sentences, to itemize the aesthetic principles — premodernist and modernist — from which each issues, and then to proceed to a great *post*modernist opening sentence and show where its aesthetics resemble and differ from those of its parents, so to speak, and those of its grandparents, respectively: "Many years later, as he faced the firing squad, Colonel Aureliano Buendia was to remember that distant afternoon when his father took him to discover ice" (Gabriel García Márquez, *One Hundred Years of Solitude*, trans. Gregory Rabassa).

Professor Graff does not do this, exactly, though no doubt he could if pressed. But I shall borrow his useful checklist of the characteristics of modernist fiction, add a few items to it, summarize as typical his and Professor Alter's differing characterizations of postmodernist fiction, disagree with them respectfully in some particulars, and then fall silent, except as a storyteller.

The ground motive of modernism, Graff asserts, was criticism of the nineteenth-century bourgeois social order and its worldview. Its artistic strategy was the self-conscious overturning of the conventions of bourgeois realism by such tactics and devices as the substitution of a "mythical" for a "realistic" method and the "manipulation of conscious parallels between contemporaneity and antiquity" (Graff is here quoting T. S. Eliot on James Joyce's *Ulysses*); also the radical disruption of the linear flow of narrative, the frustration of conventional expectations concerning unity and coherence of plot and character and the cause-and-effect "development" thereof, the deployment of ironic and ambiguous juxtapositions to call into question the moral and philosophical "meaning" of literary action, the adoption of a tone of epistemological self-mockery aimed at the naive pretensions of bourgeois rationality, the opposition of inward consciousness to rational, public, objective discourse, and an inclination to subjective distortion to point up the evanescence of the objective social world of the nineteenth-century bourgeoisie.

This checklist strikes me as reasonable, if somewhat depressing from our historical perspective. I would add to it the modernists' insistence, borrowed from their romantic forebears, on the special, usually alienated role of the artist in his society, or outside it: James Joyce's priestly, self-exiled artist-hero; Thomas Mann's artist as charlatan, or mountebank; Franz Kafka's artist as anorexic, or bug. I would add too, what is no doubt implicit in Graff's catalogue, the modernists' foregrounding of language and technique as opposed to straightforward traditional "content": We remember Thomas Mann's remark (in *Tonio Kröger*, 1903), "what an artist talks *about* is never the main point"; a remark which echoes Gustave Flaubert's to Louise Colet in 1852 — "what I could like to do . . . is write a book about nothing" — and which anticipates Alain Robbe-Grillet's *obiter dictum* of 1957: "the genuine writer has nothing to say . . . He has only a way of speaking." Roland Barthes sums up this fall from innocence and ordinary content on the part of modernist literature in *Writing Degree Zero* (1953): "the whole of literature, from Flaubert to the present day, became the problematics of language."

This is French hyperbole: It is enough to say that one cardinal preoccupation of the modernists was the problematics, not simply of language, but of the medium of literature.

Now, for Professor Alter, Professor Hassan, and others, *post*modernist fiction merely emphasizes the "performing" self-consciousness and self-reflexiveness of modernism, in a spirit of cultural subversiveness and anarchy. With varying results, they maintain, postmodernist writers write a fiction that is more and more about itself and its processes, less and less about objective reality and life in the world. For Graff, too, postmodern fiction simply carries to its logical and questionable extremes the antirationalist, antirealist, antibourgeois program of modernism, but with neither a solid adversary (the bourgeois having now everywhere co-opted the trappings of modernism and turned its defiant principles into mass-media kitsch) nor solid moorings in the quotidian realism it defines itself against. From this serious charge Graff exempts certain postmodernist satire, in particular the fiction of Donald Barthelme, Saul Bellow, and Stanley Elkin, as managing to be vitalized by the same kitschy society that is its target.

I must say that all this sounds persuasive to me — until I examine more closely what I'm so inclined to nod my head yes to.

It goes without saying that critical categories are as more or less fishy as they are less or more useful. I happen to believe that just as an excellent teacher is likely to teach well no matter what pedagogical theory he suffers from, so a gifted writer is likely to rise above what he takes to be his aesthetic principles, not to mention what *others* take to be his aesthetic principles. Indeed, I believe that a truly splendid specimen in whatever aesthetic mode will pull critical ideology along behind it, like an ocean liner trailing sea-gulls. Actual artists, actual texts, are seldom more than more or less modernist, postmodernist, formalist, symbolist, realist, surrealist, politically committed, aesthetically "pure," "experimental," regionalist, international-ist, what have you. The particular work ought always to take primacy over contexts and categories. On the other hand, art lives in human time and history, and general changes in its modes and materials and concerns, even when not obviously related to changes in technology, are doubtless as significant as the changes in a culture's general attitudes, which its arts may both inspire and reflect. Some are more or less trendy and superficial, some may be indicative of more or less deep malaises, some perhaps healthy correctives of or reactions against such malaises. In any case, we can't readily discuss what artists aspire to do and what they end up doing except in terms of aesthetic categories, and so we should look further at this approximately shared impulse called postmodernism.

In my view, if it has no other and larger possibilities than those noted by, for example, Professors Alter, Graff, and Hassan, then postmodernist writing is indeed a kind of pallid, last-ditch decadence, of no more than minor symptomatic interest. There is no lack of actual texts illustrative of this view of the "postmodernist breakthrough"; but that is only to remind us that what Paul Valéry remarked of an earlier generation applies to ours as well: "Many ape the postures of modernity, without understanding their necessity." In my view, the proper program for postmodernism is neither a mere extension of the modernist program as described above, nor a mere intensification of certain aspects of modernism, nor on the contrary a wholesale subversion or repudiation of either modernism or what I'm calling pre-modernism: "traditional" bourgeois realism.

To go back a moment to our catalogue of the field-identification marks of modernist writing: Two other conspicuous ones are not yet there acknowledged, except by implication. On the one hand, James Joyce and the other great modernists set very high standards of artistry, no doubt implicit in their preoccupation with the special remove of the artist from his or her society. On the other hand, we have their famous relative difficulty of access, inherent in their antilinearity, their aversion to conventional characterization and cause-and-effect dramaturgy, their celebration of private, subjective experience over public experience, their general inclination to "metaphoric" as against "metonymic" means. (But this difficulty is *not* inherent, it is important to note, in their high standards of craftsmanship.)

From this relative difficulty of access, what Hassan calls their aristocratic cultural spirit, comes of course the relative unpopularity of modernist fiction, outside of intellectual circles and university curricula, by contrast with the fiction of, say, Dickens, Twain, Hugo, Dostoevsky, Tolstoy. From it comes also and notoriously the engenderment of a necessary priestly industry of explicators, annotators, allusion-chasers, to mediate between the text and the reader. If we need a guide, or a guidebook, to steer us through Homer or Aeschylus, it is because the world of the text is so distant from our own, as it presumably was not from Aeschylus's and Homer's original audiences. But with *Finnegans Wake* or Ezra Pound's *Cantos* we need a guide because of the inherent and immediate difficulty of the text. We are told that Bertolt Brecht, out of socialist conviction, kept on his writing desk a toy donkey bearing the sign *Even I must understand it;* the high modernists might aptly have put on their desks a professor-of-literature doll bearing, unless its specialty happened to be the literature of high modernism, the sign *Not even I can understand it.*

I do not say this in deprecation of these great writers and their sometimes brilliant explicators. If modernist works are often forbidding and require a fair amount of help and training to appreciate, it does not follow that they are not superbly rewarding, as climbing Mount Matterhorn must be, or sailing a small boat around the world. To return to our subject: Let us agree with the commonplace that the rigidities and other limitations of nineteenth-century bourgeois realism, in the light of turn-of-the-century theories and discoveries in physics, psychology, anthropology, technology, etc., prompted or fueled the great adversary reaction called modernist art — which came to terms with our new ways of thinking about the world at the frequent expense of democratic access, of immediate or at least ready delight, and often of political responsibility (the politics of Eliot, Joyce, Pound, Nabokov, and Borges, for example, are notoriously inclined either to nonexistence or to the far right). But in North America, in western and northern Europe, in the United Kingdom, in Japan, and in some of Central and South America, at least, these nineteenth-century rigidities are virtually no more. The modernist aesthetic is in my opinion unquestionably the characteristic aesthetic of the first half of our century — and in my opinion it *belongs* to the first half of our century. The present reaction against it is perfectly understandable and to be sympathized with, both because the modernist coinages are by now more or less debased common currency and because we really don't *need* more *Finnegans Wakes* and *Pisan Cantos*, each with its staff of tenured professors to explain it to us.

But I deplore the artistic and critical cast of mind that repudiates the whole modernist enterprise as an aberration and sets to work as if it hadn't happened; that rushes back into the arms of nineteenth-century middle-class realism as if the first half of the twentieth century hadn't happened. It *did* happen: Freud and Einstein and two world wars and the Russian and sexual revolutions and automobiles and airplanes and telephones and radios and movies and urbanization, and now nuclear weaponry and television and microchip technology and the new feminism and the rest, and except as readers there's no going back to Tolstoy and Dickens. As the Russian writer Evgeny Zamyatin was already saying in the 1920s (in his essay *On Literature, Revolution, and Entropy*): "Euclid's world is very simple, and Einstein's world is very difficult; nevertheless, it is now impossible to return to Euclid's."

On the other hand, it is no longer necessary, if it ever was, to repudiate *them*, either: the great premodernists. If the modernists, carrying the torch of romanticism, taught us that linearity, rationality, consciousness, cause and effect, naive illusionism, transparent language, innocent anecdote, and middle-class moral conventions are not the whole story, then from the perspective of these closing decades of our century we may appreciate that the contraries of those things are not the whole story either. Disjunction, simultaneity, irrationalism, anti-illusionism, self-reflexiveness, medium-as-message, political olympianism, and a moral pluralism approaching moral entropy — these are not the whole story either.

A worthy program for postmodernist fiction, I believe, is the synthesis or transcension of these antitheses, which may be summed up as premodernist and modernist modes of writing. My ideal postmodernist author neither merely repudiates nor merely imitates either his twentieth-century modernist parents or his nineteenth-century premodernist grandparents. He has the first half of our century under his belt, but not on his back. Without lapsing into moral or artistic simplism, shoddy craftsmanship, Madison

Avenue venality, or either false or real naiveté, he nevertheless aspires to a fiction more democratic in its appeal than such late-modernist marvels (by my definition) as Beckett's *Texts for Nothing* or Nabokov's *Pale Fire*. He may not hope to reach and move the devotees of James Michener and Irving Wallace—not to mention the great mass of television-addicted non-readers. But he *should* hope to reach and delight, at least part of the time, beyond the circle of what Mann used to call the Early Christians: professional devotees of high art.

I feel this in particular for practitioners of the novel, a genre whose historical roots are famously and honorably in middle-class popular culture. The ideal postmodernist novel will somehow rise above the quarrel between realism and irrealism, formalism and "contentism," pure and committed literature, coterie fiction and junk fiction. Alas for professors of literature, it may not need as much *teaching* as Joyce's or Nabokov's or Pynchon's books, or some of my own. On the other hand, it will not wear its heart on its sleeve, either; at least not its whole heart. (In a recent published exchange between William Gass and John Gardner, Gardner declares that he wants everybody to love his books; Gass replies that he would no more want his books to be loved by everybody than he'd want his daughter to be loved by everybody, and suggests that Gardner is confusing love with promiscuity.) My own analogy would be with good jazz or classical music: One finds much on successive listenings or close examination of the score that one didn't catch the first time through; but the first time through should be so ravishing—and not just to specialists—that one delights in the replay.

Lest this postmodern synthesis sound both sentimental and impossible of attainment, I offer two quite different examples of works which I believe approach it, as perhaps such giants as Dickens and Cervantes may be said to anticipate it. The first and more tentative example (it is not meant to be a blockbuster) is Italo Calvino's *Cosmicomics* (1965): beautifully written, enormously appealing space-age fables—"perfect dreams," John Updike has called them—whose materials are as modern as the new cosmology and as ancient as folktales, but whose themes are love and loss, change and permanence, illusion and reality, including a good deal of specifically Italian reality. Like all fine fantasists, Calvino grounds his flights in local, palpable detail: Along with the nebulae and the black holes and the lyricism, there is a nourishing supply of pasta, bambini, and good-looking women sharply glimpsed and gone forever. A true postmodernist, Calvino keeps one foot always in the narrative past—characteristically the Italian narrative past of Boccaccio, Marco Polo, or Italian fairy tales—and one foot in, one might say, the Parisian structuralist present; one foot in fantasy, one in objective reality, etc. It is appropriate that he has, I understand, been chastised from the left by the Italian communist critics and from the right by the Italian Catholic critics; it is symptomatic that he has been praised by fellow authors as divergent as John Updike, Gore Vidal, and myself. I urge everyone to read Calvino at once, beginning with *Cosmicomics* and going right on, not only because he exemplifies my postmodernist program, but because his fiction is both delicious and high in protein.

An even better example is Gabriel García Márquez's *One Hundred Years of Solitude* (1967): as impressive a novel as has been written so far in the second half of our century and one of the splendid specimens of that splendid genre from any century. Here the synthesis of straightforwardness and artifice, realism and magic and myth, political passion and nonpolitical artistry, characterization and caricature, humor and terror, are so remarkably sustained that one recognizes with exhilaration very early on, as with *Don Quixote* and *Great Expectations* and *Huckleberry Finn*, that one is in the presence of a masterpiece not only artistically admirable, but humanly wise, lovable, literally marvelous. One had almost forgotten that new fiction could be so *wonderful* as well as so merely important. And the question whether my program for postmodernism is achievable goes happily out the window, like one of García Márquez's characters on flying carpets. Praise be to the Spanish language and imagination! As Cervantes stands as an exemplar of premodernism and a great precursor of much to come, and Jorge Luis Borges as an exemplar of *dernier cri* modernism and at the same time as a bridge between the end of the nineteenth century and the end of the twentieth, so Gabriel García Márquez is in that enviable succession: an exemplary postmodernist and a master of the storyteller's art.

A dozen years ago I published in these pages a much-misread essay called "The Literature of Exhaustion," occasioned by my admiration for the stories of Señor Borges and by my concern, in that somewhat apocalyptic place and time, for the ongoing health of narrative fiction. (The time was the latter 1960s; the place Buffalo, N.Y., on a university campus embattled by tear-gassing riot police and tear-gassed Vietnam War protesters, while from across the Peace Bridge in Canada came Professor Marshall McLuhan's siren song that we "print-oriented bastards" were obsolete.) The simple burden of my essay was that the forms and modes of art live in human history and are therefore subject to used-upness, at least in the minds of significant numbers of artists in particular times and places: in other words, that artistic conventions are liable to be retired, subverted, transcended, transformed, or even deployed against themselves to generate new and lively work. I would have thought that point unexceptionable. But a great many people—among them, I fear, Señor Borges himself—mistook me to mean that literature, at least fiction, is *kaput;* that it has all been done already; that there is nothing left for contemporary writers but to parody and travesty our great predecessors in our exhausted medium—exactly what some critics deplore as postmodernism.

That is not what I meant at all. Leaving aside the celebrated fact that, with *Don Quixote,* the novel may be said to *begin* in self-transcendent parody and has often returned to that mode for its refreshment, let me say at once and plainly that I agree with Borges that literature can never be exhausted, if only because no single literary text can ever be exhausted—its "meaning" residing as it does in its transactions with individual readers over time, space, and language. I like to remind misreaders of my earlier essay that written literature is in fact about 4,500 years old (give or take a few centuries depending on one's definition of literature), but that we have no way of knowing whether 4,500 years constitutes senility, maturity, youth, or mere infancy. The number of splendid sayable things—metaphors for the dawn or the sea, for example—is doubtless finite; it is also doubtless very large, perhaps virtually infinite. In some moods we writers may feel that Homer had it easier than we, getting there early with his rosy-fingered dawn and his wine-dark sea. We should console ourselves that one of the earliest extant literary texts (an Egyptian papyrus of ca. 2000 B.C., cited by Walter Jackson Bate in his 1970 study *The Burden of the Past and the English Poet*) is a complaint by the scribe Khakheperresenb that he has arrived on the scene too late: "Would I had phrases that are not known, utterances that are strange, in new language that has not been used, free from repetition, not an utterance that has grown stale, which men of old have spoken."

What my essay "The Literature of Exhaustion" was really about, so it seems to me now, was the effective "exhaustion" not of language or of literature, but of the aesthetic of high modernism: that admirable, not-to-be-repudiated, but essentially completed "program" of what Hugh Kenner has dubbed "the Pound era." In 1966–67 we scarcely had the term *postmodernism* in its current literary-critical usage—at least I hadn't heard it yet—but a number of us, in quite different ways and with varying combinations of intuitive response and conscious deliberation, were already well into the working out, not of the next best thing after modernism, but of the *best next* thing: what is gropingly now called postmodernist fiction; what I hope might also be thought of one day as a literature of replenishment.

14

The Blackness of Blackness: A Critique on the Sign and
the Signifying Monkey · HENRY LOUIS GATES, JR.

Signification is the Nigger's occupation. — Traditional[1]

Be careful what you do,
Or Mumbo-Jumbo, God of the Congo,
And all of the other
Gods of the Congo,
Mumbo-Jumbo will hoo-doo you,
Mumbo-Jumbo will hoo-doo you,
Mumbo-Jumbo will hoo-doo you. — Vachel Lindsay, *The Congo*

I need not trace in these pages the history of the concept of signification. Since Ferdinand de Saussure at least, signification has become a crucial aspect of much of contemporary theory. It is curious to me that this neologism in the Western tradition cuts across a term in the black vernacular tradition that is approximately two centuries old. Tales of the Signifying Monkey had their origins in slavery. Hundreds of these have been recorded since the nineteenth century. In black music, Jazz Gillum, Count Basie, Oscar Peterson, Oscar Browne, Jr., Little Willie Dixon, Nat "King" Cole, Otis Redding, Wilson Picket, and Johnny Otis — at least — have recorded songs called either "The Signifying Monkey" or simply "Signifyin(g)." My theory of interpretation, arrived at from within the black cultural matrix, is a theory of formal revisionism, it is tropological, it is often characterized by pastiche, and, most crucially, it turns on repetition of formal structures and their differences. Signification is a theory of reading that arises from Afro-American culture; learning how to signify is often part of our adolescent education. That it has not been drawn upon before as a theory of criticism attests to its sheer familiarity in the idiom. I had to step outside my culture, to defamiliarize the concept by translating it into a new mode of discourse, before I could see its potential in critical theory. My work with signification has now led me to undertake the analysis of the principles of interpretation implicit in the decoding of the signs used in the Ifá oracle, still very much alive among the Yoruba in Nigeria, in a manner only roughly related to Harold Bloom's use of the Kabbalah.

I Signifyin(g): Definitions

Perhaps only Tar Baby is as enigmatic and compelling a figure from Afro-American mythic discourse as is that oxymoron, the Signifying Monkey.[2] The ironic reversal of a received racist image in the Western imagination of the black as simianlike, the Signifying Monkey — he who dwells at the margins of discourse, ever punning, ever troping, ever embodying the ambiguities of language — is our trope for repetition and revision, indeed our trope of chiasmus itself, repeating and reversing simultaneously as he does in one deft discursive act. If Vico and Burke, or Nietzsche, de Man, and Bloom, are correct in identifying four and six master tropes, then we might think of these as the master's tropes and of signifying as the slave's trope, the trope of tropes, as Bloom characterizes metalepsis, "a trope-reversing trope, a figure of a figure." Signifying is a trope in which are subsumed several other rhetorical tropes, including metaphor, metonymy, synecdoche, and irony (the master tropes), and also hyperbole and litotes, and metalepsis (Bloom's supplement to Burke). To this list we could easily add aporia, chiasmus, and catechesis, all of which are used in the ritual of signifying.

Signifying, it is clear, in black discourse means modes of figuration itself. When one signifies, as Kimberly W. Benston puns, one "tropes-a-dope." Indeed, the black tradition itself has its own subdivisions of signifying, which we could readily identify with the typology of figures received from classical and medieval rhetoric, as Bloom has done with his "map of misprision." The black rhetorical tropes, subsumed under signifying, would include marking, loud-talking, testifying, calling out (of one's name), sounding, rapping, playing the dozens, and so on.[3]

Let us consider received definitions of the act of signifying and of black mythology's archetypal signifier, the Signifying Monkey. The Signifying Monkey is a trickster figure, of the order of the trickster figure of Yoruba mythology (*Esu-Elegbara* in Nigeria and *Legba* among the Fon in Dahomey), whose New World figurations (*Exu* in Brazil, *Echu-Elegua* in Cuba, *Papa Legba* in the pantheon of the *loa* of *Vaudou* in Haiti, and *Papa La Bas* in the *loa* of *Hoodoo* in the United States) speak eloquently of the unbroken arc of metaphysical presupposition and patterns of figuration shared through space and time among black cultures in West Africa, South America, the

Caribbean, and in the United States. These trickster figures, aspects of *Esu*, are primarily mediators: as tricksters they are mediators, and their mediations are tricks.[4]

The versions of *Esu* are all messengers of the gods: he who interprets the will of god to people, he who carries the desires of people to the gods. *Esu* is guardian of the crossroads, master of style and the stylus, phallic god of generation and fecundity, master of the mystical barrier that separates the divine from the profane worlds. He is known as the divine linguist, the keeper of *ase* (*logos*) with which Olodumare created the universe.

In Yoruba mythology, *Esu* always limps because his legs are of different lengths: one is anchored in the realm of the gods, and the other rests in this human world. The closest Western relative of *Esu*, of course, is Hermes; and, just as Hermes's role as interpreter lent his name readily to "hermeneutics," our metaphor for the study of the process of interpretation, so too can the figure of *Esu* stand as our metaphor for the act of interpretation itself for the critic of comparative black literature. In African and Latin American mythology, *Esu* is said to have taught *Ifa* how to read the signs formed by the sixteen sacred palmnuts which, when manipulated, configure into what is known as the signature of an *Odu*, two hundred and fifty-six of which comprise the corpus of *Ifa Divination*. The *Opon Ifa*, the carved wooden divination tray used in the art of interpretation, is said to contain at the center of its upper perimeter a carved image of *Esu*, meant to signify his relation to the act of interpretation, which we can translate either as *itumo* ("to unite or unknot knowledge") or as *yipada* ("to turn around or translate"). That which we now call close reading, the Yoruba call *Oda fa* ("reading the signs"). Above all else, *Esu* is the Black Interpreter, the Yoruba god of indeterminacy or *ariye-muye* (that which no sooner is held than it slips through one's fingers).[5] As Hermes is to hermeneutics, *Esu* is to *Esu tufunaalo* (bringing out the interstices of the riddle).

The *Esu* figures, among the Yoruba systems of thought in Dahomey and Nigeria, in Brazil and Cuba, in Haiti and at New Orleans, are divine; they are gods who function in sacred myths, as do characters in a narrative. *Esu*'s functional equivalent in Afro-American profane discourse is the Signifying Monkey, a figure who would seem to be distinctly Afro-American, probably derived from Cuban mythology, which generally depicts *Echu-Elegua* with a monkey at his side,[6] and who, unlike his Pan-African *Esu* cousins, exists in the discourse of mythology not primarily as a character in a narrative but rather as a vehicle for narration itself. It is from this corpus of narratives that signifying derives. The Afro-American rhetorical strategy of signifying is a rhetorical act that is not engaged in the game of information giving. Signifying turns on the play and chain of signifiers, and not on some supposedly transcendent signified. Alan Dundes suggests that the origins of signifying could "lie in African rhetoric." As anthropologists demonstrate, the Signifying Monkey is often called the Signifier, he who wreaks havoc upon the Signified. One is signified upon by the signifier. He is indeed the "signifier as such," in Julia Kristeva's phrase, "a presence that precedes the signification of object or emotion."[7]

Scholars have for some time commented upon the peculiar use of the word "signifying" in black discourse. Though sharing some connotations with the standard English-language word, "signifying" has rather unique definitions in black discourse. Roger D. Abrahams defines it as follows:

> Signifying seems to be a Negro term, in use if not in origin. It can mean any of a number of things; in the case of the toast about the signifying monkey, it certainly refers to the trickster's ability to talk with great innuendo, to carp, cajole, needle, and lie. It can mean in other instances the propensity to talk around a subject, never quite coming to the point. It can mean making fun of a person or situation. Also it can denote speaking with the hands and eyes, and in this respect encompasses a whole complex of expressions and gestures. Thus it is signifying to stir up a fight between neighbors by telling stories; it is signifying to make fun of a policeman by parodying his motions behind his back; it is signifying to ask for a piece of cake by saying, "my brother needs a piece of cake."[8]

Essentially, Abrahams concludes, signifying is a "*technique* of indirect argument or persuasion," "a language of implication," "to imply, goad, beg, boast, by *indirect* verbal or gestural means." "The name 'signifying,'" he concludes, "shows the monkey to be a trickster, signifying being the language of trickery, that set of words or gestures achieving Hamlet's 'direction through indirection.'" The monkey, in short, is not only a master of technique, as Abrahams concludes; he *is* technique, or style, or the literariness of literary language; he is the great Signifier. In this sense, one does not signify something; rather, one signifies in some way.[9]

There are thousands of "toasts" of the Signifying Monkey, most of which commence with a variant of the following formulaic lines:

> Deep down in the jungle so they say
> There's a signifying monkey down the way
> There hadn't been no disturbin' in the jungle for quite a bit,

For up jumped the monkey in the tree one day and laughed,
"I guess I'll start some shit."[10]

Endings, too, tend toward the formulaic, as in the following:

"Monkey," said the Lion,
Beat to his unbooted knees,
"You and your signifying children
Better stay up in the trees."
Which is why today
Monkey does his signifying
A-way-up out of the way."[11]

In the narrative poems, the Signifying Monkey invariably repeats to his friend, the Lion, some insult purportedly generated by their mutual friend, the Elephant. The Lion, indignant and outraged, demands an apology of the Elephant, who refuses and then trounces the Lion. The Lion, realizing that his mistake was to take the monkey literally, returns to trounce the monkey. Although anthropologists and sociolinguists have succeeded in establishing a fair sample of texts of the Signifying Monkey, they have been less successful at establishing a consensus of definitions of black signifying.

In addition to Abraham's definitions, definitions of signifying by Zora Neale Hurston, Thomas Kochman, Claudia Mitchell-Kernan, Geneva Smitherman, and Ralph Ellison are of interest here for what they reveal about the nature of Afro-American narrative parody, which I shall attempt first to define and then to employ in a reading of Ishmael Reed's *Mumbo Jumbo* as a pastiche of the Afro-American narrative tradition itself. Kochman argues that signifying depends upon the signifier *repeating* what someone else has said about a third person, in order to *reverse* the status of a relationship heretofore harmonious; signifying can also be employed to *reverse* or *undermine* pretense or even one's opinion about one's own status.[12] This use of repetition and reversal (chiasmus) constitutes an implicit parody of a subject's own complicity in illusion. Claudia Mitchell-Kernan, in perhaps the most thorough study of the concept, compares the etymology of "signifying" in black usage with usages from standard English:

What is unique in Black English usage is the way in which signifying is extended to cover a range of meanings and events which are not covered in its Standard English usage. In the Black community it is possible to say, "He is signifying" and "Stop signifying" — sentences which would be anomalous elsewhere.[13]

Mitchell-Kernan points to the ironic, or dialectic, relationship between identical terms in standard and black English, which have vastly different meanings:

> The Black concept of *signifying* incorporates essentially a folk notion that dictionary entries for words are not always sufficient for interpreting meanings or messages, or that meaning goes beyond such interpretations. Complimentary remarks may be delivered in a left-handed fashion. A particular utterance may be an insult in one context and not another. What pretends to be informative may intend to be persuasive. The hearer is thus constrained to attend to all potential meaning-carrying symbolic systems in speech events — the total universe of discourse.[14]

This is an excellent instance of the nature of signifying itself. Mitchell-Kernan refines these definitions somewhat by suggesting that the Signifying Monkey is able to signify upon the Lion only because the Lion does not understand the nature of the monkey's discourse: "There seems something of symbolic relevance from the perspective of language in this poem. The monkey and the lion do not speak the same language; the lion is not able to interpret the monkey's use of language." The monkey speaks figuratively, in a symbolic code; the lion interprets or reads literally and suffers the consequences of his folly, which is a reversal of his status as King of the Jungle. The monkey rarely acts in these narrative poems; he simply speaks. As the Signifier, he determines the actions of the Signified, the hapless Lion and the puzzled Elephant.[15]

As Mitchell-Kernan and Zora Neale Hurston attest, signifying is a sexless rhetorical game, despite the frequent use in the "masculine" versions of expletives that connote intimate relations with one's mother. Hurston, in *Mules and Men*, and Mitchell-Kernan, in her perceptive "Signifying, Loud-talking and Marking," are the first scholars to record and explicate female signifying rituals.[16] Zora Neale Hurston is the first author of the tradition to represent signifying itself as a vehicle of liberation for an oppressed woman, and as a rhetorical strategy in the narration of fiction.

Hurston, whose definition of the term in *Mules and Men* (1935) is one of the earliest in the linguistic literature, has made *Their Eyes Were Watching God* into a paradigmatic signifying text, for this novel resolves that implicit tension between the literal and the figurative contained in standard English usages of the term "signifying." *Their Eyes* represents the black trope of signifying both as thematic matter and as a rhetorical strategy of the novel itself. Janie, the protagonist, gains her voice on the porch of her husband's store, not only by engaging with the assembled men in the ritual of signifying (which her husband had expressly forbidden her to do) but also by openly signifying upon her husband's impotency. His image wounded fatally, her husband soon dies of a displaced "kidney" failure. Janie "kills" her husband rhetorically. Moreover, Hurston's masterful use of the indirect discourse allows her to signify upon the tension between the two voices of Jean Toomer's *Cane* by adding to direct and indirect speech a strategy through which she can privilege the black oral tradition, which Toomer found to be problematical and dying. Hurston's is the "speakerly text."

The text of *Their Eyes*, moreover, is itself a signifying structure, a structure of intertextual revision, because it revises key tropes and rhetorical strategies received from precursory texts, such as W. E. B. Du Bois's *A Quest of the Silver Fleece* and Toomer's *Cane*. Afro-American literary history is characterized by tertiary formal revision: Hurston's text (1937) revises Du Bois's novel (1911), and Toni Morrison in several texts revises Ellison and Hurston; similarly, Ellison (1951) revises Wright (1940, 1945), and Ishmael Reed (1972), among others, revises both. It is clear that black writers read and critique other black texts as an act of rhetorical self-definition. Our literary tradition exists because of these precisely chartable formal literary relationships.

The key aspect of signifying for Mitchell-Kernan is "its indirect intent or metaphorical reference," a rhetorical indirection which she says is "almost purely stylistic." Its art characteristics remain foregrounded. By "indirection," Mitchell-Kernan means that "the correct semantic (referential interpretation) or signification of the utterance cannot be arrived at by a consideration of the dictionary meaning of the lexical items involved and the syntactic rules for their combination alone. The apparent significance of the message differs from its real significance. The apparent meaning of the sentence signifies its actual meaning."[17]

This rhetorical naming by indirection is, of course, central to our notions of figuration, troping, and of the parody of forms, or pastiche, in evidence when one writer repeats another's structure by one of several means, including a fairly exact repetition of a given narrative or rhetorical structure, filled incongruously with a ludicrous or incongruent content. T. Thomas Fortune's "The Black Man's Burden" is an excellent example of this form of pastiche, signifying as it does upon Kipling's "White Man's Burden":

What is the Black Man's Burden,
Ye hypocrites and vile,
Ye whited sepulchres
From th' Amazon to the Nile?
What is the Black Man's Burden,
Ye Gentile parasites,
Who crush and rob your brother
Of his manhood and his rights?

Dante Gabriel Rossetti's "Uncle Ned," a dialect verse parody of Stowe's *Uncle Tom's Cabin*, is a second example:

Him tale dribble on and on widout a break,
Till you hab no eyes for to see;
When I read Chapter 4 I had got a headache;
So I had to let Chapter 4 be.

Another example of formal parody is to suggest a given structure precisely by failing to coincide with it—that is, to suggest it by dissemblance. Repetition of a form and then inversion of the same through a process of variation is central to jazz. A stellar example is John Coltrane's rendition of "My Favorite Things" compared to Julie Andrews's vapid original. Resemblance, then, can be evoked cleverly by dissemblance. Aristophanes's *The Frogs*, which parodies the styles of both Aeschylus and Euripides; Cervantes's relationship to the fiction of knight-errantry; Henry Fielding's parody of the Richardsonian novel of sentiment in *Joseph Andrews*, and Lewis Carroll's double parody in *Hiawatha's Photographing* (which draws upon Longfellow's rhythms to parody the convention of the family photograph) all come readily to mind. Ralph Ellison defines the parody aspect of signifying in several ways relevant to our discussion below of the formal parody strategies at work in Ishmael Reed's *Mumbo Jumbo*.

In his complex short story "And Hickman Arrives" (1960), Ellison's narrator defines signifying in this way:

And the two men [Daddy Hickman and Deacon Wilhite] standing side by side, the one large and dark, the other slim and light brown, the other reverends rowed behind them, their faces staring grim with engrossed attention to the reading of the Word, like judges in their carved, high-backed chairs. And the two voices beginning their call and countercall as Daddy Hickman began spelling out the text which Deacon Wilhite read, playing variations on the verses just as he did with his trombone when he really felt like signifying on a tune the choir was singing.[18]

Following this introduction, the two ministers demonstrate the definition of signification, which in turn is a signification upon the antiphonal structure of the Afro-American sermon. This parody of form is of the same order as Richard Pryor's parody of both the same sermonic structure and Stevie Wonder's "Living for the City," which he effects by speaking the lyrics of Wonder's song in the form of and with the intonation peculiar to the Afro-American sermon in his "reading" of "The Book of Wonder." Pryor's parody is a signification of the second order, revealing simultaneously the received structure of the sermon (by its presence, demystified here by its incongruous content), the structure of Wonder's music (by the absence of his form and the presence of his lyrics), and the complex yet direct formal relationship between the black sermon and Wonder's music specifically, as well as that between black sacred and secular narrative forms generally.

Ellison defines signifying in other ways as well. In his essay on Charlie Parker, entitled "On Bird, Bird-Watching, and Jazz" (1962), Ellison defines the satirical aspect of signifying as one aspect of riffing in jazz:

> But what kind of bird was Parker? Back during the thirties members of the old Blue Devils Orchestra celebrated a certain robin by playing a lugubrious little tune called "They Picked Poor Robin." It was a jazz community joke, musically an extended signifying "riff" or melodic naming of a recurrent human situation, and was played to satirize some betrayal of faith or loss of love observed from the bandstand.[19]

Here again, the parody is twofold, involving a formal parody of the melody of "They Picked Poor Robin" as well as a ritual naming, and therefore a troping, of an action observed from the bandstand.

Ellison, of course, is our Great Signifier himself, naming things by indirection and troping throughout his works. In his well-known review of LeRoi Jones's *Blues People*, Ellison defines signifying in yet a third sense, then signifies upon Jones's reading of Afro-American cultural history, which he argues is misdirected and wrongheaded. "The tremendous burden of sociology which Jones would place upon this body of music," writes Ellison, "is enough to give even the blues the blues." Ellison writes that Lydia Maria Child's title, *An Appeal in Favor of That Class of Americans called Africans*, sounds like a fine bit of contemporary ironic signifying—"*signifying*" here meaning, in the unwritten dictionary of American Negro usage, "rhetorical understatements." It tells us much of the thinking of her opposition, and it reminds us that as late as the 1890s, a time when Negro composers, singers, dancers and comedians dominated the American musical stage, popular Negro songs (including James Weldon Johnson's "Under the Bamboo Tree," now immortalized by T. S. Eliot) were commonly referred to as "Ethiopian Airs."[20]

Ellison's stress upon "the unwritten dictionary of American Negro usage" reminds us of the problem of definitions, of signification itself, when one is translating between two languages. The Signifying Monkey, perhaps appropriately, seems to dwell at this space between two linguistic domains. One wonders, incidentally, about this Afro-American figure and a possible French connection between *signe* ("sign") and *singe* ("monkey").

Ellison's definition of the relation his works bear to those of Richard Wright constitutes our definition of narrative signification, pastiche, or critical parody, although he employs none of these terms. His explanation of what we might call implicit formal criticism, however, comprises what we have sometimes called troping, after Geoffrey Hartman, and which we might take to be a profound definition of critical signification itself. Writes Ellison:

> I felt no need to attack what I considered the limitations of [Wright's] vision because I was quite impressed by what he had achieved. And in this, although I saw with the black vision of Ham, I was, I suppose, as pious as Shem and Japheth. Still I would write my own books and they would be in themselves, implicitly, criticisms of Wright's; just as all novels of a given historical moment form an argument over the nature of reality and are, to an extent, criticisms each of the other.[21]

Ellison in his fictions signifies upon Wright by parodying Wright's literary structures through repetition and difference. Although this is not the place for a close reading of this formal relationship, the complexities of the parodying can be readily suggested. The play of language, the signifying, starts with the titles. *Native Son* and *Black Boy*—both titles connoting race, self, and presence—Ellison tropes with *Invisible Man*, invisibility an ironic response of absence to the would-be presence of "blacks" and "natives," while "man" suggests a more mature, stronger status than either "sons" or "boy." Ellison signifies upon Wright's distinctive version of naturalism with a complex rendering of modernism; Wright's reacting protagonist, voiceless to the last, Ellison signifies upon with a nameless protagonist who is nothing but voice, since it is he who shapes, edits, and narrates his own tale, thereby combining action with the representation of action, thereby defining reality by its representation. This unity of presence and representation is perhaps Ellison's most subtle reversal of Wright's theory of the novel as exemplified in *Native Son*, since Bigger's voicelessness and powerlessness to act (as opposed to react) signify an absence, despite the metaphor of presence found in the novel's title; the reverse obtains in *Invisible Man*, where the absence implied by invisibility is undermined by the presence of the narrator as the narrator of his own text.

There are other aspects of critical parody at play here, too, one of the funniest being Jack's glass eye plopping into his water glass before him, which is functionally equivalent to the action of Wright's protagonist in "The Man Who Lived Underground," as he stumbles over the body of a dead baby, deep down in the sewer. It is precisely at this point in the narrative that we know Fred Daniels to be "dead, baby," in the heavy-handed way that Wright's naturalism was self-consciously symbolic. If Daniels's fate is signified by the objects over which he stumbles in the darkness of the sewer, Ellison signifies upon Wright's novella by repeating this underground scene of discovery but having his protagonist burn the bits of paper through which he has allowed himself to be defined by others. By explicitly repeating and reversing key figures of Wright's fictions, and by defining implicitly in the process of narration a sophisticated form more akin to Hurston's *Their Eyes Were Watching God*, Ellison exposes naturalism to be merely a hardened convention of representation of "the Negro problem" and perhaps part of the problem itself. I cannot emphasize enough the major import of this narrative gesture to the subsequent development of black narrative forms, since Ellison recorded a new way of seeing and defined both a new manner of representation and its relation to the concept of presence. The formal relation that Ellison bears to Wright, Ishmael Reed bears to both, but principally to Ellison. Once again, Ellison has formulated this complex and inherently polemical intertextual relationship of formal signifying, in a refutation of Irving Howe's critique of his work: "I agree with Howe that protest is an element of all art, though it does not necessarily take the form of speaking for a political or social program. It might appear in a novel as a *technical assault against the styles* which have gone before [emphasis added]."[22] This form of critical parody, of repetition and inversion, is what I define to be critical signification, or formal signifying, and is my metaphor for literary history.

This chapter is a reading of the tertiary relationship among Reed's "post-modern" *Mumbo Jumbo* as a signification upon Wright's "realism" and Ellison's "modernism." The set of intertextual relations that I chart through formal signification is related to what Mikhail Bakhtin labels double-voiced discourse, which he subdivides into parodic narration and the hidden, or internal, polemic. These two types of double-voiced discourse can merge together, as they do in *Mumbo Jumbo*. Although Bakhtin's discourse typology is familiar, let me cite his definition of hidden polemic. In hidden polemic,

> the other speech act remains outside the boundaries of the author's speech, but it is implied or alluded to in that speech. The other speech act is not reproduced with a new intention, but shapes the author's speech while remaining outside its boundaries. Such is the nature of the hidden polemic. . . .
>
> In hidden polemic the author's discourse is oriented toward its referential object, as in any other discourse, but at the same time each assertion about that object is constructed in such a way that, besides its referential meaning, the author's discourse brings a polemical attack to bear against another speech act, another assertion, on the same topic. Here one utterance focused on its referential object clashes with another utterance on the grounds of the referent itself. That other utterance is not reproduced; it is understood only in its import.[23]

Ellison's definition of the formal relationship his works bear to Wright's is a salient example of the hidden polemic: his texts clash with Wright's "on the ground of the referent itself." "As a result," Bakhtin continues, "the latter begins to influence the author's speech from within." This relationship Bakhtin calls double-voiced, whereby one speech act determines the internal structure of another, the second effecting the voice of the first, by absence, by difference.

Much of the Afro-American literary tradition can be read as successive attempts to create a new narrative space for representation of the recurring referent of Afro-American literature, the so-called black experience. Certainly, we read the relation of Sterling Brown's regionalism to Jean Toomer's lyricism in this way, Hurston's lyricism to Wright's naturalism in this way, and Ellison's modernism to Wright's naturalism in this way as well. We might represent this set of relationships in figure 1, which is intended in no sense other than to be suggestive.[24]

These relationships are reciprocal, because we are free to read in critical time machines, reading backwards, like Merlin moved through time. The

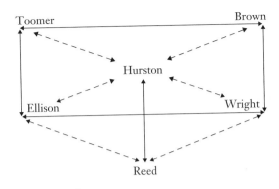

direct relation most important to my own theory of reading is the solid black line that connects Reed with Hurston. Reed and Hurston seem to relish the play of the tradition, while Reed's work seems to be a magnificently conceived play on the tradition. Both Hurston and Reed write myths of Moses, both draw upon black sacred and secular myths' discourse as metaphorical and metaphysical systems; both write self-reflexive texts which comment upon the nature of writing itself; both make use of the frame to bracket their narratives within narratives; and both are authors of fictions that I characterize as speakerly texts, texts that privilege the representation of the speaking black voice, of what the Formalists called skaz, and that Reed himself has defined as "an oral book, a talking book," a figure that occurs, remarkably enough, in four of the first five narratives in the black tradition in the eighteenth century.[25]

Reed's relation to these authors in the tradition is at all points doublevoiced, since he seems to be especially concerned with employing satire to utilize literature in what Northrop Frye calls "a special function of analysis, of breaking up the lumber of stereotypes, fossilized beliefs, superstitious terrors, crank theories, pedantic dogmatisms, oppressive fashions, and all other things that impede the free movement . . . of society."[26] Reed, of course, seems to be most concerned with the free movement of writing itself. In Reed's work, parody and hidden polemic overlap in a process Bakhtin describes thusly: "When parody becomes aware of substantial resistance, a certain forcefulness and profundity in the speech act it parodies, it takes on a new dimension of complexity via the tones of the hidden polemic. . . . A process of inner dialogization takes place within the parodic speech act."[27]

This internal dialogization can have curious implications, the most interesting of which perhaps is what Bakhtin describes as "the splitting of double-voice discourse into two speech acts, into the two entirely separate and autonomous voices." The clearest evidence that Reed in *Mumbo Jumbo* is signifying through parody as hidden polemic is his use of the two autonomous narrative voices, which he employs in the manner of, and renders through, foregrounding, to parody the two simultaneous stories of detective narration, that of the present and that of the past, in a narrative flow that moves hurriedly from cause to effect. In *Mumbo Jumbo*, however, the second narrative, that of the past, bears an ironic relation to the first narrative, that of the present, because it comments upon both the other narrative and the nature of its writing itself, in what Frye describes in another context as "the constant tendency to self-parody in satiric rhetoric which prevents even the process of writing itself from becoming an oversimplified convention or ideal."[28] Reed's rhetorical strategy assumes the form of the relationship between the text and the criticism of that text, which serves as discourse upon that text.

II "Consult the Text"[29]

With these definitions of narrative parody and critical signification as a frame, let us read Ishmael Reed's third novel, *Mumbo Jumbo*. A close reading of Reed's corpus of works suggests strongly that he seems to be concerned with the received form of the novel, with the precise rhetorical shape of the Afro-American literary tradition, and with the relation that the Afro-American tradition bears to the Western tradition. Reed's concerns, as exemplified in his narrative forms, would seem to be twofold: on the one hand with that relation his own art bears to his black literary precursors, whom we can identify to include Zora Neale Hurston, Richard Wright, James Baldwin, and Ralph Ellison, and on the other hand the process of willing into being a rhetorical structure, a literary language, replete with its own figures and tropes, but one that allows the black writer to posit a structure of feeling that simultaneously critiques both the metaphysical presuppositions inherent in Western ideas and forms of writing and the metaphorical system in which the blackness of the writer and his experience have been valorized as a "natural" absence. In the short term, that is, through six demanding novels,[30] Reed has apparently decided to criticize, through signification, what he seems to perceive to be the received and conventional structures of feeling that he has inherited from the Afro-American tradition itself, almost as if the sheer process of the analysis can clear a narrative space for his generation of writers as decidedly as Ellison's narrative response to Wright and naturalism cleared a space for Leon Forrest, Toni Morrison, Alice Walker, James Alan Mcpherson, and especially Reed himself.

By undertaking the difficult and subtle art of pastiche, Reed criticizes the Afro-American idealism of a transcendent black subject, integral and whole, self-sufficient and plentiful, the "always already" black signified, available for literary representation in received Western forms as would be the water ladled from a deep and dark well. Water can be poured into glasses or cups or canisters, but it remains water just the same. Put simply, Reed's fictions concern themselves with arguing that the so-called black experience cannot be thought of as a fluid content to be poured into received and static containers. For Reed, it is the signifier that both shapes and defines any discrete signified. And it is the signifiers of the Afro-American tradition with whom Reed is concerned.

This is not the place to read all of Reed's works against this thesis. Nevertheless, Reed's first novel lends credence to this sort of reading and also serves to create what we may call a set of generic expectations through which we read the rest of his works. His first novel, *The Free-Lance Pallbearers*, is, above all else, a parody of the confessional mode which is the fundamental, undergirding convention of Afro-American narrative, received, elaborated upon, and transmitted in a chartable heritage from Briton Hammon's captivity narrative of 1760 through the antebellum slave narratives to black autobiography into black fiction, especially the fictions of Hurston, Wright, Baldwin, and Ellison.[31] This narrative of Bukka Doopeyduk is a pastiche of the classic black narrative of the questing protagonist's "journey into the heart of whiteness"; but it parodies this narrative form by turning it inside out, exposing the character of the originals, and thereby defining their formulaic closures and disclosures. Doopeyduk's tale ends with his own crucifixion. As the narrator of his own story, therefore, Doopeyduk articulates literally from among the dead an irony implicit in all confessional and autobiographical modes, in which any author is forced by definition to imagine himself or herself to be dead. More specifically, Reed signifies upon *Black Boy* and *Go Tell It on the Mountain* in a foregrounded critique which can be read as an epigraph to the novel: "*read growing up in Soulsville first of three installments/or what it means to be a backstage darkey.*" The "scat-singing voice" that introduces the novel Reed foregrounds against the "other" voice of Doopeyduk, whose "second" voice narrates the novel's plot. Here, Reed parodies both Hurston's use of free indirect discourse in *Their Eyes Were Watching God* and Ellison's use of the foregrounded voice in the prologue and epilogue of *Invisible Man*, which frame his nameless protagonist's picaresque account of his own narrative. In *Yellow Back Radio Broke Down*, Reed more fully and successfully critiques both realism and modernism, as exemplified in a kind of writing that one character calls "those suffering books I wrote about my old neighborhood and how hard it was."[32]

Reed's third novel, *Mumbo Jumbo*, is about writing itself; not only in the figurative sense of the post-modern, self-reflexive text but also in a literal sense: "So Jes Grew is seeking its words. Its text. For what good is a liturgy without a text?" (*Mumbo Jumbo*, p. 6.) *Mumbo Jumbo* is both a book about texts and a book of texts, a composite narrative composed of subtexts, pretexts, posttexts, and narratives within narratives. It is both a definition of Afro-American culture and its deflation. "The Big Lie concerning Afro-American culture," *Mumbo Jumbo*'s dust jacket informs us, "is that it lacks a tradition." The big truth of the novel, on the other hand, is that this very tradition is as rife with hardened convention and presupposition as is the rest of the Western tradition. Even this cryptic riddle of Jes Grew and its text parodies Ellison: *Invisible Man*'s plot is set in motion with a riddle, while the theme of the relationship between words and texts echoes a key passage from Ellison's short story "And Hickman Arrives": "Good. Don't talk like I talk, talk like I *say* talk. Words are your business boy. Not just *the* word. Words are everything. The key to the Rock, the answer to the question."[33]

Let us examine the book's dust jacket. The signifying begins with the book's title. "Mumbo jumbo" is the received and ethnocentric Western designation for both the rituals of black religions and all black languages themselves. A vulgarized Western translation of a Swahili phrase (*mambo, jambo*), "mumbo jumbo," as *Webster's Third International Dictionary* defines it, connotes "language that is unnecessarily involved and difficult to understand: GIBBERISH." The *Oxford English Dictionary* cites its etymology as being "of unknown origin," implicitly serving here as the signified on which Reed's title signifies, recalling the myth of Topsy who "jes grew," with no antecedents, a phrase with which James Weldon Johnson characterizes the creative process of black sacred music. *Mumbo Jumbo*, then, signifies upon Western etymology, abusive Western practices of deflation through misnaming, as well as Johnson's specious designation of the anonymity of creation, which indeed is a major component of the Afro-American cultural tradition.

But there is more parody in this title. Whereas Ellison tropes the myth of presence in Wright's titles of *Native Son* and *Black Boy* through his title of *Invisible Man*, inverting the received would-be correlation between blackness and presence with a narrative strategy that correlates invisibility (ultimate sign of absence) with the presence of self-narration and therefore self-creation, Reed parodies all three titles by employing as his title the English-language parody of black language itself. Whereas the etymology of "mumbo jumbo" has been problematical for Western lexicographers, any Swahili speaker knows that the phrase derives from the common greeting *jambo* and its plural, *mambo*, which loosely translated means "What's happening?" Reed is also echoing Vachel Lindsay's ironic poem *The Congo*, cited as an epigraph to this essay, which proved to be so fatally influencing to the Harlem Renaissance poets, as Charles Davis has shown.[34] From its title on, the novel serves as a critique of black and Western literary forms and conventions, and complex relationships between the two.

Let us proceed with our examination of the book's cover. A repeated and reversed image of a crouching, sensuous Josephine Baker sits back to back, superimposed upon a rose. Counterposed to this image is a medallion containing a horse with two riders. These signs adumbrate the two central oppositions of the novel's complicated plot: the rose and the double image of Josephine Baker together form a cryptic *vé vé*. A *vé vé* is a key sign in Vaudou, a sign drawn on the ground with sand, cornmeal, flour, and coffee to represent the *loa*. The *loa* are the deities who comprise the pantheon of Vaudou's gods. The rose is a sign of *Ezrulie*, goddess of love, home, and purity, as are the images of Josephine Baker, who became the French goddess of love in the late 1920s, in their version of the Jazz Age. The doubled image, as if mirrored, is meant to suggest the divine crossroads, where human beings meet their fate, but also at the center of which presides the *loa* Legba (Esu), guardian of the divine crossroads, messenger of the gods, the figure representing the interpreter and interpretation itself, the muse or *loa* of the critic. It is Legba who is master of that mystical barrier that separates the divine from the profane worlds. It is this complex yet cryptic *vé vé* that is meant both to placate Legba himself and to summon his attention and integrity in a double act of criticism and interpretation: that of Reed in the process of his representation of the tradition, to be found between the covers of the book, and that of the critic's interpretation of Reed's figured interpretation.*

. . .

But just as we can define orders of multiple substitution and signification for Reed's types and caricatures, as is true of allegory generally (e.g., Von Vampton, Van Vechten, "Hinken" Knackfuss), so too can we find all sorts of consistent levels of meaning with which we could attempt to find a closure

*The following five-page discussion of *Mumbo Jumbo* has been omitted. — Editors

to the text. I shall not do that here, however; the first decade of readers of *Mumbo Jumbo* have attempted to find one-to-one correlations with great energy, decoding its allegorical structure by finding analogues between the Harlem Renaissance and the Black Arts movement, for example. As interesting as such parallel universes are, I shall not attempt such a reading here, or even engage in one more rehearsal of its complex plots, since I can in these pages assume a large measure of reader familiarity with the text. I am concerned with its status as a rhetorical structure, as a mode of narration, and with relating this mode of narration to a critique of traditional notions of closure in interpretation. For Reed's most subtle achievement in *Mumbo Jumbo* is to parody, to signify upon, the notions of closure implicit in the key texts of the Afro-American canon itself. *Mumbo Jumbo*, in contrast, is a novel that figures and glorifies indeterminacy. The novel, in this sense, stands as a profound critique and elaboration upon this convention of closure in the black novel and its metaphysical implications. In its stead, Reed posits the notion of aesthetic play: the play of the tradition, the play on the tradition, the sheer play of indeterminacy itself.**

. . .

Both Ellison and Reed, then, critique the received idea of blackness as a negative essence, as a natural, transcendent signified; but implicit in such a critique is an equally thorough critique of blackness as a presence, which is merely another transcendent signified. Such a critique, therefore, is a critique of the structure of the sign itself and constitutes a profound critique. The Black Arts movement's grand gesture was to make of the trope of blackness a trope of presence. That movement willed it to be, however, a transcendent presence. Ellison's "text for today, the 'Blackness of Blackness,'" analyzes this gesture, just as surely as does Reed's text of blackness, the "Sacred Book of Thoth." In literature, blackness is produced in the text itself only through a complex process of signification. There can be no transcendent blackness, for it cannot and does not exist beyond manifestations in specific figures. Jes Grew, put simply, cannot conjure its texts; texts, in the broadest sense of this term (Charlie Parker's music, Ellison's fictions, Romare Bearden's collages, etc.), conjure Jes Grew.

Reed has in *Mumbo Jumbo* signified upon Ellison's critique of the central presupposition of the Afro-American literary tradition, by drawing upon

**Several pages of discussion of the narrative structure of *Mumbo Jumbo*, constituting the bulk of Section III, have been omitted. — Editors

Ellison's trope as a central theme of the plot of *Mumbo Jumbo* and making explicit Ellison's implicit critique of the nature of the sign itself, of a transcendent signified, an essence, which supposedly exists prior to its figuration. Their formal relationship can only be suggested by the relation of modernism to post-modernism, two overworked terms. Blackness exists, but only as a function of its signifiers. Reed's open-ended structure and his stress on the indeterminacy of the text demand that we, as critics, in the act of reading, produce a text's signifying structure. For Reed, as for his great precursor, Ellison, figuration is indeed "the Nigger's occupation."

IV

Reed's signifying relation to Ellison is exemplified in his poem "Dualism: in ralph ellison's invisible man":

> i am outside of
> history. i wish
> i had some peanuts; it
> looks hungry there in
> its cage.
> i am inside of
> history. its
> hungrier than i
> thot.[35]

The figure of history here is the Signifying Monkey; the poem signifies upon that repeated trope of dualism figured initially in black discourse in W. E. B. Du Bois's essay "Of Our Spiritual Strivings," which forms the first chapter of *The Souls of Black Folk*. The dualism parodied by Reed's poem is that represented in the epilogue of *Invisible Man*: "now I know men are different and that all life is divided and that only in division is there true health" (p. 499). For Reed, this belief in the reality of dualism spells death. Ellison here has refigured Du Bois's trope, which bears full citation:

> After the Egyptian and Indian, the Greek and Roman, the Teuton and Mongolian, the Negro is a sort of seventh son, born with a veil, and gifted with second-sight in this American world, — a world which yields him no true self-consciousness, but only lets him see himself through the revelation of the other world. It is a peculiar sensation, this double-consciousness, this sense of always looking at one's self through the eyes of others, measur-

ing one's soul by the tape of a world that looks on in amused contempt and pity. One ever feels his twoness,—an American, a Negro; two souls, two thoughts, two unreconciled strivings; two warring ideals in one dark body, whose dogged strength alone keeps it from being torn asunder.

The history of the American Negro is the history of this strife,—this longing to attain self-conscious manhood, to merge his double self into a better and truer self. In this merging he wishes neither of the older selves to be lost.[36]

Reed's poem parodies profoundly both the figure of the black as outsider and the figure of the divided self. For, he tells us, even these are only tropes, figures of speech, rhetorical constructs like "double-consciousness," and not some preordained reality or thing. To read these figures literally, Reed tells us, is to be duped by figuration, just like the Signified Lion. Reed has secured his place in the canon precisely by his critique of the received, repeated tropes peculiar to that very canon. His works are the grand works of critical signification.

Notes

1. Quoted in Roger D. Abrahams, *Deep Down in the Jungle: Negro Narrative Folklore from the Streets of Philadelphia* (Chicago: Aldine, 1970), p. 53.

2. On "Tar Baby," see Ralph Ellison, *Shadow and Act* (New York: Vintage Books, 1964), p. 147; and Toni Morrison, *Tar Baby* (New York: Alfred A. Knopf, 1981). On the black as quasi-simian, see Jean Bodin, *Method for the Easy Comprehension of History*, trans. Beatrice Reynolds (New York: Octagon Books, 1966), p. 105; Aristotle, *Historia Animalum*, trans. D'Arcy W. Thompson, in *The Works of Aristotle*, ed. J. A. Smith and W. D. Ross (Oxford: Oxford University Press, 1910), 4:606b; Thomas Herbert, *Some Years Travels* (London: R. Everingham, 1677), pp. 16–17; John Locke, *An Essay Concerning Human Understanding* (London: A. Churchill and A. Manship, 1721), book 3, chap. 6, sect. 23.

3. Geneva Smitherman defines these and other black tropes, then traces their use in several black texts. Smitherman's work, like that of Claudia Mitchell-Kernan and Roger Abrahams, is especially significant for literary theory. See Geneva Smitherman, *Talkin' and Testifyin': The Language of Black America* (Boston: Houghton Mifflin, 1977), pp. 101–67. See notes 12 and 13 below.

4. On versions of Esu, see Robert Farris Thompson, *Black Gods and Kings* (Bloomington: Indiana University Press, 1976), pp. 4/1–4/12, and *Flash of the Spirit* (New York: Random House, 1983); Pierre Verger, *Notes sur le culte des Orisa et Vodun* (Dakar: I.F.A.N., 1957); Joan Westcott, "The Sculpture and Myths of Eshu-Elegba," *Africa* 32.4: 336–53; Leo Frobenius, *The Voice of Africa* (London: Hutchinson, 1913); Melville J. and Frances Herskovits, *Dahomean Narrative* (Evanston: Northwestern Univer-

sity Press, 1958); Wande Abimbola, *Sixteen Great Poems of Ifa* (New York: UNESCO, 1975); William R. Bascom, *Ifa Divination* (Bloomington: Indiana University Press, 1969); Ayodele Ogundipe, "Esu Elegbara: The Yoruba God of Chance and Uncertainty" (Ph.D. diss., Indiana University, 1978); E. Bolaji Idowu, *Olódùmarè: God in Yoruba Belief* (London: Longman, 1962), pp. 80–85; and Robert Pelton, *The Trickster in West Africa* (Los Angeles: University of California Press, 1980).

5. On *Esu* and indeterminacy, see Robert Plant Armstrong, *The Powers of Presence: Consciousness, Myth, and Affecting Presence* (Philadelphia: University of Pennsylvania Press, 1981), p. 4. See p. 43 for a drawing of *Opon Ifa*; and Thompson, *Black Gods and Kings*, chap. 5.

6. On *Esu* and the monkey, see Lydia Cabrera, *El Monte: Notes sobre las religiones, la magia, las supersticiones y el folklore de los negros criollos y el pueblo de Cuba* (Miami: Ediciones Universal, 1975), p. 84; and Alberto del Pozo, *Oricha* (Miami: Oricha, 1982), p. 1. On the Signifying Monkey, see Roger Abrahams, *Deep Down in the Jungle: Negro Narrative Folklore from the Streets of Philadelphia* (Chicago: Aldine, 1970), pp. 51–53, 66, 113–19, 142–47, 153–56, and especially 264; Bruce Jackson, *"Get Your Ass in the Water and Swim Like Me": Narrative Poetry from Black Oral Tradition* (Cambridge: Harvard University Press, 1974), pp. 161–80; Daryl Cumber Dance, *Shuckin' and Jivin': Folklore from Contemporary Black Americans* (Bloomington: Indiana University Press, 1978), pp. 197–99; Dennis Wepman, R. B. Newman, and M. B. Binderman, *The Life: The Lore and Folk Poetry of the Black Hustler* (Philadelphia: University of Pennsylvania Press, 1976), pp. 21–30; Lawrence W. Levine, *Black Culture and Black Consciousness: Afro-American Folk Thought from Slavery to Freedom* (New York: Oxford University Press, 1977), pp. 364, 378–80, 438; and Richard M. Dorson, *American Negro Folktales* (New York: Fawcett, 1967), pp. 98–99.

7. Julia Kristeva, *Desire in Language: A Semiotic Approach to Literature and Art* (New York: Columbia University Press, 1980), p. 31.

8. See Abrahams, *Deep Down in the Jungle*, pp. 51–53, 66, 113–19, 142–47, 153–56, and especially 264; Roger D. Abrahams, "Playing the Dozens," *Journal of American Folklore* 75 (1962): 209–20; Roger D. Abrahams, "The Changing Concept of the Negro Hero," in *The Golden Log*, ed. Moady C. Boatright, Wilson M. Hudson, and Allen Maxwell (Dallas: Texas Folklore Society, 1962), pp. 125ff; and Roger D. Abrahams, *Talking Black* (Rowley, Mass.: Newbury House, 1976).

9. Abrahams, *Deep Down in the Jungle*, pp. 51–52, 66–67, 264. Abraham's awareness of the need to define uniquely black significations is exemplary; as early as 1964, when he published the first edition of *Deep Down in the Jungle*, he saw fit to add a glossary as an appendix of "Unusual Terms and Expressions," a title that unfortunately suggests the social scientist's apologia. (Emphasis added.)

10. Quoted in Abrahams, *Deep Down in the Jungle*, p. 113. In the second line of the stanza, "motherfucker" is often substituted for "monkey."

11. "The Signifying Monkey," in *Book of Negro Folklore*, ed. Langston Hughes and Arna Bontemps (New York: Dodd, Mead, 1958), pp. 365–66.

12. On signifying as a rhetorical trope, see Smitherman, *Talkin' and Testifyin'*, pp. 101–67; Thomas Kochman, *Rappin' and Stylin' Out: Communication in Urban Black America* (Urbana: University of Illinois, 1972); and Thomas Kochman, " 'Rappin' in the

Black Ghetto," *Trans-Action* 6.4 (Feb. 1969): 32; Alan Dundes, *Mother Wit from the Laughing Barrel* (Englewood Cliffs, N.J.: Prentice-Hall, 1973), p. 310; Ethel M. Albert, "'Rhetoric,' 'Logic,' and 'Poetics' in *Burund: Culture Patterning of Speech Behavior*," in John J. Gumperz and Dell Hymes, eds., *The Ethnography of Communication*," *American Anthropologist* 66.6 (1964): 35–54. One example of signifying can be gleaned from the following anecdote. While writing this essay, I asked a colleague, Dwight Andrews, if he had heard of the Signifying Monkey as a child. "Why, no," he replied intently. "I never heard of the Signifying Monkey until I came to Yale and read about him in a book." I had been signified upon. If I had responded to Andrews, "I know what you mean; your Mama read to me from that same book the last time I was in Detroit," I would have signified upon him in return. See especially note 15 below.

13. Claudia Mitchell-Kernan, "Signifying," in Dundes, p. 313; and Claudia Mitchell-Kernan, "Signifying, Loud-Talking, and Marking," in Kochman, pp. 315–36. For Zora Neale Hurston's definition of the term, see *Mules and Men: Negro Folktales and Voodoo Practices in the South* (New York: Harper & Row, 1970), p. 161.

14. Mitchell-Kernan, "Signifying," p. 314.

15. Ibid., pp. 323–25.

16. Mitchell-Kernan, "Signifying, Loud-Talking, and Marking," pp. 315–36.

17. Mitchell-Kernan, "Signifying," p. 325.

18. Ralph Ellison, "And Hickman Arrives," in *Black Writers of America*, ed. Richard Barksdale and Keneth Kinnamon (New York: Macmillan, 1972), p. 704.

19. Ralph Ellison, "On Bird, Bird-Watching, and Jazz," *Saturday Review*, July 20, 1962, reprinted in Ellison, *Shadow and Act*, p. 231.

20. Ralph Ellison, "Blues People," in Ellison, *Shadow and Act*, pp. 249, 250. The essay was first printed in the *New York Review of Books*, Feb. 6, 1964.

21. Ralph Ellison, "The World and the Jug," in Ellison, *Shadow and Act*, p. 117. The essay appeared first in the *New Leader*, Dec. 9, 1963.

22. Ellison, *Shadow and Act*, p. 137.

23. Mikhail Bakhtin, "Discourse Typology in Prose," in *Readings in Russian Poetics: Formalist and Structuralist Views*, ed. Ladislas Matejka and Krystyna Pomorska (Cambridge: MIT Press, 1971), pp. 176–99.

24. The use of interlocking triangles as a metaphor for the intertextual relationships of the tradition is not meant to suggest any form of concrete, inflexible reality. On the contrary, it is a systematic metaphor, as René Girard puts it, "systematically pursued." As Girard says: "The triangle is no *Gestalt*. The real structures are intersubjective. They cannot be localized anywhere; *the triangle has no reality whatever; it is a systematic metaphor, systematically pursued.* Because changes of size and shape do not destroy the identity of this figure, as we will see later, the diversity as well as the unity of the works can be simultaneously illustrated. The purpose and limitations of this structural geometry may become clearer through a reference to "structural models." The triangle is a model of a sort, or rather a whole family of models. But these models are not "mechanical" like those of Claude Lévi-Strauss. They always allude to the mystery, transparent yet opaque, of human relations. All types of structural thinking assume that human reality is intelligible; it is a *logos* and, as such, *it is an incipient logic, or it degrades itself into a logic.* It can thus be systematized, at least up to a point, however unsystematic, irrational, and

chaotic it may appear even to those, or rather especially to those who operate the system" (emphasis added). René Girard, *Deceit, Desire, and the Novel: Self and Other in Literary Structure* (Baltimore: Johns Hopkins University Press, 1965), pp. 2–3.

25. For Ishmael Reed on "a talking book," see "Ishmael Reed: A Self Interview," *Black World*, June 1974, p. 25. For the slave narratives in which this figure appears, see James Albert Ukawsaw Gronniosaw, *A Narrative of the Most Remarkable Particulars of the Life of James Albert Ukawsaw Gronniosaw, An African Prince* (Bath, 1770); John Marrant, *Narrative of the Lord's Wonderful Dealings with John Marrant, a Black* (London: Gilbert and Plummer, 1785); Ottabah Cugoano, *Thoughts and Sentiments on the Evil and Wicked Traffic of the Slavery and Commerce of the Human Species* (London, 1787); and Olauduh Equino, *The Interesting Narrative of the Life of Olaudah Equino, or Gustavus Vassa, the African. Written by Himself.* (London: printed for the author, 1789).

26. Northrop Frye, *Anatomy of Criticism* (Princeton: Princeton University Press, 1971), p. 233.

27. Bakhtin, "Discourse Typology," p. 190.

28. Frye, p. 103.

29. Ellison, *Shadow and Act*, p. 140.

30. *The Free-Lance Pallbearers* (Garden City, N.Y.: Doubleday, 1967); *Yellow Back Radio Broke Down* (Garden City, N.Y.: Doubleday, 1969); *Mumbo Jumbo* (Garden City, N.Y.: Doubleday, 1972); *The Last Days of Louisiana Red* (New York: Random House, 1974); *Flight to Canada* (New York: Random House, 1976); and *The Terrible Twos* (New York: St. Martin's/Marek, 1982).

31. Neil Schmitz, "Neo-Hoodoo: The Experimental Fiction of Ishmael Reed," *20th Century Literature* 20.2 (Apr. 1974): 126–28. Schmitz's splendid reading is, I believe, the first to discuss this salient aspect of Reed's rhetorical strategy.

32. For an excellent close reading of *Yellow Back Radio Broke Down*, see Michel Fabre, "Postmodern Rhetoric in Ishmael Reed's *Yellow Back Radio Broke Down*," in *The Afro-American Novel Since 1960*, ed. Peter Bruck and Wolfgang Karrer (Amsterdam: B. R. Gruner, 1982), pp. 167–88.

33. Ellison, "And Hickman Arrives," p. 701.

34. Charles T. Davis, *Black Is the Color of the Cosmos: Essays on Black Literature and Culture, 1942–1981*, edited by Henry Louis Gates, Jr. (New York: Garland, 1982), pp. 167–233.

35. Reed, *Conjure*, p. 50.

36. W. E. B. Du Bois, *The Souls of Black Folk* (New York: Fawcett, 1961), pp. 16–17.

15

Reading for the Plot · PETER BROOKS

I

Our lives are ceaselessly intertwined with narrative, with the stories that we tell and hear told, those we dream or imagine or would like to tell, all of which are reworked in that story of our own lives that we narrate to ourselves in an episodic, sometimes semiconscious, but virtually uninterrupted monologue. We live immersed in narrative, recounting and reassessing the meaning of our past actions, anticipating the outcome of our future projects, situating ourselves at the intersection of several stories not yet completed. The narrative impulse is as old as our oldest literature: myth and folktale appear to be stories we recount in order to explain and understand where no other form of explanation will work. The desire and the competence to tell stories also reach back to an early stage in the individual's development, to about the age of three, when a child begins to show the ability to put together a narrative in coherent fashion and especially the capacity to recognize narratives, to judge their well-formedness. Children quickly become virtual Aristotelians, insisting upon any storyteller's observation of the "rules," upon proper beginnings, middles, and particularly ends. Narrative may be a special ability or competence that we learn, a certain subset of the general language code which, when mastered, allows us to summarize and retransmit narratives in other words and other languages, to transfer them into other media, while remaining recognizably faithful to the original narrative structure and message.

Narrative in fact seems to hold a special place among literary forms — as something more than a conventional "genre" — because of its potential for summary and retransmission: the fact that we can still recognize "the story" even when its medium has been considerably changed. This characteristic of narrative has led some theorists to suppose that it is itself a language, with its own code and its own rules for forming messages from the code, a hypothesis that probably does not hold up to inspection because narrative appears always to depend on some other language code in the creation of its meanings. But it does need to be considered as an operation important to all of our lives. When we "tell a story," there tends to be a shift in the register of our voices, enclosing and setting off the narrative almost in the manner of the traditional "once upon a time" and "they lived happily ever after": narrative demarcates, encloses, establishes limits, orders. And if it may be an impossibly speculative task to say what narrative itself is, it may be useful and valuable to think about the kinds of ordering it uses and creates, about the figures of design it makes. Here, I think, we can find our most useful object of attention in what has for centuries gone by the name of plot.

"Reading for the plot," we learned somewhere in the course of our schooling, is a low form of activity. Modern criticism, especially in its Anglo-American branches, has tended to take its valuations from study of the lyric, and when it has discussed narrative has emphasized questions of "point of view," "tone," "symbol," "spatial form," or "psychology." The texture of narrative has been considered most interesting insofar as it approached the density of poetry. Plot has been disdained as the element of narrative that least sets off and defines high art — indeed, plot is that which especially characterizes popular mass-consumption literature: plot is why we read *Jaws*, but not Henry James. And yet, one must in good logic argue that plot is somehow prior to those elements most discussed by most critics, since it is the very organizing line, the thread of design, that makes narrative possible because finite and comprehensible. Aristotle, of course, recognized the logical priority of plot, and a recent critical tradition, starting with the Russian formalists and coming up to the French and American "narratologists," has revived a quasi-Aristotelian sense of plot. When E. M. Forster, in the once influential *Aspects of the Novel*, asserts that Aristotle's emphasis on plot was mistaken, that our interest is not in the "imitation of an action" but rather in the "secret life which each of us lives privately," he surely begs the question, for if "secret lives" are to be narratable, they must in some sense be plotted, display a design and logic.[1]

There are evidently a number of different ways one might go about discussing the concept of plot and its function in the range of narrative forms. Plot is, first of all, a constant of all written and oral narrative, in that a narrative without at least a minimal plot would be incomprehensible. Plot is the principle of interconnectedness and intention which we cannot do without in moving through the discrete elements — incidents, episodes, actions — of a narrative: even such loosely articulated forms as the picaresque novel display devices of interconnectedness, structural repetitions that allow us to construct a whole; and we can make sense of such dense and seemingly chaotic texts as dreams because we use interpretive categories that enable us to reconstruct intentions and connections, to replot the dream as narrative. It would, then, be perfectly plausible to undertake a typology of plot and its elements from the *Iliad* and the *Odyssey* onward to the new novel and the "metafictions" of our time.[2] Yet it seems clear also that there have been some historical moments at which plot has assumed a greater importance than at others, moments in which cultures have seemed to develop an unquenchable thirst for plots and to seek the expression of central individual and collective meanings through narrative design. From sometime in the mid-eighteenth century through to the mid-twentieth century, Western societies appear to have felt an extraordinary need or desire for plots, whether in fiction, history, philosophy, or any of the social sciences, which in fact largely came into being with the Enlightenment and Romanticism. As Voltaire announced and then the Romantics confirmed, history replaces theology as the key discourse and central imagination in that historical explanation becomes nearly a necessary factor of any thought about human society: the question of what we are typically must pass through the question of where we are, which in turn is interpreted to mean, how did we get to be there? Not only history but historiography, the philosophy of history, philology, mythography, diachronic linguistics, anthropology, archaeology, and evolutionary biology all establish their claim as fields of inquiry, and all respond to the need for an explanatory narrative that seeks its authority in a return to origins and the tracing of a coherent story forward from origin to present.

The enormous narrative production of the nineteenth century may suggest an anxiety at the loss of providential plots: the plotting of the individual or social or institutional life story takes on new urgency when one no longer can look to a sacred masterplot that organizes and explains the world. The emergence of narrative plot as a dominant mode of ordering and explanation may belong to the large process of secularization, dating from the Renaissance and gathering force during the Enlightenment, which marks a falling-away from those revealed plots—the Chosen People, Redemption, the Second Coming—that appeared to subsume transitory human time to the timeless. In the last two books of *Paradise Lost*, Milton's angel Michael is able to present a full panorama of human history to Adam, concluding in redemption and a timeless future of bliss; and Adam responds:

How soon hath thy prediction, Seer Blest,
Measur'd this transient World, the Race of time,
Till time stand fixt: beyond is all abyss,
Eternity, whose end no eye can reach. (book 12, lines 553–56)

By the end of the Enlightenment, there is no longer any consensus on this prediction, and no cultural cohesion around a point of fixity which allows thought and vision so to transfix time. And this may explain the nineteenth century's obsession with questions of origin, evolution, progress, genealogy, its foregrounding of the historical narrative as par excellence the necessary mode of explanation and understanding.[3]

We still live today in the age of narrative plots, consuming avidly Harlequin romances and television serials and daily comic strips, creating and demanding narrative in the presentation of persons and news events and sports contests. For all the widely publicized nonnarrative or antinarrative forms of thought that are supposed to characterize our times, from complementarity and uncertainty in physics to the synchronic analyses of structuralism, we remain more determined by narrative than we might wish to believe. And yet, we know that with the advent of modernism came an era of suspicion toward plot, engendered perhaps by an overelaboration of and overdependence on plots in the nineteenth century. If we cannot do without plots, we nonetheless feel uneasy about them, and feel obliged to show up their arbitrariness, to parody their mechanisms while admitting our dependence on them. Until such a time as we cease to exchange understandings in the form of stories, we will need to remain dependent on the logic we use to shape and to understand stories, which is to say, dependent on plot. A reflection on plot as the syntax of a certain way of speaking our understanding of the world may tell us something about how and why we have come to stake so many of the central concerns of our society, and of our lives, on narrative.

II

These sweeping generalizations will bear more careful consideration later on. It is important at this point to consider more closely just how we intend to speak of plot, how we intend to work with it, to make it an operative analytic and critical tool in the study of narrative. I want to urge a conception of plot as something in the nature of the logic of narrative discourse, the organizing dynamic of a specific mode of human understanding. This pursuit will in a moment take us into the discussion of narrative by a number of critics (of the type recently baptized narratologists), but perhaps the best way to begin is through a brief exercise in an old and thoroughly discredited form, the plot summary, in this case of a very old story. Here, then, is the summary of a story from the Grimm brothers, known in their version as "All-Kinds-of-Fur":[4]

A dying queen makes her husband promise that he will remarry only with a woman as beautiful as she, with the same golden hair. He promises, and she dies. Time passes, and he is urged by his councilors to remarry. He looks for the dead queen's equal, but finds no one; until, years later, his eyes light on his daughter, who looks just like her mother, with the same golden hair. He will marry her, though his councilors say he must not. Pressed to answer, the daughter makes her consent contingent on the performance of three apparently impossible tasks: he must give her three dresses, one as golden as the sun, one as silvery as the moon, the third as glittering as all the stars, plus a cloak made of a thousand different furs. The king, in fact, succeeds in providing these and insists on the marriage. The daughter then flees, blackens her face and hands, covers herself with the cloak of furs, and hides in the woods, where she is captured as a strange animal by the king of another country. She goes to work as a scullery maid in his kitchens, but on three successive occasions she appears at the king's parties clothed in one of her three splendid dresses and dances with him; and three times she cooks the king's pudding and leaves in the bottom of the dish one of the tokens she has brought from home (a golden ring, a golden spinning wheel, a golden reel). On the third repetition, the king slips the ring on her finger while they are dancing, and when she returns to the kitchen, in her haste she does not blacken one hand entirely. The king searches her out, notices the white finger and its ring, seizes her hand, strips off the fur cloak to reveal the dress underneath, and the golden hair, and claims her in marriage.

What have we witnessed and understood here? How have we moved from one desire that we, like the king's councilors, know to be prohibited, to a legitimate desire whose consummation marks the end of the tale? And what is the meaning of the process lying between beginning and end—a treble testing, with the supplemental requirement of the cloak; flight and disguise (using the cloak to become subhuman, almost a beast); then a sort of striptease revelation, also treble, using the three dresses provided by the father and the three golden objects brought from home (tokens, perhaps, of the mother), followed by recognition? How have we crossed from one kingdom to another through those woods which, we must infer, border on both of them? We cannot really answer such questions, yet we would probably all agree that the middle of the tale offers a kind of minimum satisfactory process that works through the problem of desire gone wrong and brings it to its cure. It is a process in which the overly eroticized object—the daughter become object of desire to the father—loses all erotic and feminine attributes, becomes unavailable to desire, then slowly, through repetition by three (which is perhaps the minimum repetition to suggest series and process), reveals her nature as erotic object again but now in a situation where the erotic is permitted and fitting. The tale is characterized by that laconic chasteness which Walter Benjamin found characteristic of the great oral stories, a refusal of psychological explanation and motivation.[5] It matter-of-factly takes on the central issues of culture—incest, the need for exogamy—without commentary. Like a number of the Grimms' tales, it seems to ask the question, Why do girls grow up, leave their homes and their fathers, and marry other men? It answers the question without explanation, through description of what needs to happen, the process set in motion, when normal forms are threatened, go awry: as in "Hawthorn Blossom" (the Grimms' version of "Sleeping Beauty"), we are given a kind of counter-example, the working-out of an antidote. The tale appears as the species of explanation that we give when explanation, in the logical and discursive sense, seems impossible or impertinent. It thus transmits a kind of wisdom that itself concerns transmission: how we pass on what we know about how life goes forward.

Folktale and myth may be seen to show narrative as a form of thinking, a way of reasoning about a situation. As Claude Lévi-Strauss has argued, the Oedipus myth may be "about" the unsolvable problem of man's origins—born from the earth or from parents?—a "chicken or egg" problem that finds its mythic "solution" in a story about generational confusion: Oedipus violates the demarcations of generations, becomes the "impossible" combination of son/husband, father/brother, and so on, subverting (and thus perhaps reinforcing) both cultural distinctions and categories of thought. It is the ordering of the inexplicable and impossible situation as narrative that somehow mediates and forcefully connects its discrete elements, so that we accept the necessity of what cannot logically be discoursed of. Yet I don't think we do justice to our experience of "All-Kinds-of-Fur" or the Oedipus myth in reducing their narratives—as Lévi-Strauss suggests all mythic narratives can be reduced—to their "atemporal matrix structure," a set of basic cultural antinomies that the narrative mediates.[6] Nor can we, to be sure, analyze these narratives simply as a pure succession of events or happenings.

We need to recognize, for instance, that there is a dynamic logic at work in the transformations wrought between the start and the finish of "All-Kinds-of-Fur," a logic which makes sense of succession and time, and which insists that mediation of the problem posed at the outset takes time: that the meaning dealt with by narrative, and thus perhaps narrative's raison d'être, is of and in time. Plot as it interests me is not a matter of typology or of fixed structures, but rather a structuring operation peculiar to those messages that are developed through temporal succession, the instrumental logic of a specific mode of human understanding. Plot, let us say in preliminary definition, is the logic and dynamic of narrative, and narrative itself a form of understanding and explanation.

Such a conception of plot seems to be at least compatible with Aristotle's understanding of *mythos*, the term from the *Poetics* that is normally translated as "plot." It is Aristotle's claim that plot (*mythos*) and action (*praxis*) are logically prior to the other parts of dramatic fictions, including character (*ethos*). *Mythos* is defined as "the combination of the incidents, or things done in the story," and Aristotle argues that of all the parts of the story, this is the most important. It is worth quoting his claim once more:

> Tragedy is essentially an imitation not of persons but of action and life, of happiness and misery. All human happiness or misery takes the form of action; the end for which we live is a certain kind of activity, not a quality. Character gives us qualities, but it is in our actions—what we do—that we are happy or the reverse. In a play accordingly they do not act in order to portray the Characters: they include the Characters for the sake of the action. So that it is the action in it, i.e. its Fable or Plot, that is the end and purpose of the tragedy; and the end is everywhere the chief thing.[7]

Later in the same paragraph he reiterates, using an analogy that may prove helpful to thinking about plot: "We maintain, therefore, that the first essential, the life and soul, so to speak, of Tragedy is Plot; and that the Characters come second—compare the parallel in painting, where the most beautiful colours laid on without order will not give one the same pleasure as a simple black-and-white sketch of a portrait." Plot, then, is conceived to be the outline or armature of the story, that which supports and organizes the rest. From such a view, Aristotle proceeds to derive three consequences. First, the action imitated by the tragedy must be complete in itself. This in turn means that it must have a beginning, a middle, and an end—a point wholly obvious but one that will prove to have interesting effects in its applications. Finally, just as in the visual arts a whole must be of a size that can be taken in by the eye, so a plot must be "of a length to be taken in by the memory." This is important, since memory—as much in reading a novel as in seeing a play—is the key faculty in the capacity to perceive relations of beginnings, middles, and ends through time, the shaping power of narrative.

But our English term "plot" has its own semantic range, one that is interestingly broad and possibly instructive. The *Oxford English Dictionary* gives seven definitions, essentially, which the *American Heritage Dictionary* helpfully reduces to four categories:

1. (a) A small piece of ground, generally used for a specific purpose. (b) A measured area of land; lot.

2. A ground plan, as for a building; chart; diagram.

3. The series of events consisting of an outline of the action of a narrative or drama.

4. A secret plan to accomplish a hostile or illegal purpose; scheme.

There may be a subterranean logic connecting these heterogeneous meanings. Common to the original sense of the word is the idea of boundedness, demarcation, the drawing of lines to mark off and order. This easily extends to the chart or diagram of the demarcated area, which in turn modulates to the outline of the literary work. From the organized space, plot becomes the organizing line, demarcating and diagramming that which was previously undifferentiated. We might think here of the geometrical expression, plotting points, or curves, on a graph by means of coordinates, as a way of locating something, perhaps oneself. The fourth sense of the word, the scheme or conspiracy, seems to have come into English through the contaminating influence of the French *complot*, and became widely known at the time of the Gunpowder Plot. I would suggest that in modern literature this sense of plot nearly always attaches itself to the others: the organizing line of plot is more often than not some scheme or machination, a concerted plan for the accomplishment of some purpose which goes against the ostensible and dominant legalities of the fictional world, the realization of a blocked and resisted desire. Plots are not simply organizing structures, they are also intentional structures, goal-oriented and forward-moving.

Plot as we need and want the term is hence an embracing concept for the design and intention of narrative, a structure for those meanings that are developed through temporal succession, or perhaps better: a structuring operation elicited by, and made necessary by, those meanings that develop through succession and time. A further analysis of the question is suggested here by a distinction urged by the Russian formalists, that between *fabula* and *sjužet*. *Fabula* is defined as the order of events referred to by the narrative, whereas *sjužet* is the order of events presented in the narrative discourse. The distinction is one that takes on evident analytic force when one is talking about a Conrad or a Faulkner, whose dislocations of normal chronology are radical and significant, but it is no less important in thinking about apparently more straightforward narratives, since any narrative presents a selection and an ordering of material. We must, however, recognize that the apparent priority of fabula to sjužet is in the nature of a mimetic illusion, in that the fabula — "what really happened" — is in fact a mental construction that the reader derives from the sjužet, which is all that he ever directly knows. This differing status of the two terms by no means invalidates the distinction itself, which is central to our thinking about narrative and necessary to its analysis since it allows us to juxtapose two modes of order and in the juxtaposing to see how ordering takes place. In the wake of the Russian formalists, French structural analysts of narrative proposed their own pairs of terms, predominantly *histoire* (corresponding to fabula) and *récit*, or else *discours* (corresponding to sjužet). English usage has been more unsettled. "Story" and "plot" would seem to be generally acceptable renderings in most circumstances, though a structural and semiotic analysis will find advantages in the less semantically charged formulation "story" and "discourse."[8]

"Plot" in fact seems to me to cut across the fabula/sjužet distinction in that to speak of plot is to consider both story elements and their ordering. Plot could be thought of as the interpretive activity elicited by the distinction between sjužet and fabula, the way we *use* the one against the other. To keep our terms straight without sacrificing the advantages of the semantic range of "plot," let us say that we can generally understand plot to be an aspect of sjužet in that it belongs to the narrative discourse, as its active shaping force, but that it makes sense (as indeed sjužet itself principally makes sense) as it is used to reflect on fabula, as our understanding of story. Plot is thus the dynamic shaping force of the narrative discourse. I find confirmation for such a view in Paul Ricoeur's definition of plot as "the intelligible whole that governs a succession of events in any story." Ricoeur continues, using the terms "events" and "story" rather than fabula and sjužet: "This provisory definition immediately shows the plot's connecting function between an event or events and the story. A story is *made out of* events to the extent that plot *makes* events *into* a story. The plot, therefore, places us at the crossing point of temporality and narrativity."⁹ Ricoeur's emphasis on the constructive role of plot, its active, shaping function, offers a useful corrective to the structural narratologists' neglect of the dynamics of narrative and points us toward the reader's vital role in the understanding of plot.

The Russian Formalists presented what one might call a "constructivist" view of literature, calling attention to the material and the means of its making, showing how a given work is put together. "Device" is one of their favorite terms — a term for demonstrating the technical use of a given motif or incident or theme. Typical is Boris Tomachevsky's well-known illustration of the technical sense of "motivation": if a character in a play hammers a nail into the wall in act 1, then he or another character will have to hang himself from it in act 3. The work of Tomachevsky, Victor Shklovsky, and Boris Eichenbaum is invaluable to the student of narrative since it so often cuts through thematic material to show the constructed armature that supports it.¹⁰ Perhaps the instance of the Russian formalists' work most compelling for our purposes is their effort to isolate and identify the minimal units of narrative, and then to formulate the principles of their combination and interconnection. In particular, Vladimir Propp's *The Morphology of the Folktale* merits attention as an early and impressive example of what can be done to formalize and codify the study of narrative.

Faced with the mass of material collected by folklorists and the inadequacy of attempts to order it through thematic groupings or patterns of derivation, Propp began with a gesture similar to that of Ferdinand de Saussure at the inception of modern linguistics, bracketing questions of origin and derivation and reference in order to find the principles of a morphology of a given body of material. Taking some one hundred tales classified by folklorists as fairy tales, he sought to provide a description of the fairy tale according to its component parts, the relation of these parts to one another and to the tale as a whole, and hence the basis for a comparison among tales. Propp claims that the essential morphological components are function and sequence. One identifies the functions by breaking down the tale into elements defined not by theme or character but rather according to the actions performed: function is "an act of character, defined from the point of view of its significance for the course of the action."¹¹ Functions will thus appear in the analysis as labels for kinds of action, such as "interdiction," "testing," "acquisition of the magical agent," and so on; whereas sequence will concern the order of the functions, the logic of their consecution. As a result of his study, Propp with a certain bravado puts forward four theses concerning the fairy tale:

1. The functions are stable, constant elements whoever carries them out.

2. The number of functions is limited (there are just thirty-one in the Russian fairy tale).

3. The sequence of functions is always identical (not all are present in every tale, but the sequence of those present is invariable).

4. All fairy tales are of one type in regard to their structure.

Whatever the validity of Propp's theses, the concept of function, and the "functionalist" view of narrative structure it implies, stresses in a useful way the role of verbs of action as the armature of narrative, their logic and articulation and sequence. Propp suggests an approach to the analysis of narrative actions by giving precedence to *mythos* over *ethos*, indeed by abstracting plot structure from the persons who carry it out. Characters for Propp are essentially agents of the action; he reduces them to seven "dramatis personae," defined by the "spheres of influence" of the actions they perform: the Villain, the Donor, the Helper, the Princess and her Father (who together function as a single agent), the Dispatcher, the Hero, and the False Hero. The names that an individual tale will assign to these agents — and the way it may combine or divide them — are relatively unimportant, as are their attributes and motivations. What counts is their role as vehicles of the action, their placement and appearance in order to make sure that the Hero is dispatched, for instance, or that he is presented with false claims that he must expose and overcome. Propp's analysis clearly is limited by the relatively simple and formulaic nature of the narratives he discusses. Yet something like the concept of "function" may be necessary in any discussion of plot, in that it gives us a way to think about what happens in narrative from the point of view of its significance to the course of the action as a whole, the articulation of narrative as a structure of actions.

Propp's insistence on sequence and function results in a "syntagmatic" analysis, that is, one concerned with the combination of units along a horizontal axis, as in a sentence. Within French structuralism, there has rather been a strong emphasis on the "paradigmatic," an attention to the vertical axis which represents the grammar and lexicon of narrative, the elements and sets of relations which an individual narrative must call upon and activate.[12] Lévi-Strauss's interest in the "atemporal matrix structure" of narrative, the basic set of relationships which underlies and generates any given mythic narrative, is an example. So is the work of the semiotician A. J. Greimas, who takes Propp's analysis and, in the spirit of Lévi-Strauss, tries to reformulate the seven "dramatis personae" in the form of a matrix structure, a set of symmetrical oppositions which defines a kind of field of force. Greimas offers a taxonomy whose inherent tensions generate the production of narrative. It looks like this:

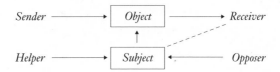

Without giving a full exposition of what Greimas calls his *modèle actantiel*— the dramatis personae have been rebaptized *actants*, emphasizing their quality of agency—one can see that the tale is conceived as a set of vectors, where the Hero's (the Subject's) search for the Object (the Princess, for instance) is helped or hindered, while the Object of the search itself (herself) is sent, or given, or put in the way of being obtained. The dotted line between Subject and Receiver indicates that very often these two coincide: the Hero is working for himself.[13]

The language used by Greimas—especially Subject and Object, but also Sender (*Destinateur*) and Receiver (*Destinataire*)—indicates that he is working also under the influence of a linguistic model, so central to structuralist thought in general. The work of Propp and other Russian formalists has proved susceptible of a reformulation by way of the linguistic model, by structuralists concerned to provide a general poetics of narrative (or "narratology"), that is, the conditions of meaning, the grammar and the syntax of narrative forms. Tzvetan Todorov (who more than anyone else introduced the ideas of the Russian formalists into French structuralism) works, for instance, from the postulate of a "universal grammar" of narrative.[14] Starting from a general analogy of narrative to a sentence writ large, Todorov postulates that the basic unit of narrative (like Propp's function) is a clause, while the agents are proper nouns, semantically void until predicated. The predicate terms are verbs (actions) and adjectives (states of being). His analysis proceeds largely with the study of verbs, the most important component of narrative, which have status (positive or negative), mood (imperative, optative, declarative, etc.), aspect (indicative, subjunctive), voice (passive or active). Clauses combine in different manners to form sequences, and complete narrative sequences are recognizable from their accomplishment of a transformation of the initial verb, now changed in status, mood, aspect, or by an added auxiliary verb.

Todorov best represents the linguistic model, applied to narrative analysis, in its most developed form. But such work is no doubt less valuable as a systematic model for analysis than as a suggestive metaphor, alerting us to the important analogies between parts of speech and parts of narrative, encouraging us to think about narrative as system, with something that approximates a grammar and rules of ordering that approximate a syntax. Perhaps the most challenging work to come out of narratology has used the linguistic model in somewhat playful ways, accepting it as a necessary basis for thought but opening up its implications in an engagement with the reading of texts. What I have most in mind here is Roland Barthes's *S/Z*, a book that combines some of the rigors of structuralist analysis, in its patient tracing of five codes through a tale broken down into 561 *lexias*, with interspersed speculative excurses on narrative and its reading.[15]

If we ask more specifically where in *S/Z* we find a notion approximating "plot," I think the answer must be: in some combination of Barthes's two irreversible codes — those that must be decoded successively, moving in one direction — the *proairetic* and the *hermeneutic*, that is: the code of actions ("Voice of the Empirical") and the code of enigmas and answers ("Voice of Truth"). The proairetic concerns the logic of actions, how their completion can be derived from their initiation, how they form sequences. The limit-case of a purely proairetic narrative would be approached by the picaresque tale, or the novel of pure adventure: narratives that give precedence to the happening. The hermeneutic code concerns rather the questions and answers that structure a story, their suspense, partial unveiling, temporary blockage, eventual resolution, with the resulting creation of a "dilatory space" — the space of suspense — which we work through toward what is felt to be, in classical narrative, the revelation of meaning that occurs when the narrative sentence reaches full predication. The clearest and purest example of the hermeneutic would no doubt be the detective story, in that everything in the story's structure, and its temporality, depends on the resolution of enigma. Plot, then, might best be thought of as an "overcoding" of the proairetic by the hermeneutic, the latter structuring the discrete elements of the former into larger interpretive wholes, working out their play of meaning and significance. If we interpret the hermeneutic to be a general gnomic code, concerned not narrowly with enigma and its resolution but broadly with our understanding of how actions come to be semiotically structured, through an interrogation of their point, their goal, their import, we find that Barthes contributes to our conception of plot as part of the dynamics of reading.

What may be most significant about *S/Z* is its break away from the somewhat rigid notion of structure to the more fluid and dynamic notion of structuration. The text is seen as a texture or weaving of codes (using the etymological sense of "text") which the reader organizes and sorts out only in provisional ways, since he never can master it completely, indeed is himself in part "undone" in his effort to unravel the text. The source of the codes is in what Barthes calls the *déjà-lu*, the already read (and the already written), in the writer's and the reader's experience of other literature, in a whole set of intertextual interlockings. In other words, structures, functions, sequences, plot, the possibility of following a narrative and making sense of it, belong to the reader's literary competence, his training as a reader of narrative.[16] The reader is in this view himself virtually a text, a composite of all that he has read, or heard read, or imagined as written. Plot, as the interplay of two of Barthes's codes, thus comes to appear one central way in which we as readers make sense, first of the text, and then, using the text as an interpretive model, of life. Plot—I continue to extrapolate from Barthes—is an interpretive structuring operation elicited, and necessitated, by those texts that we identify as narrative, where we know the meanings are developed over temporal succession in a suspense of final predication. As Barthes writes in an earlier essay ("Introduction to the Structural Analysis of Narrative"), what animates us as readers of narrative is *la passion du sens*, which I would want to translate as both the passion *for* meaning and the passion *of* meaning: the active quest of the reader for those shaping ends that, terminating the dynamic process of reading, promise to bestow meaning and significance on the beginning and the middle.[17]

But what Barthes discusses less well is the relation of the sensemaking operations of reading to codes outside the text, to the structuring of "reality" by textual systems. He tends to dismiss the referential or cultural code ("Voice of Science") as a "babble" conveying a society's received opinions and stereotypes. In particular, he does not pursue the questions of temporality raised by the irreversible nature of the proairetic and the hermeneutic codes. In the "Introduction to the Structural Analysis of Narrative," Barthes claims that time in narrative belongs only to the referent (to the fabula) and has nothing to do with the narrative discourse. And even in *S/Z*, which shows a diminished subservience to the paradigmatic model, Barthes's allegiances to the "writeable text" (*texte scriptible:* that which allows and requires the greatest constructive effort by the reader) and to the practice of "new new novelists" make him tend to disparage his irreversible codes as belonging to an outmoded ideology, and to reserve his greatest

PETER BROOKS

admiration for the symbolic ("Voice of the Text"), which allows one to enter the text anywhere and to play with its stagings of language itself.

Some correction of perspective is provided by Gérard Genette in *Narrative Discourse*, which along with the work of Todorov and Barthes constitutes the most significant contribution of the French structuralist tradition to thinking about narrative. In his careful and subtle study of the relationships among story, plot, and narrating, Genette pays close attention to the functioning of the infinitely variable gearbox that links the told to the ways of its telling, and how the narrative discourse — his principal example is Proust's *A la recherche du temps perdu* — works to subvert, replay, or even pervert the normal passages of time.[18] Noting the inescapable linearity of the linguistic signifier, Genette faces most directly the paradox of form and temporality when he points out that narrative as we commonly know it — as a book, for instance — is literally a spatial form, an object, but that its realization depends on its being gone through in sequence and succession, and that it thus metonymically "borrows" a temporality from the time of its reading: what he calls a "pseudo-time" of the text.[19]

Genette thus offers a kind of minimalist solution to the question of structure and temporality, and dissents in part from the structural narratologists' excessive emphasis on the paradigmatic, their failure to engage the movement and dynamic of narrative. Genette's solution may be too cautious. For not only does the reading of narrative take time; the time it takes, to get from beginning to end — particularly in those instances of narrative that most define our sense of the mode, nineteenth-century novels — is very much part of our sense of the narrative, what it has accomplished, what it means. Lyric poetry, we feel, strives toward an ideal simultaneity of meaning, encouraging us to read backward as well as forward (through rhyme and repetition, for instance), to grasp the whole in one visual and auditory image; and expository argument, while it can have a narrative, generally seeks to suppress its force in favor of an atemporal structure of understanding; whereas narrative stories depend on meanings delayed, partially filled in, stretched out. Unlike philosophical syllogisms, narratives ("All-Kinds-of-Fur," for example) are temporal syllogisms, concerning the connective processes of time. It is, I think, no accident that most of the great examples of narrative are long and can occupy our reading time over days or weeks or more: if we think of the effects of serialization (which, monthly, weekly, or even daily, was the medium of publication for many of the great nineteenth-century novels) we can perhaps grasp more nearly how time in the representing is felt to be a necessary analogue of time represented. As Rousseau contends in the preface to *La Nouvelle Héloïse*, a novel that in so many ways announces the nineteenth-century tradition, to understand his characters one must know them both young and old, and know them through the process of aging and change that lies in between, a process worked out over a stretch of pages.[20] And Proust's narrator says much the same thing at the end of *Le Temps retrouvé*, where — in the shadow of impending death — he resolves to dedicate himself to the creation of a novel that will, of necessity, have "the shape of time."[21]

Plot as a logic of narrative would hence seem to be analogous to the syntax of meanings that are temporally unfolded and recovered, meanings that cannot otherwise be created or understood. Genette's study of narrative discourse in reference to Proust leads him to note that one can tell a story without any reference to the place of its telling, the location from which it is proffered, but that one cannot tell a story without indications of the time of telling in relation to the told: the use of verb tenses, and their relation one to another, necessarily gives us a certain temporal place in relation to the story. Genette calls this discrepancy in the situation of time and place a "dissymmetry" of the language code itself, "the deep causes of which escape us."[22] While Genette's point is valid and important in the context of linguistics and the philosophy of language, one might note that commonsensically the deep causes are evident to the point of banality, if also rather grim: that is, man is ambulatory, but he is mortal. Temporality is a problem, and an irreducible factor of any narrative statement, in a way that location is not: "All-Kinds-of-Fur" can be articulated from anywhere, but it needs to observe the sequence of tenses and the succession of events. It is my simple conviction, then, that narrative has something to do with time-boundedness, and that plot is the internal logic of the discourse of mortality.

Walter Benjamin has made this point in the simplest and most extreme way, in claiming that what we seek in narrative fictions is that knowledge of death which is denied to us in our own lives: the death that writes *finis* to the life and therefore confers on it its meaning. "Death," says Benjamin, "is the sanction of everything that the storyteller can tell."[23] Benjamin thus advances the ultimate argument for the necessary retrospectivity of narrative: that only the end can finally determine meaning, close the sentence as a signifying totality. Many of the most suggestive analysts of narrative have shared this conviction that the end writes the beginning and shapes the middle: Propp, for instance, and Frank Kermode, and Jean-Paul Sartre, in his distinction between living and telling, argued in *La Nausée*, where in telling everything is transformed by the structuring presence of the end to come, and narrative in fact proceeds "in the reverse"; or, as Sartre puts it in respect to autobiographical narration in *Les Mots*, in order to tell his story in terms of the meaning it would acquire only at the end, "I became my own obituary."[24] These are arguments to which we will need to return in more detail. We should here note that opposed to this view stand other analysts, such as Claude Bremond, or Jean Pouillon, who many years ago argued (as a Sartrean attempting to rescue narrative from the constraints Sartre found in it) that the preterite tense used classically in the novel is decoded by the reader as a kind of present, that of an action and a significance being forged before his eyes, in his hands, so to speak.[25] It is to my mind an interesting and not wholly resolvable question how much, and in what ways, we in reading image the pastness of the action presented, in most cases, in verbs in the past tense. If on the one hand we realize the action progressively, segment by segment, as a kind of present in terms of our experience of it—the present of an argument, as in my summary of "All-Kinds-of-Fur"—do we not do so precisely in anticipation of its larger hermeneutic structuring by conclusions? We are frustrated by narrative interminable, even if we know that any termination is artificial, and that the imposition of ending may lead to that resistance to the end which Freud found in his patients and which is an important novelistic dynamic in such writers as Stendhal and Gide.[26] If the past is to be read as present, it is a curious present that we know to be past in relation to a future we know to be already in place, already in wait for us to reach it. Perhaps we would do best to speak of the *anticipation of retrospection* as our chief tool in making sense of narrative, the master trope of its strange logic. We have no doubt forgone eternal narrative ends, and even traditional nineteenth-century ends are subject to self-conscious endgames, yet still we read in a spirit of confidence, and also a state of dependence, that what remains to be read will restructure the provisional meanings of the already read.

Notes

1. E. M. Forster, *Aspects of the Novel* (New York: Harcourt, Brace, 1927), p. 126.
2. One of the ambitions of Northrop Frye in *Anatomy of Criticism* (Princeton: Princeton University Press, 1957) is to provide such a typology in his *mythoi*. Yet there is in Frye a certain confusion between mythoi as plot structures and mythoi as myths or archetypes which to my mind makes his work less valuable than it might be.
3. On historical narrative as a form of understanding, see the fine essay by Louis O. Mink, "Narrative Form as Cognitive Instrument," in *The Writing of History: Literary*

Form and Historical Understanding, ed. Robert H. Canary and Henry Kozicki (Madison: University of Wisconsin Press, 1978), pp. 129–49. Mink calls narrative "a primary and irreducible form of human comprehension" (p. 132). Of interest also is Dale H. Porter, *The Emergence of the Past* (Chicago: University of Chicago Press, 1981).

4. See "All-Kinds-of-Fur" (*Allerleirauh*), in *The Grimms' German Folk Tales*, trans. Francis P. Magoun and Alexander H. Krappe (Carbondale: Southern Illinois University Press, 1960), pp. 257–61.

5. See Walter Benjamin, "The Storyteller" (*Der Erzähler*), in *Illuminations*, trans. Harry Zohn (New York: Schocken Books, 1969), p. 91. On the place of incest and incest taboo in the Grimms' tales, see Marthe Robert, "The Grimm Brothers," in *The Child's Part*, ed. Peter Brooks (reprint, Boston: Beacon Press, 1972), pp. 44–56. One might offer the following diagram of the movement of the plot in "All-Kinds-of-Fur," from the initial overeroticization of the daughter (as the object of prohibited desires), through the underevaluation of the feminine (becoming the simulated beast), to the state of equilibrium achieved at the end: $+ + / - - / + -$. Without attaching too much importance to such a formula, one can see that it describes a process of working-out or working-through common to many tales.

6. On the Oedipus myth, see Claude Lévi-Strauss, "The Structural Study of Myth," in *Structural Anthropology* (Garden City, N.Y.: Anchor-Doubleday, 1967), pp. 202–25. On the "atemporal matrix structure," see Lévi-Strauss, "La Structure et la forme," *Cahiers de l'Institut de Science Economique Appliquée* 99, sér. M, no. 7 (1960): 29.

7. Aristotle, *Poetics*, trans. Ingram Bywater, in *Introduction to Aristotle*, 2d ed., ed. Richard McKeon (Chicago: University of Chicago Press, 1973), p. 678.

8. See Seymour Chatman, *Story and Discourse* (Ithaca: Cornell University Press, 1979). Chatman's book offers a useful summary, and attempt at synthesis, of narrative analysis in the structuralist tradition; he also gives extended bibliographical references. One can find an exposition of many of the issues that concern us here in Robert Scholes, *Structuralism in Literature* (New Haven: Yale University Press, 1974). *Fabula* and *sjužet* are rendered as "story" and "plot" by Lee T. Lemon and Marion Reis in their anthology *Russian Formalist Criticism* (Lincoln: University of Nebraska Press, 1965). Equating the fabula/sjužet distinction with story/plot is much criticized by Meir Sternberg in *Expositional Modes and Temporal Ordering in Fiction* (Baltimore: Johns Hopkins University Press, 1978), chap. 1. But Sternberg's understanding of the concept of plot is based exclusively on E. M. Forster's definition in *Aspects of the Novel*, where plot is distinguished from story by its emphasis on causality. To offer causality as the key characteristic of plot may be to fall into the error of the *post hoc ergo propter hoc*, as Roland Barthes suggests in "Introduction à l'analyse structurale des récits" (*Communications* 8 [1966], English trans. Stephen Heath, in *A Barthes Reader*, ed. Susan Sontag [New York: Hill and Wang, 1982]), and as Vladimir Propp implicitly demonstrates in *The Morphology of the Folktale*, 2d ed., trans. Laurence Scott (Austin: University of Texas Press, 1970); if plot appears to turn sequence into consequence, this may often be illusory; causality can be produced by new material, by changes in mood or atmosphere, by coincidence, by reinterpretation of the past, and so forth. Some of these issues will be taken up in chap. 10 [of *Reading for the Plot*]. Sternberg argues further that the sjužet is properly the whole of the text, whereas plot is an abstraction and reconstruction of it. But I think that sjužet

as used by such Russian formalists as Boris Tomachevsky and Victor Shklovsky is similarly an abstraction and reconstruction of the logic of the narrative text and in this sense
is quite close to Aristotle. For a useful discussion of the concept of plot, especially as
related to the notion of mimesis, see Elizabeth Dipple, *Plot* (London: Methuen, 1970).

9. Paul Ricoeur, "Narrative Time" in *On Narrative*, ed. W. J. T. Mitchell (Chicago:
University of Chicago Press, 1981), p. 167. Compare Louis O. Mink on historical
narrative, when he argues that the past "is not an untold story but can be made intelligible only as the subject of stories we tell" ("Narrative Form as Cognitive Instrument,"
p. 148). Ricoeur offers a more extended presentation of his ideas in the recent *Temps et
récit* (Paris: Editions du Seuil, 1983), which primarily concerns historical narrative and
will be followed by a second volume devoted to fictional narrative.

10. The work I refer to here is available in English translation primarily in two
anthologies: Lee T. Lemon and Marion Reis, eds., *Russian Formalist Criticism*, which
contains Tomachevsky's essay in synthesis, "Thematics"; and Ladislav Matejka and
Krystyna Pomorska, *Readings in Russian Poetics* (Cambridge: MIT Press, 1971). The
major study of the Russian formalists remains Victor Erlich, *Russian Formalism* (The
Hague: Mouton, 1955). See also the anthology in French translation edited by Tzvetan
Todorov, *Théorie de la littérature* (Paris: Editions du Seuil, 1965).

11. Propp, *The Morphology of the Folktale*, p. 21.

12. The paradigmatic axis is the "axis of selection" in Roman Jakobson's terms, the
set of rules and virtual terms that are activated along the syntagmatic axis, or "axis of
combination." For a good discussion of the uses of the two axes, see Jakobson, "Closing
Statement: Linguistics and Poetics," in *Style in Language*, ed. Thomas Sebeok (Cambridge: MIT Press, 1960), pp. 350–77.

13. See A. J. Greimas, *Sémantique structurale* (Paris: Larousse, 1966). One of Greimas's more amusing illustrations is Karl Marx's *Das Kapital*, which according to the
model gives the following "actants": Subject: Man; Object: Classless Society; Sender:
History; Receiver: Humanity; Helper: Proletariat; Opposer: Bourgeoisie.

14. See in particular Tzvetan Todorov, *Grammaire du Décameron* (The Hague:
Mouton, 1969), and the essays of Poétique de la prose (Paris: Editions du Seuil, 1971),
English trans. Richard Howard, *The Poetics of Prose* (Ithaca: Cornell University Press,
1977). On Todorov's contribution to the poetics of narrative, see Peter Brooks, "Introduction" to Todorov, *Poetics*, trans. Richard Howard (Minneapolis: University of Minnesota Press, 1981). See also Gerald Prince, *A Grammar of Stories* (The Hague: Mouton,
1973).

15. See Roland Barthes, *S/Z* (Paris: Editions du Seuil, 1970), English trans. Richard
Miller (New York: Hill and Wang, 1974).

16. The notion of "literary competence," implicit in Barthes's view of reading, is
very well discussed by Jonathan Culler in *Structuralist Poetics* (Ithaca: Cornell University
Press, 1975), pp. 113–30. Culler's book as a whole offers a lucid and useful discussion of
structuralist approaches to the study of literature.

17. Barthes, "Introduction à l'analyse structurale des récits," p. 27.

18. See Gérard Genette, "Discours du récit," in *Figures III* (Paris: Editions du Seuil,
1972), English trans. Jane Lewin, *Narrative Discourse* (Ithaca: Cornell University Press,
1980). To the histoire/récit (fabula/sjužet) distinction, Genette adds a third category,

which he calls *narration* — "narrating" — that is, the level at which narratives sometimes dramatize the means and agency (real or fictive) of their telling. This category will prove of use to us later on. On the "perversion" of time in Proust, see "Discours du récit," p. 182.

19. Genette, "Discours du récit," pp. 77–78.

20. See Jean-Jacques Rousseau, "Seconde Préface," *La Nouvelle Héloïse* (Paris: Bibliothèque de la Pléïade, 1964), p. 18.

21. Marcel Proust, *A la recherche du temps perdu* (Paris: Bibliothèque de la Pléïade, 1954), 3:1045.

22. Genette, "Discours du récit," p. 228.

23. Benjamin, "The Storyteller," p. 94.

24. See Frank Kermode, *The Sense of an Ending* (New York: Oxford University Press, 1967); Jean-Paul Sartre, *La Nausée* (Paris: Gallimard, 1947), pp. 59–60; and Sartre, *Les Mots* (Paris: Gallimard, 1968), p. 171.

25. Jean Pouillon, *Temps et roman* (Paris: Gallimard, 1946). See also Claude Bremond, *Logique du récit* (Paris: Editions du Seuil, 1973).

26. On the resistance to the end, see D. A. Miller, *Narrative and Its Discontents* (Princeton: Princeton University Press, 1981). It is to Miller that I owe the term and concept "the narratable," which will be used frequently.

The relation of past and future to present is the subject of a famous meditation by Saint Augustine, in book 11 of the *Confessions*, where he finds a "solution" to the problem by the argument that there is a present of the past, in the form of memory, and a present of the future, in the form of anticipation or awaiting — a situation that he illustrates by the example of reciting a psalm. If Augustine does not solve the problem of temporality here, he surely offers a suggestive comment on the particular temporality of recitation or reading, its play of memory and anticipation. See the very rich analysis of Augustine's meditation in Ricoeur, *Temps et récit*, pp. 19–53.

16

Breaking the Sentence; Breaking the Sequence

RACHEL BLAU DUPLESSIS

I am almost sure, I said to myself, that Mary Carmichael is playing a trick on us. For I feel as one feels on a switchback railway when the car, instead of sinking, as one has been led to expect, swerves up again. Mary is tampering with the expected sequence. First she broke the sentence; now she has broken the sequence. . . . Perhaps she had done this unconsciously, merely giving things their natural order, as a woman would, if she wrote like a woman. But the effect was somehow baffling; one could not see a wave heaping itself, a crisis coming round the next corner. . . . For whenever I was about to feel the usual things in the usual places, about love, about death, the annoying creature twitched me away, as if the important point were just a little further on. — Virginia Woolf, *A Room of One's Own* (1929)

. . . Charlotte was gazing up into the dark eyes of Redmond. "My darling," he breathed hoarsely. Strong arms lifted her, his warm lips pressed her own. . . .

   That was the way it was supposed to go, that was the way it had always gone before, but somehow it no longer felt right. I'd taken a wrong turn somewhere; there was something, some fact or clue, that I had overlooked. — Margaret Atwood, *Lady Oracle* (1976)

One approach to the feminist criticism of these modern writers is suggested in an analysis of "Mary Carmichael's first novel, *Life's Adventure*," a work and author invented by Virginia Woolf and explicated in *A Room of One's Own*.[1] This is a novel by the last of the series of ancestral mothers alluded to in the Elizabethan ballad of the Four Marys, which forms a frame for the essay. The first two are Mary Beton, with her legacy of money, and Mary Seton, who provides "room" — institutional and psychological space. Both are necessary for Mary Carmichael, the modern author, and all of them express the baffled and unmentioned Mary Hamilton, from the ages when women had no way to dissent, except through infanticide and anonymous song. Woolf scrutinizes this novel's style, plot, and purpose with a diffident casualness, finding "some fact or clue" of great importance: "Mary is tampering with the expected sequence. First she broke the sentence; now she has broken the sequence" (*AROO*, 85). In these matching statements are telescoped a poetics of rupture and critique.

The sentence broken is one that expresses "the ridicule, the censure, the assurance of inferiority" about women's cultural ineptitude and deficiencies.[2] To break the sentence rejects not grammar especially, but rhythm, pace, flow, expression: the structuring of the female voice by the male voice, female tone and manner by male expectations, female writing by male emphasis, female writing by existing conventions of gender — in short, any way in which dominant structures shape muted ones. For a woman to write, she must experiment with "altering and adapting the current sentence until she writes one that takes the natural shape of her thought without crushing or distorting it" (*G & R*, 81).[3]

At first it appeared as if Mary Carmichael would not be able to break this sentence and create her own. Her style was jerky, short, and terse, which "might mean that she was afraid of something; afraid of being called 'sentimental' perhaps; or she remembers that women's writing has been called flowery and so provides a superfluity of thorns . . . " (*AROO*, 85). Here she overcompensated for femaleness in deference to existing conventions.

But eventually, facing gender in an authentic way, the writer produces "a woman's sentence," "the psychological sentence of the feminine gender," which "is used to describe a woman's mind by a writer [Dorothy Richardson] who is neither proud nor afraid of anything that she may discover in the psychology of her sex."[4] The sentence is "psychological" not only because it deepens external realism with a picture of consciousness at work but also because it involves a critique of her own consciousness, saturated as it is with discourses of dominance.

There is nothing exclusively or essentially female about "the psychological sentence of the feminine gender," because writers of both sexes have used that "elastic" and "enveloping" form. But it is a "woman's sentence" because of its cultural and situational function, a dissension stating that women's minds and concerns have been neither completely nor accurately produced in literature as we know it. Breaking the sentence is a way of rupturing language and tradition sufficiently to invite a female slant, emphasis, or approach. Similarly there is nothing innately gendered about the signifier "I," yet in *A Room of One's Own* the speaker's "I" is both female and plural — "a woman's voice in a patriarchal literary tradition" — and another "I," shadowing the page, is "polished, learned, well-fed," an explicitly male subject speaking of and from dominance.[5]

RACHEL BLAU DUPLESSIS

Woolf's "woman's sentence," then, has its basis not in biology, but rather in cultural fearlessness, in the attitude of critique—a dissent from, a self-conscious marking of, dominant statement. It can be a stress shifting, the kind of realignment of emphasis noted by Nancy Miller, following Luce Irigaray: "an italicized version of what passes for the neutral or standard face . . . a way of marking what has already been said."[6]

A "woman's sentence" is Woolf's shorthand term for a writing unafraid of gender as an issue, undeferential to male judgment while not unaware of the complex relations between male and female. A "woman's sentence" will thus be constructed in considered indifference to the fact that the writer's vision is seen as peculiar, incompetent, marginal. So Woolf summarizes "the first great lesson" mastered by Mary Carmichael: "she wrote as a woman, but as a woman who has forgotten that she is a woman" (*AROO*, 96). The doubled emphasis on woman, yet on forgetting woman, is a significant maneuver, claiming freedom from a "tyranny of sex" that is nonetheless palpable and dominant, both negated and affirmed.[7]

In both *A Room of One's Own* and the related "Women and Fiction," Woolf criticizes women for "resenting the treatment of [their] sex and pleading for its rights," because, in her view, this threatens the poise a writer achieves by the transcending of "indignation" on the one hand and "resignation" on the other, the "too masculine" here and the "too feminine" there.[8] This movement between complicity and critique expresses Woolf's version of a doubled dynamic that is, as we shall see momentarily, characteristic of other women writers.[9]

What binds these writers is their oppositional stance to the social and cultural construction of gender.[10] This opposition has a number of origins. Perhaps the most suggestive is that of marginality in two arenas.[11] When a female writer is black (Alice Walker, Zora Neale Hurston, Gwendolyn Brooks, Toni Morrison), colonial (Olive Schreiner, Doris Lessing, Jean Rhys), Canadian (Margaret Atwood), of working-class origin (Tillie Olsen, Marge Piercy), of lesbian or bisexual orientation (H.D., Virginia Woolf, Adrienne Rich, Joanna Russ), or displaced and déclassé (Dorothy Richardson), double marginalization can be produced. Either it compels the person to negate any possibility for a critical stance, seeking instead "conformity and inclusion" because the idea of an authoritative center is defensively affirmed, or it enlivens the potential for critique by the production of an (ambiguously) nonhegemonic person, one in marginalized dialogue with the orders she may also affirm.[12]

The woman writers studied here are further unified by their interested dissent from androcentric culture in nonfictional texts: essay, memoir, polemic, and social study. The texts will be seen, case by case, to contribute to their fictional elaborations and narrative stances.[13] Hence while hardly all of the writers would describe themselves as feminists, and some, indeed, resist that term, one may assert that any female cultural practice that makes the "meaning production process" itself "the site of struggle" may be considered feminist.[14] These authors are "feminist" because they construct a variety of oppositional strategies to the depiction of gender institutions in narrative. A writer expresses dissent from an ideological formation by attacking elements of narrative that repeat, sustain, or embody the values and attitudes in question. So after breaking the sentence, a rupture with the internalization of the authorities and voices of dominance, the woman writer will create that further rupture which is a center for this book: breaking "the sequence — the expected order" (*AROO*, 95).

Breaking the sequence is a rupture in habits of narrative order, that expected story told when "love was the only possible interpreter" of women's textual lives (*AROO*, 87). In her study of *Life's Adventure*, Woolf notes that the novelist Mary Carmichael alludes to "the relationship that there may be between Chloe and Roger," but this is set aside in favor of another bond, depicted "perhaps for the first time in literature" (*AROO*, 84, 86). "Chloe liked Olivia. They shared a laboratory together," begins Woolf (*AROO*, 87). The romance names with the allusions to Shakespearean transvestite characters are very suggestive, especially as opposed to the firmly heterosexual "Roger," with a whole history of slang behind him. One of these women is married, with children; the other is not. Their work — finding a cure for pernicious anemia — may suggestively beef up women's weakness of nerve with a good dose of female bonding.

The ties between Chloe and Olivia may be homosocial or, given the subsequent sexual-cultural metaphor of exploring the "serpentine cave" of women, they may be lesbian.[15] In either case, Woolf clearly presents a nonheterosexual relation nourished by the healthy vocation of women. She is also eloquent about the meaning of these changes. The women's friendship, based on their work life, will be "more varied and lasting because it will be less personal" (*AROO*, 88). "Personal" is Woolf's word (in essays throughout the twenties) for the privatization and exclusiveness that is part of the script of heterosexual romance. So the tie between Chloe and Olivia, a model for modern women writers, makes a critique of heterosexuality and the love plot, and offers (Woolf implies) a stronger and more positive sense of female quest. One is no longer allowed to "feel the usual things in the usual places, about love, about death" (*AROO*, 95). So breaking the sequence can mean delegitimating the specific narrative and cultural orders of nineteenth-century fiction — the emphasis on successful or failed romance, the subordination of quest to love, the death of the questing female, the insertion into family life. "The important point . . . just a little further on" that Mary Carmichael pushes her reader to see might be such narrative strategies as reparenting, female bonding, including lesbian ties, mother-child dyads, brother-sister pairs, familial transpositions, the multiple individual, and the transpersonal protagonist.

This study is also designed to suggest what elements of female identity would be drawn on to make plausible the analytic assumption that there is a women's writing with a certain stance toward narrative.[16] The narrative strategies of twentieth-century writing by women are the expression of two systemic elements of female identity — a psychosexual script and a socio-cultural situation, both structured by major oscillations. The oscillations occur in the gendering process and in the hegemonic process. Oscillation is a swinging between two positions, a touching of two limits, or, alternately, a fluctuation between two purposes, states, centers, or principles. The narrative strategies I will present here all take basic elements of female identity, such as the gendering sequence, and realign their components.

The possibilities for heterosexual love and romance take shape in the object relations within the family, that is, in the ties of kinship forged between child and parent, and in the processes of gendering, all given very complete cultural and social support. As we know, there is a sequence that assists these arrangements — a psychosexual script that is one of our first dramas. The occasion of our "learning the rules of gendering and kinship" and the apparatus for the production of sexual personality is, of course, the oedipal crisis.[17]

Freudian theory, postulating the telos of "normal femininity" as the proper resolution of the oedipal crisis, bears an uncanny resemblance to the nineteenth-century endings of narrative, in which the female hero becomes a heroine and in which the conclusion of a valid love plot is the loss of any momentum of quest. The pitfalls to be avoided by a woman seeking normal femininity are very consistent with the traits of the female hero in narrative: defiance, activity, selfishness, heroic action, and identification with other women. For Freudian theory puts a high premium on female passivity and narcissism and on the "end" of husband, home, and male child. As for quest or individual aspiration, Freud poignantly realizes that the achievement of femininity has left "no paths open to [a woman] for further development; . . . [it is] as though, in fact, the difficult development which leads to femininity had exhausted all the possibilities of the individual."[18] By the repressions and sacrifices involved in becoming feminine, quest is at a dead end — a sentiment that we have seen replicated in narrative endings.

The "original bisexuality" or "bisexual disposition" of every individual is the major starting point for this account.[19] The oedipal crisis is a social process of gendering that takes "bisexual, androgynous," libidinally active, and ungendered infants and produces girls and boys, giving to the male future social and sexual domination, and to the female future domesticated status within the rules of the sex-gender system of its society.[20] Thus gender is a product. That there must be some kind of passage of an infant "into a social human being" is not at issue. It will involve the "[dialectical] process of struggle with and ultimate supersession (including integration) of symbolic figures of love, desire, and authority." As this citation from Ortner proposes, the theoretical possibility that the oedipal crisis is historically mutable must not be overlooked.[21] The drama might unfold with some alternate figures and some alternate products or emphases.

Another major element of the oedipal crisis for girls is the requisite shift of object choice from "phallic" or preoedipal mother — the mother of power — to a heterosexual object, the father. Little boys must shift generations, but not genders, in their object choice. The reason for the female shift has been contested. Freud postulated that a girl will turn from her mother, sometimes with hatred and hostility, when the mother is discovered to be bereft of the genital marker of male power. In feminist revisions of Freud, this revelation, called "penis envy" by Freud, has been viewed as the delivery of knowledge well beyond the perception of sheer genital difference, the shock of learning a whole array of psychosocial rules and orders valorizing maleness.

To Freud, the girl's tasks in the oedipal drama involve the repression of what he calls the "little man" inside her, that active, striving, clitoral self, and the repression of love for her mother, a person of her own sex. Yet even the Freudian account somewhat reluctantly presents a recurring tension between the oedipal and preoedipal phases for the female, whereas in most males (as far as the theory tells) the oedipus complex has a linear and cumulative movement. Freud has found that "Regressions to fixations at these pre-oedipal phases occur very often; in many women we actually find a repeated alternation of periods in which either masculinity or femininity has obtained the upper hand."[22] So the oedipal crisis can extend over years and follow an individual woman right into adulthood. Or, to say it another way, the "feminine" or "correct" resolution of women's gender identity comes easily unstuck and cannot be counted on.

A further elaboration of the oedipal crisis in women is available in Nancy Chodorow's analysis of mothering as a key institution in the social and psychic reproduction of gender. In her view, in the development of a girl, the preoedipal attachment to the mother is never entirely given up; it persists in coloring oedipalization, in shaping problems and issues of the female ego (boundlessness and boundary problems, "lack of separation or differentiation"), and in its influence on both the fact and the way that women mother. So while the gendering process is the "arena" where the goal of heterosexuality is "negotiated," it is also where the mother-daughter dyad and female bonding are affirmed.[23]

The narrative and cultural implications of this neo-Freudian picture of gendering are staggering. With no easy or one-directional passage to "normal femininity," women as social products are characterized by unresolved and continuous alterations between allegiance to males and to females, between heterosexuality and female-identified, lesbian, or bisexual ties. The "original bisexuality" of the individual female is not easily put to rest or resolved by one early tactical episode; rather the oscillation persists and is reconstituted in her adult identity. Further, the emotional rhythms of female identity involve repeated (and possibly even simultaneous) articulations of these two principles or states, which are taken (ideologically) as opposing poles.[24]

Twentieth-century women writers undertake a reassessment of the processes of gendering by inventing narrative strategies, especially involving sequence, character, and relationship, that neutralize, minimize, or transcend any oversimplified oedipal drama. This occurs by a recognition in various elements of narrative of the "bisexual oscillation" in the psychic makeup of characters, in the resolutions of texts, in the relationships portrayed. In twentieth-century narratives, effort is devoted to depicting masculine and feminine sides in one character — in Woolf's androgyny and in similar procedures in Richardson. Original bisexuality is extended the length of a character's life in H.D. and in Woolf. Women writers readjust the maternal and paternal in ways that unbalance the univocal sequence of object choices. This is why some female quest plots, like *To the Lighthouse* and *The Four-Gated City*, loop backward to mother-child attachments. Narratives of twentieth-century women, notably their *Künstlerromane*, may invent an interplay between the mother, the father, and the hero, in a "relational triangle."[25] These changes are often accompanied by pointed remarks about the plots, characters, and situations once expected in narrative: gender polarization, patri-sexual romantic love, the arrest of female quest, the "happy ending" — remarks that, as we shall see, underline the self-consciousness of this critique of narrative scripts and the psychosexual drama that forms them.[26]

These representations of gendering could be achieved irrespective of whether any of the authors were aware of the exact terms of Freudian theory, although no doubt a number were, or whether they explicitly con-nected their narratives to any aspect of Freud's position (something that does occur in Woolf's *Orlando*, in H.D.'s *Helen in Egypt* and *Tribute to Freud*, and in Doris Lessing's *The Golden Notebook*).[27] For women artists, this sense of "remaining in the Oedipus situation for an indefinite period" would not have to be consciously understood.[28] One may simply postulate that the habit of living with an "unresolved" oedipus complex would lead the bearer to a greater identification of the unstable elements, greater intuitive knowl-edge of these components of one's interior life.

Indeed, Freud suggests a massive slippage of effectiveness, so that the learning of the rules of gender may need a good deal of extrafamilial rein-forcement, especially where the girl is concerned. The formation of the superego — the acceptance of social rules, including those governing gen-der — is the result of "educative influences, of external intimidation threat-ening loss of love."[29] That is, education as an institution of gender, and culture as a whole, including literary products like narrative, channel the girl into dominant structures of the sex-gender system. The romance plot in narrative thus may be seen as a necessary extension of the processes of gendering, and the critique of romance that we find in twentieth-century female authors, as part of the oppositional protest lodged against both liter-ary culture and a psychosexual norm.

The psychosexual oscillation of the gendering process, so distinctly the-orized, interacts with another systemic aspect of female identity, which shows the same wavering, dialogic structure: a sociocultural oscillation of hegemonic processes. In the social and cultural arena, there is a constant repositioning between dominant and muted, hegemonic and oppositional, central and colonial, so that a woman may be described as (ambiguously) nonhegemonic or, with equal justice but less drama, as (ambiguously) hege-monic if her race, class, and sexuality are dominant. Virginia Woolf envi-sions this oscillating consciousness in *A Room of One's Own*. "It [the mind] can think back through its fathers or through its mothers, as I have said that a woman writing thinks back through her mothers. Again if one is a woman one is often surprised by a sudden splitting off of consciousness, say in walking down Whitehall, when from being the natural inheritor of that civilization, she becomes, on the contrary, outside of it, alien and critical" (*AROO*, 101). Note how Woolf passes from the oedipal-preoedipal division in object relations to the social oscillation, suggesting the relation of both processes to female identity. The debate between inheritor and critic is a movement between deep identification with dominant values and deep alienation from them. Whitehall, a street in London, is a synechdoche for British civil service and administrative agreements that endure beyond changes in specific governments, and thus is a metaphor for broad socio-cultural agreement.

The shifting into alternative perspectives is taken by Woolf as a phenomenon peculiarly resonant for a woman. Her use of the word *natural* as opposed to the word *critical* sums the process up. *Natural* is what every ideology happily claims it is; the beliefs, social practices, sense of the self are second nature, assumed. The word *critical*, however, has the force of a severe and transgressive dissent from cherished mental structures and social practices. This contradictory quiver, this social vibrato creates a critical sensibility: dissent from the culture by which women are partially nourished, to which they are connected.

A major originating moment of Woolf's "outsider's feeling" came, significantly enough, in her confrontation at the turn of the century with the banal but forceful social and romantic expectations represented by George Duckworth, her half-brother and self-appointed substitute parent. At issue was her green dress, unconventionally made of upholstery fabric. From the moment of his anger at her appearance, from her as yet muted defiance, Woolf crystallizes that hegemonic set: proper dress, patterned feminine behavior, "tea table training," the absolute necessity for romance, the "patriarchal machinery" creating rigid, polarized male and female personalities. What astonished Woolf most was the female role of passive, appreciative spectator and the acrobatic—almost Swiftean—jumping through hoops demanded of males; the whole "circus" or "required act" was accomplished with no irony or critical questioning.[30]

Many commentators on women as a group and on female identity have isolated as systemic some kind of dual relationship to the definitions offered by various dominant forces. Simone de Beauvoir sees the female child "hesitating between the role of *object*, *Other*, which is offered to her, and the assertion of her liberty" as subject.[31] John Berger argues that the "social presence" of women and their ingenuity in living in "the keeping of men" have created "two constituent yet always distinct elements of her identity as a woman": the "surveyor and the surveyed."[32] The "duality of women's position in society" is Gerda Lerner's explanation for the fact that women as a group can be both victims and upholders of the status quo: "Women live a duality—as members of the general culture and as partakers of women's culture."[33] Nancy Cott similarly views "women's group consciousness as a subculture uniquely divided against itself by ties to the dominant culture."[34] Sheila Rowbotham describes the war of parts of the self, given the attitudes of the dominant group on the Left. "One part of ourselves mocked another, we joined in the ridicule of our own aspirations. . . . Part of us leapt over into their world, part of us stayed at home. . . . We were never all together in one place, we were always in transit, immigrants into alien territory."[35] And Alice Walker, in "In Search of Our Mothers' Gardens," cites Woolf's *A Room of One's Own* to come to terms with the "contrary instincts" in certain work by black women from Phillis Wheatley to Zora Neale Hurston.[36] In sum, women writers as women negotiate with divided loyalties and doubled consciousness, both within and without a social and cultural agreement. This, in conjunction with the psychosexual oscillation, has implications for "sentence" and "sequence"—for language, ideology, and narrative.

Later in her career, Woolf continued her analysis of the source of women's sociocultural oscillation. In *Three Guineas*, Woolf finds that women's structural position enables them to take an adversarial stance to institutions of dominance. Women, she argues, are basically outsiders, formed by their nondominant ("unpaid for") education, as they observe the privileges of maleness and the sacrifices exacted from women themselves for those privileges. The lived experience of women and men even from the same social class differs so greatly that their world views and values are irreconcilably distinct: "though we look at the same things, we see them differently."[37]

Constituting a separate group within their social class, women should capitalize on this built-in zone of difference to think of themselves as an interested, coherent political bloc: an actual Society of Outsiders. They can and should refuse male society and its values (militarism, hierarchy, authoritarianism) even as they enter formerly all-male professions. And women have, Woolf is certain, less chance than men for being apologists for political, economic, and social oppression so intense that—her central point—the patriarchal politics of bourgeois liberalism is on a continuum with fascism and the authoritarian state. Being already outsiders, women should turn its negative markers ("poverty, chastity, derision, freedom from unreal loyalties") into positive markers of difference, and turn their marginal status to political advantage and analytic power (*TG*, 78).

The function of *Three Guineas* is to drive a politically motivated wedge of analysis and polemic between dominant and muted, inheritor and critic, class and gender allegiances, to try to convince educated women no longer to cooperate with the politics of their class. Indeed, in 1940 Woolf argued that women are in a position to make cross-class alliances with working-class men and women because their identification as "commoners, outsiders" will override apparent class distinctions.[38]

Yet the shift to the imperative mode and the call for a vow in *Three Guineas* betray the fact that women are not purely and simply Outsiders; otherwise one would not have to exhort them to remain so. They are, however, less integrated into the dominant orders than are men of their class. Women are a muted or subordinate part of a hegemonic process. Raymond Williams suggests that seeing hegemonic processes would be a way of visualizing culture to credit the internal debate between affirmation and critique. Hegemony includes a relationship in conflictual motion between the ideologies and practices of a dominant class or social group and the alternative practices, which may be either residual or emergent, of the muted classes or groups. Any set of hegemonic assumptions — notions orthodox in a given society and historical era — are "deeply saturating" and pervasive, "organized and lived," woven into the most private areas of our lives.[39] Still the hegemonic is always in motion, being "renewed, recreated, defended and modified."[40] These hegemonic processes are a site for both sociocultural reproduction and sociocultural dissent. The debate that women experience between the critic and the inheritor, the outsider and the privileged, the oppositional and the dominant is a major example of a hegemonic process, one whose results are evident in both social and narrative texts. Constantly reaffirmed as outsiders by others and sometimes by themselves, women's loyalties to dominance remain ambiguous, for they are not themselves in control of the processes by which they are defined.

Issues of control of voice and definition, then, allow Edwin Ardener's otherwise more static model to offer a complementary set of terms to define gender relations: the articulate or dominant men and then the nondominant or muted women. The latter term recalls the muted sonority of a musical instrument — the sound different, tamped down, repressed, but still speaking, with the speech bearing the marks of partial silencing. Interestingly, giving voice to the voiceless and making visible the invisible are two prime maneuvers in feminist poetics. As Ardener would gloss this, "The muted structures are 'there' but cannot be 'realized' in the language of the dominant structure."[41] To depict these relationships, Ardener posits two almost overlapping circles, one standing for dominant vision, the other for muted. The larger uncontested space where the circles overlap is shared by men and women in a given society as parallel inhabitants of main culture. The tiny crescent-shaped band left over for women is their zone of difference. Visualizing the relationship between dominant and muted in this fashion suggests that women can oscillate between the two parts of the circle that represents them, between difference and dominance.

The concept of a "double-consciousness" that comes from one's oscillation between a main and a muted position is not, nor could it ever be, a way of describing women exclusively, but it offers a way of seeing the identity of any group that is at least partially excluded from or marginal to the historically current system of meaning, value, and power.[42] Feminist criticism, then, may be said to begin with W. E. B. Du Bois, postulating for blacks this double consciousness, born in negotiation with hegemonic processes.

Ellen Moers analyzed distinctive female stances based not on innate or essential femininity but on the shared cultural experiences of secondary status—constraints on travel, education, social mediations of childhood and motherhood—and reflected in particular uses of certain cultural tropes, such as the Gothic, the monster, the landscape.[43] This postulate was given forceful statement by Elaine Showalter: that women are parallel to other minority groups in their subcultural position "relative to a dominant society" and that this position leads to a unity of "values, conventions, experiences and behaviors" from which women draw and to which they respond with various fictional and biographical strategies.[44] Following Showalter's emphasis on formal and biographical strategies of response, Sandra Gilbert and Susan Gubar pose a repeated and reinvoked struggle as the master plot for women of the nineteenth century: in a dynamic generational confrontation in which dominant culture is the father and women are either sage daughters or mad wives in relation to patriarchal power. A nineteenth-century woman writer is the site of an internalized cultural debate: her own rage that she cannot speak and her culture's rage that she can. This contradiction is resolved in a powerful fictional motif: the madwoman, in whom expression struggles with repression.[45]

Where a reading of twentieth-century materials necessarily differs from the nineteenth-century texts most profoundly analyzed by Showalter and Gilbert and Gubar is that, by the twentieth century, middle-class women are technically—on paper—rather more part of the economic world, rather less legally and politically circumscribed than they were in the nineteenth. This changed position does not alter the negotiation process, but it does mean that women have an interior identification with dominant values (traditionally expressed as a rejection of female specialness) as well as an understanding of muted alternatives. Dominant and muted may be more equally balanced opponents in the twentieth century than in the nineteenth.

Mary Jacobus has also noted, and made central to her analysis of women's writing, the split between alien critic and inheritor that I have taken as a key text for this book. Jacobus further argues that, given this situation, "at once within culture and outside it," a woman writer must simultaneously "challenge the terms and work within them."[46] This precisely parallels my argument—that woman is neither wholly "subcultural" nor, certainly, wholly main-cultural, but negotiates differences and sameness, marginality and inclusion in a constant dialogue, which takes shape variously in the various authors, but with one end—a rewriting of gender in dominant fiction. The two processes in concert—the gendering and the hegemonic process—create mutual reinforcement for the double consciousness of women writers. This is the social and sexual basis of the poetics of critique.[47]

All forms of dominant narrative, but especially romance, are tropes for the sex-gender system as a whole.[48] Given the ideological and affirmative functions of narrative, it is no surprise that the critique of story is a major aspect of the stories told by twentieth-century women writers. . . .[49]

Notes

1. Virginia Woolf, *A Room of One's Own* (New York: Harcourt, Brace and World, 1957); abbreviated in the text as *AROO*. The epigraphs come from pp. 85 and 95.

2. Virginia Woolf, "Women and Fiction" (1929), in *Granite and Rainbow* (New York: Harcourt, Brace, 1958), p. 80; abbreviated as *G & R*.

3. The sentence is further qualified as being "too loose, too heavy, too pompous for a woman's use" (*G & R*, 81). A parallel, but slightly softened, statement about the sentence is found in *AROO*, p. 79, and an elaboration in the 1923 review of Dorothy Richardson, "Romance and the Heart," reprinted in *Contemporary Writers: Essays on Twentieth Century Books and Authors* (New York: Harcourt Brace Jovanovich, 1965), pp. 123–25. Working with these passages, Josephine Donovan also notes that the differences between "male" and "female" sentences exist in the tone of authority, the declaration of the insider in one, the under-the-surface life in the other, which rejects the authoritarian. Donovan also links Woolf's achievements in subjective realism to her critique of gender ideologies in narrative. "Feminist Style Criticism," in *Images of Women in Fiction: Feminist Perspectives*, ed. Susan Koppelman Cornillon (Bowling Green, Ohio: Bowling Green University Popular Press, 1972), pp. 339–52. A further note on the analysis of Woolf's "sentence." In this study as a whole, I am carefully (too?) agnostic on the subject of those actual disruptions of syntax, grammar, and words more characteristic of, say, Gertrude

Stein; however, what Julia Kristeva calls the semiotic and symbolic registers may be another oscillation of dominant discourse in dialogue with marginality.

4. Richardson, "Romance and the Heart," pp. 124–25.

5. This is Nelly Furman's argument. "Textual Feminism," in *Women and Language in Literature and Society*, ed. Sally McConnell-Ginet, Ruth Borker, and Nelly Furman (New York: Praeger, 1980), pp. 50–51.

6. Nancy Miller, "Emphasis Added: Plots and Plausibilities in Women's Fiction," *PMLA* 96.1 (Jan. 1981): 38.

7. Woolf, "Women Novelists," reprinted in *Contemporary Writers*, p. 25.

8. Woolf, *Granite and Rainbow*, p. 80.

9. Here in the twenties, Woolf holds in conflictive tension her materialist and idealist views of writing. She argues that through art one may — indeed one must — transcend the cultural conditions of one's own formation. So in *A Room of One's Own*, Woolf combines a materialist analysis of the conditions that determine a woman's identity and capacity for work and an idealist vision of androgyny, a unity of the warring and unequal genders in luminous serenity. This point is made by Michele Barrett in her introduction to a collection of essays by Virginia Woolf, *Women and Writing* (New York: Harcourt Brace Jovanovich, 1979), pp. 20, 22.

10. For example, Woolf compared living with the institutions of gender as they are to living in "half-civilized barbarism," a slap at the meliorism of liberal ideology. Reply to "Affable Hawk" from the *New Statesman* of 1920, in *The Diary of Virginia Woolf, Volume Two: 1920–1924*, ed. Anne Olivier Bell and Andrew McNeillie (New York: Harcourt Brace Jovanovich, 1978), p. 342.

11. Carolyn G. Heilbrun points toward the role of double determining when she suggests that "to be a feminist one had to have an experience of being an outsider more extreme than merely being a woman." *Reinventing Womanhood* (New York: W. W. Norton, 1979), pp. 20–24. Adrienne Rich describes the tension leading to a doubled vision: "Born a white woman, Jewish or of curious mind / — twice an outsider, still believing in inclusion — " *A Wild Patience Has Taken Me This Far* (New York: W. W. Norton, 1981), p. 39.

12. Myra Jehlen, "Archimedes and the Paradox of Feminist Criticism," *Signs* 6.4 (Summer 1981): 594. Jehlen makes this point about nineteenth-century American women, attempting to explain the literature of sentiment and limited challenge that they produced. "In this society, women stand outside any of the definitions of complete being; hence perhaps the appeal to them of a literature of conformity and inclusion." "(Ambiguously) nonhegemonic" from my essay "For the Etruscans: Sexual Difference and Artistic Production — the Debate over a Female Aesthetic," in *The Future of Difference*, ed. Hester Eisenstein and Alice Jardine (Boston: G. K. Hall, 1980). A further development of the phrase "(ambiguously) nonhegemonic" is found in Margaret Homans, " 'Her Very Own Howl': The Ambiguities of Representation in Recent Women's Fiction," *Signs* 9.2 (Winter 1983): 186–205. Homans suggests that "there is a specifically gender-based alienation from language" visible in thematic treatments of language in women's fiction, which derives from "the special ambiguity of women's simultaneous participation in and exclusion from a hegemonic group," p. 205.

13. For example, Olive Schreiner, *Women and Labour*; Charlotte Perkins Gilman,

The Man-Made World; or, Our Androcentric Culture and Women and Economics; Virginia Woolf, *Three Guineas, A Room of One's Own,* and various essays; H.D., *Tribute to Freud, End to Torment,* and *The Gift;* Dorothy Richardson, essays on women; Adrienne Rich, *Of Woman Born* and *On Lies, Secrets and Silence;* Tillie Olsen, *Silences;* Doris Lessing, *A Small Personal Voice;* Alice Walker, *In Search of Our Mothers' Gardens.*

14. Annette Kuhn, *Women's Pictures: Feminism and Cinema* (London: Routledge and Kegan Paul, 1982), p. 17. The first chapter is a sterling exposition of feminist analysis of culture.

15. In the course of her research on the draft of *A Room of One's Own,* Alice Fox communicated to Jane Marcus that Woolf originally, wittily left a blank unfilled by the word *laboratory.* "Then she wrote that she was afraid to turn the page to see what they shared, and she thought of the obscenity trial for a novel." The allusion made and excised is to the contemporaneous trial of *The Well of Loneliness;* the implication that Woolf handled differently in her published text is that homophobic censorship and self-censorship alike conspire to mute discussion of relational ties between women. Jane Marcus, "Liberty, Sorority, Misogyny," in *The Representation of Women in Fiction,* ed. Carolyn G. Heilbrun and Margaret R. Higonnet (Baltimore: Johns Hopkins University Press, 1983), p. 82.

16. Elaine Showalter proposed "that the specificity of women's writing [is] not . . . a transient by-product of sexism but [is] a fundamentally and continually determining reality." "Feminist Criticism in the Wilderness," *Critical Inquiry* 8.2 (Winter 1981): 205.

17. Gayle Rubin, "The Traffic in Women: Notes on the 'Political Economy' of Sex," in *Toward an Anthropology of Women,* ed. Rayna [Rapp] Reiter (New York: Monthly Review Press, 1975), pp. 157–210.

18. Sigmund Freud, "The Psychology of Women" (1933), in *New Introductory Lectures on Psycho-Analysis,* trans. W. J. H. Sprott (New York: W. W. Norton, 1933), p. 184. The same essay is called "Femininity" in *The Standard Edition of the Complete Psychological Works of Sigmund Freud,* vol. 22, trans. James Strachey (London: Hogarth Press and The Institute of Psychoanalysis, 1964).

19. Freud, "The Psychology of Women," p. 158.

20. Rubin, "The Traffic in Women," p. 185.

21. Sherry B. Ortner, "Oedipal Father, Mother's Brother, and the Penis: A Review of Juliet Mitchell's *Psychoanalysis and Feminism,*" *Feminist Studies* 2, 2/3 (1975): 179. As Michele Barrett has remarked, "no substantial work has yet been produced that historicizes the [gendering] processes outlined in psychoanalytic theory." *Women's Oppression Today: Problems in Marxist Feminist Analysis* (London: Verso and New Left Books, 1980), p. 197.

22. Freud, "The Psychology of Women," p. 179. By female masculinity is meant the preoedipal object choice of a female; by femininity is meant the oedipal object choice of a male.

23. Nancy Chodorow, *The Reproduction of Mothering: Psychoanalysis and the Sociology of Gender* (Berkeley: University of California Press, 1978), p. 122.

24. Chodorow summarizes the female's "emotional, if not erotic bisexual oscillation between mother and father — between preoccupation with 'mother-child' issues and

'male-female' issues." *The Reproduction of Mothering*, p. 168. I am indebted to Chodorow for the concept of oscillation.

25. "The asymmetrical structure of parenting generates a female oedipus complex . . . characterized by the continuation of preoedipal attachments and preoccupations, sexual oscillation in an oedipal triangle, and the lack of either absolute change of love object or absolute oedipal resolution." Chodorow, *The Reproduction of Mothering*, pp. 133–34.

26. In an analysis related to my point here, Elizabeth Abel sees the theme and presence of same-sex friendship in literary works by women as an expression of female identity and the particularities of female oedipalization. As well, Abel offers striking remarks on the theory of literary influence that can be derived from Chodorow. "(E)Merging Identities: The Dynamics of Female Friendship in Contemporary Fiction by Women," *Signs* 6.3 (Spring 1981): 413–35.

27. For example, H.D. was psychoanalyzed by Freud, and engaged, according to Susan Friedman, in a constant interior debate with Freud on several issues, including gender. *Psyche Reborn: The Emergence of H.D.* (Bloomington: Indiana University Press, 1981). Virginia Woolf noted her "very amateurish knowledge of Freud and the psychoanalysts" and admitted that "my knowledge is merely from superficial talk." In her circle, however, the talkers might have included James Strachey, the translator of Freud's *Complete Psychological Works*, cited in note 18. *The Letters of Virginia Woolf, Volume Five: 1932–1935*, ed. Nigel Nicolson and Joanne Trautmann (New York: Harcourt Brace Jovanovich, 1979), pp. 36 and 91.

28. Freud, "The Psychology of Women," p. 177.

29. Freud, "The Passing of the Oedipus-Complex," in *Collected Papers*, vol. 2 (London: Hogarth Press, 1957), p. 275. The paper dates from 1924.

30. Virginia Woolf, *Moments of Being*, ed. Jeanne Schulkind (New York: Harcourt Brace Jovanovich, 1978), pp. 132, 129, 132.

31. Simone de Beauvoir, *The Second Sex*, trans. H. M. Parshley (New York: Bantam Books, 1972), p. 47.

32. John Berger, *Ways of Seeing* (New York: Viking Press, 1972), p. 46.

33. Gerda Lerner, *The Majority Finds Its Past: Placing Women in History* (Oxford: Oxford University Press, 1979), pp. xxi, 52.

34. Nancy Cott, "Introduction," in *Root of Bitterness: Documents of the Social History of American Women* (New York: E. P. Dutton, 1972), p. 3.

35. Sheila Rowbotham, *Women's Consciousness, Man's World* (London: Penguin, 1973), pp. 30–31.

36. Alice Walker, "In Search of Our Mothers' Gardens," in *In Search of Our Mothers' Gardens* (San Diego: Harcourt Brace Jovanovich, 1983), p. 235.

37. Virginia Woolf, *Three Guineas* (New York: Harcourt, Brace and World, 1938), p. 5. Abbreviated in the text as *TG*.

38. Virginia Woolf, "The Leaning Tower," in *The Moment and Other Essays* (New York: Harcourt Brace Jovanovich, 1948), p. 154.

39. Raymond Williams, "Base and Superstructure in Marxist Cultural Theory," *New Left Review* 82 (Nov.–Dec. 1973): 7.

40. Raymond Williams, *Marxism and Literature* (Oxford: Oxford University Press, 1977), p. 112.

41. Edwin Ardener, "The 'Problem' Revisited," a coda to "Belief and the Problem of Women," in *Perceiving Women*, ed. Shirley Ardener (New York: John Wiley and Sons, 1975), p. 22. Elaine Showalter made Ardener's analysis available to feminist criticism in "Feminist Criticism in the Wilderness," *Critical Inquiry* 8.2 (Winter 1981), especially pp. 199–201.

42. "Double-consciousness" is, in fact, the influential formulation of black identity made in 1903 by W. E. B. Du Bois in *The Souls of Black Folk* (in *Three Negro Classics*, ed. John Hope Franklin [New York: Avon Books, 1965], p. 215). "It is a peculiar sensation, the double-consciousness, this sense of always looking at one's self through the eyes of others, of measuring one's soul by the tape of a world that looks on in amused contempt and pity. One ever feels his twoness—an American, a Negro; two souls, two thoughts, two unreconciled strivings; two warring ideals in one dark body, whose dogged strength alone keeps it from being torn asunder." Richard Wright made a similar point in 1956: "First of all, my position is a split one, I'm black. I'm a man of the West. These hard facts condition, to some degree, my outlook." (*Presence Africaine* [Nov. 1956], cited in *The Black Writer in Africa and the Americas*, ed. Lloyd W. Brown [Los Angeles: Hennessey and Ingalls, 1973], p. 27).

43. Ellen Moers, *Literary Women: The Great Writers* (Garden City, N.Y.: Doubleday, 1976).

44. Elaine Showalter, *A Literature of Their Own: British Women Novelists from Brontë to Lessing* (Princeton: Princeton University Press, 1977), p. 11. The postulation of "unity" is also generally assumed in this study. However, other perspectives on women's writing might make other assumptions, now that "women's writing" is an accepted critical category.

45. Sandra M. Gilbert and Susan Gubar, *The Madwoman in the Attic: The Woman Writer and the Nineteenth-Century Literary Imagination* (New Haven: Yale University Press, 1979), p. 49.

46. Mary Jacobus, "The Difference of View," in *Women Writing and Writing about Women*, ed. Mary Jacobus (London: Croom Helm, 1979), pp. 19–20.

47. Myra Jehlen's summary of the relationship of women to culture is exemplary. Women (and perhaps some men not of the universal kind) must deal with their situation as a *pre*condition for writing about it. They have to confront the assumptions that render them a kind of fiction in themselves in that they are defined by others, as components of the language and thought of others. It hardly matters at this prior stage what a woman wants to write; its political nature is implicit in the fact that it is she (a "she") who will do it. All women's writing would thus be congenitally defiant and universally characterized by the blasphemous argument it makes in coming into being. And this would mean that the autonomous individuality of a woman's story or poem is framed by engagement, the engagement of its denial of dependence. We might think of the form this necessary denial takes (however it is individually interpreted, whether conciliatory or assertive) as analogous to genre, in being an issue, not of content, but of the structural formulation of the work's relationship to

the inherently formally patriarchal language which is the only language we have. ("Archimedes," p. 582)

The proposal this book makes for the "structural formulation" analogous to genre is the act of critique, drawing on the oscillations of female identity.

48. The sex-gender system involves a linked chain of institutions such as the sexual division of labor in production and in the socialization of children, valorized heterosexuality and the constraint on female sexuality, marriage and kinship, sexual choice and desire, gender asymmetry and polarization.

49. We have omitted a closing "survey of several contemporary works," which shows "how the critique of story is not only a thematic fact but an indication of the moral, ideological, and political desire to rescript the novel" (DuPlessis). — Editors

17

The Documentary Novel and the Problem
of Borders · BARBARA FOLEY

The documentary novel constitutes a distinct fictional kind. It locates itself near the border between factual discourse and fictive discourse, but it does not propose an eradication of that border. Rather, it purports to represent reality by means of agreed-upon conventions of fictionality, while grafting onto its fictive pact some kind of additional claim to empirical validation. Historically, this claim has taken various forms. The pseudofactual novel of the seventeenth and eighteenth centuries simulates or imitates the authentic testimony of a "real life" person; its documentary effect derives from the assertion of veracity. The historical novel of the nineteenth century takes as its referent a phase of the historical process; its documentary effect derives from the assertion of extratextual verification. The documentary novel in the modernist era bifurcates into two distinct genres. The fictional autobiography represents an artist-hero who assumes the status of a real person inhabiting an invented situation; its documentary effect derives from the assertion of the artist's claim to privileged cognition. The metahistorical novel takes as its referent a historical process that evades rational formulation; its documentary effect derives from the assertion of the very indeterminacy of factual verification. Finally, the Afro-American documentary novel represents a reality submitting human subjects to racist objectification; its documentary effect derives from the presentation of facts that subvert commonplace constructions of reality. In all its phases, then, the documentary novel aspires to tell the truth, and it associates this truth with claims to empirical validation. If it increasingly calls into question the possibility of truth-telling, this skepticism is directed more toward the ideological assumptions undergirding empiricism than toward the capacity of fictive discourse to interpret and represent its referent.

Clearly the documentary novel, as I define it in this book, is not a minor subgenre that can be readily relegated to the margins of novelistic production in any given era. On the contrary: in the seventeenth and eighteenth centuries, the documentary novel is closely aligned with writing that Lennard J. Davis calls the "news/novel discourse";[1] in the nineteenth century, the documentary novel intersects with the major tradition of realism; in the early decades of the twentieth century, it participates in the principal concerns of modernism. Much writing in the entire domain of Afro-American prose fiction has a pronounced documentary quality. Thus central texts from each phase in the history of the novel (for example, *Moll Flanders, Pamela, Waverley, Henry Esmond, Orlando, A Portrait of the Artist as a Young Man, Native Son*) can be adjudged to be documentary novels. But while the documentary novel overlaps with the mainstream tradition of the novel, it is not identical with this tradition. Rather, the documentary novel is distinguished by its insistence that it contains some kind of specific and verifiable link to the historical world. (Whether or not this link succeeds in being "extratextual" in a larger sense remains to be seen.) It implicitly claims to replicate certain features of actuality in a relatively direct and unmediated fashion; it invokes familiar novelistic conventions, but it requires the reader to accept certain textual elements — characters, incidents, or actual documents — as possessing referents in the world of the reader. The documentary novel is not superior to other modes of fictional discourse in its capacity for assertion — all fictions assert their propositional content with equal force and sincerity, I believe — but it does raise the problem of reference for explicit consideration. To investigate the truth-telling claims of the documentary novel is thus to illuminate the assertive capacities of fiction in general.

. . . Factual and fictive discourses are not immutable essences but are historically varying types of writing, signaled by, and embodied in, changing literary conventions and generated by the changing structures of historically specific relations of production and intercourse. As M. M. Bakhtin has remarked, "The boundaries between fiction and nonfiction, between literature and nonliterature and so forth are not laid up in heaven. Every specific situation is historical. And the growth of literature is not merely development and change within the fixed boundaries of any definition; the boundaries themselves are constantly changing."[2] In examining the documentary novel's protean identity, I have had to abandon many prior conceptions about what constitutes fiction, the novel, history, and the elusive quality that I am terming the "documentary" effect. Modes of discourse do not remain within "fixed boundaries"; they change as much as do the modes of social and political representation in the worlds that they take as their referents.

I have discovered, nonetheless, that the distinction between fictional discourse and its various nonfictional counterparts — history, journalism, biography, autobiography—has remained a qualitative one. The need to distinguish between narratives held to be imaginary and those held to be directly representational would seem to be not a post-Cartesian phenomenon, testifying to the alienation of subject from object, but an abiding feature of discursive production. Even in the seventeenth and eighteenth centuries, when the documentary novel possessed its most ambiguous generic identity, the issue was not that prose fiction simply blended into purportedly veracious kinds of writing but that its primary locus, the romance, could not effectively assert the kind of truth that the early pseudofactual novelists wanted to tell. The pseudofactual novel's ambiguous generic status does not mean that writers and readers of the time inhabited an ontological haze but that they felt obliged to simulate veracious discourses if they hoped to appear credible to their readers. To say, as Bakhtin does, that the borderline between fiction and nonfiction is "constantly changing" does not mean that writers have not routinely respected such a borderline; it means, on the contrary, that writers have composed their fictions in contradistinction to one or more acknowledged forms of nonfictional writing. Fiction, I would propose, is intrinsically part of a binary opposition; it is what it is by virtue of what it is not.

. . . In this prolegomenon to my central theoretical and historical discussions, I shall confront the principal claims of my adversaries by arguing on logical grounds for the superiority of a qualitative view of mimesis. (By "qualitative" I mean different in kind rather than in degree.) In so doing, I run the risk of appearing to endorse an ahistorical or essentialist view of mimesis. Certainly it is true, as we shall see, that many defenses of the uniqueness of mimesis do in fact reify the realms of fictional and nonfictional discourse and deny their continually altering character. I believe, however, that a qualitative approach to the matter of defining fictionality is consonant with the premises of a materialist literary theory, so long as we remember that binary oppositions are dialectical oppositions as well.[3]

The view that fictional and nonfictional discourse cannot be qualitatively distinguished ordinarily rests on one of three arguments. The first of these, which I shall term the "spectrum" argument, centers on the claim that the significant qualities of factuality and fictionality inhere in separate facets of a literary work, rather than in any informing paradigm, and that the task of criticism is to assess the impact of these upon the work's rhetorical effect. Thus Paul Hernadi advocates a "microstructural theory of poetic discourse," which holds that any given literary work possesses aspects of various discourses and should be analyzed not as a text unified by a single generic frame but as a unity of multiple components reflecting the richness of literary discourse in general. Hernadi repudiates the investigation of "generic conventions as reflections of historically conditioned preferences of writers and readers." Instead, he asserts, "The finest generic classifications of our time make us look beyond their immediate concerns and focus on the order of literature, not on borders between literary genres."[4] Scholes and Kellogg, in *The Nature of Narrative*, reach a similar conclusion from the opposite direction, for they insist that it is such "historically conditioned preferences" that furnish the logical basis for a nonqualitative definition of mimesis. The novel has historically synthesized two narrative impulses, they argue, one directed toward the "empirical," or historical, and the other directed toward the "fictional," or imaginary. Empirical and fictional are blended tendencies, rather than distinctive kinds; history and fantasy stand as the poles of a narrative spectrum, with different narrative forms such as autobiography, realism, and romance occupying positions at various points along the scale. The "recording of specific fact, the representation of what resembles specific fact, and the representation of generalized types of actuality," declare Scholes and Kellogg, are all to be aligned along the empirical part of the narrative spectrum.[5]

A second type of nonqualitative argument, which I shall term the "family resemblance" argument, is based upon an invocation—albeit somewhat simplified—of Ludwig Wittgenstein's theory of linguistic reference. In his discussion of the definitive characteristics of concepts such as games, Wittgenstein points out the difficulties involved in the attempt to delineate a limited set of criteria that descriptively include all activities commonly held to be games and exclude all other activities: "Consider for example the proceedings we call 'games.' . . . What is common to them all? — Don't say, there *must* be something common, or they would not be called '*games*' — but *look* and *see* whether there is anything common to all. For if you look at them you will not see something that is common to *all*, but similarities, relationships, and a whole series at that." Drawing an analogy between games and the physical traits shared by the members of the same family, Wittgenstein concludes, "We see a complicated network of similarities overlapping and crisscrossing; sometimes overall similarities, sometimes similarities of detail."[6] For Wittgenstein, no fixed set of properties defines the term "game," just as no fixed set of physical characteristics is shared by all members of the same family. For Wittgenstein, language seduces us into believing that certain words denote actually existing sets of relations, when all that these words really denote is concepts used to order the world of things.

Applied to the problem of defining mimesis, the "family resemblance" argument proposes that qualitative distinctions between factual and fictional discourse are founded upon fallacious logic. Morris Weitz, for example, invokes Wittgenstein when he asserts that all aesthetic categories, including the theory of literary kinds, are concepts with blurred edges and that it is therefore impossible to formulate a clear description of mimetic discourse. Asking himself whether an experimental fiction utilizing new kinds of referential procedures can be classified as a "novel," he observes, "What is at stake here is no factual analysis concerning necessary and sufficient properties but a decision as to whether the work under examination is similar in certain respects to other works, already called 'novels,' and consequently warrants the extension of the concept to cover the new case." Every such classificatory decision is, however, necessarily an ad hoc decision:

> "Art," itself, is an open concept. New conditions (cases) have constantly arisen and will undoubtedly constantly arise; new art forms, new movements will emerge, which will demand decisions on the part of those interested, usually professional critics, as to whether the concept should be extended or not. . . . Art, as the logic of the concept shows, has no set of necessary and sufficient properties, hence a theory of it is logically impossible and not merely factually difficult.[7]

Charles Stevenson, also invoking Wittgenstein, introduces a mathematical model to solve the problem of fictional classification. Since fictionality is signaled by a multiplicity of possibly relevant textual properties, he argues, and since no fictional work will possess all the traits associated with mimesis, fictional representation consists of a "weighted average" of mimetic elements.[8] According to Stevenson, an arithmetical computation of discernible features will yield the basis for a definitive decision about a text's qualification for membership in the class of fictions. The "family resemblance" argument claims for itself the virtues of both historicity and empirical precision: to posit a fixed set of fictional features violates not only the course of literary-historical development but also the diversity of features present in any given fictional text.

Proponents of the spectrum and family resemblance approaches to generic definition quite correctly alert us to the danger of taking fictionality to reside in an immutable set of textual properties. But their arguments are only superficially empirical and historicist. The spectrum argument conflates the necessary recognition of historical shifts in the mimetic contract with the impossibility of logical classification, thereby precluding any inquiry into the historically varying epistemological bases of generic distinctions. Scholes and Kellogg quite rightly point out that the various modes of fictional, historical, and autobiographical discourse have adopted conventions signaled by widely varying textual features, and they convincingly demonstrate that certain markers of generic identity have even reversed their functions: the unwitnessed monologue, now a sure indicator of an author's fictional intentions, was once, they show, an accepted convention of heroic history. But a recognition of the relative—that is, historically variable—nature of the fact/fiction opposition does not mean that this opposition is denied absolute status at any given historical juncture. A spectrum of empirical possibilities is not the same thing as a spectrum of discursive kinds. As Barbara Herrnstein Smith puts it, "There is no principle of relative differentiation that could allow us to speak of any given composition as 'more' or 'less' fictive . . . and thereby assign it its proper place on the continuum. The distinction between natural and fictive is absolute."[9] The spectrum argument ends up treating generic categorization as a framework imposed a posteriori by literary critics, ruling out the possibility that it may constitute a necessary basis for the contracts formed between actual writers and readers.

The central problem with the family resemblance argument is that it treats all textual elements as having an equal claim upon the reader's attention, with no single trait being privileged by convention or authorial intention to exercise a dominant influence in the reader's apprehension of the text's generic identity. The text is, quite simply, the sum of its parts; if these parts cannot add up to a sufficient total, then the text is not recognizable as a member of the family of fictions. But to maintain that separate elements in factual or fictive works signal a certain family resemblance does not imply that qualitatively defined sets of relations among these elements cannot also be uncovered. Concepts with blurred edges are not necessarily concepts that lack a principle of unity; indeed, as Wittgenstein himself pointed out, concepts such as "games," while not readily definable in descriptive terms, are easily definable in practice, since clearly people know when they are playing games and when they are not. Wittgenstein's "insight into the looseness of our concepts, and its attendant jargon of 'family resemblance,'" remarks John Searle, "should not lead us into a rejection of the very enterprise of philosophical analysis."[10]

The third type of nonqualitative argument—the one developed recently with the most vehemence—has come from poststructuralist critics, who, invoking Nietzsche, propose that all our discourses about the material world, both factual and fictive, are circumscribed by the texts we construe in relation to that world. The very act of formulating an explanatory scheme is, for Barthes and Derrida, an enterprise inevitably shaped by language and ideology and is therefore fictive, in effect if not in intent. The project of criticism should not be to perpetuate the metaphysical dualisms of Western thought—among which the opposition of fiction and nonfiction figures centrally—but to reveal the inadequacy of reductive binary oppositions that privilege the products of the "creative" imagination, relegate (non)fiction to the margins of discourse, and ignore the textuality of all writing. Thus Roland Barthes has argued that "the only feature which distinguishes historical discourse from other kinds is a paradox: the 'fact' can exist linguistically only as a term in a discourse, yet we behave as if it were a simple reproduction of something on another plane of existence altogether, some extra-structural 'reality.' Historical discourse is presumably the only kind which aims at a referent "outside" itself that can in fact never be reached." Historical discourse is, therefore, a "fake performative, in which what claims to be the descriptive element is in fact only the expression of the authoritarian nature of that particular speech-act."[11] For Barthes, the insistence upon a referent beyond textuality is not simply a gesture of epistemological naïveté: it is an act of political repression.

Derrida develops the militantly antigeneric implications of Barthes's argument. The formulation of the binary opposition fiction/nonfiction produces, for Derrida, a "hierarchical axiology" that presupposes "an origin or . . . a 'priority' held to be simple, intact, normal, pure, standard, self-identical."[12] One aspect of the opposition (in this case, fiction) is implicitly valorized, and the other (nonfiction) is defined by subordination or exclusion—that is, by nonidentity. A deconstruction of such metaphysical categories reveals that what is excluded constitutes much more than nonidentity and that identity itself—as a pure essence beyond difference—is a specious category. When brought to bear upon the theory of discursive genres, the deconstructive project therefore reveals that

the law of the law of genre . . . is a principle of contamination. . . . The trait that marks membership inevitably divides; the boundary of the set comes to form . . . an internal pocket larger than the whole; and the outcome of this division and of this overflowing remains as singular as it is limitless. . . . The principle of genre is unclassifiable, it tolls the knell of the . . . classicum, of what permits one to call out orders and to order, the manifold without a nomenclature. . . . [Genre designation] gathers together the corpus and, at the same time . . . keeps it from closing, from identifying itself with itself. This axiom of non-closure or non-fulfillment enfolds within itself the condition for the possibility and the impossibility of taxonomy.[13]

For Derrida, the very attempt to formulate genre distinctions is undermined by the subversive nature of writing, which interpenetrates among the epistemological categories that ideology sets up to delineate its terrain.

We may be grateful to Derridean deconstruction for calling our attention to the ideological agenda that is inevitably attached to the binary opposition fiction/nonfiction. . . . The common valorization of "creative" or "imaginative" writing does frequently imply a fetishization of mimetic discourse and a positivist reduction of nonfictional discourse to the unmediated reportage of "what is." But, while I would certainly agree with Barthes that historical discourse is in its way as saturated in ideology as is mimetic discourse, I would not therefore conclude that historical and mimetic discourse adopt equivalent representational procedures or constitute equivalent modes of cognition. And while I would grant Derrida's point that Western philosophy is pervaded by abstract and ahistorical oppositions that, in the guise of reflecting transcendent essences, naturalize dominant ideology, I would not therefore conclude that all inherited cognitive oppositions are equally ideological and equally fallacious. Some oppositions — between fact and fiction, for instance — describe very real (and, I believe, necessary) cognitive operations, in which actual historical people engage and have engaged. Indeed, the Derridean project itself is hardly exempt from the practice of binary opposition. Its universe is unremittingly dualistic, with the forces of logocentrism, homogeneity, and repression locked in combat with those of différance, heterogeneity, and dispersal. If we recognize, as surely we must, that certain binary oppositions have been used to legitimate a hierarchical social order, the solution is not to jettison binary opposition altogether but to formulate a binary opposition to class dominance that will carry political force. In this effort, it is not helpful to argue that all discourses are fictions or that the goal of criticism is to formulate, in Derrida's words, "undecidables" that "can no longer be included within philosophical (binary) opposition, but which, however, inhabit philosophical opposition, resisting and disorganizing it, *without ever* constituting a third term."[14] The refusal to constitute a third term cannot go very far toward dislodging the "hierarchical axiology."

It should be apparent that, when one argues for a qualitative definition of fictionality, much more than the classification of discourse is involved: at stake, ultimately, is a whole debate about the relation between—and the context of—perception and cognition. I have no wish here to extend this debate. To support my assertion that fictional and nonfictional discourses are distinguishable not in degree but in kind, however, I would point out that most twentieth-century theories of cognition—in fields from psychology to the philosophy of science to linguistics—have found it necessary to postulate that the human mind characteristically uses polarity as an essential device in gaining understanding. Any given particular must be understood as part of a larger scheme, these theories tell us, if it is to be considered at all. The possible relevance of such theories to the problem of defining fictionality should be clear: the genres of fictional discourse engage informing paradigms qualitatively different from those of the various genres of nonfictional discourse, and even a presumably verifiable fact must be framed and contextualized before its signification can be determined.

From the field of Gestalt psychology, for example, we learn that perception ordinarily operates within qualitative and totalizing frames of reference. The rabbit-duck drawing, Gestalt psychologists would tell us, has two possible, and mutually exclusive, interpretations—it is either a rabbit or a duck. The viewer can readily enough grasp both perceptual possibilities but can process only one scheme at any particular instant. Any given detail in the drawing makes sense as part of either ordering scheme, but it demands wholly different interpretations when it is "read" from each perspective. Only a prior conventional context, external to the object of perception, can provide decisive criteria for adjudging the correctness of one or another interpretation. It is impossible, concludes E. H. Gombrich of this notorious example, to see "what is 'really there,' to see the shape apart from its interpretation."[15] There are no innocent perceptions: if perception is to produce cognition, it must invoke a framework of prior assumptions about what is being seen.

Gregory Bateson and Erving Goffman have argued that a great variety of human behaviors can be explained by means of the Gestalt model. Bateson proposes that, in activities such as play, fantasy, and psychotherapy, the participants agree upon "psychological frames" that perform a "metacommunicative function," giving the receiver "instructions or aids in his attempt to understand the messages included within the frame."[16] Psychological frames are, moreover, both exclusive and inclusive, excluding certain messages by including others and vice versa: according to Bateson, Gestalt paradigms are necessary for the unambiguous signaling of complex and overdetermined meanings. Goffman examines the operations of all sorts of social codes — from body language to advertising — in terms of what he calls "primary frameworks": "Each primary framework allows its user to locate, perceive, identify and label a seemingly infinite number of concrete occurrences defined in its terms. [The user] is likely to be unaware of such organized features as the framework has and unable to describe the framework with any completeness if asked, yet these handicaps are no bar to his easily and fully applying it."[17] Primary frameworks can also be transformed, or "keyed," in such a way that almost all the elements in the original activity signal an entirely new meaning when incorporated into a keyed context. Keying involves an agreement among the parties involved to bracket the keyed activity, pretending to follow the rules of the primary framework but actually following a set of very different rules. For Bateson and Goffman, then, the entire range of human behavior, serious and playful, is regulated by conventions that bear a "metacommunicative" relation to any given activity. An activity is understood as a *kind of thing*, and it is defined largely by contradistinction to what it is not.

Turning to the field of the philosophy of science, we may note that it has become axiomatic that scientists ordinarily hypothesize generalizations and then seek out the evidence that would validate, qualify, or refute those generalizations. Early bourgeois science proposed that human beings characteristically construct conceptual categories on the basis of inductively accumulated experience — a procedure that results, in Hume's words, in "that *perfect* habit, which makes us conclude in general, that instances, of which we have no experience, must necessarily resemble those of which we have."[18] T. S. Kuhn, by contrast, cautions that "no natural history can be interpreted in the absence of at least some implicit body of intertwined theoretical and methodological belief that permits selection, evaluation, and criticism."[19] Karl Popper, who sees the growth of scientific knowledge as a process of "conjecture and refutation," holds that the mind intrinsically possesses the "expectation of finding a regularity."[20] Michael Polanyi, rejecting those versions of Gestalt psychology that describe the perceiver as a passive receiver of preformed paradigms, declares, "I am looking at Gestalt . . . as the outcome of . . . an active shaping of experience performed in the pursuit of knowledge."[21] For these theorists, the scientific method consists in the constant evaluation of explanatory frames. Particulars do not yield up their meaning; they need to be located within a qualitatively defined larger scheme if they are to possess value as evidence.

Finally, it bears noting that such concepts as "tacit knowledge" and "primary frameworks" bear a distinct resemblance to Noam Chomsky's theory of linguistic competence, which posits that native speakers of a language are governed by an "abstract system underlying behavior, a system constituted by rules that interact to determine the form and intrinsic meaning of a potentially infinite number of sentences."[22] The process of acquiring language therefore means that "a child must devise a hypothesis compatible with presented data — he must select from the store of potential grammars a specific one that is appropriate to the data available to him."[23] Whenever a speaker utters a statement, then, he or she is invoking a "deep structure" that is the basis for the statement's being coherent and comprehensible (even if the statement is new to the listener). The goal of the study of the "universal grammar" of language, Chomsky concludes, is not simply to illuminate the procedures of language acquisition and communication; it is nothing less than the discovery of the general properties of human intelligence.[24]

These various descriptions of the relation of perception to cognition could, I suppose, be taken as evidence that human intelligence can never know reality, but that it merely imposes its fictions on what it encounters. In my view, however, their implication is quite different. There is no reason to suppose that facts are created by interpretations if they are bound to them. We are free to see a duck or a rabbit, but not a giraffe; the Gestalt figure is not a Rorschach inkblot. The Copernican view of the solar system did not construct the data that rendered it a more powerful explanatory model than the Ptolemaic system. Nor is there any reason to conclude that any given "primary framework" or "tacit knowledge" or "deep structure" constitutes innate or transhistorical knowledge of a Kantian or Jungian kind. The human mind may have certain innate proclivities, but these are necessarily enacted through cognitive frames that are preeminently social constructs: the manifold variations in past and present human behavior testify to the embeddedness of any given conceptualization in a highly changeable social reality. These theories of cognition and language simply suggest that human intelligence characteristically operates in a configurational and —

indeed—binary manner. Particulars must be grasped as functional components in qualitatively defined totalities—and excluded from other possible totalities—if they are to be grasped at all.

. . .

Both fictional discourse and nonfictional discourse make use of totalizing frames analogous to those explicitly formulated by psychology, linguistics, and the philosophy of science. Any given element in a narrative . . . must be scanned and interpreted as either factual or fictive in order to be read and understood. There is no specifically linguistic essence of fictionality that is immediately perceptible in the particulars of a text. As Victor Lange aptly puts it,

> Whether or not we are in the presence of a fictional field is . . . a matter of contextual analysis; it cannot be recognized unless we examine the specific aesthetic and logical uses to which the facts that sustain it have been put. The quality of the fact itself, whether it is related to any presumed actuality or is fanciful and non-realistic, is of little concern for the determination of the fictional mode. The invented speeches in Tacitus are clearly part of a non-fictional intention; the actual letter which Rilke incorporated in *Malte Laurids Brigge* assumes, within the purposes of the novel, a distinctly fictional character.[25]

The writer assumes that the reader will possess the "competence" to know how to understand each particular, and that the "tacit knowledge" undergirding this competence is the knowledge of generic conventions shared by writer and reader alike. The nonfictional and fictional Gestalts employed by Tacitus and Rilke, respectively, are a function of the primary frameworks shared by readers of modern novels and ancient histories. I am arguing, in short, for a definition of mimesis as a contract, wherein writer and reader share an agreement about the conditions under which texts can be composed and comprehended. Even when writers take quantitative steps toward altering the terms of this agreement, they do so in the context of qualitatively defined discursive conventions. And the essence of mimesis—for it has an essence, *pace* Derrida and company—is that it is a social practice, whereby authors impart cognition of a particular kind to their readers.

The documentary novel, accordingly, is a species of fiction distinctly characterized by its adherence to referential strategies associated with nonfictional modes of discourse but also demanding to be read within a fictional Gestalt familiar to contemporaneous readers. Its dramatically altering strategies of representation do not mean that fictional discourse and nonfictional discourse are indistinguishable; they point instead to the changing terms of the fictional contract in different social formations. . . .

Notes

1. Lennard J. Davis, *Factual Fictions: The Origins of the English Novel* (New York: Columbia University Press, 1983).

2. M. M. Bakhtin, *The Dialogic Imagination: Four Essays*, ed. Michael Holquist, trans. Caryl Emerson and Michael Holquist (Austin: University of Texas Press, 1981), p. 33.

3. In chapters 1 to 4 of *Telling the Truth*, I frequently cite — and dispute — the views of critics who use the term "literature" or "poetry" where I use the term "fiction" or "mimesis." I am aware that this procedure may appear imprecise. The term "poetry," of course, often refers to verse; the term "literature" can be taken either as an honorific term denoting the quality of a text or as a highly general term denoting the whole province of "imaginative" writing — thus including a good deal of history, biography, autobiography, and journalism. In the discussions that follow, I have tried to adhere as closely as possible to the intentions of the critics cited: I have not adduced in support of my argument an opposition between "literature" and "nonliterature," for example, when its author means a distinction between "serious" and "popular" writing. It would have been incorrect, however, to confine my debates to those critics who use the terms "fiction" and "nonfiction," since critics often do mean "fictionality" when they discuss the essential feature(s) of "literary" or "poetic" discourse. For more on the definition of "literature," see the various essays in Paul Hernadi's collection *What Is Literature?* (Bloomington: Indiana University Press, 1978); Raymond Williams, *Marxism and Literature* (Oxford: Oxford University Press, 1977), pp. 45–54; and Tzvetan Todorov, "The Notion of Literature," *New Literary History* 5 (Autumn 1973): 5–16. Note, also, that I use the term "mimesis" interchangeably with "fiction." Some theorists would include under the rubric of mimesis any discourse purporting to represent reality (that is, history, biography, autobiography, and so forth) but would exclude fictions of the more romantic or fantastic variety.

4. Paul Hernadi, *Beyond Genre: New Directions in Literary Classification* (Ithaca: Cornell University Press, 1972), p. 184.

5. Robert Scholes and Robert Kellogg, *The Nature of Narrative* (New York: Oxford University Press, 1969), pp. 86–87.

6. Ludwig Wittgenstein, *Philosophical Investigations*, 3d ed., trans. G. E. M. Anscombe (New York: Macmillan, 1956), 1:secs. 66–69.

7. Morris Weitz, "The Role of Theory in Aesthetics," *Journal of Aesthetics and Art Criticism* 15 (Sept. 1956): 28, 32.

8. Charles Stevenson, "On 'What Is a Poem?'" *Philosophical Review* 66 (July 1957): 329–62. Also see N. W. Visser, "The Generic Identity of the Novel," *Novel* 2 (Winter 1978): 101–14. For a persuasive critique of the application of the "family resemblance" concept to logical problems in aesthetic theory, see Maurice Mandelbaum, "Family Resemblances and Generalization Concerning the Arts," in *Problems in Aesthetics: An*

Introductory Book of Readings, ed. Morris Weitz, 2d ed. (London: Macmillan, 1970), pp. 181–98. Mandelbaum argues that "family resemblance" theorists err in their focus upon "manifest features" rather than upon "relational attributes," which would require the critic to "consider specific art objects as having been created by someone for some actual or possible audience" (p. 187). In mathematics, as Stevenson observes, the quantitative approach to generic definition entails a repudiation of set theory. See Abraham Kaplan and H. F. Schott, "A Calculus for Empirical Classes," *Methods* 3 (1951): 165–90.

9. Barbara Herrnstein Smith, "On the Margins of Discourse," *Critical Inquiry* 1 (June 1975): 774. For a penetrating discussion of the changing boundary between autobiography and the novel, a distinction that is "dependent on distinctions between fiction and nonfiction, between rhetorical and empirical first-person narrative," see Elizabeth Bruss, *Autobiographical Acts: The Changing Situation of a Literary Genre* (Baltimore: Johns Hopkins University Press, 1976), 5–18.

10. John R. Searle, *Speech Acts: An Essay in the Philosophy of Language* (Cambridge: Cambridge University Press, 1970), 55. According to John M. Ellis, Wittgenstein's theory of language, properly understood, leads to the conclusion that literature can be qualitatively described by means of a "functional" definition. "When we seek a definition," he argues, "what we are seeking is not a statement of the feature held in common by the members of the category, but the appropriate circumstances for the use of the word and the features of those circumstances that determine the willingness or unwillingness of the speakers of the language to use the word" (*The Theory of Literary Criticism: A Logical Analysis* [Berkeley: University of California Press, 1974], p. 34). Weitz is a crude Wittgensteinian, Ellis implies, for Weitz takes the impossibility of definition as the alternative to referential definition. The value of Ellis's theory is diminished, however, by his adherence to a nonassertive view of mimesis: the functionality of literary works, it turns out, consists in their being "used by society in such a way that the text is not taken as specifically relevant to the immediate context of its origin" (p. 43).

11. Roland Barthes, "Historical Discourse," in *Introduction to Structuralism*, ed. Michael Lane (New York: Basic, 1970), pp. 153, 154–55. For an instance of the political rhetoric that critics sympathetic with poststructuralism frequently attach to their discussions of the fact/fiction distinction, compare Suzanne Gearhart: "[All theories of literature and all theories of history] have consistently sought to fix the boundary between them and to establish once and for all the specificity of the fields in one of two ways: democratically, in that each accepts a mutually agreed on boundary which grants to each its own identity and integrity; or, just as often, imperialistically, in that each tries to extend its own boundary and to invade, engulf, or encompass the other. . . . In the second [case, the other genre] is overcome, cannibalized, incorporated into the sameness of the imperializing field" (*The Open Boundary of History and Fiction: A Critical Approach to the French Enlightenment* [Princeton: Princeton University Press, 1984], p. 4).

12. Jacques Derrida, "Limited Inc abc," in *Glyph: Johns Hopkins Textual Studies* 2 (Baltimore: Johns Hopkins University Press, 1977), p. 236. See also *Positions*, trans. Alan Bass (Chicago: University of Chicago Press, 1981), pp. 39–47.

13. Derrida, "The Law of Genre," quoted in Michael Ryan, *Marxism and Deconstruction: A Critical Articulation* (Baltimore: Johns Hopkins University Press, 1982), p. 19.

14. Derrida, *Positions*, p. 43. See also my "The Politics of Deconstruction," in the special issue "Deconstruction at Yale," *Genre* 17 (Spring–Summer 1984): 113–34.

15. E. H. Gombrich, *Art and Illusion: A Study in the Psychology of Pictorial Representation* (Princeton: Princeton University Press, 1960), p. 5.

16. Gregory Bateson, "A Theory of Play and Fantasy," in his *Steps to an Ecology of Mind: Collected Essays in Anthropology, Psychiatry, Evolution, and Epistemology* (San Francisco: Chandler, 1972), pp. 187–88. For more on the relations among Gestalt frames, play and fantasy, and fictionality, see Kendall L. Walton, "Fearing Fictions," *Journal of Philosophy* 75 (Jan. 1978): 5–27.

17. Erving Goffman, *Frame Analysis: An Essay on the Organization of Experience* (Cambridge, Mass.: Harvard University Press, 1976), p. 21.

18. David Hume, *Treatise of Human Nature*, ed. L. A. Selby-Bigge (Oxford: Clarendon, 1907), p. 135. For more on Hume's inductive argument, see also 1:3, vi and 1:3, xii.

19. T. S. Kuhn, *The Structure of Scientific Revolutions*, 2d ed. (Chicago: University of Chicago Press, 1970), pp. 16–17.

20. Karl Popper, *Conjectures and Refutations: The Growth of Scientific Knowledge* (New York: Basic, 1962), p. 47.

21. Michael Polanyi, *The Tacit Dimension* (Garden City, N.Y.: Doubleday, 1966), p. 6. In citing Polanyi, Kuhn, and Popper, I do not mean to imply that I endorse the particular theories of scientific method and development that these philosophers have evolved. I am simply noting the fact that modern philosophers of science of widely varying ideological orientations, neopositivist to intuitionist, have all found it necessary to posit that thought cannot take place in the absence of informing paradigms into which data — even anomalous data — must be incorporated. For a critique of both Popper's rationalism and Kuhn's irrationalism, see Larry Laudan, *Progress and Its Problems: Toward a Theory of Scientific Growth* (Berkeley: University of California Press, 1977).

22. Noam Chomsky, *Language and Mind* (New York: Harcourt, Brace & World, 1968), p. 62.

23. Noam Chomsky, *Aspects of the Theory of Syntax* (Cambridge, Mass.: MIT Press, 1965), p. 36.

24. Chomsky, *Language and Mind*, p. 24. For an application of Chomsky's theory of "deep structure" to the problem of mobilizing and perceiving generic distinction in imaginative literature, see Sheldon Sacks, "The Psychological Implications of Generic Distinction," *Genre* 1 (1968): 106–15.

25. Victor Lange, "The Fact in Fiction," *Comparative Literature Studies* 6 (Sept. 1969): 260. For other theories of fictional discourse explicitly invoking the concept of Gestalt, see Smith, 775–76; Ralph W. Rader, "The Concept of Genre in Eighteenth-Century Studies," in *New Approaches to Eighteenth-Century Literature: Selected Papers from the English Institute* (New York: Columbia University Press, 1974), pp. 84–86; and Norman Friedman, *Form and Meaning in Fiction* (Athens: University of Georgia Press, 1975), pp. 196–97.

Politics, Literary Form, and a Feminist Poetics
of the Novel · JOANNE S. FRYE

I

As a genre, the novel is of initial interest to feminist critics because it has
some rather direct links to the kinds of discourse used in people's daily lives
and, therefore, to both interpretations and reinterpretations of women's
lives. Four prominent qualities of the novel suggest its direct connection to
life experiences: its narrative form, its flexibility, its popularity, and its concern with the individual. As a narrative form, the novel is closely tied to the
multiple narrative processes by which human beings daily shape their experience. As a flexible form, it is rather immediately responsive to patterns of
cultural change. As a popular form, it is capable of speaking to and for
people in their ordinary daily living. And as a form based in individual
experience, it is especially able to seek out new interpretations of experience
that defy the "normal." Each of these qualities participates in an initial view
of the novel as related to lived experience and peculiarly open to gender-
based interpretation.

Consider, first, the centrality of narrative to both the novel and the daily
storytelling by which people often make sense of their experience. As anthropologists have made us acutely aware, the need to narrate is an apparently pervasive human need: the need to tell stories, hear stories, read stories; the need to make sense of lived experience through setting events in
narrative relationship to each other. We use narrative to assess cause and
effect in a pattern of significance, to relate ourselves to a sense of purpose, to
claim a shared reality with other people, and to identify a specificity and a
continuity of self through memory. In short we use the process of creating
narrative shape to identify our place in the world.[1]

The need children often feel at the end of the day not just to hear a

An introductory section on theoretical issues in American feminist criticism has been
omitted. — Editors

bedtime story but also to tell the events of their own day is precisely this narrative need to give meaning and pattern to those events. Doris Lessing represents this life narrative situation vividly in her characterization of a conversation between Anna Wulf and her daughter Janet in *The Golden Notebook*. The familiar childhood plea, "Tell me a story," prompts Anna to respond, "There once was a little girl called Janet" and to proceed with the tale of "how this little girl went to school on a rainy day, did lessons, played with the other children, quarrelled with her friend." The sequence continues as, in Anna's words, "Janet eats dreamily, . . . listening while I create her day, give it form."[2] The entire process, giving form to an ordinary day, is crucial to Janet's evolving self-awareness: her attempt to place herself in the world and assess her experiences as part of a meaningful pattern.

Lessing thus draws on the common awareness of children's need for narrative pattern, their primary human relationship to storytelling. The significance of this form giving in the novel—Anna's knowledge that she creates Janet's day by giving it form—is doubly powerful because Anna herself, in recording this experience in her journal, is shaping her own experience as she tells of having shaped Janet's. Her journal serves for her the same function that the story serves for Janet. Through narrative construction, both Janet and Anna are assessing their personal experiences; through narrative construction they engage in the human process of meaning making. In doing so, they have "created" their experience as a part of an interpretive construct.

Such construction is accomplished in large measure through the identification of perceived beginnings and endings, for we assess our current situation in terms of its previous causes and its projected effects. People interpret and even choose their courses of action according to their anticipated ends: projected "conclusions" such as graduation, marriage, separations, departures, births, and deaths. All such demarcating events, in anticipation, shape the human choices prior to them and, in retrospect, shape the understanding of subsequent human experiences. Narrative construction, built as it is on the interpretation of cause and effect, beginnings and endings, becomes a primary means by which we decide what constitutes a cause or effect, a beginning or an ending. Ulric Neisser's assessment of the general process of cognition implicitly identifies how narrative becomes a cognitive instrument in our daily lives: "When we choose one *action* rather than another the embedding schema usually includes some anticipation of our own future situation; like a cognitive map it contains the ego."[3] We act, that is, according to our narrative construction of experience, future as well as past. As Barbara Hardy puts it, "In order really to live, we make up stories about ourselves and others, about the personal as well as the social past and future."[4] We create experiential narratives as a way of understanding or *making* a relationship among the events in our lives.

Narrative can thus be claimed as a crucial human means for understanding lived experience, what Louis Mink explicitly calls the "cognitive" function of narrative.[5] Although cultures vary widely in their perceptions of reality and in the symbolic systems by which they make experiences perceptible, there are no known cultures which lack storytelling as a participant in those systems. As Mink puts it, "story-telling is the most ubiquitous of human activities, and in any culture it is the form of complex discourse that is earliest accessible to children and by which they are largely acculturated";[6] like Janet, children learn how to interpret their experiences through the culturally available narrative patterns. Robert Alter makes a similar point: the human being "as the language-using animal is quintessentially a teller of tales, and narration is his [or her] way of *making* experience, or . . . of making nonverbal experience distinctly human."[7] Human beings, in other words, claim and define our experiences as our own — *make* them — through the stories by which we assign them meaning. It is in this process that narrative becomes, in Fredric Jameson's phrase, "the central function or *instance* of the human mind."[8]

Because "natural narratives and literary narratives are similar in both structure and style," as Susan Lanser reminds us,[9] the novel participates in this central human activity as both model and enactment of our daily stories. We see in the novel the kinds of interpretive patterning by which we narrate our daily experiences to each other; we learn from the novel the culturally available patterning by which to structure and understand the data of our lives. As the longest and most modern narrative form, the novel serves as a crucial exemplar for the process of interpreting and giving form to lived experience. In addition, as novelistic narrative is an agent of interpretation, it becomes as well a possible agent of *re*interpretation, not only giving form but also altering accepted forms — the process central to all feminist scholarship.

The interpretive process inherent in narrative is augmented by a second characteristic of the novel: its extraordinary flexibility as a form. Introduced as "the novel," it remains in many ways "the new." Although, as literature, the novel shares the conventional nature of all literary forms, it is incomplete to say, as Northrop Frye does, "Poetry can only be made out of other poems; novels out of other novels."[10] I would dispute such an absolute claim even with regard to poetry, but it is a still less accurate claim for novels. Quite simply, the language we use in our daily lives and in the stories we tell in our daily lives is the language predominant in most novels. As "a hybrid of narrative and discursive forms,"[11] the novel is continually bending its conventions to include issues at stake in the culture in which it was written. Walter Reed goes so far as to make this feature of the novel definitionally central: the novel, he says, is "a long prose fiction which opposes the forms of everyday life, social and psychological, to the conventional forms of literature, classical or popular, inherited from the past. The novel is a type of literature suspicious of its own literariness; it is inherently anti-traditional in its literary code."[12] He goes on to assert that the "novel explores the difference between the fictions which are enshrined in the institution of literature and the fictions, more truthful historically or merely more familiar, by which we lead our daily lives."[13] The literariness that encodes and encapsulates the novel is thus especially permeable to other cultural codes of its own time; its words carry a weight similar to the weight of words used in ordinary human efforts to communicate. It is true that the reader and writer share a sort of contractual agreement shaped by the conventions of literary genre,[14] but it is also true that they share a language coded as well to the experience of daily social life: a language with the referential impact of communication.

This is not to say that language in the novel *refers* in any direct or unitary way but rather to find in its flexibility a portion of the novel's capacity to interpret and participate in cultural change. Mikhail Bakhtin's highly suggestive analysis of the novel's development traces the historical evolution of this capacity to a developing consciousness of multiple languages—"heteroglossia"—and the resulting awareness that a given language must be seen as no more than "a working hypothesis for comprehending and expressing reality."[15] In Bakhtin's view, this human recognition that *all* language acts as hypothesis evolves into the novel's special dialogic capacity to interact with its contemporary surroundings: "an indeterminacy, a certain semantic open-endedness, a living contact with unfinished still-evolving contemporary reality (the openended present)" (p. 7). Thus does the novel reveal an "orientation that is contested, contestable and contesting" (p. 332). Thus, too, does its flexibility yield new interaction with social reality, new comprehension of cultural change. From a feminist perspective Bakhtin's analysis rings true: the novel has evolved in interaction with the social realities of women's and men's lives. But more crucially, the analysis points toward the significance of that flexibility now: the novel's dialogic capacity enables it to engage in "eternal re-thinking and re-evaluating" (p. 31) as it interacts with its social environment.

The incorporation of multiple languages in a dialogical form and the resulting openness to the languages and codes of lived experience have no doubt also contributed to the third characteristic I have claimed as vital to a feminist poetics of the novel: its evolution as a popular form in many ways prompted by and correlated to the rise in general literacy. In the eighteenth century, the century of its official birth in many literary histories, the novel was already a form available to a broad "social and educational spectrum."[16] Its growth and evolution over the subsequent two centuries, especially in its English-language versions, has depended on a broad readership and at least a partial incorporation of multi-class experience. Though its expressions have often privileged white middle-class experience and been shaped by male-dominant assumptions, its very multiplicity has opened its character-izations to a broader popular base, as its readership, at least into the mid-twentieth century, has incorporated a broad popular audience.

Many claims for the novel's feminist possibilities derive directly from the recognition of its popularity: its rise correlates with a rise in female literacy and middle-class leisure; its historical form is closely associated with varieties of personal relationships and the particularities of women's domestic and emotional lives; in comparison with other genres, a dispro-portionate number of prominent English novelists have been women, as have been a significant number of its most financially successful practi-tioners. Many historians of the novel have noted the primacy of women readers in eighteenth- and nineteenth-century authors' thinking about au-dience. Many feminist critics have noted the long and prominent associa-tion of the novel with women: as characters, as readers, as authors.[17] Decid-edly, these correlations provide rich material for feminist analysis.

The correlations, however, are not without their attendant hazards for a feminist poetics. For if the novel has grown up in association with women, it has also grown up in association with the given cultural assumptions about women's lives. A tinge of irony colors feminist claims that the domestic novel freed women to enter literature as it broke down the limits of epic form: no longer defined by the feats of the [male] hero in a mythical world of fixed values, the novel now opened extended narrative to enquire into the complex and immediate experience of women's daily lives. The claims are crucial but not yet sufficient. For the realist strand of the novel, grounded in domestic detail and personal relationships, risks assault from both sides of the straits of feminist understanding of language: appropriation into the language and sexual ideology of the status quo and separatism into the world of female "difference." One assault comes from the recognition that the realist novel will not "seem credible" if it diverges radically from "people's beliefs about reality" and is redoubled in the formulaic expressions of many overtly "popular" novels.[18] The other assault comes from the claims, built upon assumptions of "difference," that women are especially good at writing novels because of their unique gifts for observation and relationship, qualities then trivialized by a male-dominant value system.[19] Obviously, the challenges can be inverted in the hands of women choosing to value difference and seek alternative ways of expressing it, but the risk still attends the novelistic perceptions of women's lives.

The potential for irony increases when we acknowledge that, as a popular form closely associated with women and often claimed by feminist criticism, the novel seems nonetheless to resist the most urgent feminist concern: the need for cultural change and the opening of possibilities in the lives of women. Thus, in contrast to a celebratory tone in some feminist analysis, a tone of resignation or despair pervades the work of a number of other significant analysts. Nancy K. Miller, for example, concludes *The Heroine's Text* with the statement that until the culture at large changes, we must either continue to read the old plots or perhaps "stop reading novels."[20] And Myra Jehlen argues that because the novel has its ideological base in the social structures of patriarchal society, it can be of little use to feminist needs for change and of little interest to feminist writers.[21]

These crucial warnings about the confinements of the traditional realist novel are joined by a warning implicit in the general academic study of the Anglophone novel: criticism of the twentieth-century novel has canonized far more male than female novelists and has simultaneously developed a more elitist view of the novel as form. On the one hand, the realist novel, with its assumptions of a popular audience, seems doomed to reinforce the status quo; on the other hand, developments away from the realist novel seem to resist women's full participation and to deny any vital connection with immediate lives of ordinary people.

How, then, can the popularity of the novel form be a resource, rather than a liability, to a feminist poetics of the novel? One answer derives from the kind of claim that Ann Barr Snitow makes for the realist novel in implementing cultural redefinitions: "The realist novel has always been the novel of such first phases. Since the inception of the form, novels have been 'how-to' manuals for groups gathering their identity through self-description."[22]

Once a group has begun to redefine its beliefs about reality — once women have begun to reach new and shared understandings of their experience — the novel has the capacity to make those understandings available to a broad popular audience. But more than this: precisely because its flexibility interacts with its popularity, the novel is by definition disposed to incorporate developing perceptions and evolving kinds of discourse; its dialogic capacity, its openness to contemporary reality, its inclination toward a "decentering of the ideological world"[23] interact with its ties to popular and broad-based experience. It bears within its evolution as a popular form the protean capacity to resist cultural fixity and to reinterpret the lives of women. As a popular form, the novel has often tended to center in female characters and personal relationships; as a popular and flexible form, it has the capacity to criticize its historical limits and reassess the very lives it is sometimes accused of "fixing." Precisely as a popular form, the novel retains the capacity to evade the hazards of its popularity and help shape new understandings of women's lives.

A fourth characteristic, the novel's defining concern with individual experience, has similarly problematic but ultimately fruitful implications for feminist criticism, as it contributes to the novel's relationship to lived experience. The historical association of the novel with the notion of individualism has been noted by multiple analysts of the novel, with divergent measures of approval and disapproval: Walter Benjamin, Lucien Goldmann, Terence Hawkes, Edward Said, and Ian Watt, to name a few. Benjamin, for example, notes the birth of the novel in the isolated individual, as contrasted with the communal basis for storytelling.[24] More positively, Watt speaks of the subject matter of the novel as "individual self-definition,"[25] and Said calls the self the "primordial discovery of the novel."[26] This focus is, in part, because the novel, as an extended printed document, centers in the individual reader, alone with the book,[27] and in part because the idea of the novel has centered in the individuation of its characters.

An emphasis on the individual is decidedly troubling from a point of view, such as that of feminism, that views social forces as major determinants of human activity and that also rests on the need to claim a communal identity. Marxists, both feminist and nonfeminist, are central in the critique of individualism, for clear ideological and methodological reasons. Mary Poovey's Marxist feminist assessment of "the promises of love" in Jane Austen aptly identifies the problem with individualism as the view "that the personal can be kept separate from the social, that one's 'self' can be fulfilled in spite of—and in isolation from—the demands of the marketplace."[28] Such awarenesses seem to argue against any possibility of seeing the novel as participant in feminist change. Indeed, that too is one of Jehlen's conclusions in her analysis of the novel: the novel's "organically individualistic" form, she argues, is posited on "the special form that sexual hierarchy has taken in modern times"; the form itself precludes female characters from "becoming autonomous."[29]

But while such an argument is provocative, I think it is not, finally, compelling. For it requires a relatively static view of the novel, which ignores its flexibility as "the new," its capacity for self-criticism,[30] its historically persistent incorporation of multiple perceptions. Indeed, I am convinced that the novel's very basis in individualism has rich possibilities from a feminist perspective, initially because feminism, like the novel, is intimately tied to issues of individual self-definition.[31] By social definition— in which the novel has itself been historically implicated— women have been denied individual selfhood, have been refused the right to autonomous action and self-definition. As outsiders in a patriarchal culture, women have also been held in relative isolation from each other and from a sense of social consensus. Thus the need for a sense of individual strength and agency and for the inclusion of female experience in the cultural definition of the individual becomes crucial to overcoming the cultural falsification of female experience. It is in this process that the novel's centering in the individual can be especially fruitful for feminist analysis. I share Jehlen's view that the achievement of female autonomy has radical implications,[32] as does any redefinition of individualism to include female autonomy. Through its individualism, the novel opens onto a capacity to offer new narrative interpretations of the female individual, not as isolated and self-serving but as a strong and complex human being in social interaction with other human beings.

Again this capacity is not simply claimed, for the notion of the individual often brings with it associations of unity, sameness, identity as stasis— associations that can be used to limit women to an essentialist concept of femininity. In feminist as in other literary analysis, the self-evident accuracy of Bakhtin's assertion that "an individual cannot be completely incarnated into the flesh of sociohistorical categories" (p. 37) is often overlooked in the urge to systematize the functional interaction between plot and character. But because the novel's distinctive narrative form is multiple and flexible, it can yield an alternative notion of the human individual as multiple and flexible, rather than unitary and fixed. If the novelistic individual extends beyond the boundaries of our sociohistorical and linguistic categories, it follows that what Bakhtin calls "an unrealizable surplus of humanness" (p. 37) becomes a leading edge onto new possibilities in the ever-reopening future. In a feminist poetics, this notion of the individual as a defining center of the novel's narrative form frees the idea of an individual woman from established sociohistorical categories of femininity and allows the possibility for a redefined individualism. Once more Bakhtin's terms, if not his male bias, point the way.

> The epic wholeness of an individual disintegrates in a novel. . . . A crucial tension develops between the external and internal man [or woman], and as a result the subjectivity of the individual becomes an object of experimentation and representation. . . . This disintegration of the integrity that an individual had possessed in epic (and in tragedy) combines in the novel with the necessary preparatory steps toward a new, complex wholeness. (pp. 37–38)

The point to be taken here is the recognition that individualism in the novel, like the literary form itself, is a function of ceaseless and open-ended interaction. As the tension in an individual between external and internal — between established "categories" and a "surplus of humanness" — is inherent to the novel's dialogic form, so the notion of the complex and protean individual is an effect of that form.

In this sort of novelistic individualism, a feminist poetics can find a further expansion of the novel's capacity to speak to social concerns. Because the novel form is concerned with the lives of individuals, it opens immediately onto the social reality of both its author and its readers. Because it speaks from individual to individual — as Lessing says, "in a small personal voice" and "directly, in clear words"[33] — it affirms the possibility of social communication and of shared understanding. But because it is structured as process and shows us the "surplus of humanness," its individualism neither binds us to the known social reality nor limits its shared understanding to the absolutism that shadows the notion of "clear words." The novel's individualism itself can answer the feminist need to speak of women's lives and of the possibilities for changing women's lives.*

*Section II has been omitted. In it, Frye discusses the movement toward developing a feminist poetics of the novel, with special attention to Sandra Gilbert and Susan Gubar's *The Madwoman in the Attic.* — Editors

III

What we often take to be the formal conventions of the novel are more precisely those conventions that evolved as a part of the nineteenth-century novel's concern to represent social reality in a world subject to rapid shifts in shared cultural assumptions. As "truth" was under seige by the rise in scientific, industrial, economic, and eventually psychological sophistication, so the novel evolved conventions by which to assess human experience in the midst of such complexity. But, as critics such as George Levine and Robert Alter have pointed out, nineteenth-century novelists were themselves self-consciously aware that their novels were not re-presentations of reality but rather representational fictions shaped by conventions.[34] We could even say that the entire history of the novel is defined by this same tension: the urge to speak meaningfully of human experience in a social context coupled with the recognition that meaning is partial and equivocal. At any rate, the origin of the novel can be traced to this central recognition of uncertainty: a historical break with the univocal narratives of myth or epic, in which the old idea of narrative had been merged with an absolutist world view.[35]

From a feminist perspective, the break with mythic and epic visions is manifestly important to an understanding of novelistic conventions, for this break provides the initial departure from a vision of a social world in which women are mere objects of exchange in the battles among men or one in which women's only power is mysterious or magical. To depart from such narrative traditions and to enter instead a narrative of social complexity is to open the narrative possibilities evident in ordinary human interaction. By definition, the conventions of novelistic narrative initiate feminist understanding as they reject the fixity of meaning.

The positions of the two sexes in the stories of epic heroes underline the importance of relinquishing epic certainty: men fighting battles in which women serve only as booty or provocation. Helen of Troy, though most renowned, is scarcely alone either in serving this narrative function or in the mythic weight borne by the power of her beauty. Nor is Odysseus singular in encountering various and violent adventures that give shape and substance to his wanderings: as a hero of epic proportions he gains narrative presence through the completed actions of his series of conquests. Although I oversimplify to make my point, the pattern is decisive enough to need little illustration: men and women have clear sex-marked roles in the narrative forms of the epic, and for women, these roles are bound by the available images of female sexuality.

In myth and fairy tale, women are more likely to be significant agents of the tale, but here too the available roles are marked out by definitions of female sexuality and by the assumptions of univocality. It is by now nearly a cliché, evolving out of early feminist work on images of women, that these patterns of myth, legend, and fairy tale have characterized women in one of two dominant polar patterns: saint or witch, virgin or whore, angel or monster. On either side of the polarity, the vision of woman, even when she does act, is basically an objectification through her sexuality, a denial of her own complex subjective reality, a fixed perspective on her as an outsider rather than an agent of her own reality.[36] She is either the good and passive Snow White or the wicked queen her stepmother; she is Eve the temptress or she is the Virgin Mary.[37]

When the novel arises as a major narrative form, it breaks with these limitations in significant ways. As it develops what Bakhtin calls "the zone of maximal contact with the present" (p. 11), it breaks down the notions of absolute sameness in character and of absolute conclusiveness in plot.[38] In doing so it not only opens itself to notions of change and uncertainty; it also requires a reinterpretation of notions of gender. As men are no longer presented as identical with themselves, so women can no longer be easily presented as incarnations of sexually bound traits: their humanness exceeds the boundaries of sociohistorical categories.

This is why the novel's popularity, flexibility, and focus on the individual are all such powerful resources for new understandings of women's lives in the eighteenth and nineteenth centuries. This is also why the evolution of novelistic understanding turned naturally to personal relationships and hence to a more complex awareness of the dailiness of women's as well as men's lives. And this is at least one reason why women in the nineteenth century found in the novel a genre that was responsive to their own perspectives on human experience: Jane Austen, the Brontë sisters, George Eliot, and many lesser-known women novelists claimed the resources of this narrative genre to convey their own human visions.

But the sociohistorical context for these novelists remained male-dominant. They could, to some extent, write of their own experiences and perceptions but the social realities continued to set boundaries to their novelistic world. The primary arena for women's actions, in the novel as in life, was by definition domestic; and the most favored plot — also by definition — was the cultural plot for a woman's favored destiny: the "love story."

This brief historical excursus provides some explanation of why the nineteenth-century realist novel is simultaneously in favor and under attack in contemporary feminist criticism. The realist novel gave women writers access to literary voice and hence shows us the experiences of women's lives, but it also constrained their notions — and ours — of women's lives within the assumptions and values of a decidedly patriarchal society. Its conventions were both those by which women gained access to literary expression and those by which we have come to see women's lives defined as primarily domestic and relational.

But, of course, the evolution of the novel did not stop in the nineteenth century, and a feminist understanding of its resources must also take into account the issues raised by novelists of the twentieth century in interaction with their own social context. Not surprisingly, we can find in Virginia Woolf's "Modern Fiction" a crucial moment in the evolution of novelistic conventions as she rejected what she saw as the limiting conventions of novelistic form: "The writer seems constrained, not by his [or her] own free will, but by some powerful and unscrupulous tyrant who has him [or her] in thrall to provide a plot, . . . But sometimes . . . we suspect a momentary doubt, . . . Is life like this? Must novels be like this?"[39] Rejecting the realist novel, Woolf, like many another modernist, was reacting to a sense of dramatic cultural change: the breaking up of many shared cultural values, the fragmentation of modern life, the inability to trust that one's own perceptions might hold true for anyone else. She felt, too, the inadequacy of literary conventions of the realist novel to the reality of subjective experience. With the cultural change, she felt the urgency for a new literary form to characterize the altered sense of life.

Current feminist interest in Woolf has emphasized the importance of reclaiming her identity as a socialist, a political feminist, a lesbian. This is work that is extremely important and restorative after half a century of denying or obscuring these parts of her life and work. But her concern with literary conventions — her efforts at formal experimentation by which she has achieved a place as a major modernist writer — are also of crucial significance to a feminist point of view.[40] For though her observations on form are cast in a generalizing "human" context — and share, as I have said, the concerns of male modernists as well — they are of particular use in a redefinition of the novel as a way of redefining female experience. Woolf's concern was with the reshaping of novelistic conventions in order that they might better "represent" the complexities of lived experience; the modernist recognition that "life isn't like this" joins the feminist recognition that though the historical premises of "representation" are inadequate, the novel's concern to "represent" lived experience remains fundamental.[41]

To represent by redefining the premises of representation: this, then, was the problem Woolf saw in her own relationship to her social context and to novelistic conventions, as it is the problem I have made central to a feminist understanding of the novel. As Woolf was well aware, the shifting of novelistic conventions can only be an ongoing process, not something that can be accomplished by feminist fiat. But novelists have always used literary conventions and been aware that readers bring conventional expectations to their novel reading; and the self-conscious play with these expectations has participated in our sense of the novel's malleability and its potential for portraying experience in new ways. With this knowledge, contemporary feminist critics, novelists, and novel readers can follow Woolf and find in the historical shifting of these conventions a peculiarly useful access to ways of redefining our cognitive strategies: not a feminist fiat but a feminist claiming of the culturally available strategies for change.

The premises of novelistic representation are not bound by strongly defined formal conventions, but our understanding of the realist novel is nonetheless structured by novelistic conventions in four broadly defined areas: plot, character, reality, and thematic unity.[42] The modernist breaking up of the codes and expectations in these areas was a clear refusal of the world view offered in the great novels of nineteenth-century realism and a denial that that view of "reality" had a special claim on the "real." Alain Robbe-Grillet's characterization of the "old novel" is indicative of what his predecessors in the twentieth century were rejecting before him: a "Balzacian character," "chronological plot," and "transcendent humanism."[43] Furthermore, like his predecessors, he also rejects the notion that reality is "already entirely constituted" and asserts that "not only does each of us see in the world his [or her] own reality, but . . . the novel is precisely what creates it."[44] Thus the conventions of representation in the nineteenth-century novel are seen as unviable for interpreting complex lived experience, especially in the modern world.

These "old" novelistic conventions are also the conventions that have been demonstrably problematic for any view of autonomous women characters and for characterizing female experience outside the assumptions of male dominance. Women have been bound by the anticipated resolution of plot difficulties in marriage, death, or painful isolation, by the definition of character in terms of the traits of "femininity," by the presentation of reality as the relational and domestic social context that the dominant sexual ideology presumes for women, and by the coherence of the love story. Thus a feminist poetics of the novel can usefully join modernists and postmodernists in rejecting such conventions. But since the necessity of a shared community, the desire for a meaningful place in the world, and the importance of assessing actual lived experience are also central to a feminist view, much of the postmodernist movement toward self-contained structures of verbal play or Robbe-Grillet's object-centered texts will not in itself meet the feminist need for a redefined capacity to represent. A feminist poetics of the novel needs, then, to understand, to subvert, and finally to reinterpret the formal resources of novelistic representation. If we understand these conventions as having only the pretense of stability or self-assurance, we can avoid reifying them and find instead their available resources as cognitive strategies, self-consciously invoked in the attempt to interpret and represent a social experience that defies a full representation.

. . .

In a feminist redefinition of the conventions, then, social reality derives from the recognition that the structuring activity is a shared human need and is the effect of the culturally available paradigms by which people interpret the world around them. For women writers and readers the claiming of subjective experience and the development of narrative explanations for what is specifically female in that experience becomes a crucial way of identifying an altered social reality. Through a paradigm centered in female experience (thus raising to visibility, among other things, the previously invisible qualities of women's strength and agency) the novelistic claim to portray a view of social reality becomes a means of access to newly shared experience and provides the possibility, through the writer-character-reader triad, for a sense of community in the new shared reality.

In this view, it is not that there is no reality, as in extreme versions of postmodernist thought, but that the novelistic constitution of reality is a part of the endless interaction between information and interpretation by which we all live. Adding the previously obscured information of explicitly female experience requires a new interpretive paradigm for social reality; the development of new paradigms makes accessible new information. In voicing their own multiple subjective versions of the world, women thus come to identify their reality not in the "femininity" of the dominant paradigm, but in a shared basis of female experience at the heart of the sense-making process. This is a commitment not to an unchanging reality but to a reality of shared interpretation in process.

Implicit in the dialogical form of the novel, the refusals of determinate reality, character, and plot are thus all a part of the process by which women can "extend the real rather than dissolve it"[45] through renewing novelistic conventions for feminist understanding. In this context, the conventions of thematic unity operate pervasively in our reading of all the other narrative conventions and in their transfer to our reading of lives. The principle of thematic unity is the governing principle for selection of events by which the plot—or even the "story"—is constituted, of characteristics by which characters are concretized, of objects and information by which the external world is made present. In each case, the selection process for the reader reading and for the writer writing is based on the anticipation of thematic unity. Clearly the reading at which we will arrive—either of the life experience or of the novelistic world—is crucially dependent on the governing principle by which these selections are made. In the traditional portrayal of women, it is almost inevitably the defining unity of the love interest; the narrative coherence depends on our assumptions that the novelistic lives of women will be centered in their relationship to men. But through altered novelistic conventions, the shift in thematic unity, and particularly the insistence on multiple thematic unities emphasized by the modernist refusal of determinate form, enables the perception that women's lives can have multiple centers. It thus becomes possible to construct alternative thematic unities based on female autonomy and informed by female experience. The emphasis once again is on process rather than product, a further evolution of the fundamental novelistic understanding: explanatory structures have referential power and value but must always be subject to alteration.

A key agent in this contemporary reopening of conventions to process is the presence of a feminist interpretive community. In her analysis of the functioning of interpretive conventions, Jean Kennard hypothesizes that "literary conventions change when their implications conflict with the vision of experience of a new 'interpretive community.'" She argues convincingly that we must recognize the "nonliterary as well as literary influences" by which literary conventions are changed, and she suggests that contemporary feminist perspectives have enabled us to read differently the possibilities in earlier works such as *The Awakening*, even though readers of its own time could not see it as an expression of "women's search for self-fulfillment."[46] She sees this convention as operating in more recent novels first as a development of the concept of self-fulfillment and then as a convention that itself needed to be broken.

Implicit in Kennard's argument, though not actually worked out, is the recognition that such conventions create new cultural paradigms by which women readers read both novels and their lives and by which women writers read their perspectives on life into their novels. The feminist literary community thus provides a necessary link in the dialogic process involved in literary and cultural change: in perpetually evolving interchange, the culture and the individual interact through the formation and use of interpretive paradigms and with the intervention of newly evolved shared perceptions. The dominant culture text, the grid of expectations, is changed by the interpretive participation of individuals in the act of developing new shared conventions: women gain cultural support from other women and thus gain the perceptual capacities for forming new literary conventions and for reading lives in new ways.

In an early manifesto of feminist literary criticism, Adrienne Rich gave powerful definition to its experiential basis: "A radical critique of literature, feminist in its impulse, would take the work first of all as a clue to how we live, how we have been living, how we have been led to imagine ourselves, how our language has trapped as well as liberated us, how the very act of naming has been till now a male prerogative and how we can begin to see and name—and therefore live—afresh."[47] In spite of the differences among feminist critics, Rich's rationale for feminist criticism continues to define our unifying concerns: the affirmation of literature's interpretive power, the recognition of language as both constraint and liberation, the need to claim the agency of vision and voice in resistance to male dominance. Current work in feminist literary criticism seems most concerned with the difficulty of meeting these goals and with the recognition that language and literature continue to act powerfully as constraint. But even these recognitions do not require the rejection of those early values or of the experiential basis for feminist criticism; they only require that our analyses are cognizant of the complexities of literary form as it both shapes and is shaped by experience. Mary Poovey has pointed out that ideology is enabling as well as restricting;[48] so, too, is literary form as long as we recognize not only its potential imposition of stasis, but also its enabling power in yielding new understandings of women's lives.

Through claiming the novel's capacity both to "represent" and to redefine the premises of representation, a feminist poetics of the novel, then, reclaims the historical potential of the novel and addresses precisely those political concerns that gave original impetus to feminist literary criticism: the fuller understanding of women's lives and the commitment to cultural change. Eagleton's claim for the distinctiveness of feminist criticism, from which I took my point of departure in this chapter, thus becomes a claim for the "life" of literary theory rather than the "death" he proclaimed in his "obituary." What is our interest in and commitment to the study of literature? Why should we want to engage with it? Enriched by the recognitions implicit in feminist literary criticism's new sophistication, the old answer reasserts itself: because it tells us something about how we live and how we might live. It helps give us that capacity "to see and name — and therefore live — afresh."

Notes

1. My view of the human importance of narrative is pervasively indebted to Frank Kermode, *The Sense of an Ending: Studies in the Theory of Fiction* (New York: Oxford University Press, 1967). In the face of more recent work in narratology, this work retains its interest as it affirms the human and dynamic rather than the structural and static elements of narrative. For an important recent effort to restore considerations of narrative to a more dynamic awareness of human needs, see Peter Brooks, *Reading for the Plot: Design and Intention in Narrative* (Oxford: Oxford University Press, 1984).

2. Doris Lessing, *The Golden Notebook* (1962; reprint, New York: Bantam, 1973), p. 363.

3. Ulric Neisser, *Cognition and Reality: Principles and Implications of Cognitive Psychology* (San Francisco: W. H. Freeman, 1976), p. 182.

4. Barbara Hardy, "An Approach Through Narrative," in *Towards a Poetics of Fiction*, ed. Mark Spilka (Bloomington: Indiana University Press, 1977), p. 31.

5. Louis Mink, "Narrative Form as Cognitive Instrument," in *The Writings of History: Literary Form and Historical Understanding*, ed. Robert H. Canary and Henry Kozicki (Madison: University of Wisconsin Press, 1978), pp. 129–49.

6. Ibid., p. 133.

7. Robert Alter, *Partial Magic: The Novel as a Self-Conscious Genre* (1975; reprint, Berkeley: University of California Press, 1978), p. 64.

8. Fredric Jameson, *The Political Unconscious: Narrative as a Socially Symbolic Act* (Ithaca: Cornell University Press, 1981), p. 13. Cf. also Christa Wolf's impassioned conviction that "[s]torytelling is humane and achieves humane effects" and "[s]torytelling is the assignment of meaning." *Cassandra: A Novel and Four Essays*, trans. Jan Van Heurck (London: Virago, 1984), pp. 173–74.

9. Susan Sniader Lanser, *The Narrative Act: Point of View in Prose Fiction* (Princeton: Princeton University Press, 1981), p. 65.

10. Northrop Frye, *The Anatomy of Criticism* (1957; reprint, Princeton: Princeton University Press, 1971), p. 97.

11. J. Paul Hunter, "The Loneliness of the Long-Distance Reader," *Genre* 10 (Winter 1977): 481.

12. Walter Reed, "The Problem with a Poetics of the Novel," in *Towards a Poetics of Fiction*, p. 64.

13. Ibid., p. 65.

14. Cf., for example, Frye, *Anatomy of Criticism*, pp. 95–98.

15. Mikhail M. Bakhtin, *The Dialogic Imagination: Four Essays*, ed. Michael Holquist, trans. Caryl Emerson and Michael Holquist (Austin: University of Texas Press, 1981), p. 61. Subsequent references will be indicated in the text.

16. Hunter, "Loneliness," p. 459.

17. See, for example, Ellen Moers, *Literary Women: The Great Writers* (Garden City, N.Y.: Anchor Books, 1977), p. 182. See, too, Ian Watt's suggestion that the "rise of the novel . . . would seem to be connected with the much greater freedom of women in modern society." *The Rise of the Novel: Studies in Defoe, Richardson, and Fielding* (1957; reprint, Berkeley: University of California Press, 1965), p. 138.

18. Carol Pearson and Katherine Pope, *The Female Hero in American and British Literature* (New York: R. R. Bowker, 1981), p. 11; see also pp. 6–7 on the conservatism of popular literary forms.

19. See Showalter, "Women Writers and the Double Standard," in *Woman in Sexist Society: Studies in Power and Powerlessness*, ed. Vivian Gornick and B. K. Moran (1971; reprint, New York: New American Library, 1972), pp. 452–79.

20. Nancy K. Miller, *The Heroine's Text: Readings in the French and English Novel, 1722–1782* (New York: Columbia University Press, 1980), p. 158.

21. Myra Jehlen, "Archimedes and the Paradox of Feminist Criticism," *Signs* 6.4 (Summer 1981): 600. Although I disagree with a number of her major conclusions, I find Jehlen's analysis provocative and much more complex than my use of it here implies.

22. Ann Barr Snitow, "The Front Line: Notes on Sex in Novels by Women, 1969–1979," *Signs* 5.4 (Summer 1980): 705. Snitow also concludes that women novelists will continue to find "social realism" a fruitful form (p. 718).

23. See Bakhtin, *The Dialogic Imagination*, especially p. 367.

24. Walter Benjamin, "The Storyteller," in *Illuminations*, trans. Harry Zohn (New York: Schocken, 1969), p. 87.

25. Watt, "Serious Reflections on *The Rise of the Novel*," in *Towards a Poetics of Fiction*, p. 102.

26. Edward Said, *Beginnings: Intention and Method* (Baltimore: Johns Hopkins University Press, 1975), p. 141.

27. See Hunter, "Loneliness," esp. p. 471.

28. Mary Poovey, "*Persuasion* and the Promises of Love," in *The Representation of Women in Fiction*, ed. Carolyn G. Heilbrun and Margaret R. Higonnet (Baltimore: Johns Hopkins University Press, 1983), p. 172.

29. Jehlen, "Archimedes," p. 595.

30. Bakhtin speaks repeatedly of the novel's distinctive capacity to criticize itself (e.g., *The Dialogic Imagination*, pp. 6, 49, and 412).

31. I share Eagleton's view that a concern for "the experience of the human subject" is participant in the political basis of feminist criticism because "sexism and gender roles are questions which engage the deepest personal dimensions of life" (p. 149).

32. Jehlen, "Archimedes," p. 600.

33. Lessing, *A Small Personal Voice*, ed. Paul Schlueter (New York: Alfred A. Knopf, 1974), p. 21.

34. George Levine, *The Realistic Imagination: English Fiction from Frankenstein to Lady Chatterley* (Chicago: University of Chicago Press, 1981); Alter.

35. For an extended treatment of this historical break, see the essay titled "Epic and Novel: Toward a Methodology for the Study of the Novel," Bakhtin, *The Dialogic Imagination*, pp. 3–40.

36. See Sherry Ortner's anthropological analysis of women's cultural position as "both under and over (but really simply outside of) the sphere of culture's hegemony." "Is Female to Male as Nature Is to Culture?" in *Woman, Culture, and Society*, ed. Michelle Zimbalist Rosaldo and Louise Lamphere (Stanford: Stanford University Press, 1974), pp. 66–87, esp. p. 86.

37. For a powerful reading of this pattern, see Gilbert and Gubar, *The Madwoman in the Attic: The Woman Writer and the Nineteenth-Century Literary Imagination* (New Haven: Yale University Press, 1979), pp. 3–44.

38. Following Bakhtin, I recognize that "novelization" evolved gradually and was evident well before the development of what we generally recognize as the genre of the novel. See especially "From the Prehistory of Novelistic Discourse," pp. 41–83.

39. Virginia Woolf, "Modern Fiction," in *Collected Essays* (New York: Harcourt, Brace and World, 1967), 2:106.

40. Cf. Gillian Beer, "Beyond Determinism: George Eliot and Virginia Woolf," in *Women Writing and Writing about Women*: "The eschewing of plot as an aspect of her feminism" (p. 95).

41. Cf. Carolyn A. Durham's argument that women's experimental uses of narrative form, as evident in Marie Cardinal, are different from the New Novel because they are concerned with lived experience. "Feminism and Formalism: Dialectical Structures in Marie Cardinal's *Une Vie pour deux*," *Tulsa Studies in Women's Literature* 4.1 (Spring 1985): 94. I am indebted to Durham for insights in conversation on the novel and its experimental forms, as well as on feminism.

42. For analysis of more specific "codes" that can be grouped into these areas, see Barthes, "An Introduction to the Structural Analysis of Narrative," and his analysis of Balzac in *S/Z*, trans. Richard Miller (New York: Hill and Wang, 1974); see, too, Jonathan Culler's summary of structuralist codes in *Structuralist Poetics: Structuralism, Linguistics, and the Study of Literature* (Oxford: Oxford University Press, 1977), pp. 173–79; his assessment of the interaction between narrative conventions of causation is particularly suggestive (pp. 176–77).

43. Alain Robbe-Grillet, *For a New Novel: Essays on Fiction*, trans. Richard Howard (New York: Grove, 1965), p. 168.

44. Ibid., pp. 160, 161.

45. This is Robert Anchor's suggestion for what will happen if contemporary realism makes effective use of the possibilities evident in postmodernist literature. "Realism and Ideology: The Question of Order," *History and Theory* 22.2 (May 1983): 119.

46. Jean E. Kennard, "Convention Coverage or How to Read Your Own Life," *New Literary History* 13.1 (Autumn 1981): 84, 71, and 71–72, respectively.

47. Adrienne Rich, "When We Dead Awaken: Writing as Re-Vision," in *On Lies, Secrets, and Silence* (New York: Norton, 1979), p. 33.

48. Poovey, "*Persuasion* and the Promises of Love," p. 178.

19

"The Pastime of Past Time": Fiction, History,
Historiographical Metafiction · LINDA HUTCHEON

I

We theoreticians have to know the laws of the peripheral in art.
The peripheral is, in fact, the non-esthetic set.
It is connected with art, but the connection is not causal.
But to stay alive, art must have new raw materials. Infusions of the peripheral.
— Viktor Shklovsky

In the nineteenth century, at least before the rise of Ranke's "scientific history," literature and history were considered branches of the same tree of learning, a tree which sought to "interpret experience, for the purpose of guiding and elevating man" (Nye, p. 123). Then came the separation that resulted in the distinct disciplines of literary and historical studies today, despite the fact that the realist novel and Rankean historicism share many similar beliefs about the possibility of writing factually about observable reality (Hayden White, "Fictions," p. 25). However, it is this very separation of the literary and the historical that is now being challenged in the theory and art of what we seem to want to label as postmodernism. Recent postmodern readings of both history and realist fiction have focused more on what the two modes of writing share than on how they differ. They have both been seen to derive their force more from verisimilitude than from any objective truth; they are both identified as linguistic constructs, highly conventionalized in their narrative forms, and not at all transparent, either in terms of language or structure; and they appear to be equally intertextual, deploying the texts of the past within their own complex textuality. But these are also the implied teachings of what I would like to call postmodern "historiographic metafiction" — novels that are intensely self-reflexive but that also both re-introduce historical context into metafiction and problematize the entire question of historical knowledge. Like those recent theories of both history and fiction, this kind of novel — G., *Midnight's Chil-*

dren, *Ragtime*, *The French Lieutenant's Woman*, *The Name of the Rose* — forces us to recall that history and fiction are themselves historical terms and their definitions and interrelations are historically determined and vary with time (see Seamon, pp. 212–16).

In the last century, as Barbara Foley has shown, historical writing and historical novel writing influenced each other mutually: Macauley's debt to Scott was an overt one, as was Dickens's to Carlyle in *A Tale of Two Cities* (Foley, pp. 170–71). Today, the new skepticism and suspicion about the writing of history that one finds in the work of Hayden White, Michel de Certeau, Paul Veyne, Lionel Gossman, Dominick LaCapra, and others are mirrored in the challenges to historiography in novels like *Shame*, *The Public Burning*, or *A Maggot:* they share the same questioning stance toward their common use of conventions of narrative, of reference, of the inscribing of subjectivity, of their identity as textuality, and even of their implication in ideology.

In both fiction and history writing today, our confidence in empiricist and positivist epistemologies has been shaken — shaken, but perhaps not yet destroyed. And this is what accounts for the skepticism rather than any real denunciation; it also accounts for the defining paradoxes of postmodern discourses. Postmodernism is a contradictory cultural enterprise, one that is heavily implicated in that which it seeks to contest. It uses and abuses the very beliefs it takes to task; it installs and only then subverts the conventions of genre. Historiographic metafiction, for example, keeps distinct its formal autorepresentation from its historical context, and in so doing problema-tizes the very possibility of historical knowledge, because there is no recon-ciliation, no dialectic here — just unresolved contradiction.

The history of the discussion of the relation of art to historiography is therefore relevant to any poetics of postmodernism, for the separation is a traditional one, even if it is being reformulated in a different context today. To Aristotle (*Poetics*, 1451a–b), the historian could only speak of what has happened, of the particulars of the past; the poet, on the other hand, spoke of what could or might happen and so could deal more with universals. Freed of the linear succession of history writing, the poet's plot could have dif-ferent unities. This was not to say that historical events and personages could not appear in tragedy: "nothing prevents some of the things that have actually happened from being of the sort that might probably or possibly happen" (1451b). History-writing was seen to have no such conventional restraints of probability or possibility. Nevertheless, many historians since have used the techniques of fictional representation to create imaginative versions of their historical, real worlds (see Holloway; Levine; Braudy; Henderson). The postmodern novel has done the same, and the reverse. It is part of the postmodernist stand to confront the paradoxes of fictive versus historical representation, the particular vs. the general, and the present versus the past. And its confrontation is itself contradictory, for it refuses to recuperate or dissolve either side of the dichotomy, yet it is willing to exploit both.

History and fiction have always been notoriously porous genres, of course. At various times both have included in their elastic boundaries such forms as the travel tale and various versions of what we now call sociology (Veyne, p. 30). It is not surprising that there would be overlappings of concern and even mutual influences between the two genres. In the eighteenth century, the focus of this commonality of concern tended to be the relation of ethics (not factuality) to truth in narrative. Both journalism and novels could be equally "false" in ethical terms. (Only with the passing of the Acts of Parliament that defined libel did the notion of historical "fact" enter this debate [Davis].) It is not accidental that, in one critic's words, "[f]rom the start the writers of novels seemed determined to pretend that their work is not *made*, but that it simply exists" (Josipovici, p. 148); in fact, it was safer, in legal and ethical terms. Defoe's works made claims to veracity and actually convinced some readers that they were factual, but most readers today (and many then) had the pleasure of a double awareness of both fictiveness and a basis in the "real"—as do readers of contemporary historiographic metafiction.

In fact, J. M. Coetzee's recent novel, *Foe*, addresses precisely this question of the relation of "story" and "history" writing to "truth" and exclusion in the practice of Defoe. There is a direct link here to a familiar assumption of historiography: "that every history is a history of some entity which existed for a reasonable period of time, that the historian wishes to state what is literally true of it in a sense which distinguishes the historian from a teller of fictitious or mendacious stories" (Morton White, p. 4). *Foe* reveals that storytellers can certainly silence, exclude, and absent certain past events—and people—but it also suggests that historians have done the same: where are the women in the traditional histories of the eighteenth century? Coetzee offers the teasing fiction that Defoe did not write *Robinson Crusoe* from information from the historical castaway, Alexander Selkirk, or from other travel accounts, but from information given him by a subsequently "silenced" woman, Susan Barton, who had also been a castaway on "Cruso" 's [sic] island. It had been Cruso who had suggested that she tell her story to a writer who would add "a dash of colour" to her tale. She resists because she wants the "truth" told, and Cruso admits that a writer's "trade is in books, not in truth" (p. 40). But Susan sees the problem: "If I cannot come foreward, as author, and swear to the truth of my tale, what will be the worth of it? I might as well have dreamed it in a snug bed in Chichester" (p. 40).

Susan tells Foe (he added the "de" only later, and so lost Coetzee's irony) her tale and his response is that of a novelist. Susan replies: "You remarked it would have been better had Cruso rescued not only musket and powder and ball, but a carpenter's chest as well, and built himself a boat. I do not wish to be captious, but we lived on an island so buffeted by wind that there was not a tree did not grow twisted and bent" (p. 55). In frustration, she begins her own tale, "The Female Castaway, Being a True Account of a Year Spent on a Desert Island. With Many Strange Circumstances Never Hitherto Related" (p. 67), but discovers that the problems of writing history are not unlike those of writing fiction: "Are these enough strange circumstances to make a story of? How long before I am driven to invent new and stranger circumstances: the salvage of tools and muskets from Cruso's ship; the building of a boat . . . a landing by cannibals . . . ?" (p. 67). Her final decision is, however, that "what we accept in life we cannot accept in history" (p. 67) — that is, lies and fabrications.

The linking of "fictitious" to "mendacious" stories (and histories) is one that other historiographic metafictions also seem to be obsessed with: *Famous Last Words*, *Legs*, *Waterland*, and *Shame*. In the latter, Salman Rushdie's narrator addresses openly the possible objections to his position as insider/ outsider (i.e., an immigrant) writing about the events of Pakistan from England — and in English:

> *Outsider! Trespasser! You have no right to this subject!* . . . I know: nobody ever arrested me [as they did the friend of whom he has just written]. Nor are they ever likely to. *Poacher! Pirate! We reject your authority. We know you, with your foreign language wrapped around you like a flag: speaking about us in your forked tongue, what can you tell but lies?* I reply with more questions: is history to be considered the property of the participants solely? In what courts are such claims staked, what boundary commissions map out the territories? (p. 28)

The eighteenth-century concern for lies and falsity becomes a postmodern concern for the multiplicity and dispersion of truth(s), truth(s) relative to the specificity of place and culture. Yet the paradox is still there: when Pakistan was formed, the *Indian* history had to be written out of the Pakistani past. But who did this work? History was rewritten by immigrants — in Urdu and English, the imported tongues. As the narrator of *Shame* puts it, he is forced — by history — to write in "this Angrezi . . . and so for ever alter what is written" (p. 38).

There has also been another, long tradition, dating (as we have seen) from Aristotle, that makes fiction not only separate from, but also superior to, history, a mode of writing which can only narrate the contingent and particular. The romantic and modernist assertions of the autonomy and supremacy of art led, however, as Jane Tompkins has shown so convincingly, to a marginalization of literature, one that extremes of metafiction (like American surfiction) only exacerbate. Historiographic metafiction, in deliberate contrast to what I would call such late modernist radical metafiction, attempts to demarginalize the literary through confrontation with the historical, and it does so both thematically and formally.

For example, Christa Wolf's *No Place on Earth* is about the fictionalized meeting of two historical figures, dramatist Heinrich von Kleist and poet Karoline von Günderrode: "The claim that they met: a legend that suits us. The town of Winkel, on the Rhine, we saw it ourselves." The "we" of the narrating voice, in the present, underlines the metafictive historical reconstruction on the level of form. But on the thematic level too, life and art meet, for this is the theme of the novel, as Wolf's Kleist tries to break down the walls between "literary fantasies and the actualities of the world" (p. 12), contesting his colleagues' separation of poets from praxis: "Of all the people here, perhaps there is none more intimately bound to the real world than I am" (p. 82). It is he who is trying to write a romantic historical work about Robert Guiscard, Duke of Normandy. The metafictive and the historiographic also meet in the intertexts of the novel, for it is through them that Wolf fleshes out the cultural and historical context of the fictive meeting. The intertexts range from Günderrode's own letters to canonic romantic works like Hölderlin's *Hyperion*, Goethe's *Torquato Tasso*, and Brentano's *Gedichte* — but, in all, the theme is the relation, or rather the conflict, between art and history, between literature and life. This novel reminds us, as did Roland Barthes much earlier, that the nineteenth century gave birth to both the realist novel and history, two genres which share a desire to select, construct, and render self-sufficient and closed a narrative world that would be representational but still separate from changing experience and historical process. Today, history and fiction share a need, if not really a desire, to contest these very assumptions.

II

To the truth of art, external reality is irrelevant. Art creates its own reality, within which truth and the perfection of beauty is the infinite refinement of itself. History is very different. It is an empirical search for external truths, and for the best, most complete, and most profound external truths, in a maximal corresponding relationship with the absolute reality of the past events. —David Hackett Fischer

These words are not without their ironic tone, of course, as Fischer is describing what he sees as a standard historian's preconceptions about art and history. But it is not far from a description of the basic assumptions of many kinds of formalist criticism: "literature is not a discourse that can or must be false . . . it is a discourse that, precisely, cannot be subjected to the test of truth; it is neither true nor false, to raise this question has no meaning: this is what defines its very status as 'fiction'" (Todorov, p. 18). Historiographic metafiction suggests that truth and falsity may indeed not be the right terms in which to discuss fiction, but not for the reasons offered above. Postmodern novels like *Flaubert's Parrot, Famous Last Words,* and *A Maggot* imply that there are only truths in the plural, and never one truth; and there is rarely falseness per se, just other truths. Fiction and history are narratives distinguished by their frames (see Smith), frames which historiographic metafiction both asserts and then crosses. It posits both the generic contracts of fiction (as self-sufficient, autonomous metafiction) and of history. The postmodern paradoxes here are complex. The interaction of the historiographic and the metafictional foregrounds the rejection of the claims of both "authentic" representation and "inauthentic" copy alike, and the very meaning of artistic originality is as challenged as is the transparency of historic referentiality.

Postmodern fiction suggests that to re-write or to re-present the past in fiction and in history is, in both cases, to open it up to the present, to prevent it from being conclusive and teleological. Such is the teaching of novels like Susan Daitch's *L.C.,* with its double layer of historical reconstruction, both of which are presented with metafictional self-consciousness. Parts of the journal of (fictive) Lucienne Crozier, implicated yet marginalized witness of the (real) 1848 revolution in Paris, are edited and translated twice: once by Willa Rehnfield and once by her younger assistant after her death. The recent interest in archival women's history is given an interesting new twist here, for the two translations of the end of Lucienne's diary are so vastly different that the entire activity of translation, as well as research, is called into question. In the more traditional Willa's version, Lucienne dies of consumption in Algiers, abandoned by her revolutionary lover. In the version of her more radical assistant (a veteran of Berkeley in 1968, being sought by the police for a bombing), Lucienne stops writing, while also awaiting arrest for her own revolutionary activities. The only common denominator appears in the image that, in the Arab world of Algiers, Lucienne feels *like an invalid* — sequestered and marginalized.

The problematizing of the nature of historical knowledge, in novels like this or like Ian Watson's *Chekhov's Journey*, points both to the need to separate and the danger of separating fiction and history as narrative genres. This problematizing has also been in the foreground of much contemporary literary theory (on Lentricchia, de Man, and Derrida, see Parker) and philosophy of history, from Hayden White to Paul Veyne. When the latter calls history "un roman vrai" (p. 10), he is signaling the two genres' shared conventions: selection, organization, diegesis, anecdote, temporal pacing, and emplotment (p. 14, 15, 22, 29, 46–48). But this is not to say that history and fiction are part of the "same order of discourse" (Lindenberger, p. 18). They are different, though they share social, cultural, and ideological contexts, as well as formal techniques. Novels (with the exception of some extreme surfictions) incorporate social and political history to some extent, and that extent will vary (Hough, p. 113), just as historiography is often as structured, coherent, and teleological as any narrative fiction. It is not only the novel but history too that is "palpably betwixt and between" (Kermode, "Novel," p. 235). Both historians and novelists *constitute* their subjects as possible objects of narrative representation, as Hayden White ("Historical Text," p. 57) has argued (for history alone, however). And they do so by the very structures and language they use to present those subjects. In Jacques Ehrmann's extreme formulation: "[H]istory and literature have no existence in and of themselves. It is we who constitute them as the object of our understanding" (p. 153).

Postmodernism deliberately confuses the notion that history's problem is verification, while fiction's is veracity (Berthoff, p. 272). Both are signifying systems in our culture, what Doctorow once called modes of "mediating the world for the purpose of introducing meaning" ("False Documents," p. 24). And it is both the constructed, imposed nature of that meaning and the seemingly absolute necessity for us to make meaning that historiographic metafiction like Coover's *The Public Burning* reveals. This novel teaches that "history itself depends on conventions of narrative, language, and ideology in order to present an account of 'what really happened'"

(Mazurek, p. 29). Both history and fiction are cultural sign systems, ideological constructions whose ideology includes their appearance of being autonomous and self-contained. It is the metafictionality of these novels that underlines Doctorow's notion that "history is a kind of fiction in which we live and hope to survive, and fiction is a kind of speculative history . . . by which the available data for the composition is seen to be greater and more various in its sources than the historian supposes" (p. 25).

Fredric Jameson has argued that historical representation is as surely in crisis as is the linear novel, and for much the same reasons:

> The most intelligent "solution" to such a crisis does not consist in abandoning historiography altogether, as an impossible aim and an ideological category all at once, but rather — as in the modernist aesthetic itself — in reorganizing its traditional procedures on a different level. Althusser's proposal seems the wisest in this situation: as old-fashioned narrative or "realistic" historiography becomes problematic, the historian should reformulate her vocation — not any longer to produce some vivid representation of history 'as it really happened,' but rather to produce the *concept* of history. ("Periodizing," p. 180)

There is only one word I would change in this: the word "modernist" seems to me to be less apt than "postmodernist," though Jameson would never agree (see "Postmodernism and Consumer Society" and "Postmodernism or The Cultural Logic"). Postmodern historiographic metafiction has done exactly what Jameson calls for here, though it is more the problematizing than just the production of a "*concept* of history" (and fiction) that results. The two genres may be textual constructs, narratives which are both non-originary in their reliance on past intertexts and also unavoidably ideologically laden, but they do not, in historiographic metafiction at least, "adopt equivalent representational procedures or constitute equivalent modes of cognition" (Foley, p. 35). However, there are (or have been) combinations of history and fiction which do attempt such equivalence.

III

[T]he binary opposition between fiction and fact is no longer relevant: in any differential system, it is the assertion of the space *between* the entities that matters.
— Paul de Man

Perhaps. But historiographic metafiction suggests the continuing relevance of such an opposition, even if it be a problematic one. It both installs and then blurs the line between fiction and history. This kind of generic blurring has been a feature of literature back to the classical epic and the Bible (see Weinstein, p. 263), but the simultaneous assertion and crossing of boundaries is more postmodern. Umberto Eco has claimed that there are three ways to narrate the past: the romance, the swashbuckling tale, and the historical novel. He has added that it was the latter that he intended to write in *The Name of the Rose* (pp. 74–75). Historical novels, he feels, "not only identify in the past the causes of what came later, but also trace the process through which those causes began slowly to produce their effects" (p. 76). This is why his medieval characters, like John Banville's in his *Doctor Copernicus*, are made to talk like Wittgenstein. I would say, however, that this device points to a fourth way of narrating the past: historiographic metafiction — and not historical fiction — because of the intensely self-conscious way in which all this is done.

What is the difference between postmodern fiction and what we usually think of as nineteenth-century historical fiction, though its forms persist today (see Fleishman)? It is difficult to generalize about this latter complex genre because, as theorists have pointed out, history plays a great number of distinctly different roles, at different levels of generality, in its various manifestations. There seems little agreement as to whether the historical past is always presented as individualized, particularized and past (i.e., different from the present) (see Shaw, pp. 26, 48, 148) or whether that past is offered as typical and therefore present, or at least as sharing values through time with the present (Lukács). While acknowledging the difficulties of definition (see Turner; Shaw) that the historical novel shares with most genres, we might define historical fiction as that which is modeled on historiography to the extent that it is motivated and made operative by a notion of history as a shaping force (in the narrative and in human destiny) (see Fleishman). However, it is Georg Lukács's influential and more particular definition that theorists most frequently have to confront in their defining, and I am no exception.

Lukács felt that the historical novel could enact historical process by presenting a microcosm which generalizes and concentrates (p. 39). The protagonist, therefore, should be a type, a synthesis of the general and particular, of "all the humanly and socially essential determinants." From this definition, it is clear that the protagonists of historiographic metafiction are anything but types: they are the ex-centrics, the marginalized, the peripheral figures of fictional history — the Coalhouse Walkers (in *Ragtime*), the Saleem Sinais (in *Midnight's Children*), the Fevvers (in *Nights at the*

Circus). Even the historical personages take on different, particularized, and ultimately ex-centric status: Doctor Copernicus (in the novel of the same name), Houdini (in *Ragtime*), Richard Nixon (in *The Public Burning*). Historiographic metafiction espouses a postmodern ideology of pluralism and recognition of difference; "type" has little function here, except as something to be ironically undercut. The protagonist of a postmodern novel like Doctorow's *Book of Daniel* is overtly specific, individual, culturally and familially conditioned in his response to history, both public and private. The narrative form enacts the fact that Daniel is not a type of anything, no matter how much he may try to see himself as representing the New Left or his parents' cause.

Related to this notion of type is Lukács's belief that the historical novel was defined by the relative unimportance of its use of detail, which he saw as "only a means of achieving historical faithfulness, for making concretely clear the historical necessity of a concrete situation" (p. 59). Therefore, accuracy or even truth of detail was irrelevant. Many readers of historical fiction would disagree, I suspect, as have writers of it (John Williams, pp. 8–11). Postmodern fiction contests this defining characteristic in two different ways. First of all, historiographic metafiction, as we have seen, plays upon the truth and lies of the historical record. In novels like *Foe, Burning Water*, or *Famous Last Words*, certain known historical details are deliberately falsified in order to foreground the possible mnemonic failures of recorded history and the constant potential for both deliberate and inadvertent error. The second difference lies in the way in which postmodern fiction actually uses detail or historical data. Historical fiction (*pace* Lukács) usually incorporates and assimilates these data in order to lend a patina of verifiability or an air of dense specificity and particularity to the fictional world. Historiographic metafiction incorporates, but rarely assimilates the data. More often the process of *attempting* to assimilate is what is foregrounded. Historiographic metafiction acknowledges the paradox of the *reality* of the past but its (only) *textualized* accessibility to us today.

Lukács's third major defining characteristic of the historical novel is its relegation of historical personages to secondary roles. Clearly, in postmodern novels like *Doctor Copernicus, Kepler, Legs* (Jack Diamond), and *Antichthon* (Giordano Bruno), this is hardly the case. In many historical novels, the real figures of the past are deployed to validate or authenticate the fictional world by their presence, as if to hide the joins between fiction and history in a formal, ontological sleight of hand. The metafictional self-reflexivity of postmodern novels prevents any such subterfuge, and poses that ontological join as a problem: how do we know the past? what do (what can) we know of it now? Sometimes the manipulation of historical personages is so blatant and in conflict with known fact that the reader is forced to ask the reason behind, for instance, John Barth's rewriting of John Smith's rescue of Pocahontas in *The Sot-Weed Factor*. It is never too difficult to see that reason, thanks to the overt metafictionality: here, it is the demystification of the heroic — and falsifying — view of history that has passed into legend. Similarly Coover does considerable violence to the history of the Rosenbergs in *The Public Burning*, but he does so to satiric ends, in the name of social critique. I do not think that he intends to construct a wilful betrayal of politically tragic events; perhaps, however, he does want to make a connection to the real world of political action through the reader — through our awareness of the need to question received versions of history.

While the debates still rage about the definition of the historical novel, in the 1960s a new variant on the history/fiction confrontation came into being: the nonfictional novel. This differed from the treatment of recent factual events recounted as history, as in William Manchester's *The Death of a President*. It was a form of documentary narrative which deliberately used techniques of fiction in an overt manner and which usually made no pretense of objectivity of presentation. In the work of Hunter S. Thompson, Tom Wolfe, and Norman Mailer, the authorial structuring experience was often in the forefront as the new guarantee of "truth," as we watched the narrator's individual attempts to perceive and impose pattern on what he saw about him. This metafictionality and provisionality in the nonfictional novel obviously link it to historiographic metafiction, but there are, as we shall see, significant differences.

It is probably not accidental that this form of the New Journalism, as it was called, was an American phenomenon. The Vietnam War had brought with it a real distrust of official "facts" as presented by the military and the media, and the ideology of the sixties had licensed a revolt against homogenized forms of experience (Hellmann, p. 8). The result was a kind of overtly personal and provisional journalism, autobiographical in impulse and performative in impact. The famous exception was Truman Capote's *In Cold Blood*, which is a modern rewriting of the realist novel — universalist in assumptions and omniscient in narrative technique. But in works like *The Electric Kool-Aid Acid Test*, *Fear and Loathing: On the Campaign Trail '72*, and *Of a Fire on the Moon*, there was a very "sixties" kind of direct confrontation with social reality in the present (Hollowell, p. 10). The impact of the new mixing of fiction and fact is clear on popular, if not academic, history in the years following: in *John Brown's Journey*, Albert Fried broke the rules and showed the tentative groping movement of his becoming interested in his historical topic. The book is "marked by the feeling of a historian in the act of grappling with his subject" (Weber, p. 144), as the subtitle underlines: *Notes and Reflections on His America and Mine.*

The nonfictional novel of the sixties and seventies did not just record the contemporary hysteria of history, as Robert Scholes has claimed (p. 37). It did not just try to embrace "the fictional element inevitable in any reporting" and then try to imagine its "way toward the truth" (p. 37). What it did was seriously question who determined and created that truth, and it was this particular aspect of it that perhaps enabled historiographic metafiction's more paradoxical questioning. A number of critics have seen parallels in the nonfictional novel and contemporary metafiction, but they seem to disagree completely on the form that parallel takes. For one, both stress the overt, totalizing power of the imagination of the writers to create unities (Hellmann, p. 16); for another, both refuse to neutralize contingency by reducing it to unified meaning (Zavarzadeh, p. 41). I would agree with the former as a designation of the nonfictional novel, though not of all metafiction; and the latter certainly defines a lot of contemporary self-reflexive writing more accurately than it does the New Journalism. Historiographic metafiction, of course, fits both definitions: it installs totalizing order, only to contest it, by its radical provisionality, intertextuality, and, often, fragmentation. In many ways, the nonfiction novel is a late modernist creation (see Smart, p. 3) in the sense that both its self-consciousness about its writing process and its stress on subjectivity (or psychological realism) recall Woolf and Joyce's experiments with limited, depth vision in narrative, though, in the New Journalism, it is the author whose historical presence as participant authorizes subjective response. Postmodern novels like Rudy Wiebe's *The Scorched-Wood People* parody this stance, however. The participant in the historical action was real, but is still fictionalized: he is made to tell the tale of Louis Riel from a point in time *after* his own death, with the insights of retrospection and access to information he could not possibly have had as participant.

IV

History is three-dimensional. It partakes of the nature of science, art, and philosophy. — Louis Gottschalk

Historiographic metafictions raise a number of specific issues regarding the interaction of historiography and fiction that deserve more detailed study: issues surrounding the nature of identity and subjectivity; the question of reference and representation; the intertextual nature of the past; the ideological implications of writing about history; narrative emplotting; and the status of historical documents, not to mention "facts."

First of all, historiographic metafictions appear to privilege two modes of narration, both of which problematize the entire notion of subjectivity: multiple points of view (as in Thomas's *The White Hotel*) or an overtly controlling narrator (as in Swift's *Waterland*). In neither, however, do we find a subject confident of his/her ability to know the past with any certainty. This is not a transcending of history, but a problematized inscribing of subjectivity into history. In a novel like *Midnight's Children*, nothing, not even the self's physical body, survives the instability caused by the rethinking of the past in nondevelopmental, noncontinuous terms. To use the (appropriate) language of Michel Foucault, Saleem Sinai's body is exposed as "totally imprinted by history and the process of history's destruction of the body" (p. 148). Postmodernism establishes, differentiates, and then disperses stable narrative voices (and bodies) that use memory to try to make sense of the past. It both installs and then subverts traditional concepts of subjectivity; it both establishes and is capable of shattering "the unity of man's being through which it was thought that he could extend his sovereignty to the events of the past" (Foucault, p. 153). The protagonist's psychic disintegration in *Waterland* reflects this shattering; but his strong narrative voice asserts that same selfhood, in a typically postmodern and paradoxical way. The second epigraph of Swift's novel is from *Great Expectations* (a retrospectively ironic source for a book about no expectations and about the past). *Waterland* shares with Dickens's novel a locale (the marshy fenlands) and a preoccupation with the past, but Swift reveals none of Dickens's confidence that one could learn from that past. Indeed, his history teacher protagonist knows better — from both global and personal experience. This kind of intertextuality, often parodic in its ironies, is typical of postmodern fiction. It is a way of literally incorporating the textualized past into the text of the present.

Postmodern intertextuality is a formal manifestation of both a desire to close the gap between past and present for the reader and a desire to rewrite the past in a new context. It is not a modernist desire to order the present through the past or to make the present look spare in contrast to the richness of the past (see Antin, pp. 106–14). It is not an attempt to void or avoid history. Instead, it directly confronts the past of literature — and of historiography, for it too derives from other texts (documents). It uses and abuses those intertextual echoes, inscribing their powerful allusions and then subverting that power through irony. In all, there is little of the modernist sense of a unique, symbolic, visionary "work of art"; there are only texts, already written ones. Intertexts can be both historical and aesthetic in their nature and function.

To what, though, does the very language of historiographic metafiction refer? To a world of history or one of fiction? It is commonly accepted that there is a radical disjunction between the basic assumptions underlying these two notions of reference. History's referents are presumed to be real; fiction's are not. But what postmodern novels teach is that, in both cases, they actually refer at the first level to other texts: we only know the past (which really did exist) through its textualized remains. They problematize the activity of reference by refusing either to bracket the referent (as surfiction might) or to revel in it (as nonfictional novels might). This is not an emptying of the meaning of language, as Gerald Graff seems to think (p. 397). The text still communicates — in fact, it does so very didactically. There is not so much "a loss of belief in a significant external reality" (p. 403) as there is a loss of faith in our ability to (unproblematically) *know* that reality, and therefore to be able to represent it in language. Fiction and history are not different in this regard.

Historiographic metafiction also poses new questions about reference. The issue is no longer: "to what empirically real object in the past does the language of history refer?"; it is more: "to which discursive context could this language belong? to which prior textualizations must we refer?" Postmodern art is more complex and more problematic than extreme late modernist autorepresentation might suggest, with its view that there is no presence, no external truth which verifies or unifies, that there is only self-reference (Smith, pp. 8–9). Historiographic metafiction self-consciously states this, but then immediately points to the discursive nature of all reference — both literary and historiographical. The referent is always already inscribed in the discourses of our culture. This is no cause for despair; it is the text's major link with the "world," but one that acknowledges its identity as construct, rather than as simulacrum of some "real" outside. Once again, this does not deny that the past "real" existed; it only conditions our mode of knowledge of that past — we can only know it through its traces, its relics. The question of reference depends on what John Searle (p. 330) calls a shared "pretense" and what Stanley Fish calls being party to a set of "discourse agreements which are in effect decisions as to what can be stipulated as a fact" (p. 242). A "fact" is discourse-defined; an "event" is not.

Postmodern art is not so much ambiguous as it is doubled and contradictory, as can be seen in novels like Pynchon's *Gravity's Rainbow*, whose over-assertion of reference "dissipates its own referentiality" (Bradbury, p. 178). There is clearly a rethinking of the modernist tendency to move away from representation (Harkness, p. 9) by both installing it materially and subverting it. In the visual arts, as in literature, there has been a rethinking of the sign/referent relation in the face of the realization of the limits of self-reflexivity's separation from social practice (Menna, p. 10). Historiographic metafiction shows fiction to be historically conditioned and history to be discursively structured, and in the process manages to broaden the debate about the ideological implications of the Foucaldian conjunction of power and knowledge — for readers and for history itself as a discipline. As the narrator of Rushdie's *Shame* puts it: "History is natural selection. Mutant versions of the past struggle for dominance; new species of fact arise, and old saurian truths go to the wall, blindfolded and smoking last cigarettes. Only the mutations of the strong survive. The weak, the anonymous, the defeated leave few marks. . . . History loves only those who dominate her: it is a relationship of mutual enslavement" (p. 124).

The question of whose history survives is one that obsesses postmodern novels like Timothy Findley's *Famous Last Words*. In problematizing almost everything the historical novel once took for granted, historiographic metafiction destabilizes concepts of both history and fiction. The premise of postmodern fiction is the same as that articulated by Hayden White regarding history: "every representation of the past has specifiable ideological implications" (*Tropics*, p. 69). But the ideology of postmodernism is paradoxical, for it depends upon and draws its power from that which it contests. It is not truly radical; nor is it truly oppositional (as Martin, pp. 44–46, claims for the novel as a genre). But this does not mean it has no critical clout. The Epiloguist of *A Maggot* may claim that what we have read is indeed "a maggot, not an attempt, either in fact or in language, to reproduce known history" (p. 449), but that does not stop him from extended ideological analyses of eighteenth-century social, sexual, and religious history. Similarly, contemporary philosophers of history like Michel de Certeau have reminded historiographers that no research of the past is free of socio-economic, political, and cultural conditions (p. 65). Novels like *The Public Burning* or *Ragtime* do not trivialize the historical and the factual in their "game-playing" (Robertson) but rather politicize them through their meta-fictional rethinking of the epistemological and ontological relations between history and fiction. Both are acknowledged as part of larger social and cultural discourses which formalist literary criticism had formerly relegated to the extrinsic and irrelevant. This said, it is also true that it is part of the postmodern ideology not to ignore cultural bias and interpretive conventions and to question authority — even its own.

All of these issues — subjectivity, intertextuality, reference, ideology — underlie the problematized relations between history and fiction in postmodernism. But many theorists today have pointed to narrative as the one concern that envelops all of these, for the process of narrativization has come to be seen as a central form of human comprehension, of imposition of meaning and formal coherence on the chaos of events (Hayden White, "Narrativization," p. 795; Jameson, *Political*, p. 13; Mink, 132). Narrative is what translates knowing into telling (Hayden White, "Value," p. 5), and it is precisely this translation that obsesses postmodern fiction. The conventions of narrative in both historiography and novels, then, are not constraints, but enabling conditions of possibility of sense-making (Martin). Their disruption or challenging will be bound to upset such basic structuring notions as causality and logic — as happens with Oskar's drumming in *The Tin Drum*: narrative conventions are both installed and subverted. The refusal to integrate fragments (in novels like *Z.* or *The White Hotel*) is a refusal of the closure and telos which narrative usually demands (see Kermode, *Sense*). In postmodern poetry too, as Marjorie Perloff has argued, narrative is used in works like Ashbery's "They Dream Only of America" or Dorn's *Gunslinger*, but used in order to question "the very nature of the *order* that a systematic plot structure implies" (p. 158).

The issue of narrativity encompasses many others that point to the postmodern view that we can only know "reality" as it is produced and sustained by cultural representations of it (Owens, p. 21). In historiographic metafictions, these need not be directly verbal representations, for *ekphrases* (or verbal representations of visual representations) often have central representational functions. For example, in Carpentier's *Explosion in a Cathedral*, Goya's "Desastres de la guerra" series provides the works of visual art that are actually the sources of the novel's descriptions of revolutionary war. The seventh of that series, plus the "Dos de Mayo" and "Tres de Mayo," are particularly important, for their glorious associations are left aside by Carpentier, as an ironic signal of his own point of view. Of course, literary intertexts function in the narrative in a similar way. The details of Estaban and Sofía's house in Madrid come, in fact, from Torres Villaroel's *Vida*, a book which Estaban had read earlier in the novel (see Saad, pp. 120–22).

Historiographic metafictions, like both historical fiction and narrative history, cannot avoid dealing with the problem of the status of their "facts" and of the nature of their evidence, their documents. And, obviously, the related issue is that of how those documentary sources are deployed: can they be objectively, neutrally related? or does interpretation inevitably enter with narrativization? The epistemological question of how we know the past joins the ontological one of the status of the traces of that past. Needless to say, the postmodern raising of these questions offers few answers, but this provisionality does not result in some sort of historical relativism or presentism. It rejects projecting present beliefs and standards onto the past and asserts, in strong terms, the specificity and particularity of the individual past event. Nevertheless, it also realizes that we are epistemologically limited in our ability to know that past, since we are both spectators of and actors in the historical process. Historiographic metafiction suggests a distinction between "events" and "facts" that is one shared by many historians. Events are configured into facts by being related to "conceptual matrices within which they have to be imbedded if they are to count as facts" (Munz, p. 15). Historiography and fiction, as we saw earlier, *constitute* their objects of attention; in other words, they decide which events will become facts. The postmodern problematization points to our unavoidable difficulties with the concreteness of events (in the archive, we can find only their textual traces to make into facts) and their accessibility (do we have a full trace or a partial one? what has been absented, discarded as nonfact material?). Dominick LaCapra has argued that all documents or artifacts used by historians are not neutral evidence for reconstructing phenomena which are assumed to have some independent existence outside them. All documents process information and the very way in which they do so is itself a historical fact that limits the documentary conception of historical knowledge (p. 45).

I do not mean to suggest that this is a radical, new insight. In 1910, Carl Becker wrote that "the facts of history do not exist for any historian until he creates them" (p. 525), that representations of the past are selected to signify whatever the historian intends. It is this very difference between events (which have no meaning in themselves) and facts (which are given meaning) that postmodernism foregrounds. Even documents are selected as a function of a certain problem or point of view (Ricoeur, p. 108). Historiographic metafiction often points to this process by using the paratextual conventions of historiography (especially footnotes) to both inscribe and undermine the authority and objectivity of historical sources and explanations.

Unlike the documentary novel as defined by Barbara Foley, what I have been calling postmodern fiction does not "aspire to tell the truth" (Foley, p. 26) as much as to question *whose* truth gets told. It does not so much associate "this truth with claims to empirical validation" as contest the ground of any claim to such validation. How can a historian (or a novelist) check any historical account against past empirical reality in order to test its validity? Facts are not given but are constructed by the kinds of questions we ask of events (Hayden White, *Tropics*, p. 43). In the words of *Waterland*'s history teacher, the past is a "thing which cannot be eradicated, which accumulates and impinges" (p. 109). What postmodern discourses — fictive and historiographic — ask is how we know and come to terms with such a complex "thing."

Works Cited

Antin, David. "Modernism and Postmodernism: Approaching the Present in American Poetry." *Boundary 2* 1.1 (Fall 1972): 98–133.

Aristotle. *Poetics*, translated by James Hutton. London: Norton, 1982.

Barthes, Roland. *Writing Degree Zero*, translated by Annette Lavers and Colin Smith. London: Jonathan Cape, 1967.

Becker, Carl. "Detachment and the Writing of History." *Atlantic Monthly* 106 (1910): 534–36.

Berthoff, Warner. "Fiction, History, Myth: Notes toward the Discrimination of Narrative Forms." In *The Interpretation of Narrative: Theory and Practice*, edited by M. W. Bloomfield, pp. 263–87. Cambridge: Harvard University Press, 1970.

Bloomfield, M. W., ed. *The Interpretation of Narrative: Theory and Practice*. Cambridge: Harvard University Press, 1970.

Bradbury, Malcolm. *The Modern American Novel*. Oxford: Oxford University Press, 1983.

Braudy, Leo. *Narrative Form in History and Fiction: Hume, Fielding, and Gibbon*. Princeton: Princeton University Press, 1970.

Bremner, Robert H., ed. *Essays on History and Literature*. N.p.: Ohio State University Press, 1966.

Canary, Robert H., and Henry Kozicki, eds. *The Writing of History: Literary Form and Historical Understanding*. Madison: University of Wisconsin Press, 1978.

Certeau, Michel de. *L'Écriture de l'histoire*. Paris: Gallimard, 1975.

Coetzee, J. M. *Foe*. Toronto: Stoddardt, 1986.

Daitch, Susan. *L.C.* London: Virago, 1986.

Davis, Lennard. *Factual Fictions: The Origins of the English Novel.* New York: Columbia University Press, 1983.

Doctorow, E. L. "False Documents." In *E. L. Doctorow: Essays and Conversations*, edited by Richard Trenner, pp. 16–27. Princeton: Ontario Review Press, 1983.

Eco, Umberto. Postscript to *The Name of the Rose.* Trans. William Weaver. San Diego: Harcourt, Brace, Jovanovich, 1983, 1984.

Ehrmann, Jacques. "The Death of Literature." Trans. A. James Arnold. In Federman, pp. 229–53.

Federman, Raymond, ed. *Surfiction: Fiction Now . . . and Tomorrow.* 2d ed. Chicago: Swallow Press, 1981.

Fish, Stanley. *Is There a Text in This Class? The Authority of Interpretive Communities.* Cambridge: Harvard University Press, 1980.

Fleishman, Avrom. *The English Historical Novel: Walter Scott to Virginia Woolf.* Baltimore: Johns Hopkins University Press, 1971.

Fletcher, Angus, ed. *The Literature of Fact.* New York: Columbia University Press, 1976.

Foley, Barbara. *Telling the Truth: The Theory and Practice of Documentary Fiction.* Ithaca: Cornell University Press, 1986.

Foster, Hal, ed. *The Anti-Aesthetic: Essays on Postmodern Culture.* Port Townsend, Wash.: Bay Press, 1983.

Foucault, Michel. *Language, Counter-Memory, Practice.* Trans. D. F. Bouchard and S. Simon. Ithaca: Cornell University Press, 1977.

———. *This Is Not a Pipe.* Trans. and ed. James Harkness. Berkeley: University of California Press, 1982.

Fowles, John. *A Maggot.* Toronto: Collins, 1985.

Graff, Gerald. "The Myth of the Postmodernist Breakthrough." *TriQuarterly* 26 (Winter 1973): 383–417.

Harkness, James. "Translator's Introduction." In Foucault, *This Is Not a Pipe*, pp. 1–12.

Hellmann, John. *Fables of Fact: The New Journalism as New Fiction.* Urbana: University of Illinois Press, 1981.

Henderson, Harry B. *Versions of the Past: The Historical Imagination in American Fiction.* Oxford: Oxford University Press, 1974.

Holloway, John. *The Victorian Sage.* New York: Norton, 1953.

Hollowell, John. *Fact and Fiction: The New Journalism and the Nonfiction Novel.* Chapel Hill: University of North Carolina Press, 1977.

Hook, Sidney, ed. *Philosophy and History: A Symposium.* New York: New York University Press, 1963.

Hough, Graham. *An Essay on Criticism.* New York: Norton, 1966.

Jameson, Fredric. *The Political Unconscious: Narrative as a Socially Symbolic Act.* Ithaca: Cornell University Press, 1981.

———. "Postmodernism and Consumer Society." In *The Anti-Aesthetic: Essays on Postmodern Culture*, edited by Hal Foster, pp. 111–25. Port Townsend, Wash.: Bay Press, 1983.

———. "Postmodernism, or The Cultural Logic of Late Capitalism." *New Left Review* 146 (July–Aug. 1984): 53–92.

———. "Periodizing the 6os." In *The 6os Without Apology*, edited by Sohnya Sayres, et al., pp. 178–209. Minneapolis: University of Minnesota Press and *Social Text*, 1984.

Josipovici, Gabriel. *The World and the Book: A Study of Modern Fiction*. London: Macmillan, 1971.

Kermode, Frank. "Novel, History, and Type." *Novel* 1 (1968): 231–38.

———. *The Sense of an Ending*. New York: Oxford University Press, 1970.

LaCapra, Dominick. "On Grubbing in My Personal Archives: An Historiographical Exposé of Sorts (Or How I Learned to Stop Worrying and Love Transference)." *Boundary* 2, 2.3 (1985): 43–67.

Levine, George. *The Boundaries of Fiction: Carlyle, Macaulay, Newman*. Princeton: Princeton University Press, 1968.

Lindenberger, Herbert. "Toward a New History in Literary Study." *Profession* 84 (1984): 16–23.

Lukács, Georg. *The Historical Novel*. Translated by Hannah and Stanley Mitchell. London: Merlin, 1962.

Martin, Wallace. *Recent Theories of Narrative*. Ithaca: Cornell University Press, 1986.

Mazurek, Raymond A. "Metafiction, the Historical Novel, and Coover's *The Public Burning*." *Critique* 23.3 (1982): 29–42.

Menna, Filiberto. "Gli anni Settanta," *Il Verri* 1–2, 7th ser. (marzo/giugno 1984): 9–14.

Mink, Louis O. "Narrative Form as a Cognitive Instrument." In *The Writing of History: Literary Form and Historical Understanding*, edited by Robert H. Canary and Henry Kozicki, pp. 129–49. Madison: University of Wisconsin Press, 1978.

Munz, Peter. *The Shapes of Time*. Middletown, Conn.: Wesleyan University Press, 1977.

Nye, Russel B. "History and Literature: Branches of the Same Tree." In *Essays on History and Literature*, edited by Robert H. Bremner, pp. 123–59. N.p.: Ohio University Press, 1966.

Owens, Craig. "Representation, Appropriation, and Power." *Art in America* 70.5 (May 1982): 9–21.

Parker, Andrew. " 'Taking Sides' (On History): Derrida Re-Marx." *Diacritics* 11 (1981): 57–73.

Perloff, Marjorie. *The Dance of the Intellect: Studies in the Poetry of the Pound Tradition*. Cambridge: Cambridge University Press, 1985.

Ricoeur, Paul. *Time and Narrative*. Vol. 1. Translated by Kathleen McLaughlin and David Pallauer. Chicago: University of Chicago Press, 1984.

Robertson, Mary F. "Hystery, Herstory, History: 'Imagining the Real' in Thomas's *The White Hotel*." *Contemporary Literature* 25.4 (Winter 1984): 452–77.

Rushdie, Salman. *Shame*. London: Picador, 1984.

Saad, Gabriel. "L'Histoire et la révolution dans *Le Siècle des lumières*." In *Quinze Études autour de El Siglo de las luces de Alejo Carpentier*, pp. 113–22. Paris: L'Harmattan, 1983.

Sayres, Sohnya, et al., eds. *The 6os Without Apology*. Minneapolis: University of Minnesota Press and *Social Text*, 1984.

Scholes, Robert. "Double Perspective on Hysteria." *Saturday Review* 24 (Aug. 1968): 37.

Seamon, Roger G. "Narrative Practice and the Theoretical Distinction between History and Fiction." *Genre* 16 (1983): 197–218.

Searle, John. "The Logical Status of Fictional Discourse." *New Literary History* 6 (1975): 319–32.

Shaw, Harry E. *The Forms of Historical Fiction: Sir Walter Scott and His Successors.* Ithaca: Cornell University Press, 1983.

Smart, Robert Augustin. *The Nonfiction Novel.* Lanham, N.Y.: University Press of America, 1985.

Smith, Barbara Herrnstein. *On the Margins of Discourse: The Relation of Literature to Language.* Chicago: University of Chicago Press, 1978.

Swift, Graham. *Waterland.* London: Heinemann, 1983.

Todorov, Tzvetan. *Introduction to Poetics.* Translated by Richard Howard. Minneapolis: University of Minnesota Press, 1981.

Tompkins, Jane. "The Reader in History: The Changing Shape of Literary Response." In *Reader-Response Criticism: From Formalism to Post-Structuralism*, edited by Jane Tompkins, pp. 201–33. Baltimore: Johns Hopkins University Press, 1980.

———, ed. *Reader-Response Criticism: From Formalism to Post-Structuralism.* Baltimore: Johns Hopkins University Press, 1980.

Trenner, Richard, ed. *E. L. Doctorow: Essays and Conversations.* Princeton: Ontario Review Press, 1983.

Turner, Joseph W. "The Kinds of Historical Fiction." *Genre* 12 (1979): 333–55.

Veyne, Paul. *Comment on écrit l'histoire.* Paris: Seuil, 1971.

Weber, Ronald. *The Literature of Fact: Literary Nonfiction in American Writing.* Athens, Ohio: Ohio University Press, 1980.

Weinstein, Mark A. "The Creative Imagination in Fiction and History." *Genre* 9.3 (1976): 263–77.

White, Hayden. "The Fictions of Factual Representation." In *The Literature of Fact*, edited by Angus Fletcher, pp. 21–44. New York: Columbia University Press, 1976.

———. "The Historical Text as Literary Artifact." In *The Writing of History: Literary Form and Historical Understanding*, edited by Robert A. Canary and Henry Kozicki, pp. 41–62. Madison: University of Wisconsin Press, 1978.

———. *Tropics of Discourse: Essays in Cultural Criticism.* Baltimore: Johns Hopkins University Press, 1978.

———. "The Value of Narrativity in the Representation of Reality." *Critical Inquiry* 7.1 (Autumn 1980): 5–27.

———. "The Narrativization of Real Events." *Critical Inquiry* 7.4 (Summer 1981): 793–98.

White, Morton. "The Logic of Historical Narration." In *Philosophy and History: A Symposium*, edited by Sidney Hook, pp. 3–31. New York: New York University Press, 1963.

Williams, John. "Fact in Fiction: Problems for the Historical Novelist." *Denver Quarterly* 7.4 (1973): 1–12.

Wolf, Christa. *No Place on Earth.* Translated by Jan Van Heurck. New York: Farrar, Straus and Giroux, 1982.

Zavarzadeh, Mas'ud. *The Mythopoeic Reality: The Postwar American Nonfiction Novel.* Urbana: University of Illinois Press, 1976.

20

"Building Up from Fragments": The Oral
Memory Process in Some Recent African-American
Written Narratives · HELEN LOCK

Although the precise way in which memory functions is still open to question, especially in these days of contentious debate over repressed/coerced
memory, a useful distinction can be made between the differing perceptions
of the memory process generated by oral and by literate cultures. This
distinction, and, more importantly, the possibility of mediating between
these differing perceptions, has been extensively invoked by many writers of
the African diaspora for whom the process of memory is a controlling
narrative principle. Through memory, perceived in both oral and literate
terms, they aim to reconstruct the absences and silences of oral history that
are contained within the official written record.

This essay focuses specifically on recent African-American writers' re-
vival, for this same purpose, of oral perceptions of the memory process
within a literate/literary context and framework. The discussion will be
centered primarily on three novels, Toni Morrison's *Beloved* (1987), Paule
Marshall's *Praisesong for the Widow* (1983), and David Bradley's *The Chaneysville Incident* (1981). I choose these partly because of their broad familiarity as
staples of college introductory courses in African-American literature, but
also because — superficially dissimilar as they are — they are representative of
a generation of African-American literary artists whose sensibilities do not
exclude orally constituted modes of thought. This is not by any means to
suggest that they simply substitute an oral for a literate conception of memory, valorizing one and dismissing the other. To do so would be as exclusory
as the process whereby written records dismiss much of oral history. Their
aim, as African-American writers, is not to exclude either cultural tradition
but to energize the dialectic between them by reasserting — through the
medium of the written word — the value of an orally derived perception of
the workings of memory. This perception, often obscured or debased during
the ascendancy of literacy and literate thought in the twentieth century,
provides a powerful alternative means of negotiating with the past.

Literate cultures characteristically consider memory to be a rational, intellectual process. Literate, text-oriented cultures that value empirical science and verifiable fact demand of memory that it adhere to rigorous standards of exactitude and verification. Because literates think in terms of a fixed original whose total recapitulation is not only possible but desirable, "objective, deliberate, and exact recall" thus becomes the privileged definition of memory. Despite its privileged status, however, verbatim recall is not the way memory functions naturally. Recall is in fact seldom exact, but "constructed or reconstructed from a few remembered details combined with an impression left by the original. Recallers think the result is actually a reproduction of what they have retained, whereas, in fact, it has been built up from fragments."[1] Although seldom attainable, exact recall is nevertheless the desired goal. Because of the general inability of the spontaneous or subjective memory process to recuperate a fixed original, therefore, it is not valued by literate societies as it is by oral cultures.

In *The Interface between the Written and the Oral,* Jack Goody makes the important distinction "between exact recall (what psychologists often mean by 'memory') and creative reconstruction, which does not involve verbatim learning, or even imitation, but generative recall."[2] Since oral cultures characteristically conceive of time more in cyclical than linear terms, the past is not experienced as a single fixed entity, repository of unchangeable facts or "truth" — a time irrevocably gone. Thus it is recalled by memory into present consciousness not by an objective process whose results are subject to verification but by "creative reconstruction."[3] Creativity, spontaneity, intuitiveness, and subjectivity all help to provide access, through memory, to a past that does not have to be — indeed, cannot be — monolithic.

In transitional periods during which oral cultures gradually achieve literacy, we find ambiguous attitudes toward the nature of memory. For example, Frances A. Yates's *The Art of Memory* (this is still the best-known and most authoritative book on the subject, though now joined by Mary Carruthers's *Book of Memory* [1990]) described the elaborate memory arts that reached their zenith during the European Renaissance, when predominantly oral societies were becoming increasingly literate. That these arts contained components of both oral and literate conceptions of memory is made clear in a recent essay by Paul Sharrad that discusses the acknowledged debt of contemporary Caribbean writer Wilson Harris's fiction to the art of memory as Yates defines it (and as Sharrad interprets Yates's definition): "[D]espite its drive to fix everything . . . it is flexible, open to rearrangements, additions, deletions, in the light of cumulative feedback. . . .

[It is] a system which is not solely or even primarily devised as a rationalistic attempt to encompass material reality."[4] Sharrad shows the relevance and value of this mediation to the postcolonial writer whose society is undergoing a related transition: in the struggle for national self-definition, a response to the past that includes both the rational memory process and "creative reconstruction" enables the writer to look through and then beyond the written colonial record to a "subjective, tentative deconstruction of dominating presence to show the shadows of reconstructions from absence."[5]

A similar imperative informs the work of many recent African-American writers, although with a different emphasis. In the transitional period during which African Americans achieved literacy, especially in the early twentieth century, the powerful oral tradition continued to flourish, thanks both to the ambiguity of attitudes toward literacy characteristic of such periods and to varying degrees of ambivalence among African Americans about adopting the dominant culture's most privileged form of expression.[6] As it evolved, African-American literature continued to look to the oral tradition, not just for its expressive forms but for access to a past not preserved in literary form. But then, as both literacy itself and the African-American literary tradition become more firmly entrenched, so inevitably do literate definitions of the proper use of memory to access the past. This becomes especially problematic when the past in question — particularly as it pertains to slavery — becomes subsumed in the collective unconscious because it is too painful to confront directly. The linear conception of time characteristic of the literate memory process, which fixes the past unchangeably, reinforces this resistance to confrontation, because it demands that the past remain static, never to be revisited, reconfigured, or transcended. In response to this impasse, many recent African-American written narratives have sought to propose an alternative approach to the past by foregrounding the functioning of oral memory both thematically and structurally: not to recall a fixed original or a singular truth but to reconstruct and regenerate (inter)subjectively many kinds of truth. This approach ultimately enables participation in, as well as preservation of, the past, and provides the potential for its transformation and the exorcism of its pain.

Perhaps the clearest and best-known example can be found in Toni Morrison's *Beloved*. Through her central character, Sethe, Morrison coins the neologism "rememory" and implies that rememory is to be understood differently from the conventional (literate) definition of memory. It puns on the fact that to "re-member" something is to perform the act of reassembling its members, thus stressing the importance to the memory process of creative reconstruction. Rememory, in fact, evokes the more intuitive oral memory process, which both defines the characters' negotiations with the past and provides the novel's narrative and structural principle. Yet it does so within the context of a highly sophisticated literary framework.

Rememory, as Sethe expresses it, is both subjective and intersubjective: "Someday you be walking down the road and you hear something or see something going on. So clear. And you think it's you thinking it up. A thought picture. But no. It's when you bump into a rememory that belongs to someone else."[7] Rather than a solipsistic "remembering subject," Morrison envisions a remembering community of overlapping and interlocking, sometimes interdependent, consciousnesses. Rememory is also premised on a cyclical understanding of time: "Where I was before I came here, that place is real. It's never going away. Even if the whole farm—every tree and grass blade of it dies. The picture is still there and what's more, if you go there—you who never was there—if you go there and stand in the place where it was, it will happen again; it will be there for you, waiting for you" (36). "Place" is important to the visual orientation of memory, just as it was to the many *ars memorandi* Yates described, which advised memorizing ideas by associating them with different parts of physical structures.[8] Here, though, the focus is on the power of the spirit of place to evoke visual memory—again, both subjectively and intersubjectively: "Places, places are still there. If a house burns down, it's gone, but the place—the picture of it—stays, and not just in my rememory, but out there, in the world" (35–36).

Rememory, however, does not put the same premium as literate memory on the objectivity required to achieve exact recall of a fixed and verifiable original. The "truth" of the past to which rememory provides access does not take a fixed, singular form and has different implications in the present for all those—Sethe, Denver, Paul D, Stamp Paid, Baby Suggs, the women who converge on 124 at the end, and many others—who participate in the re-membering and, by doing so, reparticipate in a past that they now experience differently. In a 1987 television interview, Toni Morrison described the novel as presenting "the cumulative effect of memory and of . . . deliberately forgetting." For Sethe, in particular—whose name echoes Lethe, the mythical river of forgetfulness—*re*memory provides the key to unlocking, and ultimately transforming, a past her rational memory has repressed.

The re-membering that will enable the elements of the past to be collectively and creatively reconfigured is reflected in the structure of the narrative itself, which proceeds by "building up from fragments," shifting between present time and different points in the past as seen from multiple perspectives.[9] As Philip Page explains, "One word, detail, or image drops into their consciousness and reminds them of some part of their buried pasts. Cautiously, they relive the memory, rethinking and sometimes retelling it bit by bit, then dropping it, only to circle back to it later, with or without purpose."[10] As this process unfolds—parts of the same story are reconstructed from different points of view, new details emerge before a coherent interpretive framework can be established, and all the while Sethe is "[c]ircling [Paul D] the way she was circling the subject" (*Beloved*, 161)— perplexed readers find themselves in the position of having to join the rememberers in the act of creative reconstruction.

To extract individual meaning from the narrative, readers must enact the oral memory process by piecing together fragments, suggestions, hints, to make a whole that can never be precisely the same in each case—since one man's evocative detail is another woman's insignificant trifle—and would be diminished if it were. Morrison makes it clear that the story to be reconstructed can only be generated subjectively and intuitively and thus cannot take a final, definitive form: "To make the story appear oral, meandering, effortless, spoken—to have the reader feel the narrator without identifying that narrator, of hearing him or her knocking about, and to have the reader work with the author in the construction of the book—is what's important."[11] This complex literary text achieves its purpose, in other words, by evoking orally derived thought processes.

Each of the characters likewise re-members the story differently, though interconnectedly, according to their different needs—Denver, for example, collaborates with Beloved "to create what really happened" (78), the focus of which is the story of her own birth. For Sethe, the need is critical: first, to confront, finally, the horror of the past that her rational memory has repressed and that she has been "circling," "avoiding," "beating back the past" (73). But then, more importantly, she needs to *re-member* it. The rational memory of "what really happened" is not the whole story. When she relives the crucial scene at the end, it is through the fragmented sensory and emotional perceptions of her nonrational memory, as she confronts the man who "is coming for her best thing. She hears wings. Little hummingbirds stick needle beaks right through her headcloth into her hair and beat their wings. And if she thinks anything, it is no. No no. Nonono" (262). Through rememory the past is reconfigured. This visceral reenactment enables Sethe to see past the "facts" and place the blame for her daughter's murder where it belongs, exorcising at least part of the guilt (and, finally, the ravenous Beloved herself).

History is not repeated in this reenactment but transformed, and it is this transformative power of rememory that enables Morrison ultimately to use her novel to make restitution not just to Sethe and Beloved but by extension to all the "[d]isremembered and unaccounted for" (274) of the past—the "sixty million and more" of her headnote. The written text of *Beloved* is their memorial, supplying a voice to a silence in the oral tradition, a silence containing stories too horrible to tell ("It was not a story to pass on" [274]). The use of rememory as narrative principle, then, enables *Beloved* to mediate between past and present realities, blurring the distinction between them and re-membering the disremembered.

Although it stands as a paradigmatic example of this narrative approach to memory, *Beloved* is not its original (and will not be its final word). Among many other examples that might be discussed, one of the most pertinent is Paule Marshall's *Praisesong for the Widow*, in which the protagonist, Avey Johnson, re-members her life, undoing what it has become and reconnecting it to what she had not consciously realized it was, so that past and present lives are transformed. Like *Beloved*, the story is "built up from fragments," in this case as Avey gradually makes connections (and is guided by others to make connections) among her fragmented memories, and between these memories and her present experiences, eventually reconstructing herself as Avatara—an avatar of all the past and present consciousnesses that have contributed to the making of Avey Johnson

Avey's transformation is set in motion by a series of apparently unconnected and inexplicable sensory prompts. The overheard sound of patois in Martinique, for example, "had fleetingly called to mind the way people spoke in Tatem long ago,"[12] which in turn prompts the dream of her father's great-aunt Cuney, trying to coax and then drag Avey back to that Landing at Tatem from which the Ibos walked across the water back to Africa. Upon awakening, Avey retains the physical sensations of the fight that ensued (in front of her suburban neighborhood) as she resisted being pulled from the sophisticated, affluent life she had been conditioned to value, back to a life that values the nonmaterial and nonrational and is powerfully connected to its past. Cuney's grandmother had identified so strongly with her Ibo ancestors' rebellion that while her body might be in Tatem, "her mind was long gone with the Ibos" (39), but in the dream her descendant and namesake manifests different priorities: "Did [Cuney] really expect her to go walking over to the Landing dressed as she was? . . . With her hat and gloves on? And her fur stole draped over her arm? Avey Johnson could have laughed, the idea was so ridiculous" (40), though it is not long until "[h]er amusement began to give way to irritation" (41). That she has not fully embraced the values of her shallow suburban life, however, becomes clear the day after the dream, when the mere sight of a rich parfait causes an unshakable physical discomfort, a feeling of surfeit, which is the first clue to her subconscious dissatisfaction with a life overloaded with materialism and luxury but lacking spiritual sustenance, especially that which a reconnection with her ancestral past could bring her.

Thenceforth, after she abruptly leaves the cruise ship for reasons illdefined even to herself and embarks on a different journey that will eventually lead her to Carriacou with Lebert Joseph, Avey finds her memory constantly leading her in unexpected and unwilled directions. Her conscious, rational memory ceases to function: "[A]lthough she strained in her mind to see the [dining] room and the familiar objects there"—her silver, crystal, and china, the chandelier—"their reassuring forms refused to emerge. Instead she kept seeing with mystifying clarity the objects on display in the museum in the town of St. Pierre . . . which she had visited three days ago in Martinique" (83), objects that, bearing the scars of a volcanic eruption, are powerful reminders of the fragility and impermanence of affluent societies. Although her deliberate memory refuses to function, however, her spontaneous memory responds to a multiplicity of sensory stimuli by evoking seemingly random scenes from different points in the past: the feel of the milling crowd on the wharf, for example, their "colors and sounds" (187), remind her of her daughter's home movie, of her trip to Ghana, and then of her own childhood boat rides up the Hudson. Then the memory of the excited anticipation of the boat ride in turn evokes memories of Tatem, watching the communal ecstasy of the Ring Shout with Cuney, who had been excluded from it in punishment for "crossing her feet" (33).

Gradually, as the narrative of fragmented memories and sensations unfolds, the underlying pattern begins to emerge. Memories of the Ring Shout and of the boat ride are linked by "the same strange sensation" of

hundreds of slender threads streaming out from her navel and from the place where her heart was to enter those around her. . . . Then it would seem to her that . . . the threads didn't come from her, but from them, from everyone on the pier, including the rowdies, issuing out of their navels and hearts to stream into her. . . . While the impression lasted she would cease being herself . . . instead, for those moments; she became part of, indeed the center of, a huge wide confraternity. (190–91)

It is these connections, these "slender threads," that have been reaching out of the past to tug at her visceral memory, prompted by her subconscious need to remember both her individual and her communal identity: her need is to reconnect not only with others in her immediate past but also with all the earlier consciousnesses, the "pantheon of most ancient deities" (127) that dwell inside herself (just as in Avey's delirium Rosalie Parvay contains all the significant women of Avey's past [217], and Lebert Joseph contains an "endless array of personas" [243]).[13] Her rememory, then, will again be both subjective and intersubjective; it is evoked and shaped both by herself and by others.

Ultimately, Joseph reenacts Cuney's role in the dream by taking Avey's wrist and pulling her back toward the past. She feels "as exhausted as if she and the old man had been fighting" (184), but this time offers less resistance and allows herself to be taken on a journey that begins with a physical purging and ends with spiritual enrichment. The journey to the island (and here the spirit of place is again important: rather than "an actual place," the island seems "[s]omething conjured up perhaps to satisfy a longing and a need" [254]) in turn reenacts a more distant, ancestral memory — the Ibos' journey home — so that when Avey finally enters the dance in remembrance of the ancestors, she feels, like the Ibos, "as if the ground under her was really water" (248): she is not simply remembering but reexperiencing. The ancestors join the dance with the living: "Kin, visible, metamorphosed and invisible, repeatedly circled the cleared space together" (239). As the boundaries of time and place are erased, Avey again feels the "slender threads" of connection, as the dance is metamorphosed into the Ring Shout, and she feels reborn, "with her entire life yet to live" (249); her fellow dancers salute the deities resurrected inside her as she re-becomes the Avatara of her past, but in a new, revitalized form.

Here too, then, rememory is transformative, as Avey plans to return home to a different life and tell her story to those "lacking memory" (225), to transmit orally the story of the Ibos to rising generations. Marshall makes clear that the power of this kind of memory lies in its differentiation from conventional memory, which makes sharp distinctions between past and present, and which uses concepts such as "history" to consign people, places, and events irrecoverably and unchangeably to the past. Significantly, Avey's husband Jay, the source of her material affluence, was renowned for his "photographic memory" (92) — the epitome of exact recall. But oral, intuitive memory can evoke

> feelings that were beyond words, feelings and a host of subliminal memories that over the years had proven more durable and trustworthy than the history with its trauma and pain out of which they had come. After centuries of forgetfulness and even denial, they refused to go away. The note was a lamentation that could hardly have come from the rum keg of a drum. Its source had to be the heart, the bruised still-bleeding innermost chamber of the collective heart. (244–45)

Like Sethe, Avey had been subject to forgetfulness and denial. Like Sethe, rememory enables Avey to reconstruct the past, recover and reconnect with what is important, reject mistakes and injustices, and finally remake herself differently — not just as an individual but as a feeling part of "the collective heart."

History, "with its trauma and pain," is problematic in these texts precisely because it *is* painful: painful in its exclusions from the written historical record — the silences that *Beloved* seeks to fill — and painful in its isolation in an immutable past of so many whom the present wishes to claim and revitalize, an isolation that is the source of the sense of loss articulated by the "lamentation" Avey Johnson hears issuing from the collective heart.[14] The linear time of history fixes their fate unchangeably and precludes the transformative impulse of rememory by denying the reciprocal interaction of past and present. David Bradley's *The Chaneysville Incident*, a final example, directly addresses this issue. In this novel, a young history professor discovers he can only find meaning in his family's and community's past by abandoning the established methods of historical inquiry, and relying instead on a creative reconstruction that enables him to actively enter into and connect himself to that past, transforming the possibilities for his future.

John Washington's journey is both physically and spiritually a return to the site of his Pennsylvania childhood, initially to attend the deathbed of his father's (and his) old friend Jack. John's life has become completely disconnected from this milieu — "I knew nothing about the Hill any longer, I had made it my business not to know" — but on his arrival at the Hill, the power of the spirit of place begins to evoke initially unwilled memories: "[S]uddenly, inexplicably, I was curious, and so I thought for a moment, pulling half-remembered facts from the back of my mind."[15] His reunion with Jack revives other half-buried memories, of his own childhood and of his father, Moses Washington, and of the attempt he had made as a child to research his father's history and discover the truth about his mysterious death. The attempt had been a failure, because "I could not imagine. And if you cannot imagine, you can discover only cold facts, and more cold facts; you will never know the truth" (152). Now the adult John makes another attempt, his curiosity as a historian piqued by the fact that his father had left him a trail to follow.

In his will, Moses had bequeathed to John all his "books and records," which are not to be relinquished "until you have examined all volumes, including personal memoirs" (204). So John again attempts to decipher the written record, noting and organizing key points on index cards, which he shuffles hopelessly, failing to find connections — the trail leads him only to more "cold facts," and no closer to Moses Washington himself. He only begins to make progress when he departs from the cards and begins to talk: when he abandons the written record and begins to imaginatively reconstruct the story orally, in creative interaction with his audience, his white girlfriend, Judith (a process similar to Denver and Beloved's collaboration).[16] By thinking as a member of the collective heart, and not as a detached historian, he can reconstruct intuitively a story that takes him beyond the documented facts, beyond individual memories, beyond Moses Washington himself, and toward a personal interaction with the past of his ancestors.

The novel's narrative structure reflects this progress from fragmented "facts" toward imaginative connection. At the beginning, John is so disconnected from his family and background that his father is referred to only as "Moses Washington," without explanation. As in *Beloved*, readers find themselves in the position of trying to make their own connections, as John's narrative ranges from the present to different points in the past — prompted, for example, by memories sparked by his talks with Jack, memories of the visceral experience of hunting, or those prompted by the sight of Moses' folio — and interspersed with digressions on historical matters. This nonlinear narrative movement suggests (among other things) John's difficulty in giving a coherent shape to his memories, and in connecting them with his new discoveries.

But then gradually the initially self-sufficient first-person narrative begins to admit other voices: first Jack's lengthy tales about Moses Washington, then the voices of the Judge, Judith, and others, and ultimately the voices in the mind of the runaway slaves led by John's ancestor C. K. Washington. These voices in the wind, which have been present throughout the story (disguised in the beginning as the hum in the telephone wires, for example), and which John finally opens himself to hear, are, in Klaus Ensslen's words, "a motif which transcends rational analysis and historical quest and thereby helps to lift John's cognitive endeavor to a more imaginative and magical level where story opens into myth and assumes instinctual and somatic overtones that point away from the criteria generally accepted in Western culture, seeking connection with other cultural norms" (288). John cannot consciously summon these voices ("You can't hear them if you try. Don't try. Just listen" [*Chaneysville*, 411]), but by allowing them to speak through him, he becomes able to enter imaginatively into the story, to make an intuitive connection with his ancestors by mentally reliving their (hi)story.

The end of John's physical journey, like Avey Johnson's, marks a return: he stands on the same spot where C. K. and the runaway slaves died their heroic deaths, and where Moses reenacted their deaths through his own, in a ritual rejoining of his ancestors. The voices in the wind, which John realizes how to hear after remembering Jack's hunting advice about the necessity of intuition and identification with one's quarry ("Quit tryin' to figure where he's at an' jest follow him" [410]), give him access to years of family and community memories, which he uses to re-member the story of the fates of Moses and C. K. It is not the definitive version—in the absence of the "cold facts" of history there can be no definitive version, but as John discovered, if he has *only* cold facts as material, there can be no version at all. The story can only become coherent and meaningful to him if he reconstructs it without regard to rational analysis and lets it tell itself, relive itself, through him, in all its evocative detail ("that was how he found them, how he heard them, panting in the mist" [419])—if he lets it join him empathetically to the ancestral community.

And at the end, when he burns the index cards on which the cold facts were inscribed, he sees the transformative possibilities of the story he has creatively reconstructed, not just for the shape of the past but for the future: "[A]s I dropped the match to the wood and watched the flames go twisting, I wondered if . . . someone would understand. Not just someone: Judith" (450). There is one last potential reenactment: Judith's emulation of the white miller Liames, who, by imaginatively identifying with the runaway slaves enough to bury them according to "who loved who" (449), transcended centuries of racial conflict and antagonism. The tensions of John's relationship with Judith can be similarly transcended, if she chooses to forget history and make that empathetic leap into transformative rememory.

The narratives just discussed use the workings of the intuitive, non-rational memory to reconstruct a past that the rational memory has often chosen not to confront because of its "trauma and pain."[17] Thus these narratives do not seek its exact, accurate recuperation. Instead they illustrate how the memory process of creative reconstruction can re-member the fragments so as to transform the past and its implications, and to give it new life in the present. As Sharrad says, "The very fallibility of memory [in the literate sense] involves us in *mutual* reconstruction beyond solipsistic enclosure":[18] just as the past was shaped by many consciousnesses, so many (including the reader's) contribute in different ways to its reshaping and become active participants in stories resurrected from the grave of history. The felt need for this liberation back into the living world is, ultimately, the impulse for these novels' liberation of the oral memory process as literary narrative principle: the written text can serve to evoke all the many potential "truths" of all the unwritten stories.

Notes

1. Charles N. Cofer, Donna L. Chmielewski, and John P. Brockway, "Constructive Processes and the Structure of Human Memory," in *The Structure of Human Memory*, ed. Charles N. Cofer (San Francisco: Freeman, 1976), 191.

2. Jack Goody, *The Interface between the Written and the Oral* (Cambridge: Cambridge University Press, 1987), 180.

3. "[I]n functionally oral cultures the past is not felt as an itemized terrain, peppered with verifiable and disputed 'facts' or bits of information. It is the domain of the ancestors, a resonant source for renewing awareness of present existence, which is itself not an itemized terrain either." Walter J. Ong, *Orality and Literacy: The Technologizing of the Word* (New York: Methuen, 1982), 98.

4. Paul Sharrad, "The Art of Memory and the Liberation of History: Wilson Harris's Witnessing of Time," *Callaloo* 18, no. 1 (1995): 101.

5. Ibid., 97.

6. As Bernard W. Bell explains in *The Afro-American Novel and Its Tradition* (Amherst: University of Massachusetts Press, 1987), "[T]o cope with the complexities of their socialized ambivalence, to reconcile the tensions of their double-consciousness, the most intellectually capable and economically fortunate middle-class blacks borrowed Eurocentric forms of culture. . . . In contrast, the black majority . . . by virtue of their exclusion from full participation in the systems of the larger society were more inclined toward the alternative of the continuation and revitalization of residually oral Afrocentric forms of culture" (14–15).

7. Toni Morrison, *Beloved* (New York: NAL, 1987), 36; hereafter cited in the text.

8. The sixteenth-century Memory Theater of Giulio Camillo, as described by Frances Yates in chapter 6 of *The Art of Memory* (Chicago: University of Chicago Press, 1996), is a good example.

9. Walter Ong demonstrates that this kind of nonlinear, nonobjective structure is characteristic of oral narratives: "memory, as it guides the oral poet, often has little to do with strict linear presentation of events in temporal sequence" (*Orality and Literacy*, 147).

10. Philip Page, "Circularity in Toni Morrison's *Beloved*," *African American Review* 26, no. 1 (1992): 36.

11. Toni Morrison, "Rootedness: The Ancestor as Foundation," in *Black Women Writers (1950–1980): A Critical Evaluation*, ed. Mari Evans (Garden City: Anchor, 1984), 341.

12. Paule Marshall, *Praisesong for the Widow* (New York: Dutton, 1983), 67; hereafter cited in the text.

13. In *Moorings and Metaphors: Figures of Culture and Gender in Black Women's Literature* (New Brunswick: Rutgers University Press, 1992), Karla Holloway identifies Lebert Joseph as "the incarnation of [Avey's] ancient Ibo ancestors" (118); but he is also an incarnation of the trickster god Papa Legba (as his name suggests), clearly identified by his characteristic positioning at the crossroads with his stick, and by his shape-shifting (*Praisesong*, 232–33).

14. Arnold Rampersad has well expressed the necessity for this pain to be overcome: "Only by grappling with the meaning and legacy of slavery can the imagination, recognizing finally the temporality of the institution, begin to transcend it" ("Slavery and the Literary Imagination: Du Bois's *The Souls of Black Folk*," in *Slavery and the Literary Imagination*, ed. Deborah E. McDowell and Arnold Rampersad [Baltimore: Johns Hopkins University Press, 1989], 123).

15. David Bradley, *The Chaneysville Incident* (New York: Avon, 1981), 17; hereafter cited in the text.

16. Klaus Ensslen notes the similarity of *Chaneysville*'s structure also to Faulkner's *Absalom, Absalom!* but with a salient difference: "[W]hile Faulkner's narrators tend to become victims of their obsessive investigations into the past by getting hopelessly entangled in it, Bradley dramatizes the quest for a coherent history as instrumental in a positive reconstruction of self and community" ("Fictionalizing History: David Bradley's *The Chaneysville Incident*," *Callaloo* 11, no. 2 [1988]: 287).

17. Other narrative examples of this kind might include Morrison's *Song of Solomon* (1977), Ishmael Reed's *Mumbo Jumbo* (1972), Sherley Anne Williams's *Dessa Rose* (1986), and John Edgar Wideman's *Damballah* (1981). For this approach to memory as especially characteristic of African American women's writing, see Holloway, *Moorings and Metaphors*.

18. Sharrad, "The Art of Memory," 106; italics in original.

21

Scheherazade's Children: Magical Realism and Postmodern Fiction · WENDY B. FARIS

In 1980 John Barth rejected membership in any imaginary writers' club that did not include Gabriel García Márquez.[1] That statement, an homage directed from North to South, marks an important shift in literary relations and can serve to signal an increased worldwide recognition of magical realism—"a now widely available elixir," according to John Updike, and, as I wish to suggest here, an important component of postmodernism.[2] Very briefly, magical realism combines realism and the fantastic in such a way that magical elements grow organically out of the reality portrayed.

I invoke Scheherazade's children as its standard bearers because they might be imagined as "replenished" postmodern narrators, born of the often death-charged atmosphere of high-modernist fiction, but able somehow to pass beyond it. These narrative youths herald, perhaps, a new youth of narrative—Witold Gombrowicz proposes the slogan of "man wants to be young" to counter what he believes is the foundational nostalgia of existentialism, "man wants to be God"—and with that youth a desire for an accessibility that contrasts with the hermeticism of many modernist texts.[3] Magical realist fictions do seem more youthful and popular than their modernist predecessors, in that they often (though not always) cater with unidirectional story lines to our basic desire to hear what happens next. Thus they may be more clearly designed for the entertainment of readers. (Compare, for example, the great modernists Proust, Joyce, and Faulkner with the postmodern magical realists Günter Grass, García Márquez, and Salman Rushdie.) That the genre has been extending—often via novels—into film, including mainstream American film (*The Witches of Eastwick*, *Ironweed*, *Field of Dreams*, *Ghost*), confirms my sense of this accessibility. But what about the magic? These postmodern storytellers may need magic to battle death, a death more depersonalized even than the one their mother faced from King Shariyar; they inherit the literary memory, if not the actual experience, of death camps and totalitarian regimes, as well as the proverbial death of fiction itself. My invocation of Scheherazade's children also echoes the title of Rushdie's *Midnight's Children*, the novel that exemplifies the mode of magical realism best for my purposes here—among other reasons because it is quite real, quite magical, and not from Latin America, where the genre is usually imagined to reside. And Rushdie clearly had Scheherazade in mind in *Midnight's Children*; allusions to *The Thousand and One Nights* proliferate.

Scheherazade herself is a popular paradigm of the high modernist narrator—exhausted and threatened by death, but still inventing.[4] Scheherazade, as everyone knows, has taken up the cause of the virgins whom her father had to find for King Shariyar to sleep with every night and put to death every morning (in order to assuage his disillusionment at his wife's infidelity). Her father is in danger of being beheaded because the supply of women is running out. Scheherazade volunteers and begins to tell the king stories embedded in each other: he must wait until the next night to hear the end of a tale, by which time Scheherazade has embedded it in yet another. The king can't bear to kill her, and so she survives in this way for a thousand and one nights. By this time she has given birth to three children, at which point she confronts the king with the situation, and he relents, giving up his disillusionment and its attendant punishments. In their embedded structure, one growing out of the other, and continuing for 1,001 nights, Scheherazade's tales point up the autogenerative nature of fictions, indeed of language itself, a characteristic made more and more explicit in our post-Joycean age. In Scheherazade's tales, as in *Finnegans Wake*, language takes on magical properties to light up the nights verging on nightmares in which they are told. This generativity operates at all levels in the fictions that I am identifying as Scheherazade's children: on the structural plane with stories that grow out of other stories; on the mimetic front with characters who duplicate themselves in miraculous feats of doubling; in the metaphorical register with images that take on lives of their own and engender others beyond themselves, independent of their referential worlds.

Like many postmodern texts, these children of Scheherazade have a powerful precursor to overcome. In the case of the Latin American fiction to which the label of magical realism has most frequently been applied, that precursor is European realism—a tradition that dominated Latin American letters until midcentury and remains strong in modern and contemporary fiction. Indeed, this magical supplement to realism may have flourished in Latin America not only because it suits the climate there, as Alejo Carpentier has argued in his well-known essay on *lo real maravilloso*,[5] but also because in dismantling the imported code of realism "proper" it enabled a broader transculturation process to take place, a process within which post-colonial Latin American literature established its identity.[6] The postcolonial nature of magical realism I leave for another time, but in any case, the category of magical realism can profitably be extended to characterize a significant body of contemporary narrative in the West, to constitute, as I've suggested, a strong current in the stream of postmodernism.[7] Most importantly, magical realism seems to provide one source of the replenishment that Barth sees in contemporary fiction, a revitalizing force that comes often from the "peripheral" regions of Western culture — Latin America and the Caribbean, India, Eastern Europe, but in literary terms a periphery that has quickly become central and yet still retains the intriguing distance of that periphery. Like the frontier, like primitivism, the lure of peripheralism (more recently called by other names like the subaltern, the liminal, the marginal) dies hard, because the idea is so appealing and so central to the center's self-definition.

Geographical stylistics are problematic, but one might speculate about the existence of a tropical lush, and a northern spare, variety of this plant. In the latter cases there is less magic, and its range is more circumscribed: the programmatic magic of smell in Patrick Suskind's *Perfume*, for example, contrasts with the pervasive magic in García Márquez and Rushdie; the occasional magic of Toni Morrison's *Beloved* is somewhere in between the two.[8] Jean Weisgerber makes a similar distinction between two types of magical realism: the "scholarly" type, which "loses itself in art and conjecture to illuminate or construct a speculative universe" and which is mainly the province of European writers, and the mythic or folkloric type, mainly found in Latin America. These two strains coincide to some extent with the two types of magical realism that Roberto González Echevarría distinguishes: the epistemological, in which the marvels stem from an observer's vision, and the ontological, in which America is considered to be itself marvelous (Carpentier's lo real maravilloso).[9] The trouble is that it is often difficult to distinguish between the two strains. We can attempt it with reference to two of Cortázar's stories, otherwise quite similar. "Axolotl" is set in Paris, in the aquarium section of the Jardin des Plantes zoo, but the Axolotl itself is an American organism with a Nahua (Aztec) name, and so categories begin to crumble — just as I was about to put this story nearer the European, epistemological branch of the genre. Following my initial impulse, however, we can note that it is the narrator's identity with the amphibian that begins the magic. In "The Night Face Up," on the other hand, we might say that it is the extraordinarily strong presence of the indigenous past in modern Mexico — a more specifically American cultural phenomenon, like the atmosphere of belief in Haiti in Carpentier's *The Kingdom of This World* — that motivates the narrator's magical trip back into that past, or forward from it into the modern present. And so these categories of European versus American have a certain validity even though they are far from absolute.

In arguing that magical realism, wherever it may flourish and in whatever style, contributes significantly to postmodernism, it is useful to consider Brian McHale's idea that modernism is epistemological, concerned with questions of knowledge, while postmodernism is ontological, concerned with questions of being. (In the one we ask how we know something, and in the other we ask what it is.) McHale cleverly locates a point in Faulkner's *Absalom, Absalom!* where this line is crossed. It is the moment when Quentin and Shreve leave off their attempts to remember and reconstruct, and begin self-consciously to invent. At this point they may have moved, with Barth, from exhausted to replenished fiction. That moment of invention, the realization of an imaginary realm, can also be seen to distinguish magical realism from realism. In the former, it happens not provisionally in the voices of narrators but concretely in the reality depicted. Returning to Scheherazade and her children for a moment, we might say that though Scheherazade prefigures an ontological mode (her *being* is at stake, in her role as narrator), she is primarily concerned with epistemological questions, with figuring out how to extend her store of knowledge to stave off her death. Her children, on the other hand (whom we must imagine, as Quentin and Shreve imagine Sutpen and his offspring, since they have no substantial part in the frame of the tales), have to contend with their own narrative existence. They owe that existence to the fertility of their mother's mind (as well as to that of her body), but now they must invent their fictional identities for themselves. They come into being first as a function of Scheherazade's need to narrate, hence almost as epistemological objects, but then they must go forward as subjects, crossing into the ontological domain. And they no longer feel as did their immediate modernist predecessors, so crushed by the narrative burden of the past; somehow — and we don't quite know how — they manage to invent beyond it; the difficulty of that task is perhaps another reason why they need magic to perform it. For this literature often plays tricks; it is eminently performative.

The group of novels I had in mind most constantly as I formulated my ideas includes Gabriel García Márquez, *One Hundred Years of Solitude*

(1967), Milan Kundera, *The Book of Laughter and Forgetting* (1979), Salman Rushdie, *Midnight's Children* (1980), Robert Pinget, *That Voice* (1980), Carlos Fuentes, *Distant Relations* (1980), D. M. Thomas, *The White Hotel* (1981), William Kennedy, *Ironweed* (1983), Patrick Suskind, *Perfume* (1985), Toni Morrison, *Beloved* (1987), Laura Esquivel, *Like Water for Chocolate* (1990), and Ana Castillo, *So Far from God* (1993). Other eminent precursors and contemporaries whom I recall more peripherally are Gogol, James, Kafka, Borges, Carpentier, Paz, Cortázar, Grass, Calvino, Wilson Harris, Allende, and Ben Okri. And there are many more; the list is constantly growing. Latin American practitioners may head it — or have in the recent past — but my aim here is to extend the mode beyond that region, beyond *el boom*, which put magical realism on the map of world literature, and to keep to very recent fiction, so I include only a few Latin American works.[10] (*One Hundred Years of Solitude* is no longer "very recent," but it is too seminal to omit.) I include Pinget's *That Voice* here partly for shock value, because it is not ordinarily considered magical realist writing and is not similar to the more canonical texts in that mode. And yet for those very reasons, given its significant points of contact with magical realism via its creation of material metaphors, its use of voices from beyond the grave, and its consequent spiritual aura, *That Voice* underscores ways in which magical realism is interwoven with many strands of contemporary fiction.[11]

To begin with, it is helpful to list the primary characteristics of magical realist fiction. I suggest five: (1) The text contains an "irreducible element" of magic, something we cannot explain according to the laws of the universe as we know them.[12] In the terms of the text, magical things "really" do happen: young Victor and Andre in *Distant Relations* "really" become a twinned fetus floating in a pool; Remedios the Beauty in *One Hundred Years of Solitude* "really" does ascend heavenward; Grenouille in *Perfume* "really" distills a human scent from the bodies of virgins; Francis Phelan's dead enemies in *Ironweed* "really" do hop on the trolley he is riding and speak to him. The irreducible element says to us, in almost existential fashion, "I EKsist" — "I stick out." We might even see here the remnants of existential anguish at an un-co-optable world, but tempered by the more playful mood of surrealism. In *So Far from God*, for example, Ana Castillo specifically confirms the irreducible nature of a dead person's reappearance by verifying her sighting by several people: "Esperanza was also occasionally seen. Yes, seen, not only by La Loca, but also by Domingo who saw her from the front window. . . . And once, although she had thought at first it was a dream, Esperanza came and lay down next to her mother."[13]

Like the metaphors we shall see in a moment, which repeatedly call attention to themselves as metaphors, thus remaining partially unassimilated within the texture of the narrative, the magic in these texts refuses to be assimilated into their realism. Yet it also exists symbiotically in a foreign textual culture — a disturbing element, a grain of sand in the oyster of that realism.

Irreducible magic often means disruption of the ordinary logic of cause and effect. Lisa's pains in *The White Hotel* appear *before* she experiences the atrocities at Babi Yar that cause them and kill her. Saleem's claims in *Midnight's Children* that he caused this or that historical event — by singing a song, moving a pepper pot on a dining table — are similar logical reversals. Melquíades's manuscript turns out to be a prediction rather than just a recording of events in *One Hundred Years of Solitude*, implicitly asking whether he — and we — are the masters or the victims of our fate. Even though we may remain skeptical in the face of these proposed sequences, the enormity of the historical events, the human suffering involved in them, and the dissatisfaction we feel at the traditional ways such phenomena have been integrated into cultural logic cause us to question that logic as a result of these new fictional arrangements.

In the light of reversals of logic and irreducible elements of magic, the real as we know it may be made to seem amazing or even ridiculous. This is often because the reactions of ordinary people to these magical events reveal behaviors that we recognize and that disturb us. Grenouille's perfuming abilities and the uncannily entrancing scent he manufactures for himself are magical, but the mass hysteria that they engender and that tears him literally limb from limb and devours him at the end of the novel is real, and all-too-familiar as an analogue for the atrocities of persecution and scapegoating in recent history. Thus magic also serves the cause of satire and political commentary, as we see less seriously than in *Perfume* when the magical rebirth of La Loca in *So Far from God* serves to satirize the bureaucratic machinations of organizations. The particular one in question here is "M.O.M.A.S., Mothers of Martyrs and Saints," and it is our collective desire to codify the sacred that is satirized: "The decision as to whether a 'jito' of a M.O.M.A.S. member would be designated as a saint or a martyr was also very touchy for a lot of people. . . . Saints had the unquestionable potential of performing miracles while martyrs were simply revered and considered emissaries to the santos." However, these bureaucratic problems don't spoil the joy of the organization's annual conventions: "What a beautiful sight it all became at those reunions: 'jitos from all over the world, some transparent, some looking incarnated but you knew they weren't if you tested them in some way, like getting them to take a bite of a taquito or something when, of course, after going through all the motions like he was eating it, the taco would still be there. Although, it really wasn't such a respectable thing to do to test a santo, even if he had once been your own chiple child!"[14]

(2) Descriptions detail a strong presence of the phenomenal world — this is the realism in magical realism, distinguishing it from much fantasy and allegory, and it appears in several ways. Realistic descriptions create a fictional world that resembles the one we live in, in many instances by extensive use of detail. On the one hand, the attention to the sensory detail in this transformation represents a continuation, a renewal of the realistic tradition. But on the other hand, since in magical realist fiction, in addition to magical events (like Beloved's appearances, Frances Phelan's conversations with the dead) or phenomena (like Melquíades's manuscript, Saleem's transmitting and receiving radio head, or Grenouille's nose), the best magical realist fiction entices us with entrancing — magic — details, the magical nature of those details is a clear departure from realism. The detail is freed, in a sense, from a traditionally mimetic role to a greater extent than it has been before. This is still true even when we consider canonical realist texts from a Barthesian perspective. That perspective questions their mimetic qualities, endowing details with an *effet de réel*, which renders them principally markers that tell us not any particular information but simply that this story is real; but magical details can serve as markers that lead in the opposite direction, signaling that this might be imaginary.[15]

My second point here has to do not with description but with reference. In many cases, in magical realist fictions, we witness an idiosyncratic re-creation of historical events, but events grounded firmly in historical realities — often alternate versions of officially sanctioned accounts.[16] García Márquez's rewriting of the history of Latin America in that of Macondo, for example, including a massacre that has been elided from the public record, and the opening of *The Book of Laughter and Forgetting*, which restores a man airbrushed out of history by party doctrine, are elements distinct from the mythical components of those tales, though related to them. The combination implies that eternal mythic truths and historical events are both essential components of our collective memory. Thus these histories can include magic and folk wisdom — events told from Ursula's or Melquíades's point of view in *One Hundred Years of Solitude*, for example, and recipes and remedies in *Like Water for Chocolate* and *So Far from God*. But history is the weight that tethers the balloon of magic, and as if to warn against too great a lightness of magical being, both Fuentes and Kundera include dangerous sets of floating angels in their novels; they represent the lightness of ahistorical irresponsibility. The twin fetus at the end of *Distant Relations*, the remainder of old Heredia's desire to create an angel, floats "with a placidity that repudiates all past, all history, all repentance" — a dangerously unanchored position (225). Historical anchoring is well demonstrated in what John Foster calls "felt history," whereby a character experiences historical forces bodily.[17] This phenomenon is exaggerated and particularized in magical realist fictions. Clear examples are the coincidence of Saleem's birth with that of the nation of India, Lisa's pains that anticipate her death at Babi Yar, Grenouille's magical nose born from the smells of Renaissance Europe, the division of Fuentes's characters between Latin America and Europe.

As I have suggested, the material world is present in all its detailed and concrete variety as it is in realism — but with several differences, one of them being that objects may take on lives of their own and become magical in that way. (Here we are proceeding beyond both description and reference.) The yellow butterflies that appear with Mauricio Babilonia in *One Hundred Years of Solitude* and the basket in which Saleem travels from Bangladesh to Bombay in *Midnight's Children* are good examples, as are the shiny spherical object young Victor Heredia finds at the ruins of Xochicalco in *Distant Relations* and the door that opens at Felipe's touch in Fuentes's *Aura*. This materiality extends to word-objects as metaphors, and they too take on a special sort of textual life, reappearing over and over again until the weight of their verbal reality more than equals that of their referential function. Saleem's spittoon and the sheet through which Aadam Aziz in *Midnight's Children* first examines his future wife Naseem function in this way, as does the tick on the tree branch in *Perfume* or the recurring roses, breasts, hotels, and hair in *The White Hotel*. The part of surrealism that could be written down, its textual poetics, exploited to the fullest the magic of metaphor, foregrounding the enchanting quality of all poetry as it defies reason and logic. In taking this poetics of defamiliarization to its extreme, magical realism, as is often recognized, is a major legacy of surrealism. However, in contrast to the magical images constructed by surrealism out of ordinary objects, which aim to appear virtually unmotivated and thus programmatically resist interpretation, magical realist images, while projecting a similar initial aura of surprising craziness, tend to reveal their motivations — psychological, social, emotional, political — after some scrutiny. Thus Kafka and Gombrowicz, who actualize metaphors by projecting inner states outward, as in the case of Gregor, or public characterizations inward, as in the case of the less well known *Pornografia*, which, as Gombrowicz himself has said (in the preface), "is the grotesque story of a gentleman who becomes a child because other people treat him like one," belong here.

(3) The reader may hesitate (at one point or another) between two contradictory understandings of events—and hence experience some unsettling doubts. Much of magical realism is thus encompassed by Tzvetan Todorov's well-known formulation of the fantastic as existing during a story when a reader hesitates between the uncanny, where an event is explainable according to the laws of the natural universe as we know it, and the marvelous, which requires some alteration in those laws.[18] But this is a difficult matter because many variations exist; this hesitation disturbs the irreducible element, which is not always so easily perceived as such. And some readers in some cultures will hesitate less than others. The reader's primary doubt in most cases is between understanding an event as a character's hallucination or as a miracle. The mysterious character of Beloved in Morrison's novel of that name slithers provokingly between these two options, playing with our rationalist tendencies to recuperate, to co-opt the marvelous. Women outside of Sethe's house ask themselves, "Was it the dead daughter come back? Or a pretend? Was it whipping Sethe?" A bit farther on, "Paul D. knows Beloved is truly gone. Disappeared, some say, exploded right before their eyes. Ella is not so sure. 'Maybe,' she says, 'maybe not. Could be hiding in the trees waiting for another chance.'" And at the end of the book, we hear that "they forgot her like a bad dream." (Of course we ask ourselves whether she may have been just that.) "It took longer for those who had spoken to her, lived with her, fallen in love with her, to forget, until they realized they couldn't remember or repeat a single thing she said, and began to believe that, other than what they themselves were thinking, she hadn't said anything at all."[19]

At times like these (other examples are the yellow butterflies or Pilar Ternera's age in *One Hundred Years of Solitude*, the transformation of the pool at the automobile club in Paris into a tropical rain forest in *Distant Relations*, or Saleem's dispersal into the multitudes of India at the end of *Midnight's Children*) we hesitate. At other times we do not; in *One Hundred Years of Solitude* the flying carpets, Remedios's ascension to heaven, José Arcadio's blood traveling across Macondo and finding Ursula are clearly magic, as are the voices of Midnight's children in Saleem's head or Parvati the Witch's spiriting him from Pakistan to India in a basket. But in some cases we get there slowly, as in Felipe Montero's transformation into General Llorente in *Aura*, in the floating twins in the pool at the end of *Distant Relations*, in the growth of Grenouille's extraordinary sense of smell in *Perfume*. Another possibility is to interpret a particular bit of magic in an otherwise realistic fiction as a clear use of allegory. This interpretive strategy is tempting in Kundera's *The Book of Laughter and Forgetting*, when we see people rise above the ground in a charmed circle of ideological bliss — for Kundera an example of the "unbearable lightness" that totalitarian ideologies will tend to engender. Even so, I would argue that since the magic here is presented as such, it belongs in the mode of magical realism.

(4) We experience the closeness or near merging of two realms, two worlds.[20] We might say, as H. P. Duerr does in his *Dreamtime*, that in many of these texts "perhaps you are aware that *seeing* takes place only if you smuggle yourself in between worlds, the world of ordinary people and that of the witches."[21] The magical realist vision exists at the intersection of two worlds, at an imaginary point inside a double-sided mirror that reflects in both directions. Fluid boundaries between the worlds of the living and the dead are traced only to be crossed in *One Hundred Years of Solitude*, *Midnight's Children*, *That Voice*, *Distant Relations*, *The White Hotel*, and *Ironweed*. If fiction is exhausted in this world, then perhaps these texts create another contiguous one into which it spills over, so that it continues life beyond the grave, so to speak. From the first sentence, *Ironweed* weaves a web of connections between the lands of the living and the dead: "Riding up the winding road of Saint Agnes Cemetery in the back of the rattling old truck, Francis Phelan became aware that the dead, even more than the living, settled down in neighborhoods." Later on, Francis sees in his mind's eye "his mother and father alight from their honeymoon carriage in front of the house and . . . climb . . . the front stairs to the bedroom they would share for all the years of their marriage, the room that now was also their shared grave, a spatial duality as reasonable to Francis as the concurrence of this moment both in the immediate present of his fifty-eighth year of life and in the year before he was born."[22] Conveniently for my purposes, Kennedy has written about *Distant Relations* in terms that join his own novelistic crossing of boundaries to that of Fuentes: in *Distant Relations*, according to Kennedy, Fuentes "asserts that the various cultures are not separate but unified in dream and fantasy through history, populated by ghosts and specters who refuse to die, and who live their afterlives through endless time in ways that reshape the present."[23]

Another related boundary to be blurred is the one between fact and fiction. McHale again confirms that magical realism is central to postmodernism: in a chapter entitled "A World Next Door," he explores the generalized effect of a fantastic " 'charge' [which] seems to be diffused throughout postmodernist writing," though he claims that the hesitation in traditional fantastic writing between this world and the next has been displaced to "the confrontation between different ontological levels in the structure of texts."[24] This formulation thus stresses the magic *of* fiction rather than the magic *in* it.

(5) These fictions question received ideas about time, space, and identity. With "four years, eleven months, and two days" of rain and an insomnia plague that erases the past and hence the meaning of words, a room in which it is "always March and always Monday," José Arcadio who languishes half-dead and half-alive for years under a banana tree in the courtyard of his house, and a final whirlwind that abolishes a race's second opportunity on earth, our sense of time is shaken throughout *One Hundred Years of Solitude*. Our sense of space is similarly undermined when tropical plants grow over the Paris automobile club's pool at the end of *Distant Relations*. As Fredric Jameson sets out the project of realism, one thing it achieves is "the emergence of a new space and a new temporality." Its spatial homogeneity abolishes the older forms of sacred space; likewise the newly measuring clock and measurable routine replace "older forms of ritual, sacred, or cyclical time."[25] Even as we read Jameson's description, we sense the erosion of this program by magical realist texts — and of course by other modern and postmodern ones as well. Many magical realist fictions (like their nineteenth-century Gothic predecessors) carefully delineate sacred enclosures — Aura's house, Macondo, Saleem's pickle factory and pickle jars, Branly's house (in *Distant Relations*), Baby Suggs's leafy clearing — and then allow these sacred spaces to leak their magical narrative waters over the rest of the text and the world it describes. Magical realism reorients not only our habits of time and space but our sense of identity as well: with over five hundred children of midnight talking through his head, is Saleem himself anymore? Similarly, we ask ourselves, who is the voice in *That Voice*, and who or what are the relations in *Distant Relations*?[26] According to Linda Hutcheon, "In *The White Hotel*, the realist novel's concept of the subject, both in history and in fiction, is openly contested."[27] That contestation is all the more convincing because it comes from within; the magic contests, but it contests from within a realistically rendered historical fiction and a realistically conceived character.

As we read magical realist texts, the magic seems to grow almost imperceptibly out of the real, giving us, as Rushdie puts it, a dense "commingling of the improbable and the mundane" (4). A graphic illustration of this phenomenon, really an extension of the strong mimetic quotient of magical realism, and related to its historical dimension, is the way in which events are usually grounded textually in a traditional realistic, even an explicitly factual, manner. Felipe Montero in *Aura* reads of the magically potent job he will eventually take in a newspaper; we begin *The White Hotel* with fictional letters from Ferenczi and Freud; Rushdie situates his narrative in the events surrounding India's independence and the turmoil that followed it; Remedios the Beauty's levitation begins concretely enough, when Fernanda, as she is hanging out the laundry, feels a "delicate wind of light pull the sheets out of her hand and open them up wide."[28] Remnants of this quality, of magic's gentle blossoming out of reality, persist even when the fantastical element shows its colors quickly and clearly. In *Perfume*, for example, Jean Baptiste Grenouille, with his magically powerful and discriminating sense of smell, is born in geographical space "in Paris under the sway of a particularly fiendish stench," and in a textual time following the opening catalog of stenches "barely conceivable to us modern men and women."[29] Like the perfumers whose ranks he joins, Grenouille is a product of this smelly environment — perhaps even compensating for his mother's "utterly dulled" sense of smell (5).

Another list, of several secondary or accessory specifications, is helpful in building magical realist rooms in the postmodern house of fiction; this one is longer, more provisional, and serves less to distinguish magical realism from the rest of contemporary literature than to situate it within postmodernism and to furnish the rooms we've just constructed.

(1) Metafictional dimensions are common in contemporary magical realism: the texts provide commentaries on themselves, often complete with occasional *mises-en-abîme* — those miniature emblematic textual self-portraits. Thus the magical power of fiction itself, the capacities of mind that make it possible, and the elements out of which it is made — signs, images, metaphors, narrators, narratees — may be foregrounded. In *Distant Relations*, Fuentes refers again and again to the process of storytelling that goes on between him and the Heredias and Branly as the story of all three gets told. Near the end of the novel, we hear the narrator's anguished cry that "I didn't want to be the one who knew, the last to know, the one who receives the devil's gift and then cannot rid himself of it. I didn't want to be the one who receives and then must spend the rest of his life seeking another victim to whom to give the gift, the knowing. I did not want to be the narrator."[30] And the notion of ghosts *in* the story can be extended to encompass the

story itself. Just as Lucie Heredia seems to be Branly's ghost, and "will live the moment my friend Branly dies," so this story we are reading has been the ghost of the stories that were being told within it, and just as it dies off again as we turn the pages, so it lives in our reading of it—until . . . until . . . we kill it with a definitive interpretation (220). In *Midnight's Children*, metaphors for the making of fictions, from the partial view obtained by a Muslim doctor of his patient through a hole in a sheet, to the chutnification of history in jars that equal the novel's chapters, recur with amazing frequency: "To pickle is to give immortality, after all: fish, vegetables, fruit hang embalmed in spice-and-vinegar; a certain alteration, a slight intensification of taste, is a small matter, surely? The art is to change the flavour in degree, but not in kind; and above all (in my thirty jars and a jar) [equaling the thirty-one chapters of the novel] to give it shape and form— that is to say, meaning. (I have mentioned my fear of absurdity.)"[31] Beloved also seems to have an almost metafictional dimension to her; she seems to elicit stories at various points: " 'Tell me,' said Beloved, smiling a wide happy smile. 'Tell me your diamonds.' It became a way to feed her. . . . Sethe learned the profound satisfaction Beloved got from storytelling. . . . As she began telling about the earrings, she found herself wanting to, liking it."[32]

In the tradition of the *nouveau roman*, Pinget's *That Voice* is something of a maverick in this imaginary anthology. There, as in many of Robbe-Grillet's novels, we readers follow a voice as it articulates fragments of a potential story and induces us to participate in its composition. On the one hand, this autogenerative mode enables us to filter out the irreducible element, attributing an apparent reappearance of a dead character, for example, to the process of articulation. On the other hand, the autogenerative mode highlights the fertile magic of language itself, its capacity to create absorbing worlds out of thin event. In a similar way, when the name of Fuentes's character Artemio Cruz appears in *One Hundred Years of Solitude*, or the poet Paul Eluard in *The Book of Laughter and Forgetting*, we experience what seems to be the magical power of literary heritage—ghostly presences of a particular sort. Magical realism is not alone in contemporary literature in foregrounding metafictional concerns; on the contrary, that it does so joins it with other modern and postmodern writing. But it tends to articulate those concerns in a special light, to emphasize the magical capacities of fiction more than its dangers or its inadequacies.

(2) The reader may experience a particular kind of verbal magic—a closing of the gap between words and the world, or a demonstration of what

we might call the linguistic nature of experience. This magic happens when a metaphor is made real: we often say that blood is thicker than water, for example, and sure enough, in *One Hundred Years of Solitude*, when José Arcadio Buendía shoots himself, a trickle of his blood "came out under the door, . . . went out into the street, . . . went down steps and climbed over curbs, . . . turned a corner to the right and another to the left," and, once inside the Buendía house, hugged the walls "so as not to stain things," and came out in his mother Ursula's kitchen (129–30). When this sort of literalization happens, we may supply the words, as in this case, or the text itself may provide them: shortly before Remedios's levitation we hear that "Remedios the Beauty was not a creature of this world" (188). Similarly, in *Midnight's Children*, we hear that Saleem is "handcuffed to history," and then witness the invasion of his head by the voices of his compatriots. This linguistic magic, which runs through magical realism, thrives on the pervasive intertextual nature of much postmodern writing and the presence of intertextual bricolage. Intertextual magic in which characters from other fictions appear is relatively common, making *Don Quixote* one of our first magical realist novels. All of this celebrates the solidity of invention and takes us beyond representation conceived primarily as mimesis to re-presentation. We are surprised by the literality of the play of language in linguistically motivated fictional moments.

(3) The narrative appears to the late-twentieth-century adult readers to which it is addressed as fresh, childlike, even primitive. Wonders are recounted largely without comment, in a matter-of-fact way, accepted — presumably — as a child would accept them, without undue questioning or reflection; they thus achieve a kind of defamiliarization that appears to be natural or artless. Even *Perfume*, which pursues Grenouille's magical gifts of smell through all their marvelous variety, details them for the most part with a certain air of narrative naïveté. And Grenouille, through whose nose much of the novel is focalized (or should we say olfactorized), mixing perfumes in Baldini's shop, "looks like a child." Baldini thinks he looks "just like one of those . . . willful little prehuman creatures, who in their ostensible innocence think only of themselves" (81). Often we hear descriptions of phenomena experienced for the first time and participate in the fresh wonder of that experience. Such is the case when Grenouille first smells wood, when the Buendías discover ice or a magnifying glass or a train — "something frightful, like a kitchen dragging a village behind it" (210), one of a series of "marvelous inventions" that shook up the Macondoans so that "no one knew for certain where the limits of reality lay" (212). As if in

homage to the fresh vision of discovering ice at the start of *One Hundred Years of Solitude*, at the beginning of *Midnight's Children* we hear that as Saleem's grandfather Aadam Aziz begins a day in Kashmir, "the world was new again. After a winter's gestation in its eggshell of ice, the valley had beaked its way out into the open" (4). Kundera and Thomas, of course, present us with a different kind of freshness, the freshness of totalitarian terror — when we follow Tamina onto the dystopian island of children or Lisa into the shocking extermination at Babi Yar.

(4) Repetition as a narrative principle, in conjunction with mirrors or their analogues used symbolically or structurally, creates a magic of shifting references.[33] Saleem's life in *Midnight's Children* mirrors that of the new Indian nation with which he was born. Borges's Aleph reflects all the world and the self. In Cortázar's story "Axolotl," the aquarium wall through which the narrator watches the axolotls and through which he finally passes to become one is a kind of magical spatial mirror. Similarly, the place of Cortázar's narrator in "The Night Face Up," between modern and Aztec worlds, is a temporal double-sided mirror. In *Distant Relations* as well, the doubling of characters and stories that constitutes a mirror principle of narrative structure is reinforced by reflecting surfaces within the novel — especially windows. A similar kind of narrative mirroring structures *The White Hotel*, where the same story is retold through reflected personalities; like reflections in actual mirrors, the reflected narratives are and are not the same as the "original" ones. Moreover, in such cases, the notion of origin itself is undercut by the repetitions. The same is true of *That Voice*. As I have suggested earlier, even images participate in this process. They return with an unusual and uncanny frequency, confusing further our received notions of similarity and difference. Interestingly enough, ghosts, which figure in many magical realist fictions, or people who seem ghostly, resemble two-sided mirrors, situated between the two worlds of life and death, and hence they serve to enlarge that space of intersection where magically real fictions exist.

A variation on this mirror phenomenon is the occurrence of reversals of various kinds — plot mirroring, so to speak. This is a common feature in all literature, of course, but in these texts it occurs with particular frequency and highlights the metaphysically revisionist agenda of magical realism. In *The White Hotel*, Freud the analyst is analyzed, in a way, through Lisa's poetic narratives, which include him, and ultimately by historical events themselves, which can be seen to deconstruct his analytical system, because the personal past is ultimately not the origin of Lisa's suffering, and hence an awareness of it cannot cure her. In *Distant Relations*, Branly and Lucie Heredia change places as haunter and haunted. And at the end of the novel, the reader hears that "You are Heredia" and inherits the narrative confusion from the character Fuentes in the same way that Fuentes inherited it from Branly. So the roles of narrator and listener are reversed: if Fuentes hands us on the story, he can resume the status of listener and will no longer be condemned, as we have heard him fear earlier, to be the narrator. The powerfully charismatic perfume in Suskind's novel is manufactured by Grenouille to enhance his life; after doing just that, it causes his death. From the empowered he becomes the overpowered. Such patterns of reversal implicitly figure a lack of human control over events: what you thought you controlled controls you.[34]

(5) Metamorphoses are a relatively common event (though not as common as one might think).[35] They embody in the realm of organisms a collision of two different worlds. In *Distant Relations*, young Victor and André Heredia are changed into a sinister twin fetus — really an incomplete metamorphosis, and perhaps on one level a critique of minds that crave perfect magic. At the end of *The White Hotel*, the hellish scene of Babi Yar is metamorphosed into a kind of paradise of earthly delights. In *Midnight's Children*, Parvati the Witch changes Saleem into an invisible entity for a while. In India, of course, beliefs regarding reincarnation make metamorphoses through time particularly ubiquitous, and many of the characters in *Midnight's Children* duplicate a deity, Saleem's much-mentioned nose (to cite only one instance) corresponding to Ganesh the elephant-headed god's trunk. Saleem's "chutnification of history" — his art of transforming and preserving the chaotic passage of time and event — is more metaphorical in nature than these other examples, but similarly metamorphic in spirit.

(6) Many of these texts take a position that is antibureaucratic, and so they often use their magic against the established social order. Saleem's midnight congress is a clear alternative to the Congress Party, which the narrator seems to believe maintains a death grip on Indian political life; his magic is explicitly used against the "black widow" Gandhi's magic. The univocal authority of one voice from above is questioned by the cacophony of many voices from all over. That the rather lovable Francis Phelan in *Ironweed* is a bum, not well integrated into the capitalist system, is no accident. In *The Book of Laughter and Forgetting*, it's a bit more indirect. "Circle dancing is magic," we hear.[36] The magical levitation of party members as they dance in a ring, like the chorus of girls who agree with their teacher, has

a sinister air; the magic signals the danger of conformism, of rising on the unbearably light wings of coherent doctrine rather than being grounded in incoherent reality. As we learn in Kundera's next novel, being is unbearably light enough by nature; if we unground ourselves still further with doctrines and theories, then we float dangerously far from reality. Kundera and Rushdie, especially, create a poetics of subversion, of the non-co-optability of people, events, laughter, love, objects, even images. And with this we are back at number two on this list of secondary features, with the materiality of metaphor — with language that asserts its rights of opacity, of resistance to referentiality. Like the hat in *The Book of Laughter and Forgetting*, which floats inappropriately off a mourner's head to rest in an open grave, or Sabina's hat in *The Unbearable Lightness of Being*, which signals the nonconforming nature of Sabina's desire, this kind of language is linguistically unruly, whatever its political thematics.

Turning to that thematics for a moment, in several instances, magical realist texts are written in reaction to totalitarian regimes. Günter Grass publishes *The Tin Drum* and Suskind *Perfume* after World War II (in both cases quite a long time after, it is true, but partly in response to it and to the Nazi period in Germany); Latin American writers of magical realism criticize North American hegemony in their hemisphere; Kundera is opposed to the power of Soviet Communism; Rushdie writes *Midnight's Children* in opposition to Mrs. Gandhi's autocratic rule. Toni Morrison writes *Beloved* in direct response to the atrocities of slavery and its aftermath, and Isabel Allende builds *The House of the Spirits* in part to critique the barbarity of Pinochet's Chilean regime. These texts, which are receptive in particular ways to more than one point of view, to realistic *and* magical ways of seeing, and which open the door to other worlds, respond to a desire for narrative freedom from realism, and from a univocal narrative stance; they implicitly correspond textually in a new way to a critique of totalitarian discourses of all kinds. Scheherazade's story is relevant again here, for even though she narrated for her own life, she had the eventual welfare of her state on her shoulders as well, and her efforts liberated her country from the tyranny of King Shariyar's rule.

That realism has been a European, or first world, export, in conjunction with its mimetic program, its claim to fashioning an accurate portrait of the world, has in some instances tended to ally it with imperialism — Spanish, English, French, Russian, U.S. — endowing it with an implicitly authoritarian aura for writers in colonial situations. Taking all of this into account, we can see that magical realism does continue in the critical vein of realism, but it achieves its critical aims with different, postsurrealistic, resources and questions homogeneous systems in the name of plurality.

Jameson's discussion of realism and romance in the nineteenth century is helpful here. Jameson argues that "it is in the context of the gradual reification of realism in late capitalism that romance once again comes to be felt as the place of narrative heterogeneity and of freedom from that reality principle to which a now oppressive realistic representation is the hostage."[37] It is that "now oppressive realistic representation" that some of magical realism as an inheritor of romance disturbs. Jameson claims that in the nineteenth century, for the most part, the reinvention of romance substitutes "new positivities" like theology and psychology for the older magical content and that modernism likewise substitutes a kind of vacant expectancy (usually of city streets). Thus he believes that this new romance's "ultimate condition of figuration" is a transitional moment when two different modes of production, or of socioeconomic development, coexist.[38] Since their conflict is not yet socially manifest as such, its resolution is projected as a nostalgic or utopian harmony and hence is ultimately not politically progressive.

This is where magical realism may differ, because since we are situated clearly in reality, that harmonic world, either in the past or in the future, is not constituted, and the conflicts of political systems are more in evidence. According to Jameson, romance can make class conflict fade into bad dreams or fantastic scenarios. The irreducible element in magical realism, in conjunction with its documentary elements, may work against such fading, or co-option. Lisa's pains in *The White Hotel*, for example, are not just a bad dream but the magical premonition of a terrible, but an unmistakably real, historical nightmare. Likewise with the magical and not magical atrocities of the aftermath of partition in *Midnight's Children* or the banana company massacre in *One Hundred Years of Solitude* or the mass hysteria that devours Grenouille at the end of *Perfume*. Through that combination of history and selective magical detail (as opposed to the creation of a separate imaginary realm), magical realism moves beyond the way in which, as Jameson formulates it, in high realism and naturalism, time seems sealed off in its "perfected narrative apparatus." And, as we have been seeing, the techniques of that apparatus, "the threefold imperatives of authorial depersonalization, unity of point of view, and restriction to scenic representation," are also often disrupted by the postmodern fictional strategies of magical realist texts.[39]

As it has with other historically relevant fictions, the cultural and psychological pluralism that has inspired much magical realism can prove politically problematic. When I was working on this essay in London, the controversy over Rushdie's *Satanic Verses* was unfolding — a grisly manifestation of the collapse of a distinction between words and the world, as well as of the political and social realities Rushdie's books describe. The Rushdie-like character of the poet in *Iranian Nights* (the short drama presented at the Royal Court Theatre in London in response to the crisis) laments, "What madness have my verses unleashed? A fiction greater than any poet's imagination. Now jokes become daggers and rhymes become bullets."[40] Like their mother before them, these children of Scheherazade fear for their lives, and the linguistic magic we have been describing expands to alarming proportions. As Howard Brenton (one of the authors of the piece) puts it in an afterword, "Reality, as we know, is stranger than most fiction. The scenes we are observing could easily be excerpts from a Rushdie novel." What's more, the particular strange terror of the reality we witnessed in the Rushdie affair is precisely that it was partially engendered by a fiction.

Jean-François Lyotard ends his book *The Postmodern Condition* by responding to critiques of postmodern culture that advocate a return to referentiality, a rejection of self-referential discourses, such as those we have been discussing. Lyotard argues against our expecting a reconciliation among different language games, against hoping that a transcendental illusion will "totalize them into a real unity," because for him, "the price to pay for such an illusion is terror."[41] As I have suggested, several of these novels, most notably The *Book of Laughter and Forgetting*, *Midnight's Children*, *The White Hotel*, and *Distant Relations*, imply that the price to pay for a comforting textual univocality may be terror.

(7) In magical realist narrative, ancient systems of belief and local lore often underlie the text (more ghosts here). In the superstitious atmosphere of *Perfume*, we hear that the inhabitants of the Grasse region believed that their "only possible refuge from this monster . . . was under the . . . gaze of the Madonna"; "other, quicker wits banded together in occult groups" and hired "at great expense a certified witch from Gourdon"; "still others . . . put their money on the most modern scientific methods, magnetizing their houses, hypnotizing their daughters, gathering in their salons for secret fluidal meetings, and employing telepathy to drive off the murderer's spirit with communal thought emissions" (223). Similarly, while not specifically allied to any particular doctrine, this numinous moment in *Ironweed* occurs in the context of the provincial American Catholicism that pervades the

story: Francis at one point "felt blessed. He stared at the bathroom sink, which now had an aura of sanctity about it, its faucets sacred, its drainpipe holy, and he wondered whether everything was blessed at some point in its existence, and he concluded yes."[42] Even *That Voice* is set not in an urban area but in the countryside of France, very much within the ancient magic circle of country village lore and belief, akin in this to *The House of the Spirits*, *Beloved*, *Like Water for Chocolate*, and *So Far from God*.

Magical realism has tended to concentrate on rural settings and to rely on rural inspiration — almost a postmodern pastoralism — though *Midnight's Children* and *Distant Relations* are powerful exceptions. A character in *So Far from God*, for example, embodies a latter-day Saint Francis in the Southwest countryside. As the appropriately named Francisco secretly hides out among the agaves and hedgehog cactus to keep watch on his beloved Caridad's trailer, the narrator notes that "anyone looking up at a row of crows puffing away at cigarette butts would only be inclined to look down to see who was supplying them."[43] But this may be changing. For example, *Bigfoot Dreams*, by Francine Prose, is set in the city and uses the linguistic magic of materialized metaphor I have been describing. From the reappearance of "bigfoot" once a week in the tabloid she works for comes bigfoot's presence in Vera's mind, on the pages of her own stories, and in her world. Her writing takes the bigfoot theme a step farther than her predecessors did: she tells us that her story "'I MARRIED BIGFOOT' was a kind of landmark in Bigfoot literature, changing the focus, bringing Bigfoot home."[44] The fantastical bigfoot impulse comes home with a vengeance when a story Vera makes up turns out to be real — and she has to deal with the unsettling consequences. The kind of tabloid writing Vera does and her credulous city audiences seem likely sources for recent magical realism; they are urban, "first world," mass cultural analogues of the primitive belief systems that underlie earlier Latin American examples of magical realism.

(8) As Seymour Menton has pointed out, a Jungian rather than a Freudian perspective is common in magical realist texts; that is, the magic may be attributed to a mysterious sense of collective relatedness rather than to individual memories or dreams or visions.[45] The communal magic of storytelling figures prominently in *That Voice*, *Midnight's Children*, *Distant Relations*, *The House of the Spirits*, *Beloved*, and *So Far from God*. Furthermore, the magic in magical realism is unrepentant, unrecuperable, and thus may point toward the spiritual realms to which Jungian psychology is receptive; as we have seen, the magic cannot usually be explained away as individual or even

as collective hallucination or invention. *Beloved* takes an unusual turn here, because, as we have noted, right at the end we get what could be interpreted as a disclaimer concerning Beloved's magical existence. The people who had seen her "forgot her like a bad dream," and finally "realized they couldn't remember or repeat a single thing she said, and began to believe that, other than what they themselves were thinking, she hadn't said anything at all." In the final analysis, though, her existence remains shadowy, for we can — and perhaps should — discount this disclaimer, this after-the-fact rejection of her magic, and consider that just because the people "began to believe" this, it is only part of the whole story.

The White Hotel is particularly relevant in regard to Freud and Jung, for there, we seem at first to have the ever more analyzable dreams and hallucinations of a patient — Freud's patient, no less — but we discover in the end that her fears have magically proven to prefigure her historical circumstances, which in turn may reactivate universal archetypes. What's more, the book also seems to demonstrate in the psychological realm Gerald Graff's formulation about postmodern literature: "Whereas modernists turned to art, defined as the imposition of human order upon inhuman chaos, . . . postmodernists conclude that, under such conceptions of art and history, art provides no more consolation than any other discredited cultural institution. Postmodernism signifies that the nightmare of history, as modernist esthetic and philosophical traditions have defined history, has overtaken modernism itself."[46] In Thomas's novel, the art of psychoanalysis cannot help us with the nightmare of history.

(9) A carnivalesque spirit is common in this group of novels. Language is used extravagantly, expending its resources beyond its referential needs. These textual communities reveal economies of potlatch rather than ones characterized by a hoarding of resources. On either the level of plot or that of language — or both — they are linguistic analogues for the kinds of primitive fiestas celebrated by Mauss, Bataille, and Paz, antitheses to the more utilitarian modes of most Western capitalist enterprises, whose linguistic economies might be represented by Flaubert's notion of the *mot juste*: the one exact, economically efficient word for a particular thing.

This is Flaubert's idea, of course, not always his practice, and as Dominick LaCapra has shown, it is possible to align Flaubert's style with a carnivalesque spirit, which is embodied, among other elements, in his problematized ideal of pure art. Even so, whether or not one accepts that view of Flaubert, and taking into account LaCapra's warning about delineations of recent forms "providing an unjustified sense of originality in the present," I think we can still argue that the texts I am examining here go rather farther in the carnivalesque direction than Flaubert does.[47] Their use of magical details, especially details which are often not allegorically significant or clearly referential at first glance (even if they become so on reflection), celebrate invention moving beyond realistic representation. I am speaking comparatively here, and while Flaubert has recently been shown to be more postmodern than we might think, his texts less univocal, there are differences. Flaubert does not, for example, tell us the same story twice, from two different worlds, as does Cortázar in "The Night Face Up" (although the two views of the *commices agricoles* in *Madame Bovary* may lead to that); he does not tell us the same story from an embedded set of narrators as D. M. Thomas does in *The White Hotel* (though the shift of narrator in the first chapter of *Madame Bovary* might be seen to pave the way for such shifts); nor does he give us a vertiginous array of tenuously connected details and versions as does Pinget in *That Voice* or Fuentes in *Distant Relations*, or use the same exact image over and over again as Rushdie does with the hole in the sheet or the spittoon in *Midnight's Children* (although Emma's black wings of hair and black eyes once again can lead us toward those techniques, as can the bovine elements in *Madame Bovary* or the parrotic ones Jonathan Culler discovers in "A Simple Heart").[48]

Corresponding in the conceptual domain to what, even with all these qualifications, I believe is a generally extravagant, carnivalesque style, we can move from the grand and extravagant passions of the Buendías in *One Hundred Years of Solitude* to the love of Pedro and Tita extending over their entire lives in *Like Water for Chocolate*; these passions probably kill the characters in the end, but for the most part we feel a certain elation at their outrageousness (though that's not all we feel). The same for Tamina's nearly ludicrous (though moving) and highly romantic fidelity to her husband in *The Book of Laughter and Forgetting*; she spends more than he may have been worth, but we're glad. *Midnight's Children* is perhaps the most carnivalesque of all, in its conscious adoption of the style of a Bombay talkie — a cast of thousands, songs, dances, exaggeratedly sumptuous scenarios, horrifying blood and gore. (Carlos Fuentes's recent *Christopher Unborn* follows this same vein.) This, then, is often a baroque mode of overextension. It is appropriate here at the end of the list to invoke Scheherazade again, with her number of 1,001 — a numeral of excess, emblematic of the notion that there is always *one more*.

In conclusion, I again cite Lyotard, who characterizes the postmodern as "that which searches for new presentations . . . in order to impart a stronger sense of the unpresentable." Magical realism exemplifies this notion, first of all in its paradoxical name. Part of its attraction for postmodern writers may be its willfully oxymoronic nature, its exposing of the unpresentable, its activation of differences. *Like Water for Chocolate*, for example, ends not with the magical event of Tita and Pedro's passionate combustion, although that scene is the culmination of their love and the novel that chronicles it, but with the practical detail concerning the passing on of Tita's recipes, affirming the combination of the magical and the real in the text. Lyotard could almost be imagined to have the oppositional terms of magical realism in mind when he calls for resistance to retrogressive desires for "the realization of the fantasy to seize reality" — desires that might dissolve the delicate compound of magical realism. Using Lyotard's terms, we might say that in magical realist texts, "the answer is" to "wage a war on totality," to "be witnesses to the unpresentable" — and the irreducible; in sum, to affirm the magic of the storyteller's art, to invite Scheherazade's children over to play, whatever their ignorance of the rules of our games, and however fantastically they may be dressed.[49]

Notes

1. John Barth, "The Literature of Replenishment," *Atlantic Monthly*, January 1980, 65.

2. John Updike, "Chronicles and Processions," review of *Chronicle in Stone*, by Ismail Kadare, and *Baltasar and Blimunda*, by José Saramago, *New Yorker*, 14 March 1988, 113.

3. Witold Gombrowicz, preface to *Pornografia*, in *Ferdydurke, Pornografia, Cosmos: Three Novels by Witold Gombrowicz* (New York: Grove, 1978), 6.

4. See my article "1001 Words: Fiction Against Death," *Georgia Review* 36, no. 14 (1982): 811–30.

5. The essay formed the prologue to Carpentier's novel *El reino de este mundo* and is included in ["On the Marvelous Real in America," in *Magical Realism: Theory, History, Community*, ed. Lois Parkinson Zamora and Wendy B. Faris (Durham: Duke University Press, 1995), 75–88 — Editors].

6. In his discussion of the transculturation process in Latin American narrative, Angel Rama cites the example of García Márquez, who, according to Rama, solves the problem of joining historical realities and fantastic perspectives by recourse to oral and popular narrative structures; see *Transculturacion narrativa en America latina* (Mexico City: Siglo Veintiuno, 1982), 44–45. Magical realism has been instrumental in providing an impulse in Latin American literature that contrasts with the one Roberto González Echevarría has discussed recently as the archival; see his *Myth and Archive: A Theory of Latin American Narrative* (Cambridge: Cambridge University Press, 1990). That mode is concerned with *writing down*, this one with *rising up*. Book-length studies on magical realism in Latin American fiction are José Antonio Bravo, *Lo real maravilloso en la*

narrativa latinoamericana actual (Lima: Ediciones Unife, 1984); Irlemar Chiampi, *El realismo maravilloso* (Caracas: Monte Avila, 1983); and Graciela N. Ricci Della Grisa, *Realismo mágico y conciencia mítica en America Latina* (Buenos Aires, Fernando García Camheiro, 1985). Articles on the topic are too numerous to list; helpful essays, besides those already mentioned, include Amaryll Chanady, "The Origins and Development of Magic Realism in Latin American Fiction," in *Magic Realism and Canadian Literature*, ed. Peter Hinchcliffe and Ed Jewinski (Waterloo: University of Waterloo Press, 1986), and a series of articles in the collection *Otros mundos, otros fuegos*, ed. Donald Yates (East Lansing, Mich.: Congreso Internacional de literatura Iberoamericana, 1975). There is a bibliography in the article by Antonio Planells, "El realismo mágico ante la critica," *Chasqui* 17, no. 1 (1988): 9–23, but there exists quite a lot of recent work in this area. After formulating this notion of the magical supplement to realism, I came upon Scott Simpkins's article "Magical Strategies: The Supplement of Realism," *Twentieth Century Literature* 34, no. 11 (1988): 14054 (reprinted in modified form in this volume [*Magical Realism*, pp. 145–59 — Editors]), which uses the same term.

7. There are, of course, essential connections to be made between these magical realist texts and the particular cultural traditions and historical circumstances that produced them. Articles that describe magical realism in particular areas (besides the ones on Latin America listed earlier) include several chapters in the collection *Le réalisme magique: Roman, peinture et cinéma*, ed. Jean Weisgerber (Lausanne: L'Age d'Homme, 1987); *Magic Realism and Canadian Literature*, ed. Peter Hinchcliffe and Ed Jewinski; J. Michael Dash, "Marvelous Realism: The Way Out of Negritude," *Caribbean Studies* 13, no. 4 (1973): 57–70. I do not intend to devalue such connections, imperialistically subsuming them under one homogeneous discourse. But there is simply not enough space here to encompass them. And my aim at this point is other: to establish that despite such cultural differences and particularities, one can register significant similarities that indicate a worldwide movement of a sort. Cultural imperialisms are to be guarded against, but fear of those specters should not obscure a sense of genuine cultural community, which may eventually help us out of such imperialisms.

8. Several recent efforts to define magical realism have been rather more exclusive than this one, aiming at exactitude. See, for example, Seymour Menton, *Magic Realism Rediscovered, 1918–1981* (Philadelphia: Art Alliance Press, 1983), which concentrates on painting; and Amaryll Chanady, *Magical Realism and the Fantastic: Resolved versus Unresolved Antinomy* (New York: Garland Publishing, 1985). The general articles in the Weisgerber volume represent a more inclusive approach. My project here is similarly inclusive, given my wish to argue that magical realism is a central component of contemporary international narrative.

9. Roberto González Echevarría, "Isla a su vuela fugitiva: Carpentier y el realismo mágico," *Revista Iberoamericana* 40, no. 86 (1974): 35.

10. Cf. Isabel Allende: "What I don't believe is that the literary form often attributed to the works of . . . Latin American writers, that of magic realism, is a uniquely Latin American phenomenon. Magic realism is a literary device or a way of seeing in which there is space for the invisible forces that move the world: dreams, legends, myths, emotion, passion, history. All these forces find a place in the absurd, unexplainable aspects of magical realism. . . . Magical realism is all over the world. It is the capacity to

see and to write about all the dimensions of reality." "The Shaman and the Infidel," interview, *New Perspectives Quarterly* 8, no. 1 (1991): 54.

11. Another useful resource is the anthology *Magical Realist Fiction*, edited by Robert Young and Keith Hollaman — not only for the fiction included but for their introductory discussion as well. *Magical Realist Fiction: An Anthology*, ed. David Young and Keith Hollaman (1984; reprint, Oberlin, Ohio: Oberlin College Press, 1992).

12. The term "irreducible element" is Young and Hollaman's.

13. Ana Castillo, *So Far from God* (New York: Norton, 1993), 163.

14. Ibid., 248, 251.

15. See Roland Barthes, "L'effet de réel," *Communications* 2 (1968): 19–25.

16. For further discussion of the historical dimensions of magical realism, see Lois Parkinson Zamora, "Magic Realism and Fantastic History: Carlos Fuentes' *Terra Nostra* and Giambattista Vico's *The New Science*," *Review of Contemporary Fiction* 8, no. 2 (1988): 249–56.

17. See John Burt Foster, "Magic Realism in *The White Hotel*: Compensatory Vision and the Transformation of Classic Realism," *Southern Humanities Review* 20, no. 3 (1986): 205–19; reprinted in modified form in this volume [*Magial Realism*, pp. 267–83 — Editors].

18. See Tzvetan Todorov, *The Fantastic: A Structural Approach to a Literary Genre*, trans. Richard Howard (Ithaca: Cornell University Press, 1974), 41. Amaryll Chanady distinguishes magical realism from the fantastic by arguing that in the fantastic, because it encodes hesitation, antinomy, "the simultaneous presence of two conflicting codes in the text," remains unresolved, but that in magical realism, because the narrator's acceptance of the antinomy promotes the same acceptance in the reader, the antinomian conflict is resolved. The reason this distinction seems problematic to me is that we readers' investment in the codes of realism is still so strong that even the narrator's acceptance does not overcome it, and so the hesitation tends to remain, rather than being resolved. See Chanady, *Magical Realism and the Fantastic*, 12.

19. Toni Morrison, *Beloved* (New York: Knopf, 1987), 258, 263, 274.

20. Rawdon Wilson, following Lubomir Dolezel's analysis of Kafka's fiction as hybrid, explains how generic characters are born out of this "hybrid" fictional world of two worlds, "bizarre creatures who owe their natures to both worlds at once. . . . At such moments it seems as if two systems of possibility have enfolded each other: two kinds of cause and effect, two kinds of organism, two kinds of consequence." "The Metamorphoses of Space: Magic Realism," in Hinchcliffe and Jewinski, *Magical Realism in Canadian Literature*, p. 75; included in a revised version in this volume [*Magical Realism*, pp. 209–33 — Editors].

21. Hans Peter Duerr, *Dreamtime: Concerning the Boundary between Wilderness and Civilization*, trans. Felicitas Goodman (New York: Blackwell, 1987), 109.

22. William Kennedy, *Ironweed* (1983; New York: Penguin, 1984), 1, 97–98.

23. William Kennedy, "Carlos Fuentes: Dreaming of History," *Review of Contemporary Fiction* 8, no. 2 (1988): 236.

24. Brian McHale, *Postmodernist Fiction* (New York: Methuen, 1987), 83.

25. Fredric Jameson, "The Realist Floor-Plan," in *On Signs*, ed. Marshall Blonsky (Baltimore: Johns Hopkins University Press, 1985), 374.

26. Dupuis and Mingelgrun also argue that in magical realism, "subjectivity always ends up by transforming itself into a kind of objectivity . . . if only because the latter inevitably opens onto some general truth that transcends the individual circumstances of the hero." "Pour une poétique du réalisme magique," in Weisgerber, *Le réalisme magique*, 221.

27. As Hutcheon argues with regard to several other notions, the reality of the subject is also reaffirmed; see *A Poetics of Postmodernism: History, Theory, Fiction* (New York: Routledge, 1988), 173.

28. Gabriel García Márquez, *One Hundred Years of Solitude*, trans. Gregory Rabassa (New York: Avon, 1971), 222; hereafter cited in the text.

29. Patrick Suskind, *Perfume: The Story of a Murderer*, trans. John E. Woods (New York: Knopf, 1986), 3; hereafter cited in the text.

30. Carlos Fuentes, *Distant Relations*, trans. Margaret Sayers Peden (New York: Farrar Straus Giroux, 1982), 199; hereafter cited in the text.

31. Salman Rushdie, *Midnight's Children* (New York: Avon, 1982), 549–50; hereafter cited in the text.

32. Morrison, *Beloved*, 58.

33. Dupuis and Mingelgrun have also noted this tendency in magical realism: "Repetitions, constants, leitmotifs, resemblances, correspondences, conjunctions, mirror effects, symmetries, cyclical structures give the impression of a strange coherence among apparently different elements, spread out horizontally in time and space. Once exploited by the reader, this impression leads him to desubstantiate and to intellectualize the novelistic world to a greater extent, to lift the veil covering the 'other side' of things, in the occurrence of their 'profound reality'" ("Pour une poétique du réalisme magique," 226).

34. Isabel Allende sees magical realism as breaking away from a "way of facing reality in which the only thing one dares talk about are those things one can control. What cannot be controlled is denied." "The Shaman and the Infidel," *New Perspectives Quarterly* 8, no. 1 (1991): 55.

35. See Nancy Gray Díaz, *The Radical Self: Metamorphosis from Animal Form in Modern Latin American Literature* (Columbia: University of Missouri Press, 1988).

36. Milan Kundera, *The Book of Laughter and Forgetting*, trans. Michael Henry Heim (New York: Penguin, 1981), 63.

37. Fredric Jameson, *The Political Unconscious* (Ithaca: Cornell University Press, 1984), 104.

38. Ibid., 148.

39. Ibid., 104. Once again, Brian McHale's discussion helps place magical realism within the configurations of postmodernism. McHale claims that postmodern historical fictions—examples include Fuentes's *Terra Nostra*, Barth's *Letters* and *The Sot Weed Factor*, Coover's *The Public Burning*—are fantastic, and what's more, they foreground "the seam between historical reality and fiction" by "making the transition from one realm to the other as jarring as possible" (McHale, *Postmodern Fiction*, 90).

40. Tariq Ali and Howard Brenton, *Iranian Nights* (London: Nick Hern Books, 1989), 7.

41. Jean-François Lyotard, *The Postmodern Condition: A Report on Knowledge*, trans.

Geoff Bennington and Brian Massumi (Minneapolis: University of Minnesota Press, 1984), 82.

42. Kennedy, *Ironweed*, 171–72.

43. Castillo, *So Far from God*, 199.

44. Francine Prose, *Bigfoot Dreams* (1986; New York: Penguin, 1987), 14.

45. See Menton, *Magic Realism Rediscovered*, 13–14.

46. Gerald Graff, *Literature against Itself* (Chicago: University of Chicago Press, 1979), 55.

47. See Dominick LaCapra, "Intellectual History and Defining the Present as 'Postmodern,'" in *Innovation/Renovation: New Perspectives on the Humanities*, ed. Ihab Hassan and Sally Hassan (Madison: University of Wisconsin Press, 1983), 55.

48. See Shoshana Felman, *La folie et la chose littéraire* (Paris: Le Seuil, 1978), 165; and Jonathan Culler, "The Uses of Madame Bovary," in *Flaubert and Postmodernism*, ed. Naomi Schor and Henry F. Majewski (Lincoln: University of Nebraska Press, 1984), 6–7.

49. Lyotard, *The Postmodern Condition*, 81.

22

The Textualization of the Reader in
Magical Realist Fiction · JON THIEM

Among the mysteries of reading, the greatest is certainly its power to absorb the reader completely. — Victor Nell, *Lost in a Book*

According to Bloy, we are the versicles or words or letters of a magic book, and that incessant book is the only thing in the world; or rather it is the world.
— Jorge Luis Borges, "On the Cult of Books"

If we can treat the world as a text, as Leon Bloy did, does it follow that we can treat texts as worlds? An even bolder question: If we can literally read the text of the world, can we also enter, literally, the world of a text? An affirmative answer to the second question, which is based on the postmodern assumption that text and world are synonymous, seems preposterous. The idea that a person in the world outside a text might literally enter the world of, let us say, a fictional text is counterintuitive. Yet this very idea lies behind a distinctive magical realist topos, which I will call a "textualization."

A textualization usually occurs in one of two ways. First, a reader or sometimes an author, or even a nonreader, will be literally, and therefore magically, transported into the world of a text.[1] Here are some literary examples. In Julio Cortázar's story "The Continuity of Parks," the reader of a mystery novel is, or becomes, a character, in fact the victim, in the novel he is reading. Michael Ende's novel *The Neverending Story* has as its protagonist a boy who becomes so absorbed in reading a Tolkien-like fantasy novel that he enters its world and becomes its hero. In Woody Allen's story "The Kugelmass Episode," a professor of humanities at CCNY enters the fictional world of *Madame Bovary* and has an affair with Emma. It is, of course, a comparatist who first recognizes the unusual presence of Kugelmass in Flaubert's text.

A second type of textualization takes place when the world of a text literally intrudes into the extratextual or reader's world. In Calvino's *If on a Winter's Night a Traveler*, the first line of the eponymous inset story is a wonderful example of the second type: "The novel begins in a railway station, a locomotive huffs, steam from a piston covers the opening of the chapter, a cloud of smoke hides part of the first paragraph." Or in the same author's *Invisible Cities*, the city of Theodora, having exterminated all species of animal life, is invaded by the multitude of imaginary creatures found in the books of its library, by griffins, sphinxes, chimeras, hydras, harpies, et cetera.[2] In Borges's "Tlön, Uqbar, Orbis Tertius," the imaginary world of Tlön, about which the narrator has read so much, begins to invade and supplant the world of the narrator. And in Allen's story, Emma Bovary visits Kugelmass in New York City. A more elusive example of this type emerges in the last three pages of García Márquez's *One Hundred Years of Solitude*. There Aureliano Babilonia, the last Buendía, reads about his own life and his family's history in a manuscript written, before the events took place, by the magician Melquíades. The world of the manuscript he reads is indistinguishable from his world, the world of Macondo.

Before the twentieth century, textualization fables of either type are rare, and even in the postmodern era, that is, the postwar period, when there appears to be a spate of them, such stories are, in fact, not very frequent. Yet two of them, Allen's and Cortázar's, have achieved a kind of canonical status.[3] The purpose, though, of this essay is not so much to catalog or to explicate in detail textualization stories as to explore some of the psychological, cultural, and philosophical implications of this magical motif.

As the preceding examples suggest, this essay will focus less on the textualization of real readers (if such a thing exists) or of fictive readers (ideal, implied, etc.) than on the textualization of fictional readers, that is, readers who are already characters in the fictional world of some text and who themselves get literally absorbed into the world of fictional stories at the hypodiegetic level. Furthermore, our attention will focus primarily on the *lector in fabula*. We will pay little heed to textualizations into nonfictional texts, such as happens to Woody Allen's Kugelmass, whom we last see, alas, in a textbook of remedial Spanish, "running for his life over a barren, rocky terrain as the word '*tener*' ('to have') — a large and hairy irregular verb — raced after him on its spindly legs."[4]

I

The seeming impossibility of a textualization occurring in the world of the real reader signals the magical realist nature of this topos. To enter the world of a text literally, and not just literarily, is on the same order of impossibility as entering into the world *inside* a mirror or a painting.[5] At best you might break the mirror or poke a hole through the canvas with your finger, but with a text the very means of literal entry seem especially elusive. How *do* you get in? The mind has little other recourse than to the proverbial "black box," and indeed Kugelmass enters *Madame Bovary* through some such thing: a plywood cabinet in the office of the magician Persky.

Few writers have discussed even the possibility of a textualization, but those who have, even the most imaginative, treat such "events" as scandalous, extraordinary, unbelievable. Thus Proust in *Swann's Way* uses textualization as a metaphor to describe the astonishment of Marcel's aunt had she known Swann's true social status, namely, as a guest in the drawing rooms of counts and princes. She would, says Proust, "have found this as extraordinary as having had Ali-Baba to dinner, who, once alone, would reenter his cave resplendent with unimaginable treasures."[6] Or consider Roland Barthes on a textualization of the second type: "suffice it to imagine the disorder the most orderly narrative would create were its descriptions . . . converted into operative programs and simply *executed*. . . . [T]he novelistic real is not operable."[7]

The wondrous passage from one world to another, the interpenetration of irreconcilable worlds: such phenomena seem incredible. They also partake of a dreamlike quality that aligns them with a host of other magical realist devices and motifs. Again Proust serves us as a valuable witness. On the first page of *Swann's Way*, Marcel describes how as a child he would put down his bedtime book and enter the dreamlike state between sleep and waking. At that point he would experience the dissolution of the boundary between the self and the world of the text: "it seemed to me that it was myself the text spoke of" [il me semblait que j'étais moi-même ce don't parlait l'ouvrage] (9). Another indication of the oneiric resonance of textualization is the fact that, like so many other dream occurrences, it arises out of the literalization of a common metaphor. In English I can say, and I often do, that I have "lost myself" in a story, or that I am "totally absorbed" by a novel. Other Indo-European languages have similar idioms: "Mi perdo in un libro" or "Il libro me ha preso," an Italian will say, and a German might say, "Dieses Buch hat mich gefangen." In a textualization, the reader is literally "absorbed by" or "lost in" a fiction.

The wide diffusion of these metaphors reflects, of course, an interesting and puzzling psychological phenomenon that often occurs in the reading of fiction. To read a "gripping" story is to feel transported into its fictional world. The intensity of my identification with hero or heroine, the depth of my desire or pity or fear, the keenness of my longing to visit Middle-earth or Middlemarch impart, however briefly, the illusion that I am no longer reading but that I am actually in the story. In "The Continuity of Parks," Cortázar memorably evokes this experience of total immersion in a fictional text. His description serves as the psychological basis for the surprising textualization that concludes the story. Cortázar's reader reads a novel that spreads "its glamour over him almost at once." As he reads he tastes "the almost perverse pleasure of disengaging himself line by line from the things around him." Then comes the immersion: "Word by word, licked up by the sordid dilemma of the hero and heroine, letting himself be absorbed to the point where the images settled down and took on color and movement, he was witness to the final encounter in the mountain cabin."[8] Similarly, the author of *The Neverending Story* describes young Bastian Balthasar Bux's gradual immersion in the story, before the actual textualization occurs. The young protagonist finds it very difficult to return to reality after reading the story; he identifies strongly with Atréju, the story's hero; and he both longs and fears to enter the imaginary realm of Phantásien.

In Victor Nell's important study of the psychology of pleasure reading, *Lost in a Book*, these fictional views of reader immersion are corroborated.[9] Not only does Nell find reader "trances" similar to dream states; he also describes reader immersion in terms that could also apply to textualization. This serves to confirm the notion that textualizations dramatize an interesting psychological puzzle arising from many readers' experience: the state of being in two worlds at once, in the book and outside the book. Nell observes that "like dreaming, reading performs the prodigious task of carrying us off to other worlds" (2), and that when a person comes out of a reading trance, he or she seems to be "returning from another place" (1–2).

Nell sees reader trance as a result of pleasure reading, which he calls ludic reading. Let us say, then, that the trance of the ludic reader is the subjective mode or condition of textualization. The ludic reader longs to escape from the extratextual world into the text. Hence the pejorative expression "escapist reading." Or the ludic reader would like to have the world of the text cast its aura over the actual world, enlivening and enriching it. Textualizations in recent fiction do in fact draw on the kinds of texts that are most often the object of ludic reading: Cortázar's protagonist reads a conventional crime novel, Ende's a fantasy novel, and the Pink Panther in Kenneth Graham's textualization fable for children reads a ghost story. Kugelmass, though a professor of humanities, treats *Madame Bovary* as a cross between soft porn and soap opera. Ludic reading in particular seems to open readers to the pleasures and perils of textualization.

But the textualization of the ludic or naive reader is paradoxical, for it is as much the reader's detachment from, as his or her involvement in, the world of the text that enables the feeling of pleasure. Not being literally in the text permits the reader to enjoy the exciting and dangerous fictional world without having to suffer the consequences of living in that world. On this delicate balance between detachment and identification rests the traditional apologia for fiction reading: through it we gain experience without having to undergo the suffering and anxiety that actual experience in the extratextual world entails. In a textualization, this balance is upset. The world of the text loses its literal impenetrability. The reader loses that minimal detachment that keeps him or her out of the world of the text. The reader, in short, ceases to be reader, ceases to be invulnerable, comfortable in his or her armchair, and safely detached, and becomes instead an actor, an agent in the fictional world. As our fables of textualization show, this condition poses a serious threat not only to the reader's pleasure and the integrity of the text read but also to the reader himself.

II

Here I sit in my armchair, a comparatist, reading Cortázar's "The Continuity of Parks." I read the first sentence: "He had begun to read the novel a few days before." A few sentences later I read that the reader is "sprawled in his favorite armchair." Reading the last sentence of the story, I learn that a murderer is sneaking up behind the man in the armchair, who is reading a novel in which, at that point, a murderer is sneaking up behind a man in an armchair reading a novel. I become keenly conscious of the fact that I too am sitting in an armchair reading a story about a man in an armchair reading, who is about to be murdered. Involuntarily I turn my head and look behind me. Safe. But I have been reading a story about a man reading a story. The first man becomes, or is, the man in the story he is reading. Am I, or could I become, the man reading the story about the other man reading a story? Are we all in the same story? Are we all the same reader?

Textualization fables tend to make readers more conscious of the act of reading itself.[10] Thus a textualization is a magical realist topos that includes a pronounced metafictional dimension. As such, textualizations explicitly raise in the reader's mind the following questions: What is the ontological basis, if any, of a fictional world? What is the fictional basis of the extratextual world? What is the reader's role in *constituting* both worlds? The magical realist dimension of our motif transforms such questions into powerful fables. In Borges's "Tlön, Uqbar, Orbis Tertius," for example, the narrator reads about the imaginary country of Tlön. The intensity of his attention has the effect of causing the fictional world, literally, to intrude into his own. Conversely, when Bastian Balthasar Bux returns from his adventures in the fictional world of Phantásien, he has become a different person. Fiction has remade him. As these examples show, textualization fables take seriously, and literally, questions of how far readers may constitute fictional texts, or may be constituted by them.

We may find it helpful to consider this magical realist topos as one of the most important narrative expressions of postmodern literary theory. Both focus on the reader. As Jonathan Culler has written, contemporary critics "have concurred in casting the reader in a central role, both in theoretical discussions of literature and criticism and in interpretations of literary works."[11] With the disappearance of the author à la Barthes and with the fall of the determinate text à la Fish, it seems that criticism now is making its last stand with the reader. More than ever before, literary studies are concerned with the transformative powers of the consciousness of readers and of communities of readers, and with the bearing these powers have on defining, evaluating, misreading, and interpreting texts. From Wolfgang Iser through the whole spectrum of reader response criticism to Sandra Gilbert and Susan Gubar, theorists have taught us to be more aware of how the reader constitutes or activates the literary text.

A textualization is, in a sense, a magical literalization of a common metaphor used to describe one effect of reading, that is, "total absorption" in the story. If we move up to the level of professional literary discourse, we find that this principle of literalization still holds true. It is as if magical realist authors read and take literally the metaphors used by literary theorists. Here, for instance, is a sentence from Wolfgang Iser describing Roman Ingarden's influential theory of reading: "The literary work is more than the text, for the text only *takes on life* when it is *realized*, and furthermore the realization is by no means independent of the individual disposition of the reader." Iser goes on to say that the reader "sets the work in motion" and "animates" elements of the text.[12] None of these metaphors should be taken literally. The processes of activation and animation that Ingarden and Iser so colorfully describe take place in the reader's mind, not in the external world. Their essential point is that readers mentally fill in gaps in texts, give affect and excitement to elements of the story. In this sense, readers have to be considered producers, not just receivers, of texts.

Yet theories such as these do raise interesting questions about the extreme limits of textual activation. To what extent can a reader bring the world of a text into being? What role does reader identification or misreading play in animating texts? At one point Iser himself seems to approach the borders of magical realism when he asserts, without qualification, that "reading removes the subject-object division that constitutes all perception" (67). Fables of textualization explore the most extreme answers to such questions.

If we look, then, at these magical realist works as allegories of literary theory, what do they tell us about the nature of reader response? Or to put the question another way, what else do they reveal about the interpretative preoccupations and anxieties of our time?

Most textualizations concern characters who are engaged in reading. Postmodern theorists and writers also focus on the reader, but there is another, little acknowledged, reason that writers in particular do so. They tend to identify with the reader. This strong identification arises out of the fact that postmodern writers and readers in general share the same condition. This is the condition of belatedness. A sharp, sometimes painful feeling of belatedness is one of the defining features of the postmodern outlook, as the term "postmodern" itself suggests. The postmodern writer is acutely aware of the great achievements of his or her precursors and is an avid reader of these precursors. Often the postmodern writer is haunted by the feeling that if something has not already been written, then it is probably not worth writing. Many of the characteristic features and strategies of postmodern writing — such as the preoccupation with the past and historical representation and the reliance on quotation, pastiche, and parody — arise out of the feeling of being late and derivative.

Like the postmodern writer, the reader is also an epigone, a latecomer. Both seem to be on the receiving end of long, drawn-out developments. Both seem to occupy essentially passive positions. Both tend to see themselves as gleaners, rather than sowers or reapers. In the temporal sequence of author–text–reader, the reader comes last. The reader is thus positioned in relation to author and text as the postmodern writer is to his or her precursors and their texts. Hence the lavish attention given to the reader by quintessential postmodern writers such as Jorge Luis Borges, Umberto

Eco, and Italo Calvino. Borges, perhaps the paradigmatic postmodernist, is a good case in point. His various authorial personae, his narrators, and his protagonists are usually inveterate readers. Borges himself seems to write little, and the things he writes tend to be glosses on his reading or stories about his or his avatars' reading. Borges is, however, famous for glorifying his belatedness, his derivativeness.

The great tradition of past writing puts the postmodern writer into the position of a reader, who may be thrilled by the riches of the past or feel overwhelmed by their authority. In the reader, the postmodern writer has found an ideal figure through which to explore the splendors and miseries of belatedness.

The real task of the postmodern writer is to transcend the readerly condition, to transform his or her belatedness into something original and interesting. The magical realist textualization of the reader is in fact a figuration and parody of this writerly process. Through a textualization, the fictional reader ceases to be a reader and becomes a character in the text. The reader magically transcends his or her status as passive epigone, breaking the iron law of temporal succession. Hence the wonderful anachronism of Kugelmass popping up in Emma Bovary's bedroom. In the sequence author–text–reader, the textualized reader leaps back to the prior, more powerful, and less belated textual position. Furthermore, by thus changing the text the author has produced, the textualized reader encroaches on the authorial position and assumes to some extent the authorial function of producer of texts. The simplest way in which the reader changes the text is by appearing in it. Like the successful postmodern writer, the textualized reader transcends the readerly condition.

But in doing so, the reader becomes a rival and antagonist of the author. The textualized reader seems to represent a significant threat to the already tenuous authority of the postmodern writer. Ludic or otherwise, the lector in fabula may do to the postmodern text what the postmodern writer does to the texts he or she has read and rewritten.

This struggle or contest between author and reader, with the text as arena, may help explain the sad fate of so many textualized readers, who become victims, if not tragic figures. Kugelmass is last seen running for his life, chased by a "large, hairy irregular verb." Cortázar's reader in "Continuity of Parks" is about to become the murder victim in the world of the crime novel he reads. Borges in "Tlön, Uqbar, Orbis Tertius" laments the irrevocable destruction of the real world by the intrusive fictional world of

Orbis Tertius. And the reader-author in Duranti's *The House on Moon Lake* becomes a wraith, imprisoned in the fictional story he invented. These textualized readers never return, it seems, to the extratextual world. If textualizations are closely related to dreams, then their specific type is usually the nightmare.[13]

The authors of textualization fables usually invent readers of the ludic type. The sort of fiction these readers consume is mostly escapist, and so it seems appropriate that such readers should literally escape into the world of the text. Yet the fact that these readers' intrusions are mostly disastrous suggests that the authors of textualization fables reject naive or escapist reading as an acceptable mode of reader response. Indeed, they seem to be saying that escapist reading in this form may be hazardous to your health. Escape into the world of the text is truly the ultimate reader response: it is the most extreme one, but also the final one. Allegorically, these fables tell us that ludic reading distorts the text, if only by admitting some goofy reader into it. The strong emotional identifications that lie at the heart of escapist reading bring about a false, warped understanding of the story. True, all readers are to some extent producers of texts, but ludic readers tend to be incompetent producers. Their sudden appearance in the world of the text, which is their mode of production, establishes beyond a doubt their lack of discrimination.

Postmodern writers above all need to be concerned about the effects of ludic reading. This is because so much postmodern writing is attractive to the escapist reader. One of the most controversial aspects of postmodern fiction is its commercial viability. An astonishing number of postmodern works have become bestsellers in America — one thinks of fiction by John Fowles, Umberto Eco, García Márquez, and Milan Kundera — and this usually means that such works have succeeded in drawing large numbers of escapist readers. Many postmodern works are "double-coded."[14] One code, usually imitative of the forms of popular fiction, contributes to a wide readership and commercial success.[15] The second code, incorporating a whole range of experimental techniques and postmodern philosophical issues, is less popular and more adapted to serious readers, other writers, and those we might call the cognoscenti. Ideally, readers would relate to both code levels, but there is always the fear that the mass public will apprehend only the popular code and therefore read the work in a distortive, reductive way. The treatment of the escapist reader in textualization fables thus seems to be both an expression and an exorcism of this anxiety. The ludic reader, merrily misreading, lands in the world of the text, and his or her status as reader having thereby been eliminated, the malefactor is summarily punished.

III

The magic in magical realism emerges from the interpenetration of irreconcilable worlds. Textualization is arguably the paradigmatic topos of magical realism because of the way in which it showcases this mystifying phenomenon. Texts may encompass worlds, and worlds may be texts, but the way they come together, clash, and fuse in a textualization violates our usual sense of what is possible.

One more point before closing. Textualizations are a specific expression of the postmodern fascination with ontology, that is, the study of possible worlds. As used by Brian McHale and Thomas Pavel, the term "ontology" refers to the "theoretical description of a universe."[16] One of the central tasks of ontology in this sense is to explain how a world, such as that found in a fictional text, is constituted. Another task is, in McHale's words, the exploration of what happens when "different kinds of worlds are placed in confrontation or when boundaries between worlds are violated" (60). The violation of the boundary between the world of a fictional text and the extratextual world in textualization fables has many ramifications for inquiries into the relationships that are possible between possible worlds.[17]

As this study suggests, one of the main advantages of magical realism as a literary mode lies in its extraordinary flexibility; in its capacity to delineate, explore, and transgress boundaries. More than other modes, magical realism facilitates the fusion of possible but irreconcilable worlds. As the exemplary locus of such fusions, textualization fables will remain important sources for the study not only of postmodern poetics but also of magical realism itself.

Notes

1. How literally should we take the textualization of a real, as opposed to a fictional, author? John Barth, for instance, intrudes as a character in his "Dunyazadiad," and John Fowles does the same in *The French Lieutenant's Woman*. Cf. Francesca Duranti's *The House on Moon Lake*, where the novel's protagonist, an author-translator, gets textualized into a story of his own invention. Before the twentieth century, *Don Quixote* is perhaps the best-known locus of the textualization topos, a fact that helps explain, I think, the great appeal of this work for postmoderns. At one point Don Quixote meets Don Alvaro Tarfe, a fictional character from Avellaneda's spurious "Second Part," which Don Quixote has read (see Cervantes, part 2, chap. 72).

2. Italo Calvino, *If on a Winter's Night a Traveler*, trans. William Weaver (New York: Harcourt Brace Jovanovich, 1982); Italo Calvino, *Invisible Cities*, trans. William Weaver (New York: Harcourt Brace Jovanovich, 1974), p. 10.

3. Allen's story has, for instance, been anthologized in the *Norton Anthology of Contemporary Fiction* and in the *Norton Introduction to Fiction*. It has also been widely discussed in recent criticism, by Jonathan Culler in *On Deconstruction* and by Brian McHale in *Postmodernist Fiction*, among others. Cortázar's "Continuity of Parks" is anthologized and discussed in Brooks and Warren's influential *Understanding Fiction* and has also received a good deal of critical attention.

4. Nor will we be able to deal with the "textualization" of spectators in dramas, as occurs in Tom Stoppard's play *The Real Inspector Hound* (1969) and in the plays of Pirandello. Woody Allen, "The Kugelmass Episode," in *The Norton Introduction to Fiction* (New York: W. W. Norton, 1985), p. 512.

5. Besides *Don Quixote*, the most important antecedent of textualization is to be found in the illusions of baroque art, where an aggressive pictorial naturalism endeavors to obliterate the barriers separating spectator space and pictorial space, that is, the world outside the painting and that within it. Just as a textualization eliminates the reader by absorbing him or her into the text, so baroque illusionism works to do away with the spectator, who is compelled to become a part of, if not an actor in, the world inside the painting. The trompe l'oeil doors, the thumbs of subjects hooked around the frames of paintings, the protrusion of objects from the pictorial world into ours, the painted subjects who consciously observe the spectator—all contribute to the destruction of aesthetic distance and engender a mystique of participation.

Pictorial illusionism remains a force in the eighteenth and nineteenth centuries and contributes to the rise of the haunted portrait motif in Gothic fiction. In this early magical realist genre, illusionism is taken literally: the subjects of paintings or sculptures come to life and enter the spectator's world. In this way, Baroque illusionism served to sustain the fantasy, so compelling in the nineteenth century, that just as the artist can give his deceased subjects a kind of immortality, so can the spectator in the grip of illusion activate the artistic representation and call it back to life. The indispensable guide to this literature is Theodore Ziolkowski's *Disenchanted Images: A Literary Iconology* (Princeton: Princeton University Press, 1977).

6. Marcel Proust, *Du côté de chez Swann* (Paris: Gallimard, 1954), pp. 26–27.

7. Roland Barthes, *S/Z*, trans. R. Miller (New York: Hill and Wang, 1974), p. 80.

8. Julio Cortázar, "Continuity of Parks," trans. P. Blackburn, in *Understanding Fiction*, ed. Cleanth Brooks and Robert Penn Warren (Englewood Cliffs, N.J.: Prentice Hall, 1979), pp. 241–48.

9. Victor Nell, *Lost in a Book: The Psychology of Reading for Pleasure* (New Haven: Yale University Press, 1988), p. 73.

10. Theoretically, the awareness that we are reading should cause us to withdraw from reader trance, for one of the conditions of this state seems to be a momentary loss of consciousness that we are reading, that the fictional world is merely part of a book and therefore impenetrable. But then, with Cortázar's story at least, there is the trancelike impulse to look behind one's armchair. As if textualization had really occurred!

11. Jonathan Culler, *On Deconstruction* (Ithaca: Cornell University Press, 1982), p. 31.

12. Wolfgang Iser, "The Reading Process," in *Reader Response Criticism*, ed. Jane Tompkins (Baltimore: Johns Hopkins University Press, 1981), pp. 50–51.

13. The main exception to this pattern is Bastian Balthasar Bux, who does return to the extratextual world. For him textualization is a means of self-knowledge and self-realization. Cf. also the Pink Panther in Kenneth Graham's storybook for children. The Pink Panther makes friends with the ghost in the story into which he gets literally absorbed. It is perhaps significant that the main audience for both of these stories is juvenile.

14. See Matei Calinescu, *Five Faces of Modernity: Modernism, Avant-garde, Decadence, Kitsch, Postmodernism* (Durham, N.C.: Duke University Press, 1987), pp. 284–85.

15. The most explicit instance of a textualization as punishment for involvement in the popular code is found in Duranti's novel. The protagonist is a writer-translator who, in order to satisfy the mass reading public, fabricates an entire episode in his biography of a major fin de siècle author. The world of this fictional episode invades the translator's world, and he proceeds to become a prisoner of the fictional world. Biography, like much postmodern fiction, is regarded by many as suspect, first because of serious doubts about its claims to accurate representation, and second because of its propensity to be a popular genre.

Consider also the leftist critique of the double-coding of postmodern fiction. The argument runs that the writers of such fiction have sold out, that they have popularized and trivialized modernism for the sake of commercial success. Because such works are not sufficiently different from, or critical of, the late consumer capitalism out of which they arise, their value and their cultural usefulness are negligible.

16. Brian McHale, *Postmodernist Fiction* (New York: Methuen, 1987), p. 75.

17. For further discussion of ontology, or "possible worlds" theory, see Christine Brooke-Rose, *A Rhetoric of the Unreal* (Cambridge: Cambridge University Press, 1981); McHale, *Postmodernist Fiction*; and Thomas G. Pavel, *Fictional Worlds* (Cambridge: Harvard University Press, 1986). McHale discusses a number of textualization fables, including Cortázar's and Allen's (pp. 120–23).

23

Are Fictional Worlds Possible? · RUTH RONEN

Fictionality poses an intricate problem for literary theory because it indicates the duality inherent in the fictional universe: it is a world ontologically and epistemically separated from what is external to it, while at the same time being a world modeled in certain ways after reality. That is, fictionality stresses the autonomy and dependence of the literary system relative to other world systems.

The concept of possible worlds has become a productive and popular source for theorizing on literary fiction in recent years. A possible world is the name for a model constituted of a set of objects, related in certain ways and maintaining some relationship with the actual state of the world. Such a partial autonomy of alternative and parallel worlds, which the concept of possible worlds tries to formally define, appears as an attractive solution to the problem of fictionality. The conceptual framework connected with the notion of possible worlds thus seems at first glance to offer a new outlook on some of the pressing problems with which literary theory concerns itself: fictionality, the ontology of fictional worlds and of fictional objects, generic problems such as realism, and even the semantics of fictional narrative. My intention in this essay is to look into some aspects of possible-worlds thinking and to explore their relevance to the problem of fictionality, exposing in this way the presuppositions of theories nourished by possible-worlds concepts.

In exploring the interaction between possible worlds and fictionality, the question that poses itself is the following: To what extent is the analogy between possible and fictional worlds true to the original meaning of the concept of possible worlds? How is the concept of possible worlds actually interpreted, and what are the modifications it undergoes when transferred and adopted by the theoretical discourse on literature? My aim in this essay is to characterize the type of use that an accurate and literal understanding of possible worlds imposes on literary theory.

The first problem that arises when fictionality is defined in terms of possible worlds concerns the concept of actuality. The belief in possible worlds is based on the assumption that things might have been different and that one can describe alternative courses things might have taken. In other words, possible worlds ascribe a concrete ontological content to non-actual modalities by presenting non-actual states of affairs and alternative parallel worlds. It is a way of characterizing non-actual but concrete situations.

Fictional worlds are such non-actual states of affairs, yet assets of related objects; they are, unlike possible worlds, not "total ways the world might have been, or states or histories of the entire world."[1] It seems counter-intuitive to treat fictional worlds as non-actualized states of the world or as possible situations that did not take place. Although treating non-actual worlds in terms of concrete ontologies can offer a productive solution for the problem of fictionality, fictional worlds are not nonactual in the same sense that possible worlds are; that is, they are not alternative ways the world might have been.

A literary theory of fictionality making use of possible-worlds concepts consequently seems to require a considerable modification of the concept of actuality. Fictional worlds are, in this respect, less directly linked to the actual world than possible worlds. If we look more closely at specific versions of possible-worlds models, we discover three views on the actuality of possible states of affairs.

According to one radical view, possible worlds are as actual as the real world. Thus, according to David Lewis, who is the major proponent of such an actualism, "actual" is an indexical term, and the inhabitants of each world see their universe as the actual one.[2] To grasp this ontological extravagance of Lewis, it should be noted that for Lewis possible worlds are parallel worlds, autonomous "foreign countries" with their own laws and with an actuality of their own. Such worlds do not exist in a way that differs from the mode of existence of the actual world.

A second view is the one commonly termed "moderate realism." Possible worlds are perceived as actual worlds, but only in a restricted sense: they are components of the actual world. The actual world is a complex structure that includes both its actualized facts and also ways things might have been. The ways things might have been are composite elements of reality. If possible worlds are part of an actual-world model, one has to face the lingering question of what differentiates possible worlds from the actual state of things. Saul Kripke and Hilary Putnam, as well as other philosophers, approach the question of the mode of existence of possible worlds by claiming that possible worlds are abstract entities, hypothetical situations, not real "parallel worlds."[3] They thus differentiate between the ontology of the actual world and the ontology of hypothetical possible constructs which form the non-actualized part of the world.

The third view is the one that denies possible worlds any kind of heuristic or explanatory power, and therefore any kind of actuality. The most common ground for rejecting this notion is the argument that a belief in possible worlds assumes the existence, or at least the accessibility, of an actual world, a belief that is basically unacceptable. The myth of actuality as a constant background behind non-actual possibilities is not only part of a metaphysical stand that accepts the actual world as the best, inevitable, and only world that could have been actualized, but also part of a moderate stand that chooses to see the actual world only as a contingency. Actuality is a relative notion and is therefore indistinguishable from non-actual states of the world. This may seem to be another version of the Lewis approach, but whereas Lewis attributes absolute realism to all worlds, a philosopher like Nelson Goodman attributes existence to none. Lewis sees all worlds as equally real and concrete; Goodman sees all worlds as versions subject to radical relativism.

These three views on the heuristic significance of possible worlds, their degree of actuality, and their position in relation to the actual world already indicate the main problem in adopting this concept in the description of fictional worlds. Whereas a view of possibilism in the way Lewis proposes leads to an ontological extravagance which most philosophers disagree with, the more common conception of possible worlds as abstract entities or hypothetical states describing the ways the world might have been will not do for fiction. An absolute relativism of the kind that Goodman promotes contradicts a cultural intuitive sense of division between fiction and reality, although in certain contexts this dividing line can prove to be rather fuzzy.

Possible worlds can be conceived of as abstract constructs forming alternative world-models. As such they can allow the possibility of having a world-model empty of entities. The only restriction on constructing hypothetical world-models is their logical possibility, and it is thus logically possible to discuss in concrete terms an empty world. It is not only, as will be shown hereafter, that logical possibility is not necessarily a valid criterion in the construction of fictional worlds but also that the abstract-hypothetical nature of possible worlds, which defines their alternativeness to actuality and which allows the possibility of emptiness, contradicts the very nature of fictionality. Fictional worlds are, by definition, "pregnant" worlds, concrete constellations of objects, and not abstract constructs.[4]

The "pregnancy" of fictional worlds implies that fictional ontologies depend on the presence of concrete fictional entities; fictional worlds are worlds possessing some kind of concrete reality. Thus if one is not to use possible worlds as a metaphor, the view of possible worlds as hypothetical abstract sets does not make sense and cannot be operative in describing fictional worlds. In other words, it seems that the concept of world is used differently in each framework. Whereas in a philosophical framework, a world has the status of a conceptual construct, in literary theory, worlds are literally understood as constellations of concrete constructs.

Possible worlds are alternative worlds that allow trans-identification with actual object sets. It is possible to identify the same entity across separate worlds, although that entity can be characterized, located, or even named differently in each world. The notion of transworld identity is another aspect of possible-world framework that welcomes, and at the same time problematizes, an analogy with the notion of fictionality.

Lewis describes alternative worlds as parallel worlds or as distant planets which are necessarily autonomous. He consequently rejects transworld identifications as inconceivable and contradictory to the nature of beings. Kripke, on the other hand, claims that possible worlds are kinds of mini-worlds describing the total ways things might have been. Kripke proposes the example of a play in probabilities where two dice are thrown. The thirty-six possible states of the dice are thirty-six possible worlds. Although it is obvious that Kripke's possible mini-worlds simplify accessibility and transworld identity, it is clear already in this example why such a concept of possibilism cannot be adopted as a model for fictionality. Fictional worlds are parallel worlds and not total states of the world, and as such they are likely to raise problems that the case of the dice easily satisfies. We are more likely to identify the dice in the actual world with each of their appearances in alternative states of the world than we are to identify a Napoleon from history with his (possibly deviating) incarnation in fiction.

The main incompatibility between possible worlds and fictional worlds is revealed in the concept of possibility. Whereas the notion of possible worlds, or of non-actual states of the world, is tied to the logic and probabilities of actuality, a model for fictional worlds should be able to accommodate a logic that deviates from standard logic. Possible worlds are possible, whereas fictional worlds might be impossible. This point can be even more radically phrased. The notion of possible worlds is destined to distinguish non-actual, but possible, states of affairs from impossible ones. In a theoretical framework that should account for the fictionality of worlds, it is not only that impossibility is allowed, but that the standard of possibility is not at issue: I refer here not to the fact that fictional worlds can include supernatural elements but to the fact that contradictions do not collapse the coherence and internal truth-value of fictional worlds. A fictional character can be born on two contradicting dates, the same event can take place in two different locations simultaneously, et cetera. No sensible reader of postmodern texts rejects the worlds of these texts as impossible or incomprehensible on such grounds. Fictional worlds thus require an alternative principle, of compatibility or the like, to distinguish between "possible" and "impossible" fictional worlds.

Moreover, fictional worlds have logico-semantic properties for which standard logic cannot account. To elucidate this point, it can be instructive if we look at the problem of counterfactuals and the principle of similarity with which counterfactuals are handled. Lewis's work on counterfactuals is an attempt to explain a counterfactual situation away as a possible world more or less similar, or more or less close, to actuality. The truth of a counterfactual cannot be determined from knowledge of the truth-values of the antecedent or the consequent of a counterfactual ("If I drop the glass, it will break"). Rather, a counterfactual is true at a world just in case the consequent is true at all the nearest possible worlds in which the antecedent is true. Without going any further into this philosophical analysis, I would like to point out the way problems of inference in non-actual situations are solved by Lewis, as by other possible-worlds theorists. Lewis's treatment of counterfactuals, like Kripke's example of dice throwing, shows that we can infer or determine the truth of propositions about possible worlds by relying on their similarity or closeness to the state of affairs realized in the world. In other words, if the dice had fallen differently, no change in the laws of probability or the logic of the world would have ensued. Likewise, the notion of similarity in the cast of counterfactuals guarantees that, in the worlds closest to the actual worlds, when a glass is thrown on the floor there are no fairies to catch it before it reaches the floor, that there is a standard "terrestrial" gravity force, and that a glass cannot at the same time be safely situated on a table and in pieces on the floor.

This notion of similarity is fully manifested in the definition of possible worlds as possible worlds as maximal sets. When philosophers assume the occurrence of an alternative possible world, in which a different set of state propositions obtains (in which, for instance, the dice fell differently), all other domains of the actual world that were not contradicted by the occurrence of that possible world continue to obtain. The philosophical definition of possible worlds assumes that each world is a complete set of propositions and not a partial world consisting of those propositions explicitly asserted. This maximality of worlds is not unproblematic in itself: it implies that we can make a hypothetical local change in a world (in which the glass was situated safely elsewhere) and maximize an overall similarity to the actual world, that is, we "tinker" with the actual world at one point and then let the laws of nature operate without further interference.[5]

It is, however, the case that fictional worlds require a logic that is not the regular metalogic of nonfictional propositions, a logic including different laws of inference and of reference. Thus we cannot assume in the context of fictional worlds a maximization of sets. Reading maximal sets into fictional worlds would produce a counter-intuitive conception of fictional worlds. Fiction prevents us from reading into it a content that is not explicitly or implicitly stated by the statements of the text and that derives from what is, in this context, our irrelevant knowledge of the world. Fictional worlds thus require different laws of inference than those obtaining in our accounts of other possible worlds.

A fictional world requires a model accounting for its distinctive laws of inference and identification, distinctive both in relation to laws of the actual world and in relation to laws of non-actual and possible states of affairs. In a fictional world such as that of *Père Goriot*, we are faced with what might have happened if a character such as Rastignac was to walk the streets of Paris in the nineteenth century. The fictional world certainly clings to, and depends on, frames of actuality. Yet, at the same time, a model for fiction should account for its indispensable degree of autonomy. Fictional worlds are not part of the total histories of the world. They are not abstract hypothetical constructs but something else. Fictional worlds are related to the actual world, but they are not necessarily possible alternatives to this world. They can include impossible situations, impossible entities, and be subject to different laws of probability. Thus, Paris inhabited by fictional characters, and hypothetically furnished with impossible states, cannot be straightforwardly connected to actual Paris. The law of minimal departure is extremely problematic in fiction.[6]

The ontic nature of possible worlds is defined relative to the actual world. One of the advantages of possible worlds is that they give concrete content to the modal distinction between necessity and possibility. Thus a necessity assertion is true in all possible worlds, whereas a possible assertion is true in at least one world. The concreteness of possibilities is achieved because we assume that the world incorporates alternative ways things might have happened. This implies that, at least hypothetically, we can situate ourselves outside the actual world and examine all the possibilities that have not been actualized and determine which proposition is true in which world. Possibility is therefore a matter of comparing the states of affairs holding in different worlds, and this is one of the motivations for developing the notion of possible worlds. Yet such a notion of possibility may lead to a metaphysical Platonism of a suspicious kind, where one can be situated at an extraterrestrial standpoint, contemplating the modal structure of the universe.

Putnam, who tries to tackle this problem while retaining the concept of possible worlds, claims that the notion of "all possible worlds" raises many problems, "notably, how we are supposed to have epistemic access to this Platonic heaven of sets we pretend to be describing."[7] Putnam's solution is not to try to explain possibility with possible worlds but to define the latter as relative to a fixed language. Possible worlds defined as language-independent hypothetical situations are bound to lead to a Platonic or metaphysical view of possibilities. Another solution is, again, that of Lewis, who claims that "actual" is just the property people in each possible world attach to their world. In this way, the difficulty of accounting for a privileged overview of all possible worlds is evaded. Lewis's view makes sense when we come to deal with fictional worlds. In fiction, although readers are aware of the world's being fictional, they are willing to grant this world a certain autonomy vis-à-vis reality, to commit themselves epistemically to the laws of fiction, to suspend their disbelief. Moreover, modern literary theory regards the mimetic view, namely, that literature is a mode for directly representing or even reflecting the real world, as obsolete. In a non-mimetic framework, fiction is granted a position in relation to which the real world has no privileged position. It is recognized that modes and degrees of reliance of fictional worlds on the real world reflect different representational conventions and not a fixed similarity. The autonomy of fictional worlds, an autonomy that literary theory strives to secure, in a way works against the attempt to describe these worlds in terms of specific similarities and degrees of accessibility among worlds. Moreover, this autonomy disarms the notion of possibility in the context of fictional worlds.

Here, as in previous contexts, literary theory appears to benefit from a radical philosophical view of possible worlds rather than from more moderate views. Only when possible worlds are grasped as, to some extent, hermetic worlds in relation to which the actual world has no privilege are they likely to add explanatory power to literary theory in its dealing with worlds of fiction.

In view of the foregoing, it seems that a fictional world can be considered a possible world only in a radically modified way. The analogy between fictional worlds and possible worlds must obey severe restrictions. Consequently, "a possible world" can only be considered a metaphor for fictional existence. In examining the conceptual components that build the notion of possible worlds (the components of actuality, possibilism, concrete and abstract modes of existence, accessibility, and transworld identity), one recognizes that these are understood and interpreted differently when applied to the case of fictional worlds. One might conclude that the interdisciplinary move of possible worlds from philosophy to literary theory necessarily entails a considerable loss of original meaning.

If this is the case, the question obviously is: Why do literary theorists make use at all of possible-worlds concepts, if such concepts are at the most metaphorically adequate, or at the least very restrictedly relevant to the problem of fictionality? Which are the conceptual gains of appropriating possible worlds into discussion of fictionality? To answer this query, we should look into the nature of the larger philosophical context in which the notion of possible worlds has been developed. The possible-worlds framework reflects and is part of a broader philosophical attempt to relax the meaning of certain philosophical concepts and to propose a largely nonpositivist and nonmetaphysical framework for ubiquitous philosophical problems such as reference, truth-values, modalities, possible and nonactual existence, et cetera. This philosophical orientation suits the literary discipline engaged in an attempt to grasp the essence of fictionality.

Without going very much into the nature of this relaxation of concepts exemplified in the philosophical talk about possible worlds, I will illustrate briefly the way the notion of truth is interpreted within the possible-worlds framework. The point is that the development of logical models for possible worlds and for counterfactual situations, the attempt to examine the standard of truth in modal contexts, imposed a relaxation of truth standards. The concept of truth has undergone radical change in modern philosophy, as reflected in the move from a "correspondence theory of truth" to a "pragmatic theory of truth." This move is marked by the replacement of truth as an absolute logical standard establishing the relation between language and world with what can be described as a semiotic-oriented principle in terms of which one can describe truth relative to the way a universe of discourse is constructed and is operated. Current philosophy allows us to make valid references to objects and truthful assertions based on weaker standards of belief or of warranted assertability. Truth is not a fixed overall standard but is, rather, a changing and tentative one. It is the practical uses to which we put a statement that determine its truth-value. In our linguistic usages, we can decide whether a proposition is true or assertable even when the mode of existence of the objects to which that proposition refers is doubtful or indeterminate. Such developments open the way for considering standards of truth as internal to a universe of discourse, be it fictional or nonfictional. The strong semantic relation between words and reality is then replaced by the weaker semantic relation Rorty terms the relation of "talking about." The truth of a reference is hence determined by the very laws of discourse. The philosophical attempts to approach the truth of fiction are understandable in this context. Fiction, like possible worlds and counterfactuals, is a discourse uncommitted to actual states of affairs, and it hence requires a truth standard that will account for one's ability to refer to nonexistent objects and states. In short, truth, being one of the logical principles questioned by fiction, is already well relativized in philosophical discussions of possible worlds. The less metaphysical and rigid, the more relativized and semiotic the concept of truth has become, the more appropriate it proves to be for a definition of truth in fiction. Introducing standards of validation defined relative to a universe of discourse is one case that explains the conceptual affinity between current discussions in literary theory and the possible-worlds framework. This affinity is significant because the framework of possible worlds enables us to see worlds as semiotic models, as language-dependent constructs. If we think of possible worlds as simply possible states of affairs relative to some fixed language, and not as abstractions independent of the linguistic frame we use to talk about them, it becomes possible to identify them with semiotic conventions of world construction. At this point, the analogy between possible worlds and fictional worlds becomes apparent and productive.

Note, however, that although this is the key to understanding and promoting the talk on possible worlds in the context of a literary theory of fiction, the place of possible worlds in literary theory is a more complicated one. Possible worlds do not only attest to the feasibility of a semiotic view of worlds; if this were the case, possible worlds might have become a new version of anti-referential propensities in literary theorizing. Rather, possible-world talk in literary theory marks what Thomas Pavel has called the end of the moratorium on referential considerations.[8] Current debates in philosophy confirm this tendency, being concentrated on the question of whether "possible worlds" is a language-dependent epistemology or a language-dependent ontology. Such debates, phrased in various ways, demonstrate why the analogy between possible worlds and fictional worlds can generate research that is true to the intricate nature of both.

Notes

A later, expanded version of this essay appears as chapter 2 in the author's *Possible Worlds in Literary Theory* (Cambridge: Cambridge University Press, 1994).

1. Saul Kripke, *Naming and Necessity* (1972; Cambridge: Harvard University Press, 1980), 18.

2. David Lewis, *Counterfactuals* (Oxford: Blackwell, 1973).

3. Hilary Putnam, *Realism and Reason: Philosophical Papers*, vol. 3 (Cambridge: Cambridge University Press, 1983), 60; Kripke, *Naming and Necessity*, 16.

4. Umberto Eco, *The Role of the Reader: Explorations in the Semiotics of Texts* (Bloomington: Indiana University Press, 1979), 218.

5. Putnam, *Realism and Reason*, 60.

6. Marie-Laure Ryan, "Fiction, Non-factuals, and the Principle of Minimal Departure," *Poetics* 8 (1980): 403–22.

7. Putnam, *Realism and Reason*, 67.

8. Thomas G. Pavel, *Fictional Worlds* (Cambridge: Harvard University Press, 1986).

24

Chronoschisms · URSULA K. HEISE

Temporal Experience and Narrative Form

Theorists of narrative generally agree that time is one of the most fundamental parameters through which narrative as a genre is organized and
understood.[1] Indeed, some theorists have specifically characterized it as the
mode by which we mediate and negotiate human temporality. Paul Ricoeur,
for example, claims that "between the activity of narrating a story and the
temporal character of human experience there exists a correlation that is not
merely accidental but that presents a transcultural form of necessity. To put
it another way, *time becomes human to the extent that it is articulated through a
narrative mode, and narrative attains its full meaning when it becomes a condition
of temporal existence.*"[2] Peter Brooks points out that "[n]arrative is one of the
large categories or systems of understanding that we use in our negotiations
with reality, specifically . . . with the problem of temporality: man's time-
boundedness, his consciousness of existence within the limits of mortality.
And plot is the principal ordering force of those meanings that we try to
wrest from human temporality."[3] Similarly, Frank Kermode, in his classic
study *The Sense of an Ending*, claims that narrative endings reflect the human
need for a temporality shaped by the ordering force of the ending.[4] And
Walter Benjamin already showed in his no less famous essay "Der Erzähler"
(The Storyteller) that the narrator attains the highest degree of authority at
the moment of death.[5] Benjamin, Kermode, and Brooks all see human time
as crucially shaped by mortality. Narrative time, in their view, is a way of
confronting death through the movement toward the ending, understood
as a moment of closure that retrospectively bestows meaning on the plot.
Through the experience of reading, the readers live through the one moment in time that they cannot experience in their own lives: the moment
just beyond death, which reveals life's final pattern. Narrative, then, is a
means of bestowing meaning on one's life because it provides the possibility
of looking back at life from beyond the ending.

What makes this type of narrative theory so seductive is that it bases itself on the universal human fact of death, as did the time philosophies of Freud, Heidegger, and Sartre. But this universality is problematic insofar as it leads to the assumption that narrative as a genre is fundamentally invariant across cultures and historical periods; although its forms of appearance might change, its function for human temporal experience remains constant, and therefore narrative always retains an underlying temporal structure that defines the genre. None of these theories allows for the possibility that the human experience of time depends on cultural contexts that are themselves subject to change. Recent cultural theory has made us acutely aware that biological fact only becomes "natural" or "universal" through the operation of culture; in light of this insight, a theory of narrative that is based on an allegedly transhistorical experience of time appears questionable: the fact that mortality is a physical necessity for the individual by no means proves its universal cultural relevance. Obviously, Kermode's and Brooks' theories are not therefore "wrong," but their historical scope may be much more limited than the theorists claim.

Even in studies of the nineteenth-century novel, where the structural preeminence of the ending has generally been taken for granted, the theoretical focus on teleological form and its relation to death has come under attack. D. A. Miller, for example, points to a questioning of narrative and its conditions of existence in novelists such as Austen, Eliot, and Stendhal that accompanies and informs the narrative process even in its teleological orientation. Because of this doubt of narrative that is articulated even in the traditional novel, Miller argues, closure does not in fact have the "totalizing powers of organization" that twentieth-century narratologists have ascribed to it.[6] Dietrich Schwanitz, whose systems-theoretical approach focuses not so much on the form as on the historical function of teleological narrative, arrives at a similar conclusion. He argues that the function of narrative changes with the gradual modernization of society in the seventeenth and eighteenth centuries and the altered time sense that comes with modernity. When innovation becomes a basic principle of social and economic processes, the future can no longer be mapped out on the basis of the past but becomes unpredictable and contingent: historical time becomes asymmetrical. In this cultural framework, the novel arises as a new literary form that mediates between the past and future through the imposition of endings that give time a meaningful form but also open out onto what is to come.[7] Like D. A. Miller, then, Schwanitz implicitly questions the terminal, totalizing function that other theorists attribute to narrative endings. The contrast of his approach with more conventional narratology could not be more pronounced: whereas Benjamin, Kermode, and Brooks interpret closure as a narrative reflection of the individual's biologically closed future, Schwanitz reads it as a procedure designed to make time tellable in the face of a historical future too open and contingent to lend itself to narrative phrasing.

If the assumption that narrative form is primarily shaped by the ending does not do justice to the complexities of the conventional novel, it becomes even more problematic in twentieth-century fiction, which, as both Kermode and Brooks note, has become much more wary of teleological form and the imposition of endings.[8] Even in the high-modernist novel of the early twentieth century, endings no longer play the decisive structural role that narratology postulates. Whereas temporal succession was the principal medium of narrative meaning in the nineteenth-century novel, modernist novels tend to foreground simultaneity in their temporal organization. This emphasis on simultaneity is particularly striking in those texts that retell the same events several times from the perspective of different narrators (for example, *The Sound and the Fury* or *Absalom, Absalom!*) or that present the meandering consciousness of various characters as they confront an at least partially shared outer reality (for example, *Ulysses* or *Mrs. Dalloway*). But it also informs novels whose intense concern with the past would at first sight seem to call for a more conventionally chronological approach: in some texts, the narrator's piecemeal remembrance or retelling of past events, sometimes intermingled with perceptions from the present, turns the exploration of private memory into an exercise in narrative simultaneity (as in Proust's *A la recherche du temps perdu* or Ford's *The Good Soldier*), and in others, a sequence of events is gradually reconstructed from the accounts of a variety of narrators in such a way that eyewitness accounts of quite different moments in time are juxtaposed (as in Conrad's *Lord Jim*). Such strategies emphasize the importance of the voices or perspectives of the individual narrators or focal characters in their relations to each other over temporal sequence as a means of organizing narrative. But it is important to note that temporal succession, and more generally a coherent external reality, does in the end emerge from this juxtaposition in simultaneity: far from excluding or invalidating each other, the differing and sometimes unreliable accounts in the novels mentioned do in the end allow the reader to infer a fairly consistent story, whether it be the family history of the Compsons or the Sutpens, the events on the day of Clarissa Dalloway's party as well as those of the summer in Bourton thirty years earlier, or the fate of Jim from his abandonment of the *Patna* to his death. Different versions of events, in other words, turn out to be complementary rather than mutually exclusive.[9]

This emphasis on the simultaneity of different perspectives and moments in time as an organizational device, and the diminished importance of temporal succession as a medium of narrative meaning, closely relates to some of the problems and conflicts in the modernist conceptualization of time that I discussed in connection with Dalí's soft clocks [in an earlier section of this chapter, not reprinted here — Editors]. Clearly, many modernist novels, with their emphasis on individual psychological time, register suspicion of, and resistance to, the increasing standardization and mechanization of time in the public sphere. But it is misleading to claim that the major concern of modernist "time novels" is to provide a record of individual temporal experience in its opposition to public time, since many modernist novels in fact do not focus on one individual mind but juxtapose the memories and perceptions of several different characters (for example, any of the novels of Virginia Woolf or William Faulkner, as well as *Ulysses* or *Der Mann ohne Eigenschaften*). Through these juxtapositions, modernist novels generate a temporality that transcends the individual without obliterating it; they foreground the uniqueness of each psychological time world but in the process also open up a time beyond individual perception by allowing the readers to experience subjective temporalities other than their own and to perceive events as they appear in these different frameworks. Even though the authors may not always have intended it, the multiplicity of private temporalities that combine in the modernist novel adds up to an alternative social time, a time beyond the individual that is less alienating and impersonal than the globally standardized one of the Greenwich mean. The narrative structure of the modernist novel, then, can be quite literally understood to create a social "soft-clock" temporality against the "hard" clocks that divide public from private and scientific from commonsense temporality.

This narrative organization typically brings with it a drastic reduction in the scope of narrated time as compared to the nineteenth-century novel. Texts from Balzac to Dickens and Tolstoy had usually told stories that extended over many years, encompassing the entire life span of a character or even the life of several successive generations. Modernist novels tend to concentrate on much shorter time intervals: *The Good Soldier* narrates eleven years, Faulkner's *As I Lay Dying* a few days, *Ulysses* and *Mrs. Dalloway* one day only. Novels that do still cover a number of years tend to concentrate on a very few select scenes from this period: for example, Woolf's

To the Lighthouse, Faulkner's *The Sound and the Fury*, or Malcolm Lowry's *Under the Volcano*. Others resort to a radical fragmentation of longer time periods into tiny facets of a few hours, such as Anderson's *Winesburg, Ohio* or Dos Passos's *Manhattan Transfer*.[10] This condensation parallels the general cultural interest in speed and short time spans; but perhaps more importantly, it follows from novelists' attempt to explore the simultaneous rather than the sequential structure of time as a means of organizing narrative.

Novels from the 1950s and 1960s continue and intensify the temporal reduction characteristic of modernist narrative: Butor's *L'emploi du temps* spans twelve months; Robbe-Grillet's *Le voyeur* three days, *Les gommes* twenty-four hours; Marguerite Duras's *L'après-midi de Monsieur Andesmas* and B. S. Johnson's *The Unfortunates* describe one afternoon; Claude Mauriac's *La marquise sortit à cinq heures* one hour; Duras's *Le square* one conversation; García Márquez's *La hojarasca* thirty minutes; Mauriac's *L'agrandissement* five minutes. Most of these novels would probably be more appropriately described as "late modernist" than as "postmodernist," since they pursue goals very similar to those of modernist texts, although with more radical means: García Márquez's *La hojarasca*, for example, clearly modeled on Faulkner's narrative procedures, explores the parallel perceptions and reactions of three individuals to a single chain of events; Mauriac's *La marquise* presents the multifarious intersecting processes of thought and perception that occur around a modern city square not unlike the cityscapes of *Manhattan Transfer*, *Ulysses*, or *Mrs. Dalloway*; and B. S. Johnson's *The Unfortunates* is an exploration of human memory not in principle unlike Proust's, although Johnson uses the innovative device of the loose-leaf novel to represent physically the arbitrariness of associations as they occur in the human mind. In spite of this device, the story that emerges, no matter what page ordering is chosen, remains quite unambiguous: the narrator's memory of a close friend dying gradually of cancer. The point of the temporal experiment in these novels remains mainly psychological or, in Brian McHale's term, epistemological:[11] the narrator's goal is to explore how human perception and memory shape or distort time, and how individual temporalities are related to each other and to "objective" time.

Postmodernist novels, properly speaking, take a very different approach to time. They too present different versions of the events they describe, or piece a story together from flashbacks. But the narrative technique differs from that of high-modernist and late-modernist novels in two fundamental respects: the differing accounts or flashbacks are not linked to the voice or mind of any narrator or character configured with a view toward psychological realism, and they tell event sequences in contradictory and mutually exclusive versions that do not allow the reader to infer a coherent story and reality. In Clarence Major's *Reflex and Bone Structure*, for example, one of the protagonists, a woman named Cora, has apparently been murdered in her apartment. But repeated descriptions of her apartment and body are juxtaposed with other scenes in which Cora is not only alive and well but has affairs with various men, starts a career as a singer, and flies to foreign countries; these episodes at first sight appear to be flashbacks to earlier moments of Cora's life, until we are told that Cora dies in a plane crash on her way to Russia. Clearly, this is no longer the kind of variation that could be explained on the basis of a mingling of past and present or differing psychological realities. The reader cannot determine with certainty if any of the scenes are supposed to form part of the narrated reality, or whether they are to be understood as figments of the narrator's imagination or simple exercises of style.

The philosophy of time that underlies this type of narrative organization is prefigured most clearly in one of the most important models for postmodernist fiction, Jorge Luis Borges's short story "El jardin de senderos que se bifurcan" (The Garden of Forking Paths) from 1941. In the climactic scene of this story, the protagonist, Yu Tsun, visits the sinologist Stephen Albert and discovers that he has solved an enigma regarding the work of Yu Tsun's ancestor Ts'ui Pen. Albert explains to his visitor:

> A diferencia de Newton y de Schopenhauer, su antepasado no creía en un tiempo uniforme, absoluto. Creía en infinitas series de tiempos, en una red creciente y vertiginosa de tiempos divergentes, convergentes y paralelos. Esa trama de tiempos que se aproximan, se bifurcan, se cortan o que seculannente se ignoran, abarca *todas* las posibilidades. No existimos en la mayoría de esos tiempos; en algunos existe usted y no yo; en otros, yo, no usted; en otros, los dos. En éste, que un favorable azar me depara, usted ha llegado a mi casa; en otro, usted, al atravesar el jardín, me ha encontrado muerto; en otro, yo digo estas mismas palabras, pero soy un error, un fantasma. . . . El tiempo se bifurca perpetuamente hacia innumerables futuros.[12]
>
> [As opposed to Newton and Schopenhauer, your ancestor did not believe in a uniform, absolute time. He believed in infinite series of times, in a growing and vertiginous network of divergent, convergent and parallel times. This web of times that approach each other, bifurcate, cross or ignore each other for centuries, includes *all* possibilities. We do not exist in the majority of those times; in some you exist and not I; in others, I, not you; in [yet] others,

both of us. In this one, which a fortunate coincidence has afforded me, you have come to my house; in another, crossing the garden, you have found me dead; in [yet] another, I say these same words, but I am an error, a ghost. . . . Time bifurcates incessantly toward innumerable futures.]

When Albert explains how this philosophy relates to the incomprehensible novel Ts'ui Pen left to posterity, Yu Tsun dimly begins to perceive the existence of other temporalities that surround him and his host. "Desde ese instante, sentí a mi alrededor y en mi oscuro cuerpo una invisible, intangible pululación," he notes at first (From that moment on, I felt around me and in my dark body an invisible, intangible swarming).[13] Later this sensation becomes more concrete: "Volví a sentir esa pululacíon de que hablé. Me parecío que el húmedo jardín que rodeaba la casa estaba saturado hasta lo infinito de invisibles personas. Esas personas eran Alberto y yo, secretos, atareados y multiformes en otras dimensiones de tiempo" (I again felt that swarming I mentioned. It seemed to me that the humid garden surrounding the house was infinitely saturated with invisible persons. Those persons were Albert and I, hidden, busy and manifold in other time dimensions).[14] The alternative time dimensions Yu Tsun here dimly perceives spell out other narrative lines, many of which are incompatible with the plot as it evolves in the short story itself.

Many postmodern novels have taken up the central metaphor of Borges's seminal short story and exploited it in their narrative structure. Quite literally, it informs texts such as John Barth's short story "Lost in the Funhouse," in which every bifurcation inside the funhouse leads into a different future. But many other texts that abandon the spatial metaphor of the maze nevertheless develop story lines that exclude and invalidate each other, leaving the reader with a spectrum of possible developments rather than a single plotline. Postmodernist novels thereby project into the narrative present and past an experience of time which normally is only available for the future: time dividing and subdividing, bifurcating and branching off continuously into multiple possibilities and alternatives. It forms part of the inherent asymmetry of time that in everyday experience we envision what is to come as open and indeterminate with regard to a multiplicity of possibilities, whereas the past and present are continuously narrowed down to one temporal strand from amongst these possibilities. In the universes of postmodern novels, however, we cannot be sure even retrospectively which one of several possible developments turned from possibility to reality, let alone do we know which one is being realized in the narrative present. Through this narrative strategy, the reader is made to live in a constant retrojection of the time experience of the future; as a consequence, time in these texts appears labyrinthine in all its dimensions.

This type of textual organization is created by means of three major narrative strategies used by themselves or in combination: repetition, metalepsis, and experimental typographies. Repetition is, of course, so general a feature of literary texts that one must be cautious about claiming it as characteristic of any particular period or genre.[15] But whereas the repetition of certain plot elements and tropes occurs in all kinds of narratives from the folktale to the classical novel, many postmodern texts stand out through the insistent reiteration of identical scenes, presented in almost literally the same words every time. Only slight variations distinguish one description or account from the other, although these gradual alterations of wording or narrated elements can lead to quite disparate and even contradictory versions of what the reader must take to be the same scene or incident.

As I already indicated, the crucial difference between these almost literal repetitions and the kind of retelling one finds in the modernist novel is that in modernism, repetition and variation of the same events are motivated by the differing perspectives of the narrators or focal characters whose views they reflect. The readers may not be able to decide which versions (if any) "really" correspond to the events as they happened in the story, but based on what they find out about the focal characters, they can at least make an assessment as to what kinds of distortions are likely to have occurred in a particular retelling. Furthermore, the comparison of different narrators' accounts in a modernist novel usually allows one to form a fairly consistent picture of the events that lie behind them.[16] No such motivation, however, is normally given for postmodernist repetitions. As a consequence, it is also impossible for the reader to infer a coherent image of the actions that underlie the repetitions, since there is no criterion for evaluating the reality of any version the text happens to present. A few more examples may make this clear. Robert Coover's short story "The Elevator," for instance, consists of nothing but a series of scenes of a character taking the elevator in his office building: sometimes up, sometimes down, sometimes in the morning, sometimes in the evening, sometimes alone, sometimes in the company of colleagues, sometimes accompanied by a woman, sometimes silent, sometimes engaged in conversations with varying outcomes, or sometimes even in sex. Some of these scenes might succeed each other at different moments in time, but others are clearly mutually exclusive versions of the same elevator ride. At the end, we cannot be sure if any of the scenes even took place, or whether they were fantasies of the protagonist's or narratorial games with language. Similarly, Christine Brooke-Rose's novel *Out* [. . .] returns over and over again to a scene in which, in a futuristic world in which Africans form the uppermost social class, an elderly white man goes to ask for a job as a gardener at an African lady's manor house. In some versions of the scene, he is received by the head gardener, who is sometimes white and sometimes colored; other versions indicate that it is the gardener's wife who greets him. Sometimes the gardener is affable and shows him around the estate, but does not admit him for a job until a later season; sometimes the two get into a fight concerning their differing national and racial pasts; sometimes the gardener simply denies that the manor needs an additional employee. Along with the dialogue, descriptions of the scenery, the season, the watering of the plants, and other elements vary to such an extent that the same general setting is still recognizable, but none of the details can be held on to. The readers are left with the general impression that they are reading the same scene over and over again, but few consistent details can be relied on to prove this.

The interest of these diegetic experiments no longer lies in the exploration of what distortions or refigurations a certain sequence of events undergoes in the perception or memory of different characters. Rather, the text explores the temporal microtexture of crucial scenes in such detail that the reader is alerted to the most minute element of change. As Roland Barthes observes with regard to the works of Robbe-Grillet, time is constituted as a series of slices which *almost* exactly correspond to each other, and their temporality lies precisely in this "almost."[17] Due to this focus on the microstructure of time, what we learn is not so much how one event leads to another; in fact, the reader can never be certain whether one thing leads to another at all. Instead, the focus is on the constitution of the moment itself. Time "passes," in other words, but not in the way in which we usually understand this phrase: it does not set up any irreversible directionality but reconfigures the elements of the individual moment just enough for change to be perceptible. Instead of bridging the gap from one instant to the next, it introduces difference into the instant itself, splitting it into multiple bifurcations and virtualities.[18]

Inevitably, the insistent play on the almost same without any psychological motivation introduces a strong element of contingency into narrative. But this is no longer the kind of contingency which turned the Proustian madeleine into a vehicle of involuntary memory and heightened awareness. On the contrary, postmodernist repetition strategies seem designed precisely to preclude moments of epiphany and privileged insight, since each instant is submerged in a series of alternative versions none of which can claim priority over the others. The present is trapped in its own mutations, without any possibility of linkage to past or future, and with at best a promise of meaning that is never fulfilled. As opposed to modernist texts, then, where contingency is a force that overcomes chronoschisms and gathers temporality together, it disseminates and divides time in postmodernist novels.

This dissemination persists even when there is in fact a textual or formal principle that governs the repetition. Robbe-Grillet's *Topologie d'une cité fantôme* [. . .] revolves around a series of variations on the theme of the raped virgin. Many of these variations are motivated linguistically by the combination and recombination of a very limited number of phonetic elements that appear in such words as *vierge, vagin, vigie, navire, divin, divan, David, gravide, Diana,* and *Vanadium.* But the reason why this particular phonological set (mainly /v/, /g/, /d/, /a/, and /i/) was chosen is a purely formal one: it consists of the letters of the name *Gradiva,* which is the title of one of Robbe-Grillet's intertextual sources, as well as an anagram of the Latin word for "pregnant" that points to the text's self-generation. This matrix word could easily be replaced by any number of others: neither does there seem to be any logical necessity to any of the specific combinations the text chooses to explore, or to the sequence in which they appear. In other novels, repetition may be textually motivated by a formal principle that is either inaccessible or very difficult to guess for the reader. Brooke-Rose's *Between,* for example, systematically avoids all forms of the verb *to be,* and a fair number of repetitious scenes can be "explained" in terms of this omission — but no critic ever noticed this principle until the author herself pointed it out.[19] In either case, the order of specific scenes is not predicted even by the formal matrix, and hence the temporal development of the text remains contingent, at least as far as the reader is concerned. What postmodernist repetition creates, then, is not a temporality ruled by cause and effect, a medium of stability and continuity, but an agent of contingency and dispersion.

If certain forms of repetition disrupt the causality that was traditionally associated with temporal sequence in the novel, systematic violations of the boundary between frame narrative and embedded story destabilize another kind of conventional narrative causality: the narrator's control of the story. The nesting of diegetic levels or *recursion* is, of course, not specific to postmodernist novels, or indeed to the novel at all. In its technical mathematical sense, *recursion* refers to the repeated application of a rule or routine to the variable values of a function. But as a structural pattern, it can be found in a much wider variety of information practices and sign systems, such as the embedding of sentences in natural languages or the modulation of a tune across different keys in music.[20] In literature, the embedding of stories within stories and of plays within plays is the most obvious corresponding form. This type of pattern in itself does not necessarily cause any disruption of linear time; instead, time simply seems to be suspended at one level while it proceeds at another. But certain strategies of recursion can nevertheless blur or block temporal progression: for example, switches of level may occur so frequently that it becomes difficult for the reader to remember and piece together the fragmented pieces of each story line.[21] [. . .] A similar blurring of the time sense sets in when different levels of the nested structure resemble each other closely enough that at least a temporary confusion becomes possible; in other words, when some form of *mise en abyme* is involved.[22] And linear temporality may collapse completely when, as is frequently the case in postmodern fiction, the boundaries between nesting and nested text are crossed by characters or other textual elements that "migrate" from the embedded story and participate in the framing events, in a process which Gérard Genette has called "metalepsis."[23] A concise example of this is Julio Cortázar's short story "Continuidad de los parques," in which a man sits down in a green velvet armchair to read the story of a married woman and her lover who are planning to murder the woman's husband. As they penetrate into the house to carry out their plan, they open a door and find the husband reading in a green velvet armchair: the reader in the frame narrative is suddenly no longer outside the story he reads, but involved in it; he literally becomes its victim.

Recursion and metalepsis crucially shape a great number of postmodern novels — Fowles's *The French Lieutenant's Woman*, Federman's *Double or Nothing*, B. S. Johnson's *Christie Malry's Own Double-Entry*, Brook-Rose's *Thru*, Calvino's *If on a Winter's Night a Traveler*, Barth's "Menelaiad" and the stories in *Chimera*, Robbe-Grillet's *La maison de rendez-vous* and *Topologie d'une cité fantôme*, and many others play with the multiplication of diegetic levels and their transgression.[24] To see how this splitting of the narrative thread into a multiplicity of levels affects time, we must return to our earlier observation that the experience of temporal continuity depends on our ability to construct events in succession at a similar scale or a similar level of abstraction.[25] Narrative leaps between diegetic levels prevent exactly that, since framed and framing story cannot normally be construed as pertaining to the same time sequence: while events proceed at one level, they are suspended at the other levels until the narrative focus returns to them. But to say this is to simplify the temporal processes that occur during the reading of framed stories. For the reader, the embedded narrative is intercalated between two moments of the main story and serves to dilate that instant "in between." This fact can sometimes be foregrounded in the story itself: the most famous example is the series of stories Scheherazade tells in *The Arabian Nights* to extend the duration of her life, which is to end along with her storytelling. Recursion, in other words, is a means of articulating a temporal interval through a narrative that is not its own but that of another moment in time: that is, of giving it a structure of meaning while "at the same time" leaving it semantically empty as an interval of pure chronology, since nothing can happen in the frame narrative while the framed story is being told. Recursion figures the moment as what it is not, replacing it by the story of another moment; somewhat paradoxically, it becomes narrative by not being narrated.

If recursive processes are carried far enough, they can produce texts in which there are still distinct nesting levels, but no single "monitoring level" at which the nesting "bottoms out": a visual example of such a "heterarchy" without the oriented layering characteristic of a hierarchy is M. C. Escher's painting of two hands which draw each other, since neither one can unambiguously be claimed for the status of "picture within the picture."[26] In narrative, an analogous structure would be that of Coleman Dowell's novel *Island People*, in which one of the characters not only emerges from an embedded story to converse with the narrator, but even takes over the writing of the latter's journals and narratives; some of these revolve around a character bearing the same name as the narrator, so that in the end it becomes practically impossible to decide who has invented whom.[27] In such inversions of cause and effect, the directionality of time comes into question along with the authority of the narrator. However, as Douglas Hofstadter points out, there is an inherent limit to this type of experiment, since it always ends up reconfirming the authority of one narrator who *does* remain at a so-called "inviolate level" outside the heterarchy. The reader knows that characters can only emerge from stories and talk back to narrators *in stories*, and so the questioning of narratorial authority within the story ultimately confirms the existence of such authority outside it.[28] But knowing this does not help the reader untangle the text's temporal loops, although it does foreground their textual nature.

In literary narrative, repetitions and recursions are articulated by means of written language. Print typography and the book format place a number of "natural" constraints on how temporality can be presented, and some postmodern texts foreground and exploit these particular constraints in ways that were common in avant-garde poetry of the early twentieth century but did not make their way into fiction until the 1960s. Written language, especially when configured in narrative structures, is forced to present time in a medium that operates on the basis of discrete, digital units: words. Punctuation, articulation in sentences, and the division of longer texts into numbered pages impose further boundaries and discontinuities on what Bergson and many modernist writers conceived of as the uninterrupted flow of *durée*. When postmodernist texts do away with punctuation, they tend to replace it with typographic devices that foreground linguistic discontinuity even more dramatically: Beckett's *How It Is*, for example, [. . .] suspends punctuation and capitalization only to divide each of its pages into approximately equal blocks of text and blank space. Raymond Federman's *Double or Nothing* goes even further by configuring the typography of every single one of its almost two hundred pages differently, breaking down paragraphs and sentences into other, visually motivated units. Brooke-Rose's *Thru* contains pages that are configured in crossword-puzzle fashion, so that the reader is forced not only to take in every word individually but even to break it down into its constituent letters, which form part of several differently oriented words at the same time. William Gass's *Willie Masters' Lonesome Wife* incorporates photographs and the "accidental" ring-shaped marks of glasses into its print configuration and divides some pages into two or three typographically distinct areas, each of which follows a different narrative strand. The reader must choose which story line to follow and then is forced to flip back and forth through the text to catch up on the other strands. These experiments put postmodern fiction at the opposite extreme of texts such as Molly Bloom's monologue at the end of *Ulysses*, which in its suspension of syntax and punctuation attempts to come as close as possible to representing the uninterrupted flow of time and mind. Contemporary texts, on the contrary, disarticulate time into moments through their nonlinear typography and suggest that every page can be read following a variety of itineraries.

Such strategies of "concrete prose"[29] transform temporal processes into visual and spatial objects, and in this respect it makes sense to speak of a postmodern tendency toward the spatialization of time that is quite unlike the metaphoric spatialization Joseph Frank claimed was characteristic of high-modernist poetry and novels.[30] These typographical structures remain strictly local, however, since principles of printed configuration can, in most cases, be formulated only for very restricted passages, not for the text as a whole. In the reading process, the foregrounded spatiality of print is thereby itself subjected to the discontinuity of change, and to a contingency that makes it impossible for the reader even to predict what the next page will look like, let alone the text in its entirety. The typographical configuration of some postmodern novels, then, contributes to the fracturing of narrative time into alternative temporal universes.

The three narrative strategies I have discussed — repetition, metalepsis and "concrete" typography — do not always occur together, and they are often complemented by other, more author-specific techniques, some of which I will analyze in later chapters. But all of them crucially contribute to a specifically postmodernist articulation of narrative time. Four general characteristics define this time sense. First, postmodernist novels focus on the moment or the narrative present at the expense of larger temporal developments, not unlike modernist novels. Second, the moment is not envisioned as a self-identical instant of presence but as partaking of or leading to an indefinite number of different, alternative, sometimes mutually exclusive temporalities, which, as I suggested, can be understood as a projection of the temporal mode of the future into the past and present. Third, the juxtaposition of alternative plot developments and the metaleptic crossing of boundaries between diegetic levels leads to a double symmetrization of time and causation: on one hand, the temporal ordering of events becomes considerably less important than it was in the conventional and the high-modernist novel; and on the other, the hierarchical logic of the relationship between narrator and narrated material becomes susceptible to inversion, so that characters gain access to and alter the world of the narrator just as the latter shapes that of the characters. Fourth, none of these infractions of classical narrative logic are justified in terms of the psychology of the human mind, as they were, for the most part, in the modernist novel; postmodernist narrative time is detached from any specific human observer, and in some cases is not meant to represent any temporality other than that of the text at all.

Clearly, the reduction of temporal scope in the postmodernist novel forms part of a more general culture of time that has become wary of hypostatizing long-term historical patterns and developments. The focus on the present, the moment now at hand, also seems to link metafiction firmly to contemporary media and consumer culture with its relentless emphasis on the present as the only time phase available for gratification, planification, and control. But in this context, differences in temporal philosophy also emerge very strikingly. Even a first reading of Beckett, Perec, Robbe-Grillet, Arno Schmidt, or Luisa Valenzuela reveals that their novels resist easy consumption and immediate gratification in a way that distinguishes them sharply from the kinds of narrative that typically occur in magazine, film, television, video, and advertising production; the difficulty and sometimes even the tedium of such a first reading bears witness to narrative organization that does not lend itself to fast assimilation and easy retelling. This difficulty does not provide a basis for judging the aesthetic value of such fiction in comparison to other forms of contemporary narrative, but it does point to a different type of time structure that does not put the present at the reader's disposal. On the contrary, the moment becomes increasingly difficult to grasp as it is split into multiple versions of itself, embedded in intricate and sometimes logically impossible recursion structures, and fractured into experimental typographical configurations. Similarly, this kind of temporality does not allow for privileged instants of epiphany, visions of coherence, or unmediated access to the past as one finds them in many modernist novels; the narrative organization systematically prevents any such privileging, since any epiphany attained in a specific episode might be canceled out by a subsequent, different version of the same episode. By refusing to compensate the absence of long-term narrative developments with the self-presence of the individual moment, postmodernist narrative form resists the cultural fixation on the now.

Whether the labyrinthine vision of multiple temporalities that many postmodern novels offer presents any genuine alternative to this fixation, however, is more difficult to say. Very strikingly, the multiplicity of temporal universes in these novels does not seem to lead to a wider spectrum of plot possibilities and a vastly enriched narrative repertoire, but on the contrary to the almost obsessive repetition of a relatively restricted inventory of scenes and, even in texts with wildly proliferating plots such as those of Thomas Pynchon, to a pervasive sense of paranoia and control. Perhaps with such restrictions in mind, Gary Saul Morson accuses the Borgesian time concept of being even more ferociously determinist than the conventional linear one, since the individual in Borges encounters the multiplicity of temporal universes without having any part in shaping them through his intentionality and agency.[31] Certainly, postmodernist novels do not generally make any attempt to celebrate the freedom of the individual either in their content or in their organization; their protagonists tend to appear as victims rather than as beneficiaries of multiplicity and ambiguity. But these postmodernist characters are not conceived mimetically as "realist," self-possessed individuals with the ability to intend and act in the first place; frequently, they appear as partly human and partly linguistic constructs and sometimes have the paradoxical capability of recognizing themselves as textual entities: the protagonist of Ronald Sukenick's *Out*, for example, changes names and identity in almost every chapter, the I-narrators of some of Robbe-Grillet's later novels switch name and gender repeatedly, and B. S. Johnson's Christie Malry talks back to his creator knowing full well that he is a character in a novel. But even if we assumed with Morson that metafictional novels relied on rationally and realistically conceived characters who find themselves in a deterministic universe, the question remains whether the text as such could be considered determinist if it juxtaposes several universes that take the same events to different outcomes, and gives none of them ontological priority over the others. It is precisely this kind of juxtaposition that opens up interpretive possibilities for the reader and manifold layers of textual self-referentiality that cannot appropriately be called determinist.

It would be more accurate to say that novels with titles such as *In Transit*, *Between*, or *How It Is*, in analyzing the constant emergence of the moment out of different histories, languages, voices, images, or identities, explore the temporal interplay between determinism and indeterminacy, or between causality and contingency. This exploratory intent shapes narrative procedures which treat episodes that already form part of the narrated past as if they were still part of the indeterminate possibilities and hypothetical alternatives of the future: the determinacy of the material of the past is subjected to the indeterminacy of the future mode in such a way that a finite narrative repertoire can be deployed in infinite variations. The same intent also underlies other strategies that characterize not only the novel but other art forms: intertextual appropriation of previous artworks and aesthetic forms that is turned into a procedure of innovation, pastiche, and the deliberate cultivation of plagiarism obey the same temporal principle.[32] The difficulty of envisioning the future that characterizes the historical imagination as well as the invention of literary narrative is, in the realm of art at least, transformed into a new way of articulating the past and present not in terms of sequentiality but in terms of an often deliberately paradoxical and self-contradictory simultaneity.

The temporal structure of the postmodernist novel, then, is a way of dealing aesthetically with an altered culture of time in which access to the past and especially to the future appears more limited than before in cultural self-awareness. If the teleological form of the nineteenth-century novel mediated the relationship between past and future in an era in which the future had become unpredictable on the basis of past social patterns, the postmodernist novel confronts the more radically contingent future of Western societies in the late twentieth century by projecting the temporal mode of the future into the narrative present and past. Narrative, in other words, takes on the temporal structure of a future that can no longer be envisioned without great difficulty, so that the time experience of the future is displaced into the reading experience. The novels of Thomas Pynchon and Christine Brooke-Rose that I will discuss, *Gravity's Rainbow* and *Out*, show this very clearly, since their protagonists' loss of a vision for the future is accompanied by a narrative present constantly splitting into alternative and incompatible versions of itself. Brooke-Rose's *Out* and Bruce Sterling's *Schismatrix* [. . .] are in fact science fiction novels that quite literally propose a version of the future: but in this case, a version of the future that is highly aware of the difficulties of articulating any such version, and that incorporates these difficulties into the novel's narrative organization (in Brooke-Rose's case) or into its thematic frame of reference (in Sterling's case). Contingency is made narratable not by its conversion into teleological form, as in the nineteenth-century novel, or by its recuperation through the human mind, as in the high-modernist novel, but through its displacement from the future to the present and past.

One might argue that this displacement is in essence an escapist strategy designed to help narrative literature avoid the more difficult task of projecting avenues into the future, at least in the imaginative realm. This critique is, in my view, justified and perhaps helps to explain why authors who assign to their fictions the task of overt social and political intervention have tended to rely less on metafictional strategies than some of those authors whose main goal is aesthetic innovation, although the boundary between the two groups is by no means clear-cut. I would hold against this critique, however, that if metafictional texts are escapist in this particular sense, they in no way offer an easy escape. The difficulties that many postmodernist texts cause in their reading are not just self-serving intricacies but provide a basis for reflecting on the interplay of determinism and indeterminacy, or causality and contingency, in our temporal experience. In this sense, their project parallels that of theories of complexity and nonlinear dynamics that have emerged in the natural sciences in the last twenty years, which equally aim to explore the relationship between the predictable and the unpredictable in the evolution of systems over time. Texts such as Sterling's

Schismatrix make this parallel explicit by incorporating some of these scientific theories into the narrative plot, but even the great majority of postmodernist texts that make no direct reference to such theories participate in their project through their specific type of narrative organization. Viewed from this perspective, what appears to be a lack of social or political project is quite possibly due to a higher level of abstraction in the approach postmodernist novels take to the problem of contemporary history.

Historicizing Posthistory

Somewhat simplistically, one could say that postmodernist texts take to the extreme a narrative technique that was typical of high-modernist novels, the juxtaposed accounts of identical events by different characters, but strip it of the element of human observation: what is left are contradictory accounts without any overarching psychological motivation.[33] The preceding analysis of the organization of narrative time indicates the reasons for this development. On one hand, in novels that are concerned with the way in which events at widely diverging time scales relate to each other, the human time dimension may lose its preeminence because humans have only mediated access to developments at other time scales. On the other hand, if the peculiar time structures of postmodernist novels should be understood as projections of the future mode into the present and past, as I have argued, this precludes a consistent observer position, since by definition the future cannot be accessed and observed directly. These two points may become clearer when we look at an example, John Barth's short story "Menelaiad" from *Lost in the Funhouse.*

At first sight, the "Menelaiad," a postmodernist retelling of Menelaus's unhappy marriage to Helen and its consequences, displays a very tidy symmetrical organization: it consists of fourteen numbered sections divided in two sets. The first set of sections, numbered 1 to 7, leads the reader backward in time from the period after the Trojan war, when Menelaus has long been reunited with Helen, to the first days of their marriage; every time Menelaus tells a part of his story, he is asked by his listener(s) first to narrate a previous episode, so that each section is also embedded in the previous one. In the story, this progressive embedding is signaled by an additional pair of quotation marks for every level. The second set, numbered 7 to 1, takes the reader forward in time again to the narrative present, and progressively out of the nested narrative frames. But in fact, this perfect numerical order only camouflages a temporal and causal chaos in which neither time references nor diegetic levels can be identified at all.[34] To begin with, the reader does not know and never finds out what moment of his long story Menelaus's voice really speaks from. In the first embedded text, Menelaus observes:

> "One evening, embracing in our bed, I dreamed I was back in the wooden horse, Waiting for midnight. Laocoön's spear still stuck in our flank . . . But in the horse, while smart Odysseus held shut our mouths, I dreamed I was home in bed before Paris and the war, our wedding night . . . Now I wonder which dream dreamed which, which Menelaus never woke and now dreams both.
>
> "And when I was on the beach at Pharos, seven years lost en route from Troy, clinging miserably to Proteus for direction, he prophesied a day when I'd sit in my house at last, drink wine with the sons of dead comrades, and tell their dads' tales; my good wife would . . . dutifully pour the wine. That scene glowed so in my heart . . . and the Nile-murk on my tongue turned sweet. But then it seems to me I'm home in Sparta, talking to Nestor's boy or Odysseus's; Helen's put something in the wine again . . . and the tale I tell so grips me, I'm back in the cave once more with the Old Man of the Sea."[35]

This introductory passage makes it impossible for the reader to decide which of the scenes whose chronological order seems so transparent in the successive embeddings actually lies in the past, and which still in the future for the narrating voice. The present eludes the reader's grasp because what we take to be the present at one moment may be a memory that Menelaus looks back on from a later stage, or an image of the future he creates out of Proteus's prediction. Menelaus, whose history is reconstructed in this elaborate textual and temporal structure, really turns out to be a paradigmatically "posthistorical" figure whose past, present, and future all appear in some sense simultaneous and therefore cannot be apprehended historically.

The only meaning the notion of "present" still has in these circumstances is that it is the attempt to grasp the present; this insight emerges from the double vertigo that overcomes Menelaus during his drawn-out struggle with Proteus on the beach at Pharos. His first realization in this fight, during which Proteus successively turns into different kinds of animals, into saltwater, into a tree, and finally into an old man, is a properly temporal one. It occurs to him that Proteus, not bound by the same time scale as Menelaus, might remain in one shape for longer than Menelaus can hold on: " " " 'My problem was, I'd leisure to think. My time was mortal, Proteus's im-; what if he merely treed it a season or two till I let go?" ' " " [36]

Reflected in Menelaus's dealings with gods and demigods, we here encounter precisely the problem of disparate time scales we earlier discussed as part of the postmodern scientific *Weltbild*, the idea that present events might be taking place at a time scale that is simply inaccessible to human perception and manipulation. This consideration ultimately renders even human time incomprehensible to Menelaus:

> " ' "What was it anyhow I held? If Proteus once was Old Man of the Sea and now Proteus was a tree, then Proteus was neither, only Proteus; what I held were dreams. But if a real Old Man of the Sea had really been succeeded by real water and the rest, then the dream was Proteus. And Menelaus! For I changed too as the long day passed: changed my mind, replaced myself, grew older. How hold on until the 'old' (which is to say the young) Menelaus rebecame himself?" ' "[37]

Proteus's successive metamorphoses become, for Menelaus, metaphors of human change through time; and yet they are ironic metaphors, since they imply a reversibility that human temporality lacks. But both the metamorphoses and human aging disperse identity over time, and this process continues even when Proteus finally returns to his shape as an old man and asks Menelaus to let him go. As Menelaus refuses, Proteus angrily points out to him that nothing proves that Menelaus is in fact holding Proteus at that very moment at all, since Proteus himself might well have turned into Menelaus, and indeed into Menelaus holding Proteus. This is the second moment of vertigo in the struggle: under Menelaus's very eyes, the present splits into two different versions of itself, and he has no way of deciding which is the "real" one. As a consequence, he becomes unable to affirm anything at all about the present moment, except that it is the instant in which he attempts to grasp the present, and Proteus becomes the figure for the multiple temporalities in which Menelaus loses himself.

He loses himself not only in the sense of being deprived of a clear sense of his own identity; he also, quite literally, turns from a human being into a voice that may be no more than a tape recording. This voice, finally without quotation marks, narrates the beginning and ending of the short story, referring to Menelaus sometimes in the first and sometimes in the third person. "No matter; this isn't the voice of Menelaus; this voice *is* Menelaus, all there is of him," this speech without speaker affirms at the beginning.[38] And at the end it explains: "When I understood that Proteus somewhere on the beach became Menelaus holding the Old Man of the Sea, Menelaus ceased. Then I understood further how Proteus thus also was as such no more, being as possibly Menelaus's attempt to hold him, the tale of that vain attempt, the voice that tells it."[39] The "I" by this time has become an unidentifiable amalgam of Proteus and Menelaus, a voice detached from either character that refers to both of them in the third person. The "history" of Menelaus, then, in a movement that emerges from and repeats the moment in which Proteus turns into Menelaus holding Proteus, has here generated the voice that tells it. This voice, however, has more affinities with a pre-recorded program than a human storyteller; at the very beginning, it declares, "When I'm switched on I tell my tale, the one I know, How Menelaus Became Immortal, but I don't know it," a phrasing that suggests a radio or a tape recorder.[40] Menelaus's immortality depends on the elimination of his identity as a human being: the story can only be told because Menelaus's and Proteus's identities have disappeared, but this disappearance is also what the story is about and aims to achieve.

Barth's short story makes explicit what is implied in other texts with similar organizational patterns. Proteus, the figure who has privileged access to the future, prophesies to Menelaus what is to come; but far from clarifying Menelaus's future, these prophecies instead make his past and present indistinguishable from it and fracture Menelaus's identity to the point where his text is all that remains of him, since he cannot retain a stable self in Protean time. The voice that is "switched on" is all that is left of the high-modernist exploration of consciousness and memory. Where past and present are structured like the future, there is no room for human observers, who in the process of observation would be constantly fractured into multiple versions of themselves: hence the strangely inconsistent, self-contradictory, or disintegrating narrators that characterize many postmodern novels. There is not, in other words, a perspective with the distance that would make it possible to transform this sort of time into conventional narrative or historical form.

If indeed the changes in narrative organization I have discussed are related to more general developments in the Western culture of time, these difficulties associated with the position of the narrator must lead one also to question the position of the critic who analyzes cultural and literary phenomena, and the temporal orientation that guides this analysis. Some theorists see something akin to paradox in the attempt to account historically for a culture that resists the concept of history. Katherine Hayles, for example, claims that "[a]nalyzing postmodernism . . . amounts to writing the history of no history. In an important sense, to write the history of postmodernism is to indulge in anachronism."[41] One might want to hold against this claim that a method of study is not obligated to replicate the structural features of the object of study: the post- or antihistorical dimensions of postmodern culture do not automatically force an analysis of this culture to proceed post- or antihistorically itself. As Andreas Huyssen notes, "the waning of historical consciousness is itself a historically explainable phenomenon."[42] Nevertheless, one must ask to what extent a literary or cultural analysis should insist on establishing historical coherence by outlining, for example, the transition from high-modernist to postmodernist art, when postmodernist artifacts stress the impossibility or irrelevance of such coherence.

A full answer to this question can probably not be given without a detailed examination of the theoretical foundations and procedures of literary history, a project that lies beyond the scope of this book. But it is worth noting that a concept such as that of posthistory, even as it declares the end of conventional temporality and indeed the end of ending, relies itself to some extent at least on the conventional narrative mechanism of closure to structure time: placing oneself at or after the end of history provides one with a vantage point from which past time becomes narratable because it is concluded, and hence allows the observer to contemplate it from the distance afforded by closure. One may regret this as a methodological anachronism, but clearly any historical approach requires some mechanism whereby the observer gains distance from the time period to be described, as Fredric Jameson points out: "Historicity is . . . neither a representation of the past nor a representation of the future (although its various forms *use* such representations): it can first and foremost be defined as a perception of the present as history; that is, as a relationship to the present which somehow defamiliarizes it and allows us that distance from immediacy which is at length characterized as a historical perspective."[43] The paradox of the multiple alternative temporalities that structure postmodern novels lies in the fact that they make conventional observer positions impossible, but precisely thereby do achieve the defamiliarization that creates a distance from the present. This kind of distancing certainly does not lead directly to anything like a historical perspective, but at the very least it allows one to reflect on the possibility of different and perhaps alternative histories to frame the present, which themselves have to be evaluated with critical distance. Whether the historicization of contemporary posthistory that has been proposed here does justice to its object can only be judged with such distance — among others, that of time.

Notes

Bracketed ellipses indicate deletion of internal cross-references that appeared in the original.

1. For classical studies on the relationship between time and narrative, see M. M. Bakhtin, "Forms of Time and of the Chronotope in the Novel," in *The Dialogic Imagination: Four Essays*, trans. Caryl Emerson and Michael Holquist, ed. Michael Holquist (Austin: University of Texas Press, 1981), 84–258; E. M. Forster, *Aspects of the Novel* (San Diego: Harcourt Brace Jovanovich, 1985), 83–103; Eleanor N. Hutchens, "The Novel as Chronomorph," *Novel* 5 (1972): 215–24; A. A. Mendilow, *Time and the Novel* (New York: Humanities Press, 1972); Hans Meyerhoff, *Time in Literature* (Berkeley: University of California Press, 1955); Jean Pouillon, *Temps et roman* (Paris: Gallimard, 1946); Georges Poulet, *Etudes sur le temps humain* (Paris: Rocher, 1976). A fully articulated structuralist theory of narrative time is presented in Gérard Genette, *Narrative Discourse: An Essay in Method*, trans. Jane E. Lewin (Ithaca: Cornell University Press, 1980).

2. Paul Ricoeur, *Time and Narrative*, vol. 1, trans. Kathleen McLaughlin and David Pellauer (Chicago: University of Chicago Press, 1984), 52; italics in original.

3. Peter Brooks, *Reading for the Plot: Design and Intention in Narrative* (New York: Random House, 1985), xi.

4. Frank Kermode, *The Sense of an Ending* (London: Oxford University Press, 1967), 3–31.

5. Walter Benjamin, "Der Erzähler," in *Illuminationen: Ausgewählte Schriften*, ed. Siegfried Unseld (Frankfurt: Suhrkamp, 1961), 409–36. See also Garrett Stewart's study, *Death Sentences: Styles of Dying in British Fiction* (Cambridge: Harvard University Press, 1984), which explores the relationship between narrative and death in texts from Dickens to Beckett.

6. D. A. Miller, *Narrative and Its Discontents: Problems of Closure in the Traditional Novel* (Princeton: Princeton University Press, 1981), xiii–xiv.

7. Dietrich Schwanitz, *Systemtheorie und Literatur: Ein neues Paradigma* (Opladen: Westdeutscher Verlag, 1990), 152–68. Schwanitz's paradigm for such endings is the love story, which ends when the hero and heroine are about to get married: the story of their mutual discovery comes to a meaningful end at the same time that the story opens out onto the prospect of their future life together (168–88). On the relation of modernization processes and the changed vision of the future they bring about, see also Niklas Luhmann, "The Future Cannot Begin: Temporal Structures in Modern Society," *Social Research* 43 (1976): 130–52; Anthony Giddens, *Consequences of Modernity* (Stanford: Stanford University Press, 1990), 50–51; and Reinhart Koselleck, *Vergangene Zukunft: Zur Semantik geschichtlicher Zeiten*, 2nd ed. (Frankfurt: Suhrkamp, 1992).

8. Kermode, *Sense*, 4; Brooks, *Reading*, 313–14.

9. This is also Brian McHale's understanding of perspectivism in modernist fiction; see "Modernist Reading, Postmodern Text: The Case of *Gravity's Rainbow*," in *Constructing Postmodernism* (London: Routledge, 1992), 64–66.

10. Dario Villanueva describes "temporal reduction" as one of the hallmarks of twentieth-century fiction and gives a detailed classification of its different types as well as

an abundance of examples in *Estructura y tiempo reducido en la novela* (Valencia: Bello, 1977).

11. Brian McHale, *Postmodernist Fiction* (New York: Methuen, 1987), 9–11.

12. Jorge Luis Borges, "El jardín de senderos que se bifurcan," in *Ficciones*, 12th ed. (Madrid: Alianza, 1984), 114–15; translation mine, italics in original.

13. Ibid., 113.

14. Ibid., 115.

15. Brooks, *Reading*, 99; see also J. Hillis Miller, *Fiction and Repetition: Seven English Novels* (Cambridge: Harvard University Press, 1982), 2–3, 5–6.

16. McHale, "Modernist Reading," 64–66.

17. Roland Barthes, "Littérature objective," in *Essais critiques* (Paris: Le Seuil, 1964), 36.

18. The critique of the present and the self-identical now that is articulated through these narrative strategies is comparable in some of its aspects to the one carried out by Jacques Derrida in his critique of Husserl's time philosophy: see *"Ousia* and Gramme: Note on a Note from *Being and Time,"* in *Margins of Philosophy*, trans. Alan Bass (Chicago: University of Chicago Press, 1982), 29–67; and *Speech and Phenomena and Other Essays on Husserl's Theory of Signs*, trans. David B. Allison (Evanston: Northwestern University Press, 1973). For a close analysis and critique of Derrida's argument concerning Husserl and Heidegger, see David Wood, *The Deconstruction of Time* (Atlantic Highlands: Humanities Press International, 1989), 111–33, 251–64, 267–77.

19. Christine Brooke-Rose, "Illicitations," *Review of Contemporary Fiction* 9, no. 3 (1989): 102–3; see also "Conversation with Christine Brooke-Rose," with Ellen G. Friedman and Miriam Fuchs, *Utterly Other Discourse: The Texts of Christine Brooke-Rose*, ed. Ellen G. Friedman and Richard Martin (Normal: Dalkey Archive Press, 1995), 32–33.

20. Douglas R. Hofstadter, *Gödel, Escher, Bach: An Eternal Golden Braid* (New York: Vintage, 1980), 127–52.

21. McHale, *Postmodernist Fiction*, 113.

22. Hofstadter, *Gödel, Escher, Bach*, 128. The classical study of *mise en abyme* is Lucien Dällenbach's *Le récit spéculaire: Essai sur la mise en abyme* (Paris: Le Seuil, 1977); see also Jean Ricardou, *Problèmes du nouveau roman* (Paris: Le Seuil, 1967), 171–90.

23. Gérard Genette, *Narrative Discourse: An Essay in Method*, trans. Jane E. Lewin (Ithaca: Cornell University Press, 1980), 234–37.

24. For a more detailed discussion see McHale, *Postmodernist Fiction*, 112–30.

25. See Wolf-Dieter Stempel, "Möglichkeiten einer Darstellung der Diachronie in narrativen Texten," in *Zeitgestaltung in der Erzählkunst*, ed. Alexander Ritter (Darmstadt: Wissenschaftliche Buchgesellschaft, 1978), 303.

26. Hofstadter, *Gödel, Escher, Bach*, 133–34.

27. For a more detailed analysis of *Island People*'s metaleptic structure, see my article "Time Frames: Temporality and Narration in Coleman Dowell's *Island People*," *Journal of Narrative Technique* 21 (1991): 274–88.

28. Hofstadter, *Gödel, Escher, Bach*, 688–89.

29. See McHale, *Postmodernist Fiction*, 184–87.

30. Joseph Frank, "Spatial Form in Modern Literature," in *The Idea of Spatial Form* (New Brunswick: Rutgers University Press, 1991), 3–66.

31. Gary Saul Morson, *Narrative and Freedom* (New Haven: Yale University Press, 1994), 227–33.

32. Fredric Jameson, *Postmodernism, or The Cultural Logic of Late Capitalism* (Durham: Duke University Press, 1991), 17–18, 286. See also Raymond Federman, "Imagination as Plagiarism," *New Literary History* 7 (1975–1976): 563–78; and Douglas Crimp, "Appropriating Appropriation," in *Image Scavengers: Photography*, ed. Paula Marincola (Institute of Contemporary Art/University of Pennsylvania Press, 1982), 27–34.

33. Brian McHale makes a related point in "Modernist Reading" when he analyzes the ways in which, in *Gravity's Rainbow*, events and phenomena that characters perceive are later invalidated by the narrator, by other events, or by their belated attribution to a character's dreams, fantasies, or hallucinations: in either case, it becomes impossible to construct a coherent fictional universe through the thoughts and perceptions of the characters, whereas this construction is possible in most modernist novels (64–73).

34. Aleid Fokkema analyzes structures of recursion in *Lost in the Funhouse* and discusses how in the "Menelaiad," the intervention of certain characters at narrative levels other than their own leads to chronological paradoxes ("Gödel, Escher, Barth: Variations on a Triangle," *Delta* 21 [1985]: 65–78). See also Beth A. Boehm's analysis of the relationship between storyteller and audience in the "Menelaiad" ("Educating Readers: Creating New Expectations in *Lost in the Funhouse*," in *Reading Narrative: Form, Ethics, Ideology*, ed. James Phelan [Columbus: Ohio State University Press, 1989], 109–13).

35. Barth, "Menelaiad," in *Lost in the Funhouse: Fiction for Print, Tape, Live Voice* (New York: Bantam, 1969), 127–28.

36. Ibid., 138.

37. Ibid.

38. Ibid., 127; italics in original.

39. Ibid., 161.

40. Ibid., 127. In the "Author's Note" that precedes the short stories of *Lost in the Funhouse*, Barth footnotes several of the stories by saying that they were intended for a recorded voice: "'Menelaiad,' though suggestive of a recorded authorial monologue, depends for clarity on the reader's eye and may be said to have been composed for 'printed voice'" (ix). Walter Verschueren sees the "great accomplishment of the 'Menelaiad'.. in the intermediate and ambivalent level of the tape discourse . . . its project can be described as the attempt by the voice of the tape discourse to recover, in a purity and uniqueness of context, the intentional consciousness of the original speech act" ("'Voice, Tape, Writing': Original Repetition in *Lost in the Funhouse* [Beyond Phenomenology: Barth's 'Menelaiad']," *Delta* 21 [1985]: 80).

41. N. Katherine Hayles, *Chaos Bound: Orderly Disorder in Contemporary Literature and Science* (Ithaca: Cornell University Press, 1990), 281. Lutz Niethammer circumvents this paradox by arguing that it will be up to others to judge "de[n] Reflex des Historikers, Posthistoire zu historisieren" [the reflex of the historian to historicize posthistory] (*Posthistoire: Ist die Geschichte zu Ende?* [Reinbek: Rowohlt, 1989], 10).

42. *Twilight Memories: Marking Time in a Culture of Amnesia* (New York: Routledge, 1995), 9.

43. Jameson, *Postmodernism*, 284; italics in original.

25

Queering Narratology · SUSAN S. LANSER

The narrator of Jeanette Winterson's *Written on the Body* (1992) is in love with a married woman. Hardly a new topic, hardly tellable by some narratological criteria, but for the novel's narrative voice. For the unnamed autodiegetic narrator of *Written on the Body* is never identified as male or female. That silence and the extent to which it destabilizes both textuality and sexuality drive this novel at least as much as its surface plot. As I contemplate the field of feminist narratology which has emerged in the past decade and which comes of age with this volume [*Ambiguous Discourses*, ed. Kathy Mezei — Editors], *Written on the Body* leads me to new and similarly destabilizing inquiries. In what ways, I wonder, might this text's silence be a matter for narratology? How, indeed, might sex, gender, and sexuality function as elements of a narrative poetics, and why have these categories remained on the margins of narratological inquiry?

To be sure, over this decade, narratology has become more complex in its understandings of textual production and correspondingly more flexible about what constitutes its field. Yet the sex and gender (let alone the sexuality) of textual personae have not been graciously welcomed as elements of narratology; they have been relegated to the sphere of "interpretation," which is often considered a "temptation" into which narratology must be careful not to "fall."[1] Even feminist narratology, my own work included, has tended to focus on women writers or female narrators without asking how the variables "sex," "gender," and "sexuality" might operate in narrative more generally.

Taking my cue from a 1995 essay by Gerald Prince to which I have responded elsewhere, I want to argue here for the inclusion of sex, gender, and sexuality as important, intersecting elements of narrative poetics, even within conventional definitions of the field.[2] I will claim that just as Proust's *A la recherche du temps perdu* fostered Genette's identification of certain narrative conventions and transgressions and Balzac's *Sarrasine* fostered Barthes's formulation of narrative codes, *Written on the Body* points to aspects of narrative that are "proper" to narratology in its classical sense, that is, to "the (structuralist-inspired) theory of narrative," which "studies the nature, form, and functioning of narrative (regardless of medium of representation)" and examines "what all and only narratives have in common (at the level of story, narrating, and their relations) as well as what enables them to be different from one another, and it attempts to account for the ability to produce and understand them."[3] Setting aside the phrase "all and only" as a criterion that, as Prince himself has asserted, has consistently been violated even by the earliest and most renowned of narratologists,[4] I will argue that the categories sex/gender/sexuality interact with other narratological elements from narrative person to paralepsis to reliability in ways that I will only begin to suggest here. At the same time, the "application" of the categories of sex, gender, and sexuality to actual texts calls profoundly into question the separation of text from context and grammar from culture and threatens the viability of binary systems on which narratology "proper" tends to insist.

The complexities posed by sexual categories begin to emerge in the very attempt to define them for narratological purposes. Feminist theorists of the 1970s and 1980s usually distinguished "sex" from "gender" by designating "sex" as a biological category and "gender" as a social one. More recent theorists such as Judith Butler have successfully deconstructed this opposition by arguing that "sex" is itself a culturally constructed category as much constituted by "gender" as "gender" is constituted by sex.[5] Language, I suggest, further complicates this dynamic — and differently so according to whether and how sex is grammatically and hence culturally marked. When I say "she" in English, I am usually referring to animate creatures or sometimes to objects that have been grammatically gendered through cultural practice (for example a ship, a country, the moon). When I say "elle" in French or "ella" in Spanish, however, I may be referring to any number of objects, animate or inanimate, even to objects that might be biologically sexed as male; for example, "personne" (person) in French is feminine. And in German I might use the neuter form, nonexistent in French and Spanish and used in English almost exclusively (except derogatorily) for nonhumans, to name a young or unmarried female (das Mädchen). These linguistic phenomena, which obviously have ramifications far beyond the scope of this inquiry, are already, I submit, ever so slightly *queer*: sexually transgressive, undercutting their own apparent binaries.

Keeping this fluidity in mind, for the purposes of this essay I will use the term "sex" to designate the formal identification of a represented human entity as male or female. I will use "gender" to designate characteristics constructed in and by texts that implicate—but do not prove—a male or female identity by drawing on cultural codes that conventionally signify masculinity or femininity: codes such as proper names and metonymic references to clothing, activities, and behaviors. And I will use "sexuality" to designate erotic orientation or identity particularly with respect to object choice. I am assuming that readers routinely attribute a sex to narrators and characters and that they do so both through explicit linguistic markers such as "he" and "she" (or "the man" and "the woman"), through gendered codes that vary historically and culturally but are nonetheless present at least in all language cultures of the so-called West, and sometimes also through presumptions of (hetero)sexuality. Although the narrator's *sex* is never identified in *Written on the Body*, for example, that absence surely does not stop readers from looking for *gender* markers through which to constitute that narrator's sex and with it his/her sexuality—and hence to stabilize the text. It so happens that in this case Winterson has elided from the novel virtually every possible gendered identifier; only the most conventional of readers—readers unable to imagine that a woman could wield a hammer, urinate out of doors, deride marriage, hit a man, or make love to other women—would insist that this narrator is gendered male. For other readers, the markings of gender in *Written on the Body* will be as elusive as the markings of sex.

In positing a process by which readers use gender and sexuality to infer the sex of an author, narrator, or character, I want also, then, to stress the instability of such a project. To take a mundane example, someone reading a book's acknowledgments for clues to the sex of an author with an ambiguous first name might look for a thank-you to the author's husband or wife. That gay and lesbian couples sometimes now use these spousal designations undercuts any construction of sex that the reader might make on such a basis and shows that it is as tenuous to infer sex from sexuality or gender as it is to infer gender from sex or sexuality. But this only complicates and does not halt the project by which readers, I argue, conventionally seek to attribute sex to textual personae, if only to be able to speak about them in a binary-inflected language, but probably also from profound anxiety. This anxiety is precisely what makes *Written on the Body* so compelling a narrative.

Taking sex, then, to mean very simply the linguistic marking of a textual persona as male or female, I want to argue that sex is a far more integral and important component of narrative than narratologists have recognized. For, as *Written on the Body* starkly reminds us, there is not only the question of which sex is designated but also the prior question of whether sex is designated at all. Sex is surely a common if not constant element of narrative, in other words, once we include its *absence* as a narratological variable. Once sex becomes a category for narratology, we can identify different modes of narrative according to the ways in which they conventionally deploy or elide markings of sex.

I will begin this enterprise by suggesting that sex is intimately connected to the narratological category that Gérard Genette has called narrative "person" and is differently constituted in homodiegetic and heterodiegetic narratives, at least in European-language texts. Let me posit a basic narrative convention: a narrator's sex is normatively unmarked in heterodiegetic narratives and normatively marked in autodiegetic texts. That is, the vast majority of heterodiegetic narrators of European-language texts do not mark themselves on the basis of sex. This absence of sex marking does not mean that sex and gender fail to signify in heterodiegetic texts, for as I have been suggesting, there is also the question, to which I return later, of the *reader's* construction of sex through what s/he takes to be signs of gender. Moreover, cases in which heterodiegetic narrators mark their sex do exist; the narrators of *Tom Jones* and *Vanity Fair* explicitly refer to themselves as men. But even a heterodiegetic narrator who employs first-person pronouns may, in virtually all European languages, safely employ a range of *narrative* acts without identifying him- or herself by sex. The narrator of *Northanger Abbey*, for example, undertakes a broad range of speech acts without designating her sex, though arguably she does implicate a gender identity by deriding the productions of men and praising the works of women novelists. Some of George Eliot's early narrators, in contrast, adopt gendered allusions to implicate themselves as male.

Although the narrator's sex is normally unmarked in heterodiegetic texts, sex is routinely marked in most homodiegetic and virtually all autodiegetic narratives of any length. Granted, all of us could construct brief autodiegetic texts in which the narrator's sex is not manifest, but it is rare for an extended autodiegetic narrative to elide all markers of both sex and gender. Not all autodiegetic narratives mark the narrator's sex explicitly: names, clothing, and physical attributes — characteristics of *gender* — do indeed, as I have been suggesting, allow or encourage readers to construct assumptions about a narrator's *sex*. I would suggest, however, that while sex may appear initially as an open question, heterosexual presumptions operate as designators for a narrator's or character's *sexuality* unless an alternative sexuality is explicitly marked. In order to test and expand these assumptions about narrative, one might fruitfully classify and study autodiegetic narratives for their various configurations — and elisions — of markers of sex, gender, and sexuality.

My reading of *Written on the Body* suggests that a considerable degree of information has to be omitted from an autodiegetic narrative for both sex and gender to remain unmarked. Such information — including, of course, the primary omission of sex itself — would seem to constitute what Genette has called a *paralepsis*: the underreporting of information that would conventionally be provided by a particular narrator or focalizer. Paralepsis (or ellipsis in general) then becomes, along with narrative person, another narratological category that interacts with sex, gender, and sexuality. In *Written on the Body*, for example, we never learn the narrator's name, his/her physical appearance, or physical details about how his/her lovers make love to him/her, though we know the names and sexes of the lovers, their physical appearances, and physical details about how he/she makes love to them. Since much of *Written on the Body* is *about* the body, the elided physical descriptions of the narrator are not insignificant, a fact of which the narrator is well aware: "Written on the body is a secret code only visible in certain lights; the accumulations of a lifetime gather there. In places the palimpsest is so heavily worked that the letters feel like braille. I like to keep my body rolled up away from prying eyes. Never unfold too much, tell the whole story."[6]

The absence of information about a narrator's sex raises productive questions too about the relationship readers construct between the narrator and the implied author of a text. I have suggested elsewhere my own perplexity as to whether and when the marking of an author's sex (on the title page or book cover) serves implicitly to mark the sex of a sexually unmarked narrator or whether a normative masculinity overrides that link. For example, if *Pride and Prejudice* is "by a lady," is the narrator assumed to be female, or is even a narrator constructed by a female author read as male? (Or, I would now add, is such a narrator conceptualized in this age of electronic voice synthesis as a sexless "it"?) And what about the case of autodiegetic narrators, whom college-trained readers of literature, at least, have learned not to equate with their authors? Would *Written on the Body*, for example, be assumed to have a female narrator because it is written by "Jeanette Winterson"? If so, would the text from the start be read as a lesbian narrative? Or would normative heterosexuality prevail, particularly for a reader unfamiliar with Winterson's previous novels, such that the unsexed narrator would be read as male and, for the first half of the novel, the question of a possible lesbian relationship would never arise?

I allude to the first half of the novel because *Written on the Body* also takes a narrative swerve in which sexuality ruptures the conventional system by which readers attempt to determine sex on the basis of gender clues. For readers who recognize that the narrator's sex is unmarked (rather than simply constructing the narrator as a heterosexual male or as a lesbian woman), *Written on the Body* creates a tension between two narrative scenarios. In both, the beloved is married, and narrative conflict centers first around whether Louise will leave her husband Elgin, a brilliant cancer researcher, and later on the effects of the narrator's decision to flee from Louise when she/he hears that Louise has leukemia so that Louise will return to Elgin, who claims that she will die without the care that he has the power to arrange or to obstruct. For a reader open to the possibility of both narratives, the tension between the two narrative scenarios rises and falls, I suggest, according to the represented content: rising, for example, during a physical fight between the narrator and Elgin, during the narrator's musings about the negative aspects of marriage in general, or during descriptions of lovemaking, and falling, perhaps, when the focal issue is whether Louise will leave Elgin. To the extent that sex and gender matter for interpretation, the nonmarking of sex yields, in some sense, two narrative texts. Moreover, the narrative opens questions about the relationship between sex and gender in ways that allow the reader to test his or her own assumptions repeatedly.

Then, at a point midway through the novel, the text takes another informational swerve: the narrator who is in love with Louise talks about a male boyfriend called "Crazy Frank." Now we do have certain information, not about the narrator's sex, but about his/her bisexuality. The nonmarking of sex yields somewhat in importance to a new category, sexuality, that had been hitherto unmarked. How does the insertion of this new formal element — undeniable queerness — affect the signification of the narrator's unmarked sex and gender? Little, perhaps, if the narrator had been read originally as lesbian; more, perhaps, if the narrator had been read as a straight man. For the new information erases the possibility that *Written on the Body* is the story of a strictly heterosexual male in love with a married woman and hence erases one standard age-old scenario of Western literature. *Written on the Body*, whatever the sex of its narrator, is a queer novel with a queer plot.

For me, *Written on the Body* also ruptures presumed links between sex, gender, and sexuality with respect to other, seemingly more conventional texts. I said earlier that in autodiegetic narratives the narrator's sex may be marked explicitly, or it may be capable of construction through markings of gender. But what if these gender markings *do not signify* the conventionally implied sex? What if the narrator in pants is a woman, or the narrator named Mary a drag queen? Lesbian and gay writers have indeed exploited these possibilities of gender bending for cover or for play; is it not possible that readers have made conventional assumptions about sex and sexuality in texts that do not explicitly mark these categories? What if we are dealing in these cases with "queer" narratives that we have been duped into constructing as sexually conventional on the basis of binary oppositions or gendered conventionalities? What if a straight-seeming narrative lends itself to a queer reading? A sexually conscious narratology offers the possibility of identifying texts according to the intersecting systems of sex, gender, and sexuality that they do and do not make possible.

The categories of sex, gender, and sexuality raise questions about narrative reliability as well. Prince argues in "On Narratology," for example, that a narrator's geographical information may be "no less correct" for his being a psychopath. But there are myriad other, grayer areas of "fact" — for example, the narrator's "factual" statement about another character's behaviors — on which doubt might well be cast were the narrator a psychopath. Prince further suggests that a narrator's authority is weakened by a "point of view designated as (suspiciously) subjective." But what determines the suspicious subjectivity of that narrative voice? Certainly, as early criticism of a novel like *Jane Eyre* gives evidence, there was a time not far distant when all women narrators were suspect for presumed subjectivity. If a heterosexual and heterosexist reader were to construct the narrator of *Written on the Body* as queer whatever his/her sex, that reader might also decide that the point of view of the narrator was suspiciously subjective about everything to do with love and desire — which are what this book is all about. Would that reader not perhaps consider unreliable the narrator's claim to have left Louise in hopes that she would in this way be able to benefit from her husband's medical connections and expertise?

Sex/gender/sexuality might also, then, constitute a category of reliability — or, conversely, reliability might be another subcategory of sex/gender/sexuality that works itself out in narratological terms. Indeed, narratological definitions of reliability, including the one I offered in *The Narrative Act*,[7] are perilously tautological: if a reliable narrator is one who behaves "in accordance with the implied author's norms," and an unreliable narrator is one "whose values (tastes, judgments, moral sense) diverge from those of the implied author,"[8] how, in the ordinary processing of narrative, would one know the implied author's norms *except* by constructing them oneself from the values one *thinks* this author *ought* to hold? A sexually conservative reader of *Written on the Body* — fortified, perhaps, by the evidence of Winterson's previous novels, *Oranges Are Not the Only Fruit* (1985), *The Passion* (1988), and *Sexing the Cherry* (1989) — might well decide that the norms of the implied author "Jeanette Winterson" are decadent or diseased and the author's judgments therefore unreliable. In this case a narrator who would technically be considered reliable by standard definitions — because the narrator's norms are consistent with those of the implied author — might well be judged unreliable by readers whose values diverge from those of "Winterson."

Narratological distinctions of sex, gender, and sexuality may also differentiate texts by both language and medium. European languages permit considerably greater sexual ambiguity in the construction of narrators than of represented characters because the first person is less sex-specific than the third. But even with regard to narrators, the language of representation is a significant variable. *Written on the Body* is an Anglophone text, and I imagine that translators will have difficulty rendering it into any number of languages. On the very first page, for example, the narrator says, "I am alone"; in many Indo-European languages, this simple clause would require a masculine or feminine adjective, as subsequent clauses would require numerous other sex-specific adjectives and predicates that are not inflected in the English text. Such languages might, then, require even deeper ellipses for maintenance of the text's silence about its narrator's sex. Languages without grammatical gender, on the other hand, might allow much more latitude than English in constructing an autodiegetic narrator without a sex. American Sign Language would give even the represented character a gender-neutral identity, because ASL does not use gendered pronouns at all.

And while I would not want to insist that the absence of sex marking in autodiegetic narrative is exclusive to verbal texts, I think it would be extremely difficult to maintain such an absence in a visual text. Two recent films, *Orlando* and *The Crying Game*, are instructive even though their ambiguities of sex, gender, and sexuality occur not in narrators but in characters. Most viewers of the film version of *Orlando* to whom I have spoken had difficulty imagining Tilda Swinton as a male either in voice or body; only the "ellipsis" of never representing the "male" Orlando without full dress maintained the illusion that Orlando was a man. In Woolf's novel, on the other hand, there is not only no difficulty naming Orlando as male, but there is none of the prolepsis (foreshadowing) that occurred for viewers of the film who recognized (or knew ahead of time) that the person playing Orlando was female. *The Crying Game* represents a related if somewhat different case: in the film, Dill, the cross-dressed male marked as "she," appeared visually — at least to most viewers — to be female. Dill is revealed only midway through the film to be biologically male: thus Dill is marked mimetically as female in *gender*, although Dill's body comes to be marked as male in *sex*. This queering of the filmic narrative occurs with the unveiling of the body; what the film does not permit is for Dill to be *un*known in sex in a way that a written account might have allowed — I think, for example, of Balzac's *Sarrasine*. All of which is simply to say that what Prince calls the "expressive possibilities" of different "media of manifestation" are fascinatingly addressed by the insertion of sex/gender/sexuality as questions for narratology.⁹ How, indeed, would *Written on the Body* be translated into film?

The narrative complexities that result from sex, gender, and sexuality also bear on the question of tellability that some narratologists have addressed. *Written on the Body* entails three plot possibilities, two by inference ("The man loves a married woman" and "The woman loves a married woman") and one empirically verifiable ("A person of indeterminate sex loves a married woman"). Of the three, the first version seems to me the least conflict intense for a homophobic culture, the second more conflict intense, and the third different in kind because it inserts a metaplot in which additional narrative tension is generated precisely by the excitement to know whether the narrator in love with the married woman is male or female.

My point in raising these possibilities is not to suggest that narratology can *decide* these questions, just as it cannot decide the effects of metalepsis or unreliability. My point is that sex, gender, and sexuality constitute narratologically significant elements that intersect with other textual aspects to illuminate "the nature, form, and functioning of narrative," to describe commonalities and differences among narratives, and to account for readers' "ability to produce and understand them." But narratological attention to sex, gender, and sexuality also makes a strong case for a *contextual* poetics: for the impossibility of reading any narrative without considering the cultural conventions in which the narrative operates. Narratology has been nervous about such a blurring of the sharp boundaries of textuality, as it has been nervous about the related "slide" from poetics to interpretation to which the strong narratologist will not "yield." Is it possible that these resistances — to interpretation, contextuality, and sex/gender/sexuality — stem from the same anxiety?

With one last, playful evocation of *Written on the Body*, I want to suggest that narratological practice has to do not only with science but also with desire. What we choose to support, to write about, to imagine — even in narratology — seems to me as much a function of our own desire as of any incontrovertible evidence that a particular aspect of narrative is (im)proper or (ir)relevant. By resisting the notion that the text is merely an agglomeration of formal elements, the introduction of sex and gender, like the introduction of contextuality and with it of questions that have previously been associated only with interpretation, threatens the "purity" of the narratological enterprise. For some of the most interesting elements of narrative are indeed as maddeningly difficult to pin down as Winterson's narrator's sex. Perhaps, then, to embrace questions of sex, gender, and sexuality is to end up "queering" narratology in another sense: to let it deviate from the straight-and-narrow path of structuralism's binaries into a more dauntingly indeterminate terrain. Indeed, if, as some postmodern theorists contend, sex has been the binary on which all other binaries have been constituted, then the dismantling of this binary through the recognition of queerness — a queerness that, I have suggested, is already implicated in the grammars of apparently binary languages — threatens all other binaries and with it other structural certainties.

At this time when lesbian, gay, and queer studies are burgeoning, *Written on the Body* leads me to imagine that there might eventually be a queer narratology in which questions of sexuality and the challenges sexuality poses to conventions of sex and gender become a telescope through which to seek narrative elements not before attended to or attended to differently. In this context, I can't resist noting that the texts on which Barthes and Genette expend their own narratological energies, respectively *Sarrasine* and *A la recherche*, are, like *Written on the Body*, queer texts, and I would suggest that both Genette and (especially) Barthes "yield to the interpretive temptation" in delightful and illuminating ways.[10] Instead of worrying about poetical improprieties, I hope we will welcome other such efforts much as biologists might welcome the opportunity for deep-water expeditions or accounts of them, reveling in what can be learned and experienced and willing to worry later about sifting the theoretical from the praxeological, the textual from the contextual, the narratological from the interpretive. Or, to close with the final words of Jeanette Winterson's narrator, whose sex is forever a mystery: "Hurry now, it's getting late. I don't know if this is a happy ending but here we are let loose in open fields" (190).

Notes

1. See, for example, Nilli Diengott, "Narratology and Feminism," *Style* 22, no. 1 (1986): 42–50; and Gerald Prince, "On Narratology: Criteria, Corpus, Context," *Narrative* 3, no. 1 (January 1995): 73–84.

2. In "On Narratology," Prince endorses in theory the inclusion of "gender" as an element of narrative poetics but stops short of embracing feminist narratology. For my response to this essay, see my "Sexing the Narrative: Propriety, Desire, and the Engendering of Narratology," *Narrative* 3, no. 1 (January 1995): 85–94.

3. Gerald Prince, *Dictionary of Narratology* (Lincoln: University of Nebraska Press, 1987), 65.

4. As Prince has recognized in his own more recent work, one element of the classical definition has been observed consistently in the breach (and, I would add, evoked only to keep certain issues fenced out of narratology): the dictate that narratology explore "what *all and only* narratives have in common" (italics mine). To follow such a dictum would long ago have reduced narratology to a far more restrictive science than its most classical practitioners have constructed; as Prince notes, key narratological elements such as focalization, character, and description are hardly restricted to narrative. Nor, indeed, is voice: a lyric poem, for example, is said to manifest "voice," although the "speaker" is conventionally called a "persona" rather than a "narrator." Prince seems to propose a criterion of significance in place of distinctiveness: elements called into play in the relationship between story and discourse, or elements such as focalization and voice that are relevant to the "nature, form, and functioning of narrative," are worth the attention of narratologists. Likewise, narratology has always paid attention to many features that do not necessarily appear in all narratives. Such transgressive elements as metalepsis and paralepsis, which Gérard Genette has identified and discussed at some length, occur in relatively few narratives—far fewer, I hope to demonstrate, than are implicated by questions of sex.

5. Judith Butler, *Gender Trouble: Feminism and the Subversion of Identity* (New York: Routledge, 1990), 6–9, 36–38.

6. Jeanette Winterson, *Written on the Body* (New York: Alfred A. Knopf, 1993), 89; hereafter cited in the text.

7. Susan S. Lanser, *The Narrative Act: Point of View in Prose in Fiction* (Princeton: Princeton University Press, 1981).

8. Prince, *Dictionary of Narratology*, 101.

9. Ibid., 79.

10. Ibid., 82.

26

A Brief Story of Postmodern Plot

CATHERINE BURGASS

There is perhaps likely to be a general quickening of interest in the concepts of time and history toward the end of a millennium. Stephen Hawking's bestseller *A Brief History of Time* (1988), which explains to the nonspecialist the complex physics of time and space, is a manifestation of this interest. Without attempting to trace in any detail connections between scientific theories of time and those in the wider cultural context, Hawking was working on a theory that posited the dissolution of the time boundaries of the universe (its beginning and end) in the 1970s, the time that literary theorists were deconstructing the idea of linear time and novelists dramatizing this chronological confusion.[1] Postmodern fiction is often and appropriately characterized by a concern with ontological categories, an exploration of the boundaries between fact and fiction, the world and the text. Lyotard makes the basic or commonplace distinction "between the time it takes the painter to paint the picture (time of 'production'), the time required to look at and understand the work (time of 'consumption'), the time to which the work refers (a moment, a scene, a situation, a sequence of events: the time of the diegetic referent, of the story told by the picture)," stating: "This principle, childish as its ambitions may be, should allow us to isolate different 'sites of time.' "[2] Childish or not, postmodern theorists are often too credulous of postmodern literature's ability to disturb the reader's ontological categories, including the distinction between real time and time in a parallel fictional world, because they fail to put themselves in the position of the naive (nonacademic or recreational) reader whose literary competence facilitates the absorption of metafictive elements into the fictional world. The novels discussed hereafter deconstruct linear time through thematic and plot devices, but it will be argued that where postmodern plot disrupts causality and coherence to a significant extent, the *story* (here meaning both the temporal-causal chain of events and *yarn*) will suffer, as will its potential to disrupt ontological-chronological categories.

The concept of linear time, or classical time, can be found in Aristotle's

Physics, although its very existence as a divisible entity is immediately called into question: "The following considerations would make one suspect that it either does not exist at all or barely, and in the obscure way. One part of it has been and is not, while the other is going to be and is not yet. Yet time — both infinite time and any time you like to take — is made up of these."[3] This time can be objectively measured because "change is always faster or slower, whereas time is not; for fast and slow are defined by time — fast is what moves much in short time, slow is what moves little in a long time; but time is not defined by time, by being either a certain amount or a certain kind of it" (371). It is, however, dependent on motion: "For it is by means of the body that is carried along that we become aware of the before and after in the motion, and if we regard these as countable we get the 'now'" (372). This "'now' is the link of time, as has been said (for it connects past and future time), and it is a limit of time (for it is the beginning of the one and the end of the other)" (375). The fact that this "now" is both "link" and "limit" is highly significant for any deconstruction of time, since it functions both to separate and to mediate the binary opposition of past and future. In fact, Aristotle raises, though he does not finally endorse, the possibility of a radical deconstruction of linear time when he remarks: "If coincidence in time (i.e., being neither prior nor posterior) means to be in one and the same 'now,' then, if both what is before and what is after are in the same 'now,' things which happened ten thousand years ago would be simultaneous with what has happened today, and nothing would be before or after anything else" (370).

The argument cited against this notion rests on the relation of time to space: "The distinction of before and after holds primarily, then, in place" (371). The concept of linear time, the progression from past to present to future, is one that has been challenged by quantum physics but remains dominant in both the scientific and the popular imagination. For Derrida, however, whose fame rests on combining the spatial difference of structuralist linguistics with temporal difference in poststructuralist *différance*, linear time is no longer tenable because of its reliance on binary oppositions: "At the point at which the concept of *différance* and the chain attached to it, intervenes, all the conceptual oppositions of metaphysics (signifier/signified; sensible/intelligible; writing/speech; passivity/activity etc.) — to the extent that they ultimately refer to the presence of something present . . . become nonpertinent."[4] In "Spectres of Marx," Derrida questions the notion that the past and the future are mutually exclusive: "Before knowing whether one can differentiate between the spectre of the past and the spectre of the future . . . one must ask oneself whether the *spectrality effect* does not consist in undoing this opposition, or even this dialectic, between actual, effective presence and its other."[5] The "spectre" of Marx functions rather like *différance* here, as the mobile force used to deconstruct the binary of linear history.

There is a clear connection between theories of time and theories of plot for the banal reason that plot represents events which happen over time. Aristotle's theory of plot, as formulated in the *Poetics*, is coherent with his linear theory of time: "Tragedy is an imitation of an action that is complete in itself, as a whole of some magnitude; for a whole may be of no magnitude to speak of. Now a whole is that which has beginning, middle, and end."[6] It is also causal: "A beginning is that which is not itself necessarily after anything else, and which has naturally something else after it; an end is that which is naturally after something itself, either as its necessary or usual consequent, and with nothing else after it; and a middle, that which is by nature after one thing and has also another after it" (2321). Aristotle's model for plot is so structurally similar to his model of time that it appears to ignore the most common of plot devices, such as analepsis, and to confine itself to *story* or the temporal-causal raw material of fiction as defined by the Russian formalists. Derrida's theory of "writing" can be found in his discussion of Heidegger's *Being and Time* and depends on *différance*: "Such a *différance* would at once, again, give us to think a writing without presence and without absence, without history, without cause, without *archia*, without *telos*, a writing that absolutely upsets all dialectics, all theology, all teleology, all ontology."[7] This model of writing suggests a radical dissolution of story.

Plot has always entailed arranging or deranging linear chronology, the significant disruption of the temporal-causal story, but before the twentieth century this artifice was not generally foregrounded. In most narratives the disruption of linear time is naturalized, for example through the memory of a character, or is a familiar device like the explanatory aside by an omniscient narrator characteristic of nineteenth-century realism. Even modernist fiction, which demonstrated an increasing preoccupation with time in its experiments with plot, did so in the service of realistic representation. Virginia Woolf's *Mrs. Dalloway* contrasts subjective and objective time: the disjunction between the former and the latter is signified by the chimes of Big Ben slicing into Clarissa's consciousness. Woolf wrote of her "tunnelling method," which relies heavily on analepsis but is motivated by memory.

These plot devices are distinctive, but not deliberately foregrounded, since their purpose is to render faithfully internal consciousness, including the perception of time.

In postmodern fiction, thematic and plot devices are designed specifically to question linear history and temporality. Gabriel García Márquez's *One Hundred Years of Solitude* (1967) is the story of the Buendía family over six generations and one hundred years until its final extinction, whose plot demonstrates a characteristic circularity. At the close of the novel, Aureliano Buendía finds a history of his family in the form of a prophecy written one hundred years ago of the next hundred years, that is the book the reader has just been reading. The text Aureliano reads is in code, "based on the fact that Melquíades [the prophet-historian] had not put events in the order of man's conventional time, but had concentrated a century of daily episodes in such a way that they coexisted in one instant."[8] This is an ideal to which a real plot cannot conform; although the story is peopled with revenants, and history keeps repeating itself in successive generations of the Buendía family, it is, like Salman Rushdie's *Midnight's Children* (1981), conventionally chronological. As Aureliano, fascinated, reads more quickly, he hastens his own death as the real and fictional story come to a simultaneous close. This device could be read as metafictive, but the novel belongs to the tradition of magical realism, and its treatment of time is naturalized within this genre. The conclusion of the novel does not so much deconstruct the time of the story as bend it in a circle, effectively sealing the self-contained fictional world.

Midnight's Children has elements of magical realism but has also been defined by Linda Hutcheon as a "historiographic metafiction," a genre that foregrounds the narrative construction of history in direct opposition to those early-eighteenth-century fictions, such as *Robinson Crusoe*, which claimed to be real histories and were sometimes accepted as such. It is also engaged in a discussion of narrative technique. As the title *Midnight's Children* suggests, time is thematized; the narrator Saleem Sinai was born "once upon a time. . . . And the time? The time matters, too. Well then: at night. No, it's important to be more . . . On the stroke of midnight, as a matter of fact. Clock-hands joined palms in respectful greeting as I came."[9] (This time is significant because it was the hour of India's independence.) However, the narrator muses: "Time has been an unsteady affair, in my experience, not a thing to be relied upon. It could even be partitioned: the clocks in Pakistan would run half an hour ahead of their Indian counterparts"

(459). Postmodern fiction tends to favor relative time over subjective time and to question the very possibility of objective time and measurement. Plot is discussed in metafictional passages; the narrator-protagonist is relating his story to his consort Padma, the naive reader incarnate, who believes Saleem's narrative to be factual, history rather than story. Saleem particularly notes Padma's reactions to the metafictive elements of his narrative: "Padma has started getting irritated whenever my narration becomes self-conscious" (65). He modifies his style of storytelling accordingly: "I must return (Padma is frowning) to the banal chain of cause-and-effect" (295). These metafictive passages accurately describe the actual plot structure; although they represent time out of narrative time and remind the reader that "distortions are inevitable," the story is related broadly chronologically, and the present of the telling is fictionalized to the extent that it is not likely to shatter the boundaries of the fictional world.

Kurt Vonnegut's *Slaughterhouse-Five* (1968) also thematizes the writing of history, this time of the Second World War, particularly the bombing of Dresden. It opens with a qualified truth claim: "All this happened, more or less. The war parts, anyway, are pretty much true."[10] This parodies the eighteenth-century novelistic convention, as does the title page. Time is predictably unpredictable, even for the narrator, who experiences a conflict between subjective and objective time: "The time would not pass. . . . The second hand on my watch would twitch once, and a year would pass, and then it would twitch again" (20). It is another framed narrative whose end is prefigured in its beginning as the narrator tells us that the story he is going to tell begins like this:

> Listen:
> *Billy Pilgrim has come unstuck in time.*
> It ends like this:
> *Poo-tee-weet?* (22)

And so it does.

The narrator proceeds to relate the fantastic tale of Billy Pilgrim, wartime chaplain's assistant and time traveler. Aristotle's scenario where "nothing would be before or after anything else" is dramatized as the hero is abducted by benevolent aliens, for whom "all moments, past, present, and future, always have existed, always will exist. The Tralfamadorians can look at all the different moments. . . . They can see how permanent all the moments are, and they can look at any moment that interests them. It is just an illusion we have here on Earth that one moment follows another one, like beads on a string" (27).

This picture of time has its origins in Einstein's general theory of relativity (1915), a radical revision of Newtonian physics, contemporaneous with modernism, which presents the universe in terms of a four-dimensional space-time continuum, although it does not directly challenge the idea of linear time. Tralfamadorian plot construction is coherent with four-dimensional time; their novels are emphatically anti-Aristotelian and bear a singular resemblance both to Derrida's idea of writing and to Melquíades's fictional technique in *One Hundred Years of Solitude*. They are laid out in clumps of symbols which are read "all at once, not one after the other. There isn't any particular relationship between all the messages. . . . There is no beginning, no middle, no end, no suspense, no moral, no causes, no effects. What we love in our books are the depths of many marvelous moments seen all at one time" (88). Conventional plot is considered in the initial framing chapter of *Slaughterhouse-Five*, where the narrator discusses one version of the story that he has outlined in crayon on a roll of wallpaper:

> I used my daughter's crayons, a different color for each main character. One end of the wallpaper was the beginning of the story, and the other end was the end, and then there was all that middle part, which was the middle. And the blue line met the red line and then the yellow line, and the yellow line stopped because the character represented by the yellow line was dead. And so on. (5)

The real plot of *Slaughterhouse-Five* is somewhere between the Aristotelian plot and Derrida's "writing" or the narrator's plot diagram and a Tralfamadorian novel. The postmodern plot and reading experience cannot match Derrida's ideal because the earthling cannot read or write the scenes or symbols of the novel simultaneously. If we were to attempt to draw a real plot diagram of *Slaughterhouse-Five* in crayon, it would resemble colored spaghetti. But although its jumps in time are more frequent and abrupt than those in either *Midnight's Children* or *One Hundred Years of Solitude*, the prolepsis and analepsis are still *realistically* motivated by Billy Pilgrim's travel backward and forward in time, which is itself naturalized by his abduction by the Tralfamadorians or, if you cannot stomach that, by his madness, caused by a bump on the head in an airplane crash. The narrator describes himself "as a trafficker in climaxes and thrills and characterization and wonderful dialogue and suspense" (5). *Slaughterhouse-Five* is another highly *readable* novel where cause and effect still operate, and even though the conclusion is written in the introduction, the writer cannot dispense with suspense, because the reader does not know for sure whether or how that conclusion is reached until he or she reaches it in real time.

According to John North, Stephen Hawking's deconstruction of the boundaries of time can be described in terms of a circular, self-contained universe that has no beginning or end. Possibly the replacement of linear time with circular or deconstructed time in postmodern theory and fiction is a manifestation of the fear of death, and these alternative narratives of time function to replace the religious narratives of immortality that have been discredited in a godless world. The Tralfamadorians have no such fear of death precisely because they can see the fourth dimension: "When a Tralfamadorian sees a corpse, all he thinks is that the dead person is in a bad condition in that particular moment, but that the same person is just fine in plenty of other moments" (27). Billy Pilgrim tries to spread the Tralfamadorian gospel, at one point speaking at a radio conference on the death of the novel, at another reassuring a little boy he is fitting for glasses that his dead father is really alive in other moments. Paul Ricoeur suggests in *Time and Narrative* that it is through narrative that we humanize time and resolve the disjunction between our necessarily limited experience and the scientific idea of time. Both Hawking's theory and the fourth dimension as depicted in Vonnegut's novel are imaginative constructions to the extent that finity bounds human experience, but they are read in different ways: one as scientific exposition, the other for its entertainment value.

Clearly, beginnings and endings have a special function in postmodern metafiction, marking the entrance and exit of the fictional world and its parallel time. There is a structural circularity in these novels that confounds linear time: the end of *Midnight's Children* returns to the present of the telling, a not unconventional plot device, but also foretells the future; the ending of *One Hundred Years of Solitude* is more complex as Aureliano reads his future in a historical document. The narrator of *Slaughterhouse-Five* is particularly taken with songs whose last line repeats the first line "and so on to infinity," like the story of Billy Pilgrim (3). Derrida turns deconstruction on narrative time in "The Law of Genre," an analysis of Blanchot's *La folie du jour*, which includes in its final paragraphs its first line. Derrida reads this as a deconstruction of linear time:

> These first words mark a collapse that is . . . unsuitable within a linear order of succession, within a spatial or temporal sequentiality, within an objectifiable topology or chronology. One sees . . . reads the crumbling of an upper

boundary. . . . Suddenly, this upper or initial boundary, which is commonly called the first line of a book is forming a pocket inside the corpus. It is taking the form of an *invagination* through which the trait of the first line, the borderline, splits while remaining the same and traverses yet also bounds the corpus.[11]

This symbolizes the deconstruction of narrative chronology. However, this kind of metafiction could just as easily be read as reinforcing the self-containment of the fictional world together with its particular chronology in an infinite *loop*.

The final novel, Italo Calvino's *If on a winter's night a traveller* (1979), is the most radically and structurally metafictive. On the penultimate page the reader is asked, "Do you believe that every story must have a beginning and an end?"[12] The novel plays mercilessly with the Aristotelian notion of plot. It opens: "You are about to begin reading Italo Calvino's new novel, *If on a winter's night a traveler.*" The *story* is enclosed within a full frame and ends in the same manner: "And you say, 'just a moment, I've almost finished *If on a winter's night a traveler* by Italo Calvino'" (205). But unlike the traditional frame that gently leads the reader into and out of the narrative, Calvino's is structurally closer to Derrida's *parergon* or chiasmus, a deconstructed, collapsed, or "invaginated" frame that is both inside and outside the body proper of the text.[13] Calvino intersperses metafictive (numbered) chapters with named chapters that parody various genres. The numbered chapters, which form a continuous narrative, are addressed to "you," the Reader, and in this metafictional story, "you" read the first (named) chapter, "If on a winter's night a traveller," but find that the book has been wrongly bound and "you" have in fact been reading the first chapter of a different novel. "You" then return to the publisher for a copy of this book and are issued with a similarly deceptively bound but different novel, and so it goes on. The metafictive chapters parody the classic romance as "you," the Reader, and Ludmilla, the "Other Reader," meet, overcome various obstacles, and finally get married.

There is some debate as to the metafictive power of this text. For Welch Everman, "the work goes beyond itself, beyond its printed text and into the text of the Reader's (real) world. This novel is purposely literary, and yet it wants to push against the limits of the literary and break through to a place beyond language."[14] Peter Lamarque and Stein Olsen read the opening frame in a similarly dualistic way: "The first sentence is both true and fictional in intent."[15] Elizabeth Ermarth maintains that postmodern novels, unlike conventional linear narratives, foreground the experience of reading as a continual present.[16] Although the reader of *If on a winter's night a traveller* is addressed as "you," because he is inscribed in the text he can be read as an entirely fictional character. Linda Hutcheon concedes, "The reader is . . . a function implicit in the text, an element of the narrative situation. No specific real person is meant."[17] Elizabeth Dipple more pertinently points to the fact that the reader of *If on a winter's night a traveller* is a particular fictional character.[18] In spite of the documented assimilation by a wider nonscientific public of radical new theories of time and the assertions of literary theorists that metafiction disrupts ontological categories, in practice it is only academics who are consistently self-conscious enough to read metafiction as persistently disruptive. *Real* readers can often quickly neutralize metafictional devices so that their ontological (and chronological categories) remain intact. This is something recognized by Lamarque and Olsen, who maintain that fact is largely irrelevant to literature because factual inference is blocked by what they call the "fictive stance" (88). The fact that readers temporarily suspend disbelief and imaginatively enter the alternative fictional world, with its alternative temporality, renders them immune to metafiction.

Theoretical attempts to establish the ontologically disruptive capacity of metafiction are doomed to failure because of the primacy of context in interpretation, but one can predict that the power of metafiction will be drastically reduced if the reader is already familiar with the technique. Many readers are, not only because metafiction was a highly popular literary mode during the 1970s and 1980s, but because it has a long history, its origins in the British novel being almost contemporaneous with the birth of the genre. At one point in the archetypal eighteenth-century metafiction, *Tristram Shandy*, the narrator parodies the plot devices of the novel:

> I am this month one whole year older than I was this time twelve-month; and having got, as you perceive, almost into the middle of my fourth volume — and no farther than to my first day's life — 'tis demonstrative that I have three hundred and sixty-four days more life to write just now, than when I first set out; so that instead of advancing, as a common writer, in my work with what I have been doing at it — on the contrary, I am just thrown so many volumes back.[19]

Such metafictive devices foreground plot design as *If on a winter's night a traveller* foregrounds real (reading) time, but neither effectively compromises the simple fact that realism and reality are not identical, that literary and literal truth are different, and that real time and narrative time run parallel and are therefore separate.

There is one factor that tends not to be considered when discussing the potential of metafiction to disrupt ontological-chronological boundaries: where story is subordinated and there is no compensation for the loss of the readerly pleasure of *consumption*, there is even less likelihood that the ordinary reader's sense of separate worlds will be compromised because such novels are likely to remain unread. The reader of Calvino's novel might be able to fictionalize "you" but for the fact that the novel is rebarbative in other ways. At one point "you" remark that "this is a novel where, once you have got into it, you want to go forward, without stopping" (64), but its structure prevents this as each false fictional start is arrested, suspended, and then succeeded by another. *If on a winter's night a traveller* would be likely to irritate or frustrate a recreational reader to the point that he or she stops without going forward and simply puts the book down. A comment on Alphonse Allais's *Une drame bien parisien* by Umberto Eco seems applicable to Calvino's text: "The naive reader will be unable to enjoy the story (he will suffer a final uneasiness), but the critical reader will succeed only by enjoying the defeat of the former."[20] According to the rather bossy narrator of Calvino's novel,

> The dimension of time has been shattered, we cannot love or think except in fragments of time each of which goes off along its own trajectory and immediately disappears. We can rediscover the continuity of time only in the novels of that period when time no longer seemed stopped and did not yet seem to have exploded, a period that lasted no more than a hundred years. (13)

In spite of some jibes at humorless theorists, *If on a winter's night a traveller* neatly illustrates and even incorporates postmodern theory by means of a highly innovative arrangement of temporal-causal events, but at the expense of old-fashioned storytelling. *Slaughterhouse-Five*, *Midnight's Children*, and *One Hundred Years of Solitude*, on the other hand, play with time, but their respective stories are neither subsumed nor exploded by their postmodern plots.

Notes

1. See John North, *The Fontana History of Astronomy and Cosmology* (London: Fontana, 1994), pp. 611–12.

2. Jean-François Lyotard, *The Inhuman: Reflections on Time*, trans. Geoffrey Bennington and Rachel Bowlby (Cambridge: Polity Press, 1993), p. 78.

3. *The Complete Works of Aristotle*, ed. Jonathan Barnes, 2 vols. (Oxford: Princeton University Press, 1984), vol. 1, p. 370.

4. Jacques Derrida, *Positions*, trans. Alan Bass (London: Athlone Press, 1987), p. 29.

5. Jacques Derrida, "Spectres of Marx," *New Left Review* 205 (May–June 1994): p. 36.

6. *The Complete Works of Aristotle*, vol. 2, p. 2321.

7. Jacques Derrida, *Margins of Philosophy*, trans. Alan Bass (London: Harvester Wheatsheaf, 1982), p. 67.

8. Gabriel García Márquez, *One Hundred Years of Solitude*, trans. Gregory Rabassa (New York: Bard, 1971), p. 382.

9. Salman Rushdie, *Midnight's Children* (London: Cape, 1981; London: Pan, 1982), p. 9.

10. Kurt Vonnegut, *Slaughterhouse-Five* (New York: Dell, 1968), p. 1.

11. Jacques Derrida, *Acts of Literature*, ed. Derek Attridge (London: Routledge, 1992), p. 236.

12. *If on a winter's night a traveller*, trans. William Weaver (London: Picador, 1982), p. 204. [The UK edition of this translation uses British spelling in the title, "traveller," but retains American spelling in the text, "traveler." — Editors]

13. For a discussion of the parergon, see Jacques Derrida, *The Truth in Painting*, trans. Geoff Bennington and Ian McLeod (London: University of Chicago Press, 1987), p. 61; see also *Acts of Literature*, pp. 236–38.

14. Welch Everman, *Who Says This? The Authority of the Author, the Discourse, and the Reader* (Carbondale: Southern Illinois University Press, 1988), p. 122.

15. Peter Lamarque and Stein Haugom Olsen, *Truth, Fiction, and Literature: A Philosophical Perspective* (Oxford: Clarendon Press, 1994), p. 66.

16. Elizabeth Deeds Ermarth, "The Crisis of Realism in Postmodern Time," in *Realism and Representation: Essays on the Problem of Realism in Relation to Science, Literature, and Culture*, ed. George Levine (Madison: University of Wisconsin Press, 1993), pp. 214–24.

17. Linda Hutcheon, *Narcissistic Narrative: The Metafictional Paradox* (London: Methuen, 1984), p. 139.

18. Elizabeth Dipple, *The Unresolvable Plot: Reading Contemporary Fiction* (London: Routledge, 1988), p. 107.

19. Laurence Sterne, *The Life and Opinions of Tristram Shandy* (1759–1767; New York: Random, 1950), pp. 295–96.

20. Umberto Eco, *The Role of the Reader: Explorations in the Semiotics of Texts* (Bloomington: Indiana University Press, 1984), p. 10.

27

On Voice · JOHN BRENKMAN

1.

I intend in this essay on "voice" in the novel to sharpen the difference between narrative theory and novel theory as antagonistic genres of criticism. Their antagonism is not, of course, absolute. The development of literary criticism since the early twentieth century is the product of the cross-fertilization as well as the conflict between formalism and antiformalism. Formalist narrative theory has often enriched nonformalist novel theory. Structuralism not only gave birth to narratology but also profoundly affected novel theorists, for example, Fredric Jameson in *Marxism and Form* and *The Political Unconscious*, Franco Moretti in *The Way of the World*, and Nancy Armstrong in *Desire and Domestic Fiction*. Other theorists have sought to synthesize rhetorical or linguistic formalisms into projects in novel theory, from Wayne Booth's *Rhetoric of Fiction* to Roland Barthes's *S/Z*.[1] Indeed, the neglect of form in more recent criticism is a result in part of the fact that no new formalism has emerged since structuralism to challenge those trends which, while opening new perspectives on the politics and cultural contexts of literature, have drifted more and more into thematic, even allegorical, criticism. A new formalism would be welcome today — for its insights and as something to contend against.

The principal strength of novel theory lies in its tendency to conceive the novel as a specific cultural and literary form, as when Moretti analyzes the form of the bildungsroman from Goethe to Flaubert in cultural rather than formalist categories. His thesis is that as "Europe plunges into modernity, but without possessing a culture of modernity," it finds in "youth" a "material sign" to represent the "spiritual content" of modernity.[2] "The new and destabilizing forces of capitalism impose a hitherto unknown mobility" but also give "rise to unexpected hopes, thereby generating an interiority not only fuller than before, but also . . . perennially dissatisfied and restless" (4). Youth, shed of many of its actual features, becomes a culturally potent symbol capable of designating at once this mobility and this restless, dissatisfied interiority. "If youth, therefore, achieves its symbolic centrality, and the great narrative of the Bildungsroman comes into being, this is because Europe has to attach a meaning, not so much to youth, as to modernity. . . . Youth is, so to speak, modernity's essence, the sign of a world that seeks its meaning in the future rather than in the past" (5). The cultural symbolization of modernity as youth generates the formal possibilities of the bildungsroman, but at the same time it creates the genre's formal limit and inner contradiction: the brevity of youth "forces the a priori establishment of a formal constraint" (the story cannot proceed beyond the protagonist's maturation); consequently, the bildungsroman's means of representing modernity tends to betray the "intrinsically boundless dynamism" of the modernity it is called upon to represent in the first place (6). To examine how the different trends within the bildungsroman cope with this latent contradiction in the form, Moretti foregrounds the problem of plot and draws extensively on analytic models developed by narrative theory and narratology. His work remains within the critical tradition of novel theory, however, because its formal-structural analysis of plot strategies is ancillary to the social-symbolic determinations of the bildungsroman's form, origins, inner contradictions, cultural value, and aesthetic effects.

Novel theory diverges sharply from narrative theory when it comes to understanding the novel's relation to the folktale and other popular fiction, such as romances or detective novels. For narrative theory, all these narrative forms have the same, or at least homologous, elements and structuring principles. The novel is a variant of narrative in general. Not so, in the eyes of novel theory. Whereas structuralism takes Propp's *Morphology of the Folk Tale* as its inaugural model for a structural analysis of all narrative, including the novel, Bakhtin considers the folktale a "primary genre" that the novel reinscribes — rewrites and reaccentuates — according to its own specifically novelistic imperatives and purposes. As for popular fiction — and by extension other narrative forms that emerge alongside the history of the modern novel, like cinema — Bakhtin and the early Lukács insist that these popular and mass-cultural forms are derivatives and artistic reductions of the novel form itself, not equivalent or parallel developments. Lukács makes the following assertion in the context of assessing why critics in the early twentieth century failed to grasp the aesthetic importance of the novel compared to genres like epic, poetry, and tragedy whose origins lay in the premodern world:

The novel, in contrast to other genres whose existence resides within the finished form, appears as something in process of becoming. That is why, from the artistic viewpoint, the novel is the most hazardous genre, and why it has been described as only half an art by many who equate having a problematic with being problematic. The description may seem convincing because the novel—unlike other genres—has a caricatural twin almost indistinguishable from itself in all inessential formal characteristics: the entertainment novel, which has all the outward features of the novel but which, in essence, is bound to nothing and based on nothing, i.e., is entirely meaningless; superficial likeness can almost lead to the caricature being mistaken for the real thing. But a closer look will always, in any concrete case, reveal the caricature for what it is.[3]

Bakhtin, who cuts a much wider swath than Lukács in defining the novel and views folkloric and popular culture as a source of the novel's aesthetic, holds much the same view of the relation of the novel to its derivatives and caricature. Valuation is integral to novel theory's understanding of literary forms. By contrast, narrative theory and narratology aspire to a value-neutral conception of narrative; indeed, going back to the seminal issues of the French journal *Communications*, structuralist narrative theory gaily combines Raymond Roussel and Ian Fleming, La Princesse de Clèves and France-Soir, Flaubert and Bororo myth, to banish aesthetic value from narrative analysis.[4]

The tendency of novel theory to define the novel as a genre that is sui generis does lead to certain impasses and quandaries, whether in the theory of the novel as such or of a subgenre like the bildungsroman. The novel theorist ties the interpretation of the literary form to a particular historical and philosophical understanding of the salient features of modern society and culture; inevitably, the evaluation of the form has to exclude or devalue certain works and tendencies. *The Theory of the Novel* concludes with a reflection on Dostoevsky as a limit-case that cannot be comprehended within Lukács's own conception of modernity and the novel: "He, and the form he created, lie outside the scope of this book. Dostoevsky did not write novels . . . !"[5] For Lukács, Dostoevsky was strictly speaking uninterpretable, an incomprehensible dead end within the modern world or a harbinger of something new that only "later artists will one day weave into a great unity" (153). Moretti delineates the complexities of the bildungsroman with extraordinary subtlety and precision and yet, because of the very understanding of history and culture that his reading unfolds, is led to disqualify the English tradition, from Austen and the Brontës to Dickens, as failed or flawed attempts to realize the genre's possibilities. His valuations, inseparable from his historical-cultural interpretation of the genre's form, open onto controversy as dramatically as Lukács's exclusion of Dostoevsky. Bakhtin's placing of Dostoevsky at the very heart of the modern novel, or feminist critics' revaluation of English courtship and marriage novels, suggests the sorts of controversy to which novel theory is intrinsically prone.

Narrative theory is spared such difficulties. In construing its object as narrative structures, strategies, and functions without regard to the kind of discourse in which they occur, it achieves a self-consistent critical language unencumbered by the need to assess either the aesthetic or the social value of the novel or to account for its contradictory imperatives. The self-consistency of narrative theory is not, however, a point in its favor. On the contrary. For isn't the moment one's thought begins to match up perfectly to its object the exact moment to doubt its truthfulness? For me, an indelible lesson taught by Paul de Man is to recognize that it is in the nature of literary works and interpretation that every genuine critical understanding arrives at its maximum insight only to disclose its ineradicable blind spot.[6]

2.

The general antagonism between novel theory and narrative theory takes on a new urgency in light of the tendency in several recent novelists to cast the narrative voice as the writer, not a narrator in the sense of a storyteller or observer or presiding consciousness. In their work, narration is an act of writing, not storytelling. That a novel is a product of writing is hardly controversial. It is a self-evident fact known to all readers. But novelists who foreground the act of writing seem to challenge a set of well-entrenched narrative conventions and reading habits that have been variously codified in twentieth-century criticism.

According to those conventions, habits, and codes, narration takes place in an imaginary space. The first-person narrator, even if a participant in the story, recounts it from a fictive place unlocated in concrete space and time. Where is Pip when he recounts his encounter with the convict, his days at Miss Havisham's, or his arrival in London? The question is superfluous, indeed silly. In third-person narrations, from *Madame Bovary* to *A Portrait of the Artist as a Young Man*, the supposed narrator occupies an imaginary space in the simple sense that he does not "exist," either on the plane of reality of the story or that of the book. This creation of an imaginary space of narration is a complex stylization, a kind of rhetorical zone in which the narrator "recounts" events — actions, emotions, thoughts — as though he or she has "observed" them, though no such space of witness exists within or outside the story told. That we accept this rhetoric of recounting and observing, this imaginary space from which someone who is no one addresses us, is at the very least a significant achievement in our modern capacity for alienation.

For that very reason, the novel form bugged Walter Benjamin, who saw the rise of the novel as the death of genuine storytelling and, with it, of the very capacity to communicate one's experiences and wisdom, the kind of experience and wisdom that accumulated, according to his archetypes, in the lives of sailors, farmers, travelers, and urban craftsmen. Modern critics have on the whole, unlike Benjamin, embraced the alienations of the novel but then set about to describe and codify narrative conventions so as to tame these alienations into structured unities in the name of various values: aesthetic mastery, impersonality, objectivity, irony, judgment, controlling consciousness, and so on.

Our whole conceptualization of narrator and implied author has generated a rich vocabulary for clarifying narrational structures, but there is something amiss in it, for it ultimately neglects the specificity of novelistic writing. An implied author occupies a perspective; an author engages in an act of writing. Narrative theory in effect reduces the act of writing, that is, the actual author's practice, to nothing more than the process of creating the implied author, who is then stationed as the outer limit of the narrative theorist's interpretive and analytical attention. What, then, is at stake when contemporary novelists reverse this scheme and identify narration with writing, evacuating or overrunning that imaginary space in which we read — or hear — an implied author or narrator addressing us? The purposes and effects of novelists' foregrounding of writing are extremely varied, as are the stylistic and formal challenges posed by their active interrogation of the imaginary space of narration.

3.

Salman Rushdie writes a Menippean voice in *Shame*, riding roughshod over tropes of invention and tropes of representation: "The country in this story is not Pakistan, or not quite. . . . My story, my fictional country exist, like myself, at a slight angle to reality."[7] He opens avenues of commentary with essayistic asides on politics and history and mulls over the plot choices he makes and the nuances of the theme of shame. At one point, he tells how a character in the novel was inspired by the story of a Pakistani girl in London murdered by her father for "making love to a white boy":

> My Sufiya Zinobia grew out of the corpse of that murdered girl. . . . I even went so far as to give the dead girl a name: Anahita Muhammad, known as Anna. . . . But finally she eluded me, she became a ghost, and I realized that to write about her, about shame, I would have to go back East, to let the idea breathe its favourite air. Anna, deported, repatriated to a country she had never seen, caught brain-fever and turned into a sort of idiot.
>
> Why did I do that to her? (124–25)

The mixing of fantastic and realistic modes in Rushdie, the ragged edges he makes between invention and representation, has been generally described as magical realism or metafiction. I think both descriptions are misleading, though the influence of Gabriel García Márquez or Thomas Pynchon on Rushdie is undeniable. García Márquez's magical realism works by making the connection between the fantastic and the realistic seamless; he narrates utterly implausible and plausible events alike in the style of verisimilitude. He creates the unified sense of a world which is neither mundane nor fanciful because both at once. Rushdie, by contrast, spins fantastical episodes as imaginative and comic commentary on social realities. It is in that sense that he revives Menippean satire within contemporary fiction. By the same token, he does not write metafiction in the sense contemporary criticism gives the term. The passage about the creation of Sufiya Zinobia does not draw you into an epistemological paradox about the possibilities of knowing or representing reality. It jarringly layers the real-world sources of the story and its elaboration into a full-blown fictional tale and signals the yet more complex historical referent of that tale. That the London news story the writer says he read may itself be a fabrication is moot. In foregrounding the act of writing, with its heterogeneous sources and referents, Rushdie is recovering the Menippean tradition, which, through Rabelais, Sterne, and Dostoevsky, has shadowed other developments in the history of the novel.

Rushdie exemplifies the tendency in twentieth-century fiction that Milan Kundera identifies as a spiraling back to formal possibilities of "the nearly forgotten aesthetic of the novel previous to the nineteenth century."[8] In

Rushdie's recovery of Menippean satire—with its mixture of fantasy and reality, comic exaggeration, intellectual parody, social commentary—the voice of the novel emerges as the writer's creation, putting his intentions and purposes openly at stake in the narration itself.

4.

Christa Wolf's novel *Patterns of Childhood* is unmistakably autobiographical, but it is not narrated autobiographically. It alternates among three distinct time frames and different voices. The main story is presented in the third person as the story of a young girl named Nelly Jordan, her parents, and her younger brother Lutz. Nelly, like Christa Wolf, is born in 1929 and hence four years old when the Nazis come to power and sixteen at the end of the war. She lives in the German town of L. The second time frame is the summer of 1971 during a trip the writer takes to her birthplace in the Polish town of G., formerly the German town of L. She is accompanied by her husband and daughter and her younger brother Lutz. This narrative is told in the second person in the form of a memoir the writer addresses to herself. The third strand is likewise in the second person and is presented as the diary the writer keeps during the composition of the novel, from 1972 to 1974.

The project first arose years earlier when Frankfurt students avidly following the Auschwitz trial disturbed the writer's assumption that only the older generation of Germans had secrets from the Nazi era: "You were unprepared for their demand that you yield your secret. . . . As though you could be relieved of the duty to lay a hand upon your own childhood."[9] But she was unable to begin the writing until she recast the story that was emerging from her own remembering as someone else's life story. Hence third-person narration: "Gradually, as the months went by, the dilemma crystallized: to remain speechless, or else live in the third person" (3). Remaining speechless was, she says, impossible, living in the third person merely strange.

Next she planned a novel written completely in the third person, presumably shuttling between a woman's trip in 1971 to her birthplace and the story of her childhood there during the Third Reich, minus the writer's diary. "The sudden switch from the third to the second person (which only seems to be closer to the first)" came "the morning after a vivid dream" (118), in which she discovers a mysterious object and tricks someone into believing that it is the thing she had been entrusted with and was then accused of stealing; by finding this mysterious object, she proves she had merely forgotten about it: "a true memory lapse!" (119). The writer takes the dream as a warning against her assumption that the child whose experience the adult seeks to remember and the adult herself must be, or can become, the same. Some discoveries, like the mysterious object in the dream, have the feel of memory lapses but are in fact hoaxes that merely exonerate the one who "remembers." So just as the writer is stymied in speechlessness in the face of first-person narration, she now rejects the purely third-person narration because it presumes an identity between child and adult and does not guard the writer herself against turning memories and memory lapses into a hoax. Therein lies the dilemma of Wolf's search for Nelly Jordan. To find her, she must sharpen the estrangement: "That's when you had to realize that you could never again be her ally, that you were an intruding stranger pursuing not a more or less well-marked trail but actually the child herself" (119).

The therapeutic expectation of modern autobiography is jeopardized in *Patterns of Childhood*. Not only does autobiography suppose the power to recover forgotten traumas, suppressed desire, and the oldest misunderstandings, but the very process of recovering them is supposed to secure and deepen one's identity. As Wolf's novel delves into the adolescent Nelly's relationship to Dr. Julianne Strauch—her inspiring teacher, role model, love object, and a devoted Nazi—the crisis of the writer's relation to her character reaches a new extreme. What the writer's memory recovers is how thoroughly Nelly's schooling in the values that the writer now most prizes within herself, independence and self-respect as a woman, come from her devotion to Julianne and enthusiastic participation in Hitler Youth. The more the writer discovers the entanglement of Nazism and everyday life, ideology, and identity, the less her life returns to her as her own. There is no bridge between her past and present: "The closer she gets to you in time, the less familiar she becomes" (211). The novelistic strategy of estrangement, originally undertaken through the splitting of voices in order to overcome speechlessness and bad faith, does not open any dialectic path to overcoming a lived estrangement; indeed, the writer's estrangement from her own elaborately disclosed past has found form in this stylistic experiment, but not a healing transcendence. In the end, she asks, "And the past, which can still split the first person into the second and the third—has its hegemony been broken? Will the voices be still?" She answers, "I don't know" (406).

5.

The voice of Toni Morrison's *Jazz* is an I-narrator who has no role in the story, nor even an identity, though her verbal style, recollections, and familiarity with events and surroundings place her in the same Harlem of the 1920s as the characters. She belongs to the neighborhood, but her omniscience exceeds what even the most inveterate busybody could acquire in gossip and talk. And yet nothing in the text raises questions about her reliability in the conventional sense.

When the final chapter uncovers a turbulence in the relation between the voice and the characters, it also makes evident something that is palpable throughout the novel: the novel's voice is an amalgam of the unidentified neighbor and the writer. Writer, not "implied author," because the chapter explores the making of the characters and story, not merely the "observation" and "recounting" of them: "Pain. I seem to have an affection, a kind of sweettooth for it. . . . I break lives to prove I can mend them back again."[10] The difference between the neighbor and the writer is not a structured separation of "narrator" and "implied author," for they confront the same crisis when faced with the story's outcome, and they articulate the same sentences, share the same voice. Their difference is more akin to the two sides of a Möbius strip: the neighbor is a gossip and chronicler who embellishes what she knows about the protagonists up to the crisis point where their actions throw in doubt her speculations about their inner reality and their fate; the writer is a creator who has made characters who, against her own expectation, resist the fate to which the story seems to destine them. Thus neighbor and writer admit (in one voice) to misunderstanding Joe and Violet: "I was sure one would kill the other" (220).

The moral pattern inscribed in the story of Joe and Violet Trace suggests an unexpiated violence that inevitably spawns more violence. Joe's murder of his young lover Dorcas is never comprehended or forgiven, and Violet's mad attempt to disfigure the dead girl's face is followed by her yet madder act of setting Dorcas's photograph on the mantel in an uncanny homage meant to remind Joe of what he can never undo, and ambiguously give Violet herself an image of the daughter she lost long ago in miscarriage, a daughter Joe never wanted. Neighbor and writer have read in these bluesy actions auguries of recurrent violence: "So I missed it altogether. I was so sure one would kill the other. I waited for it so I could describe it. I was so sure it would happen. That the past was an abused record with no choice but to repeat itself at the crack and no power on earth could lift the arm that held the needle" (220). The moral inevitability of the agon between Joe and Violet is thwarted, as this bluesman and blueswoman do an improvisation of their own, eluding the outcome that the novel's voice was prepared for: "I was so sure, and they danced and walked all over me. Busy, they were, busy being original, complicated, changeable—human, I guess you'd say, while I was the predictable one, confused in my solitude into arrogance, thinking my space, my view was the only one that was or that mattered" (220).

What is this solitude and arrogance, this space and view, if not the solitary space and arrogant view of omniscience? Morrison is interrogating what cannot be known of another—whether a character in a novel or the troubled couple across the street—just as Christa Wolf is interrogating what cannot be known of oneself. "I got so aroused while meddling, while finger-shaping, I overreached and missed the obvious. I was watching the streets, thrilled by the buildings pressing and pressed by stone; so glad to be looking out and in on things I dismissed what went on in heart-pockets closed to me" (Morrison, 220–21).

There is no novel without omniscience, yet every omniscience is limited; therefore there is no omniscience. Our readerly obsession with authorial judgments, psychological and moral, ideological and political, easily misses this paradox inherent in novel writing. For to create a character is also to create the heart-pockets closed to writer and reader alike. Morrison is not simply playing a narratological game here, though it would be easy to describe it as such by claiming that she has her narrator marvel at the mystery of the characters in order to "motivate" or rationalize an ending in which those characters slip the yoke that the story's logic enticed the reader into expecting.

The mystery of character, however, belongs to novelistic truth rather than narratological lie, and novelists frequently remark on their sense of a character's relative opacity and separateness from them. "My characters always begin by being an enigma to me," says Nadine Gordimer. "I know something about them. And then as the novel, the story, develops I learn more. I don't know how. I don't have a preconceived idea of everything that they are."[11] Her novels frequently internalize this always incomplete probing by presenting the main character obliquely—Rosa in *Burger's Daughter*, Hillela in *A Sport of Nature*, Duncan in *The House Gun*—as a puzzle the other characters struggle to comprehend.[12] Characters also recoil on their authors in the wake of writing; when Elias Canetti finished *Auto-da-Fé*, he fell into confused remorse and guilt for inventing the death by fire that was his protagonist Kien's fate.[13] The limits or gaps in omniscience are in fact part of the very shape of the making of characters; the precise nature of the limit acquires significance within a novel's larger patterns and purposes. Remarking on the "sudden illumination" that marks "the metamorphoses of Tolstoy's characters," Kundera writes, "Pierre Bezukhov is transformed from an atheist into a believer with astonishing ease. All it takes is for him to be shaken up by the break with his wife and to encounter at a post house a traveling Freemason who talks to him. That ease is not due to lightweight capriciousness. Rather, it shows us that visible change was prepared by a hidden, unconscious process, which suddenly bursts into broad daylight."[14]

In *Jazz*, the dimension of Joe and Violet that the story's moral design could not bring to light is designated "something rogue." Their survival together entails "something rogue. Something else you have to figure in before you can figure it out" (228). The narrative crisis dramatized in the final chapter touches on the cultural and historical project Morrison poses for herself in writing *Jazz*. The novel's larger project is to create a vision of the African American lifeworld of Harlem in the 1920s. The architecture and rhythm of city life, the historical awareness of black migrants, war veterans, and riot victims, and the constant presence of jazz in the culture of everyday life are the rich and rugged components of this represented lifeworld.

In Joe and Violet's story of love and violence, craziness and survival, Morrison sets out to render a blues story novelistically. There is a rift, however, between novelistic design and the blues aesthetic. "It never occurred to me that they were . . . putting their lives together in ways I never dreamed of" (221); their survival is an improvised dance: "they danced and walked all over me" (220). The voice Morrison stylizes in *Jazz* — the neighbor busying herself with other people's pain and the writer in search of a historical lifeworld that beckons just beyond the reach of her own experience — this voice posits her own understanding of the blues and sees it exceeded by what's unseen: "I started out believing that life was made just so the world would have some way to think about itself, but that it had gone awry with humans because flesh, pinioned by misery, hangs on to it with pleasure. . . . I don't believe that anymore. Something is missing there. Something rogue. Something else you have to figure in before you can figure it out" (227–28).

6.

Two originators of novel theory, the early Lukács and Bakhtin, do not presuppose an imaginary space of narration. They look at narration from the standpoint of writing. Rather than treating the novel as a type of narrative among others (myth, folktale, film, and so on), as narrative theory and narratology do, the novel theorists consider the novel a specific, though diverse and polyglot, cultural form and social practice. Its aesthetic is incommensurable with that of other narrative arts.

Lukács approaches the act of novelistic writing in his densely dialectic account of irony in *The Theory of the Novel.* I will quote the central passage and then gloss it:

> Irony in the novel signifies an interior diversion of the normatively creative subject into a subjectivity as interiority, which opposes power complexes that are alien to it and which strives to imprint the contents of its longing upon the alien world, and a subjectivity which sees through the abstract, and therefore, limited nature of the mutually alien worlds of subject and object, understands these worlds by seeing their limitations as necessary conditions of their existence and, by thus seeing through them, allows the duality of the world to subsist. At the same time the creative subjectivity glimpses a unified world in the mutual relativity of elements essentially alien to one another, and gives form to this world.[15]

To paraphrase: novelistic irony is attained as the writing subject splits in two, becoming (1) the protagonist's inner striving and desire, whose efforts are represented in story coming up against the limits of the social world, political forces beyond his control, the will of others, and so on; and (2) the novel's voice, which, unlike the protagonist, (a) sees through the abstractness of the conflict between the latter's inner world and the outer world; (b) understands that the outer world is necessarily meaningless because without any animating orientation and that the subject's inner animation is necessarily blind to the way of the world; and therefore (c) negates neither inner nor outer reality in favor of the other. At the same time, the creative subject who has thus split in two in making the novel (d) glimpses and (e) gives form to this unified world of mutually antagonistic subjective and objective forces.

According to Lukács, the subject who achieves this form-giving glimpse recognizes "the antagonistic nature of the inner and outer worlds . . . as necessary." Who, then, is this subject? Certainly not a presiding consciousness, since it does not contemplatively possess these necessarily antagonistic, mutually relative worlds. And not an implied author, whether conceived as an omniscient judge of inner and outer realities or as an effect of textuality. Lukács insists, on the contrary, that this subject "is just as empirical — just as much part of the outside world, confined in its own interiority — as the characters which have become its object" (75). This subject is the writer.

Bakhtin likewise insists on the empirical existence and worldly practice of the writer. The essential reference point of novel theory for Bakhtin is the process of composition; he conceives of the novel as discourse, an act of communication ventured in, and venturing to alter, concrete public spheres. The composition or construction of a novel takes as its raw material a variety of discourses active in society at large and revoices them. In the terms he developed in the essay "The Problem of Speech Genres," these preexisting social discourses are "primary genres" — for example, "the rejoinder in dialogue, everyday stories, letters, diaries, minutes, and so forth" — which "secondary, complex genres," like novels, "play out."[16] The novel engages the sociality of communication on, as it were, two fronts: on the one hand, it incorporates into its very construction discourses originating in several social contexts, public and private; and on the other hand, it addresses itself to, and intervenes in, an actual public realm.

As part of his account of the voicing a novel acquires in this layering of discourse, Bakhtin gives a more ample and variegated account of narrational structures than any other twentieth-century critic. He details a wealth of literary "conventions and semi-conventions" through which novelists create "images of substitute authors, editors, and various kinds of narrators" (98). He does not, however, then conceptualize the novel as those Chinese boxes by which narrative theory encases story and character inside the box of narrator-narratee and then encases that box within the implied author-implied reader box, leaving the writer and the reader mysteriously outside the narrative boxes altogether. On the contrary, Bakhtin insists that "the most complex and ultracomposite work of a secondary genre" — like a novel — "as a whole (viewed as a whole) is a single integrated real utterance that has a real author and real addressees whom this author perceives and imagines" (98–99).

Bakhtin does not attribute to the real author anything like sovereignty over the discourse he or she produces. Like Lukács, though with a significantly different analysis of the novel form, Bakhtin locates the writer's subjectivity in the social practice of writing. On the one hand, the author is "the creator of the work itself, although he is located outside the chronotopes represented in his work, he is as it were tangential to them. We meet him (that is, we sense his activity) most of all in the composition of the work";[17] and on the other hand, the author is present in the "accentuations," "accents," "refracted" intentions, with which he or she inflects the contentious dialogical play of the social discourses within the work.

While Bakhtin locates the writer's empirical existence in the composition and communicative action of the novel within what Hannah Arendt calls the worldly space of the public realm,[18] Lukács locates it in the practice of novelistic irony. As creator, the writer puts his or her own subjectivity in play by projecting it into the interiority of the character enmeshed in the social world represented in the novel. As observer, the writer attains the irony by which he or she "sees through," "understands," "recognizes," "glimpses," and "gives form" to the relation of protagonist and society, inner and outer reality. As creator, the writer draws on his or her own inner reality, fully as finite and enmeshed in outer reality as the character's; as observer, the writer's understandings are as worldly and fragile as any act of understanding. In Lukács's words: "In the novel the subject, as observer and creator, is compelled by irony to apply its recognition of the world to itself and to treat itself, like its own creatures, as a free object of free irony."[19]

Neither Lukács nor Bakhtin brackets or boxes out the real author in accounting for the form of the novel. Therein lies another crucial difference between novel theory and narrative theory; novel theory is as preoccupied with form as narrative theory is, but it has a nonformalist conception of form. Narrative theory's formalism, in eschewing the real author, the empirical subject who writes, installs a semblance of authorial consciousness far more sovereign and unified than anything Lukács or Bakhtin could fathom. Narrator-narratee and implied author–implied reader preside over homogeneous worlds of representation and meaning, neatly removed from the antagonistic unity that the Lukácsian subject glimpses between inner and outer worlds and from the public world in which the Bakhtinian author inflects contentious discourses with particular values, judgments, and perspectives.

Glimpse and inflection — these terms suggestively affirm that the ultimate manifestation of the writer's presence in the novel, whether conceived as the attainment of irony or as the communication of intention, is partial, finite, even precarious, because it dwells in the empirical world of experience and communication. The more fully the writer's subjectivity and the actual act of novelistic writing are accounted for, the less writing and reading are idealized. Criticism needs to reaffirm this worldly space of the novel rather than the imaginary space of narrative.

7.

Where, then, did the regulative, homogeneous conception of narrative voice come from? What are the sources of our critical and readerly habit of bracketing out the writer and boxing in narrators and implied authors? Like most critical concepts and terms, the current vocabulary of narrative voice is a response to specific innovations and conventions in the history of fiction itself. The languages of criticism are prepared by the language of literature.

Edgar Allan Poe's innovations in narrative form crucially consolidated the conventions that fix the narrator in an imaginary space. His first-person narrators typically address their story to a hypothetical listener, in the sense that there is no interlocutor on the same plane of reality or representation as the narrator himself. It is this void marking the absence or sheer hypothesis of a listener that narrative theory fills, rather pointlessly in my view, with the theoretical postulate of a "narratee." That Poe's innovations took place in short stories rather than novels suggests how far-reaching those innovations were, how much control over the composition of prose was required to effect a structured distinction between narrator and (implied) author and uphold it through an entire narrative.

In "The Black Cat," the narrator himself occupies a concrete space and time: he is in his jail cell on the eve of his execution. And there is the fiction that he is writing — "the most wild yet most homely narrative which I am about to pen"[20] — but as with Poe's other first-person narrators, there is no one to receive this narrative on the same plane of reality as the narrator.

The creation of a voice that sustains a consistent distinction between narrator and author is far more than a matter of distinct identities. Innumerable earlier narrative styles would avoid confusing the author with a narrator on the verge of death. Poe's achievement lies in organizing every element of the story into a pattern that makes the author/narrator distinction central to the story's total aesthetic, moral, and thematic effect. Just as he advocates in his essay "The Poetic Principle" an aesthetic whose unity of effect and affect is impossible to achieve in a long poem, his prose aesthetic found its appropriate boundaries in the short story form rather than the novel. But the stylistic innovations and conventions he established through that form profoundly influenced the novel and novel criticism.

The organizing principle that structures voice in "The Black Cat" lies in the logic governing the sequence of events, the "chain of facts" in the narrator's words, through which the story unfolds. "I am above the weakness of seeking to establish a sequence of cause and effect, between the disaster and the atrocity," the narrator insists. "But I am detailing a chain of facts — and wish not to leave even a possible link imperfect" (225). The narrator is the protagonist of an uncanny story, a "most wild yet most homely narrative," but he repudiates superstition, like the belief that black cats are "witches in disguise," to explain the happenings in his story, and he affirms that he is not mad. Yet he knows it will take "some intellect more calm, more logical, and far less excitable than my own" to see "nothing more than an ordinary succession of very natural causes and effects" in the details that fill the narrator himself with "horror" and "awe" (223). This allusion to another understanding signals the two tiers of perspective essential to the work's ultimate effect.

The "chain of facts" — this "series of mere household events" whose "consequences" have "terrified," "tortured," and "destroyed" the narrator (223) — acquires its uncanniness as the mere events begin to repeat or allude to one another. The narrator, recounting how the "disease" of alcohol altered his personality, tells of the cruelties he increasingly directed at his wife and their several pets. In the first sequence of events, one night he turns on his favorite pet, the black cat, and "deliberately cuts one of its eyes from its socket" (224); some while later, in a second fit, he kills the cat by hanging it from a tree in the yard; soon thereafter, the house is destroyed by fire, and when the narrator joins the neighbors gathered around the ruins the next morning he discovers they are staring in amazement at "the figure of a gigantic cat," noose around its neck, embedded in the house's one remaining wall (225). This uncanny return of the cat, the sign of his crime, sets in motion the struggle of reason with conscience, science with fancy:

> When I first beheld this apparition — for I could scarcely regard it as less — my wonder and my terror were extreme. But at length reflection came to my aid. The cat, I remembered, had been hung in a garden adjacent to the house. Upon the alarm of fire, this garden had been immediately filled by the crowd — by some one of whom the animal must have been cut from the tree and thrown, through an open window, into my chamber. This had probably been done with the view of arousing me from sleep. The falling of other

walls had compressed the victim of my cruelty into the substance of the freshly-spread plaster; the lime of which, with the flames, and the ammonia from the carcass, had accomplished the portraiture as I saw it.

Although I thus readily accounted to my reason, if not altogether to my conscience, for the startling fact just detailed, it did not the less fail to make a deep impression upon my fancy. (225–26)

The narrator's experience of dread begins with the second sequence of events. Wanting to replace the pet he's killed, he purchases another black cat one night at a tavern, a cat as large as the first and resembling him except for an "indefinite splotch of white" on its breast. Next morning, however, the narrator discovers that this cat, "like Pluto, . . . also had been deprived of one of its eyes." His dread intensifies to torment when his wife points out that the cat's white markings are the image "of the GALLOWS! — oh, mournful and terrible engine of Horror and of Crime — of Agony and of Death!" (227). Faced with these signs of his previous crimes, the narrator acquires a "hatred of all things and of all mankind," more and more directing his fury at his wife. One day as they are going down to the cellar, the cat follows them and nearly trips him; "forgetting in my wrath the childish dread which had hitherto stayed my hand," he picks up an axe and aims at the cat. "But this blow was arrested by the hand of my wife. Goaded by the interference into a rage more than demoniacal, I withdrew my arm from her grasp and buried the axe in her brain. She fell dead upon the spot without a groan" (228). He decides to pull out the bricks from a cellar wall that "had lately been plastered," place the corpse within, and repair the wall. When the police come to investigate the wife's absence a few days later, they search the entire house, including the cellar; satisfied, they are about to leave when the narrator — "in the rabid desire to say something easily" — remarks on the construction of the house and raps on the wall where his wife is buried. A "voice from within the tomb" answers, "quickly swelling into one long, loud, and continuous scream, utterly anomalous and inhuman." The police tear down the wall, revealing the corpse. "Upon its head, with red extended mouth and solitary eye of fire, sat the hideous beast whose craft had seduced me into murder, and whose informing voice had consigned me to the hangman. I had walled the monster up within the tomb" (230).

So ends the narration, the sign of the narrator's crime once again returning to him, the howling of the walled-in cat repeating, down to the details of plaster and fire, the hanged cat's return in the wall of the ruined house. The two sequences are a series of mere facts:

(I)

(1) cuts out cat's eye (2) hangs cat (3) cat embedded in the wall.

(II)

(4) one-eyed cat (5) gallows markings (6) kills wife (7) cat howls in wall.

Through the workings of sheer chance and happenstance, these events fall into a pattern in which each crime returns in a sign of the crime; moreover, the second sequence of events reiterates the first:

(I)

(1) cuts out cat's eye crime.

(2) hangs cat crime.

(3) cat embedded in wall sign of crime (2).

(II)

(4) one-eyed cat sign of crime (1).

(5) gallows markings sign of crime (2).

(6) kills wife crime.

(7) cat howls in wall sign of crime (3) (6).

The sense of fatality so important in Poe culminates in the fact that the narrator's imminent encounter with the hangman gathers up the imagery of noose and gallows into a kind of final manifestation of the symbolic in the real:

(III)

(8) He is to hang 2, 3, 5, 6.

As in the E. T. A. Hoffmann tale Freud analyzes,[21] Poe here produces the uncanny by projecting a set of symbolic equivalences and doublings onto the plane of the character's reality. The symbolic happens as the real, not in the mode of a symbolically rich universe realizing itself in events as is the case with myth, fairy tale, or providential history, but in the disenchanted world of "natural causes and effects," the "chain of facts," "a series of mere household events." The uncanny requires the "homely narrative" as its base.

The structured distinction between narrator and (implied) author, I want to suggest, is not primarily a matter of identity or personality. In this story it lies, rather, in the distinction between two attitudes toward the uncanny play of the symbolic and the real. For the narrator, the uncanny is an experience of dread, the moral dread of the criminal whose psychology is Poe's principal theme and fascination. The narrator's reason struggles almost helplessly against the feeling of a supernatural force which even at the last moment prevents him from recognizing his own agency in his crime: "the hideous beast whose craft had seduced me into murder" (230).

What then is the second, differentiated attitude, the one we now so commonly attribute to the implied author? My quarrel with the narrator/implied author formula is that it reduces the author's activity to contemplation. Accordingly, "The Black Cat" would be construed as a story recounted by a narrator contemplated by an implied author. But to get at what's going on, let's restate this from the standpoint of writing rather than contemplation: the author writes the narrator telling a story. What needs to be described is this process of writing the narrator telling. Poe projects the symbolic plane of doublings, signs, repetitions, and equivalences onto the plane of the narrator's reality. The two structurally distinct attitudes are the result. For counterposed to the dread evoked for the narrator by the interpenetration of the symbolic and the real is the aesthetic mastery of the writing itself, a mastery in which the prevalence of the symbolic over the real occurs without recourse to superstition, magic, or providence, without, that is, challenging "natural causes and effects." The unity of effect which is the aim of Poe's aesthetic takes the form in "The Black Cat" of the simultaneity and differentiation of moral dread and aesthetic mastery. More precisely, the dread is evoked and mastered within the aesthetic attitude, that frisson of fascination with horror that replicates in reverse the narrator's own transfixed horror at his fate. Poe's act of writing-the-narrator telling is the stylization that creates this effect, transforming horror into fascination, dread into aesthetic contemplation. It is this contemplative attitude that narrative criticism has codified into the normative stance of the implied author and implied reader.

8.

Poe's achievement is immense, and if my hypothesis is correct that it established the conventions of the imaginary space of narration and the structured distinction of narrator and (implied) author, it has had a profound effect on reading habits and criticism. When Bakhtin surveys the long history of the novel, taking stock of its stylistic variability, he assesses the role of "posited authors," storytellers, and first-person narrators in light of an aesthetic very different from Poe's. "The speech of such narrators is always another's speech (as regards the real or potential direct discourse of the author) and in another's language (i.e., insofar as it is a particular variant of the literary language that clashes with the language of the narrator). . . . All forms involving a narrator or a posited author signify to one degree or another by their presence the author's freedom from a unitary and singular language, a freedom connected with the relativity of literary and language systems; such forms open up the possibility of never having to define oneself in language, the possibility of translating one's own intentions from one linguistic system to another."[22]

Bakhtin thus sees in the flexibility and relativity of "double-voiced" narrations the writer's leeway to experiment with his or her commitment to the norms and meanings of a particular discourse. Keying on the resources that such "a refracting of authorial intentions" affords the comic novel in particular, he stresses the "variety of different distances between distinct aspects of the narrator's language and the author's language" (315). Poe's innovative stylization turns the relativity of double voice to a more regulated, unified purpose. He renders it "monological" in Bakhtin's terms or "parsimoniously plural" to borrow Roland Barthes's term in *S/Z*. The underlying discourses of confession, gothic tale, psychology, and criminology are blended into the two-tiered attitude that fixes the author's relation to the narrator as contemplative aesthetic mastery. In demanding unity of effect and affect, Poe's aesthetic represents an innovation in prose fiction and at the same time a narrowing of its vocal variability or plurality.

Benjamin counts Poe among his valued storytellers. This seems wrong to me on Benjamin's own terms. The storyteller's "gift is the ability to relate his life; his distinction, to be able to tell his entire life. The storyteller: he is the man who could let the wick of his life be consumed completely by the gentle flame of his story."[23] Poe? Benjamin is, I think, lured into feeding his nostalgia for storytelling with Poe's stories because their first-person narrators and their brevity seem to fit his notion of the immediacy between teller and listeners. The novel is the death of storytelling in Benjamin's view because it separates tellers and listeners from one another through the mediation of print: "The storyteller takes what he tells from experience — his own or that reported by others. And he in turn makes it the experience of those who are listening to his tale. The novelist has isolated himself. The birthplace of the novel is the solitary individual, who is no longer able to express himself by giving examples of his most important concerns, is himself uncounseled, and cannot counsel others" (87). But the mediation of print affects the inner form of Poe's stories as much as the novels Benjamin has in mind. Moreover, the stylization through which Poe writes the storyteller precisely isolates the storyteller in an experience that is not communicated and shared so much as simulated and mastered in the aesthetic contemplation of reading. This stylization henceforth became available to modern novelists as a technique of aesthetic distance.

As a matter of literary history, Poe is part of the development of the novel, not the preservation of storytelling, at least not in Benjamin's sense. But this touches on the deeper problem in Benjamin's historical claims. Bakhtin is truer to the history of the novel in seeing it as a continual appropriation of other social discourses, including the whole array of storytelling modes. The mediations of print and novelistic writing do not kill storytelling but appropriate and transform it in keeping with the exigencies of the modern forms and institutions of publicness. The nature of such novelistic appropriations and transformations is not uniform. Benjamin's theoretical error is in supplying a single interpretation of the difference between storytelling and novel, setting a categorical divide between them.

His historical error is in supposing that the rise of the novel extinguishes storytelling from modern culture and social life. The ongoing development of the novel belies the declaration of the death of storytelling, just as it belies the many declarations of the death of the novel itself. The novel form continues to replenish itself and transform its own modes of cultural commentary by drawing on living — or disappearing — practices of storytelling in the construction of novelistic narratives. The sheer diversity of the appropriations suggests the complexity of the contemporary novel's interaction with oral culture and the lifeworlds within which it flourishes. Maxine Hong Kingston draws on the "talk-stories" of immigrant Chinese life in America in constructing the innovative narration of *The Woman Warrior*. John Edgar Wideman's Homewood trilogy elaborates its narratives and voicings out of the vernacular discourse of the black ghetto he writes about. Several strands of magical realism reinscribe the storytelling styles and norms of preliterate cultures in order to represent a profoundly modern experience of historical memory and change. The Indonesian novelist Pramoedya Ananta Toer "drafted" *The Buru Quartet* while a political prisoner by entertaining his fellow inmates with stories and then writing these tales down to make a complex historical bildungsroman spanning several decades of Indonesian history; the very composition of his novel joins the storytelling context of prison life and the publicness of print culture, in defiance of the deformation of the public sphere by political repression and censorship.[24]

9.

Benjamin pegs Flaubert's *The Sentimental Education* as the supreme example
of the novel in its utter negation of storytelling, citing and commenting on
the closing passage in which Frederic and Deslauriers, middle-aged and
shorn of all their aspirations and dreams, recall the boyhood episode in
which they sneaked into the local bordello, presented the patronne with
flowers, and then immediately fled: " 'That may have been,' said Frederic
when they had finished, 'the finest thing in our lives.' 'Yes, you may be
right,' said Deslauriers, 'that was perhaps the finest thing in our lives.' "[25]
With such an insight, the novel reaches an end which is more proper to it, in
a stricter sense, than to any story. Actually there is no story for which the
question as to how it continued would not be legitimate. The novelist, on
the other hand, cannot hope to take the smallest step beyond that limit at
which he invites the reader to a divinatory revelation of the meaning of life
by writing "Finis."[26]

Benjamin pits the novelist's "meaning of life" against the storyteller's
"moral of the story"; the latter's wisdom stands off against the former's
perplexity: the novel's "quest for 'the meaning of life' is no more than the
initial expression of perplexity with which its reader sees himself living this
written life." In Flaubert, "the meaning which the bourgeois age found in
its behavior at the beginning of its decline has settled like sediment in the
cup of life" (99). But Flaubert's "Finis" is even more pointedly ironic, more
novelistic, than Benjamin claims. The finest moment that Frederic and
Deslauriers here recall takes place three years before the beginning of the
novel! It is outside the quest to which Flaubert gives form.

The irony is directed at Frederic insofar as he cannot in the end grasp any
value in his life except outside the "adventure of interiority" (Lukács) in
which his longings and actions have taken place. At the same time, however,
the irony turns back on the writer's own ironic subjectivity, rendering him
"as observer and creator . . . a free object of free irony," for the very form he
has given the quest threatens to collapse from its inability to bestow a
meaning. Flaubertian irony lies in this vibration between Frederic's empty
gesture of endowing his life with meaning and the writer's inability to extract a meaning from his own full rendering of that life. In reducing this
permanent oscillation and uncertainty to some generalized life perplexity
endemic to the novel as a bourgeois form, Benjamin misses the deeper
validity of the novel as a form of social and cultural criticism, in Flaubert's
case a criticism of the bourgeois lifeworld itself.

Benjamin misses the critical force of the novel because he takes its commodity form in the marketplace and its exfoliation of modern individuality as mere symptoms of capitalism. According to his history of forms, the novel is wedged between storytelling and the cinema, his nostalgia for storytelling counterbalanced by his utopian expectations for film. The ongoing interaction of storytelling, novel, and mechanical reproduction has proved more complex, more nonsynchronous, than predicted by Benjamin, who matched these different forms of cultural production to precapitalist, capitalist, and postcapitalist lifeworlds respectively. Leaving aside that the survival of capitalism incorporated the film form as a major component of consumer culture (a historical development long recognized as qualifying the hopes Benjamin so boldly expressed in "The Work of Art in the Age of Mechanical Reproduction"), the novel form itself has drawn, in its spiraling fashion, more fully on the entire tradition of the novel than did its nineteenth-century antecedents and has by the same token undergone unprecedented transformations in response to the mass media.

10.

To illustrate my point, I want to take up an unlikely example to counter Benjamin's sense of the novel form, namely, Norman Mailer's *The Executioner's Song*. This "true-crime" documentary novel explodes the categories by which Benjamin divides the novel from storytelling and from mechanical reproduction. In the process, it also achieves one of the most startling innovations in novelistic voice in contemporary literature.

The making of the book was no ordinary work of journalism. The journalist-entrepreneur Lawrence Schiller — whose most recent contribution to American culture was peddling exclusive photos of O.J. Simpson's arrival home after his acquittal — saw an opportunity for magazine articles and a film or book in the story of Gary Gilmore as soon as Gilmore began opposing any appeal or stay of his death sentence for two murders in Utah in 1976. He would become the first person executed in the United States since the Supreme Court lifted its long-standing ban on capital punishment. Schiller negotiated exclusive rights to the stories of virtually everyone involved in the case, from Gilmore and his girlfriend Nicole Barrett and their families and friends to the widows of the two victims. He set about taping scores of interviews and exercised considerable control over the media's access to personal testimonies, private letters, and interviews. He created the oral archive of the Gilmore case, and it wasn't until a month after

Gilmore's death that Schiller made the deal for Mailer to write the book. Mailer came to the project in the role of a hack.

Mailer's achievement as a writer in *The Executioner's Song* begins with his mastery of the sheer bulk of material, some 15,000 pages of interview transcripts, in addition to news stories, court records, and Gilmore's autopsy. From these raw materials, Mailer constructs a narrative that turns around two profoundly troubling enigmas: the mentality of a sociopath whose own suffering and sensitivity, especially in his love for Nicole, can never be squared with his capacity to kill two people without motive or passion or remorse; and the mentality of a society that gleefully regresses to the rationalized irrationality of capital punishment, an irrationality made all the more glaring by Gilmore's own insistence that he die.

The principles of construction at Mailer's disposal are thoroughly novelistic. He plots a multi-character story, moving apace through the nine months between Gilmore's release from an Illinois penitentiary and his execution in Utah, while braiding into that narrative the history of several of the characters. He holds the narrative together with the love story of Nicole and Gary, a story replete with menace, alcohol, sexual freedom and sexual dysfunction, tender letters, belief in reincarnation, and an abortive suicide pact.

What makes the novel, however, is its voice. Among Flaubert's indelible contributions to the novel form is free indirect style, with its unlimited flexibility in evoking the subjectivity, the interiority and inner speech, of a character within the objectifying trajectory of third-person narration. The whole of *The Executioner's Song* is written in free indirect style. The underlying discourse of the characters comes from the 15,000 pages of transcript. Section by section, sometimes paragraph by paragraph, the source of the story switches from one character to another. Mailer's prose is inflected with their perceptions and idioms. Written with lightning speed to meet the demands of a book market that might quickly tire of the Gilmore case, the novel's scope and texture are made possible by the interviews. The writing depends on storytelling and on the mechanical reproduction by which those stories were recorded. The everyday storytelling of the small-town, working-class people who knew Gilmore during his brief time in Utah is the mainspring of the narration. Mailer brings to his retranscriptions the flattening tone and deadpan concision that give the novel's voice its relative consistency across the multiple voices, in keeping with the norms of both journalism and Flaubertian free indirect style.

There is one storyteller who is indispensable to the narrative as a whole and whose voice resonates most centrally throughout, Nicole Barrett. Her life story, that of a free spirit in love with a succession of bad men, and the honesty with which she details the romance and hard facts of her relationship with Gary create a language that Norman Mailer couldn't possibly invent, though he can write it:

> Then she thought of the night up in the hills behind the nuthouse when she wondered if he was a magnet to evil spirits. Maybe he had to act that nasty to keep things off. The idea didn't cheer her. He could get meaner and meaner if that was the truth.
>
> Around midnight, Nicole was feeling awfully cooped up with Gary.
>
> She found herself thinking of Barrett. It kept working away in her. There had also been a letter from Kip that afternoon but she kept thinking about Barrett and Rosebeth.
>
> She hadn't even wanted to open Kip's letter, and when she did, he wrote that he wanted her to come back. The letter left her feeling crowded. It was like the past was coming back. Hampton, of all people, was going around with her sister April. Everybody, Nicole decided, was fucking with her head.
>
> All the while she was having these thoughts, Gary had been sitting at her feet. Now he had to pick this moment to look up with all the light of love shining in his eyes. "Baby," he said, "I really love you all the way and forever." She looked back. "Yeah," she said, "and so do seven other motherfuckers."
>
> Gary hit her. It was the first time, and he hit her hard. She didn't feel the pain so much as the shock and then the disappointment. It always ended the same way. They hit you when they felt like it.[27]

Who can deny this storyteller her experience and wisdom? Contrary to Benjamin's diagnosis, the novel has proved capable not only of maintaining its vitality in the age of mechanical reproduction but also of preserving the very possibility of communicating experience that he nostalgically associated with storytelling.

11.

Throughout this essay, I have mixed metaphors in my use of the terms "voice" and "writing." I have argued that novelistic narration should be approached as an act of writing, but I have also retained the ambiguous concept of voice. Though the language of criticism is necessarily metaphorical, not all metaphors are created equal when it comes to their use and analytic power. Let me conclude, then, with a reflection on these two terms.

"Writing" is on the face of it a literal rather than metaphorical term. And indeed I hold the view, which I associate with the work of Bakhtin and Raymond Williams, that "literature," broadly defined, is the social practice of writing and therefore inseparable from the social history of literacy.[28] Nevertheless, poststructuralism threw a wrench into every purely empirical sense of "writing," beginning with Jacques Derrida's huge claim in *Of Grammatology* that Western philosophy conceptualizes speech and writing as opposites and then freights the concept of writing with whatever features of language are deemed errant and recalcitrant to the reigning metaphysical idea of the nature of language. De Man's *Allegories of Reading* and Derrida's own work as a literary critic, especially in the essays on Plato, Mallarmé, and Philippe Sollers in *La dissémination*, revolutionized literary studies by showing that metaphors of writing are so integral to every practice of writing that it is impossible to say what writing is — as artistic activity, social practice, or vocation — without entering the metaphorical or figurative labyrinth of the written text.[29]

When Rushdie writes the story of his fictional Sufiya Zinobia from a news item; when Wolf writes her autobiography by turning the "I" inside-out into third-person novel and second-person diary and memoir; when Morrison writes the story of Joe and Violet up to a denouement she does not foresee or fully comprehend; when Mailer writes hundreds of tape-recorded interviews about actual events into a unified novel in free indirect style — the critic cannot say what "to write" means except by struggling to grasp writing at once as social practice and metaphor-laden textuality.

"Voice" is overtly metaphorical and has acquired connotations ranging from onto-theological presence to the linguistic technicalities of grammatical mood. Yet it has distinctive advantages over other widely used terms in novel criticism. Unlike "presiding consciousness," it does not presuppose what shape the subjectivity of writing and reading actually takes, or ought to take, in novels. Unlike "point of view" or "perspective," it does not import a visual metaphor into the account of a phenomenon of language. Narratology's recourse to the visual metaphor is somewhat surprising. Gérard Genette's goal in *Narrative Discourse* is to describe every aspect of the art of narration in rigorously linguistic and rhetorical terms, but when faced with novelistic prose's capacity to create a voice that can simultaneously convey, usually tacitly, someone else's attitude, responses, perceptions, vocabulary, or manner of speaking, he turns to a distinction between the narrative's "voice" and the one who sees or perceives.[30] This distinction gets worked up into a full-blown scheme in Mieke Bal's theory of "focalization," which she intends to clarify the "distinction between, on the one hand, the vision through which the events are presented and, on the other, the identity of the voice that is verbalizing that vision. To put it more simply: . . . between those who see and those who speak."[31] But is it really a clarification? In keeping with the boxes-within-boxes approach to narration, "focalization" theory uncritically recycles Cartesian *res mentis* and *res extensa* as though every layer — or box — of narration establishes a homogeneous relation between a perceiving subject and a world available to perception. Moreover, as I argued earlier, narrative theory thus grounds its critical categories in the created world of the novel (the world of the "story" in narratological terms) at the expense of the world of the "discourse." Novel theory, by contrast, starts from this latter world, the actual worldliness of the novelist's creative subjectivity and practice and of the novel's cultural origins and uses.

It is significant that narrative theory's commitment to linguistic and rhetorical rigor breaks down right where the problem of pinpointing the subject of novelistic narration encounters a multiplication of subjects (writer or implied author? implied author or narrator? narrator or character? voice or "focalizor"?). The palpable but indistinct intersubjectivity so essential to the stylistic complexity of novels haunts narrative theory. It cannot penetrate the shadowy world of narrators and characters because it eschews from the outset the concrete subject of novelistic writing, that is, the writer in all his or her overdetermined empirical-social-linguistic existence.

Narrative theory draws on structuralist linguistics to outline the relation of the subject of the *énonciation* (speech event) to the *énoncé* (narrated event) but misses the most pertinent implications of the idea that the subject of the énonciation is referred to by means of the so-called shifters, principally, the pronoun "I." In Emile Benveniste's formulation, "I" is a signifier in the énoncé that refers to the subject of the énonciation; it is completely devoid of semantic content, since it refers to this speaker only because it refers to whoever is speaking. The linguistic marker of identity is anonymous. What follows from this? Structuralist narrative theory and narratology conclude that the subject is therefore but an effect of discourse or the outer limit of the narrative boxes and therefore moot. I think that Benveniste implies, rather, that the subject of the énonciation is at once the referent of an empty signifier and the concrete subject who produces the discourse. Therefore we only glimpse this subject's presence fleetingly in the movement of his or her énonciation as a whole.

Here Bakhtin's insistence that "the real unit of speech communication" is the "utterance" takes on its full import for literary studies.[32] An utterance — or "speech event" (énonciation) in structuralist terminology — is de-marcated in the moment it tacitly calls for a response; its length can vary "from the single-word rejoinder to a large novel" (81–82). It is in that sense that the subjectivity of the writer can only be glimpsed in the reader's responsiveness to the movement of the utterance as a whole. The aesthetics of the novel turn on this worldly relation between concrete subjects. The critical categories of novel theory and narrative theory traverse "discourse" and "story" in opposite directions. In the analysis of first-person narratives, it is the difference between "a story recounted by a narrator contemplated by an implied author" and "the author writing the narrator telling a story." The worldliness of writers and readers, which remains the bracketed-out limit of narrative theory, is the starting point of novel theory. "Of course," writes Bakhtin, "these real people, the authors and the listeners or readers, may be . . . located in differing time-spaces, sometimes separated from each other by centuries and by great spatial distances, but nevertheless they are all located in a real, unitary and as yet incomplete historical world set off by a sharp and categorical boundary from the represented world in the text."[33]

At stake is how criticism understands literary creativity. I follow Bakh-tin's assertion that the "real, unitary and as yet incomplete historical world" is "the world that creates the text, for all its aspects — the reality reflected in the text, the authors creating the text, the performers of the text (if they exist) and finally the listeners or readers who re-create and in so doing renew the text — participate equally in the creation of the represented world of the text. Out of the actual chronotopes of our world (which serve as the source of representation) emerge the reflected and created chronotopes of the world represented in the work (in the text)" (253). Because he does not separate language from its worldliness, Bakhtin does not put the reality that creates the text or the reality to which it refers outside language. Reality is not extratextual. As I argue in "On Innovation," the realist imperative continues to animate the contemporary novel's formal and stylistic inno-vations.[34] Unlike narrative theory, which often seeks to reconnect formal structures and social categories after having strictly separated them, novel theory is not constrained to smuggle social reality back into textual analysis.

Moreover, because novel theory starts from the worldly intersubjectiv-ity of writing and reading, it eliminates the need for dubious categories like "vision" or "focalization" to fit intersubjectivity into novelistic prose, whether the shadowy intersubjectivity of free indirect third-person narra-tion or the relatively delimited intersubjectivity of unreliable first-person narrations. For Bakhtin, language is in essence intersubjective, lying "on the borderline between oneself and the other. The word in language is half someone else's. It becomes one's own only when the speaker populates it with his own intention, his own accent, when he appropriates the word, adapting it to his own semantic and expressive intention."[35] The novelist's stylistic achievement of "double voicing," however masterful, derives from the existential condition of every speaking being: no one ever truly originates or masters speech.

In such a conception, novel theory deploys the metaphorical concept of "voice" without falling prey to the metaphysics of presence that deconstruction decries or to the simulated Cartesianism of narratology's narrators and narratees, speakers and "focalizors." At the same time, it does not repudiate the common use of the metaphor, as when we say that an author has created a "distinctive voice" or that a work of prose "has a voice." Such statements may seem naively intuitive, but they in fact point the way to questions that criticism has still barely explored. For example, how does a writer's stylistic realization of a "voice" shape the interplay of identity and anonymity intrinsic to language? And how does our aesthetic response to novelistic "voice" relate to the everyday experience of recognizing someone's voice, even to the experiences of infancy that lead Jacques Lacan to say that the voice is a primordial libidinal object?[36] "We always arrive, in the final analysis," Bakhtin was not afraid to say, "at the human voice, which is to say we come up against the human being."[37]

Notes

1. Fredric Jameson, *Marxism and Form: Twentieth-Century Dialectical Theories of Literature* (Princeton: Princeton University Press, 1971), and *The Political Unconscious: Narrative as Socially Symbolic Act* (Ithaca: Cornell University Press, 1981); Franco Moretti, *The Way of the World: The "Bildungsroman" in European Culture* (New York: Verso, 1987); Nancy Armstrong, *Desire and Domestic Fiction: A Political History of the Novel* (New York: Oxford University Press, 1987); Wayne C. Booth, *The Rhetoric of Fiction* (Chicago: University of Chicago Press, 1961); Roland Barthes, *S/Z*, trans. Richard Miller (New York: Farrar, Straus and Giroux, 1974).

2. Moretti, *The Way of the World*, 5.

3. Georg Lukács, *The Theory of the Novel*, trans. Anna Bostock (Cambridge: MIT Press, 1971), 72–73.

4. *Communications* 8 (Paris: Editions du Seuil, 1966); *Communications* 11 (Paris: Editions du Seuil, 1968).

5. Lukács, *Theory of the Novel*, 152.

6. See Paul de Man, *Blindness and Insight: Essays in the Rhetoric of Contemporary Criticism*, 2nd ed. (Minneapolis: University of Minnesota Press, 1983).

7. Salman Rushdie, *Shame* (New York: Alfred A. Knopf, 1983), 23–24.

8. Milan Kundera, *Testaments Betrayed: An Essay in Nine Parts*, trans. Linda Asher (New York: HarperCollins, 1995), 74. Also see Kundera, *The Art of the Novel*, trans. Linda Asher (New York: Harper and Row, 1988).

9. Christa Wolf, *Patterns of Childhood*, trans. Ursule Molinaro and Hedwig Rappolt (New York: Farrar, Straus and Giroux, 1980), 248.

10. Toni Morrison, *Jazz* (New York: Alfred A. Knopf, 1992), 219; hereafter cited in the text.

11. Nadine Gordimer, "Family Plots," interview with John Brenkman, *Artforum International: Bookforum*, spring 1998, 21.

12. Nadine Gordimer, *Burger's Daughter* (New York: Penguin, 1980), *The House Gun* (New York: Farrar, Straus and Giroux, 1997), and *A Sport of Nature* (New York: Penguin, 1988).

13. Elias Canetti, *Auto-da-Fé*, trans. C. V. Wedgwood (New York: Continuum, 1981); also see Canetti, "The First Book: Auto-da-Fé," in *The Conscience of Words*, trans. Joachim Neugroschel (New York: Farrar, Straus and Giroux, 1984), 203–13.

14. Kundera, *Testaments Betrayed*, 215.

15. Lukács, *Theory of the Novel*, 74–75.

16. M. M. Bakhtin, "The Problem of Speech Genres," in *Speech Genres and Other Late Essays*, ed. Caryl Emerson and Michael Holquist, trans. Vern W. McGee (Austin: University of Texas Press, 1986), 98.

17. M. M. Bakhtin, *The Dialogic Imagination: Four Essays*, ed. Caryl Emerson and Michael Holquist, trans. Michael Holquist (Austin: University of Texas Press, 1981), 254.

18. See Hannah Arendt, *Between Past and Future: Eight Exercises in Political Thought* (New York: Penguin, 1977), and *The Human Condition* (Chicago: University of Chicago Press, 1958).

19. Lukács, *Theory of the Novel*, 75.

20. Edgar Allan Poe, "The Black Cat," in *The Complete Tales and Poems of Edgar Allan Poe*, ed. Hervey Allen (New York: Modern Library, 1938), 223.

21. See Sigmund Freud, "The Uncanny," in *The Standard Edition of the Complete Psychological Works of Sigmund Freud*, ed. and trans. James Strachey, vol. 17 (London: Hogarth Press, 1955), 219–56.

22. Bakhtin, *The Dialogic Imagination*, 313–15.

23. Walter Benjamin, *Illuminations*, ed. Hannah Arendt, trans. Harry Zohn (New York: Schocken, 1969), 108–9.

24. See Maxine Hong Kingston, *The Woman Warrior: Memoirs of a Girlhood among Ghosts* (New York: Alfred A. Knopf, 1976); John Edgar Wideman, *Damballah* (New York: Avon, 1981), *Hiding Place* (New York: Avon, 1981), and *Sent for You Yesterday* (New York: Avon, 1983) (the three volumes are reprinted in *The Homewood Books* [Pittsburgh: University of Pittsburgh Press, 1992]); Pramoedya Ananta Toer, *The Buru Quartet*, trans. Max Lane (New York: Penguin, 1990).

25. Gustave Flaubert, *Sentimental Education*, trans. Robert Baldick (New York: Penguin, 1964).

26. Benjamin, *Illuminations*, 100.

27. Norman Mailer, *The Executioner's Song* (New York: Warner Books, 1980), 158.

28. See Raymond Williams, *Writing in Society* (London: Verso, 1983).

29. Jacques Derrida, *La dissémination* (Paris: Editions du Seuil, 1972), and *Of Grammatology*, trans. Gayatri Chakravorty Spivak (Baltimore: Johns Hopkins University Press, 1976); Paul de Man, *Allegories of Reading: Figural Language in Rousseau, Nietzsche, Rilke, and Proust* (New Haven: Yale University Press, 1979).

30. See Gérard Genette, *Narrative Discourse: An Essay in Method*, trans. Jane E. Lewin (Ithaca: Cornell University Press, 1980).

31. Mieke Bal, *Narratology: Introduction to the Theory of Narrative*, trans. Christine van Boheemen (Toronto: University of Toronto Press, 1985), 100–101.

32. Bakhtin, *Speech Genres*, 71.

33. Bakhtin, *The Dialogic Imagination*, 253.

34. John Brenkman, "On Innovation," unpublished essay, 2001.

35. Bakhtin, *The Dialogic Imagination*, 293.

36. See Jacques Lacan, *Le séminaire, livre XI: Les quatre concepts fondamentaux de la psychanalyse*, ed. Jacques-Alain Miller (Paris: Editions du Seuil, 1973).

37. Bakhtin, *The Dialogic Imagination*, 252–53.

28

What Interactive Narratives Do That Print Narratives Cannot · J. YELLOWLEES DOUGLAS

I only wish I could write with both hands so as not to forget one thing while I am saying another. — Saint Teresa, *The Complete Works of St. Teresa of Jesus*

If written language is itself relentlessly linear and sequential,[1] how can hypertext be "nonsequential writing with reader-controlled links," as Ted Nelson, who both created the concept and coined the term, has argued?[2] How can we read or write nonsequentially, since language, by definition, is sequential? Many definitions of hypertext include this emphasis on nonsequentiality, as does the succinct definition put forward by George Landow and Paul Delany in their introduction to *Hypermedia and Literary Studies*: "Hypertext can be composed, and read, nonsequentially; it is a variable structure, composed of blocks of text . . . and the electronic links that join them."[3] But these definitions are slightly misleading, since both hypertext fiction and digital narratives enable readers to experience their contents in a variety of sequences — as Nelson himself acknowledges in *Literary Machines*.[4] As definitions go, those that emphasize nonsequentiality are also rather restrictive, since they tend to set hypertext and hypermedia off from print in a kind of binary opposition: if print is both linear and relentlessly sequential, it follows, then, that hypertext and hypermedia must be non-linear and nonsequential.

The dilemma in most short, succinct definitions of hypertext lies in the definition of the word *sequence*. As used in the foregoing definitions, *sequence* and *sequential* denote a singular, fixed, continuous, and authoritative order of reading and writing. But *sequence* can also mean "a following of one thing after another; succession; arrangement; a related or continuous series," according to the likes of the *American Heritage Dictionary*. In this context, it becomes significant that the Latin root of *sequence*, *sequi*, means simply "to follow." All interactive narratives have sequences — some of them more disorienting than others, granted — making the medium, if anything, poly-sequential. The process of reading interactive narratives themselves is, as hypertext theorist John Slatin has noted, discontinuous, nonlinear, and often associative — but hardly nonsequential. His interpretation of hypertext accommodates Nelson's definition of "nonsequential writing" by inferring that Nelson meant "writing in that the logical connections between elements are primarily associative rather than syllogistic, as [they are] in conventional text," which closely corresponds to Bush's vision of the original Memex as well as the way in which most readers experience hypertext fiction.[5]

Arriving at brief and succinct definitions of an entire medium in a single sentence or even a mere phrase, at any rate, is more reductive than illuminating, a little like describing a book as "pages containing text that follows a fixed, linear order." While that might work perfectly well in describing instructions on how to operate your VCR, it doesn't quite cut it when it comes to nailing down the works of William Burroughs, nor does it account for the chapters on whales in *Moby-Dick* or the likes of either *Hopscotch* or Barthes's *The Pleasure of the Text*. Moreover, it is not likely that anyone currently attempting to describe hypertext fiction, a medium that is only beginning to toddle through its infancy, is going to hit on an illuminating or time-resistant definition. Not only are the aesthetics and conventions of the medium evolving, but the technology itself is also still developing, as is its content, which currently borrows from genre and avant-garde print fiction, cinema, *Adventure* and arcade games, and graphic novels like *Maus*.

Further, [. . .] critics, blinded by the small number of early works, have mistaken the hallmarks of a single type or genre of hypertext fiction for the defining characteristics of all present and future works within the medium.[6] This accounts partly for Birkerts's and Miller's flat rejections of hypertext fiction's aesthetic possibilities — although both critiques were probably also influenced by flawed assumptions about digital narratives threatening to replace print stories and novels. But this tendency to conflate early work and the aesthetic possibilities of the medium also sheds light on the puzzling critiques of hypertext fiction from otherwise insightful theorists like Janet Murray, who equates "literary hypertext" with postmodern narratives that refuse to " 'privilege' any one order or reading or interpretive framework" and end up "privileging confusion itself."[7] If the earliest examples of hypertext fiction happen to represent the sophisticated play with chronology, completeness, and closure that draws many of its precedents from avant-garde print genres, it hardly follows that all hypertext fiction will resist privileging one reading of character or one set of choices for navigation through its network of potential narratives, or even that authors will plump for the conspicuously postmodern over, say, the hallmarks of the mystery, the hard-boiled detective story, or science fiction. Print fiction, after all, is hardly a monolithic entity: for every *Great Expectations* or *Persuasion* that Birkerts and Miller wish to defend from the onslaught of digital narratives, there are scores of Harlequin romances, John Grisham thrillers, and Danielle Steel paperbacks that readers consume in a matter of hours and scarcely recall a week later. Print fiction means an abundance of genres and categories—*The Crying of Lot 49* existing alongside *Princess Daisy*, *The Bridges of Madison County* outselling *Middlemarch*, just as cinema includes both *The Magnificent Ambersons* and *Dumb and Dumber*, for all it may pain critics to admit it. This much is certain: the examples we have before us are only a beginning, the early efforts of writers who grew up with the singularity, linearity, and fixity of print. Imagine someone supplying an accurate definition of the content and aesthetic possibilities of all television programs once and for all during the Milton Berle era, when television borrowed heavily from vaudeville and theater, and you will have the right idea. For the purposes of investigating how readers experience and interpret interactive narratives in the here and now, it is far better for us to define just what hypertext fiction and digital narratives are, and what they can do, by examining just what they do that print does not—or cannot—do.

Interactive Narratives Have No Singular, Definitive Beginnings and Endings

"Begin at the beginning," the King said gravely, "then proceed straight through to the end. Then stop."—Alice in Wonderland

Readers of print narratives generally begin reading where print begins on the first page of the book, story, or article and proceed straight through the text to the end. Although reading print narratives involves readers' thumbing back through the pages to clarify an impression or recall a name and a continual looking forward or predicting what will happen next, we nonetheless move more or less straightforwardly through *Pride and Prejudice* or *Huckleberry Finn*.[8] That is not to say that it is impossible to begin reading *The Great Gatsby* at the point where Daisy and Gatsby are reunited for the first time in Nick's living room. But the reader who begins reading a print narrative in medias res is placed in a situation somewhat analogous to a filmgoer who has arrived in the darkened cinema forty minutes into a feature. Placed in these circumstances, we struggle merely to establish who is who and understand just what is taking place—and we bring to the text none of the opinions, expectations, conclusions, or, for that matter, pleasures that would otherwise be available to us had we followed the narrative from its beginning. The reader's gradual progression from beginning to end follows a carefully scripted route that ensures "the reader does indeed get from the beginning to the end in the way the writer wants him or her to get there."[9]

While many digital narratives begin with a scene or sequence that establishes both the identity of the user as part of an intrigue or quest and the parameters for the plot, most hypertext narratives have no single beginning. In Stuart Moulthrop's *Victory Garden*, readers are confronted with, among a multitude of possible ways of entering the hypertext, three lists that seem to represent a sort of table of contents: "Places to Be," "Paths to Explore," and "Paths to Deplore." Unlike a table of contents, however, these lists do not represent a hierarchical map of the narrative, providing readers with a preview of the topics they will explore during their reading and the order in which they will experience them.[10] The first place or path in the list has no priority over any of the others—readers will not necessarily encounter it first in the course of their reading and need not encounter it at all. Each of the words or phrases instead acts as a contact point for readers entering the narrative. By choosing an intriguing word or particularly interesting phrase, even constructing a sentence out of a set of choices that Moulthrop supplies, readers find themselves launched on one of the many paths through the text. In print narratives, reading the table of contents—if there is one—is generally irrelevant to our experience of the narrative itself: our reading experience begins with the first words of the narrative and is completed by the last words on the last page. In *Victory Garden* and most hypertext fiction, however, readers have to begin making choices about their interests and the directions in which they wish to pursue them right from square one.

More strikingly, interactive narratives have no single ending. *Victory Garden* has six different points of closure, while Michael Joyce's *afternoon* has five or more—depending on the order in which the reader explores the narrative space—since the sequence in which places are read determines whether or not readers can move beyond certain decision points in the narrative. And though the plot's puzzles, twists, and challenges in both *Gadget* and *Douglas Adams' Starship Titanic* culminate in a single endgame sequence that ratifies the reader's success in having solved the story's central puzzle, *Obsidian* challenges readers to allow the Conductor to live—resulting in the world as we know it being remade—or to destroy the

Conductor and the Ceres Project and save the world. After making one last decision in *Obsidian*, readers still have opportunities to view the outcomes of the alternative scenario. More satisfying still are *Myst*'s three distinct endings that accompany readers' decisions to believe Achenar's, Sirrus's, or Atrus's version of events, and the eight potential endings to *Titanic: Adventure out of Time*. Deciding when the narrative has finished becomes a function of readers deciding when they have had enough, or of understanding the story as a structure that, as Jay Bolter notes, can "embrace contradictory outcomes."[11] Or, as one student reader of interactive narratives realized, as he completed a series of readings of *afternoon*:

> We have spent our whole lives reading stories for some kind of end, some sort of completion or goal that is reached by the characters in the story. . . . I realized this goal is not actually reached by the character, rather it is reached by our own selves. . . . [It] occurs when we have decided for ourselves that we can put down the story and be content with our interpretation of it. When we feel satisfied that we have gotten enough from the story, we are complete.[12]

This particular sense of an ending is, however, by no means unique to interactive narratives. Although print narratives physically end, literary conventions dictate that endings satisfy or in some way reply to expectations raised during the course of the narrative. As psycholinguists studying print stories have noted: "episodes end where the desired state of change occurs or clearly fails. In most stories, goals are satisfied and when goal satisfaction occurs, the protagonist engages in no further action."[13] In Stuart Moulthrop's interactive fantasy "Forking Paths," based on the Jorge Luis Borges short story "The Garden of Forking Paths," readers can experience no fewer than twelve separate instances of what we might call "points of closure" — places where the projected goals of the protagonist involved in a particular narrative strand are satisfied, or where the tensions or conflicts that have given rise to the narrative strand are resolved.

The multiplicity of narrative strands, the plethora of points of closure, the increased difficulty of reading interactive narratives — as we shall discover in the next chapters — can combine to stretch the time required to read an interactive novella like *Victory Garden*, with nearly a thousand segments of text and more than twenty-eight hundred links, to seventy hours. Compare this with the time required for the average reader to consume a three-hundred-page novel, generally anywhere from six to twelve hours.[14] Even a hypertext fiction as brief as Joyce's "Twelve Blue," with ninety-six segments of text bound by 269 links, contains multiple sequences that feed into other strands, crisscross them, loop endlessly, or arrive at points of closure, with no single reading exhausting the branching and combinatory possibilities of the text. Unlike print narratives, where each chapter builds upon the preceding one and leads to a single, determinate conclusion, the narrative strands in hypertexts can lead to numerous points of closure without satisfying the reader. Or the reader can be satisfied without reaching any point of closure at all.

Readers of Interactive Narratives Can Proceed Only on the Basis of Choices They Make

As noted in the previous chapter, in the past twenty years the concept of reading as a passive activity has become theoretically passé, an untenable stance held strictly by the unenlightened. Readers are now seen as breathing life into texts, reifying, or concretizing their possibilities — even receiving the text by creating it, in an effort nearly tantamount to that exerted by the author. As Barthes argues in "The Death of the Author,"

> [A] text is made of multiple writings, drawn from many cultures and entering into mutual relations of dialogue, parody, contestation, but there is one place where this multiplicity is focused and that place is the reader, not . . . the author. . . . [T]o give writing its future . . . the birth of the reader must be at the cost of the death of the Author.[15]

Yet reading print narratives is far from being a *literally* interactive activity, if we examine existing definitions of interactivity. Media theorist Andy Lippman of the Massachusetts Institute of Technology's Media Lab has succinctly defined *interactivity* as "mutual and simultaneous activity on the part of two participants, usually working toward some goal, but not necessarily" — a definition that can be met admirably thus far only by something as technologically unremarkable as human conversation.[16] For this "mutual and simultaneous activity" to be truly interactive, however, it must also, Lippman believes, contain a few other components.

Interruptibility: participants should be theoretically able to trade roles during the interaction, as speakers do in conversation, and not simply take turns in occupying the more active or more passive roles in the interaction.

Fine granularity: actors should not have to wait for the "end" of something to interact, with true interactivity being interruptible at the granularity level of a single word.

Graceful degradation: the parties involved can still continue the interaction without interruption, even if non sequiturs or unanswerable queries or requests enter into it.

Limited look-ahead: goals and outcomes in the interaction cannot be completely predetermined at the outset of the activity by either of the two parties, with the interaction created "on the fly," or coming into being only at the moment gestures, words, or actions are expressed.

Absence of a single, clear-cut default path or action: parties in the interaction cannot have definite recourse to a single or "default" path, one available to them throughout the interaction without their having to make any active decisions for interaction.

The impression of an infinite database: actors in an interaction need to be able to make decisions and take action from a wide range of seemingly endless possibilities.

When we converse, we stop or talk across each other (interruptibility) — often in the midst of a word or phrase (fine granularity) — and ask each other questions to which our partner may not have answers or even introduce non sequiturs into the conversation (graceful degradation). We can refuse to be cast in the role of cynic or idealist as we engage in an informal, conversational debate (no default), change subjects abruptly or follow an unforeseen shift in the direction of the conversation (limited look-ahead). Unless we find ourselves in the company of a true veteran bore, we seldom operate under the impression that our "database," the store of subjects and material from which we draw the shared opinions, emotions, and ideas that form the basis of the conversation, is anything but unlimited.

But according to this model of interaction, the average reader poring over *Jane Eyre* or *Ulysses* is placed in the position of someone listening to a monologue. We can interrupt only by closing the book or allowing our attention to wander, so the granularity to our interruption is the entire book itself. There is *only* one path through all but the most experimental of print narratives (these exceptions include *The Pleasure of the Text* or Julio Cortázar's *Hopscotch*, as we shall see). And if I try to focus only on the references to material wealth in *The Great Gatsby* — leaping from Daisy's voice sounding "like money" to a street vendor's absurd resemblance to John D. Rockefeller — my interaction with the novel will not simply degrade decidedly ungracefully, it will very likely collapse into mere incomprehension. My look-ahead is also completely determinate and limited. If I become impatient with the unfolding of Agatha Christie's narrative *The Murder of Roger Ackroyd*, I can simply skip forward to the end and find out who bumped off Roger Ackroyd, and no matter where I pause to skip ahead—whether I stop at chapter 4 or 24, the murderer will always be the narrator. And, of course, my "database" will always be confined to the words in print enclosed between two covers, even if the significance of the text and the repertoire of interpretive strategies available to me were to embrace the entire existing literary canon.

Conversely, when readers open most interactive narratives, they can begin making decisions about where to move and what to read right from the outset, even, as in *Victory Garden*, right from the text's title. Most segments feature text that has individual words or phrases linked to other places or icons that act as navigational tools: arrows representing forward and backward movement, a feature of many hypertext narratives; the map of the United States and highway icons in "Trip"; a schematic map that recalls the London Underground journey planner and a map of the passengers in each car in 253; the map of the ship in *Titanic*; a Mood Bar™ in *Midnight Stranger* that invites users to respond to characters by indicating green, amber, or red hues—presumably representing repartee that will push the conversation along, shift it into idle, or halt it in its tracks.[17] Unless segments are chained in a sequence with no options for navigation within each segment, readers can interrupt most interactive narratives within each segment—clicking on a word in *afternoon* or one of the brightly colored threads in "Twelve Blue," wandering up and down the seemingly endless corridors of *Titanic*, twisting doorknobs at random. The words, paths, and actions available as "interruptions," however, are chosen in advance by the author of the interactive narrative and not by the reader—an aspect of hypertext fiction that Espen Aarseth claims mitigates the medium's possibilities for bona fide interactivity, classifying it, instead, [. . .] as "participation, play, or even use."[18]

Furthermore, interactive narratives typically represent a spectrum of dialogues between reader and author anticipated in advance by the author, eliminating any possibility of graceful degradation. If I ponder the relationship between the unfaithful husbands and wives in *afternoon* and those in *WOE*, neither narrative can answer my query. Even the bots in *Starship Titanic*—ostensibly armed with thousands of lines of dialogue that should, at the very least, enable them to respond to the words and sentences typed in by users—respond to lines within highly confined scripts. Insult Nobby, the elevator bot, and he cries, "Wot? Wot?"—the same response he'll also supply to a dozen other queries and statements. Pose a question to the snippy deskbot, and she replies tartly, "I'll ask the questions here," before proceeding with queries that you must answer according to a script; refuse to answer them or supply an answer different from those she obviously seeks, and you are doomed to listening to them repeated over and over again, ad nauseam. For all the developers of *Starship Titanic* may have labored for weeks over the bots' scripts, the main interaction remains between user and the tools necessary to defuse the bomb aboard the ship, replace Titania's head, and route the ship successfully home again, with the bots remaining intermediaries, obstacles, or helpmates in each of these tasks. And contrary to Murray's belief that devices like *Midnight Stranger*'s Mood Bar™ make for less-obtrusive interfaces for interaction, it can feel downright eerie to have a traveling businesswoman come on to you merely because you answered a seemingly innocuous query with a tap on the green end of the spectrum, particularly when you, the reader, are straight, female, and merely trying to locate the whereabouts of a mysterious intergalactic object.[19] Whenever interactions have been designed, the methods and consequences of interrupting them can feel more than a little limited or contrived.

Still, readers can meander around an interactive narrative in a manner not possible in print or cinema: in both *Titanic* narratives, I can wander around the transatlantic liner or the intergalactic spaceship at my leisure, examining objects, riding the elevators, making small talk with staff. As you amble around exploring, however, you eventually become aware that your actions have become decoupled from all aspects of the plot. Unlike a train jumping the tracks, however, your actions do not bring all potential for interaction with the text to a screeching halt. Your aimless explorations do, however, contain you within a temporal and plotless limbo, where time stands still and your interactions with bots, crew members, or passengers become severely restricted, if not impossible.[20]

While interactive narratives do not generally reward random explorations of the text—except when they happen to intersect with the plot's challenges and conundrums by pure chance—they offer readers a series of options for experiencing the plot, rather than the singular skein that connects print novels and stories.[21] On the no-default continuum, interactive narratives fall somewhere between the no-default absolute of conversation, where conversationalists may gamely try to answer you or listen even when you suddenly shunt the topic under discussion to something completely different, and the default-only mode of films—even on DVD or videodisc—where viewing segments of narrative in random orders makes a hash equally of plot, characters' motivations, causes, and effects.

In Web- and disk-based hypertext fiction, defaults generally take the form of arrow keys and represent the strongest links between one segment and another, usually tied together causally. In one scene in Carolyn Guyer's *Quibbling*, clicking on the Storyspace path key, an arrow takes the reader from the segment where one character pries open a cigar box to the next segment in the sequence, where he hesitates as he opens it, and on to the next segment, where he peers inside. These links are called "defaults" in Storyspace terminology because they represent the action taken when readers choose to explore what may "come next," instead of choosing named paths to other segments from a menu or following links between segments connected by words in the text. Web-based hypertexts like "Trip" sometimes use default links to tie together narrative sequences that run to two or three segments so that readers experience and enjoy set pieces and vignettes as unbroken strings. Disk-based hypertexts, depending on the author's particular designs for potential interactions, may feature default links to and from virtually every segment of text, so that when readers reach the place "I call Lolly" in *afternoon* or "The End" in "I Have Said Nothing," the absence of a default can signal a potential ending of the narrative or a spot at which the readers must pause, reconnoiter, and decide whether — and how — to continue reading.

Even the presence of clear-cut links between causal sequences — or a single, clear-cut path through an entire narrative — does not provide a singular, authoritative version of the text that maintains priority over others. Defaults in *afternoon*, *WOE*, and *Victory Garden* do not provide a "master" version of the text.[22] Often, defaults deliberately play off readers' expectations, as in *WOE*, where readers using defaults shuttle between places describing passionate lovemaking between two couples. Because the default seems like the simplest and, therefore, most direct link between places, we assume that the stroking and groaning taking place between an unnamed couple in the first place we encounter belong to the same couple engaging in postcoital talk and smoking in the second. Since default connections do not involve us in the overt, more obtrusive acts of finding links in the text or choosing paths from a menu, hypertext readers may be tempted to see defaults as equivalents to the linear and singular connections characteristic of print. We discover this assumption with a jolt when we find that the couple in the first place consists of husband and wife, and, in the second, of the same husband and his wife's best friend. Default connections can jar readers, leap between narrative strands, and overturn predictions just as often as they can seamlessly move readers from one place to the next.

The impression of an unlimited database is not as impossible to convey as it may at first appear. The interactive narrative and simulation created by Mark Bernstein and Erin Sweeney, *The Election of 1912*, has 169 nodes containing information on the people, issues, and contexts surrounding the election, connected by an average of 4.3 links per node. Because this number of nodes can be comprehensively explored in one or two reading sessions, the database can seem conspicuously limited to readers. Yet when these links and nodes are explored in the course of the decision making and planning involved in the simulated election of 1912 — where readers manage Teddy Roosevelt's third-party campaign and enjoy a shot at changing history — the database seems considerably larger than a book of a comparable number of words. Because the information in each node appears in a dramatically different context, depending on the uses that the actor in the simulation finds for it, the database can appear to be double or triple its actual size.

The size of a database, the amount of information you have to potentially interact with, also depends on the number of pathways you can take through it. If you need to resort to the "back" option every time you want to explore more of a Web-based fiction, for example, your sense of the database can seem every bit as limited as it seems in *Gadget*, a highly atmospheric digital narrative that involves a comet hurtling toward the earth, a clutch of scientists creating retro machines straight out of *Brazil*, and a narrative that seems to lead almost inevitably to train stations regardless of the latest twist in plot. In *Gadget* the master narrative steers your experience ever forward, seamlessly, invisibly, through a world of train stations that recall the Gare du Nord and Waterloo Station — mammoth spaces that dwarf football fields in which you sometimes discover your only navigational option involves strolling over to a phone booth where your alter ego's detective superior, Slowslop, just happens to be waiting on the other end of the line. If the train pauses at the station before your assigned stop and you do not deign to step down from the car and stroll over to a bystander on the platform — who, not coincidentally, has a tidbit of information about the scientist you are stalking — the narrative stops dead. Most digital narratives are built around a quest, whether for the identity of a killer or artifacts collected on a grown-up version of a treasure hunt, providing a set of purposes that inform the narrative, propelling both it and the reader forward. The quest also, conveniently and not merely incidentally, enables designers to limit the characters, spaces, and scenarios populating the narrative.

Grail-less *Gadget*, which requires its readers merely to keep going through the narrative, is, however, more immersive than *Myst* or *Obsidian* because its readers seldom need to pause and think purposively about the plot, plan some strategic swordplay, or collect the obligatory artifacts that litter so many digital narratives. Ironically, *Gadget* derives its ability to lure readers into the externally oblivious, trancelike state of ludic reading precisely because its database is severely limited: you do not need to poke around the hotel for a map that will let you locate the train station. In fact, if you do not pause for a word with the clerk hovering over the reception desk, you cannot leave the hotel, let alone get to the train station, because the clerk conveniently has your ticket. Pick up the ticket, and the entire scene dissolves gently to the train station, segueing to the spot where a ticket agent retrieves the ticket from you. Likewise, if you attempt to leave the cavernous Museum train station without a second conversation with the distinctly odd-looking character lingering by the steps, your cursor will not turn into the directional arrow enabling you to navigate down the stairs and out of the building. Occasionally, the participatory and immersive aspects of interactivity can become mutually exclusive, one reason a narrative with a small database and virtually illusory choices for navigation should nonetheless seem peculiarly compelling, even entrancing.

What is striking about narratives like *Gadget* is that too much participation, too many gadgets to collect and assignations to keep and bad guys to sock, detracts from the immersiveness of digital environments, the very feature that Murray believes represents their single most valuable aspect. Constant demands for input or inputs that are frustrated—as when, for example, players thrash around *Myst*'s landscape, clicking wildly and randomly in the fervent hope the shape of their cursors will change and permit them to move forward in the narrative—can remind readers that they are grappling with a narrative designed by others, disrupting their suspension of disbelief in the same way that difficult texts do: requiring frequent pauses, reflection, even regressing over pages already read.

Paradoxically, genre fiction and interactive narratives like *Gadget* that are not terribly interactive fill readers' cognitive capacities more completely than difficult texts; familiar plot conventions and characters considerably speed the pace of reading and absorption, placing a far heavier continuous load on readers' attention.[23] Authors may use default options to privilege some linkings in the text over others, saving the fates, for example, of characters until readers know them sufficiently well for their victories or deaths to matter. Authors may use defaults to remove readers' concerns about actions and paths taken, thereby deepening their immersion in the narrative. And sometimes they use defaults to limit the amount of sheer data any interactive narrative must include to produce even a small simulacrum of a mere wedge of the world.

Finally, interactive narratives offer a very tangible sense of limited look-ahead, because navigational choices always depend on where you are and where you have already been. Occasionally, since connections between places can crisscross each other in a truly tangled skein, readers attempting to re-create an earlier reading exactly, by using, say, the "back" option on their Web browser, can find it well-nigh impossible without following a list of their previous navigational choices. You cannot be entirely certain, either, that your carefully considered choice has not triggered a connection randomly—as it can in Storyspace narratives when the author creates more than one default branching out from a single place—so that the same answer to the same question does not yield the same reply. This makes your reading of hypertext fiction a far less predictable matter than conversation with most people, even those you know only slenderly, since most of us exchange words according to highly structured conventions that extend from gripes about the weather to a confession of the strangers-on-a-train variety made aboard the Twentieth Century Limited. That means that while our look-ahead in conversation is limited—even if I have already agreed with my partner not to mention the Clintons, the stock market, or whether the Rolling Stones should throw in the towel and retire—I also cannot begin to see what is coming next when, for example, you start talking about the War of Jenkins' Ear. When I read *afternoon*, though, I have no way of knowing where the narrative may branch next, where any of the connections I choose may take me, or how long my reading of the text will take (which can last as long as my eyes hold up). As far as the limited look-ahead corollary goes, where interactive narratives are concerned, you *can* have too much of a good thing.

On the other hand, some hypertext fiction provides readers with the kind of overview impossible in a face-to-face exchange, via functions like the cognitive maps in Storyspace that act as schematic drawings of all possible versions of the text you might experience if you persevere long enough. As I pursue a narrative strand in *WOE* concerning the couplings and uncouplings of the adulterous foursome, I discover that all are connected by a single path named "Relic" and that, by selecting "Relic" from the Path menu each time it appears, I can watch the four come together in various combinations throughout their daily lives. When I encounter the place called "We," I stumble across a concluding sentence that reads "a happy ending," something that seems entirely at odds with the heavy sense of foreboding that seems to hang over the characters. When my desperate search for any further places on the "Relic" strand proves fruitless and subsequent browsing through a succession of nodes yields no further trace of the "Relic" foursome, I quickly switch to the Storyspace cognitive map and find "Relic" at last: a chain of places tidily laid out within a single, confining space and connected by path arrows labeled "a story" that ends with the place "We." The "happy ending," it turns out in this version, really was an ending, which makes me reconsider if the adjective, then, should be read ironically after all — an interpretation possible only through my using the map of the text to gain an Olympian perspective over the entire thing, what Jay Bolter has called a "structure of possible structures."[24] Like a topographic map of an unfamiliar island, the cognitive map of *WOE* eases the limitations of my look-ahead, providing me with vague suggestions about which directions might prove the most fruitful for further, dedicated exploration.

Interactive Narrative Segments Exist in a Network of Interconnections Mapped in Virtual, Three-Dimensional Space

It is not necessary to pore over cognitive maps, or any map at all, to encounter interactive narratives as structures suspended in virtual, three-dimensional space. In a look at the interpretive strategies used by readers of his own "Forking Paths," Moulthrop discovered that maps are not essential to navigation through hypertext space, but that readers of hypertext fiction seldom read without an awareness of the virtual, three-dimensional arrangement of the places they read. Back when he was still adapting the hypertext to the fledgling Storyspace interface, Moulthrop casually provided me a copy of "Forking Paths" — which I took straight into a freshman expository writing workshop I was then teaching at New York University. Dividing the class in half, I asked students to retell what they thought happened in the texts they read, then handed out photocopies of Borges's short story "The Garden of Forking Paths," and diskettes with copies of Moulthrop's hypertext. Still unpublished, "Forking Paths" is a hypertext fantasy built around a skeletal arrangement of the Borges short story, with fully fledged narratives branching off from each of the episodes and scenarios depicted in the original print fiction. Intending to invite readers to become coauthors of "Forking Paths," Moulthrop had omitted default connections and relied entirely on links, joining places through words or phrases in the text of each place. This, he explains, seemed logical to him, because "stories are a dialectic of continuity and closure, each fragmentary unit of the text (word, sentence, page, scene) yielding to the next in a chain of substitutions or metonymies that builds toward a final realization of the narrative as a whole, or a metaphor."[25] Although he acknowledges that the readers may have been somewhat disabled by the lack of instructions (which were still being written for "Forking Paths"), when he read their written responses to his hypertext, he discovered the antithesis of what he had anticipated. Instead of engaging the text at the local level and reaching what critic Peter Brooks has described as a metaphor for the text through following a chain of metonymies, my students gave up attempting to discover matches between their choices of words to form likely links between places and the words Moulthrop used to link them.[26] Amid all the complaints, however, one enterprising reader hit on navigation buttons that enabled him to move up, down, left, or right from the place he was stuck in. Others followed suit, exploring the hypertext outside the connections Moulthrop had mapped for them. As a result, their discussions of the narrative strands and the narrative as a structural whole reflected their awareness of moving through this virtual space, much as Greek and Roman rhetoricians once mentally strolled through their elaborate memory palaces. Inverting the relationship between metonymy and metaphor implicit in conventional print narratives, my students

> were plotting their own readings through a cartographic space, hoping to discover a design which, though it was in no way "promised," might prove to be buried or scattered in the text. The map, which represents the text as totality or metaphor, was not something to be reached through the devious paths of discursive metonymy, rather it was a primary conceptual framework, providing the essential categories of "right," "left," "up," and "down" by which these readers oriented themselves.[27]

As Jay Bolter argues, "topographic" writers in print — Sterne, Joyce, Borges, and Cortázar, who have created narratives that explore, exploit, and chafe at the confines of printed space — are "difficult" writers.[28] What makes them difficult is their self-conscious absorption with the act of writing itself and the problematic relationship among narrator, text, and reader, since their print texts work strenuously — and ultimately unsuccessfully — against the medium in which they were conceived. This is largely because spatial relations in print narratives — or the "spatial form" lauded by Joseph Frank and his critical successors — are very much like spatial relations in the cinema, where we see three dimensions represented and projected on a flat, two-dimensional plane.[29] We understand that the placement of the objects, characters, and events represented in print narratives has significance in terms of our understanding of the entire work, but this understanding is not necessary to our ability to proceed through the text itself (although, upon seeing his first film, an actor once reported, he and the other children watching it in the humid island cinema ran out into the alleyway behind the screen in search of the police car that had raced from one side of the screen to the other). Our awareness of print space, containing two potential dimensions, and of cinema, three dimensions projected onto two, is intrinsic to our reading experiences of both media.[30] In hypertext narratives, however, this awareness is inextricably wedded to our "reading" of the text itself, because the burden of interactivity and the continual necessity to choose directions for movement never allows us to forget that we are reading by navigating through virtual, three-dimensional space.

Interactive Narratives Have Many Orders in Which They Can Be Read Coherently

As Richard Lanham has observed, digital media—such as digitized films and interactive narratives—have no "final cut."[31] This means they have no singular, definitive beginnings, middles, or endings, but also that no single, definite order of reading is given priority over the others that exist alongside it. There is also no single story, and contrary to our expectations based on reading print narratives, readings do not simply provide varying versions of this story or collection of stories. As Jay Bolter has argued, each reading generates or determines the story as it proceeds: "[T]here is no story at all; there are only readings. . . . [T]he story is the sum of all its readings. . . . Each reading is a different turning within a universe of paths set up by the author."[32]

In *afternoon*, some readings represent alternative voices or perspectives on the narrative, with the changes in narrative perspective made separate and discrete by electronic space. The narrative strands in *Victory Garden* involve political developments during the Nixon, Reagan, and Bush eras, paralleling and crisscrossing each other as they follow a few weeks in the lives of nine characters. In "Twelve Blue," narrative strands represent the perspectives and experience of each character, each strand corresponding to the brightly colored threads that cross, arch, and dip across a blue field, a visual corollary to the voices and stories contained in the narrative that touch each other when stories meet or fray at the ends as stories begin to wind down. In some instances, the readings themselves may constitute mutually exclusive representations of the same set of circumstances with radically different outcomes, as readers can discover in both *afternoon* and "I Have Said Nothing." Like these hypertext writers, Faulkner once attempted in print to separate the different perspectives in *The Sound and the Fury* with something more than the conventional options of white space or discrete chapters. When, however, he indicated to his publisher that he wanted each represented by different colors of ink, Random House shuddered at the cost and refused.[33]

When you read hypertext narratives, you also have the option of limiting your experience of the text to the pursuit of narrative strands that you find particularly intriguing. If I want to trot after the romance burgeoning between Nick Carraway and Jordan Baker in *The Great Gatsby*, I have to read, or browse through, or skim the entire novel in order to pursue the romance that mirrors Gatsby's involvement with Daisy. And, of course, this narrative strand, like the episode narrated by Jordan, is but a fragment of the total novel — a particle that is comprehensible and meaningful only in the context of the novel as a whole. Yet I can simply pursue the tortuous relationships between the unfaithful wives and husbands of *WOE* or focus my readings on the relationships between Emily, Victor, and Jude as I make my way through *Victory Garden*. In some instances, focusing on the stories and strands of particular interest may be relatively easy, with the options for navigation through the narrative made accessible through lists, as in *Victory Garden*, or by way of cognitive maps that enable readers to arrive at a place by pointing at it with a cursor. At other times, however, following a single narrative strand can involve a complicated process of selecting paths by trial and error, or determining which path or place names document certain narrative episodes and strands. Regardless of whether the process of following the chosen narrative strand is easy or incredibly difficult, readers of hypertext narratives can coherently experience these texts in a variety of different orders and sequences without doing violence to the narratives, stories, or meaning of the hypertext as a whole.

The Language in Interactive Narratives Appears Less Determinate than the Language Present in Print Pages

Most obviously, interactive narratives embrace a far wider and less determinate spectrum of meanings than print narratives because few readers will experience identical readings of texts that can have thousands of connections between thousands of segments of text, which can be as brief as a single word or as long as pages of print text. The more links, or decision points, each reader must confront in the course of navigating through the narrative, the less singular and determinate the meaning of the hypertext narrative as a whole, because no single path through the text has priority over all others.

Yet the indeterminacy of interactive narratives also exists in a far more fundamental sense than this. In most hypertexts, a majority of the nodes will appear in more than one context as a point along two, three, or more paths. The metaphor for hypertext is, after all, not a flowchart but a web that acknowledges the myriad of associative, syllogistic, sequential, and metatextual connections between words, phrases, paragraphs, and episodes. To be comprehensible, print paragraphs need only to build off the paragraphs that have preceded them and prepare the reader for what is yet to come. Print narratives can use paragraphs and transitions toward creating a sequence that both directs the reader's experience of the material forward and seems like the most authoritative, and even the only possible, sequence for structuring the material.[34] But hypertext fiction seems to work in the opposite direction. Ideally, print paragraphs and transitions close off alternative directions and work to eliminate any suggestion of other potential sequences that might have been created from the same material—so that readers do not end up stopping in the middle of a paragraph like this one to reflect on all the other ways these same details might be construed. But nodes or windows in hypertext fiction must, by their very nature, prove comprehensible in more than one sequence or order. Instead of closing off any suggestion of alternative orders or perspectives, the text contained in each segment must appear sufficiently open-ended to provide links to other segments in the narrative. This, de facto, fosters an additional level of indeterminacy generally rare in print narratives—although it does appear in avant-garde and experimental forms of print narratives like *The Alexandria Quartet*, *Hopscotch*, and *The Pleasure of the Text*.

Print Precursors and Hypertext Fiction

At present, existing hypertext fiction resembles two of the divergent modes explored in avant-garde or experimental fiction: what we might call "narratives of multiplicity" and "mosaic narratives." Mosaic print narratives, such as Lawrence Durrell's *Alexandria Quartet*, Julio Cortázar's *Hopscotch*, and Barthes's *The Pleasure of the Text* consist of narrative fragments, conflicting perspectives, interruptions, and ellipses that impel readers to painstakingly piece together a sense of the narrative, with its full meaning apparent only when viewed as an assembled mosaic, a structure embracing all its fragments.

At a local level, a mosaic narrative such as *The Alexandria Quartet* presents its readers with more determinacy than *The Pleasure of the Text*. That is, Durrell's novel consists of a set of four novels, each of which can stand as a discrete, independent text on its own, and each seems perfectly conventional and self-contained when read separately. Unlike trilogies or tetralogies that merely feature the same bit of geographic territory or the same cast of characters, *The Alexandria Quartet* novels relate the same set of events from the perspective of the different players involved. Even readers of *Justine*, the version of events narrated by the naive Darley, can feel their experience of the novel is perfectly complete when they reach the ending. Yet as you move from *Justine* to the last of the novels, *Clea*, your view of events begins to burrow beneath the skin of the world according to Darley and the worlds known by Balthazar, Mountolive, and Clea, the most informed of the four narrators. By the time you reach the end of *Clea*, the observations made by Darley in *Justine* that had seemed so straightforward and reliable can end up seeming a little like Benjy's in *The Sound and the Fury*. What had appeared perfectly accurate in even *Balthazar* and *Mountolive*, when read against Clea's supplementary version of events, brims with ambiguities, ellipses, and unanswered questions, making you wonder how you had ever accepted it as a fully fledged account in the first place. Balthazar's story points up how hopelessly uninformed Darley's grasp of reality is and positions itself as an authoritative supplement to it. Balthazar's representation of Nessim's proposal to Justine, meant to provide us with insight into their relationship, insists that Nessim is hopelessly infatuated and Justine ruthlessly pragmatic:

> After a long moment of thought, he picked up the polished telephone and dialled Capodistria's number. "Da Capo," he said quietly. "You remember my plans for marrying Justine? All is well." He replaced the receiver slowly, as if it weighed a ton, and sat staring at his own reflection in the polished desk.[35]

Hundreds of pages later, in *Mountolive*, you may find yourself wondering just how penetrating Balthazar's insight was when you encounter the same scene again:

[A]fter a long moment of thought, [he] picked up the polished telephone and dialled Capodistria's number. "Da Capo," he said quietly, "you remember my plans for marrying Justine? All is well. We have a new ally. I want you to be the first to announce it to the committee. I think now they will show no more reservation about my not being a Jew — since I am to be married to one."[36]

Plainly, Balthazar's story about the personal relationship between Nessim and Justine cannot do full justice to the complexity of their passionate political and strategic alliance, and our understanding of the entire world of *The Alexandria Quartet* shifts dramatically from the inclusion of a mere three sentences. Our faith in the accuracy and authenticity of Balthazar's account, which presented itself as more complete than Darley's, is tattered well before the close of *Mountolive*, just as the value of the Mountolive section declines seriously the further we proceed through Clea's. You could not, however, save yourself the effort of reading all four novels simply by beginning with Clea's account — that would be rather like chipping a diamond apart so you could admire the slender sliver of its face and lose the pleasure of peering beyond it into depths emphasized by precisely cut facets.

The pleasure of reading Durrell's tetralogy is not unlike the pleasure in listening to Bach's *Goldberg Variations*, where you are dazzled by just how richly evocative a few seemingly simple phrases can be — here sequence is everything. In Barthes's *The Pleasure of the Text*, sequence apparently means nothing: the book itself is a succession of fragments, ordered alphabetically. While the segments are tagged with titles in the book's table of contents, the reader in the throes of absorbing the text has no such assistance, only a scattering of typographical marks and white space to indicate the division between fragments. Together these pieces represent Barthes's erotics of the text, yet no single fragment maintains priority over the others, and even the most vigilant readers will not find any transitions to transport them easily and painlessly into the next segment. As Barthes notes in one such segment, "[A]ll the logical small change is in the interstices. . . . [T]he narrative is dismantled yet the story is still readable."[37]

The Pleasure of the Text offers the same lack of definitive beginnings, middles, and endings, and singular, definitive paths through the narrative, you would discover in hypertext narratives. Likewise, Durrell's *Alexandria Quartet* presents readers with the discrete, separate, and entirely self-contained narrative perspectives that you could encounter in the likes of Moulthrop's *Victory Garden* or Joyce's *WOE* or *afternoon*. Yet each of

Barthes's segments and Durrell's chapters builds off the others in a highly determinate way impossible in hypertext fiction. Read in a random, reverse-alphabetic order, Barthes's meditations on the act of reading do not bear upon one another any differently than they might if you were to explore the text from front to back, or to weave your own path through the book. If there are alternative ways of assembling Barthes's erotics of text, other orders awaiting liberation from the linearity of conventional print, they do not crowd the surface of the text or shout at you from its pages, which are, after all, still relentlessly linear. Similarly, Durrell's presentation of four sequential narratives traces and retraces the same events in a chrono-logical order that removes any ambiguity from your immediate experience of the narrative. As you ponder the entire construction in retrospect in light of what you have learned by the end of *Clea*, what is striking is not how ambiguous or incomplete events seem (since the version presented in *Clea* fills in any last vestiges of ambiguity or openness) but how obtuse or slen-der a grasp any of the observers has on the complexity of the whole. At no point in the throes of peering over Darley's shoulder, though, or reading Balthazar's notes, are you invited to mull over what might be missing from their depictions of events: ambiguity here is something you are free to realize had been present only after a fully informed, detailed account has banished it forever.

Just as you are not aware, the first time you happen upon Nessim's tele-phone conversation, that you are not getting the whole picture (nor that you are going to see it replayed again somewhat differently), you probably would not find one particular passage in *afternoon* remarkable the first time you run across it. In it, the protagonist and sometime narrator, Peter, shares lunch with his employer, Wert. There is a bit of badinage, some sexual innuendo reserved for the waitress, and then Wert springs a question on Peter:

> He asks slowly, savoring the question, dragging it out devilishly, meeting my eyes.
> "How . . . would you feel if I slept with your ex-wife?"
> It is foolish. She detests young men.[38]

The second time you read this, however, you might be convinced that you had read a different passage, and by the third or fourth time, you might find yourself trying desperately to locate these different spots that sound awfully similar but seem to mean entirely different things. In one narrative strand, this segment crops up amid Wert's clowning around over lunch, emphasiz-ing his immaturity around women. In another, Wert poses the question to

Peter playfully, to distract him from his concern over the whereabouts of his missing son and estranged wife, who he believes may have been injured in a car accident earlier that day. Encountered in yet another context, the passage occurs in the context of Peter's fling with a fellow employee, Nausicaa, and Peter sees Wert's question as evidence of his boss's jealousy over their involvement. Later, the lunch date and conversation reappear after a narrative strand couched in Nausicaa's own perspective, which reveals that she is sleeping with *both* Wert and Peter, making Wert's query something of a game of cat's-paw. "I'm sleeping with your lover," Wert seems to be thinking, so he follows the line of thought to a position he perceives as more daring: "What if I were sleeping with your ex-wife?" But if you reach a segment called "white afternoon," having visited a fairly detailed series of places, you will discover that Wert and Peter's ex-wife, Lisa, have been seen together by Peter himself, although Peter cannot be certain that they are involved with each other. When the lunchtime conversation reappears, after this last revelation, Wert's query is a very real question indeed.

What is striking about the way *afternoon* works is that there is only one passage involved here — and the language within it is as fixed as on any printed page. Although the contexts may alter its meaning drastically with each new appearance, the language itself stays the same, unlike Durrell's quartet of novels, where he can manipulate our perspective on events only by a combination of ellipsis and supplement. Yet the language itself is not indeterminate: readers seeking a precedent for the "he," "my," and "she" that occur in the text need look no further than the preceding or succeeding segments. In all the contexts in which this place appears, it is clear that the "he" posing the question is Wert, the ex-wife or "she" in question is Lisa, and the "you" who thinks the question is foolish is Peter.

In *WOE* Joyce further capitalizes on the indeterminacy of hypertext narratives to induce a reading experience that approximates a trompe l'oeil, where your interpretation of what is happening in a narrative sequence disintegrates just as you finish reading it. It would not normally occur to you to wonder if the "he" you have been reading about is the selfsame "he" a few paragraphs later, but *WOE* springs its surprises on you by switching the identities of pronoun precedents in midstream. You can never be certain who the "he" and "she" are in a particular passage — to brilliant effect, since several of the narrative strands in *WOE* involve romantic attachments between two couples closely allied by both friendship and infidelity.

The other form of print narrative that thrives on indeterminacy, the narrative of multiplicity, is produced by writers who have chafed at the way confines of printed space preclude multiple, mutually exclusive representations of a single set of events. Robert Coover's "Babysitter," and "The Elevator" from *Pricksongs and Descants*, Borges's "The Garden of Forking Paths," and Fowles's *French Lieutenant's Woman*, all engaging and entirely successful works of fiction when read at face value, are also as much about the experience of multiplicity and simultaneity and the way these are represented in print as they are about their ostensible subjects.

Fowles's *French Lieutenant's Woman*, for example, features three endings: a parody of the tidy-but-breathless tying up of loose ends so characteristic of the Victorian novel; a happy but conventional resolution of the tortured relationship between Charles and Sarah; and a more complex, "modern" resolution that serves to deconstruct the paternalistic perspective of the traditional Victorian novel of love and marriage. Not surprisingly, none of the three endings is compatible with another. Tellingly, the modern, deconstructive episode comes last in print — which can be said to provide this last "ending" with priority over those preceding it — just as the "ending" that occurs midway through the book has its authoritativeness somewhat undermined by the bulging stack of unread pages remaining after it.

More radically, Coover's "The Babysitter" features 105 narrative segments that begin as nine separate and distinct narrative strands framed from nine different perspectives, becoming less distinguishable from one another as the narrative proceeds. Mutually exclusive versions of events begin unfolding one after the other, sometimes feeding clearly into each other. The passages depicting husband Harry's first sexual musings on the babysitter and wife Dolly's bitter thoughts about marriage occur sequentially in time, united by Dolly's question "What do you think of our babysitter?" which appears in both segments. By the time the reader has reached a section where the babysitter screams after discovering herself watched from a window, however, it is not clear whether the perspective originates in her boyfriend's fantasies about her or in Harry's idylls of seducing her. In the segment that immediately follows it, the babysitter's scream metamorphoses into an indignant shriek as the children she is supposed to be supervising whisk the bath towel away from her wet body after she leaves the bathtub to answer a phone call. The phrase "she screams" is identical in both passages, but the context and narrative strands in which it is embedded are mutually exclusive representations of a single moment in time. In the narrative universe of "The Babysitter," all possibilities are realized, with actions, thoughts, idylls, and snatches of television programs offering an equal, textual tangibility. In the end, however, all this burgeoning and splintering of perspectives converges in two episodes. One neatly resolves the wild and mutually exclusive seduction, rape, and murder scenes by depicting the babysitter waking up from a dream amid a setting so orderly that even the Tucker family dishes have been washed and put away. The other represents a conflation of all the narrative strands in a single, final, wild conclusion: the Tucker children are dead; the babysitter is a drowned corpse in the bathtub; Mr. Tucker has fled the scene; and Dolly cannot get out of her girdle.[39] The wild improbability and satirical tone of the last segment and the suggestion, in the passage that precedes it, that everything in the narrative belonged to one vast, distended dream also tend to undermine the "reality" and priority of any single narrative segment or sequence.

When print narratives attempt to resist the physicality of print by increasing the number of stories, narrative strands, and potential points of closure — as is the case with the likes of "The Babysitter," Sterne's *Tristram Shandy*, or Borges's "The Garden of Forking Paths" — the medium inevitably resists, making the reading experience and the significance of the narrative itself a meditation on the confines of print space. In "The Garden of Forking Paths," for example, master spy Yu Tsun is introduced by Sinologist Stephen Albert to the concept of the labyrinth, once discovered by his illustrious grandfather Ts'ui Pen. The embodiment of an "infinite series of times . . . a network of diverging, converging and parallel times . . . [that] embraces *every* possibility,"[40] the labyrinth represents an alternative universe where mutually exclusive possibilities exist alongside one another, producing a space in which, as Albert himself notes, Yu and Albert can simultaneously be both friends and mortal enemies. Yu is, of course, both to Albert. As the grandson of Ts'ui Pen, he shares Albert's most valued interests; as a German spy who must kill Albert to signal the location of a British armaments site in France, he is also his most deadly enemy. With the arrival of the British captain pursuing Yu, however, the German spy shoots Albert, and the infinite possibilities hinted at in the story are, ironically, reduced to a single, sordid conclusion — death.

Seeing the story as an example of topographic writing struggling against the confines of print, Stuart Moulthrop sought to liberate the Borges story by splitting the original story into hypertext nodes, then grafting onto each node a series of narrative strands.[41] Following certain links introduces you to a narrative involving Stephen Albert's former lover or thrusts you onto the trail of Yu's German intelligence chief, Viktor Runeberg. You might follow Yu, Captain Richard Madden, and Albert through the labyrinth in the garden and experience no fewer than twelve separate permutations on the ending to the original Borges tale. Or you might explore retellings of narrative events plucked from the original story from entirely new points of view, unexpected reversals in character traits and motives, and even playful, metatextual commentary on interactivity itself. In Moulthrop's garden, Yu Tsun murders Stephen Albert; Albert and Yu stroll peaceably into the labyrinth together; Yu disappears from pursuer Richard Madden in the midst of the labyrinth; and Albert garrotes Yu — a true realization of the "infinite but limited" labyrinth of possibilities that exist in the heap of contradictory drafts that constituted the Garden of Forking Paths created by Ts'ui Pen.

Similarly, in Michael Joyce's *afternoon*, car accidents occur, seem to have occurred, may possibly have occurred, and never occurred. The narrator, Peter, has an affair with Nausicaa but also does not have an affair. His employer, Wert, is faithful to his wife, is having an affair with Nausicaa, and may well have had an affair with Peter's ex-wife, Lisa — or none of the above. Peter loses his son, fears him dead or seriously injured, and begins a frenetic search for him in some readings of *afternoon*. In others, he simply goes about his daily business. "The story," Jay Bolter has noted, "does and does not end."[42] There is a challenge implicit in any reading of these highly indeterminate narratives that embody a dense thicket of possibilities without giving priority to any one of them, a requirement that we learn to read "multiply," as Bolter insists (144), aware that a single perspective on any set of circumstances can never do full justice to the complexity and contingency of even a fictional world dreamed up by a single author.

All right, you may be wondering, so interactive narratives do not have singular or definite beginnings or endings, and readers can proceed through them only by making choices about what they have read or what they would like to read . . . but how on earth do you know when the story is over? How do you know when it is finished, when you are finished? Most of us have, at one time or another, flinched at the credits scrolling up the screen, wondering how the story could be over when so many loose ends were left dangling so teasingly. We are accustomed to dealing with texts that end more prematurely than their stories would seem to, but what do we do with a text that, a bit like a book made of sand, has pages we cannot properly count and nothing like end titles or hard covers to contain it? And when you stop reading, what is really finished: the stories — or you?

Notes

Bracketed ellipses indicate deletion of internal cross-references that appeared in the original.

1. Walter J. Ong, *Orality and Literacy: The Technologizing of the Word* (London: Methuen, 1981), 102–3.

2. Jay David Bolter, "Topographic Writing: Hypertext and the Electronic Writing Space," in *Hypermedia and Literary Studies*, ed. Paul Delany and George P. Landow (Cambridge: MIT Press, 1991), 105.

3. George P. Landow, "Hypertext, Hypermedia, and Literary Studies: The State of the Art," in Delany and Landow, *Hypermedia and Literary Studies*, 3.

4. Theodor Holm Nelson, *Literary Machines* (Bellevue, Wash.: OWL Systems, 1987), 1.

5. John M. Slatin, "Reading Hypertext: Order and Coherence in a New Medium," *College English* 52, no. 8 (1990): 876. More recent definitions of hypertext also emphasize the medium's multilinear and multisequential aspects. See George P. Landow, *Hypertext: The Convergence of Contemporary Critical Theory and Technology* (Baltimore: Johns Hopkins University Press, 1992), 4.

6. I use the term *medium* in a way analogous to its use in painting — where artists work with oil, pastels, watercolors, or etchings, the different tools causing them to render vastly different effects. At the same time, painting generally is also a medium, as the term is used to refer to media like radio, television, and film. Similarly, as used here, the medium for hypertext fiction is different from that used in creating and reading digital narratives — and digital environments are also the medium in which writers like Joyce and Moulthrop create interactive narratives.

7. Janet H. Murray, *Hamlet on the Holodeck: The Future of Narrative in Cyberspace* (New York: Free Press, 1997), 133.

8. See Slatin, "Reading Hypertext," 871. See also Frank Smith, *Understanding Reading: A Psycholinguistic Analysis of Reading and Learning to Read*, 3rd ed. (New York: Holt, Rinehart and Winston, 1982), 76–77.

9. Slatin, "Reading Hypertext," 871.

10. Bolter discusses tables of contents as print examples of hierarchical maps in *Writing Space: The Computer, Hypertext, and the History of Writing* (Hillsdale, N.J.: Lawrence Erlbaum Associates, 1991), 22.

11. Bolter, *Writing Space*, 124.

12. Student Andrew Sussman, quoted in Stuart Moulthrop and Nancy Kaplan, "Something to Imagine: Literature, Composition, and Interactive Fiction," *Computers and Composition* 9, no. 1 (1991): 16.

13. Tom Trabasso, Tom Secco, and Paul Van Den Broek, "Causal Cohesion and Story Coherence," in *Learning and Comprehension of Text*, ed. Heinz Mandl, Nancy L. Stein, and Tom Trabasso (Hillsdale, N.J.: Lawrence Erlbaum Associates, 1984), 87.

14. Richard Ziegfeld, "Interactive Fiction: A New Literary Genre?" *New Literary History* 20 (1989): 363.

15. Roland Barthes, "Death of the Author," in *Image-Music-Text*, trans. Stephen Heath (New York: Hill and Wang, 1977), 148.

16. Lippman is quoted in Stewart Brand, *The Media Lab: Inventing the Future at MIT* (New York: Viking, 1987), 46–49.

17. I discuss the Mood Bar™ as interface more fully in "Virtual Intimacy™ and the Male Gaze Cubed: Interacting with Narratives on CD-ROM," *Leonardo* 29, no. 3 (1996): 207–13.

18. Espen J. Aarseth, *Cybertext: Perspectives on Ergodic Literature* (Baltimore: Johns Hopkins University Press, 1997), 49.

19. Murray argues, "If we ask the interactor to pick from a menu of things to say, we limit agency and remind them of the fourth wall. Some CD-ROM stories give the interactor the task of deciding the mood or tone of a spoken response rather than picking a statement from a list of possible things to say. This is a more promising route because it seems less mechanical, although the mood selector is often a menu on a slider bar that is outside the story" (*Hamlet on the Holodeck*, 190–91).

20. *Titanic*'s narratives suggest that you have jumped tracks by, for example, barring access to the First Class lounge or Café Parisien through your steward's telling you repeatedly that both rooms are closed and showing you the door. Narratives like *Gadget* bar your exit from the story's railway stations and museums until you milk all the requisite clues from each scene. Others, such as *Midnight Stranger*, shuttle the reader into empty comedy clubs and restaurants where there is nobody to interact with, while narratives like *Who Killed Taylor French?* hustle you along with gentle prods from your assistant, chewings out by a police superior, and a loudly ticking clock signifying how little time remains before you need to swear out a warrant for your suspect's arrest.

21. In *The Last Express*, discussed at length in chapter 7, however, there is no "dead zone": anywhere you wander on the train at any time provides opportunities for interactions with other characters. If, for example, you do not choose to sleep during the small hours, you can still interact with characters on board the Orient Express—if they are also awake—and suffer the repercussions of sleep deprivation the following day.

22. Michael Joyce, "Selfish Interactions: Subversive Texts and the Multiple Novel," in *Of Two Minds: Hypertext Pedagogy and Poetics* (Ann Arbor: University of Michigan Press, 1995), 144.

23. B. K. Britton, A. Piha, J. Davis, and E. Wehausen, "Reading and Cognitive Capacity Usage: Adjunct Question Effects," *Memory and Cognition* 6 (1978): 266–73.

24. Bolter, *Writing Space*, 144.

25. Stuart Moulthrop, "Reading from the Map: Metonymy and Metaphor in the Fiction of Forking Paths," in Delany and Landow, *Hypermedia and Literary Studies*, 127.

26. Peter Brooks, *Reading for the Plot: Design and Intention in Narrative* (New York: Vintage, 1985), 23.

27. Moulthrop, "Reading from the Map," 128.

28. Bolter, *Writing Space*, 143.

29. Joseph Frank, "Spatial Form in Modern Literature," in *Essentials of the Theory of Fiction*, 3rd ed., Michael J. Hoffman and Patrick D. Murphy (Durham: Duke University Press, 2005), 61–73.

30. See W. J. T. Mitchell, "Spatial Form in Literature: Toward a General Theory," in *The Language of Images*, ed. W. J. T. Mitchell (Chicago: University of Chicago Press, 1980), 284. See also Jeffrey R. Smitten, "Spatial Form and Narrative Theory," in *Spatial*

Form in Narrative, ed. Jeffrey R. Smitten and Ann Daghistany (Ithaca: Cornell University Press, 1981), 9–20.

31. Richard Lanham, "The Electronic Word: Literary Study and the Digital Revolution," *New Literary History* 20 (1989): 269.

32. Bolter, *Writing Space*, 124–25.

33. Ziegfeld, "Interactive Fiction," 352.

34. Slatin, "Reading Hypertext," 872.

35. Lawrence Durrell, *The Alexandria Quartet* (London: Faber and Faber, 1962), 249.

36. Durrell, *The Alexandria Quartet*, 555.

37. Roland Barthes, *The Pleasure of the Text*, trans. Richard Miller (New York: Hill and Wang, 1975), 9.

38. Michael Joyce, *afternoon, a story* (Cambridge, Mass.: Eastgate Systems, 1990), "asks."

39. Robert Coover, "The Babysitter," in *Pricksongs and Descants* (New York: Plume, 1969), 239.

40. Jorge Luis Borges, "The Garden of Forking Paths," in *Fictions*, trans. Anthony Kerrigan (London: John Calder, 1985), 91.

41. Moulthrop, "Reading from the Map," 124.

42. Bolter, *Writing Space*, 143.

29

A Media Migration: Toward a Potential Literature

JOSEPH TABBI

A central argument in this book [*Cognitive Fictions*] has been that, at the turn of a century when literature has been engaged in an ongoing intermedial struggle for representational primacy, the new media can help us to see the older, printed book in fresh ways. Throughout the exposition, I have tried to avoid the notion, which has unfortunately polarized much of the debate, that hypertext and hypermedia imply the demise of the printed book. Instead I want to suggest that even if the inscription, storage, and dissemination of information increasingly happens in electronic writing spaces (a transformation that is by now well under way), and even if reading itself is done on screens rather than on the printed page, that will not mean the end of the book so much as a return to its beginnings, when print was not yet a dominant medium and when textual authority, even the identity of authors and the stability of the bound text, was not so firmly established.

From an aesthetic standpoint, the idea of a migration toward the virtual (with nomadic meanderings back and forth across a boundary rather than one medium *replacing* an earlier medium) has the advantage of letting us recognize the centrality of certain narrative features that have long been marginalized or forgotten — so secure is our faith in the book's fixity and the singular authority of its author. Features that tend to be associated with avant-garde or experimental texts — reflexive identity formations, intertextual collaborations, nonlinear or multilinear narrative action, concretism, and the involvement of readers in the act of creation — can again be seen to have been always present in print texts of any literary interest. Moreover (and this is what initially got me interested, in the summer of 1995, in the hands-on construction of a literary Web site) the new media have forced a reconsideration of exactly how narrative, whether in print or on the screen, represents thought and constructs subjectivity. Because hypertext and hypermedia turn "cognitive theorizing into concrete practice" — to the point that many of their early promoters tried, too hastily, to equate computer networks with neural networks in the brain — the introduction of computers into literary study has given new life to formal and materialist approaches.[1] A mind is not a computer; but one thing that unites literature, computer science, and cognitive psychology is a new appreciation of the *embodiment* of each of these ways of knowing, down to the material substrate whose differentiations enable the emergence of higher-level structures of meaning. One can study the structures, as media theory studies hardware and cognitive science studies modules in the brain. Or one can study consciousness, using either the methods of second-order observation theory or phenomenological approaches to the reflective subject. One cannot, however, map consciousness onto cognition or derive communications from hardware. What one can do — the approach taken in this book — is to fluctuate between these incompatible theories in the hope of accommodating linear writing to multilinear thought, the conscious mind to the unreflective medial ecology.

The word *hypertext* itself, which Ted Nelson defined as nonsequential writing organized in blocks through electronic links, is often meant to supplant some supposed traditional (but, in reality, largely mythical) notion of narrative as a linear, page by page movement from definite beginnings through intermediate complications to an ultimate resolution (in death, marriage, or — more often in recent narratives — frozen social and economic mobility). Novelistic endings are supposedly made palpable and poetic closure reinforced by the diminished number of bound pages as we finish reading a book, a material satisfaction that is not possible in the Web's open network. And yet at any point within a print narrative, this inevitability may be resisted or put off in ways that depend on syntactic, semantic, and symbolical structures much more than the particular lexical coding — that is, the arrangement of words or word groups that can be identified and accessed electronically in any order, or in no order at all. It is telling, I think, that Nelson chose the word *lexia* to designate reading units in hypertext, since it is only at the lexical level that (barring puns and other accidents, oversights, or willful wordplay) readers can be fairly sure of a one-to-one correspondence between words and their cumulative meanings. If books could be neutralized in this way, according to a referential model of knowledge as information extraction, they would easily be displaced by a nonsequential technology.

But that's not how books work — not when a passage can be *gone back to* with a flip of pages that, while reading, is often easier than retracing the branching pathways through a hypertext. The book, as N. Katherine Hayles has pointed out, is as yet a more efficient random access device

(RAD) than any electronic hypertext, and I might mention here that the computer's ability to hold any given trajectory in digital memory is actually less helpful, to me, than my own visual memory of where a word or phrase happened to appear on a page within a particular section of a book. My students, who sometimes find electronic search routines less of a bother, are perhaps less likely to rely on such visual memory, but with the right kind of narrative repetitions and cognitive reinforcement, even the flipping of pages can be avoided. It would seem, then, that the celebrated nonlinearity of hypertext is in large part a literalization (at the level of tagged word groups) of mental connections that readers learn to make, one way or another, when reading fiction or poetry in print. Through a kind of flickering or oscillating attention, such connections can easily take place across many pages, or within the space of a single phrase; they enable a poem or a narrative to take shape in the mind of a reader, and this mental picture — "a network of possibilities rather than a preset sequence of events"[2] — is rarely congruent with the progressive continuity of lines following lines and pages stacked on pages through the course of a book.

Strictly speaking, it is only *after* the reader stops reading that the hypertext link becomes useful, not for establishing a narrative or poetic sequence, but for producing and retrieving information, and finding pathways through lexia that have already been mapped out by the author during composition or the reader during previous readings. Francis Crick has noted the overemphasis on parallel distributing processes (PDP) in the brain, when what is needed, even at the level of recognizing letters on a page, is a serial process capable of holding the reader's attention: "I suspect," Crick writes, "that what is missing may be a mechanism of *attention*. Attention is likely to be a *serial* process working on top of the highly parallel PDP processes."[3] Even in those literary works such as *Wittgenstein's Mistress* or *Ghosts* whose processing across separate sites resembles distributed cognition,[4] data is both patterned *and* sequential, distributed *and* differential: indeed, one argument of this book has been that consciousness in such fiction emerges precisely out of the tensions and interactions between these modes.

As claims for the brain's distributed nature may distract from attention-holding processes that are likely to be serial in nature, claims for hypertext as a superior medium of associative connection too often ignore the actual language in which any text is written. Even the relative ease with which one can enter a hypertext at any point, in a structure whose visible outline has several immediate points of entry, has its analogues in print narrative. The start of a discourse in medias res, for example, is a device that never waited on hypertext; it was in fact originally an epic convention that got carried over from orality into print. Similarly, the conflation of beginnings and endings within a single print paragraph can make the newfound ability to start anywhere and then jump from one passage to another seem arbitrary by comparison. It is easy to cite examples in printed texts when one thinks one has reached an end — say, after a treacherous stretch of driving in bad weather — only to find that one is in fact just beginning:

> The rain had stopped. I could forget about the curved warning signs; the gently winding road, which conformed so gratifyingly to my map, would dry fast. I settled back in the driver's seat and accelerated. The steering wheel came off in my hand.[5]

The mention of a map, in these fine opening lines from Harry Mathews's *The Journalist*, raises many questions relevant to the cognitive mapping that one seeks when reading pages and viewing screens. Conformity to a map is a gratifying, precise, but necessarily false illusion, because one-to-one correspondences, whether lexical or topographical, fail to describe the ongoing mental activity that actually generates much of our perception of a text or a passing landscape. Given enough rules of mapping, anything can be mapped onto anything; but one never knows all the mappings that are going on in one's own mind and through one's own body. For practical aesthetic purposes, the fewer the rules, the better — hence the gratification in reading minimal fictions by, for example, Jorge Luis Borges. The power of a minimal mapping is precisely that it makes a world (if not "the" world) knowable against the background of multiple unknown mappings in the unconscious. Mapping generates order within a noisy environment; but noise is precisely what Mathews's driver is forced to confront, in all its unknowability, at the moment the steering wheel comes off in his hand. No longer able to distinguish between what is inside and outside, his sense of a personal identity is revealed to have been, at every moment and without his knowing it, a cognitive fiction, which is to say, the fiction that consciousness is very closely connected to what our minds and bodies are procedurally doing at any moment:

> The possibility had always been real. You never had to remind yourself. And it remains real. At such a moment, who are you? Where are you? You cannot dismiss the question by observing that "you" have become a mere object manipulated by the indifferent laws of physics. One part of you says that; another part listens. What and where are they? What and where is your identity? (3)

A part of us speaks and another part listens, as if our very sense of a stable and continuous self were nothing but a *narrative* that we tell ourselves, a world fiction that under normal circumstances seems continuous enough and linear, but which is more likely a set of multiple narratives variously linked in concatenations that the brain can search through and recall in a moment. These links are decidedly nonlinear, accompanied by analogies, puns, rhymes, and associations that generally remain unconscious — except in literature, art, or more immediately defamiliarizing experiences such as can result from a sudden change in our environment, the disengagement of self and world at the moment the steering wheel comes off in our hand. Then our sense of self can be revealed as fundamentally fragmented and permeable, a webwork of signs and divergent discourses vying for attention (and continuing to jostle with one another in our minds, after they have receded from consciousness).

Losing the distinction between inside and outside, Mathews's journalist creates another distinction that allows him to displace unanswerable questions by taking note of the questions themselves:

> Set down such questions here. "Set down" also means "stop lugging around," as with a suitcase full of bricks. Speculation can dissolve ordinary things into purest uncertainty. Of course, uncertainty has a truth of its own — there are moments when I "honestly" can't tell a concert grand from an elephant.

At such moments we may sense, without directly observing, the cognitive complexity in an act of recognition. The journalist's response, once again, is to appreciate "finding ordinary things in their ordinary places" and to notice, by noting down, the remarks people around him make:

> Paying the attention needed to retain the words let me see the speakers in a vividly spatial way. It brought them in from the flat screen of what surrounds me, which usually looks impenetrable no matter how near it is. I felt closer to them.

A cognitive fiction that reestablishes relationships out of indistinct environments, Mathews's project, it seems to me, is worth bringing to the computer "screen" where writing has its nearest proximity to the medial environment.

Words that Yield: To Frames that Form

"Hypertext has gone through a few phases: as a system for maximizing on the research efforts of military scientists via a network of microfiche machines; as a global archive of everything ever; and — never trust a writer who insists on telling you that you are also the author — as a neato apotheosis of 'contemporary literary theory.' "[6] So writes Internet activist Matt Fuller, in a piece for *lo fi*, the net art locator, where hypertext is regarded not as a revolutionary medium to end all media but as a way of framing patterned and sequential materials: "text as data and text as language." The hypertext reader is not an author (as was often claimed) but rather a rearranger of materials the author has selected and arranged. The hypertextually constructed Internet may become the nearest thing we have to an archive of "everything ever" (which is also the dream of Mathews's journalist), but that's not where its cognitive potential lies. Rather, hypertext finds its nearest analogue to cognitive activity in its powers of *selection* — its mindlike ability not to jump around at random but to create a unity within the impossible plenitude of the World Wide Web. It is often forgotten that Ted Nelson designed his initial *Xanadu*™ system (with its ever-present trademark symbol) not in order to *preserve* an archive but rather to *select* documents for present uses. It is true that he sought to make permanent the products of "thoughts and minds" that themselves "do not last,"[7] but he also left room in his system for contingency and openness by recognizing the need to kill off information ("untruth") in order to free up capacities for debates over what counts as the truth: "The important thing about science," Nelson wrote in "Computer Lib/Dream Machines," "is not that everything will be known, or that everything unanimously believed by scientists is necessarily true, but that science contains a *system* for seeking untruth and purging it" (156). Toward this collaborative truth, Nelson conceived his literary machine not as a network of neutral citations or footnotes but as a way of bringing a series of target texts bodily into an author's work-in-progress. What is stored becomes meaningful only by being *restored* in the present, as the mind recalls its store of memories, or as a music DJ mixes a sample. And what lives in the archive does so only for as long as it is shared and debated by researchers past and present who are ready to trust each other as independent truth-seekers.

And hypertext links? Links are easy; trustworthy links, hard:

The words lie there and they may be lies. They lie on the page. They are little worms. Once she dreamed, on the night before a reading she was to give, that rather than words on paper, there were tiny objects linked one to another, which she had to decipher instantly and turn into words, sentences, a story, flawlessly, of course. Funny fear of the blank page. Didn't she recently explain that writing was erasure, because the words were already there, already in the world, that the page wasn't blank.[8]

The protohypertextual quality of Lynne Tillman's conception of language, the psychological block that the blank page inspires, and a lost objectivity that has separated the word from the world have been features in each of the works discussed in this book. Each narrative under consideration has found a way of opening the block by reestablishing a nearness to words that would otherwise lose their referential power and become interacting objects endlessly recombining outside of conscious control. Hypertext blocks, like mental modules, are powerful precisely because they work below the level of consciousness; they are place markers or self-contained mental tasks capable of being called up and run at any moment — thought at the speed of light. What distinguishes the aesthetic use of such objects, however, is the artist's ability not simply to create from them a passive memory or written record, but rather a transformation within the virtual realm. Thus N. Katherine Hayles cites the cognitive work by Cees van Leeuwen, Ilse Verstijnen, and Paul Heckert on the role of material objects in the creation of art:

> When an artist creates a sketch of a work she intends to implement more fully in another medium (for example, a sketch of an oil painting), the sketch does much more than function as external memory to remind the artist what she intended. Rather, the sketch enters actively into the cognitive process of artistic creation. As the artist works with the sketch, erasing lines, drawing arrows, rearranging objects and so forth, the external object becomes part of her extended mind, not just recording her thoughts but transforming her thoughts.[9]

In fiction, too, as work intended for a print medium is remediated within electronic writing spaces, acts of enregistration and composition become themselves narrative objects. Literary note taking in such an environment is no longer a mere preparation for a realist presentation; it is rather itself a cognitive realism, continuous with the larger discourse network but more aware of itself *as* a notation system. (Friedrich Kittler's term for discourse networks, *Aufschreibsysteme*, means literally "noting-down systems"; the word's origin in the schizoid writings of Dr. Schreber is wholly consistent with the obsessive note taking we've seen in narratives by Tillman, Mathews, Markson, and Auster.)

With this visual example, we can perhaps begin to specify what it is that changes fundamentally when we move from print to hypertext reading. In hypertext we are given a multiplicity of sources and texts for browsing, so that image and narrative, the verbal and the visual, all exist on the same plane; even the near and the far, as hypertext poet Stephanie Strickland has written, are "equally present, and equally speedily present."[10] Where a book can *refer* to the texts and images that it cites, directing readers toward a plane of meaning that is not identical with the plane of the printed page, a Web page can, in theory, actually present its electronic citations directly, through the clickable link or mouseover view that brings the environment into the screen space. The screen and the environment exist on the same plane, as a set of overlapping pages with continually shifting margins. This simultaneity allows readers to select elements from within the discourse environment that will count as meaningful; it creates a pattern that readers, or the author at a later time, can *return* to, but differently, when encountering similar events and patterns later on. The outside is thus ready at any moment to match up with the inside, present notations are posted forward for future processing, and this permeability, more than the actuality of any particular link or set of links, seems to me to be definitive of reading in electronic environments.

To the extent that we have hypertext only through a series of mediations — our screen that brings the environment *in*, our browsing software, the electronic desktop that requires us to customize image and text for further processing, and so on — we are likely to be that much more aware of our collaborative activity while reading. Far from confirming readers in a central and authorlike authority, the hypertext composition "literally opens up" the space in which the reader coexists with the materials being read. Stephanie Strickland describes this readerly disorientation in an essay published concurrently with her hypertext poem sequence *True North*:

> Released from the printed page into this floating space, readers are often uneasy. What is the poem? Is it the sum of every possible way to proceed, the sequence of such journeys, or one particular path privileged as a saved reading? Only slowly does one assimilate the truth that one may return each time differently.[11]

With the environmental interruption of cognitive illusions of continuity comes a relocation of meaning making in the hands and eyes and ears of the reader, who now seeks to be simultaneously "in touch and in control" of both the hypertext and its environment (to cite the title of another Strickland essay).[12] For this to happen, the evolving hypertext must create its environment even as the hypertext reader draws material from the environment — a "floating space" that lacks all distinction until a selection is made. Instead of a uniform surround, this created environment is then a product of selections that determine which, out of all possible, objects and Web sites will be significant within the reader's own writing space. In this respect (and not in naive equations of two very different associative mechanisms), hypertext is "mindlike," because the mind, too, like any organism, admits only those aspects of the environment that it is structurally *able* to process. A successful hypertext construction will be, therefore, not an accumulation of objects and texts defined indexically as some sort of preexisting information network; it will be, rather, a set of dovetailing or complementary *structures*, which have cognitive meaning to the extent that these structures are brought out, sequentially and associatively, in the process of linking.

It could well be that a perceived lack of a true cognitive dimension in hypertext is behind critical calls for a "rhetoric or stylistics of departure and arrival" (van Looy) oriented toward aspects of the target text that are structurally and thematically relevant to the source text currently on the screen. As Jan van Looy writes in his "Conclusion: Toward a Hyperfiction Poetics," "the notion of *'words that yield'* has to be elaborated [by the author]. . . . In the same way as a full stop and a capital letter signal the beginning of the next sentence, links should inform the reader of their presence and their aim, and suggest a destination." The link, then, is not so much a mode of neutral connectivity as an active device that *enframes*; it is the bounded place where readers create a literary and visual system that would otherwise exist as an indistinguishable mass or unknown domain of automatic functioning. The visual representation of such navigational and framing devices is *the* point at which narrative and graphic arts are likely to converge in hypertext writing. But apart from this necessary convergence of image and text, enframement can also happen at the level of words themselves. Tillman enacts the necessity of selective attention, the permeability of inside and outside and their mutual self-creation, by having the individual words of her narrative literally "yield" not arbitrarily to another set of chunked words but to the multiple meanings and differential structures that each word possesses by the fact that it functions within a grammar.

In "To Find Words," which opens the collection *The Madame Realism Complex*, Tillman's protagonist is a young author named, improbably, Paige

Turner, who cannot "pretend to believe in words and in the power of stories" and so determines to write instead about writing itself. Her narrative alternates between third-person views of Paige, direct presentations out of the literal pages in her notebook, and first-person commentaries by a narrator with access to Paige's thoughts. To herself, Paige defines her ambitions as an author in the barest material terms: "to find words and place them in sentences in a certain order. Syntax." That's what Paige *thinks*; the sentence she goes on to *write* has to do with "a sin tax in the U.S. on liquor and cigarettes."[13] This happens throughout the narrative, as the words found by the narrator are continually taken over and reappropriated by the character, and vice versa. At issue is the relation between the thought track that runs through every one of Tillman's essay-narratives (whether presented as fiction or nonfiction) and the texts that her protagonists are working on — or, when the protagonists are nonwriters, between the self and the voices and human visitors who "become phrases in [the] body" (33). In one formulation, Paige speaks of the relation between conscious and unconscious thought:

> It is in the unconscious [Paige writes] that fantasy, moments of the day, and memory live, a reservoir for the poetry of the world. Is everything else prose? Is what's conscious ordinary prose, the prose of the world?

But the formulation is rejected, as the narrator, ever ready to turn on a pun, responds:

> Or, I tease, the pose of the world. She is preparing much too neatly the world she knows — I nearly wrote word for world — from the world she doesn't know, the one that owns her and to which she is a slave. She is a slave to what she can't remember and doesn't know and she is a slave to what she remembers and what she thinks she knows. Her education has damaged her in ways she does not even know. (26)

Paige does not know what she does not know; an eye does not see what it does not see; and "the world is what one does not perceive when one perceives it":[14] such truisms characterize all systems. But the narrator, Paige's creator who exists at a later stage in her literary career and cognitive development, presumably *does* know. Between the various narrative levels, first- and third-person narration, early and later development, the author who writes a draft and the same author (now a reader) who revises, we can perceive what the character wishing to be an author cannot see: for example, the educational system and ready-made fund of cultural memories that enslave her because she knows no other possibilities. The words she knows *are* her world.

Like all writers, Paige longs to find a voice and a style — to make music with words. Yet the words she succeeds in finding are consistently turned into other words by the narrator, or the same word is given a different meaning. Syntax becomes sin tax; prose is unmasked as a mere pose, so that the limitations inherent in the words Paige uses can be, not overcome, but reinscribed within a new perspective. "She imagines the inside is the outside. She is greedy for everything," and so she will eventually transform the boundary between herself and her environment into a division *within herself*: "She opens her mouth wide. If words could make wishes come true. If wishes were horses she'd ride away" (18). Paige, of course, knows that words are not wishes, as Oedipa Maas [in Thomas Pynchon's *The Crying of Lot 49* — Editors] discovers that a sign is not what it is: unlike a digital tape whose meaning and function are identical with its coding, or a "complexity" that is "its own best — shortest — description,"[15] neither spoken words nor material signs have the power to do what they say; they can only create alternate worlds inside the speaker or writer. Each world Paige might inhabit or Oedipa might project is a different constellation of words with its own articulation and its own blind spots that can only be displaced by finding other words and (not finding) other blind spots.

To be sure, most print fiction tries to suppress narrative self-consciousness in the interest of immersing readers more fully in a *story*. Similarly, enormous sums of money are currently being spent in making virtual reality environments as transparent and immersive as possible, so that we might move through them with a feeling of verisimilitude. It was not always so in the computer business, as changes in the meaning assigned to the word *transparency* might indicate. At first, the word was used to mean that a user was *close* to the operating system (such that one tells the machine to do things in ways that it really does do things). Today *transparency* more often means that the operating system is *invisible* and so what's transparent is the machine itself — a window manufactured out of opacity (hence Microsoft's Windows). A steam locomotive displays its power in its massive crankshafts and wheels; the transparent case of an iMac displays nothing operative. But consider how the word *transparent* is used by a computer scientist actually involved in making decisions at the level of operations:

> Lentz did a good job of making the hardware transparent to me. He hooked
> up topologies the culmination of a decade or more of tinkering. He ex-

plained every link in the process. . . . The gist consisted of vectors. A stimulus vector, converted by the net's self-reorganization into a response vector.
We started with a three-deep array of neurodes, enough for a test start. Each
field was the size of the net that had learned to pronounce English. Imple-
mentation A would be spared this task. Lentz wired it to a canned speech
synthesis routine. We worked at the level not of phonemes but of whole
words.[16]

Which is to say that the task had been modularized, such that with each
move to the next level, from phonemes to whole words to sentences to
entire texts, the previous level would be absorbed into a more comprehensive operation.

By actually imagining those aspects of a cognitive system that have sunk
below the level of operational awareness, a small number of contemporary
novelists and poets are creating a new order of realism in fiction and poetry,
akin to functionalism in technological design and operational-minimalism
in painting, that makes a frank admission of its own materiality and so
establishes a ground on which authors and readers can meet as equals and
communicate without false illusions. Mathews works within this neomate-
rialist climate, as do most of the Oulipo members with whom he is associated. Georges Perec had written a novel, *La Disparition*, without using the
letter *e* (the novel has been translated into English, a language where not
even the article "the" is allowed, under the punning title, *A Void*). Italo
Calvino arranged the chapters for *Invisible Cities* according to a mathematical formula in which the chapters, like cities, build themselves up by numbers 1, 21, 321, 4321, and then erase themselves in inverse order: 5432, 543,
54, 5; Raymond Queneau proposed ten sonnets, each of whose fourteen
lines could be arranged in any order, producing 10^{14} or *Cent mille milliards de
poems* (one hundred thousand billion poems). This is not automatic writing;
rather, it is writing under constraint. Such work does not give over the
creative process to either the unconscious or mathematical formalisms but
rather forces the co-conscious, language-based, composing mind to put
itself into contact with formal and procedural conditions that are always
present, always constraining, supporting, tweaking, and unconsciously controlling the creative process. The only difference is that the Oulipian follows self-set rules, constraints of one's own making, and so learns how
autonomy produces results that are not entirely under authorial control.
From a cognitive perspective, such writing is significant in that it recognizes
the thousands of ways that conscious experience "is constantly influencing

and being influenced by many unconscious processes" involving perception and action, thought and emotions, as well as the computational and recursive routines that support the construction of even the simplest sentence.[17]

Although for more than thirty years the Oulipo group has devoted themselves, ostensibly, to researching past literary forms and making them available to the public, few of these forms have ever been used beyond the moment of their "discovery" — and this is possibly the best thing about the Oulipo and what distinguishes their art from mere formalism. For what signifies is the cognitive and combinatorial *potential* that is held in the forms, not the form itself, which can go back on the shelf with all the other dusty books and dusty bottles the moment it is perceived or identified *as* a form. (The same is true of invented forms and self-imposed constraints: Mathews, for example, has never found it necessary to reveal the constraint under which he wrote his most Oulipian novel, *Cigarettes*. And who has yet noticed that his very short story, "Mr. Smathers," though published online in paragraph form, is actually a sestina?)

The Journal of the Journal

That we know the world only through particular frameworks, categorizations, and preestablished expectations is brought home to readers by the very look of *The Journalist*, in which paragraphs are numbered, and then renumbered and subdivided in an elaborate and doomed attempt to match the language to the atomistic world of facts and perceptions. The project is doomed because, unlike the semiotic model of a network of signifiers linked with each other and their signifieds, the identity of the world is a composite of attributes that only come into existence *as they are observed*. Even the shoes that the journalist's colleagues wear to work or the sunlight falling across an office worker's telephone become distinct (and thus capable of relating to one another) only as they are newly noted in the journal; only then do they "emerge from the strangeness of systems outside" the journalist's control, as the clarity of his own evolving system plunges endlessly into the obscurity of these "systems outside."[18]

As noted attributes take form in clusters shaped in a network of coded relations, Mathews's novel spirals away from any notion of journal writing as the objective reporting of some preexisting world; only in the notation are objects and events "naturalized" (9). At the same time, the novel also avoids attributing purposeful creation to the writer/observer. Instead, as the narrator discovers to his surprise, the journal has a life of its own, its purpose the mere reflection and reproduction of the categories with which he approaches the world. This narrator, the "journalist" of the title, has been advised by his doctor to jot down "everything" that happens to him (8), "from how much he has spent on books and movies to what he eats" (dust jacket). But "everything," he soon discovers, is already caught up in its own networks of relations, and each item can belong to more than one category and can operate at several different levels. Initially he tries to distinguish "between fact and speculation, between what is external and verifiable and what is subjective," but this does not prevent the one from mingling into the other (20); at the start he considers "a separate notebook for dreams" (4); as he gets into the project he makes "a further division into what concerns others and what concerns only myself" (32). Indeed, as distinctions noted down in the journal continue to proliferate and the act of recording makes ever greater demands on his time, lived experience and the record of the experience converge, and the notation system itself expands to the point where it ceases to be meaningful to speak of a life "outside" the system. So logical and calm are the notes that, although readers are given plenty of indications as to the journalist's deteriorating state, we are as surprised as he is when he breaks from his obsession long enough to observe himself: "when I heard a dry noise above my head, like a cracking in the ceiling boards: I saw myself as if through an eye in the ceiling, fidgeting and sweating like a demented inmate, a disgrace. I calmed down" (129).

This is an astonishing moment, and not because, while reading, we are unaware of the narrator's growing obsession and mental stress. His literary decorum matches a poise typical of Mathews, even as his protagonist steals into a closet in order to toss rolls of toilet paper down the air shaft of his office building and later neglects to change out of his soiled white suit after a fall and lapse of consciousness during a nighttime prowl. He does allow himself to make a mental note: "I must get back early in the morning and straighten up" (173). But of course he does no such thing. In the morning he will be writing in the journal and recording these very actions. The journalist is interested in the illusion of control, never the actual manipulation of reality, which is "the world's, not mine" (154). At no time does the journalist apply any of his numerous and detailed acts of self-observation to the improvement of his condition.[19] For no sooner does he reflect back on himself than he retreats from the self-observation into the security of the note-taking system. *Because* such acts are recorded entirely from within this system, however, we accept his state as "natural." To the extent that we enter the fiction, we accommodate ourselves to it, like a live fish adjusting its body

JOSEPH TABBI

temperature to a surrounding fluid, not noticing that it is slowly boiling or becoming frozen. In essence, by accepting the terms of Mathews's fiction, we enter something very like the "floating space" that Strickland speaks of in electronic environments, before that environment is articulated and made active by the reader's selective engagements and disengagements. For the journalist, and for "us," the journal's reader, the outside world *does not exist*—except as it conforms to the selections and identifications that the journalist's mental state disposes him to make.

Even more significant for the narrative structure than this (quickly suppressed) moment of self-consciousness is the decision that can be felt pulling at him from the start, to replace the proliferating petty differences noted down in his journal with a single global distinction: he will move the system one level up, applying the idea of the journal to itself. Here is how he explains his decision to write a "journal of the journal": "What I discovered is this: all the care I have brought to organizing this journal has been misspent; my laborious classifications have proved worthless; my efforts at competence are an illusion. Why? Because I have left out the chief activity of my life and the chief fact of my project: the keeping of this journal" (190–91). From here, it is only one small step to the next and final logical level at which we as readers experience a book titled *The Journalist*, when Mathews's narrator admits to "a closeted vision, that of writing a novel—a novel about someone whose passion is keeping a journal" (209).

In numerous essays and interviews, Mathews has held that the role of the author is to provide materials that readers can then use as a means of creation.[20] In literary studies, such a position has been made to seem marginal and exceptional. To contain the self-consciousness and radical contingency that must pervade the creative act at every moment, mainstream writing programs tend to regard a fundamental *condition* as a *technique*, and novels explicitly concerned with reflexive identity-making are most often filed away (and largely forgotten) under the subcategory "metafiction." That literature has thus largely marginalized its own reflexivity (in favor of some liberal humanist ideal of authorial self-possession or narrative "voice") is all the more surprising given that it is a field whose subject is homogeneous with its object, in that both literature and criticism (that is, writing about writing) are conducted in the same medium, and not infrequently by the same person at the moment of composition. This point is brought home to Mathews's journalist when he discovers the necessity of keeping a "journal of the journal." In all he has been doing up to that point, he has left out his own controlling presence—a control, however, that emanates not from the mind of the journalist himself but the communicative network that he deploys. Only now, when he is in fact losing his grip, does he accord the writing itself its "supreme place" and so reestablish a complex conceptual autonomy:

> My work is not for "the world" (by that I mean *anybody* else) or for me (I hardly have time to read what I've written). It's for "It." "Its" fugitive name does not matter. I've called it truth, and before that reality; since it is never to be completely obtained, it may be beyond naming altogether. (200)

(Mathews's journalist, appropriately, is himself never named in the novel.)

Paul Harris nonetheless suggests a name that is appropriate not only for Mathews's novel but for all constraint-driven narrative, in print or hypertext: "The potential of constrained writing," Harris notes, "is that it ends up an autopoietic writing machine."[21] Autopoiesis — literally, self-making — describes "a form of system organization where the system as a whole produces and replaces its own components and differentiates itself from its surrounding environment on a continual basis."[22] In Mathews's case, the "it" that is both self and not-self, a unity that consists of reciprocal perturbations between system and environment, is a kind of machine for "generating linguistic distinction 'in a linguistic domain.' "[2] "It's for 'It' ": the "work" is for its own sake; the system is working hard just to keep working, conservatively cycling within its own logic and oblivious to any environment; but the work, "it," is also for the sign, "It," presented here as absolutely arbitrary and "beyond naming altogether." "A sign is not what it is," William S. Wilson has written (in correspondence from February to October 1999), putting much the same pressure on that single small word, the place where an autopoietic writing system draws a distinction with its environment and then folds that distinction back within itself.

The discovery that "the main story of the journal is the journal itself" (191) is the trigger point, in Mathews, of narrative applied to itself. A new level of sustainability emerges when a referential notion (the journal) becomes an object in itself, an element that is made to migrate from "outside" to "inside" the journal. Only through such a reversal of target and source can the journal's system differentiate internally, and so redraw its border with the outside, "lived," world. After "the J of J quandary" (218) reveals to him the futility of his efforts up to that point, the journalist is unsure how to go on: "How," he asks, "could I grasp the problem from inside the system it had demolished? I had to invent a new approach and context" (212). Should he draft a separate journal "duplicating each existing category with its journalistic parallel: the first records an event, while the second records the event of its recording" (191), and so forth? At one point he purchases a tape recorder, thinking that the machine will solve the quandary by recording "the recorder as well as what *he* was recording" (218). But there is no automatic solution to be had by simply switching to an alternative medium: the journalist soon resorts to his "customary tools" (219), pencil and paper, but he uses the journal differently now that he is newly aware of its medial support. Before the calamitous scene that provokes his final collapse, he begins to note down the positions and dispositions of the people closest to him: his wife, son, brother- and sister-in-law, and best friend. Instead of continued speculation about motives (and the extrapolation from "complex theories of behavior"), he creates a category for "snoopery" that allows him to classify his material "by situations rather than by persons" (212). Having become aware of the limits of his own position, he turns his attention to each person, noting their actions not as "the work of individuals" but as "collaborations," a composite of conjoined identities that further reveal the self's elusiveness:

And who else, and what else? No one else matters, and these are all joined against me: Daisy with Paul, Colette with Gert, Daisy and Paul with Colette and Gert, with Jago picking up the tab, and here I sit holding the steering wheel that long ago came off in my hands. (218)

Letting go of his own first-order controlling consciousness, the journalist discovers another key feature of autopoietic theory: the second-order observation by differently positioned observers, each one displacing and correcting for the others' blind spots.

It is while spying on each of them — as they, in turn, are spying on each other before they become aware of his presence — that the journalist collapses in his sister-in-law Colette's garden. While there, he sees enough to revise completely the picture he has had of these people, their motives, and the import of their actions: instead of conspiring "against" him (218), each one has been generously concerned for his welfare. Their separate secrecies have concerned themselves only, just as his own mental life, as recorded in the journal, concerns him alone. They, of course, also have relationships with one another, and with him too, but these latter he has consistently misread as a result of his own too perspicuous attentions, which, like the all-absorbing attention he gives to the journal, only isolate him within his own self-created meanings. Only by losing himself does he recognize the *necessity* of the social; only by withdrawing, at the end, and by separating his writing from a society of real and objective other people different from himself, does he recognize their love that is unconditional and unwritten.

At the hospital where he has been institutionalized, he is not allowed to write in the journal, and he reacts by refusing to speak. His separate encounters with visitors are observed and presented in the manner of a third-person clinical report — an apparent objectivity that is, however, signaled as yet another journalistic invention by a small, momentary, shift to the first person. When an orderly at the hospital asks "the patient" if he wants to hear a story,

> The patient declined the first subjects proposed: the impoverished artist who inherits a rich man's finery; the worker's son who becomes a world-class violinist only to ruin his career by gambling; the abandoned little girl who every night sneaks into the houses of the wealthy. My hesitation in rejecting the last subject led the orderly to think that another children's story might be acceptable. He suggested the tale of "Michael the Orphan," and to this I agreed.
>
> What then took place marked an evolution in the patient's condition, to what effect it is too early to say . . . (235)

The story opens: "*Once upon a time and a very good time, monkey chew tobacco and spit white lime, once upon a time there was a young boy named Michael*" (236). Hearing these lines and the opening scene (in which Michael, leaving home at the age of nine, gets off an express train), the journalist then begins to interrupt with words of his own — or perhaps words from another, remembered story — adding characters, objects, and events as the orderly goes on reading. With this small and mutually distanced dialogue, a modest hypertextual collaboration, the novel reaches a kind of closure impossible from within the journalist's earlier elaborated system of notation and classification. The first-order system gives way to a more properly narrative apparatus, reflexivity and circularity turn into forward movement, and the act of turning inward is replaced by the turning of pages in a book. The journalist is now poised for *reentry* into his environment at another level, in a wholeness of interiority and exteriority and a dialogue that is not so much a communication between two people as a creation of a new narrative object outside either one of them, and outside any inscription in the book they are reading.

Smoke and Perfume

If the small shift back to the first person at the end of *The Journalist* indicates the persistence, in Mathews, of the controlling subject of phenomenological reflection, the subject's status *as a fiction* is equally evident—particularly if we look to the subject for a ground or basis for the narrative we've been reading. If at the novel's conclusion the journalist is without speech and is unable to write in his journal, who, then, has provided those journal entries up to the point where he gave up control over his production? No answer is forthcoming, either from within the fiction or from the more general structure of autopoietic systems. Because the movement from level to metalevel is a difference that can have no actual equivalent in reality (the narrator cannot be at the same time both a character *and* the author of the book), the self-generated difference functions at a wholly mental level. It's for "It," but "It" is no less "real" for that. Neither the sign nor what the sign points to is real: what is real is the *difference* inherent in such self-reference. This operational reality, at the heart of cognitive fictions, is also consistent with how neurobiology regards the construction of reality in the brain, which is based largely on "self-perception and on self-established differences that have no actual equivalent in reality."[24] The realism of cognitive fictions is then of a piece with the illusory nature of cognition.

Notes

1. Jan van Looy, "Authoring as Architecture: Toward a Hyperfiction Poetics," 2.2.2.1, http://www.jan.vanlooy.net. On the "false analogy" linking minds and digital computers, see Gerald Edelman, *Bright Air, Brilliant Fire: On the Matter of the Mind* (New York: Basic Books, 1992), 218–27.

2. N. Katherine Hayles, "The Transformation of Narrative and the Materiality of Hypertext," *Narrative*, January 2000, 21.

3. Francis Crick, *What Mad Pursuit: A Personal View of Scientific Discovery* (New York: Basic Books, 1988), 160.

4. See Paul Auster, *Ghosts* (Los Angeles: Sun and Moon Press, 1986); and David Markson, *Wittgenstein's Mistress* (Normal, Ill.: Dalkey Archive Press, 1988).

5. Harry Mathews, *The Journalist* (1994; Normal, Ill.: Dalkey Archive Press, 1997), 1.

6. Matt Fuller, review of hypertext Web sites in *lo fi* [Net art locator], http://www.low-fi.org.uk.

7. Ted Nelson, "Computer Lib/Dream Machines," in *Multimedia: From Wagner to Virtual Reality*, ed. Randall Packer and Ken Jordan (New York: Norton, 2001), 157. Also see Nelson, *Literary Machines* (Theodor H. Nelson, 1984).

8. Lynne Tillman, "To Find Words," in *The Madame Realism Complex* (New York: Semiotext[e], 1992), 22.

9. Hayles, "Transformation of Narrative," 31.

10. Stephanie Strickland, "Poetry in the Electronic Environment," *Electronic Book Review*, spring 1999.

11. Strickland, "Poetry in the Electronic Environment." See also Strickland's *True North* (South Bend, Ind.: Notre Dame University Press, 1997; hypertext published in 1998 by Eastgate Systems).

12. Stephanie Strickland, "To Be Both in Touch and in Control," *Electronic Book Review*, spring 1999.

13. Tillman, "To Find Words," 17; hereafter cited in the text.

14. See Niklas Luhmann, *Essays on Self-Reference* (New York: Columbia University Press, 1990).

15. Strickland, "Figures of Speech," in *True North*.

16. Richard Powers, *Galatea 2.2* (New York: Farrar, Straus and Giroux, 1995), 71–72.

17. Gerald Edelman and Giulio Tononi, *A Universe of Consciousness: How Matter Becomes Imagination* (New York: Basic Books, 2000), 177.

18. Mathews, *The Journalist*, 9; hereafter cited in the text.

19. The journalist is true to those psychoses in which the patient, while perfectly capable of "reality testing," evidences no inclination to it (a condition we have seen noted by Louis Sass in *Madness and Modernism* and exemplified by the narrator in *Wittgenstein's Mistress*). See Louis Sass, *Madness and Modernism: Insanity in the Light of Modern Art, Literature, and Thought* (New York: Basic Books, 1992).

20. Lynne Tillman, "Harry Mathews by Lynne Tillman," in *Bomb Interviews*, ed. Betsy Sussler (San Francisco: City Lights, 1992), 29.

21. Paul Harris, "Harry Mathews's Al Gore Rhythms," *Electronic Book Review*, spring 1999.

22. Joel Slayton and Geri Wittig, "Ontology of Organization as System," paper presented in conjunction with the release of the C5 SoftSub data-mining freeware application at *Ars Electronica: OpenX*, http://www.c5corp.com/softsub.

23. Slayton and Wittig, "Ontology of Organization as System."

24. Dietrich Schwanitz, "Systems Theory According to Niklas Luhmann — Its Environment and Conceptual Strategies," *Cultural Critique*, spring 1995, 140.

M. M. BAKHTIN (1895–1975) has become famous as the founder of the dialogic method in literary criticism and philosophy, as developed in books and essays written over a sixty-year period. He is the author of such works as *The Dialogic Imagination* (trans. 1981), *Problems of Dostoevsky's Poetics* (trans. 1984), *Speech Genres and other Late Essays* (trans. 1986), and *Toward a Philosophy of the Act* (trans. 1993).

JOHN BARTH (b. 1930), a professor emeritus at Johns Hopkins University, has been hailed as one of the leading "postmodernists" in the United States, having published such novels as *Giles Goat-Boy* (1966), *The End of the Road* (1967), *Sabbatical: A Romance* (1982), and *Coming Soon!!! A Narrative* (2002).

ROLAND BARTHES (1915–1980) gained an extraordinary reputation as a brilliant, prolific, and eclectic cultural critic. Identified with a number of critical movements, his method always remained uniquely individual in such works as *Writing Degree Zero*, the source for this essay (1953; trans. 1967), *The Pleasure of the Text* (1973; trans. 1975), *S/Z* (1970; trans. 1974), *Mythologies* (1957; trans. 1972), and *Camera Lucida* (1980; trans. 1981).

WAYNE BOOTH (b. 1921) is a professor of English emeritus at the University of Chicago. In addition to the classic of literary criticism, *The Rhetoric of Fiction* (rev. 1983), he has published numerous other critical works, including *A Rhetoric of Irony* (1974), *Critical Understanding: The Powers and Limits of Pluralism* (1979), and *The Company We Keep* (1988).

JOHN BRENKMAN is Distinguished Professor of English and Comparative Literature at the CUNY Graduate Center and Baruch College. He has published *Culture and Domination* (1987) and *Straight Male Modern* (1993).

PETER BROOKS (b. 1938) is Sterling Professor of Comparative Literature and French at Yale University. In addition to *Reading for the Plot* (1984), from which this chapter is taken, he has also written *Body Work* (1993) and *Troubling Confessions: Speaking Guilt in Law and Literature* (2000), and other works of literary criticism.

CATHERINE BURGASS taught for several years as a lecturer in twentieth-century literature in English at the University of Liverpool. She is the author of *A.S. Byatt's "Possession": A Reader's Guide* and *Challenging Theory: Discipline After Deconstruction*, as well as several other essays on postmodern fiction in addition to the one reprinted here.

SEYMOUR CHATMAN (b. 1928) is a professor emeritus of rhetoric at the University of California, Berkeley. He has also published, among other books, *Coming to Terms: The Rhetoric of Narrative in Fiction and Film* (1990) and *Reading Narrative Fiction* (1992).

J. YELLOWLEES DOUGLAS is an associate professor of English and associate director of the University Writing Program at the University of Florida. In addition to *The End of Books –Or Books Without End?* (2000), from which this excerpt is taken, Douglas has also written *I Have Said Nothing*, a hypertext fiction.

RACHEL BLAU DUPLESSIS, a professor of English at Temple University, is both a poet and critic. In 2001 she published *Drafts 1–38, Toll*, a collection of long poems, and *Genders, Races, and Religious Cultures in Modern American Poetry, 1908–1934*, a work of literary criticism. Her other poetry includes *Tabula Rosa* (1987) and her other criticism includes *Writing Beyond the Ending* (1985), from which this excerpt is taken.

WENDY B. FARIS is a professor of English and comparative literature at the University of Texas, Arlington. Among other works, she has written *Labyrinths of Language: Symbolic Landscapes and Narrative Design in Modern Fiction* (1988) and *Ordinary Enchantments: Magical Realism and the Remystification of Narrative* (2004), and has edited, with Lois Parkinson Zamora, *Magical Realism: Theory, History, Community* (1995), in which this essay originally appeared.

BARBARA FOLEY (b. 1948) is a professor of English at Rutgers University, Newark. In addition to *Telling the Truth* (1986), from which this excerpt is taken, she has also written *Radical Representations: Politics and Form in U.S. Proletarian Fiction, 1929–1991* (2003).

E. M. FORSTER (1879–1970) was a major English prose stylist in novel, short story, and literary essay. His most famous novels are *A Room with a View* (1908), *Howards End* (1910), and *A Passage to India* (1924). Many of his best essays are collected in *Arbinger Harvest* (1936).

JOSEPH FRANK (b. 1918) is a professor emeritus of Slavic and comparative literature at Stanford University. He has elaborated on his concept of "Spatial Form in Modern Literature" most recently in *The Idea of Spatial Form: Essays on Literature and Culture* (1991). In 1976 he published the first volume of a planned five-volume biography of Dostoevsky, which he completed with the publication of *The Mantle of the Prophet* (2003).

JOANNE S. FRYE (b. 1944) is a professor of English at the College of Wooster. She has written *Tillie Olsen: A Study of the Short Fiction* (1995), in addition to *Living Stories, Telling Lives* (1986), from which this excerpt is taken.

WILLIAM H. GASS (b. 1924) taught philosophy at Washington University, St. Louis, for many years. He is well known as a novelist and a literary critic, having written such works as *Omensetter's Luck* (1966), *In the Heart of the Heart of the Country* (1968), *Fiction and the Figures of Life* (1970), from which this essay is taken, and most recently, *Tests of Time: Essays* (2003).

HENRY LOUIS GATES, JR., is W. E. B. DuBois Professor of Humanities and Chair of the Afro-American Studies Department at Harvard University. The essay excerpted here from *Figures in Black* (1987) originally appeared in *Critical Inquiry*. He has written such books as *The Signifying Monkey* (1988) and *Loose Cannons: Notes on the Culture Wars* (1992), and edited and coedited numerous volumes, including *Black Literature and Literary Theory* (1984), *Reading Black, Reading Feminist* (1990), and *The Norton Anthology of African American Literature* (1996).

GÉRARD GENETTE (b. 1930) is a French critic and rhetorician, whose *Narrative Discourse* has been recognized as a major document of French structuralism. In addition to that work, his criticism has been translated into other books, such as *Figures of Literary Discourse* (1982) and *The Architext: An Introduction* (1992),

URSULA K. HEISE is an associate professor of English and comparative literature at Stanford University. She specializes in contemporary fiction and poetry and is the author of *Chronoschisms* (1997), from which this excerpt is taken. She is currently completing a book entitled *World-Wide Webs: Global Ecology and the Cultural Imagination*.

LINDA HUTCHEON (b. 1947) is a professor of English and comparative literature at the University of Toronto. A major theorist and critic of the postmodern, she has published numerous books, including *A Theory of Parody* (1985), *A Poetics of Postmodernism* (1988), *The Politics of Postmodernism* (1989), and *Irony's Edge: The Theory and Politics of Irony* (1994).

HENRY JAMES (1843–1916) is best known for many novels that have become classics of English language literature, including *The American* (1877), *Portrait of a Lady* (1881), and *The Ambassadors* (1903). He has also left us a legacy of novellas and short stories, such as *Daisy Miller* (1879), *The Turn of the Screw* (1898), and *The Beast in the Jungle* (1903). Much of his literary criticism can be found in *The Art of the Novel* (1934) and *The Future of the Novel* (1956).

SUSAN S. LANSER is a professor of English and director of women's studies at Brandeis University. She is the author of *The Narrative Act* (1981), *Fictions of Authority: Women Writers and Narrative Voice* (1992), and numerous articles on feminist narratology. She has also coedited, with the Folger Collective, *Women Critics, 1660–1820* (1996).

HELEN LOCK is a professor of English at the University of Louisiana, Monroe. She has published *A Case of Mis-taken Identity: Detective Undercurrents in Recent African-American Fiction* (1994).

GEORG LUKÁCS (1885–1971), a leading Marxist literary theorist, was born in Budapest. He returned there from Moscow after World War II to become professor of aesthetics at the University of Budapest. Although *Studies in European Realism* was the first of his Marixst books to be translated into English, his pre-Marxist work, *The Theory of the Novel* (1920; trans. 1971), is perhaps the most popular of his translated work.

RUTH RONEN is an associate professor of poetics and comparative literature at Tel Aviv University. She has written *Possible Worlds in Literary Theory* (1994) and *Representing the Real* (2002).

JOSEPH TABBI is an associate professor of English at the University of Illinois, Chicago. He has written *Postmodern Sublime* (1995) and *Cognitive Fictions* (2002), from which this excerpt is taken. He has also edited and introduced William Gaddis's last fiction and collected nonfiction.

JON THIEM is a professor of English at Colorado State University, where he teaches courses in European literature and myth. He has edited *Lorenzo de'Medici: Selected Poems and Prose* (1991) and coedited, with Pat McKee, *Real Life: Ten Stories of Aging* (1994).

TZVETAN TODOROV, born in 1939 in Sofia, Bulgaria, is a professor of aesthetics at the Centre National de la Recherche Scientifique, Paris. He is the author of numerous books, including *Symbolism and Interpretation* (trans. 1983), *Mikhail Bakhtin: The Dialogical Principle* (trans. 1984), *The Conquest of America: The Question of the Other* (trans. 1984), *Genres of Discourse* (trans. 1990), and *Imperfect Garden: The Legacy of Humanism* (trans. 2002).

VIRGINIA WOOLF (1882–1941) is best known as the author of such modernist novels as *Mrs. Dalloway* (1925), *To the Lighthouse* (1927), and *The Waves* (1931). She was also a prolific essayist, literary critic, major feminist theorist—as in *A Room of One's Own* (1929), diarist, and letter writer, as well as being a member of the Bloomsbury Group of British intellectuals. "Mr. Bennet and Mrs. Brown" appears in her collection *The Captain's Death Bed and Other Essays* (1950).

MICHAEL J. HOFFMAN is a professor emeritus of English at the University of California, Davis. He is the author of *Critical Essays on Gertrude Stein* (1986), *Gertrude Stein* (1976), *The Subversive Vision* (1972), *The Buddy System* (1971), and *The Development of Abstractionism in the Writings of Gertrude Stein* (1966). He is the coeditor, with Patrick D. Murphy, of *Critical Essays on American Modernism* (1992).

PATRICK D. MURPHY is a professor of English at the University of Central Florida. He is the author of *Farther Afield in the Study of Nature-Oriented Literature* (2000), *A Place for Wayfaring: The Poetry and Prose of Gary Snyder* (2000), *Literature, Nature, and Other: Ecofeminist Critiques* (1995), and *Understanding Gary Snyder* (1992). He is the editor of *The Literature of Nature: An International Sourcebook* (1998); *Staging the Impossible: The Fantastic Mode in Modern Drama* (1992); and *Critical Essays on Gary Snyder* (1991). He is the coeditor of *Ecofeminist Literary Criticism and Pedagogy*, with Greta Gaard (1998); *American Panorama: An English at Your Fingertips Reader*, with the University of the Ryukyus Textbook Editorial Committee (Tokyo, 1998); *Handbook of Chinese Popular Culture*, with Dingbo Wu (1994); *Critical Essays on American Modernism*, with Michael J. Hoffman (1992); *The Poetic Fantastic: Studies in an Evolving Genre*, with Vernon Hyles (1989); and *Science Fiction from China: Eight Stories*, with Dingbo Wu (1989).

Library of Congress Cataloging-in-Publication Data
Essentials of the theory of fiction / edited by Michael J. Hoffman and Patrick D. Murphy. — 3rd ed.
p. cm.
Includes bibliographical references and index.
ISBN 0-8223-3509-3 (alk. paper)
ISBN 0-8223-3521-2 (pbk. : alk. paper)
1. Fiction — History and criticism — Theory, etc. I. Hoffman, Michael J., 1939– II. Murphy, Patrick D., 1951–
PN3331.E87 2005
809.3 — dc22   2004024770